# MARKETING:
## Contemporary Concepts and Practices

**William F. Schoell** and **Thomas T. Ivy**
University of Southern Mississippi

**ALLYN AND BACON, INC.**
Boston   London   Sydney   Toronto

Production Editor: Elaine Ober
Manufacturing Buyer: Patricia Hart
Managing Editor: Michael E. Meehan

**Library of Congress Cataloging in Publication Data**

Schoell, William F.
  Marketing: contemporary concepts and practices.

  Includes indexes.
  1. Marketing.    I.  Ivy, Thomas T    II.   Title.
HF5415.S357      658.8        81-10973
ISBN 0-205-07656-4          AACR2

Printed in the United States of America.
10  9  8  7  6  5  4  3  2  1  86  85  84  82

## Credits:

**Chapter 1:** p. 19—*Marketing molehills.* Reprinted from *Marketing News*, May 18, 1979, published by the American Marketing Association. p. 22—Photo reprinted courtesy of the House of Seagram.

**Chapter 2:** p. 38—Reprinted with permission of United Energy Resources, Inc., Houston, Texas. p. 40—*Monthly Labor Review* vol. 90–104, (Washington, D.C.: Bureau of Labor Statistics, 1967–1981). p. 45—Reprinted with permission of Harris Corporation, Melbourne, Florida. p. 49—Reprinted from the September 1, 1980 issue of *Business Week* by special permission, © 1980 by McGraw-Hill, Inc. New York, NY 10020. All rights reserved. p. 50—© 1980, The Warner & Swasey Company, Cleveland, Ohio. Reprinted with permission. p. 56—Reprinted from the January 27, 1975 issue of *Business Week* by special

permission, © 1980 by McGraw-Hill, Inc. New York, NY 10020. All rights reserved.

**Chapter 3:** p. 74—*Current Population Reports*, Series P–25, No. 640 (Washington, D.C.: U.S. Bureau of the Census, 1979). p. 79—*Statistical Abstract of the United States, 1979*, 100th ed. (Washington, D.C.: U.S. Bureau of the Census, 1979), p. 440. p. 81—Reprinted with permission of Atlantic Richfield Company. p. 83—*Statistical Abstract of the United States, 1979*, 100th ed. (Washington, D.C.: U.S. Bureau of American Express Company. p. 85—*Statistical Abstract of the United States, 1979*, 100th ed. (Washington, D.C.: U.S. Bureau of the Census, 1979), p. 452. p. 87—Reprinted by permission from *Sales & Marketing Management* magazine. Copyright 1980. p. 89—Reprinted with permission of Volvo of America Corporation, Rockleigh, New

To
Rosie, Shannon, Bryan, Edith, and Bill, Jr.
Sarah, Stephanie, and Brody

# Brief Contents

# Contents

Section VI **Promotion 477**

## Section VII  Price 581

# Preface

Not long ago, marketing was low on the list of important business functions. Production and finance, for example, almost always preceded it in perceived importance to business success. Marketing simply meant finding buyers for a firm's products and moving those products to the buyers.

In fact, it was not until the middle of this century that business people began to recognize marketing's importance. That recognition fostered a gradual movement from a production orientation to a marketing orientation in many companies. The revolutionary new idea was that businesses exist mainly to satisfy their customers—that is how they will profit most over the long haul.

Today more than ever before, effective marketing is recognized as an essential ingredient in the successful operation of any type of organization, including business firms, governments, nonprofit organizations, and individuals. It is not unusual, today, to hear the statement "We need to do a better job of marketing ourselves" from college and university presidents, hospital administrators, heads of government bureaus and agencies, police chiefs, museum directors, politicians, and spokespersons for charitable organizations and churches. As marketing has become more essential to the successful operation of all types of organizations, it has become more complex, more controversial, more challenging, more dynamic, more socially responsive, and perhaps most importantly, infinitely more interesting and exciting.

Considerable marketing effort preceded and accompanied the writing and production of this text. We began by surveying students and instructors in introductory marketing courses concerning what they wanted in a basic marketing text. Based on the results, we realized that students in the course have various backgrounds and academic majors. We learned that some of them are not business majors, many are not marketing majors, and many are employed full- or part-time. The average age of the students also seems to be rising. Finally, it became clear that today's students demand more of the texts they use and are not hesitant to complain about texts to their instructors.

What about the instructors? We found that many are teaching larger sections, many are having to perform an increasing variety of nonteaching activities, and they want a text that has no gaps in coverage. They want a basic, but comprehensive, text that is teachable, contemporary, relevant, and presents marketing as a dynamic, interesting, and exciting discipline.

Thus our primary mission in *Marketing: Contemporary Concepts and Practices* is to convey the excitement of marketing and provide students with a basic understanding of fundamental marketing concepts and how they are applied in contemporary marketing practice. Some students will have little or no previous formal exposure to marketing other than through their roles as consumers. Others, as we said earlier, will be employed full- or part-time. This text should be relevant and useful to both groups. We make no assumptions regarding any prerequisite work experience or college courses.

This text presents concepts in adequate breadth to give a comprehensive overview of the marketing discipline. They also are presented in sufficient depth to develop and maintain the interest of students who have had some on-the-job exposure to marketing, whether in a business or nonbusiness organization. Numerous examples of real world marketing practices illustrate the application of the concepts.

Marketing is the process of managing effort, in a dynamic environment and in a socially responsible manner, to facilitate exchange relationships that match an organization's capabilities and resources with the wants of selected market targets. Although it views marketing as a process of managing effort, this is not a marketing management text. You will get a taste of marketing management and decision making, for example, from the chapters on selecting market targets and developing and managing marketing mixes. Matching an organiztion's capabilities and resources with the wants of selected market targets is a major task of marketing. All organizations have limited capabilities and resources which they must direct toward satisfying target groups' wants.

As we suggested earlier, the marketing process occurs in a dynamic environment whose pace of change has accelerated in recent years. This has been accompanied by an equally rapid change in marketing practice. You will encounter frequent references to this environment and see how it affects, and is affected, by marketing practices.

The issue of social responsibility is an important part of this change. More than ever before society is holding marketers accountable for their actions. Thus some marketing practices that may have been acceptable only a few years ago may be unacceptable today. Marketing is no longer a simple matter of stimulating demand without regard to customer and social welfare. This makes marketing decision making more complex and requires marketers to consider the social consequences of their decisions.

Because instructors want a text that will facilitate teaching, learning, and comprehension, we focused a great deal of effort on organizing the material in a logical and straightforward manner. The text is organized into eight sections. We introduce a basic model in Chapter 1 to link them together. Each section begins with a preview of the material to be covered in the related chapters.

Section One traces the evolution of marketing and presents an overview of the marketing process and its environment. Section Two focuses on the American consumer market, its buying decisions and behavior, and the industrial market, with its buying decisions and behavior. Section Three examines how a marketing organiztion matches its capabilities and resources with the wants of its market targets. The focus is on the analysis of market opportunity, the selection of market targets, and marketing research. Sections Four through Seven develop the concept of the marketing mix in detail. The product component is the central concern in Section Four, the distribution component is covered in Section Five, the promotion component is examined in Section Six, and the price component is analyzed in Section Seven. Section Eight focuses specifically on international marketing.

Each chapter opens with a set of objectives you should be able to accomplish after completing the chapter, and a list of the chapter's key concepts. These concepts are listed in the order of their appearance in the chapter and are highlighted in the margins where they are introduced into the discussion.

Following the list of key concepts is a brief attention-getter. Some are vignettes, some raise contemporary issues related to the chapter content, and some seek to stimulate thinking about how marketing affects our daily lives. Next is a short introduction to the chapter material. Each chapter includes numerous examples, tables, and figures to enrich discussion, and a summary outlines the chapter's main points and provides a brief look ahead to the next one. Each chapter ends with two types of questions. The review questions are a good tool for self-testing. They can be answered directly from material presented in the chapter. The discussion questions require more original input from you. Their purpose is to stimulate critical thinking, application, and discussion.

In addition to various supplements for the instructor, a *Study Guide* is available to reinforce text discussion for students. Many of the exercises permit self-testing.

We sincerely want to encourage both students and instructors to send us their comments regarding the text and its supplements. That type of feedback from you will help us in future editions to do a better job of satisfying your need for an up-to-date marketing text that is relevant, teachable, and learnable.

# Acknowledgements

We are grateful to the following reviewers for their thoughtful and helpful suggestions during the development of this text:

Beverlee Anderson
  University of Kansas—Lawrence
William Ash
  California State University—Long Beach
William N. Curtis
  University of Nebraska—Lincoln
Ralph DiPietro
  Montclair State College
Charles H. Dufton
  Northeastern University
Robert F. Dyer
  George Washington University
Thomas V. Greer
  University of Maryland
Jim L. Grimm
  Illinois State University
Roy R. Grundy
  College of DuPage
Franklin S. Houston
  Temple University
Howard T. Kubota
  San Bernardino Valley College
Ray McAlister
  North Texas State University
Suzanne McCall
  East Texas State University
Suzanne McWhorter
  North Texas State University
John R. Nevin
  University of Wisconsin—Madison
Stan Reid
  Syracuse University

Joseph T. Straub
  Valencia Community College
John A. Weber
  University of Notre Dame
Garvin F. Williams
  Bucks County Community College
Frederick Wiseman
  Northeastern University

We also owe special thanks to the following people at Allyn and Bacon, Inc.: Michael E. Meehan, managing editor; Wayne Froelich, series editor; Allen Workman, developmental editor; and Elaine Ober, production editor.

We are indebted to Pam Rockwell, our copyeditor, and Christine Lebednik, who helped us in securing permissions.

Finally, to our families, we owe special personal thanks for their patience, sacrifices, understanding, and encouragement.

We would also like to thank the following people who graciously offered suggestions by replying to questionnaires distributed by the Allyn and Bacon sales representatives. Their comments were gratefully received, carefully read, and implemented wherever possible.

John C. Hafer
  University of Nebraska—Omaha
William Branner
  Creighton College
Robert Atkins
  Ouachita Baptist University
Leonard Kreitz
  Rio Hondo College
Eugene Britt
  Grossmont College

Jerry DeHay
  East Texas State University
Ira Dolich
  University of Nebraska—Lincoln
William Knoke
  California State University, Los Angeles
Jean Lindahl
  University of South Dakota
H. R. Muller
  Salisbury State College
H. Jean Waldrop
  California State University, Los Angeles
Bernard Codner
  California State University, Los Angeles
Paul McElhenney
  California State University, Los Angeles
Don Altman
  Abilene Christian University

Robert Sutton
  University of Iowa
John C. Rogers
  Texas Christian University
Dick Hansen
  Southern Methodist University
Phillip McVey
  University of Nebraska—Lincoln
Philip Downs
  Florida State University
Gemmey Allen
  Mount View College
Larry Beck
  Richland Community College
Suzanne McCall
  East Texas State University
Billy Frederick
  Northeast Louisiana University

# Marketing:
## Contemporary Concepts and Practices

# Section I
# **Background**

The two chapters in Section I set the stage for our discussion of contemporary marketing. In Chapter 1 we will learn that marketing exists at two levels, the macro and the micro levels. All countries need a marketing system to resolve the basic problem of allocating their limited resources to satisfy the unlimited wants of society. A marketing system provides a way to organize production and consumption activities. This economy-wide perspective of marketing is called macro marketing. Micro marketing, on the other hand, focuses on the marketing effort of individual marketers—business firms, nonprofit organizations, and individuals.

Chapter 2 discusses the environmental setting within which the marketing process takes place. This environment includes economic, competitive, technological, sociocultural and ethical, and political and legal factors that basically are beyond the marketer's control. They are uncontrollable variables in the marketing environment.

# Chapter 1

# What Is Marketing?

**OBJECTIVES**

*After reading this chapter you should be able to*

1. distinguish between macro and micro marketing.

2. identify and give examples of the marketing functions and five types of utility.

3. contrast production and marketing orientations.

4. discuss marketing management's role in the company's mission.

5. interrelate the selection of the market target and the development of the marketing mix.

6. identify the elements of the marketing mix and the variables in the marketing environment.

**KEY CONCEPTS**

*Look for these terms as you read the chapter:*

Macro Marketing
Consumer Sovereignty
Micro Marketing
Social Marketing
Utility
Marketing Functions
Marketing
Consumerism
Marketing Concept
Production Orientation
Societal Marketing Concept
Company Mission
Marketing Management
Marketing Objectives
Marketing Strategy
Market Target
Market Offering
Marketing Mix
Environmental Variables

*Government-run stores in Russia experienced a major shortage of cosmetics in 1977 because Russian cosmetics plants met only half the production quota set for them by the government. A huge black market developed to help satisfy the demand for cosmetics. An enterprising Russian plumber decided to get into the cosmetics business. He ground different colors of children's chalk to make eyeshadow, made nail polish from furniture lacquer sprinkled with metal filings for sparkle, and made mascara from black ink and shoe polish. His prices were three times higher than the prices set by the government and he was arrested for profiteering.\**

*The plumber recognized the existence of an unsatisfied consumer want and tried to satisfy it in order to make a profit. He became a marketer on his own initiative. His behavior would have been perfectly legal in the United States. In our competitive system his prices would have been regulated by the marketplace, not the government. He was arrested, however, because the marketing system in the Soviet Union does not operate like ours. The Soviet government decides what products will be produced and the quantities that will be produced. In the United States consumers basically determine what will be produced through their buying decisions. Within very broad limits, marketers in the United States are free to try to satisfy consumer wants as consumers express their wants through their buying decisions.*

This chapter begins with a look at marketing on the macro level. A marketing system is a society's way of organizing its productive resources to satisfy society's objectives. Such systems are necessary in all economic systems whether they are free-enterprise, socialist, or communist systems, but they can be very different types.

The marketing system's objectives are set basically by the government in the Soviet Union. The political leaders determine the objectives and manage the system to achieve them. In the United States the marketing system's objectives are set basically by consumers, who decide how society's productive resources will be used through their buying decisions in the marketplace.

We will then begin to examine marketing on the micro level, or marketing from the organization's perspective. The ideas discussed are applicable to all individuals and organizations (profit and nonprofit) that seek to accomplish objectives. Micro marketing effort occurs within the macro marketing system.

Tracing the evolution of marketing as it has developed in the United States helps to place contemporary marketing into proper perspective. Marketing has undergone a great deal of change over the years—evolutionary, but perhaps also revolutionary change. The macro system impacts on micro marketing effort and macro-micro interests do overlap,

\*Source: "Black Market Cosmetics Big in Russia," *The Times-Picayune,* December 11, 1978, sec. 3, p. 6.

and sometimes conflict. Tradeoffs are inherent in achieving micro objectives within the framework of macro objectives. This will become clearer in our discussion of the societal marketing concept. We also will give a brief overview of how an organization manages its marketing effort through marketing management.

## MACRO MARKETING SYSTEMS

All economies need a macro marketing system to cope with the economic problem of satisfying unlimited human wants with limited resources.[1] **Macro marketing** is the process in an economic system that organizes productive resources to produce a flow of products that satisfies the system's objectives.

    Coping with the economic problem requires decisions about how an economy's productive resources will be used. Decisions must be made about what to produce, how to produce it, how much to produce, and where and how this output which includes both products and services will be distributed among people for consumption.[2] Societies have always faced this problem and still do. Three basic types of economic systems have evolved for coping with these decisions: (1) tradition-controlled systems, (2) consumer-controlled systems, and (3) state-controlled systems.

**macro marketing**

### Tradition-Controlled Systems

Tradition-controlled systems use long-established customs and environmental adaptations in dealing with the economic problem. Custom and age-old adaptations to desert conditions lead some Arabs to follow their herds in a nomadic way of life in preference to a sedentary, agricultural way of life. Over the centuries such herders have devised tried-and-true patterns of settling temporarily in small groups close to a source of water and pasture for their animals. Increasing productivity through raising crops would require new resource development and a great upheaval in cultural traditions. Similarly, small-scale subsistence farming still is traditional in some areas of Mexico. The small scale of these farms would make it uneconomical to try boosting productivity through the use of technology. Increasing the size of the typical farm would cause massive disruptions in traditional ways of life. Many small farmers would have to leave farming, but job opportunities elsewhere are lacking. People's demands in such traditional systems tend not to fluctuate and old patterns change very little.

### Consumer-Controlled Systems

Consumers' demands are the deciding factor in how the economy will cope with the economic problem in consumer-controlled systems. According to the concept of **consumer sovereignty**, consumers are at the center of the economic system. They are free to buy whatever products

**consumer sovereignty**

are available to meet their demands and to buy from whichever sellers they prefer. The producers' reaction to consumer demand determines how productive resources will be used. Thus the system ultimately is regulated by the balance of consumer decisions to buy or not buy the products offered for sale by all the profit-seeking business firms. Firms that do the best job of offering consumers what they want are the ones that make the most profit. In a purely capitalist system no one guarantees that a firm will be profitable. It must cater to customers' wants or it will go out of business. The system relies on the laws of supply and demand to keep it in self-regulating balance. Macro system objectives are the outgrowth of a basically unregulated market mechanism. They are not set by the government.

## State-Controlled Systems

Government decides how the economy will cope with the economic problem in state-controlled systems. When Cambodia fell to the communist Khmer Rouge in 1975, the new government ordered middle- and upper-class city dwellers to leave the cities to work on farms. This, in part, was the government's way of coping with the scarcity of food. In state-controlled systems government controls social and economic decision making through central planning. It owns the means of production, drafts a master plan of what it wants to accomplish, and attempts to manage the economy directly to reach the plan's goals. In other words, government tries to determine the economy's rate of growth, how productive resources will be used, what will be produced, and how the products produced will be divided among the people. Government regulates supply and demand in its effort to accomplish the macro system objectives which it has set. Individual producers and consumers have no voice in running the economy, except possibly through their voting privileges.

## Real-World Economic Systems

No real-world economic system, however, is purely tradition- , consumer- , or state-controlled. For example, the oil riches of the Arab nations have led some of them to modify many traditional values and customs, such as antimaterialism and noninvolvement with foreigners. There also are degrees of state control among communist nations. There is more government control in Albania than in Czechoslovakia. In recent years governments in some communist countries such as China and the Soviet Union have given consumers more voice in economic affairs and have permitted private ownership of some firms to ensure higher production of quality products. Consumers, nevertheless, play a much lesser role in economic decision making than they do in consumer-controlled systems.

But our economic system is not directed solely by consumers. Business firms, government, and consumers participate in economic decision making in our mixed system. For example, Chrysler Corporation was granted loan guarantees by the federal government several years ago to help keep the firm intact despite sagging sales of its new cars. Tradeoffs such as this reinforce the notion that ours is not a purely consumer-controlled marketing system. We will return to this issue of macro-micro objectives later in the chapter's discussion of the societal marketing concept.

## MICRO MARKETING

All marketers need an awareness and understanding of the macro marketing system. This helps them in planning and managing their individual marketing efforts within the larger macro system and in recognizing how the macro system impacts on their efforts. **Micro marketing** focuses on the marketing effort of a particular individual, business firm, or any other type of marketing organization. An understanding of micro marketing is important to all individuals and organizations that seek to accomplish goals, not only to business firms. Job applicants market themselves to job interviewers, and candidates for public office market themselves to voters. Churches, labor unions, and the American Red Cross are examples of nonprofit organizations that also market themselves. The Army, Navy, and Air Force also use micro marketing to attract recruits.

micro marketing

Thus marketing isn't just for business firms. In fact, social ideas and causes also are marketed. **"Social marketing** is the design, implementation, and control of programs seeking to increase the acceptability of a social idea, cause, or practice in a target group(s)."[3] Examples are safe driving, family planning, blood donation, church attendance, and support of higher education.[4]

social marketing

A state university markets its offerings to present and prospective students. It also markets itself to the state college board to increase its financial support, and to other groups such as state legislators (who determine how much money the state college board will receive for higher education) and corporate contributors. Although the costs and benefits may be reckoned somewhat differently for nonprofit organizations than for profit-seeking business firms, the underlying elements of marketing strategy still are comparable. Thus the main concern in this text is the marketing organization's effort to match its capabilities and resources with its present and potential customers' wants. The term *customers*, as used here, includes people who buy the organization's products, whether those products are cars, the idea of safe driving, or a political candidate.

### Creating Utility Within Macro and Micro Marketing Systems

Products that satisfy human wants have **utility.** *Utility* means usefulness. Production activity creates a product that is in a useable form in relation to a specific person's want at a particular point in time. Suppose you

utility

want a ten-pound bag of crushed ice to cool drinks in an ice chest. The manager of a local convenience store may be willing to give you free of charge ten pounds of water, but this will have little utility for you. On the other hand, the manager will want to be paid for the bag of ice and you will be willing to pay for it if you are hot and thirsty. Value has been added to the water by production activity—making it available in the form you desire, crushed ice. You will exchange some of your money for the store's crushed ice.

Look at Figure 1–1. On the first level are limited resources and unlimited wants. As we said earlier, a macro marketing system is created by a society to deal with the economic problem of satisfying unlimited human wants with limited resources.

But we cannot make resources satisfy wants unless someone makes it happen. Someone has to organize these resources for production activity. Furthermore, the people who perceive that the products produced will satisfy their wants must be able to get them. Thus, on the second level of Figure 1–1, we begin with the extraction of raw materials and agricultural production. These outputs are exchanged, for money, with people who will process, fabricate, and manufacture them into products that, in turn, are exchanged for money with resellers. In the end, the

**Figure 1–1.  The purpose of a macro marketing system**

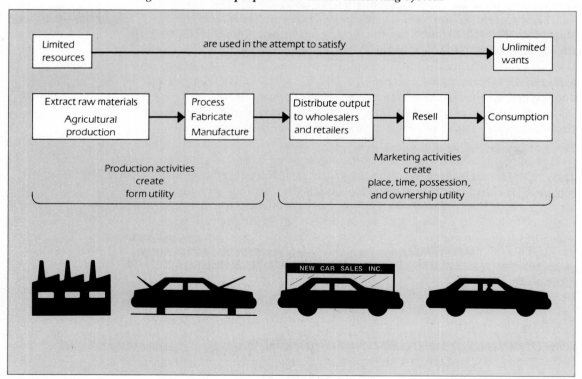

products are made available to consumers for consumption when they exchange money with resellers.

**The Exchange Process and Marketing Functions**

Suppose you are an early cavedweller who produces everything you consume. You are entirely self-sufficient and totally independent. Gradually, however, you leave your cave and form villages with other people. This creates an opportunity for trade, or exchange, that can be realized if the villagers practice specialization, or division of labor. If each person concentrates on producing what he or she can produce best, surpluses, exchange, and economic growth might result. In the process, however, you become dependent on the productive efforts of other specialists.

The division of labor results from the villagers' perceiving the opportunity to exchange. A person who has grain but no cattle, for example, might exchange grain with somebody else who has cattle but no grain. This possibility for exchange creates the opportunity for specialization, advances in productivity, surpluses, and economic growth. Exchange is a contributor to surpluses and economic growth, not a result of them. In our highly interdependent economy many thousands of production specialists exchange their products with thousands of others. Ford Motor Company, for example, exchanges money for plastics, steel, glass, paint, and products produced by thousands of other production specialists.

**Marketing functions** are necessary to create utility and facilitate exchange. We will discuss the marketing functions listed in Table 1–1 throughout the text. Although these functions cannot be eliminated, they can be shifted and shared among participants in a macro marketing system. The participants include producers, wholesalers, retailers, and consumers, as shown on the second level of Figure 1–1.

marketing functions

Consider the storage function. Campbell Soup Company may sell through a wholesaler to many retailers. Campbell does not need to store

***Table 1–1.*** *The marketing functions*

| Function | Nature |
|---|---|
| 1. Buying or leasing | 1. Defining needs, selecting sources of supply, testing products, and transferring title or use rights (leasing). |
| 2. Selling or leasing | 2. Locating buyers, stimulating demand, negotiating terms of sale or lease. |
| 3. Transportation | 3. Moving people to products or products to people. |
| 4. Storage | 4. Holding and protecting products to create time utility. |
| 5. Standardization | 5. Establishing grades to which products can be assigned. |
| 6. Grading | 6. Sorting products according to established standards. |
| 7. Financing | 7. Providing and managing money needed to get products to customers; possession utility. |
| 8. Risk taking | 8. Assuming, transferring, and controlling risk associated with marketing products. |
| 9. Market information | 9. Gathering, analyzing, and communicating data as a base for decision making. |

large quantities of soup at the factory because soup can be stored in the wholesaler's warehouse. The need for storage is not eliminated. The storage function, however, is shifted from the manufacturer to the wholesaler.

In Figure 1–1, we start out on level one with the economic problem and cope with it through the processes of specialization and exchange (level two). Production and marketing activities create utility, as shown on level three.

### How Marketing Functions Create Utility

As we said earlier, products that satisfy human wants have utility. We can distinguish five types of utility: (1) form, (2) place, (3) time, (4) possession, and (5) ownership. (See Figure 1–1, level three).

**Form Utility.** Production activity creates form utility, or a product that is in a useable form in relation to a specific person's want at a particular point in time. In the earlier example, the ice manufacturer created form utility by making ice from water. Car makers create form utility by combining raw materials through production activities to create a car that you can drive.

**Place and Time Utility.** Making products available where and when consumers want to buy them creates place and time utility. A finished car in an assembly plant in Detroit on April 15 has form utility, but it is not useful to a person in Chicago who wants to buy it on April 15 in a Chicago dealer's showroom.

**Possession and Ownership Utility.** Sales transactions create possession and ownership utilities. The dealer transfers possession of the car to the buyer. If it is bought on credit, transfer of ownership (title) may not occur until the buyer makes the final monthly payment. Marketing activities also create value by adding place, time, possession, and ownership utilities. The five types of utility are explained further in Figure 1–2.

Some people underestimate the importance of time, place, possession, and ownership utility. They admit the importance of form utility but do not fully appreciate the importance of the other four types.[5] "Society honors those who build better mousetraps but suspects those who market mousetraps better."[6] Actually, marketing is a sort of catalyst that makes the total utility of a product a reality for consumers.

As is evident in Figure 1–1, marketing activites are part of the macro marketing system. Marketers must understand where their particular activities fit into the macro system and how that system may impact on their respective marketing efforts. The next section focuses on the marketing process in the United States.

### Defining the Marketing Process

Prior to the early twentieth century, marketing was a branch of economics—distribution. Economics is a broad discipline that includes labor

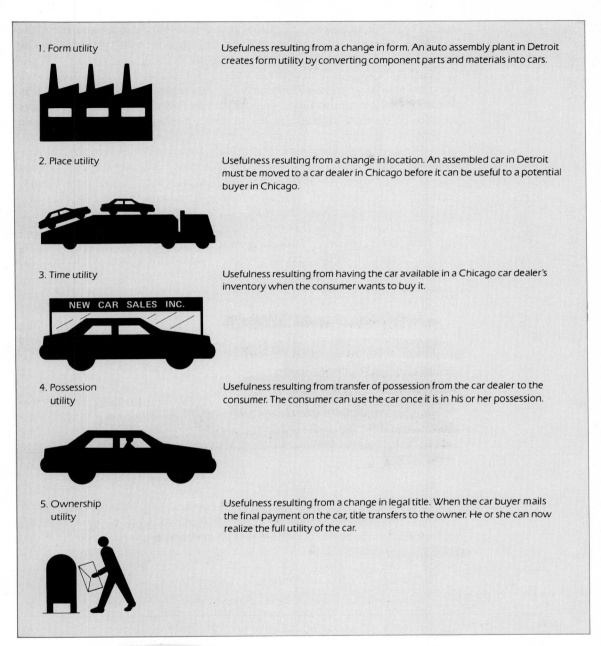

1. Form utility — Usefulness resulting from a change in form. An auto assembly plant in Detroit creates form utility by converting component parts and materials into cars.

2. Place utility — Usefulness resulting from a change in location. An assembled car in Detroit must be moved to a car dealer in Chicago before it can be useful to a potential buyer in Chicago.

3. Time utility — Usefulness resulting from having the car available in a Chicago car dealer's inventory when the consumer wants to buy it.

4. Possession utility — Usefulness resulting from transfer of possession from the car dealer to the consumer. The consumer can use the car once it is in his or her possession.

5. Ownership utility — Usefulness resulting from a change in legal title. When the car buyer mails the final payment on the car, title transfers to the owner. He or she can now realize the full utility of the car.

*Figure 1–2.* **The five types of utility**

economics, economic development, and public finance. Furthermore, many economists are concerned mainly with developing theory. Some of these theories make simplistic assumptions about some of the most important real-world activities that marketers must perform. This is not a criticism of theory.   But marketers are practitioners and the study of marketing can help us to understand and improve real-world marketing practices.

For example, some economic theorists assume that consumers have perfect knowledge about competitive products and that products will flow automatically from producers to consumers.   Marketers, however, know they must inform consumers about new products through advertising campaigns and personal selling efforts.   Marketers also know they must create and manage distribution channels to get products from producers to consumers.   Even the Coca-Cola Company cannot rely on "natural forces" to accomplish the marketing job for Coke.   The firm spends millions of dollars every year advertising Coke and manages a huge network of bottlers to distribute it.

As our economy became more complex, marketing became a separate and applied discipline.   Marketing courses started to appear at the college level in the early 1900s.   As an integrative discipline, marketing borrows concepts, theories, techniques, and practices from other disciplines, such as economics, sociology, anthropology, political science, psychology, and social psychology.

marketing     As this book defines it, **marketing**

is the process of managing effort
in a dynamic environment
in a socially responsible manner
to facilitate exchange relationships
which match an organization's capabilities and resources
with the wants of selected market targets (present and potential customers).

**Managing Effort.**   Managing effort refers to the performance of activities designed to facilitate exchange.   These activities might include conducting marketing research, studying consumer behavior, developing new products, evaluating advertising campaigns, selecting retailers, and motivating salespersons.   These and other marketing activities are discussed in the text.

**Operating Within a Dynamic Environment.**   Marketing occurs within an environmental setting that is subject to change.   Laws, administrative agency rulings, cultural values, ethical values, technology, and the level of economic activity are external variables over which the participants in an exchange relationship may have little, if any, control. These variables exist in the macro environment and impact on the marketer's marketing effort.   Thus, as we said earlier, marketers must understand the nature of the macro marketing system within which they operate.

**Behaving in a Socially Responsible Manner.**   The participants in an exchange relationship have responsibilities to groups other than themselves, such as society in general. Marketing is social, as well as economic, in nature. Again, micro marketing effort occurs within a macro marketing system and marketers must recognize the interdependence. We will return to this later in the chapter when we discuss the societal marketing concept.

**Participating in Exchange Relationships.** An exchange relationship requires that a potential buyer and a potential seller be prepared to interact for the purpose of exchange (trade, buy, lease). Each has something that may be valuable to the other, each is free to agree or disagree to exchange, and each is able to make available what he or she has to offer to the other party.[7]

An exchange relationship, however, does not require the participants to exchange. For example, an exchange relationship exists if a potential buyer and seller are negotiating the sale of a car. If they cannot agree on the price, exchange will not occur. There is no transaction between them—no trading of values. The potential buyer did not get the potential seller's car and the potential seller did not get any of the potential buyer's money, or anything else of value. The potential seller, however, did engage in marketing effort in trying to create a transaction by, for example, placing an ad in the newspaper, setting a minimum acceptable price, and so on. The marketing functions (see Table 1–1) must be performed if utility is to be created and exchange is to occur.

**Engaging in the Matching Process.** The organization directs its capabilities and resources to create products that match the wants of selected market targets. If this results in exchange, transactions will occur. The matching process involves the creation of utility.

## Why Study Marketing?

Marketing activities generate new investment in developing products to satisfy consumer wants. This leads to economic growth. On the average, if an American household spends $900 per month of its after-tax income on products, about $450 goes to cover the cost of marketing those products. Understanding the nature of these marketing activities may help you form your own conclusions about whether these costs are too high and, if so, how they might be reduced.

A profit-seeking business firm or a nonprofit organization must cater to customer or client or member wants or else it may not be as profitable or successful as it could be. Sales revenue is the ultimate source of a business firm's profit. Nonprofit organizations must market themselves to their contributors and other publics. Both types of organizations must understand marketing activities if they are to be effective. They also must understand where and how they fit into the macro marketing system.

Roughly one-third of the American labor force is engaged in performing a wide variety of such marketing activities as retailing, wholesaling, marketing research, packaging, and advertising. The study of marketing may suggest several career options to you.

**Table 1–2.** *Approaches to the study of marketing*

| *Approach* | *Reasoning* |
|---|---|
| 1. Commodity | The nature of marketing varies so much for different commodities that it must be studied from the perspective of individual commodities. Generalizations about the marketing process can be formulated by studying various commodities. |
| 2. Functional | Attention centers on classifying and studying the functions performed in transferring products from producer to consumer. (See Table 1–1.) |
| 3. Institutional | The institutions (wholesalers, retailers, etc.) involved in the marketing system are the basis for studying marketing. |
| 4. Managerial | Production, marketing, finance, and personnel management are basic functions of business firms. Each should be approached from a managerial, or decision-making, perspective. |
| 5. Systems | Marketing is a subsystem within the firm, which is, in turn, a subsystem of its industry. The industry is a subsystem of the socioeconomic system. Complex interrelationships exist among all systems and their component subsystems. Marketing should be studied from a systems perspective. |
| 6. Societal | Marketing is a social as well as an economic institution. It must serve the wants of society if it is to remain a viable institution. |

Finally, marketing activities often are controversial. Complaints about misleading advertisements, poor product quality, inadequate product safety, high prices, too much materialism, and lack of concern about ecology are directed primarily at marketing. We will explore these and other criticisms throughout the text to help us weigh the pros and cons of alternative ways of dealing with them.

Several approaches to the study of marketing are discussed in Table 1–2. In order to present a realistic and useful introduction to marketing, this text will borrow from the various approaches. We want to present our readers a well-balanced picture with enough breadth of coverage and depth of detail to understand the contemporary marketing process.[8]

## MARKETING'S EVOLUTION

Marketing in the United States has evolved through several rather distinct eras. These are depicted in Figure 1–3.

### The Subsistence Era

During the subsistence era America's pioneer families had to scratch a subsistence from the soil. Each family's major concern was to produce enough for survival because it could consume only what it had produced for itself. Each raised its own crops, built its own home, hunted and fished, and even made its own tools. Producer and consumer were the same.

## The Made-to-Order Era

The growth of small towns during the made-to-order era brought together people with different skills who could engage in exchange beyond the immediate family. Thus production and consumption became separate activities. Shoemakers, for example, could specialize in making shoes because they could buy other products from other production specialists, such as blacksmiths and wagon makers. Ordinarily, production was undertaken by artisans only on receipt of orders from customers (job order production). Customers told producers exactly what they wanted and producers offered them custom-tailored products. Production was more important than selling because the products were sold before they were produced.

## The Early Production-for-Market Era

During the early production-for-market era many producers began to realize that they lost valuable production time by delaying production activity until orders had been received from customers. Job order production, therefore, gradually began to be replaced by speculative production. Producers began making products in advance of customer orders. Producers had to speculate about which products would sell because products no longer were tailor-made to individual customer specifications. This was not a major problem, however, since producers and customers were located nearby. Nor was overproduction a problem because technology was crude and most businesses were small. Production, therefore, still remained more important than selling.

*Figure 1–3. The evolution of the marketing era*

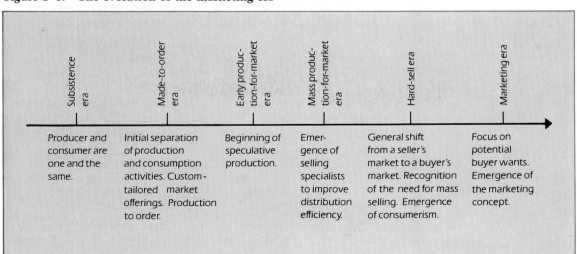

## The Mass Production-for-Market Era

Beginning in the second half of the nineteenth century the United States entered the mass production-for-market era. The Industrial Revolution was under way. The concept of interchangeable parts originated in this era.

The basic idea of mass production is that unit costs of production will decline as the volume of output increases. But declining unit cost of production is meaningless if the output cannot be sold. Producers, therefore, had to sell to a greater number of customers than was available in their local market areas. They began turning the selling job over to wholesalers and retailers, who became selling specialists for production specialists. These selling specialists found new customers for producers.

During this period, which lasted until the early twentieth century, the term *marketing* came into use. The emphasis was on improving the efficiency of the distribution process—getting products to customers more efficiently. The American Marketing Association's definition of marketing probably has its roots in this period: "the performance of business activities that direct the flow of goods and services from producer to consumer or user."[9]

## The Hard-Sell Era

Producer efforts to achieve lower unit costs of production led them to realize that production economies hinged on sales efficiency. The selling task could not be left entirely to wholesalers and retailers. Producers also had to assume some responsibility for selling their products. Mass selling was necessary to support mass production.

During the early part of this hard-sell era there was a shift in many industries from a seller's market (demand greater than supply) to a buyer's market (supply greater than demand) due in part to the economies of mass production. Maximizing sales volume became the main goal of producers, who began using persuasive advertising and hard-sell techniques to move their inventories. In many cases, marketers ignored customer wants and began using deceptive ads and questionable sales techniques to help sell their products. This resulted in the emergence of consumerism.

consumerism

**Consumerism** is a movement to strengthen the power of consumers relative to the power of manufacturers and sellers. Our first consumer movement occurred in the early 1900s. Upton Sinclair's book *The Jungle* (1906) exposed the filthy conditions in meat packing plants and stimulated consumer protest that led to passage in 1906 of the Pure Food and Drug Act and the Meat Inspection Act. This movement showed that the marketing system required some government regulation to protect consumers.

A second consumerist era began in the 1930s. Stuart Chase and F. J. Schlink's book, *Your Money's Worth* (1934), criticized hard-sell tactics, such as deceptive, misleading, and fraudulent advertising, and it helped secure passage of the Wheeler-Lea Act. This act gives a government agency, the Federal Trade Commission (FTC), power to prosecute firms that use deceptive ads and other deceptive sales practices.

Consumerism declined as the United States entered World War II. Consumer products were very scarce during the war because production lines were converted to military production. This meant the return of a seller's market (demand greater than supply). After the war, consumers were anxious to spend money on the consumer products that began appearing as we shifted from a war to a peacetime economy.[10]

## The Marketing Era

Many firms and industries once again faced a buyer's market during the middle of the twentieth century. Producers began to recognize the advantage of the close customer contact that had existed during the made-to-order era. But direct seller-buyer contact became less practical as firms grew larger, and producers had to research the market and study consumer behavior to learn about potential customers' wants.

Sellers focused on their need to move inventory during the hard-sell era. In the marketing era sellers began to focus on the potential buyer's wants by producing products that those buyers wanted.[11] Whereas selling focuses on the seller's needs, marketing focuses on the potential customer's wants. The marketing concept was born during this marketing era.

## THE MARKETING CONCEPT

The idea that a firm exists to serve its present and potential customers, a management philosophy that advocates customer orientation, is called the **marketing concept**.[12] Customers are the focal point for all decision making in the firm, and all functional areas (production, marketing, finance, engineering, etc.) are geared to providing customer satisfaction, thereby helping to ensure a satisfactory rate of return on the owners' investment. The marketing concept has replaced a production orientation in many firms.

marketing
concept

According to the systems view of management, a firm should operate as a unified system.[13] This view underlies the marketing concept. All departments and personnel in the firm should work to accomplish the goal of customer satisfaction at an acceptable rate of return on the owners' investment.

This systems view is essential to the successful implementation of the marketing concept. For example, a firm's engineering department may think its goal is to design engineering marvels. Chrysler's Airflow models of the 1930s, for example, were designed to minimize wind resistance. But many potential buyers thought the cars did not look right and they did not buy them. Similarly, the production department may think its only goal is to maximize manufacturing efficiency. In 1977 General Motors (GM) marketed some Oldsmobiles that were equipped with Chevrolet engines.   Although this may have eased some production problems, it cost GM millions of dollars to settle lawsuits by unhappy buyers of Oldsmobiles that had Chevrolet engines.

**production orientation**

For convenience we can refer to these nonmarketing orientations as a **production orientation.**   This orientation does not recognize that a firm is first and foremost in the business of satisfying present and potential customers.

Summing up, the marketing concept is a philosophy of management that advocates (1) present and potential customer orientation from the top to the bottom of the firm, (2) the systems view of management, and (3) earning a satisfactory rate of return on the owners' investment in the firm.

## Production vs. Marketing Orientation

Production comes first in production-oriented firms and marketing simply means selling products that are produced.   The focus is on the producer's need to move inventory. (See Figure 1–4.) Present and potential customers' wants come first in marketing-oriented firms.   These firms research the market to (1) learn what potential customers want, (2) identify profitable market segments (potential customer groups), and (3) tailor market offerings for these market segments.   We will discuss market segmentation in Chapter 8 and marketing research in Chapter 9.

Research of potential customer wants is the starting place in relating a firm to the market, or matching its resources and capabilities to potential customer requirements.   (See Figure 1–4.)   The underlying belief is that it is easier to market a product that potential customers really want than it is to make a product and then convince potential buyers that this product is what they want.   Although research does not guarantee success, the odds favor firms that try to learn what potential customers want before they produce products.

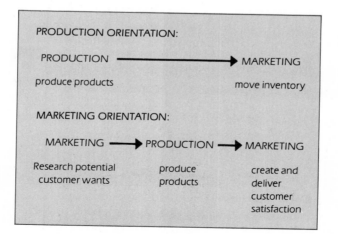

*Figure 1–4. Comparison of production and marketing orientation*

Budget Rent-A-Car Corporation's research showed that consumers who rent cars rank travel directions as their second highest need. As a result, the firm developed a program that gives its customers preprinted, clear-cut directions.[14] Conair Corporation's research showed that many consumers wanted to buy pistol-grip hairdryers. Before Conair's product was introduced on the market, only professional beauticians used pistol-grip hairdryers.

A custom tailor of men's suits still offers the same degree of customer orientation that existed in the made-to-order era. But most marketers now produce in anticipation of orders, often on a mass-production basis. Mass production, however, is not at odds with the marketing concept. Marketing-oriented, mass-production firms try to identify market segments composed of people who have highly similar characteristics and wants. These firms know they cannot offer a custom-tailored product for each customer. They also know that one product probably will not satisfy everybody. Instead, they lump together people whose wants are very similar, and if the resulting segment is large enough, a product can be mass produced to satisfy them. The potential customer, however, still comes first.

*"I don't care what the market research shows, I say consumers won't buy a self-propelled, battery-operated, microwave snow-melting machine."*

Source: *Marketing Molehills*, American Marketing Association.

Ford Motor Company can mass produce its various models because the market segment for each model is large enough. If Ford produced only one model many people would never be Ford customers. On the other hand, if Ford offered only custom-tailored cars it would have even fewer customers because the cars would be very expensive.

## Implementing the Marketing Concept

The marketing concept will accomplish nothing for a firm until it is put into practice. Among the incentives to do this are more intense competition for customers, the growing selectivity of buyers in making purchasing decisions, the potential for more government regulation of marketing activities and practices, and the need to develop customer loyalty and to realize the firm's profit goals.

The firm seeks to match market opportunity with marketing effort. It researches the market to identify unsatisfied wants that it can satisfy, at an acceptable profit, with its capabilities and resources. Firms that do the best job of offering customers what they want will profit most. (See Figure 1–5.)

The firm's chief executive officer (CEO) must understand the philosophy and get all company personnel committed to making it work by convincing them that the firm is in business to create satisfaction for its customers.[15] An information system helps the firm to know its customers' wants. But the more production oriented a firm is, the tougher the implementation effort. This is especially true when the firm man-

*Figure 1–5.* **The marketing task**

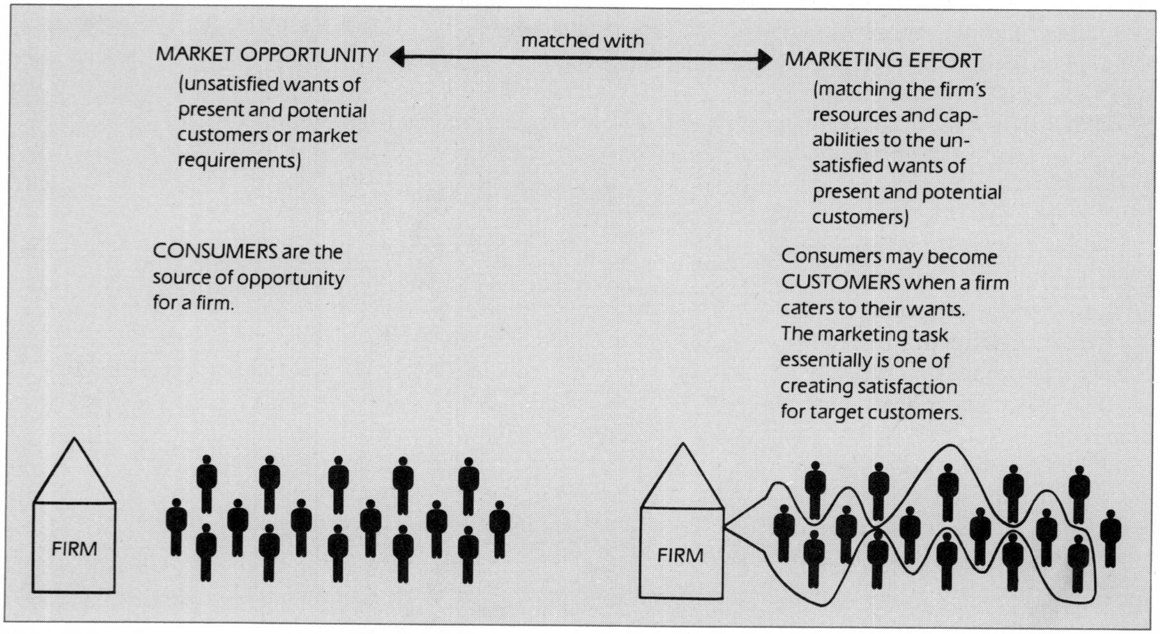

MARKET OPPORTUNITY
(unsatisfied wants of present and potential customers or market requirements)

matched with

MARKETING EFFORT
(matching the firm's resources and capabilities to the unsatisfied wants of present and potential customers)

CONSUMERS are the source of opportunity for a firm.

Consumers may become CUSTOMERS when a firm caters to their wants. The marketing task essentially is one of creating satisfaction for target customers.

FIRM

FIRM

ages to survive because the owners are willing to accept a lower rate of return on their investment and top management is unwilling to assume the risk of changing the firm's orientation. As long as the firm is earning acceptable profits, the CEO may be unwilling to risk change. Reductions in sales and/or profit sometimes are needed to bring about change.

On the other hand, the more a firm operates as a unified system, the better the chances of implementing the concept.[16] All personnel are working to create customer satisfaction in order to achieve profit.

## A New Marketing Concept?

Societies evaluate and regulate the marketing system differently. Marketing activities in some less-developed countries resemble those of the premarketing era in the United States. For example, products such as eyebrow pencils containing lead and baby bottles made with polyvinyl chloride are marketed in some less-developed countries although they are banned in the United States.

Various groups within a society also place different demands on the marketing system. Some Americans think the system's basic task is to stimulate the demand for products so our economy will grow. Some other groups want the system to help us enjoy a higher quality of life, for example, by reorienting our preferences for convenience foods like instant breakfasts, disposable products like paper diapers and wiping cloths, and conspicuous consumption—buying products like gas-guzzling cars mainly to impress other people with our wealth and good taste. These people expect marketers to consider society's well-being in their decision making. Tradeoffs are necessary between macro and micro objectives—between societal objectives and those of individual marketing organizations.

Some people, therefore, think the traditional marketing concept focuses too much on selected customer wants at the expense of societal well-being.[17] A beverage firm that packages cola in disposable aluminum pop-top cans may be satisfying its customers but is this in society's long-run best interests? Nonusers also bear the costs of cleaning up the litter that careless people create with throwaway cans. Cigarette manufacturers may be satisfying their customers but what about the rights of nonsmokers? Manufacturers of children's breakfast cereals often package the cereal sugar coated. Parents can prepare breakfast faster, which can be important when both work outside the home. But are these firms offering nutritious food that is in the long-run best interest of the consumers? What about using up so much aluminum foil, plastic wrap, and other materials to package cereal? What about advertising to young children?

As we said earlier, our macro marketing system basically is a consumer-controlled system. Thus marketers traditionally have assumed that individual consumers are the best judge of what is good for them. Otherwise, the question arises as to who is the best judge of the consumer's long-run welfare. Among people who raise the issue there is no generally acceptable answer. Some of them advocate significant change

*An ad advocating socially responsible behavior*

Source: Photo courtesy of The House of Seagram

in our macro marketing system, such as giving greater control to government in resource allocation decisions. Some others would prefer a lessening of government regulation and greater consumer control.

Societal marketing, however, requires marketers to make socially responsible decisions.[18] The **societal marketing concept** means that marketers have to strike a balance among (1) their customers' wants, (2) their customers' long-run best interests, (3) the society's long-run best interests, and (4) the firm's return-on-investment goal.[19]

**societal marketing concept**

This concept is even tougher to implement than the traditional marketing concept. However, the so-called "citizen consumer" has been emerging.[20] Such a consumer's buying behavior is not concerned only with his or her personal satisfaction. Because citizen consumers consider the rights of others in using the products they buy, they may make it easier for firms to implement the societal marketing concept. Thus after years of health warnings many people are against smoking and some restaurants require separate seating of smokers and nonsmokers.

As we have seen, marketing is a process that requires management. Marketing management plans, implements, and controls a firm's marketing effort.

## MARKETING MANAGEMENT

A firm's top management is responsible for formulating its mission—what it wants to become. This mission underlies all company planning. It is within the constraints set by the **company mission** that marketing planning occurs.[21] Three major variables affect the formulation of a firm's mission: (1) its resources and capabilities, (2) its environment, and (3) market requirements.

**company mission**

In formulating its mission statement top management states what the firm's line of business should be—how its resources and capabilities should be used to satisfy which market requirements. Paper Mate, a division of Gillette Company, at one time was in the business of marketing writing instruments. But when top management decided to buy out Liquid Paper Corporation, a maker of typewriter correction fluid and ribbons, its line of business was broadened beyond writing instruments. Holiday Inns, Inc., on the other hand, narrowed its scope when it sold its Continental Trailways subsidiary to focus its effort more specifically on the hospitality industry.

The decision to satisfy certain market requirements involves a commitment of resources to the effort. Many firms conduct company audits to analyze the strengths and weaknesses of their resources and capabilities. This helps them to build on their strengths and to avoid trying to satisfy market requirements which they lack the capability to satisfy. A company audit may indicate that some products are tying up more of the firm's resources than is justified by the rate of return on investment. General Motors sold its Frigidaire appliance business to White Consolidated Industries in 1979. GM's decision was prompted by the fact that the Frigidaire Division was contributing only a very small percentage to GM's revenues.

Every firm's resources and capabilities are limited. Two firms, however, may have the same kind and amount of resources but one may be able to develop more capability through better management. It can define its mission more broadly. Top management makes decisions about a firm's mission and also determines the part different departments (personnel, production, engineering, finance, and marketing) will play in carrying it out. Thus **marketing management's** role in a firm depends largely on whether top management is basically production or marketing oriented and how well this orientation permeates the firm.

marketing
management

In a production-oriented firm, production and finance are considered more important than marketing in carrying out the firm's mission. The top marketing executive, who may be just a sales manager, performs a service function for the firm by managing the salesforce. In a marketing-oriented firm, one executive is in charge of the firm's entire marketing effort—sales, advertising, marketing research, product design, etc. This marketing manager reports to the firm's CEO, and the advertising manager, the sales manager, and so on report to the marketing manager.

## The Task of Marketing Management

Management involves (1) planning (setting up a plan), (2) implementing (carrying out the plan), and (3) controlling (comparing actual results to plans).

Planning means setting goals, or standards of performance, and developing plans for reaching them. A plan is a blueprint that states what is to be accomplished and how it is to be accomplished.

Implementing means (1) organizing a structure that relates personnel

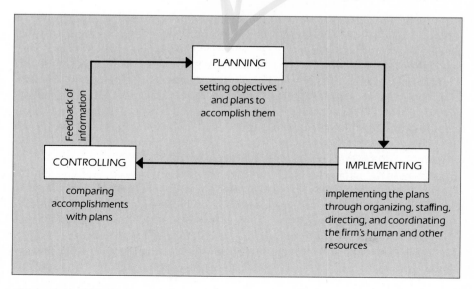

*Figure 1–6.*
*The management*
*job*

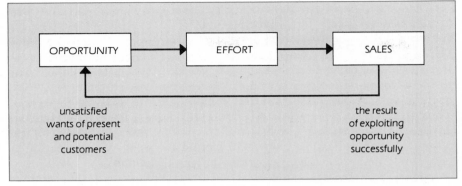

**Figure 1–7.**
**The management job in marketing: PLANNING, IMPLEMENTING, and CONTROLLING**

Diagram boxes: OPPORTUNITY → EFFORT → SALES

unsatisfied
wants of present
and potential
customers

the result
of exploiting
opportunity
successfully

and other resources to the activities needed to reach the planning goals, (2) staffing the firm with personnel, (3) directing their efforts to accomplish goals, and (4) coordinating their activities.

Controlling means regulating operations so the performance standards set by the plan are met. Figure 1–6 shows the interrelationships among these tasks.

Market opportunity (unsatisfied present and potential customer wants) results in sales; the firm achieves its marketing goals if marketing management can match that market opportunity with the proper marketing effort. Rent-A-Wreck, Lease-A-Lemon, and Ugly-Duckling-Rent-A-Car are three firms that recognized opportunity to lease and rent used cars to people who wanted to pay lower rates than those charged by firms that rent and lease new cars. Notice in Figure 1–7 that success in exploiting opportunity creates further opportunity.

### Marketing Planning

Marketing planning involves developing marketing objectives and strategies. Strategies are plans for accomplishing objectives. Thus although two firms may have the same marketing objective, they may use different strategies to reach that objective. Maytag and Whirlpool may both want to increase sales. Whirlpool's strategy includes producing appliances under the brand names of retailers such as Sears. Maytag sells only Maytag-branded appliances.

**Developing Marketing Objectives.** Marketing planning is based on clearly stated **marketing objectives** that fit within the framework of company-wide objectives. Marketing planning is handicapped by nonmarketing-oriented company-wide objectives. Marketing objectives should be: (1) clearly stated in writing, (2) specific, and (3) stated in terms of a specific time frame. People accountable for reaching objectives are more committed to them when they are written. A specific objective "to increase our market share by 20 percent during the next twelve months" is better than the general objective "to increase our profit by selling more."

marketing
objectives

Marketing objectives, however, may be stated vaguely when it is hard to measure how well they are being met. For example, advertising objectives may not be quantified because it is hard to measure advertising results. On the other hand, electronic data processing (EDP) has made it easier and cheaper to gather and process large amounts of data. The result is that marketers sometimes overemphasize the quantitative aspects in setting objectives and underemphasize the qualitative aspects. Thus although an advertising objective "to increase sales by 10 percent during the coming year" lends itself to measurement, it is just as important that the ad campaign present factual and relevant information to help consumers make more informed buying decisions.

marketing<br>strategy

**Developing Marketing Strategy.** In developing **marketing strategy** the marketing manager (1) selects the market target and (2) develops the marketing mix. These are not independent tasks. They are interrelated and interdependent.

Selecting a market target without considering the firm's resources and capabilities to satisfy it is a mistake. Reader's Digest Association's basic strength is repackaging the creativity of others. The company failed in its attempt to market a woman's magazine in Spain.[22] Developing a marketing mix that makes good use of the firm's resources and capabilities but does not satisfy the market target also is a mistake. Green Giant Company's Oven Crock baked beans failed to satisfy its market target. The firm's research showed that people who like heavily

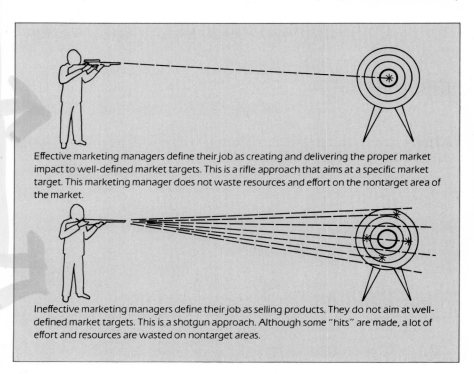

Effective marketing managers define their job as creating and delivering the proper market impact to well-defined market targets. This is a rifle approach that aims at a specific market target. This marketing manager does not waste resources and effort on the nontarget area of the market.

Ineffective marketing managers define their job as selling products. They do not aim at well-defined market targets. This is a shotgun approach. Although some "hits" are made, a lot of effort and resources are wasted on nontarget areas.

*Figure 1–8.*
*The market target*

flavored baked beans prefer to add their own spices to regular canned baked beans.   Oven Crock baked beans came presweetened in the can.[23]

### Selecting the Market Target

A marketing-oriented firm is in business to create satisfaction for its present and potential customers, its **market target.**  This target is made up of people whose characteristics and wants are very similar.   The firm's resources and capabilities are directed to satisfying its market target. (See Figure 1–8.)   We will discuss the consumer market in the United States in Chapter 3 and the specifics of market-target selection in Chapter 8.   The role of marketing research in the selection process is discussed in Chapter 9.

    A manufacturer of kitchen matches may define its target very broadly, while a marketer of diamond and gold cigarette lighters may define its target very narrowly.   Practically every household buys matches but only a small percentage of them is likely to buy jeweled cigarette lighters.

*market target*

### Developing the Marketing Mix

The **market offering** is what a firm creates to satisfy target customer wants.   It is the overall result of the combination of elements in the marketing mix: (1) product, (2) place, (3) promotion, and (4) price.

    The "4 Ps" (the elements of the **marketing mix** or the controllable variables) are mixed to create a blend that satisfies target-customer wants and helps the firm to achieve its marketing objectives in a socially responsible manner.[24]   These 4 Ps can be blended in many ways but decisions on all elements are made at the same time.   (See Figure 1–9.)

*market offering*

*marketing mix*

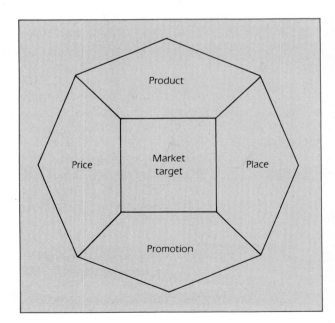

**Figure 1–9.   The marketing mix**
*A well-blended marketing mix means the right product is in the right place at the right time at the right price and present and potential customers know about it. The marketing manager mixes the ingredients of the marketing mix to develop a customer-satisfying blend.*

A watch manufacturer like Rolex that is trying to serve a market target of quality-conscious buyers would produce a high-quality prestige watch. But suppose ads for the watch feature low price and easy availability in supermarkets and variety stores. The elements in this marketing mix are not blended properly because ads for prestige products do not stress low price nor are the products sold in supermarkets and variety stores.

**The Product Element.** A product can be a physical item (a car), a service (car wash), a combination of them (a new car and dealer preparation), or an idea or a cause (safe driving). Although the activities involved in producing product items are production activities, marketing activities, such as the study of consumer behavior, influence what products a firm will make and their design. Other marketing-related product decisions include product warranties, service policies, packaging, branding, and new product development. The "total product" is a marketer's primary vehicle for delivering customer satisfactions. It is much more than the physical product. Consider cosmetics purchased by men and women. On the average only eight cents of the sales revenues cosmetics manufacturers receive is needed to pay for the ingredients.[25] Few people would argue that a person who buys cosmetics is buying only the ingredients.

The manager of a McDonald's restaurant in the Southwest had an in-depth understanding of the total product. The outlet was near a military base that forbade GIs to enter public places in their fatigues. The manager, therefore, opened a drive-through window to serve them. Women in curlers and housecoats also could buy Big Macs without having to enter the restaurant.[26] Drive-through windows soon were added to countless other fast-food restaurants in the area.

**The Place Element.** The place element involves distribution—creating time and place utility by having the product available when and where target customers want it. Public libraries use bookmobiles to increase the distribution of their product. Sears was the first retailer to sell life insurance in retail stores. For manufacturers, distribution may involve selecting wholesalers and retailers to resell the product. Physically moving the products toward the customer also involves transportation and warehousing decisions.

Most toy makers distribute their products through toy shops and department stores. But R. Dakin and Company distributes 60 percent of its output of stuffed toys through a variety of outlets in which it faces less competition from other toy makers. These outlets include airport and hospital gift shops, restaurants, amusement parks, stationery shops, drugstores, and banks.[27]

**The Promotion Element.** Promotion involves informing, persuading, and/or reminding target customers about the organization and its products and/or services. The promotional mix includes advertising, personal selling, sales promotion, publicity, and public relations.

The Lung Association uses TV ads to inform and remind people about the dangers of smoking—"It's a matter of life and breath"—and to persuade them to stop smoking. Toro Company used to be known mainly for its lawnmowers. Heavy advertising of the firm's name has helped it to become better known by consumers and has aided Toro's introduction of other products, such as snow throwers and garden hoses that wind up automatically.

**The Price Element.** The price element involves setting a basic price for the product and policies concerning trade-in allowances, discounts, etc. Since many people associate high prices with high quality, and low prices with low quality, a firm's pricing decisions can affect a product's image. Puritan Fashions Corporation traditionally was a maker of low-priced apparel. In the late 1970s the firm introduced jeans bearing the label of fashion designer Calvin Klein. The designer jeans brought a much higher price and Puritan started phasing out its low-priced jeans.

Using price to gain a competitive edge over rival products can set off

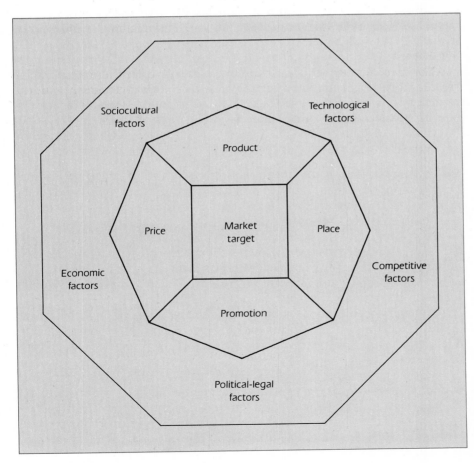

*Figure 1–10.*
*The marketing mix and the marketing environment*

fierce price competition. The Gillette Company began marketing pocket calculators in 1974 and digital watches in 1976 but dropped both products largely because of stiff competition that drove prices way down. Prices must always be set to provide a profit to the firm.

### The Uncontrollable Variables

environmental variables

As we said earlier, every marketing organization operates within a macro marketing system. No firm exists in a vacuum. The second major set of variables the marketing manager faces are the uncontrollable, or **environmental variables,** which include factors in the (1) economic, (2) competitive, (3) technological, (4) sociocultural and ethical, and (5) political-legal environment.

For example, firms in the fast-food industry in recent years have had to contend with environmental realities that include rising construction costs, beef prices, interest rates, and the minimum wage. The high cost of fuel has hurt firms like Winnebago and other marketers of recreational vehicles. Some firms have been unable to cope and have gone out of business. Changes in American cultural values probably were a factor in the decision of Holiday Inns, Inc. and Ramada Inns, Inc. to open hotel casinos.

Just as the controllable variables are not always totally controllable, neither are the uncontrollable variables always totally uncontrollable. For example, when proposed new laws will limit management's ability to make decisions, firms and their trade associations often lobby against passage of these laws. (See Figure 1–10.)

## SUMMARY AND LOOK AHEAD

All economies need a macro marketing system to organize productive resources and produce a flow of products that satisfies the system's objectives. The consumer is at the center of the system in consumer-controlled systems. Our system basically is consumer controlled.

Production activities create form utility and marketing activities create place, time, possession, and ownership utilities. Utility means usefulness. Creating utility and facilitating exchange require the performance of marketing functions that can be shifted and shared among the participants in the system, but they cannot be eliminated.

Micro marketing focuses on the marketing effort of a particular individual, business firm, or any other type of marketing organization. Social marketing is concerned with the marketing of social ideas, causes, or practices.

Marketing can be defined as the process of managing effort, in a dynamic environment, in a socially responsible manner, to facilitate exchange relationships which match an organization's capabilities and resources with the wants of selected market targets. In this book we will borrow from the commodity, functional, institutional, managerial, systems, and societal approaches to the study of marketing and also borrow concepts and techniques from other disciplines, such as economics and psychology.

The marketing concept has evolved through several eras. During the made-to-order era many products were made to individual customer specifications. But mass-production technology replaced job-order production with speculative production, and some production-oriented firms forgot that they were in the business of creating customer satisfaction. The marketing concept was born during the marketing era toward the middle of the twentieth century. It focuses on the need to provide customer satisfaction at a satisfactory profit.

Some people now question whether the traditional marketing concept is still valid. They prefer the societal marketing concept, which requires a firm to strike a balance among (1) their customers' wants, (2) their customers' long-run best interests, (3) the society's long-run best interests, and (4) the firm's return-on-investment goal.

Marketing management is accountable for developing marketing objectives and marketing strategy. These objectives should be clearly stated in writing, specific, and stated in terms of a specific time frame. Strategy development involves selecting the market target and developing the marketing mix. The market target is the group of present and potential customers to whom a firm directs its marketing effort. The marketing mix is the blend of the product, place, promotion, and price variables.

Marketing effort occurs in a dynamic environment. The uncontrollable variables include economic, competitive, technological, sociocultural and ethical, and political and legal factors. This environment is the subject of our next chapter.

## REVIEW QUESTIONS

1. What is macro marketing?

2. Do all economies need a macro marketing system? Explain.

3. Contrast: (a) tradition-controlled economic systems, (b) consumer-controlled economic systems, and (c) state-controlled economic systems.

4. What is consumer sovereignty?

5. Identify and discuss the five types of utility.

6. Identify and discuss four marketing functions. Can they be eliminated? Why or why not? Can they create utility? Explain.

7. What is micro marketing?

8. Define social marketing.

9. Is marketing an integrative discipline? Explain.

10. State the definition of marketing that is used in the text.

11. Contrast the commodity and the functional approaches to the study of marketing.

12. Identify and discuss the "eras" that preceded the marketing era.

13. What is consumerism?

14. What is the marketing concept?

15. Give an example of production orientation.

16. How does the societal marketing concept differ from the traditional marketing concept?

17. Identify and discuss the three major variables that affect the formulation of a firm's mission.

18. Should a marketing manager consider the

selection of the market target and the development of the marketing mix to be independent of each other? Why or why not?

**19.** What is a market target?

## DISCUSSION QUESTIONS

**1.** How do marketing activities add value to products that have only form utility?

**2.** Is it practical for churches and candidates for public office to think of themselves as marketers?

**3.** Do consumers have an obligation to practice socially responsible consumption?

**20.** Identify and discuss the elements in the marketing mix.

**21.** Identify the uncontrollable variables in the marketing environment.

**4.** Can consumers do anything to reduce the cost of marketing?

**5.** What market offering are you receiving when you pay your college tuition?

**6.** What sort of utilities are created by McDonald's restaurants?

## NOTES

1. See Reed Moyer, *Macro Marketing: A Social Perspective* (New York: John Wiley & Sons, Inc., 1972); John F. Grashof and Alan P. Kelman, *Introduction to Macro-Marketing* (Columbus, Ohio: Grid, Inc., 1973); Bruce Gunn, "The Macro-Marketing System—An Analog Model," *Marquette Business Review*, Spring, 1976, pp. 1–11; and Robert Bartels and Roger L. Jenkins, "Macromarketing," *Journal of Marketing*, October, 1977, pp. 17–20

2. We usually think of physical objects like washing machines and a package of corn flakes as products while we think of intangible things like haircuts and dental work as services. Throughout the text the term *product* will be used in place of product and/or service. The differences between physical products and intangible services are discussed in Chapter 10.

3. Philip Kotler, *Marketing Mangement: Analysis, Planning, and Control*, 3d ed. (Englewood Cliffs, N.J.: Prentice-Hall, Inc., 1976), p. 495.

4. See Philip Kotler and Gerald Zaltman, "Social Marketing: An Approach to Planned Social Change," *Journal of Marketing*, July, 1971, pp. 3–12; William A. Mindak and H. Malcolm Bybee, "Marketing's Application to Fund Raising," *Journal of Marketing*, July, 1971, pp. 13–18; Gerald Zaltman and Ilan Vertinsky, "Health Service Marketing: A Suggested Model," *Journal of Marketing*, July, 1971, pp. 19–27; Adel I. El-Ansary and Oscar E. Kramer, Jr., "Social Marketing: The Family Planning Experience," *Journal of Marketing*, July, 1973, pp. 1–7; David J. Luck, "Social Marketing: Confusion Compounded," *Journal of Marketing*, October, 1974, pp. 70–72; Stephen W. Brown, George D. Downing, and William V. Stephenson, "Strategies for Marketing a Community," *Arizona Business*, April, 1976, pp. 3–8; Franklin S. Houston and Richard E. Homans, "Public Agency Marketing: Pitfalls and Problems," *MSU Business Topics*, Summer, 1977, pp. 36–40; Donald F. Dixon, "The Poverty of Social Marketing," *MSU Business Topics*, Summer, 1978, pp. 50–56; Thomas J. C. Raymond and Stephen A. Greyser, "The Business of Managing the Arts," *Harvard Business Review*,

July–August, 1978, pp. 123–132; Stephen W. Brown and Bruce J. Walker, "University Marketing Can Begin with Departments of Marketing," *Akron Business and Economic Review*, Fall, 1978, pp. 20–23; Philip Kotler, "Strategies for Introducing Marketing into Nonprofit Organizations," *Journal of Marketing*, January, 1979, pp. 37–44; Gene R. Laczniak, Robert F. Lusch, and Patrick E. Murphy, "Social Marketing: Its Ethical Dimensions," *Journal of Marketing*, Spring, 1979, pp. 29–36; Robert F. Lusch, Gene R. Laczniak, and Patrick E. Murphy, "The 'Ethics of Social Ideas' versus the 'Ethics of Marketing Social Ideas,'" *Journal of Consumer Affairs*, Summer, 1980, pp. 156–164; and Karen F. A. Fox and Philip Kotler, "The Marketing of Social Causes: The First 10 Years," *Journal of Marketing*, Fall, 1980, pp. 24–33.

5. See Donald F. Dixon, "Prejudice v. Marketing? An Examination of Some Historical Sources," *Akron Business & Economic Review*, Fall, 1979, pp. 37–42.

6. Robert L. Steiner, "The Prejudice against Marketing," *Journal of Marketing*, July, 1976, p. 2.

7. For discussion of exchange as a central concept in marketing, see Richard P. Bagozzi, "Marketing as Exchange," *Journal of Marketing*, October, 1975, pp. 32–39. Also see Donald P. Robin, "A Useful Scope for Marketing," *Journal of the Academy of Marketing Science*, Summer, 1978, pp. 228–238.

8. For discussion of the integration of the functional and systems approaches, see Richard J. Lewis and Leo G. Erickson, "Marketing Functions and Marketing Systems: A Synthesis," *Journal of Marketing*, July, 1969, pp. 10–14.

9. Committee on Definitions, *Marketing Definitions: A Glossary of Marketing Terms* (Chicago: American Marketing Association, 1960), p. 15.

10. We will discuss modern consumerism in Chapter 2.

11. See Philip Kotler, "From Sales Obsession to Marketing Effectiveness," *Harvard Business Review*, November–December, 1977, pp. 67–75.

12. See Fred J. Borch, "The Marketing Philosophy

as a Way of Business Life," *The Marketing Concept: Its Meaning to Mangement* (New York: American Management Association, Marketing Series, No. 99, 1957), pp. 3–5; Richard T. Hise, "Have Manufacturing Firms Adopted the Marketing Concept?" *Journal of Marketing*, July, 1965, pp. 9–12; Richard R. Weeks and William J. Marks, "The Marketing Concept in Historical Perspective," *Business and Society*, Spring, 1969, pp. 24–32; Hiram C. Barksdale and Bill Darden, "Marketers' Attitudes toward the Marketing Concept," *Journal of Marketing*, October, 1971, pp. 28–36; Carlton P. McNamara, "The Present Status of the Marketing Concept," *Journal of Marketing*, January, 1972, pp. 50–57; H. Robert Dodge, "The Marketing Concept—Philosophy or Operation?" *Mid-South Quarterly Business Review*, April, 1973, pp. 8–11; and Hiram C. Barksdale, William J. Kelley, and Ian MacFarlane, "The Marketing Concept in the U.S. and the U.S.S.R.: An Historical Analysis," *Journal of the Academy of Marketing Science*, Fall, 1978, pp. 258–277.

13.  See Lee Adler, "Systems Approach to Marketing," *Harvard Business Review*, May–June, 1967, pp. 105–118.

14.  "Budget 'Attacks' Hertz with Military Marketing Strategy," *Marketing News*, January 25, 1980, p. 8.

15.  See Robert J. Keith, "The Marketing Revolution," *Journal of Marketing*, January, 1960, pp. 35–38.

16.  See Leonard L. Berry, "The Marketing Concept: Some Preach It; Others Practice It," *Arizona Business Bulletin*, April, 1969, pp. 94–102; Dennis F. Healy, "What Next? Is the Marketing Orientation the Next Step in the Course of Organizational Evolution?" *Marquette Business Review*, Summer, 1975, pp. 98–104; and Robert W. Stampfl, "Structural Constraints, Consumerism, and the Marketing Concept," *MSU Business Topics*, Spring, 1978, pp. 5–16.

17.  See Martin L. Bell and C. William Emory, "The Faltering Marketing Concept," *Journal of Marketing*, October, 1971, pp. 37–45.

18.  See Laurence P. Feldman, "Societal Adaptation: A New Challenge for Marketing," *Journal of Marketing*, July, 1971, pp. 54–60, and Adel I. El-Ansary, "Societal Marketing: A Strategic View of the Marketing Mix in the 1970s," *Journal of the Academy of Marketing Science*, Fall, 1974, pp. 553–556.

19.  The following articles provide insight into the controversy surrounding the scope of marketing and the remarketing concept: Philip Kotler and Sidney J. Levy, "Broadening the Concept of Marketing," *Journal of Marketing*, January, 1969, pp. 10–15; William Lazer, "Marketing's Changing Social Relationships," *Journal of Marketing*, January, 1969, pp. 3–9; David J. Luck, "Broadening the Concept of Marketing—Too Far," and Philip Kotler and Sidney J. Levy, "A New Form of Marketing Myopia: Rejoinder to Professor Luck," *Journal of Marketing*, July, 1969, pp. 53–57; Sidney J. Levy and Philip Kotler, "Beyond Marketing: The Furthering Concept," *California Management Review*, Winter, 1969, pp. 67–73; Robert J. Lavidge, "The Growing Responsibilities of Marketing," *Journal of Marketing*, January,

1970, pp. 25–28; Leslie M. Dawson, "Marketing Science in the Age of Aquarius," *Journal of Marketing*, July, 1971, pp. 66–72; Philip Kotler, "A Generic Concept of Marketing," *Journal of Marketing*, April, 1972, pp. 46–54; Philip Kotler, "Defining the Limits of Marketing," *1972 Fall Conference Proceedings* (Chicago: American Marketing Association, 1973), pp. 48–56; Ben M. Enis, "Deepening the Concept of Marketing," *Journal of Marketing*, October, 1973, pp. 57–62; Adel I. El-Ansary, "Towards a Definition of Social and Societal Marketing," *Journal of the Academy of Marketing Science*, Spring, 1974, pp. 316–321; A. B. Blankenship and John H. Holmes, "Will Shortages Bankrupt the Marketing Concept?" *MSU Business Topics*, Spring, 1974, pp. 13–18; F. Kelly Shuptrine and Frank A. Osmanski, "Marketing's Changing Role: Expanding or Contracting?" *Journal of Marketing*, April, 1975, pp. 58–66; Richard M. Bessom, "New Challenges for Marketing," *Arizona Business*, November, 1975, pp. 11–17; Shelby D. Hunt, "The Nature and Scope of Marketing," *Journal of Marketing*, July, 1976, pp. 17–28; Johan Arndt, "How Broad Should the Marketing Concept Be?" *Journal of Marketing*, January, 1978, pp. 101–103.

20.  See Thomas C. Kinnear, James R. Taylor, and Sadrudin A. Ahmed, "Ecologically Concerned Consumers: Who Are They?" *Journal of Marketing*, April, 1974, pp. 20–24; Frederick E. Webster, Jr., "Determining the Characteristics of the Socially Conscious Consumer," *Journal of Consumer Research*, December, 1975, pp. 188–196; Robert N. Mayer, "The Socially Conscious Consumer—Another Look at the Data," *Journal of Consumer Research*, September, 1976, pp. 113–115; and Stephen W. Brown, Zohrab S. Denurdjian, and Sandra E. McKay, "The Consumer in an Era of Shortages," *MSU Business Topics*, Spring, 1977, pp. 49–53.

21.  For an interesting perspective on the company mission, see Theodore Levitt, "Marketing Myopia," *Harvard Business Review*, September–October, 1975, pp. 26–39.

22.  "Reader's Digest: Modernizing the Beat of a Different Drummer," *Business Week*, March 5, 1979, p. 98.

23.  "There's No Way to Tell If a New Food Product Will Please the Public," *Wall Street Journal*, February 26, 1980, p. 21.

24.  See Neil H. Borden, "The Concept of the Marketing Mix," *Journal of Advertising Research*, June, 1964, pp. 2–7; and Harry A. Lipson and Fred D. Reynolds, "The Concept of the Marketing Mix: Its Development, Uses, and Applications," *MSU Business Topics*, Winter, 1970, pp. 73–80.   The term *4Ps* was coined by E. Jerome McCarthy; see E. Jerome McCarthy, *Basic Marketing*, 6th ed. (Homewood, Ill.: Richard D. Irwin, Inc., 1978).

25.  "Cosmetics: Kiss & Sell," *Time*, December 11, 1978, p. 94.

26.  "Still the Champion," *Time*, April 25, 1977, p. 77.

27.  "R. Dakin: Marketing Old-Style Toys through Offbeat Outlets," *Business Week*, December 24, 1979, p. 94.

# Chapter 2

# The Marketing Environment

**OBJECTIVES**

*After reading this chapter you should be able to*

1. identify and discuss the stages of the business cycle.

2. identify and discuss four basic types of market structure.

3. discuss technology from society's and the marketer's perspective.

4. compare the traditional and the professional-managerial business ethics.

5. identify and discuss important federal anti-trust laws and their significance for marketers.

**KEY CONCEPTS**

*Look for these terms as you read the chapter:*

Business Cycle
Demarketing
Pure Competition
Monopolistic Competition
Oligopoly
Nonprice Competition
Pure Monopoly
Differential Advantage
Market Niche
Innovation
Traditional Business Ethic
Professional-Managerial Ethic
Antitrust Laws
Exclusive Dealing Contract
Tying Contract
Vertical Territorial Restriction
Horizontal Territorial Restriction
Price Discrimination
Brokerage Allowance
Promotional Allowance
Unfair Trade Practices Acts

*Major airlines begin offering numerous types of discount fares as the Civil Aeronautics Board (CAB) moves to deregulate the airlines.*

*Ford and General Motors announce plant closings and layoffs as sales fall and inventories rise because of the recession.*

*IBM and Exxon plan to compete with each other in the market for the high-technology office of the future.*

*Credit card companies ask consumers to use their credit cards only for emergencies.*

*Price-fixing scheme results in suits totaling millions of dollars.*

*The above could have been captions for newspaper articles during recent years. They all deal with elements in the marketing environment. Although factors in this environment are beyond the marketer's control, they do affect decision making.*

As we have seen in Chapter 1, marketing occurs within a dynamic environment. Marketing managers must understand this environment to develop effective marketing strategies.

This chapter discusses the elements in the marketing environment: the economic, competitive, technological, sociocultural and ethical, and political and legal factors. Although we will discuss them one at a time, these factors are in dynamic interaction in the real world. They are interrelated. Let's begin with the economic environment.

## THE ECONOMIC ENVIRONMENT

Although the overall economic environment at any given time is beyond the firm's control, it is a major factor in planning marketing strategy.

### The Business Cycle

The level of business activity in most countries fluctuates over time. These changes are called the **business cycle.** They occur in four stages: (1) prosperity (boom), (2) recession (slowdown), (3) depression (bust), and (4) recovery (upswing). (See Figure 2–1.) This happens because of variations in the overall supply of and demand for products, the ability and willingness of consumers to buy products and of businesses to invest in new plants and equipment, the volume of consumer spending, employment levels, interest rates, and government spending and tax policies.

business cycle

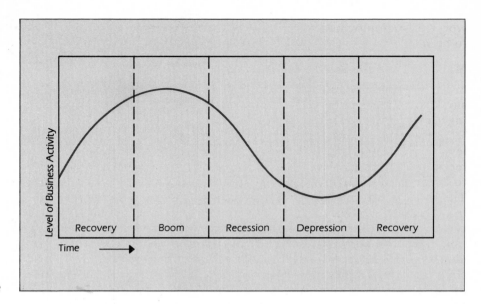

*Figure 2–1.*
*The business cycle*

The demand for most products is strong during prosperity. Consumers are in a buying mood because they feel secure in their jobs and have confidence in the future. Marketers are introducing new products and expanding advertising. Government policies also seem favorable to continued expansion of the economy.

No boom is permanent, however, and there are many factors that can turn a boom into a recession. Extreme optimism among consumers and marketers during the boom may lead some marketers to oversupply the market. Inventories build up and current production is cut back, resulting in rising unemployment, declining buying power, and reduced consumer and business spending. Consumer spending patterns also change. Some consumers may eat out less in order to stretch their dollars, especially when the recession is accompanied by rapidly rising prices for the products consumers buy (inflation). Some also postpone buying durable products like furniture and cars because they do not want to overextend themselves when the future is so uncertain.

A very deep and long-lasting recession, such as that during the 1930s, is called a depression. Many firms go out of business, unemployment is very high, consumer buying power is way down, new business investment dries up, and extreme pessimism exists among consumers and marketers. Consumers are not buying cars and car makers are not buying steel.

A recession (or depression) can turn into a recovery for any of a number of reasons. Government, for example, can engage in heavy deficit spending to create jobs for unemployed workers, which leads to increased consumer buying and declining inventories. Some firms rehire laid-off workers, unemployment begins falling, and consumer confidence starts to build.

### Marketing and the Economic Environment

In recent years marketers, at times, have faced problems related to recessions, materials and energy shortages, inflation, high interest rates, and high unemployment in the economy.

**Recession.** Consumers doubt their ability to maintain accustomed levels of consumption and may try to save more and spend less in a recession. This increases pessimism among marketers and often leads to reduced investment in new product development and advertising. The onset of a recession can play havoc with a firm's marketing plans. In the early 1970s Sears was trying to increase its appeal to more affluent two-income families by stocking higher-priced apparel. But the fashion image Sears was trying to create confused many of its customers, who did not think of Sears as a store that sells fashion apparel. Thus they shopped at other stores for fashion apparel. Meanwhile, it also lost some other customers who were trying to stretch their buying power during the 1974–75 recession to discount merchandisers such as Kmart.

All marketers, of course, are not affected equally by recessions. Products like Hamburger Helper sell better during recessions than during more prosperous periods when consumers can afford higher-priced meals. The easier it is to postpone buying a product the more likely its sales will decline during a recession. Purchases of durable products like cars, furniture, and new homes are easier to postpone than purchases of nondurable products like basic food products. On the other hand, sales of big-ticket items like houses pick up rapidly during a recovery. This may not be true for everyday necessities.

Firms, however, can respond to recession creatively and explore new opportunities for sales rather than slashing promotion, marketing research, and new product development as some marketers try to do.[1] For example, marketers of durable products like home freezers can change their promotion to focus on the consumer's problems in coping with the recession. Consumers become more value conscious and marketers could advertise that freezers help them save money on food bills, rather than stressing the convenience of owning a freezer. Radial tire marketers often stress the fuel-saving feature of radials in their ads.

The home-improvement market usually is countercyclical because sales pick up during recessions. When people cannot afford new homes they tend to repair and remodel their present homes, often doing the work themselves. Stanley Works, a marketer of tools for professional carpenters, redesigned some of its tools to sell them at lower prices to homeowners who do their own remodeling during recessions and periods of high interest rates on home mortgages.

**Shortages.** Product shortages also affect consumers and marketers.[2] Some consumers reduce their use of or stop buying products that are in

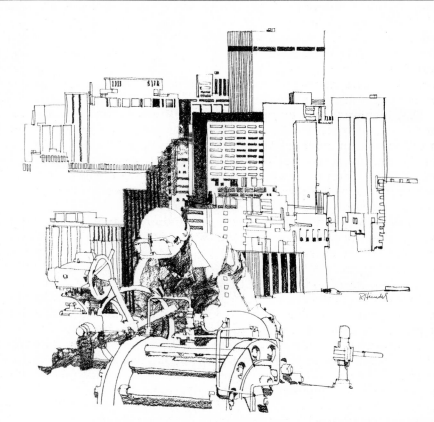

# CONSERVATION CAN SAVE
## ENOUGH GAS FOR A CITY

Every cubic foot of natural gas wasted is energy gone forever — energy that American homes and industry cannot afford to lose. Not only because it is a limited resource, but also because the increase in natural gas prices has given this fuel a value it never had before.

Right now the short term supply outlook appears reasonably good. No one really knows how much gas remains to be discovered by a revitalized national exploration effort, but it is expected to extend natural gas reserves into the next century.

As a nation, however, we're still using up more gas than we're adding to our national reserves. We've been doing this for more than a decade. Under such circumstances, conservation assumes an unprece-

dented importance.

Diligent conservation, shared by a conscientious citizenry and industry, can save enough gas to run a plant or a city. While United Gas is using every means available to attach new gas supplies to its system, consumers can help. Frugality in the use of our natural resources can be highly beneficial.

Many years ago the nation in general paid little attention to the conservation of a resource that was so cheap. But the price of natural gas has risen — and is still rising — toward its true value. It isn't cheap anymore. And as this cost continues to rise, the cost of waste rises with it.

Waste doesn't have to happen.

## UNITED GAS PIPE LINE COMPANY
A UNITED ENERGY RESOURCES, INC. COMPANY
. . . where the search for new energy never stops.

*An example of demarketing*

Source: United Energy Resources, Inc.

short supply, while others try to hoard them to offset expected future price increases. Examples from recent years include meat, sugar, and coffee. Consumers who expect these shortages to be long lasting may alter their buying habits and perhaps even their lifestyles. Price increases caused by shortages lead some people to switch to substitutes. Some people have even had their cars and pickup trucks modified to use propane instead of gasoline or diesel fuel.

The high price of gasoline has indeed changed our driving habits and the high price of electricity, natural gas, and heating oil has contributed to the growth in the Sunbelt states. The high price of beet and cane sugar has led many food and beverage producers to switch to high-fructose corn syrup. The high price of silver was a major factor that led the 3M Company to develop a new type of film for use in the offset-printing process. The product is made with another metal.

Disposable products have given way to recyclable products in some cases. Our entire convenience-disposable mentality is being affected. The high cost of energy leads marketers of houses and cars to design in energy efficiency. Ads for cars used to stress horsepower and roominess but present-day ads stress fuel economy. How much our lifestyles will be changed by product shortages depends a lot on our ability to develop and apply new technology, mainly in the energy field, and to substitute plentiful raw materials for scarce ones in production operations.

Along with providing substitutes, alternative strategies for coping with shortages may include attempts by marketers to reduce the demand for their products. This is called **demarketing**.[3] Electric and natural **demarketing** gas utilities are demarketing when they run ads urging customers to reduce their use of electricity and natural gas. Pennsylvania Power and Light Company, for example, will not serve new homes or commercial buildings unless they are insulated properly to save energy.

Intermittent and protracted shortages of products can lead to changes in a firm's mission. Peoples Gas Company began operations in 1850 as a supplier of manufactured gas to consumers in a Chicago neighborhood but has grown into a large and diversified energy company, Peoples Energy Corporation. Many former oil companies also have become energy companies. Oil companies are not in the solar, nuclear, and geothermal energy business, but energy companies are.

**Inflation.** The declining buying power of money due to inflation has been a major problem during recent years.[4] (See Table 2–1.) Consumers who expect inflation to continue and to get worse develop an inflationary psychology. They spend their money faster because today's prices look like bargains compared to tomorrow's expected prices. They also turn to credit to help them maintain their standard of living in the face of rapidly rising prices. The use of consumer credit reached such proportions in 1980 that the President of the United States instituted consumer credit controls to reduce credit purchases, which were contributing to the high inflation rate. Many credit-issuing companies were required to set aside 15 percent of new credit balances in noninterest bearing

**Table 2–1.** *Purchasing power of the consumer dollar (1967 = $1.00)*

| | |
|---|---|
| 1967 | $1.00 |
| 1968 | 0.960 |
| 1969 | 0.911 |
| 1970 | 0.860 |
| 1971 | 0.824 |
| 1972 | 0.798 |
| 1973 | 0.751 |
| 1974 | 0.677 |
| 1975 | 0.620 |
| 1976 | 0.587 |
| 1977 | 0.551 |
| 1978 | 0.512 |
| 1979 | 0.459 |
| (Aug.) 1980 | 0.401 |
| (Jan.) 1981 | 0.384 |

Source: *Monthly Labor Review.*

accounts at Federal Reserve banks. Some firms like Mobil Corporation even stopped processing applications for credit cards.

The big boom in antiques and collectibles has been helped by consumer desire to offset the effects of inflation. Marketers of collectibles, such as the Franklin Mint, antique dealers, and jewelry stores, sell products that buyers hope will increase in value over the years.

Computer manufacturers used to offset inflation's effects on production costs with new technology. More recently, however, production costs have been going up faster than the cost savings realized from applying new technology. The result is higher prices for computer hardware, software, and maintenance services.

Rapid inflation also may lead some consumers to do without products they used to consider necessities. Electric toothbrushes, knives, and can openers, for example, may become luxuries. Ads stressing convenience may be less effective than ads stressing the idea of gift giving for consumers who think these products are too extravagent to buy for themselves.

## THE COMPETITIVE ENVIRONMENT

Our macro marketing system is based on competition, and business firms within the system compete for customer buying power. But what is competition?[5] Roughly five hundred firms have engaged in tire manufacturing in the United States since 1900 but only eight major manufacturers remain. Of the hundreds of breweries that used to exist, only about forty remain. Is this the result of competition and, if so, is it a desirable result?

Public policymakers are responsible for setting and maintaining the rules that make our marketing system competitive. They act on the belief that a large number of competitors ensures lower prices and better products for consumers. Thus we have laws to prevent monopolies.

Marketers, on the other hand, take a micro view of competition. They look at it as rivalry among firms for customer patronage. More efficient firms will survive at the expense of less efficient ones. The nature of this rivalry depends largely on the type of market structure in which the firm operates.

## Market Structures

A marketing manager's objectives and strategies are affected by the market structure in which the firm operates. The market structure also determines the number and type of competitors the marketer faces and their marketing behavior. Whereas a tobacco grower may be in competition with thousands of other small growers, there are only a few, but large, cigarette manufacturers.

Four basic types of market structure are (1) pure competition, (2) monopolistic competition, (3) oligopoly, and (4) pure monopoly.

**Pure competition** means (1) many small sellers, no one of which has much effect on total industry supply and the product's market price, (2) many small buyers, no one of which has much effect on total market demand and the product's market price, (3) a homogeneous product—all firms in a given industry offer the same product, (4) easy entry into and exit from the industry by competitors, (5) all buyers buy and all sellers sell under the same conditions, and (6) perfect information in the hands of buyers and sellers.

Pure competition, of course, does not exist in the real world. Buyers and sellers do not have perfect information, different brands within a product category are not homogeneous, all buyers and sellers do not operate under the same conditions, and so on.

**Monopolistic competition** means there are many sellers but each seller's brand within a product category is unique. The more that a seller's brand differs from rival brands, the more control that seller has over its price because buyers perceive no close substitutes for it. They have to buy it from that seller. Marketers devote a lot of effort to creating differences between their brands and rival brands. Monopolistic competition also is very common in retailing. Clothing stores, for example, often compete on the basis of their different product lines and the services they offer.

**Oligopoly** means a small number of large and interdependent firms. The actions of one firm tend to affect directly the others in the industry. Each firm has a large number of the industry's customers and each tries to anticipate what the others will do. Kellogg, General Mills, and Gen-

*pure competition*

*monopolistic competition*

*oligopoly*

eral Foods, for example, together account for roughly 86 percent of sales of ready-to-eat breakfast cereals.[6]

Price competition typically is not much in evidence in oligopoly. A firm may avoid raising its price if it fears rivals will not follow. It might lose customers who think the different brands really are alike. If one firm cuts its price and the others follow, a price war could result. Thus prices can remain fairly stable without illegal price fixing because the rivals recognize their interdependence. In some cases there is a price leader whom all firms follow on price changes.

**nonprice competition**

Oligopolists engage mainly in **nonprice competition.** They stress nonprice elements in their marketing mixes. In differentiated oligopoly buyers perceive differences among brands. Examples are cars and household appliances. In undifferentiated oligopoly buyers perceive brands to be pretty much the same. Examples are steel and cement. Appliance makers differentiate their brands through product design and advertising, whereas cement producers stress factors like quick delivery. Entry into oligopolistic industries is tough because of the high cost. For example, it has been estimated that a firm would need to make a $150 million investment to enter the cereal industry.[7] Firms already in the industry must invest $20 million to launch a new brand of cereal.[8]

**pure monopoly**

**Pure monopoly** is the opposite of pure competition. One seller sells a product for which there are no close substitutes and people who want it must pay the seller's set price. This is why monopolies such as telephone, gas, and electric utilities are regulated by government. They are monopolies because society believes it is more efficient, for example, to have one company lay cables than fifty companies lay fifty sets of cables.

**Table 2–2.** *Important characteristics of four types of market structure*

| Market Structure | Number of Sellers | Size of Sellers | Control over Price | Product | Entry into Industry |
|---|---|---|---|---|---|
| Pure competition | many | small | none | homogeneous | easy |
| Monopolistic competition | many | varies | depends on extent of differentiation | differentiated | relatively easy |
| Differentiated oligopoly | small | large | considerable (prices tend to be stable) | differentiated | difficult |
| Undifferentiated oligopoly | small | large | considerable (prices tend to be stable) | fairly homogeneous | difficult |
| Pure monopoly | one | varies | maximum control | no close substitutes | difficult |

Entry of a new firm into a monopolistic industry is tough because of the seller's exclusive patent rights to the product, the seller's present market dominance, or the high cost of setting up plants. The seller might advertise its product to convince people there are no substitutes for it and/or to expand demand for it. This makes it even harder for rivals to enter the market. Table 2–2 summarizes the important characteristics of the four types of market structure we have discussed.

## Marketing and the Competitive Environment

Since buyers can spend their money as they see fit, all marketers compete for customer buying power. In general they can compete on a price basis, a nonprice basis, or a combination of both.

Consumerists and public policymakers prefer price competition. Many marketers do, in fact, compete mainly on the basis of price, as newspaper ads for supermarkets and discount stores suggest. They rely on lower prices to attract customers.

Marketers, however, generally place equal emphasis on nonprice competition. They want to create a lasting **differential advantage** over their rivals. Their market offerings are different from those of rivals. If they rely only on lower prices to achieve this advantage, it will not last long because it often is easy for rivals to match a firm's lower prices.

Nonprice competition means marketers try to create a differential advantage by stressing nonprice elements in their marketing mixes. For many products some consumers think style, quality, product warranty, extended shopping hours, and so on are more important than price. Firms competing to serve them might stress product superiority by investing in product improvements. This type of difference is harder for rivals to match than a price cut. Procter & Gamble, for example, has changed its Tide detergent fifty-seven times between 1947 (the year it was introduced) and 1980.[9]

Critics of nonprice competition say many firms spend too much on ad campaigns to convince people that one brand is better than a rival brand. They argue that these firms should cut their prices instead of spending money on ads or making minor product changes. But marketers say better-designed and higher-quality products give them an advantage and argue that better products are as good for consumer welfare as lower prices. Furthermore, advertising may help increase the demand for a product, which could lead to economies in large-scale production and marketing. Some of these cost savings could be passed on to customers.

**Creating a Differential Advantage.** A marketer has two basic options in dealing with competitors. One is to do as they are doing—imitation. Thus some small fast-food restaurants try to imitate Burger King or McDonald's.

The other approach is to create a differential advantage by doing things differently. This might involve serving different market targets and/or

differential
advantage

developing totally different market offerings. Household appliances used to be sold only in appliance stores and department stores that offered many services such as credit and delivery. Discounters appeared, dropped many of these services, and underpriced their rivals. This competitive action led to a competitive reaction—many department stores and appliance stores dropped some services and cut their prices.

**market niche**

Creating a differential advantage involves positioning a firm in a niche in the market. A **market niche** is a hollow spot in the market that is not being satisfied. By carving out a niche and positioning itself within that niche, a firm becomes the source of unique satisfaction for its customers and enjoys some degree of insulation from rivals. Miller Brewing Company identified the low-calorie beer segment in 1974 and began marketing Miller Lite. It was not until 1977 that Anheuser-Busch, Inc. entered with its Natural Light.

## THE TECHNOLOGICAL ENVIRONMENT

Technology means knowledge to do new or old tasks in a better way. An invention results from applying technology to develop a new product, process, or idea. Introducing inventions in the marketplace is called

**innovation**

innovation. Technology, by itself, is neutral in its effects on humankind but its application can have good and/or bad effects.

Americans twenty-five years ago did not drink freeze-dried coffee, eat low-cholesterol margarine, or cook with microwave ovens or Teflon-coated pots and pans. There were no eight-track tapes, supersonic airliners, or electronic pocket calculators. Innovation has given us a greater quantity of products to consume. In some cases our quality of life is higher, and in other cases it may be lower.

Nevertheless, many Americans expect technology to solve social problems produced by past applications of technology. For example, junk foods probably contribute to making some of us overweight. But instead of cutting down consumption of these products, many consumers expect pharmaceutical firms to introduce new diet aids.

Social values influence, and are influenced by, technology. The desire for a low-cost way to control population growth led to the birth control pill, which has affected our lifestyles and social values. But society has become more intolerant of innovations that adversely affect it, and there is a growing need for technological assessment by businesses. This involves the difficult task of forecasting the effects of applying new technology on the firm, its customers, its rivals, and society in general. If the negative effects are expected to outweigh the positive effects, the technology should not be developed.

### Marketing and Technology

Technological developments affect marketing in many ways.

**The Company Mission.** Technological developments can cause problems and/or create opportunities for marketers. NCR Corporation

# HARRIS technology on the job

**In printing equipment,** Harris Corporation produces a broad range of web offset presses, bindery and mailroom systems for newspapers, magazines, business forms and commercial printers.

HARRIS Densicontrol System at
Arcata Corporation's Pacific Press Division
electronically pre-sets press ink mechanism

With computer-controlled makeready and operating systems, HARRIS presses get up to speed faster and provide better and more consistent print quality. Reducing waste. Boosting productivity...*and* profits.

HARRIS technology works worldwide—in communication equipment, information systems, government systems, semiconductors and printing equipment. For information, write: Harris Corporation, Melbourne, Florida 32919.

*An ad that suggests the importance of technology to a firm and its customers*
Source: Harris Corporation

(formerly the National Cash Register Company) was an established leader in marketing mechanical cash registers and accounting machines but it began losing sales when electronic data processing (EDP) made mechanical processes practically obsolete. NCR has broadened its mission and positioned itself in the computer industry by producing electronic data-processing equipment. Olivetti, Europe's largest maker of office machines, started phasing out its line of ordinary electric typewriters when the firm decided to enter the electronic office market and began marketing electronic typewriters.

**Product Innovation.** Marketing helps to deliver the benefits of new technology to society. Miniaturization in electronics made possible the big boom in pocket calculators and video recording and playback systems. The semiconductor, used in making minicomputers, also has enabled toy makers to produce an almost endless variety of electronic toys. But the introduction of closed-circuit TVs and other electronic security devices caused problems for firms in the uniformed guard industry.

A good marriage between technology and marketing is important. Transferring technological know-how into marketable products requires a good marketing organization. This is one reason many inventors sell their ideas to larger marketing organizations. They lack the know-how to market their products.

**Distribution and Pricing.** New technology also affects distribution and pricing activities. The Universal Product Code (UPC) enables supermarkets to automate checkout stands. In an automated checkout system a computer and its memory are tied to the checkout stands. The prices of all products in the supermarket are stored in the computer's memory. Each checkout has an electronic terminal, a scanner, and a display screen. As each product passes over the scanner a laser light reads the UPC symbol and relays the information to the supermarket's computer. The computer shows the product's name and the price on the display screen, prints it on a receipt for the shopper, and deducts from inventory each product that is sold—all in a fraction of a second.[10]

This example illustrates another important point. Marketers often have to educate their salespeople and customers about the benefits of innovation. Air freight companies have been educating shippers about the cost savings possible from using air freight for certain types of shipments. High technology firms like Xerox also educate their sales personnel and target customers about their new products. Marketers of sophisticated office-automation products are recognizing the need to support their users by offering training programs.

**Promotion.** New technology also is evident in communicating with target customers. Computer-controlled typing and printing systems enable marketers to mail out promotional letters that appear to be individually typed. Consumers who have complaints about Whirlpool products can call a toll-free consumer Cool-Line.[11] The revolution in telecommunications promises to bring even more dramatic changes in promotional tools and techniques.

**Differential Advantage.** A firm may achieve a differential advantage over its rivals by pioneering new production and marketing technology. Dr. E. H. Land's pioneering technology in instant photography enabled Polaroid to enter an industry that had been dominated by Kodak. But new technology becomes old with the passage of time. Thus Kodak has become a rival of Polaroid in instant photography. Kodak recognized the fallacy of its old idea that photography and instant photography were two separate markets.

## THE SOCIOCULTURAL AND ETHICAL ENVIRONMENT

Culture refers to how people in a society adapt to their environment. It is their distinctive way of life. Art, morals, ethics, customs, laws, and beliefs are elements of a culture. A society's cultural values put limits on what firms can do. Different groups in society also put pressure on firms to influence their behavior. Examples are consumer groups, conservation groups, and women's rights groups. These pressures can affect a firm's mission, its selection of market targets, and its other marketing decisions.[12]

### Business Ethics

Business ethics deal with principles and practices that are judgments about what is "right" and "wrong." Some people think business behavior is ethical if it is legal. Others believe it must adhere to the Golden Rule to be ethical. There also is controversy whether business behavior should conform to the strict letter of the law or to the more general spirit of the law. This is important because some laws that pertain to marketing practices are vague about which types of activities are illegal.

Many criticisms about business ethics grow out of marketing practices. Misleading ads, high prices, and low product quality are examples. Marketing provides the most direct link between a firm and its customers and marketers play a major role in establishing the ethical conduct of businesses.[13]

**Social Responsibility.** Businesses serve society by making products that people want. This creates jobs and provides tax revenues for government to use in attacking social problems. Business firms, therefore, help society even if they do not become involved directly in solving social problems.

Two general points of view about the obligations of American business to society are the traditional business ethic and the professional-managerial ethic. According to the **traditional business ethic,** business decisions are based on their short-run effects on profit. A good decision is one that produces measurable profit in the short run.

According to the **professional-managerial ethic,** business managers represent the interests of stockholders, customers, employees, the general public, and other groups.[14] Decisions are weighed in terms of longer-

traditional business ethic

professional-managerial ethic

range company welfare, not short-run profit. So a firm is successful when it contributes to social welfare, thus assuring long-run profit growth.

The traditional marketing concept emphasizes customer satisfaction as the key to making a profit. The societal marketing concept recognizes that groups other than a firm's customers must be considered in decision making. It stresses social responsibility—a long-run view of company, customer, and societal welfare.[15] Table 2–3 indicates several reasons business firms are concerned about social responsibility.

What constitutes socially responsible behavior, however, is not always simple to determine. For example, a few years ago several makers of powdered infant formula began marketing the product in less-developed countries. They perceived an opportunity to satisfy a consumer and a societal need at a profit. Mothers who are unable to breast-feed because of malnutrition or disease often substitute sugar water for breast milk, which contributes to the high infant mortality rate in less-developed countries. Infant formula would be better for babies than sugar water. Critics, however, said advertising the infant formula led some people to believe that the product was superior to breast milk and using the product also was perceived to have status value. Critics also argued that advertising the product to poor and illiterate parents in rural areas was not socially responsible because these parents could not follow label directions for preparing the formula and they often mixed the powder with impure water, thus causing infants to become ill. The controversy led to efforts by the World Health Organization and other groups to prescribe an international code to limit the marketing of the product in less-developed countries.

**Table 2–3.** *Some reasons businesses are concerned about social responsibility*

1. Declining confidence among many Americans in big institutions like corporations, labor unions, and government. Business firms cannot survive if people do not have confidence in them.
2. The increasing professionalization of management. Owner-managers tend to be interested mainly in short-run profits. Professional managers take a longer-run view of profit.
3. Growing acceptance of the systems view of the firm. The firm is part of a larger environment, and the firm and its environment are interdependent.
4. Rising expectations of Americans about their rights as consumers. Efforts to do away with racial, sexual, and other types of discrimination have lifted the expectations of millions of consumers and they have become more demanding of business.
5. The increasing authority with which consumer advocates speak for the consuming public. Their efforts have helped to pass laws that require a higher level of concern for the public good in business decision making.
6. The increasing willingness of regulatory agencies to represent and protect consumer interests in the buyer-seller relationship. The old idea of "let the buyer beware" has given way to "let the seller beware."

## THE POLITICAL-LEGAL ENVIRONMENT

The relationship between government and business during most of our history was based on the philosophy of laissez faire, or "let businesses compete." Government allowed rivals to compete without regulation. This approach worked rather well when firms were small and products were simple. But as firms got larger, technology advanced, and products became more complex, government began its growing role in regulating business activity. Laws were passed to maintain a competitive marketplace and to regulate marketing activities.

Politics and laws are parts of a country's culture. The political climate affects the types of laws that are passed and their enforcement. Recent consumer laws reflect more political concern with protecting

**Table 2–4.**  *The top 20 corporate law departments*

|    | Company | Number of lawyers |
|----|---------|-------------------|
| 1  | American Telephone & Telegraph | 902* |
| 2  | Exxon | 384 |
| 3  | General Electric | 302 |
| 4  | Prudential Insurance | 202 |
| 5  | Du Pont | 194 |
| 6  | Mobil Oil | 188 |
| 7  | Standard Oil (Indiana) | 179 |
| 8  | General Motors | 159 |
| 9  | Gulf Oil | 152 |
| 10 | BankAmerica | 150 |
| 11 | Hartford Insurance Group | 140 |
| 12 | International Business Machines | 138 |
| 13 | Atlantic Richfield | 138 |
| 14 | Sears Roebuck | 131 |
| 15 | Westinghouse Electric | 129 |
| 16 | Ford Motor | 110 |
| 17 | Union Carbide | 108 |
| 18 | Shell Oil | 104 |
| 19 | United Technologies | 104 |
| 20 | Texaco | 101 |

*Includes lawyers at all divisions and operating companies
Data: Law and Business Inc. BW
Source: *Business Week.*

# Government
## ~~of the people,~~
## ~~by the people,~~
## ~~for the people,~~
# shall not perish...

When Lincoln mourned at Gettysburg, he pleaded for the preservation of a fragile thread of government struggling to connect the diverse interests of the nation.

Today, our government is hardly a fragile thread. With more than 400 federal agencies writing 25,000 new regulations each year, it's more like a ball of twine that totally surrounds, binds and touches upon every aspect of our lives.

Lincoln would be pleased to see that the men at Gettysburg did not die in vain; that in fact the union has survived.

But we think that he would speak out to warn the people for whom this government was founded and preserved that they are about to lose control of it. To the un-elected and unchecked bureaucracy it has spawned.

Let us dedicate ourselves to insuring that Lincoln's union survives in the manner he intended. That his words are not deleted by some federal agency to conform to the latest government regulation.

Inspector gages turret clearance of W-3050 turret punch press on assembly floor. A product of the Wiedemann Division, King of Prussia, PA, the W-3050 features 30-ton punching capacity with a hit rate of 175 per minute.

## WARNER & SWASEY
Productivity equipment and systems in machine tools, textile and construction machinery

© 1979 THE WARNER & SWASEY COMPANY    Executive Offices 11000 Cedar Avenue, Cleveland, Ohio 44106

---

*Government regulation of business activity has increased over the years*
Source: © 1980, The Warner & Swasey Company, Cleveland, Ohio.

consumers than sellers, which is in sharp contrast to some earlier laws that generally favored sellers.

## Marketing and the Law

Many laws and administrative agencies regulate marketing practices. Marketers also must keep abreast of court interpretations of laws and the extent to which the laws are enforced. Thus marketing managers often turn to their firms' legal departments for counsel in decision making.

Legislation and administrative rulings affect marketing in two basic ways. First, they may restrict the marketer's ability to do certain things, such as misleading advertising and deceptive pricing, in order to preserve competition and protect consumers. Second, they may create market opportunity. The Federal Communications Commission (FCC) ruling that telephone subscribers could buy their own phones and connect competitive products to American Telephone and Telegraph's wires created opportunity for many firms. The Federal Trade Commission (FTC) ruling that preempted all state bans on price advertising of eyeglasses opened the market to discount drug chains such as the Jack Eckerd Corporation.

Firms do what they can to influence the political-legal environment. Executives appear before legislative committees and regulatory agencies to give their views on proposed laws or enforcement procedures.[16] Firms and their trade associations also engage in lobbying. There are limits, however. Federal laws have been passed to prevent abuses of such activities as lobbying and making campaign contributions to candidates for public office.

## Federal Laws

**The Sherman Act.** Common law is based on custom and previous court decisions. Statutory law is written, or codified, law. Prior to the Sherman Act of 1890 the courts relied mainly on the common law to protect competition. But the Industrial Revolution brought great change to the world of business. Factories replaced home workshops, local markets grew into regional and national markets, and big business trusts tried to monopolize industry during the late 1880s. State laws and the common law were not enough to protect competition.

The Sherman Act sets forth our national policy of maintaining a competitive marketing system. It outlaws "every contract, combination, or conspiracy in restraint of trade" and monopolies and attempts to monopolize trade or commerce. But what constitutes a monopoly is subject to court interpretation. For example, in 1945 the United States Supreme Court ruled that the Aluminum Company of America's 90 percent market share made it a monopoly. In 1962 it ruled that a merger between Brown Shoe Company and Kinney Shoe Corporation would not be allowed because the firm would have 5 percent of the market for women's and children's shoes.

Berkey Photo brought an antitrust suit against Eastman Kodak Company in 1973. Berkey alleged that Kodak's introduction of the pocket

Instamatic camera and 110 film without advance notice to its competitors amounted to unlawful monopolization because of Kodak's dominant market position when it launched the camera in 1972. The camera used special-sized cartridge film that other camera makers' models could not use. A court of appeals rejected Berkey's contention in 1979, after Berkey had won triple damages in a federal district court in 1978. The United States Supreme Court refused to review the decision of the appeals court.[17]

The Federal Trade Commission (FTC), along with the Department of Justice, also is responsible for enforcing antitrust legislation. In 1978 the FTC staff issued a complaint charging that Du Pont used unfair competition to keep the price of a paint pigment low enough to discourage competitors from entering the market but high enough to finance expansion of Du Pont's production capacity. An FTC administrative law judge rejected those charges in 1979 and said Du Pont's success was due to efficient planning and the application of technological advantage. In 1980 the FTC in a major statement of its antitrust policy ruled that actions that could lead to a monopoly are not illegal if they are the result of competition based on technological advantage.[18]

**antitrust laws**

The Sherman Act was the first of our **antitrust laws.** Others include the Clayton Act, the Federal Trade Commission Act, the Wheeler-Lea Act, the Robinson-Patman Act, the Celler-Kefauver Act, and the FTC Improvement Act.[19] (See Table 2–5.)

**Table 2–5.** *Major antitrust laws*

| Date | Act | Provisions |
|------|-----|------------|
| 1890 | Sherman Act | Outlaws every contract, combination, or conspiracy in restraint of trade, monopolies, and attempts to monopolize trade or commerce |
| 1914 | Clayton Act | Sherman Act amendment that spells out actions that are illegal if they substantially lessen competition or tend to create a monopoly |
| 1914 | Federal Trade Commission (FTC) Act | Makes unlawful unfair methods of competition in commerce if they injure a competitor |
| 1936 | Robinson-Patman Act | Clayton Act amendment dealing with price discrimination, brokerage allowances, and promotional allowances |
| 1938 | Wheeler-Lea Act | FTC Act amendment that makes unlawful unfair or deceptive acts or practices in commerce if they injure consumers |
| 1950 | Celler-Kefauver Act | Clayton Act amendment that allows the FTC to prevent asset acquisition mergers if the effect may be to substantially lessen competition or tend to create a monopoly |
| 1975 | FTC Improvement Act | Strengthens the FTC's ability to protect consumers |

**The Clayton Act.** Under the Sherman Act the courts did not consider the future effects of currently legal activities. Thus a firm could engage in activities that did not violate the act directly, even though the effect of those activities might lead to a violation. The Clayton Act of 1914 amends the Sherman Act and spells out activities that are illegal if they "substantially lessen competition or tend to create a monopoly."

**The Federal Trade Commission (FTC) Act.** The FTC Act of 1914 outlaws all business practices that injure competition, even if they do not tend toward monopoly or restraint of trade. "Unfair methods of competition in commerce" are illegal. The FTC was created to enforce the act and to help the Department of Justice to enforce laws pertaining to business practices. The FTC is a major regulator of marketing practices, as we will see throughout this text.

**The Wheeler-Lea Act.** The effectiveness of the FTC, however, was limited because the courts said they, not the FTC, would decide the meaning of "unfair methods of competition." Also, a business practice had to injure a competitor before it could be held to be unfair. The Wheeler-Lea Act of 1938 amends the FTC Act and makes illegal "unfair or deceptive acts or practices in commerce" regardless of whether injury occurs to one or more competitors. The FTC can take action against acts or practices that injure consumers, even if they do not affect competition. This puts the FTC in the business of protecting consumers. The FTC Improvement Act of 1975 expands the FTC's authority.[20] It also strengthens its ability to protect consumers.

The FTC can issue cease and desist orders against a firm that uses unfair or deceptive practices. The firm can choose to enter into a consent decree in which it does not admit guilt but agrees to abide by the order. Otherwise, the firm can appeal the order to a federal court. In 1976 the FTC issued a complaint charging Levi Strauss and Company with illegally fixing the retail prices of blue jeans and other clothing. The firm entered a consent decree in 1978 and stopped making price recommendations to retailers. One result was that price wars broke out in some cities among stores that sold Levi's.

The FTC in recent years has been involved in several controversial issues. For example, in May 1980 both houses of Congress failed to provide funding for the FTC, and its 1,600 employees started to shut down operations. Some people in Congress were angered over FTC proposals, including increased control of TV advertising to children. Congressional funding was restored several days later.

**The Robinson-Patman Act.** During the Great Depression of the 1930s big grocery chains that bought products in large volume demanded big discounts from manufacturers. They could, therefore, sell their merchandise at lower prices than small grocery stores that did not qualify for these discounts. This forced many small stores out of business and contributed to passage of an amendment to the Clayton Act, the Robinson-Patman Act of 1936. Although it is the single most important federal law for marketing, it is confusing and unclear, as we will see later in this chapter after discussing how the antitrust laws affect marketing.[21]

*Merger restrictions.* A merger means one firm acquires the stock or assets of another firm and controls it. The Clayton Act prohibits a firm in interstate commerce from acquiring the stock of a competitor in the same industry where the effect "may be to substantially lessen competition or tend to create a monopoly." This is called a horizontal merger.

Several years ago Bic Pen Corporation wanted to buy American Safety Razor Company from Philip Morris, Inc. Bic had introduced its Bic disposable razor and wanted a wider line of blades. Philip Morris was willing to sell but the deal was called off when the FTC filed an antimerger complaint under the Clayton Act.

The Clayton Act, however, did not outlaw mergers by acquiring a competitor's assets. The Celler-Kefauver Act (the Antimerger Act) of 1950 allows the FTC to prevent these types of mergers if the effect "may be to substantially lessen competition or tend to create a monopoly." In addition to horizontal mergers it also can seek to prevent vertical and conglomerate mergers. A vertical merger involves firms at different levels in a marketing channel, such as a manufacturer merging with its wholesaler. A conglomerate merger involves firms in different industries.

Mergers have come under closer scrutiny by the federal government in recent years and this has affected the missions of some firms. For example, Bic dropped its plans to market a wider line of razor blades and Philip Morris decided to close down the American Safety Razor plant. Philip Morris wanted to focus its effort more on marketing its brands of cigarettes and Miller beer. Some people in Congress favor stopping all mergers between firms that have more than $2 billion in sales or assets and forcing other sizable firms to prove there is a significant social benefit to their acquiring another firm with similar market power before the merger would be allowed.

*Product and distribution restrictions.* The Clayton Act also outlaws several types of product and distribution restrictions if they tend to lessen competition substantially. Exclusive dealing contracts and tying contracts are two types of product restrictions.[22]

**exclusive dealing contract**

In an **exclusive dealing contract** the seller forbids its resellers (wholesalers and/or retailers) to handle competitive products. The goal is to force the resellers to concentrate their efforts on that seller's product. Such a prohibition may violate the Clayton Act.

**tying contract**

In a **tying contract** the seller requires the lessee or buyer of a product to buy some of the seller's other products in order to be able to buy the desired product. IBM, for example, used to require firms leasing its computers also to buy their punch cards from IBM. Some manufacturers require resellers to stock their slow-moving products as a condition of selling them fast-moving ones. Tying contracts also have been popular in franchising agreements. In the past, a franchisee legally could be required to buy supplies from the franchisor, even if the franchisee could get a better price elsewhere. Now a franchisee who can get a better price without sacrificing the quality of the product he or she sells can buy from any supplier. In general, tying contracts are illegal if they lessen competition.

The customer-territory restriction is a type of vertical or horizontal distribution restriction.[23] In a **vertical territorial restriction** suppliers restrict their resellers' sales territories, such as a manufacturer restricting a retailer's sales territory. The retailer faces no competition in its territory from other retailers carrying this brand. The goal is to allow the retailer to concentrate on competing with other brands. The courts tend to accept this line of reasoning when the manufacturer is relatively small.

In a **horizontal territorial restriction,** resellers agree not to compete with each other in selling products from the same manufacturer. This is illegal.

*Price discrimination.* Suppose a manufacturer wants to sell the same product to two different wholesalers at different prices. This is called differential pricing, or price differentiation. The wholesaler who is expected to do the better job of selling the product gets the lower price. This is illegal if it gives a manufacturer's reseller or an industrial buyer an advantage over its other resellers or industrial buyers who are in competition with them. Price differentiation becomes **price discrimination.** Different prices could be charged, however, if the manufacturer's customers are not in competition with each other.

Price discrimination is illegal under the Clayton Act when its effect "may be to substantially lessen competition or tend to create a monopoly." The courts, however, held that the Clayton Act did not cover buyers who were injured by a seller's discriminatory pricing practices. The courts sought to protect competition, not individual competitors.

Under the Robinson-Patman Act, charging different prices to competitive buyers of "commodities of like grade and quality" is illegal when the effect may be to injure competition. The act covers injury to individual customers as well as injury to competition in general. Manufacturers and their resellers and industrial buyers who compete with one another can be prosecuted if they enter into discriminatory contracts knowingly.

Price differentials, however, may be legal when any of the following conditions are met: (1) they do not injure competition; (2) they result from cost differences in selling to different customers; (3) they are used to sell perishable or obsolete products; (4) they are offered in good faith to meet a competitor's equally low price; or (5) they are offered to customers who do not compete with each other. In some cases the cost and "good faith" defenses are unacceptable to the courts.[24]

*Brokerage allowances.* A **brokerage allowance** is a discount allowed to a broker (a type of wholesaler) for its services. During the 1930s many big grocery chains that bought directly from manufacturers demanded these allowances. They wanted the same discount brokers received when they bought products from manufacturers and resold them to

----

**vertical territorial restriction**

**horizontal territorial restriction**

**price discrimination**

**brokerage allowance**

smaller grocery stores.   Under the Robinson-Patman Act brokerage fees are illegal if offered to big chains that do their own buying rather than use an independent broker.   They can only be offered to independent brokers.   Whether this helps consumers or inefficient smaller firms is open to debate.

promotional<br>allowance

*Promotional allowances.*   Sellers also are prohibited from offering various types of **promotional allowances** unless they offer them to all customers "on proportionally equal terms."   Examples are push money offered to resellers to provide extra selling effort for the manufacturer's product, point-of-purchase displays, and advertising allowances.   A canned foods manufacturer might offer a big grocery chain an advertising allowance of 5 percent off the cost of its purchase to use in advertising the product.   Under the Robinson-Patman Act, the seller must inform and offer the same percentage to all competing buyers.[25]

## State Laws

The federal laws we have discussed apply only to firms engaged in interstate commerce (commerce between states).   Many states have laws that cover firms engaged in intrastate commerce (commerce within a state).[26]

unfair trade prac-<br>tices acts

More than half the states have **unfair trade practices acts.**   These prohibit retailers and wholesalers from selling below cost, or below cost plus a required percentage markup.   These laws vary but the minimum required markup usually is 6 percent for retailers and 2 percent for wholesalers.   The laws usually are not enforced vigorously.

**Table 2–6.**   *Ten don'ts of antitrust*

*Warnings that companies most frequently issue to employees to keep them in compliance with antitrust laws:*

1. Don't discuss with customers the price your company will charge others.
2. Don't attend meetings with competitors (including trade association gatherings) at which pricing is discussed.   If you find yourself in such a session, walk out.
3. Don't give favored treatment to your own subsidiaries and affiliates.
4. Don't enter into agreements or gentlemen's understandings on discounts, terms or conditions of sale, profits or profit margins, shares of the market, bids or the intent to bid, rejection or termination of customers, sales territories or markets.
5. Don't use one product as bait for selling another.
6. Don't require a customer to buy a product only from you.
7. Don't forget to consider state antitrust laws as well as the federal statutes.
8. Don't disparage a competitor's product unless you have specific proof that your statements are true.   This is an unfair method of competition.
9. Don't make either sales or purchases conditional on the other party making reciprocal purchases from or sales to your company.
10. Don't hesitate to consult with a company lawyer if you have any doubt about the legality of a practice.   Antitrust laws are wide-ranging, complex, and subject to changing interpretations.

Source: *Business Week.*

Blue laws prohibit certain types of businesses from opening on Sunday or regulate the types of products that can be sold on Sunday. Small convenience food stores can open on Sundays in some areas but large supermarkets cannot. Selling hardware items is illegal on Sundays in some states. Some states allow individual communities to set their own blue laws under local option.

State public service commissions regulate the intrastate marketing operations of telephone companies, railroads, truck lines, and gas and electric utilities. Rates and services are regulated.

## Consumer Protection Legislation

The most recent consumerism era began in 1962 when President John F. Kennedy set forth four consumer rights: (1) the right to choose from an adequate number of products; (2) the right to be informed of all the important facts about products, such as price, durability, and safety hazards; (3) the right to be heard by producers and government when treated unfairly or when a question or complaint arises; and (4) the right to safety in the use of all products.

Rachel Carson's *Silent Spring* (1962) attacked the irresponsible use of pesticides, and Ralph Nader's *Unsafe at Any Speed* (1965) attacked the

**Table 2–7.** *Examples of federal consumer protection agencies*

| Agency | Consumer Protection |
|---|---|
| Interstate Commerce Commission | Regulates rates and trade practices of interstate transportation firms. |
| Department of Agriculture | Sets inspection and labeling standards for dairy products, eggs, meat, and other food products. |
| Postal Service | Seeks to prevent the use of the mail for promoting fraudulent selling schemes. |
| Federal Trade Commission | Promotes and protects free and fair competition, investigates false and deceptive advertising, and enforces truthful labeling laws. |
| Federal Power Commission | Controls water power resources and regulates interstate electric and natural gas utilities. |
| Food and Drug Administration | Enforces laws relating to the purity and truthful labeling of food, drugs, and cosmetics. |
| Securities and Exchange Commission | Oversees the operation of the securities exchanges and the issuance and sales of corporate securities to help prevent fraud. |
| National Highway Traffic Safety Administration | Sets motor vehicle safety standards. |
| Environmental Protection Agency | Sets and enforces standards of quality on air, water, and other environmental elements. |
| Consumer Product Safety Commission | Helps prevent unsafe products from reaching the market. |

defects in the Corvair auto. Nader has served as the central figure in the present consumerist era and has helped to pass laws relating to packaging, product safety, warranties, and information on consumer financing plans.[27] In the 1930s consumer protection was a secondary purpose of laws passed to help small firms survive the Depression and competition from big firms. The main purpose of recent consumer laws is to protect consumers. (See Table 2–7.)

**Marketers and Consumerism.** Some marketers perceive consumerism as a threat to free enterprise, some see it as a passing annoyance that can be dealt with by lobbying and good public relations, and some see it as a valid reflection of consumer dissatisfaction.[28] Modern consumerism has adapted and grown to encompass equal opportunity, product safety, product warranties, honest advertising, child protection, full disclosure by lenders, fair packaging and labeling, and other consumer interests. Perhaps consumerism has become a permanent part of the marketing environment.

Local, state, and federal laws and their interpretation by the courts have become more consumer oriented. Consider the concept of product liability. In the past consumers injured by using a product had little chance of winning a lawsuit against the manufacturer unless they had entered into direct buying contracts with that firm. Even then there was the defense that the firm had used reasonable care in designing and making the product. More recently, the courts have been using the concept of strict liability under which manufacturers and their resellers are liable for defective products that injure consumers. This makes it easier for consumers to win their cases.

Every state provides some protection against consumer fraud through the state attorney general's office. Many states also have some form of consumer representation in the governor's office.

## Living Within the Law

A firm may violate the law intentionally if it believes the chances of getting caught are slim or the penalty is minor. This, of course, is not in the firm's long-run best interest.

Unintentional violations often result from ignorance of the law. Thus many firms have legal staffs to keep up with new laws and court interpretations. Government agencies such as the FTC try to help by issuing guidelines.

Absence of or vagueness in laws pertaining to marketing activities may lead firms to practice self-regulation either on an individual firm basis or through their trade associations. Gillette, for example, stopped using fluorocarbon propellants long before it was required to by law. TV stations that are members of the National Association of Broadcasters pledge to abide by certain standards in children's programing and advertising. Voluntary efforts like these may make the passage of some additional laws to regulate marketing activities unnecessary.

## SUMMARY AND LOOK AHEAD

Marketing managers develop their marketing strategies within an environmental setting that basically is beyond their control. The variables are in dynamic interaction and include economic, competitive, technological, sociocultural and ethical, and political and legal factors.

Marketers must cope with the business cycle and its four stages of prosperity, recession, depression, and recovery. Public policymakers tend to equate a greater number of competitors with a more competitive system. Marketers view competition as rivalry for customer patronage. Superior marketers may increase their market shares at the expense of rivals. This can reduce the number of competitors in an industry and lead to antitrust action by government.

Pure competition, pure monopoly, monopolistic competition, and oligopoly are four basic types of market structure. Pure competition really does not exist in the United States. Government regulations have also, practically speaking, prevented the establishment of pure monopoly. Most real-world market structures are closer to monopolistic competition and oligopoly. Nonprice competition can be very important in developing differential advantage for a firm.

Businesses spend billions of dollars every year to develop new products and improve existing ones. During recessions they tend to spend more on improving established products, whereas they tend to stress new product development during boom periods. Ecology and quality-of-life considerations, however, have made technological assessment more important. This demonstrates how interrelated the environmental variables are.

Our modern marketing system has evolved away from laissez faire toward greater government regulation. Federal antitrust laws are important constraints within which marketing managers must operate. They affect decision making about a firm's mission and its selection of market targets and marketing mixes. Our political-legal system also favors the furtherance of the goals of consumerism.

The next section of this text examines the nature of markets, which are the source of market opportunity. Chapter 3 looks at the American consumer market.

## REVIEW QUESTIONS

1. Identify and discuss the four stages in the business cycle.

2. Contrast the views of competition held by public policymakers and by marketers.

3. Identify and discuss the four major types of market structures.

4. Contrast price and nonprice competition.

5. Give examples that show how technology can affect each element in the marketing mix.

6. Contrast the traditional and the professional-managerial ethic and the traditional and the societal marketing concept.

7. Discuss the two basic ways legislation affects marketing.

**8.** In what major way did the Clayton Act amend the Sherman Act?

**9.** Explain how the Wheeler-Lea Act puts the Federal Trade Commission in the business of protecting consumers.

**10.** Distinguish between an exclusive dealing contract and a tying contract.

**11.** What does the Robinson-Patman Act say about (a) price discrimination, (b) brokerage allowances, and (c) promotional allowances?

**12.** What are unfair trade practices acts?

**13.** Identify and discuss the four rights of consumers set out by President Kennedy in 1962.

## DISCUSSION QUESTIONS

**1.** Suppose a firm's customer orientation enables it to achieve a virtual monopoly. Should it be permitted to maintain its monopoly power?

**2.** Which is better for consumers, price or nonprice competition?

**3.** How does positioning itself into a market niche help to insulate a firm from competitors?

**4.** Has the application of new technology during the past decade raised or lowered the quality of life of the average American?

**5.** How is technological assessment related to the societal marketing concept?

**6.** Has the Robinson-Patman Act outlived its usefulness?

**7.** Do state unfair practices acts that set minimum required markups for retailers promote or hinder competition?

**8.** Has consumerism become a permanent force in American society?

**9.** Do government regulatory agencies function mainly to protect consumers or the business firms they are supposed to regulate?

## NOTES

1. See "Marketing in a Recession: Comments from Our Readers," *Journal of Marketing*, July, 1975, pp. 78–79; and Mordechai E. Kreinin, "Inflation, Recession, and Stagflation," *MSU Business Topics*, Winter, 1975, pp. 5–18.
2. See Eugene J. Kelley and L. Rusty Scheewe, "Buyer Behavior in a Stagflation/Shortages Economy," *Journal of Marketing*, April, 1975, pp. 44–50.
3. See Philip Kotler and Sidney J. Levy, "Demarketing, Yes Demarketing," *Harvard Business Review*, November–December, 1971, pp. 74–80; Philip Kotler, "Marketing During Periods of Shortage," *Journal of Marketing*, July, 1974, pp. 20–29; Theodore Levitt, "Marketing Tactics in a Time of Shortages," *Harvard Business Review*, November–December, 1974, pp. 6–7; David Cullwick, "Positioning Demarketing Strategy," *Journal of Marketing*, April, 1975, pp. 51–57; and Stanley J. Shapiro, "Marketing in a Conserver Society," *Business Horizons*, April, 1978, pp. 3–13.
4. See Fabian Linden, "Budget Message: Stretch It!" *Across the Board*, May, 1979, pp. 51–54.
5. See Michael E. Porter, "How Competitive Forces Shape Strategy," *Harvard Business Review*, March–April, 1979, pp. 137–145.

6. "Too Many Cereals for the FTC," *Business Week*, March 20, 1978, p. 166.
7. Ibid., p. 171
8. "Kellogg: Still the Cereal People," *Business Week*, November 26, 1979, p. 83.
9. "At Procter & Gamble, Success Is Largely Due to Heeding Consumer," *Wall Street Journal*, April 29, 1980, p. 24.
10. This is also discussed in Chapter 9.
11. For discussion of telephone calls to a hotline sponsored by a state's attorney general's office, see Steven L. Diamond, Scott Ward, and Ronald Faber, "Consumer Problems and Consumerism: Analysis of Calls to a Consumer Hotline," *Journal of Marketing*, January, 1976, pp. 58–62. Also see F. Kelly Shuptrine, "Consumer Protection Communications," *Marquette Business Review*, Spring, 1975, pp. 1–8.
12. One author cites six societal values that are shaping the course of history in the United States: (1) the youth movement; (2) the consumer protection movement; (3) the ecology movement; (4) the civil rights movement; (5) the women's liberation movement; and (6) the egalitarian movement. See Alfred L. Seelye, "Societal Changes and Business-Government

Relationships," *MSU Business Topics*, Autumn, 1975, pp. 5–11.

13. See O. C. Ferrell and K. Mark Weaver, "Ethical Beliefs of Marketing Managers," *Journal of Marketing*, July, 1978, pp. 69–73.

14. See Committee for Economic Development, *Social Responsibility of Business Corporations* (New York: 1971).

15. See Betsy D. Gelb and Richard H. Brien, "Survival and Social Responsibility: Themes for Marketing Education and Management," *Journal of Marketing*, April, 1971, pp. 3–9; Raymond A. Bauer, "The Corporate Social Audit: Getting on the Learning Curve," *California Management Review*, Fall, 1973, pp. 5–10; S. Kerry Cooper and Mitchell H. Raiborn, "Accounting for Corporate Social Responsibility," *MSU Business Topics*, Spring, 1974, pp. 19–26; M. Neil Browne and Paul F. Haas, "Social Responsibility: The Uncertain Hypothesis," *MSU Business Topics*, Summer, 1974, pp. 47–51; Frank H. Cassell, "The Social Cost of Doing Business," *MSU Business Topics*, Autumn, 1974, pp. 19–26; Ramon J. Aldag and Donald W. Jackson, Jr., "A Managerial Framework for Social Decision Making," *MSU Business Topics*, Spring, 1975, pp. 33–40; Michael M. Pearson, "The Motivation of Social Responsibility," *Bulletin of Business Research*, May, 1975, pp. 1–3; Keith Davis, "Five Propositions for Social Responsibility," *Business Horizons*, August, 1975, pp. 5–10; Clint B. Tankersley, "A Comparison of Evaluations of Social Responsibility: Students vs. Businessmen," *Akron Business and Economic Review*, Fall, 1975, pp. 48–51; Steven C. Dilley, "External Reporting of Social Responsibility," *MSU Business Topics*, Autumn, 1975, pp. 5–25; Butler D. Shaffer, "The Social Responsibility of Business: A Dissent," *Business and Society*, Spring, 1977, pp. 11–18; Kenneth E. Miller and Frederick D. Sturdivant, "Consumer Responses to Socially Questionable Corporate Behavior: An Empirical Test," *Journal of Consumer Research*, June, 1977, pp. 1–7; and Rogene A. Buchholz, "An Alternative to Social Responsibility," *MSU Business Topics*, Summer, 1977, pp. 12–16.

16. For discussion of the use of marketing research as an input to public policy decision making by regulatory agencies, see Paul N. Bloom and Nikhilesh Dholakia, "Marketing Behavior and Public Policy: Some Unexplored Territory," *Journal of Marketing*, October, 1973, pp. 63–67; William L. Wilkie and David M. Gardner, "The Role of Marketing Research in Public Policy," *Journal of Marketing*, January, 1974, pp. 38–47; J. R. Brent Ritchie and Roger J. LaBrèque, "Marketing Research and Public Policy: A Functional Perspective," *Journal of Marketing*, July, 1975, pp. 12–19; and Robert F. Dyer and Terence A. Shimp, "Enhancing the Role of Marketing Research in Public Policy Decision Making," *Journal of Marketing*, January, 1977, pp. 63–67.

17. "Kodak's Win," *Time*, July 9, 1979, pp. 49–50; and "High Court's Latest Term Aided Business, Although Justices Avoided Stereotyping," *Wall Street Journal*, July 7, 1980, p. 4.

18. "FTC Dismisses Charges Against Du Pont in Major Statement of Its Antitrust Policy," *Wall Street Journal*, October 28, 1980, p. 5.

19. See G. David Hughes, "Antitrust Caveats for the Marketing Planner," *Harvard Business Review*, March–April, 1978, pp. 40–58.

20. See Gerald G. Udell and Philip J. Fischer, "The FTC Improvement Act," *Journal of Marketing*, April, 1977, pp. 81–86.

21. See Ray Werner, "Robinson-Patman: Purchasing's Responsibility Still Unclear," *Journal of Purchasing and Materials Management*, Spring, 1978, pp. 12–15.

22. See William L. Trombetta and Albert L. Page, "The Channel Control Issue Under Scrutiny," *Journal of Retailing*, Summer, 1978, pp. 43–58.

23. See James R. Burley, "Territorial Restriction in Distribution Systems: Current Legal Developments," *Journal of Marketing*, October, 1975, pp. 52–56; and Louis W. Stern, Oriye Agodo, and Fuat A. Firat, "Territorial Restrictions in Distribution: A Case Analysis," *Journal of Marketing*, April, 1976, pp. 69–75.

24. See B. J. Linder and Allan H. Savage, "Price Discrimination and Cost Defense—Change Ahead?" *MSU Business Topics*, Summer, 1971, pp. 21–26.

25. For discussion of U.S. Supreme Court decisions pertaining to territorial allocation systems, pricing practices, exclusive dealing and tying contracts, the Robinson-Patman Act, and mergers, see Ray O. Werner, "Marketing and the U.S. Supreme Court, 1968–1974," *Journal of Marketing*, January, 1977, pp. 32–43.

26. See Gary T. Ford, "State Characteristics Affecting the Passage of Consumer Legislation," *Journal of Consumer Affairs*, Summer, 1977, pp. 177–182; and Gary T. Ford, "Adoption of Consumer Policies by States: Some Empirical Perspectives," *Journal of Marketing Research*, February, 1978, pp. 49–57.

27. See Robert O. Herrmann and Rex. H. Warland, "Nader's Support: Its Sources and Concerns," *Journal of Consumer Affairs*, Summer, 1976, pp. 1–18.

28. For further reading on consumerism, see George S. Day and David A. Aaker, "A Guide to Consumerism," *Journal of Marketing*, July, 1970, pp. 12–19; Richard H. Buskirk and James T. Rothe, "Consumerism: An Interpretation," *Journal of Marketing*, October, 1970, pp. 61–65; Robert O. Herrmann, "Consumerism: Its Goals, Organizations and Future," *Journal of Marketing*, October, 1970, pp. 55–60; H. Bruce Palmer, "Consumerism: The Business of Business," *Michigan Business Review*, July, 1971, pp. 12–17; Philip Kotler, "What Consumerism Means for Marketers," *Harvard Business Review*, May–June, 1972, pp. 48–57; Gary M. Grikscheit and Kent L. Granzin, "Who Are the Consumerists?" *Journal of Business Research*, January, 1975, pp. 1–12; Hiram C. Barksdale and Warren A. French, "Response to Consumerism: How Change Is Perceived by Both Sides," *MSU Business Topics*, Spring, 1975, pp. 55–67; Gregory M. Gazda and David R. Gourley, "Attitudes of Businessmen, Consumers, and Consumerists toward Consumerism," *Journal of Consumer Affairs*, Winter, 1975, pp. 176–186; Alan R. Andreasen, "The Differing Nature of Consumerism in the Ghetto,"

*Journal of Consumer Affairs*, Winter, 1976, pp. 179–190; and Thomas J. Stanley and Larry M. Robinson, "Opinions on Consumer Issues: A Review of Recent Studies of Executives and Consumers," *Journal of Consumer Affairs*, Summer, 1980, pp. 207–220.

29.  Marketers also can make a positive response to consumerism by helping to educate consumers to be more informed consumers.   See Wesley D. Seitz, "Consumer Education as the Means to Attain Efficient Market Performance," *Journal of Consumer Affairs*, Winter, 1972, pp. 198–208; Gerhard W. H. Scherf, "Consumer Education as a Means of Alleviating Dissatisfaction," *Journal of Consumer Affairs*, Summer, 1974, pp. 61–75; Paul N. Bloom and Mark J. Silver, "Consumer Education: Marketers Take Heed," *Harvard Business Review*, January–February, 1976, pp. 38–42; Paul N. Bloom, "How Marketers Can Help Consumer Educators," *Journal of Consumer Affairs*, December, 1976, pp. 91–96; and Frederick W. Langrehr and J. Barry Mason, "The Development and Implementation of the Concept of Consumer Education," *Journal of Consumer Affairs*, Winter, 1977, pp. 63–79.

# Section II
# Markets and Buyer Behavior

The focus of marketing effort is the market. A market exists when there are people who have desires, buying power, the willingness to give up buying power to satisfy their desires, and the authority to buy.

In Chapter 3 we examine the American consumer market. It is made up of more than 225 million ultimate consumers who buy products for their personal or household use. We will study this market in terms of population characteristics, buying power, and expenditure patterns.

Chapters 4, 5, and 6 discuss buyer behavior. Chapter 4 discusses consumer buying decisions. Chapter 5 examines intrapersonal influences on consumer behavior such as motivation, perception, cognition, and learning. Chapter 6 focuses on interpersonal influences such as the family and social and cultural factors.

Chapter 7 looks at the industrial market and the behavior of industrial buyers. Unlike ultimate consumers, industrial buyers do not buy products for their personal or household consumption. They buy products to use in making other products for resale or for use in conducting their operations.

Discussion of foreign markets is reserved for Chapter 23 to enable us to develop a deeper understanding of the marketing process before facing international markets.

Chapter 3

# The American Consumer Market

**OBJECTIVES**
*After reading this chapter you should be able to*

1. distinguish between ultimate consumers and industrial users.

2. identify and discuss the five requirements for the existence of a market.

3. identify and discuss the three main dimensions of the ultimate consumer market that are important to marketers.

4. give examples of population changes that are important to marketers and show why they are important.

5. identify and discuss the three main sources of consumer buying power.

6. distinguish among disposable, discretionary, and real income.

7. distinguish between the economic and psychological dimensions of buying power.

**KEY CONCEPTS**
*Look for these terms as you read the chapter:*
  Ultimate Consumers
  Industrial Users
  Market
  Demography
  Zero Population Growth (ZPG)
  Standard Metropolitan Statistical Areas
   (SMSAs)
  Household
  Liquid Wealth
  Nonliquid Wealth
  Installment Credit
  Noninstallment Credit
  Disposable Income
  Discretionary Income
  Real Income
  Engel's Laws

*Marketers need to keep a close watch on changes in our lifestyles because those changes can have a great impact on selecting market targets and developing marketing mixes. One good source of data is census data. Our government reports more data on its citizens than any other government in the world. It can be very useful to marketers. Consider a few examples.*

*Recent census data show a big increase in the number of households in which both spouses are employed. That could be important for marketers who run daytime TV commercials on the soap operas. For one thing, they may not be reaching all the potential customers they want to reach. Perhaps they will want to shift some commercials to nighttime TV. It also might mean something to electric utilities. Perhaps dual-earner households will keep their homes warmer during the day in summer and cooler during the day in winter while they are away at work. That might reduce the need for new generating capacity.*

*What about the rising divorce rate? One married couple may share only one refrigerator, one house or apartment, and one car. Two divorced persons will need one of each.*

*What about the increasing number of children under eighteen years of age who live with only the mother rather than two parents? Might that mean less money available for spending on those children? Could it be significant to toy marketers?*

*People also are marrying later in life. Should life insurance companies expect that some insurance policy purchases will be postponed? Should they devote more effort to educating young singles about the need for life and hospitalization insurance?*

Marketing-oriented firms focus on satisfying present and potential customers. They select their market targets and develop customer-satisfying marketing mixes. As we saw in Chapter 1 a market target is made up of people whose characteristics and wants are very similar. Thus marketers need information about the characteristics of the people who are potentially includable in their market targets.

The 1980 Census counted 226.5 million people. But, of course, not all of them are potential customers for all marketers. General Motors knows that most of them cannot afford to buy a Cadillac. Thus GM wants information on the population's buying power by area of residence. It may want to avoid opening Cadillac dealerships in areas where the average family's income is under $10,000.

On the other hand, practically everybody is a potential Coke drinker. But the Coca-Cola Company also is interested in the changing composition of our population. Teen-agers are the heaviest drinkers of soft drinks. In developing its product offering, Coke is well aware of the fact that the number of teen-agers in our population is declining while the number of middle-aged people is increasing. Perhaps this is one reason the company has started marketing wine.

Other data about our population are important to marketers also. A marketer of outdoor furniture can do a better job of focusing its marketing effort if it is aware of the movement of some people from the Snowbelt states to the Sunbelt states. People who live in warmer climates buy more outdoor furniture than do people in colder climates. In this chapter, therefore, we will take a close look at the consumer market in the United States.

## WHAT IS A MARKET?

Before we discuss what a market is we should first make clear that there are two basic types of markets—consumer markets and industrial markets. This distinction is important.

**Ultimate consumers** buy and/or use products for their personal and/or household use. Together they make up the consumer market. Babies consume food their parents buy and people receive Christmas gifts from friends outside their immediate households. Women buy about 95 percent of men's cosmetics as presents for fathers, husbands, and boyfriends.[1] The consumer, therefore, is not always the buyer but all individuals are ultimate consumers.

ultimate consumers

**Industrial users** buy products to use in making other products for resale or for use in conducting their operations. They do not buy for personal and/or household use. The Boeing Company buys metal to make planes, farmers buy fertilizer for use in commercial farming, retailers buy cash registers to conduct their operations, hospitals buy bed sheets, and the United States Navy buys ships. Together they make up the industrial market, which we will discuss in Chapter 7.

industrial users

Now, consider these statements:

"I am going to the market to buy groceries."
"How is the market for new cars this year?"
"Are people in the Houston market spending as much as last year?"
"Are you in the market for a new home?"
"What's the stock market doing today?"

These are only a few of the ways we use the term *market*. To a marketer, however, a **market** means:

market

1. people (as individuals or as members of organizations)
2. people with desires
3. people with buying power to satisfy their desires
4. people who are willing to give up some buying power to satisfy their desires
5. people who are eligible to become customers because they are authorized to buy

All five requirements must be met before a marketer has a market. Only then does effective demand exist for a product. (See Figure 3–1.) Mar-

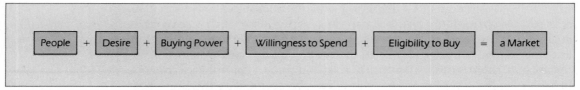

*Figure 3–1. Requirements for a market*

kets also are dynamic, not static. They change over time and marketers must stay alert to these changes by anticipating them as much as possible.

## People

The number of people in a market is a major determinant of market potential for many products, especially those that many people consider necessities. Thus the more people, the more loaves of bread a baker probably will sell. Marketers of necessities like a growing population.

Marketers also are interested in changes in the population's makeup. A declining number of births may mean reduced sales of baby food, whereas longer life expectancy may mean increased sales of geriatric foods.

*People*, as used here, means ultimate consumers and industrial users but our main concern in this chapter is ultimate consumers.

## People with Desires

A marketer, of course, is interested mainly in people who are potential buyers of his or her product. People must desire the product to at least minimally qualify for inclusion in that marketer's market. Nonsmokers are not in the market for cigarette marketers; people who want single-family houses are not in the market for condominium developers; and hard-rock fans are not in the market for tickets to the Metropolitan Opera. A university that tries to recruit high school graduates will find that some do not want to go to college. These people are nonprospects for these marketers.

Marketers, of course, try to influence consumer desires. Cigarette marketers advertise smoking as enjoyable, condominium developers stress security and freedom from yard maintenance, opera is touted as culturally enriching, and university recruiters compare lifetime earnings of college and noncollege graduates. Advertising and personal selling are used to help create desire for products and to persuade us to buy.

## People with Buying Power

Many people would like to own a new Rolls-Royce but only a few can afford one. The third requirement for a market is people with enough buying power to satisfy their desire for a product. Consumers make liberal use of bank credit cards (Visa and MasterCard) and travel and entertainment cards (Carte Blanche and American Express) in addition to cash to buy products. Roughly half of American households use Visa and MasterCard cards. Many also have charge accounts and credit cards at retail stores, buy on installment contracts, and borrow from many types of financial institutions to buy today and pay tomorrow.

Aggregate consumer buying power is a major factor that affects the business cycle. Government tries to protect consumers from major losses in buying power to prevent violent ups and downs in the cycle. Social Security payments to disabled workers help protect their incomes. Other examples are federal and state programs such as workers' compensation insurance, the food stamp program, and public housing programs. Company and union pension plans also provide a cushion against dramatic decreases in income when workers retire.

## People Who Are Willing to Buy

Even if some people desire a product and have the needed buying power, a market still may not exist. They must be willing to give up some buying power to buy the product. Sales of power boats and recreational vehicles in some recent years have been hurt by consumer fears about fuel availability and cost.

Advertising can help to build desire for a product and willingness to spend for it. The success of Perrier water is due in no small part to advertising. Credit also expands buying power in the short run and increases the willingness of people to buy. People in their early twenties and thirties generally save less than older people because their incomes tend to be lower. They are heavy users of credit to buy homes and durable products like appliances, furniture, and cars. Consumer credit controls such as those imposed in early 1980 by the President can significantly reduce ability and willingness to buy.

Since most of us have more desires than we can afford to satisfy, we rank them in terms of their importance. The more effectively marketers match their market offerings to consumer desires, the more willing consumers are to buy them. All marketing mix elements can help to build consumer willingness to buy. Marketers of home smoke alarms recognized this several years ago. Within one year of the nuclear accident at Three Mile Island near Harrisburg, Pennsylvania, radiation detector kits also were on the market for consumers to buy.

## People with Eligibility to Buy

Suppose some people desire a product, have the buying power to buy it, and are willing to buy it. There still may be no market for it if the people are not eligible to become customers. People below a certain age are not included in the market for X-rated movies, adult magazines, and liquor. Age and health status may affect a person's eligibility to buy life insurance. Likewise, a driver's accident record may affect his or her eligibility to buy auto insurance. People below the legal age to contract are ineligible for credit.

## THE CONSUMER MARKET

As we said earlier, marketers study population characteristics to do a more effective job of defining their market targets and developing satisfying marketing mixes. Retailers, for example, are looking closely at the big bulge in our population that will occur in the thirty-five–forty-four age group during the 1980s. People in this age group are heavy users of credit.

James Cash Penney's original "cash only" policy probably did not exclude too many people from his market target. Years ago people were used to paying cash. But in 1979 J.C. Penney became the first national retailer other than discount stores to accept Visa cards in its stores. This provided credit in Penney stores to people who did not have J.C. Penney credit cards. Could it be that awareness of the increase in the number of middle-aged consumers and the fact that they are heavy users of credit played some part in Penney's decision to start accepting Visa and also MasterCard?

Likewise, is it possible that awareness of the aging baby-boom generation is affecting the selection of market targets and development of marketing mixes of a wide variety of marketers? Could it help to explain why Geritol now often features women in their thirties and forties in its ads? These women are not elderly but they do constitute a huge potential market for the product. Ads for vitamins, skin creams, figure salons, and diet colas also now often feature women in that same age bracket. The age of fashion models also seems to be edging up in recent years.

As we said earlier the five requirements for the existence of a market are (1) people, (2) desire, (3) buying power, (4) willingness to buy, and (5) eligibility to buy. Thus the rest of the chapter focuses on an analysis of (1) population, (2) buying power, and (3) willingness to buy. Our purpose in discussing these market dimensions is to show how marketers can use this knowledge to do a more effective job of selecting market targets and

*Table 3–1.* *Three key market dimensions*

| | |
|---|---|
| Population: | Attitudes about population growth |
| | Population shifts |
| | Age distribution |
| | Sex distribution |
| | Ethnic distribution |
| | Households |
| Buying Power: | Current income |
| | Accumulated wealth |
| | Credit |
| | Inflation |
| | Ethnic distribution |
| | Regional distribution |
| Willingness to buy: | Expenditure patterns |

developing satisfying marketing mixes. Table 3–1 gives an overview of the major components we will discuss under each of the three key market dimensions.

## POPULATION

The term *population* means the number of people who live in a certain place at a given time. Marketers need data about the people in their market targets. **Demography** is the study of population statistics, such as the number of births, deaths, marriages, and age groupings. As we will see in greater detail in Chapter 8, marketers use demographic statistics in selecting their market targets and in identifying trends. For example, Fisher-Price began preparing plans to market toys for older children after its demographic analysis showed that preschool children, its traditional target, were declining as a proportion of our population. Thus the firm wanted to seek growth in age brackets that were growing.

demography

A nation's population is determined by the number of (1) births, (2) deaths, (3) immigrants, and (4) emigrants. A natural increase occurs when the number of live births exceeds the number of deaths during a period of time. The natural increase in our population is due mainly to the long-term decrease in the infant mortality rate and the long-term increase in life expectancy. Although we can exercise more control over the birth rate, it is harder to predict than the death rate. Life expectancy increases mainly as a result of breakthroughs in medical science. Changes in the death rate, therefore, occur in minor increments over time. This is why the death rate is more predictable than the birth rate.

Immigration occurs when people move into a country from elsewhere. Emigration occurs when people leave a country to live elsewhere. There is much more immigration to than emigration from the United States. Legal immigration is controlled through legislation but illegal immigration has been a problem in recent years. It is anticipated that roughly 400,000 immigrants per year will come to the United States during the 1980s and that this will account for about 20 percent of the increase in our population. Estimates of aliens living illegally in this country range up to 12 million people.[2]

### Attitudes About Population Growth

When the United States was a farming economy the typical family was larger than it is today. Children who worked on farms were earning assets. Industrialization, however, caused many people to leave farms for cities. Children of office or factory workers in cities do not work on farms and it costs more to rear children in urban areas. Furthermore, prior to Social Security, children also often were considered a type of insurance. They were expected to provide for their elderly parents. But Social Security has helped to weaken this cultural value. Thus the fertility rate (number of births per 1,000 women of childbearing age) has declined during many recent years in the United States.

What does this mean to marketers? Consider, for example, the boom in retirement communities in states like Arkansas, Florida, and Arizona. Instead of moving in with their children, these retirees moved to communities that were specifically developed to cater to retirees' wants. Likewise, many banks, savings and loan associations, and insurance companies have put together savings and insurance programs that help ensure prospective retirees they will have adequate funds to enjoy their retirement years. Thus a change in our cultural values gave rise to a potential market target that had to be identified by alert marketers.

During the Great Depression of the 1930s there was a big drop in the birthrate. But immediately after World War II there was a baby boom. The baby boom generation includes people who were born between 1946 and 1966. These people represent a big bulge in our population and they are studied very carefully by marketers. In 1960, for example, the oldest baby boom children were fourteen years old and 26.2 percent of our population was between fifteen and thirty-four years old. By 1980, the oldest baby boom children were thirty-four years old and 35 percent of our population was between fifteen and thirty-four years old. The aging of the baby boom children means greater demand for housing, furniture, appliances, and financial services.

We sometimes refer to 1976 as the baby bust because the birthrate was exceptionally low, due in part perhaps to the 1974–75 recession. But the economic recovery that began in 1976 contributed to an increase in the birthrate in 1977.

**zero population growth (ZPG)**

The overall declining rate of increase in our population has been due mainly to the declining birthrate. The United States someday may reach the point of **zero population growth (ZPG)** at which our population would level off. There is some concern about overpopulation in the face of increasingly scarce natural resources. The women's rights movement also has shown that women can enjoy fulfilling lives without having children. Couples are marrying later in life and having fewer children. They can afford more expensive homes, cars, furnishings, and vacations and marketers of these products are targeting their efforts to them.[3]

Gerber Products Company used to say "Babies are our business, our only business" but dropped the latter phrase when it started marketing life insurance to older people with the slogan "Gerber now babies the over-50s." Many other firms that traditionally relied on a constantly and rapidly growing population also have rethought their company missions and marketing strategies. Thus some toy makers that marketed toys exclusively for small children have also begun marketing adult toys and games.

Vaccines for diseases like mumps, polio, and measles are taken in childhood and they last a lifetime. Marketers face a market whose growth is limited to increases in the birthrate and some have decided to discontinue marketing these products. Hershey Foods Corporation, which did not advertise at all until 1969, has since targeted a lot of its advertising to adults. Walt Disney Productions used to produce only

G-rated movies but has offered some PG-rated movies to appeal to the heavy moviegoers in the eighteen-to-thirty age bracket. Colleges also are increasingly turning to marketing as the baby boom has gone bust. They are targeting more to older people as the number of eighteen-to-twenty-two-year-olds decreases. Thus there has been a boom in weekend colleges, night schools, and extension programs.

Consider a marketer of baby beds, a durable product. This product usually is bought by a couple when the first baby arrives. If they have a second and a third child, the same bed can be passed down and used by those babies. But the trend toward smaller families has a much greater effect on marketers of nondurable products like baby food and disposable diapers.

Marketers, however, have to keep up-to-date on population data. For example, during the 1980s the increase in the number of women of childbearing age could offset a low birthrate, if in fact the rate remains low. Perhaps women who have postponed having children will decide to have them in the 1980s. In fact, both the birthrate and the fertility rate increased slightly in 1980. There were 16.2 live births per 1,000 population, a 3 percent increase over 1979. There were 69.2 births per 1,000 women of childbearing age (fifteen to forty-four).

## Population Shifts

Population shifts also are important to marketers. Many downtown merchants in our older cities grasped the significance of people moving to the suburbs and started opening branch stores in the suburbs during the 1950s. Marketers of snow blowers probably are watching closely the movement of people to the Sunbelt states in more recent years.

We traditionally have been a very mobile people.[4] For example, during recent years roughly one out of five families moves from one county to another once in five years. But there are some signs that the willingness and ability of people to move may be declining. Working wives, concern about the quality of life, high mortgage interest rates, and a growing proportion of middle-aged people (the least likely to move) are only a few factors that may reduce the mobility of American families. Again, marketers constantly must keep alert to changing demographics.

Two types of population shifts in the United States are especially important: (1) movement from rural to urban areas and movement within urban areas and (2) movement from region to region.

**Urbanization.** There has been a long-term movement of Americans from rural to urban areas—from farm to city. The U.S. Bureau of the Census lists 310 **standard metropolitan statistical areas (SMSAs).** An SMSA is an area that includes a central city (or twin cities) with a population of 50,000 or more and the surrounding counties that are economically and socially integrated with it. Roughly three out of four Americans live in metropolitan areas.

Marketers of specialized services, such as a poodle clipping service, want to target their offerings in heavily populated areas. Huge shopping

standard metropolitan statistical areas (SMSAs)

**Table 3–2.** *Percent distribution of population by residence and region*

| Residence | U.S. | Northeast | North Central | South | West |
|---|---|---|---|---|---|
| Large metropolitan | 39 | 58 | 39 | 22 | 45 |
| Other metropolitan | 34 | 28 | 30 | 42 | 36 |
| Nonmetropolitan | 27 | 14 | 31 | 36 | 20 |

Source: *Current Population Reports.*

centers also require a large and concentrated population. But marketers in SMSAs also typically have to contend with more competition. The higher population density and higher household incomes attract competitors. Thus some discount chains, for example, prefer to locate their stores in smaller communities.

**Interurbia.** Our largest SMSAs are clustered in the North Central states and on the east and west coasts. (See Table 3–2.) The U.S. Bureau of the Census also recognizes sixteen standard consolidated statistical areas (SCSAs), each of which is made up of an SMSA that has at least one million people and one or more adjoining SMSAs that are socially and economically integrated with it. Roughly one-third of our population lives in these SCSAs.

Some SMSAs have grown toward one another, thereby creating interurbia. J. Walter Thompson Company, a large advertising agency, has coined the term *megalopolis* to describe interurbia. An example is the "Eastern corridor" that includes Boston, New York, Baltimore, Philadelphia, Washington, D.C., and their suburbs. This megalopolis accounts for only about 5 or 6 percent of the land area of the United States but is home to roughly 20 percent of our population.

**Central City Outmigration.** During the 1950s the Atlanta SMSA's population was heavily concentrated in the central city. Between 1970 and 1980, however, the central city lost 15 percent of its population while the SMSA grew by 44 percent and included fifteen counties. If you owned a department store in downtown Atlanta, you probably would have seriously considered opening branches in the rapidly growing suburbs. The same pattern prevails in our other SMSAs. The central cities are losing population while their suburbs are growing.

Over half the people in our SMSAs live in the suburbs. They tend to be young, white, middle-income people who want to raise their children in the suburbs. Although many work in the city, they live in suburban bedroom communities and shop mostly in suburban shopping centers. Marketers must stay alert to such shifts. For example, suburbanites tend to spend more than central city dwellers on lawn equipment, patio furniture, home tennis courts, and swimming pools.

Immediately after World War II Sears and Montgomery Ward were about equal in size but by the end of the 1970s Sears' sales were three times bigger. One reason was Ward's slow move to the suburbs during the postwar economic boom.

The tax bases of central cities tend to shrink as low-income and retired people account for a growing percentage of their population. Many city governments try to reduce spending by cutting back on city services. One result is that downtown shopping areas often tend to deteriorate. This, in turn, causes some retailers to leave the area and others to redefine their market targets. For example, some clothing stores may begin stocking cheaper lines of clothing. Central city mayors often favor city-suburb planning and levying a city income tax on commuters who work in the city but live in the suburbs. Suburbanites often resist, however. This is one reason federal assistance programs for central cities were begun.

The political boundaries between cities and suburbs are less important to marketers than the social and economic differences between city dwellers and suburbanites.[5] Income and family size, for example, tend to be larger for suburban families. Some retailers have left downtown shopping districts for suburban shopping centers, but others have seen that the growing percentage of low-income people in central cities means opportunity for furniture rental and low-cost housing.

**Central City Inmigration.** In recent years there has been some movement of people back to the city. This process is called *gentrification* and is especially visible in cities like Washington, D.C. Some movers are affluent young families, some are singles, and some are people who moved to the suburbs to start their families but return after the children leave home ("empty nesters").

Many of the younger resettlers buy and renovate houses in older neighborhoods. They often find this cheaper than buying new homes and it may reduce the cost of commuting to work. The empty nesters often move into condominiums or apartments to escape home and yard maintenance problems; they trade the lawnmower for central city attractions like theaters, operas, and medical centers. The nostalgia craze and federally sponsored revitalization demonstration projects are other factors in the gentrification process.

**Deurbanization.** The United States is an urban nation. But in recent years some people in rural areas and small towns are choosing to stay there to enjoy "the good life." Several government programs focus on making small-town life more attractive to help reduce overcrowding in big SMSAs.

Some people also are moving from the SMSAs (urban flight) to rural areas and small towns to escape big-city headaches like traffic congestion, pollution, crime, city taxes, and other problems associated with urban sprawl. They often take lower-paying jobs to be able to move. Some business firms also are moving to smaller cities and towns for some of the same reasons.

### Regional Shifts

Roughly four out of ten Americans live in the densely populated East–North Central states (Ohio, Indiana, Illinois, Michigan, and Wisconsin) and the Middle Atlantic states (New York, New Jersey, and Pennsylvania). On the other hand, the Mountain states (Montana, Idaho, Wyoming, Colorado, New Mexico, Arizona, Utah, and Nevada) account for only about 5 percent of our population. Some of these states are very thinly populated. (See Figure 3–2.)

Marketers tend to prefer densely populated regions and states because of the relative ease and low cost of serving customers. But this can lead to overlooking opportunity in less-populated areas. Wal-Mart Stores Inc. is a discount chain that operates stores in towns with populations of

*Figure 3–2.  **Geographic distribution of the population of the United States***

| State by State | 1980 Population | State by State | 1980 Population |
|---|---|---|---|
| Alabama | 3,863,698 | Michigan | 9,236,891 |
| Alaska | 400,331 | Minnesota | 4,068,856 |
| Arizona | 2,714,013 | Mississippi | 2,503,250 |
| Arkansas | 2,280,687 | Missouri | 4,901,678 |
| California | 23,510,372 | Montana | 783,674 |
| Colorado | 2,877,726 | Nebraska | 1,564,727 |
| Connecticut | 3,096,951 | Nevada | 800,312 |
| Delaware | 594,779 | New Hampshire | 919,114 |
| Dist. of Columbia | 635,233 | New Jersey | 7,335,808 |
| Florida | 9,579,495 | New Mexico | 1,290,551 |
| Georgia | 5,396,425 | New York | 17,557,288 |
| Hawaii | 964,624 | North Carolina | 5,846,159 |
| Idaho | 943,629 | North Dakota | 652,437 |
| Illinois | 11,321,350 | Ohio | 10,758,421 |
| Indiana | 5,454,154 | Oklahoma | 2,998,519 |
| Iowa | 2,908,797 | Oregon | 2,617,444 |
| Kansas | 2,355,536 | Pennsylvania | 11,824,561 |
| Kentucky | 3,642,143 | Rhode Island | 945,761 |
| Louisiana | 4,194,299 | South Carolina | 3,067,061 |
| Maine | 1,123,560 | South Dakota | 687,643 |
| Maryland | 4,193,378 | Tennessee | 4,539,834 |
| Massachusetts | 5,728,288 | Texas | 14,152,339 |

25,000 or less in the South Central states. These are the types of towns many large discount chains have tended to avoid.

More than half our people live in the West and South. The 1980 Census showed that every one of the twenty-five fastest-growing SMSAs during the 1970s was in the South or West. Five cities in the Southwest are among the nation's top ten in population: San Diego and Los Angeles, California, and San Antonio, Houston, and Dallas, Texas.

**The Sunbelt.** The older, industrialized East–North Central and Middle Atlantic states are losing population to the Sunbelt states in the South and Southwest. The reasons are varied but include the desire to escape crime, high taxes, and high costs of living and to enjoy a higher quality of life in a warmer climate.

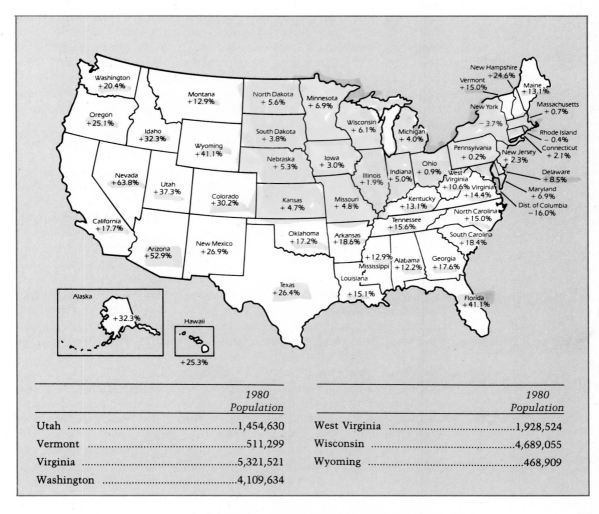

| | 1980 Population | | 1980 Population |
|---|---|---|---|
| Utah | 1,454,630 | West Virginia | 1,928,524 |
| Vermont | 511,299 | Wisconsin | 4,689,055 |
| Virginia | 5,321,521 | Wyoming | 468,909 |
| Washington | 4,109,634 | | |

Industry also has been migrating to the Sunbelt. The reasons include lower taxes, less unionization, lower energy costs, and, perhaps, greater labor productivity. The business boom in the Sunbelt is not due only to firms leaving the older industrialized states; many newly established firms are choosing to locate there also. This increasing economic power is having a political impact as Sunbelt states are increasing their seats in Congress at the expense of states in the Northeast and Midwest.[6]

As we said earlier, Americans are a mobile people. "The age group that likes to move the most is between 25 and 29. Since the peak year for births in the U.S. was 1961, when 4,350,000 children were born, the biggest outward surge is yet to come."[7]

### Age Distribution

Age, of course, affects buying behavior. Only 5 percent of males under age fifty-five smoke cigars while 11 percent of males over fifty-five smoke cigars. This fact led Consolidated Cigar Company to introduce new products, such as an odorless cigar, to appeal to the under-fifty-five segment.[8] The heaviest consumers of soda pop are ten to twenty-four years of age. Their numbers are expected to decline during the 1980s while the twenty-five-to-forty age group is expected to increase. Thus, as we said earlier, the Coca-Cola Company has entered the wine business and firms that used to market only pop wines are expanding their offerings to include other wines.

A changing age distribution creates both opportunity and problems for marketers and so they are interested in the age breakdown of the population. Table 3–3 shows the population of the United States broken down by age groups for 1977 and Census Bureau projections for the year 1987. Notice the declining number of teen-agers both in absolute numbers and as a percentage of total population. This means potential problems for fast-food restaurants in hiring part-time workers, slackening demand for high schools, soft drinks, records, lower-priced stereos, and other teen-oriented products. Several years ago Levi Strauss and Company started marketing jeans that are bigger in the seat and thigh areas for men well past their teen-age years and early twenties. Jostens, Inc. is the nation's biggest marketer of high school class rings and yearbooks. Declining high school enrollments were a factor in the firm's decision to run ads in the *Wall Street Journal* advertising college rings to executives who did not buy them while they were in college.[9]

Table 3–3 also shows that the older middle-aged groups, mainly people born during the Great Depression, will decline slightly in numbers. The young middle-aged group, traditionally the biggest-spending age group, will increase in absolute numbers and as a percentage of total population. This group includes the earliest arrivals during the postwar baby boom. Most of the growth in the young adult group will occur in the upper range of the twenty-one-to-thirty-four age bracket. Some of these people were the last arrivals in the postwar baby boom.

**Table 3–3.** *Age distribution of the United States population, 1977 and 1987 (projected)*

| Age group | 1977 pop. in millions | % of total pop. | 1987 pop. in millions | % of total pop. | % change in numbers 1977–1987 |
|---|---|---|---|---|---|
| Children under 13 | 43.9 | 20.25 | 48.9 | 20.49 | + 11.39% |
| Teen-agers 13–20 | 29.3 | 13.51 | 24.2 | 10.14 | − 17.41% |
| Young adults 21–34 | 53.2 | 24.54 | 60.2 | 25.23 | + 13.16% |
| Young middle age 35–49 | 35.0 | 16.14 | 45.7 | 19.15 | + 30.57% |
| Older middle age 50–64 | 32.2 | 14.85 | 32.0 | 13.41 | − 0.62% |
| Elderly 65 and over | 23.2 | 10.70 | 27.6 | 11.57 | + 18.96% |

Source: U.S. Bureau of the Census.

Better health care delivery to a greater percentage of elderly Americans will cause the elderly group to increase by 19 percent. The median age of Americans by the year 2000 is projected to be thirty-five, up from twenty-eight in 1970 and thirty in 1980. This reflects the "graying of America."[10] Demand for products like digestive aids, decaffeinated coffee, bran cereals, and laxatives will increase and, as we suggested earlier, there may be some decline in the youth orientation of some ad campaigns. An ad for Clairol's Silk and Silver hair coloring from recent years featured an older woman under the headline "Free, Grey, and 51."

During the 1980s the fastest-growing segment of our population will be people twenty-five to fifty. People under twenty-five will decline in absolute numbers during the early 1980s. Think of the implications for marketers of cereals. Average yearly consumption of cereals per capita for people under twenty-five is eleven pounds. For people twenty-five to fifty it is less than half that amount.[11]

## Sex Distribution

Traditional sex barriers to consumption of products like colognes and facial creams are falling. Changes in traditional sex roles also are important. The growing percentage of male grocery shoppers, for example, has great meaning to supermarket operators and packagers of food products. In 1977 the Gillette Company merged its Personal Care Division (mostly female products) with its Toiletries Division (mostly male products) to form a consolidated Personal Care Division. It also launched Ultra Max in 1977, a shampoo targeted to the unisex market.[12]

There are about 95 males per 100 females in the United States. But the number of males per 100 females decreases as age increases. For example, there are about 70 males for every 100 females in the sixty-five-and-over age group. Thus we see banks and savings and loan associations targeting more marketing effort to older women who live alone.

## Ethnic Distribution

Would the marketer of a food product targeted to Hispanics benefit from knowing that Cuban-Americans are heavily concentrated in Miami and the rest of southern Florida? Would that marketer also benefit from knowing that Hispanics are the largest minority group in Los Angeles, or that Puerto Ricans are mostly concentrated in New York City, or that Mexican-Americans are mostly concentrated in the Southwestern states?

Many people think of the United States as a great "melting pot" in which all people basically are alike. But this is an inaccurate view. Even within the Hispanic group, there are differences. Consider, for example, an adhesive bandage marketer who wanted to reach the large and growing Hispanic market in the United States with Spanish-language commercials on TV. The product was recommended for use on *conquitos* on children's knees. Cuban-Americans translated the word to mean "little scratches" but Mexican-Americans translated it to mean "little coconuts."[13]

In other words, many subcultures exist within the dominant American culture. Examples are Hispanics and black Americans. Ours is a pluralistic society. Our single largest ethnic group, blacks, accounts for roughly 12 percent of our population. Blacks no longer are as concentrated in the southern states as they were prior to World War II. Just a little over half of American blacks now live in the South. Thus marketers who sell to blacks have expanded distribution into other areas, especially in the central cities of large SMSAs in the East–North Central and Middle Atlantic states. Blacks also live mostly in our central cities. They account for only 6 percent of our total suburban population.

The fastest-growing ethnic group in the United States is Hispanics. At some point in the 1980s they may outnumber blacks. As the bandage marketer discovered, there can be a language barrier between English-speaking marketers and Hispanics and among Hispanic groups themselves. Surely the "melting pot" view of the market can cause problems for marketers.

There are also other ethnic groups in the United States. The important point for marketers is that buying behavior and product preferences often differ among various ethnic groups and within those groups, as well as from those of people in the dominant American culture. Marketers must consider this in developing market offerings. Thus Del

## Thirty percent of all Los Angeles schoolchildren are learning a second language.    English.

Almost half of all elementary schoolchildren in the Los Angeles Unified School District are Hispanic. Over two-thirds of these children speak Spanish as their first language.

Surprised? You shouldn't be. Just look at California's Spanish heritage. And Spanish-flavored culture.

Atlantic Richfield believes Hispanics will play a very important role in Southern California's future. Consider the demographics.

There are over four million Hispanics living in Los Angeles, Orange, Riverside, San Bernardino, and Ventura counties. Over seventy percent of them live in husband-wife households, and more than half of these families bring home two paychecks. That kind of industriousness means upward mobility. (Hispanics already constitute a $12 billion market in these five counties alone.) And the Hispanic population is growing twice as fast as the rest of the population.

Atlantic Richfield believes that whatever your business plans, you should take the Hispanic community into account. You can't afford to ignore their buying power. Their influence. And their leadership.

**ARCO**
Atlantic Richfield Company

*The population of the United States is not homogeneous*
Source: Atlantic Richfield Company.

Monte recently entered the ethnic foods market with a line of Mexican foods.

### Households

household

A **household** is made up of all persons who live in a housing unit such as an apartment, a mobile home, or a house. How important to General Electric and State Farm Insurance Company is the fact that the percentage increase in households has been greater than the percentage increase in our population during recent years? Would not a high household-formation rate mean greater demand for home owners' and renters' insurance, auto insurance, and household appliances?

The reasons for the big increase in the household-formation rate relate to changes in our lifestyles. They include older surviving spouses living alone and older children leaving home to set up their own households. Slightly more than half our households consist of one or two people. This reflects the declining birth rate, the growing divorce rate, and living-together arrangements. A married couple, for example, that lives together counts as one household. If they divorce and set up their own individual living arrangements, two households are created.

Again, however, marketers must keep up-to-date on demographic data. For example, the onset of recession and high unemployment in early 1980 led to some reduction in the number of American households as some people moved in with relatives or friends to cut living costs. Thus there may be some decline in the current percentage (roughly 20 percent) of one-person households.

## BUYING POWER

As we said earlier, the number of people ten to twenty-four years of age will decline during the 1980s. So why did Consumers Union, the publisher of *Consumer Reports*, start a new bimonthly magazine, *Penny Power*, in 1980? This magazine is targeted to children eight to twelve years old and is intended to help them become more informed consumers. Could it be that children in that age group do make significant expenditures or influence the purchase of products ranging from breakfast cereals to sophisticated electronic toys? Could it be that they have a lot of buying power?

Because of escalating mortgage interest rates, inflation, and recession the housing industry has been in a slump in many recent years. Were it not for the big increase in dual-earner families, the housing market would have been even more depressed. Families in which both spouses are employed now outnumber those in which only one spouse is employed.

Household buying power comes from three main sources: (1) current income, (2) accumulated wealth (or assets), and (3)credit.

**Table 3–4.** *Percentage of aggregate income received by each fifth and the top 5 percent of U.S. families in selected years*

| Percentage of families | 1950 | 1955 | 1960 | 1965 | 1970 | 1975 | 1977 |
|---|---|---|---|---|---|---|---|
| Lowest fifth | 4.5 | 4.8 | 4.8 | 5.2 | 5.4 | 5.4 | 5.2 |
| Second fifth | 12.0 | 12.3 | 12.2 | 12.2 | 12.2 | 11.8 | 11.6 |
| Middle fifth | 17.4 | 17.8 | 17.8 | 17.8 | 17.6 | 17.6 | 17.5 |
| Fourth fifth | 23.4 | 23.7 | 24.0 | 23.9 | 23.8 | 24.1 | 24.2 |
| Highest fifth | 42.7 | 41.3 | 41.3 | 40.9 | 40.9 | 41.1 | 41.5 |
| Top 5 percent | 17.3 | 16.4 | 15.9 | 15.5 | 15.6 | 15.5 | 15.7 |

Source: *Statistical Abstract of the United States.*

## Current Income

Current income, the major source of buying power for Americans, is not distributed evenly among our households. The data in Table 3–4 show that total income is becoming more evenly divided among American households. But the change toward more equal distribution is proceeding so slowly that there is relatively little discernible effect from a marketing or a social standpoint. Families in the top fifth, for example, have almost 7½ times as much income as those in the bottom fifth.

## Accumulated Wealth

Accumulated wealth is another important component of consumer buying power in the United States. It can be liquid or nonliquid.

**Liquid wealth** such as checking and savings accounts, money in credit    liquid wealth
unions, government bonds, and corporate securities that are traded on stock exchanges can be converted quickly into cash for making purchases. It often is used to make down payments on durable purchases like appliances and furniture. It may be stored up for specific purchases like college education and/or for contingencies like hospital bills. Liquid wealth also is distributed unevenly among American households.

**Nonliquid wealth,** such as a family's equity in its home, cannot be    nonliquid wealth
converted as quickly into buying power as liquid wealth. Future generations often benefit from accumulated wealth, particularly nonliquid wealth, when it is willed to them upon the death of their parents. It is buying power that is shifted to succeeding generations.

In the United States taxes impact mainly on income, not on wealth. People who favor heavier taxation on wealth as a means of redistributing it say this would reduce poverty and expand the market for many products. Of course it also might reduce the market for luxury products. Opponents argue that a person's wealth tends to be in proportion to his

# We're issuing American Express Cards the way we always have.

# Responsibly.

American Express isn't suddenly limiting the number of new Cards we issue.

There always have been limitations. Not everyone who applies for an American Express® Card gets one.

We look for financial responsibility in potential Cardmembers. It's essential, because of the wide-ranging charge opportunities we offer coupled with the fact that Cardmembers are expected to pay their bill in full every month.

We don't offer revolving, open-end credit. In fact, we're not really a credit card. We're a charge card with many services, conveniences and privileges.

If this is the kind of card that makes sense for you, call 800-528-8000 and we'll send you an application.

*An ad that appeared in April 1980 after the government imposed consumer credit controls*

or her contribution to society's productivity.    Thus nonliquid wealth also is distributed unevenly among American households.

## Credit

When sources of consumer credit are willing to increase lending, total consumer buying power increases, at least in the short run.    When they are less willing to lend, total consumer buying power declines.    The President of the United States imposed consumer credit controls in early 1980.    This made it harder for consumers to get credit and had great meaning to retailers like J.C. Penney, the third largest retailer in the nation, which was making about 43 percent of its sales on credit.[14]

**Installment credit** requires making regular monthly payments (installments) on credit purchases.    It is very important in buying consumer durables such as furniture and cars.

**Noninstallment credit** requires paying charge purchases off within thirty days of the date the statement arrives.    Table 3–5 shows two important trends in consumer credit: (1) big growth in the total volume of credit and (2) faster growth of installment credit than noninstallment credit.

Some people say using credit amounts to using tomorrow's buying power today and that it cannot expand consumer buying power over the long run.    Other people say it expands consumer buying power because credit buyers may be willing to work more to pay their bills on time.[15]    Some families, as we said earlier, can buy expensive homes only because both spouses are willing to work to meet the notes.    About 60 percent of all first-time home buyers are families in which both spouses work. The percentage may increase as home mortgage interest rates and construction costs escalate.

## Buying Power and Inflation

Three types of income are important to marketers: (1) disposable income, (2) discretionary income, and (3) real income.

**Disposable income** is the amount of buying power available to consumers from current sources.    Basically, it is their current income (salaries, wages, interest on savings accounts, rental income, dividends on

*installment credit*

*noninstallment credit*

*disposable income*

**Table 3–5.**  *Consumer credit (in billions of dollars) for selected years*

|  | 1950 | 1960 | 1965 | 1970 | 1975 | 1978 |
|---|---|---|---|---|---|---|
| Total credit outstanding | 25.6 | 65.1 | 103.3 | 143.1 | 223.3 | 339.9 |
| Percent of disposable income | 12.0 | 18.5 | 21.0 | 20.4 | 19.8 | 22.4 |
| Installment | 15.5 | 45.1 | 73.9 | 105.5 | 172.4 | 275.6 |
| Noninstallment | 10.1 | 20.0 | 29.4 | 37.6 | 50.9 | 64.3 |

Source: *Statistical Abstract of the United States.*

stock, interest on bonds) minus the taxes they pay. What is left can be spent on necessities and luxuries.

discretionary
income
real income

**Discretionary income** is disposable income minus expenditures for necessities. It can be spent on luxury products.

**Real income** is current income, adjusted for inflation, to express the real buying power of current income. Suppose a family's income in current dollars in one year is $10,000. It stays the same in current dollars the next year. But if the Consumer Price Index went up 10 percent, real income in the second year is 10 percent less than the current income figure.

Our progressive federal income tax causes consumers in higher income brackets to pay higher taxes. Suppose your income one year is $10,000 and it increases to $11,000 the next year. If the inflation rate is 10 percent, your real income in the second year is $9,900 ($11,000 minus 10 percent). Your real income before taxes went down. If the extra $1,000 in income shifts you to a higher income tax bracket, your real income after taxes is even less.

People living on fixed incomes, such as many retired people, suffer most from inflation. Their buying power diminishes as inflation continues. It appears that some inflation has become a rather permanent fixture in the American economy and government and business recognize it. Thus Social Security payments have been tied to the Consumer Price Index, as are wages of workers whose union contracts have escalator clauses. But there also is a concerted effort by the federal government to bring inflation under control. Thus some people favor removing or reducing cost-of-living adjustments for Social Security recipients. Think of what that might mean to marketers who focus their efforts on the elderly.

### Ethnic Distribution of Buying Power

Income is distributed unevenly among American households regardless of ethnic group. But there also are differences among ethnic groups. For example, in 1979 the median family income was $19,684. For whites, it was $20,520. For Hispanics, it was $14,320 (70 percent of $20,520). For blacks, it was $11,650 (57 percent of $20,520). Overall, 11.6 percent of the population, or 25.2 million persons, were below the poverty line ($7,412 for an urban family of four).[16] Marketers must be aware of such data in selecting their market targets.

---

**Table 3–6.** *How states compare in median EBI per household*

Note: Median EBI per household means there are as many households above the stated income figure as below it. It is a more reliable indicator of buying power than average EBI per household because the latter includes income from nonhousehold sources, such as institutions and military barracks, hence will always be a higher figure than the median one. The year 1977 was chosen for computing % growth because that is the year in which the most recent Census of Retail Trade was taken.

| Rank | State | Median Effective Buying Income Per Household | % Growth 1977-79 |
|---|---|---|---|
| 1. | Alaska | $26,107 | +18.4% |
| 2. | Hawaii | 22,991 | +26.8 |
| 3. | New Jersey | 21,771 | +17.9 |
| 4. | Illinois | 21,054 | +16.4 |
| 5. | Connecticut | 20,815 | +17.8 |
| 6. | Michigan | 20,091 | +13.5 |
| 7. | Nevada | 19,680 | +19.1 |
| 8. | Washington | 19,417 | +23.4 |
| 9. | Ohio | 19,274 | +18.3 |
| 10. | Wyoming | 19,199 | +27.9 |
| 11. | Delaware | 19,195 | +17.4 |
| 12. | Maryland | 19,179 | +16.9 |
| 13. | Indiana | 19,118 | +20.6 |
| 14. | Minnesota | 18,852 | +27.6 |
| 15. | California | 18,811 | +20.4 |
| 16. | Iowa | 18,779 | +26.4 |
| 17. | Massachusetts | 18,730 | +18.7 |
| 18. | Wisconsin | 18,617 | +18.9 |
| 19. | Pennsylvania | 18,265 | +17.2 |
| 20. | Texas | 18,135 | +25.2 |
| 21. | Utah | 18,126 | +22.6 |
| 22. | New Hampshire | 18,087 | +19.9 |
| 23. | Colorado | 18,060 | +25.1 |
|  | U.S. | 17,924 | +19.4 |
| 24. | Kansas | 17,829 | +23.6 |
| 25. | Rhode Island | 17,699 | +14.1 |
| 26. | Arizona | 17,691 | +28.7 |
| 27. | New York | 17,487 | +14.3 |
| 28. | Nebraska | 17,334 | +22.9 |
| 29. | Dist. of Columbia | 17,315 | +14.7 |
| 30. | Virginia | 17,288 | +19.0 |
| 31. | Oregon | 17,162 | +23.3 |
| 32. | North Dakota | 16,724 | +30.3 |
| 33. | Missouri | 16,416 | +20.9 |
| 34. | Idaho | 16,407 | +18.5 |
| 35. | Louisiana | 16,119 | +22.5 |
| 36. | West Virginia | 15,801 | +23.3 |
| 37. | North Carolina | 15,741 | +18.9 |
| 38. | South Carolina | 15,689 | +20.5 |
| 39. | South Dakota | 15,683 | +40.7 |
| 40. | New Mexico | 15,635 | +25.6 |
| 41. | Georgia | 15,608 | +15.0 |
| 42. | Vermont | 15,555 | +19.4 |
| 43. | Maine | 15,479 | +15.6 |
| 44. | Kentucky | 15,388 | +21.4 |
| 45. | Florida | 14,915 | +23.2 |
| 46. | Tennessee | 14,833 | +16.8 |
| 47. | Montana | 14,813 | +17.4 |
| 48. | Oklahoma | 14,634 | +22.5 |
| 49. | Alabama | 14,267 | +16.8 |
| 50. | Arkansas | 13,150 | +17.7 |
| 51. | Mississippi | 12,776 | +15.7 |

Source: *Sales & Marketing Management's 1980 Survey of Buying Power.*

### Regional Distribution of Buying Power

Buying power is not distributed evenly among the different regions nor among and within the states. Families in the Northeast, for example, have more buying power than families in the Southeast. In 1940 per capita income in the poorest one-fifth of the states was 36 percent of that in the richest one-fifth. The corresponding percentage in 1978 was 72 percent.[17] Thus the income gap among the states is narrowing.

The South experienced outmigration of poor families during many recent decades. Many of these people moved to the West, Northeast, and Midwest. But in recent years the situation is changing. There is more inmigration than outmigration of poor people in the South. Meanwhile, the West continues to gain poor people while the Northeast and Midwest are losing them.[18] Marketers have to keep this in mind when contemplating market opportunities in various regions of the country. Thus the population increase in the Sunbelt is not due only to more affluent families moving there. Marketers must continually study current and projected income and buying power statistics in their market areas.

One source of data many marketers use is *Sales & Marketing Management* magazine's annual *Survey of Buying Power*. Table 3–6 is taken from this source. It shows how states compared in median effective buying income (EBI) in 1979. Essentially, EBI is disposable personal income minus compensation paid to military and diplomatic personnel stationed overseas.[19]

### WILLINGNESS TO BUY

Buying power affects our ability and willingness to buy. Ability to buy is the economic dimension of buying power. Willingness to buy is the psychological dimension.

Families ordinarily can derive more buying power from their income when they are confident about the future. They tend to be willing to spend more of their income. Consumers who lack confidence tend to save more and spend less because they are worried about unemployment and recession. Bread and milk are bought out of necessity but many other products will sell only if consumers are in a buying mood. This is why marketers engage in research to gauge consumer confidence in the economy.

The Survey Research Center at the University of Michigan, the Commercial Credit Corporation, and The Conference Board, Inc. are three consumer pollsters that survey consumer buying intentions.[20] They have a good record for accurately forecasting actual expenditure patterns for consumer durables and industrial products.

American consumers historically have reacted to inflation by reducing spending and increasing savings. In the middle of 1978 the Survey Research Center found consumer confidence at a very low level. They

# ART, REAL ESTATE, GOLD. AND VOLVOS?

There are still a few investments left today that are worth making. And these three people know them when they see them. That's why they all own Volvos.

They not only consider Volvo a safe car to be in; they also consider it a safe place to put their money. Maybe that's because over the last two years the dollar invested in a Volvo has held its value better than the dollar in your pocket.*

So right now, a two-year-old Volvo could actually be worth more than it originally cost.

Of course if you're shrewd enough to invest in a Volvo, it's unlikely you'll want to turn it over so quickly. Because a Volvo is made to last a long time. (The life expectancy of a Volvo is now up to 17.9 years in Sweden.)

And with the money you might save by not buying a new car every few years, you can make another investment as worthwhile as your Volvo. Like art, real estate or gold.

**VOLVO**
A car you can believe in.

Joseph Eliasoph, art dealer

Ruth Baskow, real estate agent

RARE COINS
123

Sheldon Rosenblatt, coin dealer

*Based on a comparison between the consumer price index for the first 11 months of 1977 vs. 1979 and depreciation of a 2-year-old Volvo. © 1980 VOLVO OF AMERICA CORPORATION.

*An ad that makes an investment appeal*
Source: Volvo of America Corporation.

doubted government's ability to control inflation.  But they were willing to buy houses and cars because they expected prices to go even higher, and they were buying silverware and jewelry because they figured these products retained real value.[21]  But by 1980 consumer credit controls and heavy indebtedness by consumers had begun to take their toll and consumer spending started to decline, thereby helping to bring on a recession.

Nevertheless, the average consumer today has to work fewer hours than consumers in the past to buy many, if not most, of the same products. This means real income has increased over the long haul.

### Expenditure Patterns

The first work published on consumer spending patterns dates back to the mid-nineteenth century when a German statistician, Ernst Engel, reported on the spending patterns of working-class families.  He found that as a family's income rises, expenditures for most categories also will rise.  Notice, however, that the following generalizations, often called **Engel's laws,** focus on what happens to the *percentages* of income spent on certain categories as a family's income increases.

**Engel's laws**

As income increases the percentage spent on

1. food will decrease.
2. housing and household operation will remain constant.
3. all other categories (such as clothing, transportation, recreation, health, and education, will increase, as will the amount saved.

Engel developed these laws from studies of individual families who were moving from one income group to another.  They cannot, however, predict what will happen to consumer expenditure patterns of an entire nation as gross national product (GNP) changes.  Modern marketers have more detailed aggregate expenditure data for making these predictions.

*"I now pronounce you a two-spouse working household."*

Source: *Wall Street Journal.*

**Table 3–7.** *Personal consumption expenditures for selected years*

| Expenditures | 1950 | 1955 | 1960 | 1965 | 1970 | 1975 | 1977 |
|---|---|---|---|---|---|---|---|
| Total consumption (in billions of $) | 192.2 | 253.7 | 324.9 | 430.2 | 618.8 | 979.1 | 1,206.5 |
| Percentage due to: | | | | | | | |
| Food, beverages, and tobacco | 30.3 | 28.5 | 27.1 | 24.9 | 23.8 | 22.9 | 21.7 |
| Clothing, accessories, and jewelry | 12.3 | 11.0 | 9.9 | 9.4 | 9.0 | 8.4 | 7.9 |
| Personal care | 1.3 | 1.4 | 1.6 | 1.8 | 1.8 | 1.5 | 1.4 |
| Housing | 11.3 | 13.5 | 14.8 | 15.2 | 15.2 | 15.3 | 15.3 |
| Household operations | 15.2 | 14.6 | 14.2 | 14.2 | 14.2 | 14.5 | 14.7 |
| Medical care | 4.7 | 5.2 | 6.2 | 7.0 | 8.1 | 9.1 | 9.8 |
| Personal business | 3.4 | 3.7 | 4.4 | 4.6 | 5.1 | 5.3 | 5.0 |
| Transportation | 13.2 | 13.6 | 13.1 | 13.5 | 12.6 | 12.8 | 14.3 |
| Recreation | 5.8 | 5.6 | 5.5 | 6.0 | 6.6 | 6.8 | 6.7 |
| Other | 2.4 | 2.9 | 3.3 | 3.4 | 3.7 | 3.4 | 3.2 |

Source: *Statistical Abstract of the United States.*

One way to gauge consumer willingness to buy is to study what they are buying. Consumer spending can be divided into spending on (1) durables (cars and household appliances), (2) nondurables (food and clothing), and (3) services (entertainment and medical care).

Various government departments, business magazines, and trade associations report statistics on spending patterns by expense categories such as housing, transportation, and recreation. These data often are broken down by family income groupings.

The data in Table 3–7 show a decreasing percentage of total consumption expenditures for food, beverages, and tobacco and for clothing, accessories, and jewelry. The data also show an increasing percentage spent for housing, medical care, and personal business.

A lot of attention has been given in recent years to expenditure patterns of families in which both spouses work.[22] Dual-earner families used to be mostly associated with lower- and middle-income groups. Now they are increasingly common among higher-income families. They spend more than single-earner families on household help, furniture, kitchen appliances, cars, and travel. They also spend more than other affluent people on golf, tennis, and swimming club memberships and they entertain at home less.

## SUMMARY AND LOOK AHEAD

The two basic types of markets are ultimate consumer markets and industrial user markets. Ultimate consumers buy and/or use products for their personal and/or household use. Industrial users buy products to use in making other products for resale or for use in conducting their operations.

A market means the same thing as effective demand. A market exists for a product when people desire it, have buying power and the willingness to use it to satisfy that desire, and are eligible to buy it.

The population of the United States is distributed unevenly among the states and marketers must be aware of population shifts. These include the movement of people to the Sunbelt states, the migration of people into our SMSAs, and the movement of people within our SMSAs. The age, sex, and ethnic distribution of the population also is important to marketers.

The three main sources of buying power are current income, accumulated wealth, and credit. Current income is the major source for American consumers but credit also is very important. Buying power declines during inflation and willingness to buy depends a lot on consumer confidence in the outlook for the economy. This is especially true for products that are not necessities.

Three basic types of income are important to marketers: (1) disposable income, (2) discretionary income, and (3) real income. Inflation's effect on buying power is especially serious for people who live on fixed incomes. Consumer buying power in the United States is distributed unequally among households, regions, and ethnic groups.

Consumer spending can be divided into spending on (1) durable products, (2) nondurable products, and (3) services. Marketers give a lot of attention to expenditure patterns of households and surveys of consumer intentions to buy.

In the next chapter we will begin our dicussion of consumer behavior. The focus is on consumer buying decisions.

## REVIEW QUESTIONS

**1.** What determines whether a buyer is an ultimate consumer or an industrial user? Explain.

**2.** Identify and discuss the five major requirements for the existence of a market.

**3.** Give three examples of government programs that help protect some consumers against losses in buying power.

**4.** Give an example that shows how a firm might increase the effective buying power of its target customers.

**5.** Identify the three main dimensions of the ultimate consumer market.

**6.** Identify and discuss the four key factors that determine a nation's population.

**7.** Why is the birthrate more controllable, but harder to predict, than the death rate?

**8.** What factors help to explain a declining birthrate in the United States?

**9.** What is an SMSA? Discuss the population movements within our SMSAs.

**10.** Should marketers look at the United States as a great "melting pot" in which all people basically are alike? Explain.

**11.** Why has the percentage increase in the number of households been greater than the percentage increase in our population during some recent years?

**12.** Identify and discuss the three main sources of consumer buying power.

**13.** Distinguish between installment and non-installment credit. Which type has experienced the greater growth during recent decades?

**14.** Define: (a) disposable income, (b) discretionary income, and (c) real income.

**15.** Is income in the United States distributed evenly by region, by ethnic group, and among households? Explain.

**16.** Distinguish between the economic and the psychological dimensions of buying power.

**17.** Discuss Engel's laws and their implications for marketers.

## DISCUSSION QUESTIONS

**1.** Some TV commercials and magazine ads may stimulate desire for products among consumers who cannot afford to buy them. Is this desirable?

**2.** Are Americans too free and easy with their use of credit?

**3.** Organized crime thrives on selling products that many Americans are prohibited from buying, such as lottery tickets and addictive drugs. Should

laws that prohibit the legal marketing of these products be eliminated?

**4.** What effects might a trend toward smaller families have on marketers of (a) refrigerators, (b) cars, (c) houses, and (d) medical insurance policies?

**5.** Mandatory retirement for most workers at age sixty-five has been abolished. How might this affect the development of marketing strategies?

## NOTES

1. "Cosmetics: Kiss and Sell," *Time*, December 11, 1978, p. 88.
2. "Decade's Boom in Prime-Age Consumers Will Offer Vast Opportunities for Business," *Wall Street Journal*, June 26, 1980, p. 23.
3. See Roxann A. Van Dusen and Eleanor Bernert Sheldon, "The Changing Status of American Women: A Life Cycle Perspective," *American Psychologist*, February, 1976, pp. 106–116; Rena Bartos, "The Moving Target: The Impact of Women's Employment on Consumer Behavior," *Journal of Marketing*, July, 1977, pp. 31–37; and Suzanne H. McCall, "Meet the 'Workwife'," *Journal of Marketing*, July, 1977, pp. 55–65.
4. See Vance Packard, *A Nation of Strangers* (New York: David McKay Company, 1972).
5. See Juan de Torres, "The New Reality of Major U.S. Metro-Areas," *Conference Board Record*, June, 1975, pp. 54–61; Fabian Linden, "The Changing Cities and Suburbs," *Conference Board Record*, February, 1976, pp. 14–17; and Juan de Torres, "The New Pattern of Urban Migration," *Conference Board Record*, May, 1976, pp. 28–34.
6. See Kirkpatrick Sales, *Power Shift: The Rise of the Southern Rim and Its Challenge to the Eastern Establishment* (New York: Random House, 1975).

7. "Americans on the Move," *Time*, March 15, 1976, p. 64.
8. "Consolidated Cigar: Reversing a Decline by Appealing to Youth," *Business Week*, July 30, 1979, pp. 88–89.
9. "Jostens: A School Supplier Stays with Basics as Enrollment Declines," *Business Week*, April 21, 1980, p. 129.
10. See Betsy D. Gelb, "Exploring the Gray Market Segment," *MSU Business Topics*, Spring, 1978, pp. 41–48; and Rena Bartos, "Over 49: The Invisible Consumer Market," *Harvard Business Review*, January–February, 1980, pp. 140–148.
11. "Kellogg: Still the Cereal People," *Business Week*, November 26, 1979, p. 81.
12. "Gillette: A New Shampoo Aims for More of the Unisex Market," *Business Week*, April 3, 1978, pp. 96–97.
13. "Firms Seek to Tighten Links with Hispanics as Buyers and Workers," *Wall Street Journal*, November 10, 1980, p. 14.
14. "J.C. Penney Solicits Credit Card Customers Despite Tougher Tests," *Wall Street Journal*, April 24, 1980, p. 32.
15. One study found that heavy and light users

of credit feel that credit enables them to increase their short- and long-run ability to buy products. See Gordon L. Wise, Herbert E. Brown, and Myron K. Cox, "Profiling the Heavy Users of Consumer Credit," *Journal of Consumer Credit Management*, Spring, 1977, pp. 116–123.

16. "Family Median Income Climbed a Scant 0.3% after Inflation in 1979," *Wall Street Journal*, October 23, 1980, p. 14.

17. "Study Shows Income Gap Is Closing Among States, *Wall Street Journal*, April 16, 1980, p. 28.

18. "Sunbelt and Suburbia Still Strong Magnets for Migrating Americans During Decade," *Wall Street Journal*, July 2, 1980, p. 19.

19. "EFFECTIVE BUYING INCOME (EBI). A classification exclusively developed by Sales & Marketing Management, it is personal income less personal tax and nontax payments. Personal income is the aggregate of wages and salaries, other labor income (such as employer contributions to private pension funds), proprietors' income, rental income (which includes imputed rental income of owner-occupants of nonfarm dwellings), dividends paid by corporations, personal interest income from all sources, and transfer payments (such as pensions and welfare assistance). Deducted from this total are personal taxes (federal, state, and local), nontax payments (such as fines, fees, penalties),

and personal contributions for social insurance. The resultant figure is commonly known as "disposable personal income." Market Statistics, the research division of Bill Communications that prepares the *Survey* data, removes from this figure compensation paid to military and diplomatic personnel stationed overseas to arrive at Effective Buying Income.

"Effective Buying Income is a bulk measurement of market potential. It indicates the general ability to buy and is essential in comparing, selecting, and grouping markets on that basis. But for products that appeal to specific income classes, the percent of households by Effective Buying Income group should be considered." *Sales & Marketing Management*, July 28, 1980, p. A-34.

20. For discussion of the Survey Research Center at the University of Michigan, see Lee Smith, "The Economist Who Polls Consumers," *Dun's Review*, April, 1976, pp. 68–70.

21. "The Customer Holds the Key," *Time*, August 7, 1978, p. 62.

22. See Susan Edmiston, "Love, Honor and Earn: The Two-Income Marriage," *Working Woman*, November, 1976, pp. 28–32; and Walter Kiechel, III, "Two-Income Families Will Reshape the Consumer Markets," *Fortune*, March 10, 1980, pp. 110–114, 117, 119–120.

Chapter 4

# Consumer Buying Decisions

**OBJECTIVES**

*After reading this chapter you should be able to*

1. contrast programed and nonprogramed decisions.

2. tell how consumers and marketers attempt to reduce cognitive dissonance.

3. explain how programed decisions can become nonprogramed.

4. explain the relationship between brand loyalty and the stability of the product category.

5. give examples of how marketers use personality and attitude data in making decisions.

**KEY CONCEPTS**

*Look for these terms as you read the*

Nonprogramed Decisions
Deficits List
Use System
Information Processing
Buying Alternative
Cognitive Dissonance
Programed Decisions
Economic Importance
Psychological Importance
Purchase Frequency
Lifestyle
Fully Programed Decisions
Personality
Attitudes
Product Diffusion

*Why are some beer drinkers intensely loyal to their brands and buy them out of habit while some others buy unbranded (generic) beer at the supermarket?*

*What about the effects of changing lifestyles on consumer buying decisions?  Some Heublein ads for Harveys Bristol Cream sherry, for example, feature a woman talking on the phone with a friend.  "A few years ago, it wasn't considered respectable for a woman to ask a man over for a drink.  But I figure when I'm serving Harveys Bristol Cream, it's more than just respectable, it's downright upright."*

*Consider also the effects on consumer buying decisions of reported research findings that appear to link cholesterol with heart disease, sugar with various health problems, and nitrates with cancer.  Why will some consumers stop buying products that represent a possible health hazard while some others will shrug the reports off and continue to consume these products?*

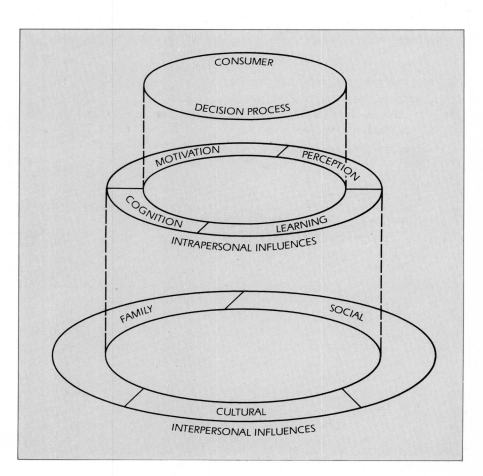

**Figure 4–1.
A model of the consumer decision process**

Ordinarily there are many differences in the ways consumers make buying decisions. Some people buy some products out of habit whereas others go through an involved decision process in buying those same products. Even when people appear to make a decision in the same way, the importance of some factors in their choices may vary. For example, two consumers may need new tires. They consult friends and *Consumer Reports*, comparison shop five stores, and finally buy the same brand. But they may have very different reasons for their choices. One may be looking for safety features and product warranty while the other may be more interested in mileage, price, and appearance.

Figure 4–1 is a simplified model of the consumer decision process and the factors that influence it. This chapter deals with consumer buying decisions. Although others may actually use the product or make the purchase, understanding the person who makes the buying decision is most important to marketers. Chapters 5 and 6 will discuss the intrapersonal and interpersonal influences on these decisions. We will focus more specifically on industrial buyer behavior in Chapter 7.

Consumer decisions can be divided roughly into two types, nonprogramed and programed. Let's begin with nonprogramed decisions.

## NONPROGRAMED DECISIONS  New Task

**Nonprogramed decisions** are those that consumers have not worked out a routine method of handling. To make these decisions, consumers engage in problem-solving behavior aimed at filling gaps in their assortment of products. They are in an active learning situation and are receptive to information about products and brands—where they are available, their prices, and so on. Information from advertising, brochures, friends and relatives, store personnel, the Better Business Bureau, and *Consumer Reports* may be sought and used in the decision process. Providing information to help consumers make nonprogramed decisions is part of the marketing effort.

nonprogramed
decisions

Modified

### Characteristics of Nonprogramed Decisions

Decisions that the consumer has never made before are nonprogramed. For example, newlyweds who are buying furniture and appliances for the first time are making nonprogramed decisions.

Some decisions, however, can be nonprogramed even though they have been made before. Nonprogramed decisions are made when buying products that are hard to compare and products that are seldom bought. It is hard to compare brands of tires, stereo equipment, life insurance, and upholstered furniture, and consumers often make choices based on features that are unrelated to product performance. Most people cannot tell which of two stereo amplifiers is better simply by looking at them, and technical information about them is hard to understand. Consumers buy other products such as refrigerators, garden hoses, and luggage so seldom that the buying decision remains nonprogramed. Over time, product requirements change along with the relative ranking of different brands in a product category. This is why the decision to buy these products usually is nonprogramed.

Truly important decisions hardly ever become programed. Those that involve a lot of money in relation to a consumer's disposable income or are considered important for other reasons generally are nonprogramed. Buying a house or choosing a suit are nonprogramed decisions for most people.

**Stages of Nonprogramed Decisions**

Figure 4–2 lists the stages in making nonprogramed decisions. Few people, however, actually perform all the activities in this step-by-step sequence. A consumer may perform several at the same time, ignore and not perform some, or perhaps not go through this process at all.

**Awareness of Needs.** Your buying behavior results from deficits or excesses in your assortment of products. Awareness of these conditions may range from a vague feeling of dissatisfaction to a clear, readily stated desire. You constantly scan your situation to identify imbalances in your assortment and assign them priority rankings. If you were asked, you could make a list of needs in the form of products you need to get. A college student, for example, produced the **deficits list** shown below in about five minutes. The highest-priority items are listed first.

deficits list

1. Ban roll-on deodorant
2. A blouse to wear with my blue skirt
3. A gift for mother
4. A notebook
5. Eyeshadow (new shade)
6. Pantyhose
7. A new pair of shoes

The deficits list and the priorities assigned to items on it result from the student's assessment of her situation at the moment the list was prepared. Changes in her situation would affect the items included on the list and their priorities. The list might have been different had she prepared it an hour earlier. Such lists are changing continually and they do not always predict buying behavior.

Factors that can lead to changes in a person's deficits and their priority ranking include (1) exposure to new products or information, (2) using up the supply of a regularly used product, (3) more money to spend, (4) changes in social activities, (5) changes in goals, and (6) mood changes.

The list also shows that a person's awareness of deficits varies. The deodorant is listed by brand name but the gift for mother is vague. People entering nonprogramed decisions often cannot specify more than a product category. Thus a person who for the first time is considering the purchase of a pair of binoculars probably will not be aware of the various brands available or details about product features.

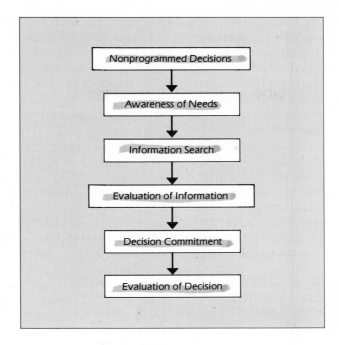

*Figure 4–2.*
*Stages of*
*nonprogramed*
*decisions*

The product, or categories of products, included in such a list depends largely on your familiarity with the products you use to satisfy your needs. Products that fit into familiar use systems are more likely to be included than products that fit new use systems. **A use system** is all the activities and objects necessary to use a product to do something. Innovative products (those that fit new use systems) are not as likely to be included on a deficits list. A new brand of toothpaste, for example, is more likely to be included than a Water Pik.

use system

**Information Search.** Consumers start searching for information when they recognize a need for which there is no predetermined buying solution.[1] They may recall prior experiences in similar buying decisions or the experience of friends in making a similar decision. The more similar the decision is to previous ones, the more likely it will be based on information they already have. But if the decision is not similar they search for more information from external sources such as family members, ads, and salespersons.

In general, consumers will seek more information when they feel a decision is important.[2] Importance is judged in terms of economic, psychological, and time considerations. The more money involved relative to one's disposable income, the greater the perceived psychological risk in making the decision, and the longer the period the product will have to be used, the more information the consumer will seek. Also, more information is sought when a person's prior experiences do not fit the decision at hand.

The information search focuses on several elements of the decision process. A decision is needed concerning the general product category (or categories) that will fill the deficits. For example, decisions about social activities involve different product categories than the gift for mother. Once a product category (or categories) is decided on, effort shifts to gathering information on specific products in the category (or categories). Then information is gathered for comparing price, quality, manufacturer, and retailer services.

Most consumers, however, do not sequence their information search in this exact fashion. They may shop a store to look at one product and try to find alternatives, gathering information as they go. They may explore one product fully if the needed information is readily available and give less attention to others. Consumers become upset when products are available but information about them is lacking, when they see ads on TV for products that are not available locally, and when retail store personnel lack product knowledge. Printed information at the point of purchase, proper coordination of the promotion and distribution elements of the marketing mix, and sales training programs can reduce this frustration.

**Evaluation of Information.** It is almost impossible for consumers to pay attention to all the product information that is directed to them every day. But they have to process the information before making a buying decision.[3] **Information processing** requires (1) categorizing and arranging information, (2) establishing criteria for judging the accuracy or usefulness of information, (3) establishing criteria to decide among purchase alternatives, (4) making a commitment to a purchase alternative, and (5) evaluating the decision. Although these steps are discussed in the order listed they do not necessarily occur in that order. (See Figure 4–3.)

information processing

Consumers get information about products in bits and pieces from different sources and sort it into categories such as price, durability, and safety. The categories vary among products and consumers. The ones consumers use depend on their prior experiences and what they learn in gathering information. Suppose you want to buy a riding lawn mower. You may bring to the decision situation habitually used categories to sort information on price, service, and warranty. Additional categories such as motor horsepower and number of gears may be added by talking with other people and comparing models.

Consumers sort information about product alternatives to make comparisons. Information that does not fit the categories they are using may be ignored. Information from different sources also may be treated differently. Friends may be a more or less important source than ads, depending on how reliable and credible they have been in the past and how well consumers can sort the information into the categories they are using.[4] A person may rely on ads to learn about new products but rely on a friend's advice about product durability. Information in ads may be discounted if it is inconsistent with that provided by friends.

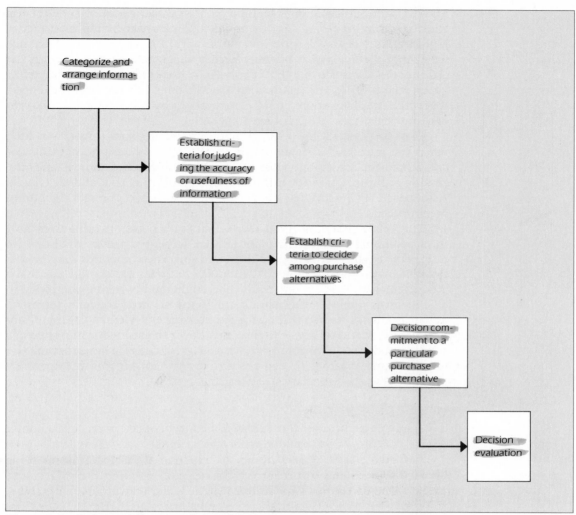

*Figure 4–3. Information processing activities*

**Decision Commitment.** Gathering, processing, and evaluating information about buying decisions takes time, energy, and money.[5] At some point the consumer must stop and make a commitment to a course of action. This may involve a commitment to a buying alternative, deciding not to buy, or deciding to rethink the need situation to find other solutions.

A **buying alternative** for a consumer product means the product itself, package, store, and method of purchase. In nonprogramed decisions the alternative picked is the one that appears best for the consumer's situation. This usually involves a tradeoff between product features and other factors—"satisficing" in decision making.[6] The consumer makes a de-

buying
alternative

cision that represents an acceptable compromise regarding product features and other factors. For example, a person may be willing to pay a higher price to get a washing machine with a gentle cycle. Although we cannot predict which buying alternative a consumer will choose, the one most likely is the one that involves the least risk, such as alternatives about which he or she has information or ones previously experienced. If several alternatives are equally attractive, the consequences of buying one and rejecting the others are considered.

**Decision Evaluation.** Information processing activities do not stop when the purchase is made. The results of the decision are evaluated and stored for future reference. Thus they affect the sources and processing of information for future decisions. If the product does what it is supposed to do the decision is judged to be a good one and the choice is reinforced.

The information received while making a decision influences how the consumer evaluates the product after buying it. If he or she is led to expect it will do things which it will not, the consumer may be dissatisfied with a good product. Marketers, therefore, should not make product claims that cannot readily be confirmed by using the product, regardless of whether the claims are based on the product's technical features or what its use will do for the consumer's social standing. Unfortunately, marketers have little control over the social meanings people give to products. Some people may be dissatisfied with a toothpaste that lives up to its claim for reducing cavities but does not increase their sex appeal as ads for other brands claim.

### Cognitive Dissonance

cognitive
dissonance

It is harder to evaluate the decision's consequences when a consumer selects one of several equally attractive alternatives. This leads to an uncomfortable state of psychological tension—**cognitive dissonance**—a feeling of uneasiness which arises when you choose one alternative and reject others that are equally attractive.[7] The consumer, in effect, asks, "Did I do the right thing?"

The amount of dissonance is determined by (1) the similarity of the alternatives, (2) the economic and psychological importance of the decision, (3) the quality and quantity of information available before making the decision, and (4) the extent to which the considered alternatives perform the same function. The more similar the alternatives and the greater the decision's importance, the greater the dissonance. The less information available about alternatives and the less the alternatives perform the same function, the greater the dissonance.

Consider the potential of the following incidents to create cognitive dissonance among a group of new car buyers. In 1978 Chrysler Corporation launched the first American-made subcompacts with front-wheel drive, the Omni and the Horizon. *Motor Trend* named Omni-Horizon the "car of the year." *Road and Track* and *Car and Driver* also had favorable comments.

But after running its tests on a special track Consumers Union reported in its *Consumer Reports* that four Omni-Horizons had failed two tests for stability and handling at expressway speeds. A rival of Consumers Union, Consumers' Research, also ran its own tests under normal road conditions. Omni-Horizon passed.

The issue finally went to the National Highway Traffic Safety Administration (NHTSA). After conducting the same tests as Consumers Union, NHTSA announced the same results. But NHTSA ruled that the cars were every bit as safe as Chrysler had contended. According to NHTSA, the tests Consumers Union had run were irrelevant to driving situations motorists encounter in the real world.

**How Consumers Reduce Dissonance.** Many nonprogramed decisions produce dissonance. Consumers try to reduce it and reassure themselves they made the right decision by reevaluating information obtained prior to the decision and searching for more information. They may (1) deny or distort information, (2) seek confirming opinions from others, (3) discredit the information source, (4) minimize the issue's importance, or (5) change the overall evaluation of the chosen alternative.

Suppose you believe Toyotas, Hondas, and Datsuns are equally attractive but you buy a Toyota. You may lower the overall appeal that the Honda and Datsun had for you by changing positive characteristics to negative ones and rejecting some of the positive information because of its source. You might turn to other Toyota owners to reinforce your decision, or simply conclude there are no real differences among the three makes.

If you cannot distort, reevaluate, or discredit the information you obtained before making the decision, you may seek new information. But your search for and use of information after the decision is biased. Favorable information is readily used but positive information about Hondas and Datsuns and negative information about Toyotas is ignored or discounted. You also will notice more Toyotas on the highway and pay more attention to Toyota ads.

The bias is magnified when the purchase is followed by poor product performance. If your Toyota performs poorly after repeated service, you may reduce dissonance in the only way left—by admitting you made a mistake. This massive reevaluation of the whole decision process is painful and has major consequences on the decision-making process you will use in the future.

**How Marketers Can Help Reduce Dissonance.** Marketers can help consumers reduce dissonance by (1) providing information consumers can use to reduce it and (2) ensuring that poor product performance is corrected as soon as possible. Marketers can use postpurchase communications such as letters and brochures to help buyers reduce dissonance.[8] Many car dealers send reassuring letters to new car buyers. Procter & Gamble's products carry a toll-free phone number on the package or label. Consumers can call in their praise or complaints about the products immediately rather than take the time to write to Procter & Gamble.

# How a phone call got a part-time bachelor off the hook.

*Based on an actual call made to the toll-free 24-hour Whirlpool Cool-Line® service.*

(Telephone Rings)

**Cool-Line Consultant:** Whirlpool Cool-Line. May I help you?

**Man:** If you don't she's going to kill me.

**Consultant:** What happened?

**Man:** It's our new self-cleaning oven. I think I ruined it. What can I do?

**Consultant:** We're here to help. Tell me about it.

**Man:** My wife is in the hospital. So for a week I've been batching it. Today she's coming home. So I decided to clean the oven for her. I turned the knob to CLEAN, but the oven won't heat up. And the oven door won't close. Can I get a serviceman out here fast?

**Consultant:** You really don't have to call a Whirlpool franchised Tech-Care® representative. Even though your warranty does cover it.

**Man:** I can never understand warranties.

**Consultant:** Ours are written so you can. But I think we can fix that oven over the phone. When a self-cleaning oven is turned to CLEAN, an automatic safety arm hooks the door closed. If your oven door wasn't closed when you turned it to CLEAN, the arm's blocking the door open.

**Man:** How can I get the door closed?

**Consultant:** Look on the edge of the oven for a small button. It operates the oven light and is part of the safety interlock system. Push the button in until you hear the motor stop running.

**Man:** Okay, the motor's running. Now it stopped.

**Consultant:** With the button still pushed in, turn the control dial back to OFF. The lock should retract.

**Man:** It's working! Now the door closes.

**Consultant:** Your oven will heat up, too.

**Man:** You really saved me. Now I've got to pick up my wife and . . . new baby.

**Consultant:** Call again if we can help with your Whirlpool appliances. And congratulations on your baby.

This is the kind of two-way communication we've been having with our Whirlpool Cool-Line service for the past eleven years. It's just one example of the continuing concern we have for customers who purchase quality Whirlpool appliances.

If you ever have a question or problem with your Whirlpool appliance, call our toll-free 24-hour Cool-Line service at 800-253-1301. In Alaska and Hawaii, the number is 800-253-1121. In Michigan, call 800-632-2243.

**Whirlpool**
Home Appliances
Quality. Our way of life.

*Whirlpool's Cool-Line helps in reducing cognitive dissonance*
Source: Whirlpool Corporation

In 1980 the firm phoned or visited 1.5 million people to ask them about their likes and dislikes concerning its products. Inquiries, complaints, and other contacts that are initiated by consumers are handled by the sixty employees who staff Procter & Gamble's consumer services department.[9]

The more times a consumer makes a buying decision that is confirmed by good consequences, the greater the chance the decision will become programed. Dissonance that is not reduced, however, leads to future nonprogramed decisions about products in that category.

## PROGRAMED DECISIONS

Consumers, of course, make many purchases without engaging in the process we have described. Many purchases are handled routinely. **Programed decisions** are the end result of the learning process consumers engage in when making nonprogramed decisions.

programed
decisions

### Characteristics of Programed Decisions

Programed decisions differ from nonprogramed decisions in that they (1) usually involve simple decision products, (2) usually are not very important in an economic and psychological sense, and (3) have a high purchase frequency.

**Simple Decision Products.** Toothpaste, toilet soap, cigarettes, and breakfast cereals are programed decisions for most consumers. These are noncomplex products, their functions usually are clear-cut, and their important features are evident.

**Little Economic and Psychological Risk.** Programed decisions usually involve little economic and psychological risk. But this does not mean the consumer considers the brand of soap or cigarettes to be unimportant. It only means the risk involved in this decision is minimal. At worst, the buyer of an unsatisfactory brand of toothpaste throws away a half-used tube and buys a different brand. But quite the opposite is true if a person buys an unsatisfactory home or car. The effects can be long lasting.

As we said earlier **economic importance** depends on the product's cost in relation to the consumer's disposable income. It must be judged from each consumer's frame of reference. Thus expensive products may be considered economically unimportant by some consumers.

economic
importance

On the other hand, **psychological importance,** is related to the purposes for which the product will be used (its function) and the social consequences of using it. This also must be judged from the consumer's frame of reference. The reactions of others to the use of Colgate toothpaste rather than Crest would be negligible since few people can observe which brand the consumer uses. Social value is minimal and the decision is unimportant in terms of social risk.

psychological
importance

Products with high visibility to other people (social value) are not as likely to become programed decisions because of the increased risk.[10]

Women ordinarily do not develop strong loyalty to brands of dresses because fashion changes constantly and there are undesirable styles in every brand. Clothing is highly visible to others and there is a lot of social risk in each purchase decision.

The functional aspects of a product that affect its psychological importance are the consequences of using a product that performs poorly. The consequences of using a faulty electric blanket or a faulty gas furnace are severe. If the consumer will be stuck with an inferior product for a long time after buying it, the decision is less likely to become programed. Once an initial satisfactory decision is made, however, many psychologically important decisions are programed as a way of reducing risk.

**High Purchase Frequency.** Frequently purchased products usually are handled in a programed way to save time and effort. But frequency is now an exact concept. Some consumers buy a large number of units of a product at one time. Others buy smaller amounts more often. It is not clear whether the number of units purchased during a period of time or the actual number of times the consumer buys the product is the more accurate measure of **purchase frequency.**

purchase
frequency

Consider the effects of purchase frequency on the tendency of buying decisions to become programed. The stability of the product category comes into play here. The faster new products are introduced and changes are made in existing products within a category, the higher the purchase frequency needed for the buying decision to become programed. For example, in the 1940s there were 3 major brands of cigarettes, Camels, Lucky Strike, and Chesterfield. Now there are more than 160 brands.

Decisions also become programed in stable product categories with low buying frequencies. Writing instruments used to be a very stable product category and pencil and pen makers relied on strong habitual purchases by consumers. The introduction and improvement of many types of disposable ballpoint and fiber tip pens and Paper Mate's Eraser Mate, an erasable ink pen, changed this. Programed buying decisions, in cases like this, are relatively short-lived because they must be re-evaluated constantly in view of the new products that appear.

Buying decisions that involve simple, unimportant, and/or frequently purchased products, therefore, usually become programed. Let's look at how consumers handle these decisions.

### Consumer Behavior in Programed Decisions

The programed decision sequence shown in Figure 4–4 is much simpler than that for nonprogramed decisions. Consumers making programed decisions exhibit three characteristics: (1) their behavior is under external stimulus control, (2) they are not receptive to new information, and (3) their behavior will be relatively consistent in making these decisions.

**External Stimulus Control.** If you are aware of a need you buy the product that satisfies the need. Often you become aware of the need on seeing the normally purchased product. In other words, you may be

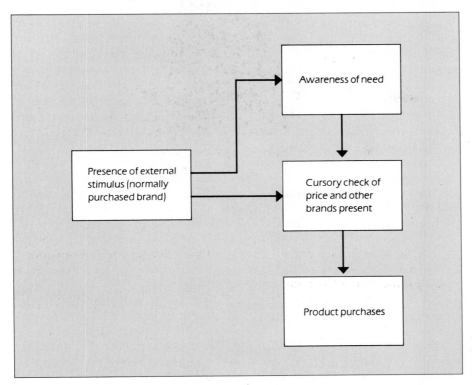

Figure 4–4.
Decision sequence
in programed
decisions

aware of the need before going shopping or realize the need on seeing your normally purchased product while shopping. The same product may be bought on either basis at different times. Staple products and impulse products, as we will see in Chapter 10, are examples.

**Not Receptive to New Information.** A programed decision does not involve much thinking by the consumer. It does not involve new learning; it is the result of earlier learning. This means the consumer is not actively receptive to new information. He or she buys out of force of habit. When Anheuser-Busch discovered that many consumers simply requested "light" beer and were served Miller's Lite brand, it started an ad campaign to get its target customers to request "Natural" instead of a "light" beer. Anheuser-Busch's brand name is "Natural Light."

Ads and point-of-purchase displays by competing brands generally have no effect on consumers making programed decisions because they are geared to pay attention to only a few specific types of information.[11] They filter out information about other brands. This makes it hard to switch brand-loyal customers. They simply do not see the information or else they consider it irrelevant to their buying situation. Product and store loyalty are well-developed programed decisions to buy a particular brand or to buy from a particular store. Figure 4–5 illustrates the ten-

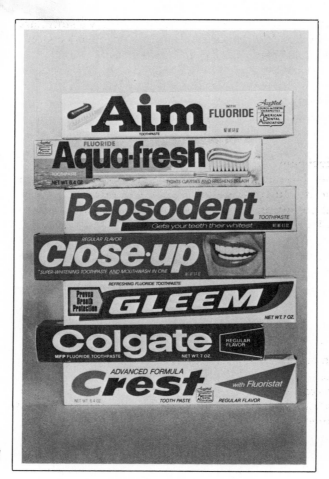

*Figure 4–5.*
*Perception of*
*normally purchased*
*brand*

dency to see only information that is relevant. As you glance at the tubes of toothpaste you will first notice the brand you normally use.

Another reason people are not receptive to new information is that it takes time and effort. Most people will not take the time and exert the effort unless there is a very good reason. How a person sees an object, situation, or event becomes habitual and resistant to change.

The information search and processing that do occur in programed decisions usually are limited to cursory checks of different sizes and styles of the product or of nearby competing brands. This minimal effort is not a real consideration of alternative products. It is a casual check to make sure that price and other product features are within a reasonable range. This, however, does not occur when the decision is fully programed and includes both brand and store. Such a programed decision may be stated, "Buy Crest toothpaste at Gibson's Discount Store when I go to get macrame supplies."

**Relatively Consistent Behavior.**   Your **lifestyle** is simply a summary lifestyle statement of the way you handle a large number of programed decisions. Programed decisions for a number of different product categories will be relatively similiar.   Your tendency to buy several types of toilet articles at discount stores instead of at supermarkets or drugstores may be characteristic of your buying habits.   It may reflect your strategy of finding the lowest price for normally purchased products or the desire to find a convenient place to buy a number of items at one time.   Thus your behavior is relatively consistent in making these programed decisions.

**Fully programed decisions** are more than just store or brand loyalty. fully programed decisions Only when the consumer has habitual answers for the following questions about a buying decision is it fully programed:   (1) what brand?   (2) what store?   (3) under what conditions?   (4) what price?   (5) what payment terms?   (6) other products bought at the same time?   This degree of programing is rare among consumers.   In industrial marketing, however, reorders of some raw materials and supplies such as light bulbs and cleaning compounds may be this fully programed.   As we will see in Chapter 7, they may be so fully programed that computers handle the placement of orders.

## SHIFTS IN TYPES OF DECISIONS

How nonprogramed and programed decisions are made often is called the product adoption process.   We will discuss this process in greater detail in Chapter 10.   Traditional stages are:   (1) awareness, (2) interest, (3) evaluation, (4) trial, and (5) adoption.[12]   Nonprogramed decisions include all these stages.   Programed decisions are a later part of the adoption stage. A consumer's adoption of a product, however, does not end the decision process.

The division of buying decisions into programed and nonprogramed is not permanent.   Successful nonprogramed decisions become programed if they are repeated often enough under the right conditions. Programed decisions also can become nonprogramed if (1) new products become available, (2) you have used your brand for a long time and are tired of it, (3) people whose opinions you respect suggest new ways of doing something, and (4) your living situation changes a great deal.[13]

A consumer's brand loyalty depends somewhat on the stability of the product category.   If the brands competing with your brand do not change you probably will continue to buy it.   But when new brands come out or old ones are improved your decision may become nonprogramed. These changes in the competition create a new decision situation and may affect your brand loyalty.   For many years amateur photographers in the United States were very loyal to Polaroid and Kodak cameras. Japanese marketers were targeting their 35mm cameras to professional photographers, not amateurs.   But in 1979 Canon, Nikon, Olympus, Minolta, and Pentax started targeting low-priced 35mm cameras to amateur photographers, thereby causing some brand switching.

Most consumers occasionally try brands other than their normally used brand. You may have done this simply because you wanted to try something different. Your programed decision may become nonprogramed if the brands you tried seem better than your regular one. Programed decisions also often become nonprogramed when others tell us there is a better way to handle the buying decision, especially if the advice comes from people whose opinions we respect.

People grow and change throughout their lives. More money available for a decision may result in a new decision. Cadillac and Lincoln had record sales in the late 1970s because they were able to entice some traditional buyers of Oldsmobiles and Fords to trade up. Decreasing buying power has the opposite effect. Whereas the luxury car share of the market normally is 5.5 percent, it was 7 percent in the late 1970s. But the recession that started in 1980 decreased the share to about 4 percent by May 1980. Some potential buyers of luxury cars also were afraid of being perceived as greedy.[14]

## PERSONALITY AND ATTITUDES IN BUYING DECISIONS

Marketers have suspected for a long time that personality and attitudes influence what consumers buy and how they make buying decisions. Some studies using personality and attitude inventories have demonstrated relationships between these factors and what consumers will do in the marketplace. Others have not.[15]

personality

**Personality** is the relatively permanent tendency to behave in a consistent way in certain situations. We infer personality data from people's reports of their typical behaviors and concerns on personality inventories and try to predict how they will behave based on these reports.

attitudes

**Attitudes,** an important part of personality concepts, are predispositions to feel, believe, or behave in certain ways. It is assumed that how a person feels, thinks, and behaves are related. If we can get a measure of how consumers think and feel about a situation, we sometimes can predict what they will do. Psychographic analysis is used to determine these relationships. In this procedure consumers report their attitudes, interests, and opinions. Together they describe the consumer's lifestyle and the role a given product plays in that lifestyle. Differences in lifestyles between users and nonusers of products, for example, are important factors in developing marketing strategy.

Marketers use personality and attitude data to (1) understand the product diffusion process, (2) identify market segments, and (3) develop marketing mixes.[16]

### The Product Diffusion Process

product diffusion

**Product diffusion** is the spread of a new product or new use for an existing product throughout a society. Figure 4–6 depicts the traditional view

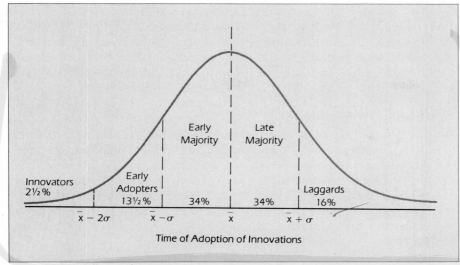

Source: Rogers, *Diffusion of Innovations*.

Figure 4–6.
The product
diffusion process

of the diffusion process, the categories of adopters, and the percentage of adopters that fall into each category.

On the surface it would appear that innovators, those who first try new products, would be different in their attitudes and personality traits from laggards, those who adopt products very late. There is, however, no general personality pattern for innovators or laggards. As we will see in Chapter 6 the differences in their behavior can be more easily predicted and explained by using social class, income levels, and status positions in reference groups. These characteristics seem to be more related to the degree of risk taking, or lack of it, in buying decisions. A person may be an innovator for one product and a laggard for another. We will discuss the diffusion process again in Chapter 10.

We do know, however, that some people are habitual risk takers. They always are trying new ideas, experiences, and products. Others are consistently cautious in their approach to any decision or action. Being the first to buy a new product such as a food processor, trash compactor, synthetic motor oil, or home computer, or only buying long-established products would be extensions of these habitual behavior patterns (personality traits). Such people, however, would represent only a small portion of those considered to be innovators or laggards for any one new product. It is likely that social class and cultural differences between innovators and laggards will exist because they affect people's contact with each other—and how quickly they will be exposed to new products.

### Identifying Market Segments

Personality and attitude data help in identifying market segments for existing products. For example, heavy and light users of a product probably will see and use it in different ways and buy it for different reasons. Personality and attitudes are an influence on these differences. By identifying these relationships through psychographic analysis the marketer can decide what features to add to an existing product to make it more appealing to different market segments, light and moderate users, and perhaps even nonusers. We will discuss this in greater detail in Chapter 8.

### Developing Product Strategy

New products also can be designed for specific market segments that are dissatisfied with an existing product that cannot be modified. A product's final form often is determined by personality and attitude data. Procter & Gamble's research, for example, showed that many potential customers of its Downy fabric softener disliked having to go to the washing machine during the rinse cycle to pour in Downy. The firm could not solve the problem by modifying Downy so it developed Bounce. Unlike Downy, Bounce is used in the clothes dryer.[17]

If the personality characteristics and attitudes of a market segment are known, the preferences for alternative product designs can be tested by using a small sample of people. This concept testing, as we will see in Chapter 11, saves money and lowers the risk in introducing new products. Concept testing indicated to Airwick Industries that its new product, Carpet Fresh, would sell better if its original granular form were changed to a more powdery form. Consumers were afraid the granules would lodge under their furniture.[18]

Personality and attitude data also can be used to determine other products that present customers might use. A manufacturer of four-wheel-drive recreational vehicles might also decide to acquire or expand into other areas such as hunting gear, camping equipment, and guns based on its knowledge of its present customers. Of course, this decision would also depend on the firm's desire to diversify, technical expertise, and unused production capacity.

### Developing Distribution Strategy

Lifestyle studies can help marketers in developing distribution strategies, such as the location of branch banks. People bank either where they work, where they shop, or where they live. By knowing which market segments prefer which location, marketers know where to locate branches.

Products designed to appeal to certain market segments usually must be placed in certain types of stores. Designer label jeans, for example, probably would not sell well in discount department stores. Some products—carpet shampoo machines, for example—may be marketed through a variety of stores such as drugstores, discount stores, supermarkets, and hardware stores. Different market segments may look for the product in very different types of stores. Perhaps a segment of highly mobile consumers would prefer to rent such a machine at a rental store rather than buy it.

### Developing Promotion Strategy

A marketer who fully understands the role a product plays in the consumer's life and the meanings assigned to it is better able to select an appropriate promotion strategy. Media, ad appeals, and the decision to use certain magazines and radio stations, for example, should reflect the personality and attitude characteristics of target customers. To reach outdoor-type, aggressive men, we would select magazines they read such as *True*, *Field & Stream*, and *Sports Illustrated*. Ads for this group might appear during football games or other programs that would fit their interests.

### Developing Price Strategy

As we will see in Chapter 20, some consumers are more price conscious than others. Some comparison shop for prices while others do not. A market segment's sensitivity to price differences may limit the marketer's pricing strategy options.

Some consumers develop a decision strategy related to price. Some may buy middle-of-the-line appliances, for example, while some others buy the top-of-the-line models and still others buy the bottom-of-the line models. Price also often has to reflect consumer attitudes regarding how much a product is worth. We will also discuss this price-quality relationship in Chapter 20.

### SUMMARY AND LOOK AHEAD

Consumer buying decisions are either nonprogramed or programed. Nonprogramed decisions are those a consumer has not worked out a routine method of handling. Buying decisions for products that are hard to compare, are bought infrequently, or are very important usually are nonprogramed. They are problem-solving behavior in which the consumer searches actively for and evaluates information from many sources, makes a commitment, and evaluates the results of his or her decision. The stages in making nonprogramed decisions are: (1) awareness of needs, (2) information search, (3) evaluation of information, (4) decision commitment, and (5) evaluation of decision.

Cognitive dissonance, an uncomfortable state of psychological tension, often arises after a consumer selects one of several equally attractive purchase alternatives. In effect, the consumer questions the wisdom of the decision. Consumers try to reduce dissonance, for example, by denying or distorting information or seeking confirming opinions from others. Marketers can help consumers reduce dissonance by, for example, providing information consumers can use to reduce it or by ensuring that poor product performance is corrected quickly.

The more times a consumer makes a buying decision that is confirmed by good consequences, the more likely the decision will become programed. Programed decisions are the end result of the learning process consumers engage in when making nonprogramed decisions. They usually involve simple decision products, are not very important in an economic or psychological sense, and have a high purchase frequency. A decision becomes programed gradually, perhaps to the extent that the entire decision process, including the product, store, and buying procedure, becomes habitual.

Advertising and other attempts to influence the consumer's behavior may be largely unsuccessful except when the consumer is tired of the normally purchased brand, his or her living conditions have changed, and/ or the product category is unstable. Under these conditions programed decisions can shift to a nonprogramed status.

Personality is the relatively permanent tendency to behave in a consistent way in certain situations. Attitudes are an important part of personality concepts. They are predispositions to feel, believe, or behave in certain ways. Marketers use personality and attitude data to understand the product diffusion process, identify market segments, and develop marketing mixes.

In the next chapter we will discuss factors in the individual consumer that affect his or her consumer behavior.

## REVIEW QUESTIONS

1. Contrast programed and nonprogramed decisions.

2. Identify and discuss the stages in the nonprogramed decision process.

3. What factors might lead to changes in a consumer's deficits list?

4. What factors influence the amount of information a consumer will seek while making a nonprogramed decision?

5. What activities are involved in information processing?

6. What is meant by buying alternative?

7. Do information processing activities stop when a purchase is made? Explain.

8. What is cognitive dissonance? What fac-
tors determine the amount of dissonance and how can it be reduced?

9. Discuss the economic and psychological importance of a product.

10. What is a fully programed decision? Are these decisions more likely in industrial or consumer products marketing? Explain.

11. Under what conditions are programed buying decisions likely to become nonprogramed?

12. What are innovators and laggards? Is there a general personality pattern for either group? Explain.

13. What is the product diffusion process?

14. Give examples of how marketers use personality and attitude data.

## DISCUSSION QUESTIONS

1. Are purchase decisions for men's colognes more likely to be programed or nonprogramed?

2. Is there any difference between brand loyalty and a programed decision?

3. Are consumer decisions ever perfect?

4. Would you advertise to consumers who make programed decisions for a competitor's brand?

5. Can marketers control the social meanings consumers give their products?

# NOTES

1. See Alan R. Andreasen and Brian T. Ratchford, "Factors Affecting Consumers' Use of Information Sources," *Journal of Business Research*, August, 1976, pp. 197–212.

2. For discussion of the problems in measuring the amount of information consumers seek before buying, see Joseph W. Newman and Bradley D. Lockman, "Measuring Prepurchase Information Seeking," *Journal of Consumer Research*, December, 1975, pp. 216–222.

3. The strategies consumers use to acquire information are affected by the structure of the information presented. See James R. Bettman and Pradeep Kakkar, "Effects of Information Presentation Format on Consumer Information Acquisition Strategies," *Journal of Consumer Research*, March, 1977, pp. 223–240.

4. See Ruby Roy Dholakia and Brian Sternthal, "Highly Credible Sources: Persuasive Facilitators or Persuasive Liabilities?" *Journal of Consumer Research*, March, 1977, pp. 223–232.

5. For further discussion of information processing, see Robert E. Burnkrant, "A Motivational Model of Information Processing Intensity," *Journal of Consumer Research*, June, 1976, pp. 21–30.

6. See J. Paul Peter and Lawrence K. Tarpey, Sr., "A Comparative Analysis of Three Consumer Decision Strategies," *Journal of Consumer Research*, June, 1975, pp. 29–37.

7. See Leon Festinger, *A Theory of Cognitive Dissonance* (Stanford, Cal.: Stanford University Press, 1957). Also see Sadaomi Oshikawa, "Can Cognitive Dissonance Theory Explain Consumer Behavior?" *Journal of Marketing*, October, 1969, pp. 44–49; and Michael B. Menasco and Del I. Hawkins, "A Field Test of the Relationship between Cognitive Dissonance and State Anxiety," *Journal of Marketing Research*, November, 1978, pp. 650–655.

8. See Richard J. Lutz, "An Experimental Investigation of Causal Relations among Cognitions, Affect and Behavioral Intention," *Journal of Consumer Research*, March, 1977, pp. 197–208; and Elden M. Wirtz and Kenneth E. Miller, "The Effect of Post-Purchase Communication on Consumer Satisfaction and Consumer Recommendation of the Retailer," *Journal of Retailing*, Summer, 1977, pp. 39–46.

9. "At Procter & Gamble, Success Is Largely Due to Heeding Consumer," *Wall Street Journal*, April 29, 1980, p. 24.

10. For discussion of the relationship between the social visibility of a product and the types of information sources consumers use, see Donald N. Granbois and Patricia L. Braden, "Good Consumership in Household Appliance Purchasing," *Journal of Business Research*, May, 1976, pp. 103–116.

11. See Jacob Jacoby, George J. Szybillo, and Jacqueline Busato-Schach, "Information Acquisition Behavior in Brand Choice Situations," *Journal of Consumer Research*, March, 1977, pp. 209–216.

12. Everett M. Rogers, *Diffusion of Innovations* (New York: Free Press, 1962), pp. 81–86.

13. For discussion of the differences in buying behavior between initial and repeat purchasers and the reasons they should be treated as distinct market segments, see Igal Ayal, "Trial and Repeat Buying—The Case for Separate Consideration," *Journal of the Academy of Marketing Science*, Summer, 1974, pp. 413–431.

14. "Luxury Car Sales Skid to New Lows," *Business Week*, May 19, 1980, pp. 35–36.

15. See Harold W. Berkman and Christopher C. Gilson, *Consumer Behavior: Concepts and Strategies* (Boston, Mass.: Kent Publishing Company, 1981), pp. 276–332.

16. See Michael B. Mazis, Olli T. Ahtola, and R. Eugene Klippel, "A Comparison of Four Multi-Attribute Models in the Prediction of Consumer Attitudes," *Journal of Consumer Research*, June, 1975, pp. 38–52; William J. McGuire, "Some Internal Psychological Factors Influencing Consumer Choice," *Journal of Consumer Research*, March, 1976, pp. 302–319; and Robert J. Paul, "Personality Analysis as a Predictor of Consumer Decision Patterns," *Marquette Business Review*, Fall, 1976, pp. 112–117.

17. "At Procter & Gamble, Success Is Largely Due to Heeding Consumer," *Wall Street Journal*, April 29, 1980, p. 24.

18. "Airwick's Discovery of New Markets Pays Off," *Business Week*, June 16, 1980, p. 140.

# Chapter 5

# Intrapersonal Influences on Consumer Behavior

**OBJECTIVES**

*After reading this chapter you should be able to*

1. explain how needs motivate behavior.

2. explain the difference between deficit and excess motivation and give marketing examples of each.

3. define developmental tasks and show how marketers can use them.

4. identify the factors that affect perception.

5. identify two types of meanings products have and give examples of each.

6. explain how consumer behavior is learned.

**KEY CONCEPTS**

*Look for these terms as you read the chapter:*

Tension Reduction
Hierarchy of Needs
Multiple Determination of Behavior
Optimal Stimulation Maintenance
Developmental Tasks
Perception
Weber's Law
Subliminal Stimuli
Perceptual Sets
Closure
Cognitive Systems
Functional Meanings
Subjective Meanings
Empathy
Semantic Differential Scales
Learning
Extinction
Generalization
Discrimination Training
Oscillation Responses
Vicarious Reinforcement

*How consumers perceive products is important to marketers. For example, most of us believe the redder meat is, the fresher it is. Thus some meat counters in supermarkets have red lights shining on the displayed packages of meat. Margarine is actually a colorless product; marketers have added yellow coloring to make it look like butter. It was no easy task to convince consumers that a low-sudsing detergent could clean clothes. Many consumers associated plenty of suds with cleaning power. The same was true of cold-water detergents.*

*Quaker State motor oil enjoys strong brand loyalty. Many people associate it with the Pennsylvania-grade variety of crude oil, a light, greenish crude which was used in refining the first motor oils. Thus some other oil companies that use crude from other areas add green dye to it to give it a greenish color.\**

*Finally, consider the problems faced by the earliest marketers of microwave ovens. Many people suspected the product of being dangerous because of radiation leakage. Marketers had to address themselves to this problem before they could focus on the product's benefits.*

In this chapter we will study the intrapersonal factors that affect consumer behavior. Intrapersonal factors are those that are specific to an individual's psychological make-up. These factors affect how a person becomes aware of imbalances in his or her assortment of products, processes data from the environment, and assigns meaning to the data based on the consequences of behavior. They are the individual's unique contributions to the buying process. In the discussion of factors that affect consumer behavior we will deal with motivation, perception, cognition, and learning.

## MOTIVATION

There is general agreement that consumer behavior is stimulated by internal and external conditions and is goal oriented. Consumers are motivated to seek ways to satisfy specific goals. The process of motivation has been explained in three ways: (1) tension reduction, (2) optimal stimulation maintenance, and (3) developmental tasks. Together these ideas form a useful framework for marketers.

### Tension Reduction

When you lack satisfactions in your environment you have an uncomfortable build-up of tension that stimulates action to reduce it **(tension reduction).** The goal of behavior is to reduce tension to its lowest level. Thirst, for example, is a build-up of tension that leads a person to drink.

    How strong a need is (the amount of tension) depends on (1) the length

tension reduction

*"Quaker State Hurt by Drop in Use of Cars," *Wall Street Journal,* December 11, 1980, p. 27.

of time since satisfaction and (2) the nature of the need. The longer a need has gone unsatisfied, the greater the tension. These needs are more important in determining behavior than those that have been recently satisfied. Stronger (prepotent) needs produce more tension and must be satisfied before other needs can influence behavior. The strongest needs relate directly to a person's survival. Abraham Maslow listed and arranged five categories of needs into a hierarchy according to strength. (See Table 5–1.) The physiological needs, such as the needs for food and shelter, are the strongest.

**hierarchy of needs**

The elements in the **hierarchy of needs** are clusters of specific needs. Thus safety needs include physical safety and ensuring that sources of satisfaction for the physiological needs will be available in the future. Purchasing apartments with security services, life insurance, and gold coins or bullion is related to these needs.

But some needs do not fit neatly into the hierarchy. Cognitive needs, such as the need for consistency between thoughts (cognitive consistency), the need for complete stimulus patterns (closure), and the need for new stimulation (curiosity), also are important motivators of behavior. Territoriality, the need to claim and protect physical space as one's own, is another example. Cognitive needs are reflected in such products as puzzles, electronic games, and coordinated clothing and such marketing practices as informative ad campaigns and shortened versions of advertising jingles. Marketing responses to territorial needs also include products, such as hedges and fences, and marketing practices, such as advertising appeals based on privacy.

A second problem with the needs hierarchy is that there seldom is a one-to-one relationship between needs and behavior. Needs do not always result in a corresponding behavior for a number of reasons. You may not be aware the needs are present, or you may be aware of them but attribute your dissatisfaction to the wrong needs, or you may be aware

**Table 5–1.** *Maslow's hierarchy of needs*

| | |
|---|---|
| 1. Physiological needs | Acid-base balance, salt, water, temperature, sleep, oxygen, sex, protein |
| 2. Safety needs | Physical safety, ensuring future sources of satisfaction for physiological needs and familiar surroundings |
| 3. Love needs | To love another person, to be loved by at least one other person, to establish love relationships, to maintain love relationships |
| 4. Esteem needs | Realistic high evaluation of one's self, realistic high evaluation by others, ability to cope with demands, achievement, group membership |
| 5. Self-actualization needs | To develop one's potential, to feel at one with the universe |

Source: Maslow, "A Theory of Human Motivation," *Psychological Review.*

of certain needs, perceive them correctly, and still not take action to satisfy them, or you may be aware of the means to satisfy these needs but lack the resources to obtain them. Most behaviors are caused by several needs operating together. The behavior that results satisfies several needs at the same time. This is called **multiple determination of behavior.** A woman who buys a winter dress may be satisfying physiological and esteem needs at the same time. She selects it for the probable reactions of friends as well as its style and warmth.

multiple determination of behavior

A third problem is that weaker needs may determine behavior when other stronger needs are present. A person may forgo food to buy a new suit. The esteem or safety needs are the major determiners of this behavior even though they are less prepotent than the need for food. It is as if the person expects satisfactions for physiological needs to be available once less prepotent needs are satisfied.

Finally, some behavior cannot be explained in terms of tension reduction. Riding a roller coaster or eating exotic food does not reduce tension.

### Optimal Stimulation Maintenance

The needs hierarchy's usefulness to marketers is improved by changing the concept of tension reduction to **optimal stimulation maintenance** (homeostasis). According to this concept any stimulus that varies from an optimal level can cause behavior. The optimal level of stimulation varies for different types of stimuli and individuals. An optimal level of background music for a teen-ager who is studying, for example, probably is much higher than that for an adult performing similar mental work. This view of needs can explain behaviors that increase or decrease stimulation.[1] (See Figure 5–1.)

optimal stimulation maintenance

There are many products that increase stimulation. For example, Ultrabrite toothpaste leaves a tingling sensation in the mouth. Several

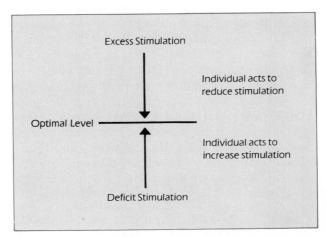

Figure 5–1.
*Optimal stimulation maintenance*

years ago General Foods introduced Pop Rocks, a carbonated candy that also left a tingling sensation.   Vacations in New York City are especially stimulating to people from small towns.   Canada Dry and Perrier water are sparkling waters and Coast soap is promoted as refreshing.

Needs that are normally met by tension reduction can also be described as excess stimulation.   External stimuli that are too strong are also examples of excess stimulation.   Changing channels when annoying commercials come on and using air fresheners, mouthwash, and deodorant are behaviors motivated by excess external stimulation.   Miller beer's "When it's time to relax" theme also is based on the appeal of reducing the excess stimulation some workers receive on the job.

The optimal stimulation maintenance view of needs helps in understanding how many products satisfy needs.   But it is not specific enough to help marketers generate new product ideas or guide their day-to-day decision making.

### Developmental Tasks

developmental<br>tasks Society and culture do not create needs but they do determine how consumers will satisfy basic needs.   These social and cultural demands on behavior are called developmental tasks.   From birth to death we pass through a series of periods during which we must learn to satisfy basic needs in appropriate ways.   Although the basic needs remain the same throughout life, how they are satisfied depends largely on a person's stage of development.

The sequence of development and the developmental tasks at each stage are roughly the same for everyone.   A person who does not learn how to cope with the developmental tasks of one stage will have trouble progressing to the next stage.   The ages given for each developmental stage in Table 5–2 are approximate since some persons complete a stage much earlier than others.

Marketers can use this view of motivation to generate new product ideas and select ad appeals.   If you want to know what consumers will buy or what will gain their attention, you must know what they are trying to accomplish.   Developmental tasks give us insight into a consumer's major concerns at each stage and what those concerns will be in the future.   For example, during adolescence esteem needs are met by same-sex peer groups.   During young adulthood they are met by career success and civic group memberships.

Consider the developmental tasks of the decline period.   Persons sixty-five or older must learn to cope with many changes in their living conditions.   Some may be retiring and will have a lot of free time. Travel, hobbies, and volunteer work can fill it.   Older people also have a hard time doing some tasks because of reduced physical vigor.   Sweeping and mopping are tough chores for people with heart trouble.   Zipping up a dress with a back zipper and bending over to plug in a vacuum cleaner are hard for people with arthritis.   Climbing stairs, moving

**Table 5–2.** *Developmental stages and tasks*

| | *Life Stages* | *Developmental Tasks* |
|---|---|---|
| Growth | Infancy (birth–3 years) | Learning to eat solid food and feed self, control elimination, manipulate objects, walk, explore surroundings, communicate |
| | Early Childhood (3–6 years) | Learning to play and share with others, dress self, follow verbal instructions, pay attention, become independent; developing sense of self and realistic concepts of world |
| Exploration | Later Childhood (6–12 years) | Learning to be a student, help others, develop a set of values, to read and calculate, delay satisfaction of needs, control emotions, do chores, deal with abstract concepts, give self to others |
| | Early Adolescence (12–14 years) | Learning to belong in groups, control impulses, be positive toward work, study, organize time, develop new values |
| | Later Adolescence (15–19 years) | Learning to move from group to individual relationship, cut parents' apron strings, establish an identity as a worker, cooperate with others, date and relate to opposite sex |
| Establishment | Exploration Young Adulthood (20–30 years) | Learning to take risks; commit self to goals, career, partner; be adequate parent; give without expecting something in return; value consistent decisions |
| | Realization (30–50 years) | Learning to be inner directed, interdependent, emotionally flexible; developing problem-solving techniques; leadership, helping, creative, accomplishment roles; objectivity, logical analysis; concentration; empathy; tolerance for ambiguity |
| Maintenance | Stabilization (50–65 years) | Learning to be aware of change; have attitude of tentativeness; develop broad intellectual curiosity, realistic idealism, time perspective, sensitivity to younger people; exercise leadership positions; cope with authority and prestige |
| Decline | Examination (65 + years) | Learning to cope with death, retirement, reduced physical vigor; adjust to retirement and reduced income, death of spouse; relate to peers; use leisure time; cope with nonauthority; care for the aging body |

Adapted from Blocher, *Developmental Counseling.*

chairs, or lifting flower pots is hard on people with back problems. Dresses with front zippers, houses with electrical outlets at waist level, lightweight furniture, built-in vacuum cleaner systems, and no-wax floors are products that recognize these physical limitations.

There is a lot of controversy about rational and emotional buying motives. Many people think economic motives are rational and all other motives are emotional. The developmental task view does away with this problem. Behavior is rational if it leads to the achievement of the appropriate developmental task.

We must make inferences, or guesses, about the causes of behavior based on observation since we cannot tell what goes on in a consumer's head. Our guesses are better when we understand what the consumer is trying to accomplish and how he or she "sees" a situation.

## PERCEPTION

perception

You are bombarded constantly by an ever-changing flow of stimuli, many of which are irrelevant to the tasks you are trying to accomplish. You cannot give meaning to them all or even admit them to awareness. **Perception** is the process that enables you to filter relevant stimuli from your environment, admit this raw sensory data to awareness, and organize it so meaning may be assigned to it. Perception must occur before you can interpret the objects and events in your environment.

You are not a passive receiver of stimulation, however. You change and reorganize it to be consistent with your own knowledge, goals, and experiences. Your behavior, therefore, is determined by how you perceive your environment and not by what is really there. Consumer behavior is a product of the stimuli consumers select to pay attention to and how they transform, organize, and interpret them. Properties of the stimulus (stimulus factors) and personal characteristics (personal factors) affect perception.

### Stimulus Factors

Stimulus factors that affect perception include (1) presence of color, (2) context, (3) location, (4) intensity, and (5) consistency. They determine whether you will pay attention to something and how you will see it.

**Color and Context.** Color ads in magazines usually receive more attention than black-and-white ads, but not always. The context in which an ad appears affects the attention-producing value of color.[2] Figure 5–2 shows how the ratio of color to black-and-white ads in a

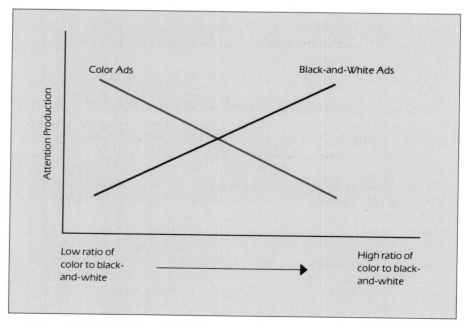

*Figure 5–2.*
*Effects of context*
*on the attention*
*value of color*

magazine may affect color's ability to elicit added attention. When the ratio of color to black-and-white ads is high, black-and-white ads actually may receive more attention. In this case the context of the stimulus is more important than the presence or absence of color. The context provided by other pages in a magazine is also a factor. *The New Yorker* magazine is printed in three columns that are broken by black-and-white cartoons; there are no color photographs on these pages. This helps to produce attention for color ads. The decision to use color or black-and-white ads depends on factors such as cost and the value of color to the product. Unless the added attention-producing value of color offsets the added cost, black-and-white ads should be used.

**Location.** The location of a stimulus influences whether you will pay attention to it. When several stimuli are similar, those that have certain locations are more likely to be seen than others. Products slightly below eye level on grocery shelves are noticed better than products located elsewhere. Ads on the top half of a magazine page are noticed more than those on the bottom half, and ads on the left are noticed more than those on the right.

**Intensity.** The greater the stimulus intensity the more attention it will produce. Loudness, weight, sweetness, and size are intensity dimensions. But the relationship between attention and stimulus intensity is not one-to-one. Doubling the size of a cereal package, for example, will not double the attention it receives.

**Consistency.** Consistency of the stimulus also affects how much attention it will get. Stimuli that remain unchanged in intensity soon lose their attention-producing value because of adaptation. Ads produce less attention with repeated use.[3] Changing a stimulus to which a person has adapted restores its attention-producing value. The amount of change needed depends on the intensity of the stimulus where change takes place. **Weber's law** summarizes this relationship:[4]

Weber's law

$$\frac{\Delta I}{I} = K$$

$\Delta I$ is the smallest increase in the stimulus that will be noticeably different from the previous intensity. $I$ is the intensity of the stimulus where the change is to take place. K is a constant (an average for the general population) for the sensory mode (sight, sound, taste, smell, and feel) stimulated.

Consumers often judge the quality of upholstered chairs in terms of weight—the heavier, the better. A firm that wants to make its chairs seem higher in quality could increase the chair's weight. Figure 5–3 summarizes the absolute size of the change needed at different weight levels, assuming a K value of 20 percent. The heavier the chair, the greater the change needed to make it noticeably heavier. The just-noticed difference (j.n.d.) is the change needed to make the chair noticeably heavier.

Changes in the stimulus intensity that are less than a j.n.d. will not

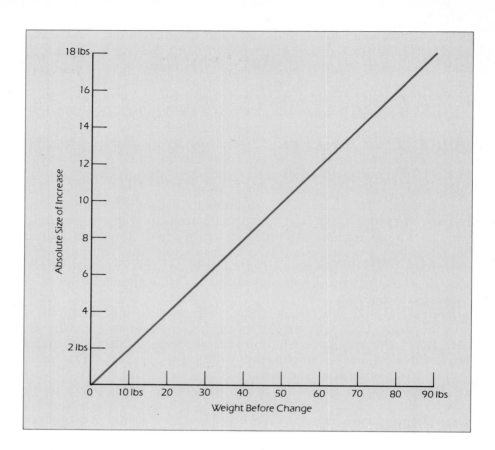

*Figure 5–3.*
*Absolute size of*
*the just-noticed*
*difference*

be noticed.    Consider a marketer of a soft drink whose sales are off.    A survey shows that 99 percent of the respondents gave "lack of sweetness" as the reason for not buying that brand.    It contains 14.2 grams of sugar while the leading seller has 15.1 grams.    By computing a j.n.d. using a constant for taste perception (K value) of 10 percent, the marketer discovers there is no perceptible difference in sweetness between the two brands.    Consumer perceptions of the marketer's brand are thus likely to be due to image rather than to real differences in sweetness.    Making it sweeter probably will not increase sales.

Marketers do reformulate their products from time to time to stimulate interest in them.    For example, the Coca-Cola Company introduced Mr. Pibb in 1973 and reformulated it in 1980 to appeal more to teen-agers and homemakers who wanted a less sweet taste.    Schlitz Brewing Company lost customers after it changed the formula and taste of its beer in the 1970s and in recent years the firm has attempted to improve the taste. In 1979 it reformulated and repackaged its Schlitz Light.

The j.n.d. concept also often holds true in price perception.    A two-cent change in the price of a pack of gum will be more likely to produce attention than a two-cent change in the price of a man's shirt.

## Personal Factors

Personal factors that influence perception include (1) accuracy of the sensory processes, (2) motivation, (3) previous experiences with the same or similar stimuli, and (4) emotions.

**Accuracy of Sensory Processes.** Stimuli above or below certain intensity levels cannot be perceived by the average person. The upper and lower thresholds of perception also vary from person to person depending on the accuracy of their receptors for the sensory mode. Some people have hearing and vision problems. Without hearing aids and glasses their world is very different from that of people with normal hearing and vision. Stimuli presented above the upper threshold or below the lower threshold do not produce awareness.

Some consumers have innate ability to perceive stimuli that others cannot. Some consumers of saccharin-sweetened soft drinks complain the drinks taste bitter. *The Sensory Service*, a newsletter published by MPI Marketing Research that covers developments in sensory research that have relevance for marketers, has reported recent research indicating that a genetic ability to taste $6-n$-propylthiouracil, a bitter substance, determines whether people will perceive saccharin as bitter.[5]

Marketing uses of the knowledge of thresholds include subliminal advertising, product differentiation, and discrimination experiments. Attempts have been made to use **subliminal stimuli** (stimuli below the lower threshold of perception) to trigger buying behavior. In one case in the 1950s messages were flashed on a movie screen urging viewers to drink cola and eat popcorn. When these messages were flashed for fractions of a second cola and popcorn sales increased greatly. This led some people to believe consumers could be manipulated without being aware of it. But more recent tests have indicated that subliminal stimulation is not useful to marketers because (1) subliminal stimuli are weak in comparison to other stimuli, (2) stimuli below the lower threshold for

**subliminal stimuli**

*"Incredible! The bottom line does say 'SALE'!"*

Source: *The Better Half*, The Register and Tribune Syndicate, Inc.

some people would be apparent to others, and (3) only a small amount of information can be transmitted by subliminal stimuli.[6]

A major concern in product management is that rival brands often are so similar that the only difference is their brand names, and those that are noticeably different have an advantage. Miller Brewing Company's choice of the Lowenbrau brand name for one of its beers probably helped to set it apart by making it appear to be an imported beer with a distinctively different taste. In fact, Anheuser-Busch complained about Miller's advertising, which allegedly suggested that Löwenbräu was imported although it was brewed in the United States. Subsequent advertising of Lowenbrau made clear that it was domestically brewed, but still claimed a distinctively different taste.

Marketers often use blind tests to see if consumers can detect differences among brands. The "Pepsi Challenge" ad campaign of recent years features the use of a blind test between Pepsi and Coke. If a person cannot identify the brand he or she normally uses when the label is removed or covered up, that person's preference is due to something other than the product's make-up. Cola, cigarettes, and beer are a few of the products many consumers cannot discriminate among.

**Motivation.** Objects or events related to what you are trying to accomplish receive more attention than others. Your needs or motives filter the stimulation coming in from the environment.

You may travel the same route to school each day and pass several shops. Ordinarily you are unaware of them but today is your mother's birthday and you have not bought a gift for her. Thus you notice a gift shop for the first time and decide to stop. The stimulus factors of the gift shop have remained constant, but today they produce awareness. This change in the gift shop's attention-producing value is due to motivation.

Motivation makes you more sensitive to stimuli that are related to your needs at the moment. This selective nature of perception causes problems in planning ad campaigns, selecting market targets for a new product, and presenting product advantages to a shopper.[7] If what a salesperson says about a product is unrelated to what you are trying to accomplish, it will be filtered out.

**Previous Experience.** How you transform, organize, or complete incomplete stimulus patterns depends a lot on your prior experiences. This especially is true of programed decisions. You tend to perceive stimuli in habitual ways that are called **perceptual sets.** Information about products is screened against them. Stimuli that fit are admitted to awareness and assigned meaning. Those that do not fit are not admitted to awareness or they are reorganized and changed to fit your perceptual sets. Meanings are assigned on the basis of these distorted data.

Brand and company images often are the result of your perceptual sets. Your experience with a product or firm is filtered against your perceptual sets (image). If these experiences do not fit your expectations, you reorganize them by selecting those parts that fit and ignoring the

perceptual sets

# Now you can copy both sides of this page without

# turning it over.

**The Xerox 5600. You put in a two-sided original, and get back a two-sided copy. Automatically.**

If you copy from two-sided originals, you've turned to the right copier.

The Xerox 5600 is the only one that lets you copy a two-sided original without having to:

(1) copy one side,
(2) turn the original over, and
(3) copy the other side.

The 5600 does it all in (1) step, automatically.

It also collates your copies into nice, neat sets, automatically. And even staples them, automatically.

For more information, call us at 800-648-5600 (operator 263)?

We'll show you how a Xerox 5600 lets you do something more productive than turn over originals.

Namely, reduce office turnover by 100%.

## XEROX

***An ad that illustrates the use of closure.***
Source: Xerox Corporation.

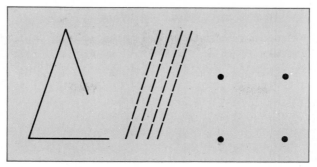

**Figure 5–4.
Closure**

rest.   Positive perceptual sets predispose you to good experiences with a product.   Negative ones predispose you to bad experiences.   If you have a negative set you discount good experiences as inaccurate.   This is why advertising may fail to switch customers who are loyal to a brand and why bad store images are hard to change.

Your tendency to fill in missing parts of an incomplete stimulus pattern is called **closure.** You search your prior experiences with similar stimuli and use them to complete the stimulus pattern.   In Figure 5–4 because of closure you see a triangle, four parallel lines, and a square. An incomplete stimulus pattern produces a lot of attention.   If you know how to complete it you will do so automatically, thereby paying attention to it.   A person is almost compelled to finish "Volkswagen does it . . . ."   The Xerox ad is also a good example of closure.

*closure*

**Emotions.**   Emotions affect the perceptual processes in two ways. First, emotions limit the external stimuli that are admitted to awareness. People experiencing strong emotions focus on what is taking place internally.   Anger, fear, and love are strong emotions and only those parts of the environment that are relevant to them are admitted to awareness. Thus a salesperson will have a tough time communicating with a prospect who has just received upsetting news.

Second, emotions increase the attention-producing value of certain stimulus patterns. Angry consumers are very sensitive to treatment by store personnel when returning purchases.   Annoying ads often are remembered because of their association with strong emotional reactions.

## COGNITION

Once raw sensory data have been organized, transformed, or completed through the perceptual processes, consumers assign meanings to the stimulus pattern.   The meanings attached to experiences are called *cognitions.* All consumers have unique **cognitive systems** with which they interpret information about products.   It is an organized and integrated system of thoughts, feelings, and beliefs developed through their own experiences and those of others.[8]   This system is consistent over time and is composed of two types of meanings, functional and subjective.

*cognitive systems*

## Functional Meanings

functional
meanings

A product's **functional meanings** reflect how well it will do something for you. They are an objective assessment of the product's quality, price, and utility. Most consumers agree on the functional meanings of products because they are shared readily. Even new uses for products can be adopted without much trouble. Consumers quickly accepted the new functional meanings for dried soup as a basis for making snack dips and Arm & Hammer baking soda as a deodorizer for refrigerators and kitty litter boxes.

Several years ago General Electric announced its development of a new household light bulb that lasts five times longer and uses only one-third as much electricity as ordinary bulbs. But the firm decided to test market the product before introducing it on the market. General Electric felt it faced a real marketing challenge in persuading consumers to spend ten dollars for the bulb and it wanted to study consumer response to the new product.

## Subjective Meanings

subjective
meanings

Those meanings consumers give to products that are unrelated to their intended functions are **subjective meanings.** They include the cultural and social value of products. Products often are symbols that communicate meaning to other people. In recent years, sales of unassembled furniture have increased. The buyers are interested in function and utility. Traditional furniture often is marketed on the basis of aesthetic appeal and prestige. Two types of subjective meanings are (1) social and (2) symbolic.

**Social Meaning.** Marketers often are faced with consumer behavior that appears illogical. After looking at several brooches in a discount store, a woman selects one and seems to consider it appropriate. Its price is seven dollars. But after thinking about it for fifteen minutes, she returns it to the tray and leaves the store. A few days later in an exclusive department store she sees the same brooch, looks at it for a moment, and buys it for fifteen dollars.

From an external frame of reference she made an irrational decision. But if the marketer could enter her frame of reference and discover the meanings she is attaching to this experience, her behavior might make

empathy

sense. **Empathy** is the ability to enter another person's frame of reference (cognitive system). It is the only real way a consumer's subjective meanings can be understood. The woman may have wanted to give the brooch as a gift and thus did not want to buy it from a discount store. This is an example of the social meaning of products.

**Symbolic Meaning.** You may not be able to identify the symbolic meanings you attach to products. You may want a product without knowing why. For example, you may buy a pair of boots even though you have no occasion to wear them. Symbolic meaning is important in product design, ad campaigns, and understanding why consumers reject certain products.

Fashion designer Ralph Lauren pioneered the Western look in high fashion that was popular in the late 1970s and early 1980s. The movie *The Urban Cowboy* was an outgrowth of the Western look. Both Western clothing and riding mechanical bulls are loaded with symbolic meaning.

Four product characteristics are related to symbolic meaning: (1) activity, (2) form, (3) color, and (4) shape.

The activities associated with using a product can have symbolic meaning and the meanings attached to these activities can influence buying behavior. Bathing is a symbolic activity that often is interpreted as washing away one's guilt. Bath products can be promoted as cleaning agents to capitalize on both functional and symbolic meanings.

The form of a product or an ad influences the meaning attached to it. When bourbon sales started falling off and wine sales rose, ads for Old Forester bourbon began depicting the bottle resting on its side just as wine is stored. The marketer wanted to get across the idea that its product was made like a good wine. The California Prune Advisory Board found that the wrinkled form and pits of their product had very negative meanings for many consumers—old age, laxative, and unpleasant to eat. Removal of the pit and a stress on youth has increased acceptance of prunes.

Colors also have symbolic meaning. The earth colors brown and brick red are considered masculine; greens and some blues, feminine. Brown and Williamson Tobacco Company ran market tests on thirty-three packages before choosing the blue, gold, and red colors on its Viceroy Rich Lights package. Red packs connote strong flavor, green packs connote coolness or menthol, and white packs connote low tar.[9] Colors also denote weight, harshness, and freshness. Bread, butter, and milk may be made to appear richer by adding yellow food coloring. But marketing uses of color must operate within the law, especially the use of color additives for food products.

The shape of certain products affects consumers' choices. Shape preferences symbolize the consumer's perceptions of himself or herself. Products such as neckties, knives, and guns have symbolic shapes. The shapes of packages for some colognes and deodorants also have symbolic meanings.

### Measurement of Consumer Meaning

Marketers want to know what meanings consumers attach to their products or firms to develop better ad campaigns and more satisfying products. For example, research has shown that consumers feel "bigger is better" for airlines. This was a factor in Allegheney Airlines' decision to change its name to USAir.[10] To determine how consumers interpret their ex-

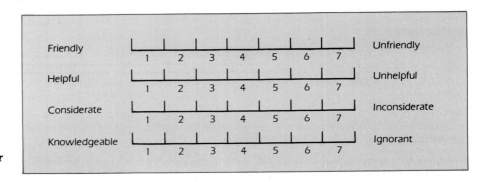

*Figure 5–5.*
*Use of semantic*
*differential to*
*measure consumer*
*perceptions*

periences with a product, brand, or firm marketers use (1) projective techniques and (2) semantic differential scales.

**Projective Techniques.** Projective techniques help in measuring a product's symbolic meanings. For example, the meanings attached to instant coffee were measured by giving two groups of people shopping lists that were identical except for the type of coffee listed (instant vs. drip grind). The two groups were then asked to describe the person who bought these groceries. Differences in their descriptions were attributed to the type of coffee on the lists. Shoppers with the instant coffee on the list were perceived to be lazy and poor homemakers. This study was published in 1950.[11] In a repeat of this experiment published in 1970 homemakers who used drip-grind coffee were seen as old-fashioned.[12]

Another projective technique is the use of cartoons or pictures to determine the symbolic meaning of a brand name. Two groups might be given cartoons or pictures of a situation. The product would be identified by brand name in one picture but not in the other. Any differences in the descriptions of the person who would buy each product would thus be due to the meanings the subjects attach to the brand name. We will discuss projective techniques again in Chapter 9.

**Semantic Differential Scales.** The meanings consumers attach to products, brand names, or companies can be measured by **semantic differential scales.**[13] The consumer, presented with pairs of antonyms (opposites), rates the product or firm on a seven-point scale between them. Specific aspects of the brand or firm can be measured, and comparisons can be made with other brands and firms. Consumer reactions to store layout, store personnel, product assortment, and pricing policies also can be measured individually by retailers. Figure 5–5 shows some of the scales that could be used to measure consumer reactions to store personnel.

**semantic differ-
ential scales**

## LEARNING

Learning is the process by which consumer behavior develops and changes as the consumer's conditions change. Understanding this process helps marketers to understand and influence consumer behavior. Promotional efforts, planning new products, and developing company and brand images are based on learning.[14]

Several years ago, the Pillsbury Company was planning to market a new product, a high-quality frozen croissant. Consumer taste tests were very encouraging but people did not know when to eat the product—at dinner or at breakfast. Pillsbury decided to drop the product rather than educate consumers about its consumption.[15]

### Reinforcement

**Learning** is a relatively permanent change in behavior that is influenced by the consequences of behavior. If behavior leads to desirable consequences, consumers tend to behave the same way the next time the situation occurs. Otherwise, the behavior will be replaced by some other response.

*learning*

Consumers adjust their behavior according to its consequences. If you make a trial purchase of a laundry detergent that does not do a good job, you probably will not buy it again. If a retail clerk laughs at you for asking a question about a product, you are not likely to ask another question. Marketers try to make customers' first experience with their products or firms satisfying, or else customers may not remain customers. This concern about the consequences of behavior is one reason marketers attempt to help customers reduce the dissonance that some decisions create.

Learning occurs gradually. The more times a response to a stimulus is repeated with reinforcement, the more likely it will be made when the stimulus situation occurs again. This relationship is shown in Figure

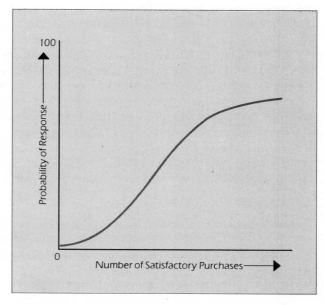

*Figure 5–6.*
*The learning curve*

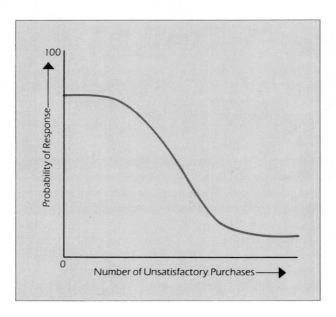

*Figure 5–7.*
*The extinction*
*curve*

5–6.   Repetition is how brand or company loyalty develops and the basic method by which consumer decisions become programed (habitual). You usually repeat purchases of brands because you have been rewarded. These brands can be arranged in a hierarchy based on the number of satisfactory purchases.   Those that have rewarded you most are most likely to be bought.

extinction

A well-established buying habit is weakened by unsatisfactory experiences.   This is called **extinction.**   (See Figure 5–7.)   Although you may not switch to some other brand or store after one bad experience, the more of them you have the less likely you will buy that brand or shop at that store again.[16]   Thus if you occasionally get a poorly cooked steak at your favorite restaurant, you are likely to discount it and continue to eat there.   But if you regularly get poorly cooked food, you will switch restaurants.

Old habits are not broken as fast as new ones because new habits have not been repeated so often.   Customers may switch to a new brand for a while and then switch back to the old brand as the big advertising push for the new one slacks off.   Older brands, therefore, require less advertising than newer brands to keep their market share.

### Generalization and Discrimination

generalization

**Generalization** is the tendency to exhibit the same response to new stimulus situations that are like old ones.   The more similar a new stimulus is to the original, the more likely the same response will occur.   (See Figure 5–8.)

If you buy Coke and are satisfied, you may generalize the same re-

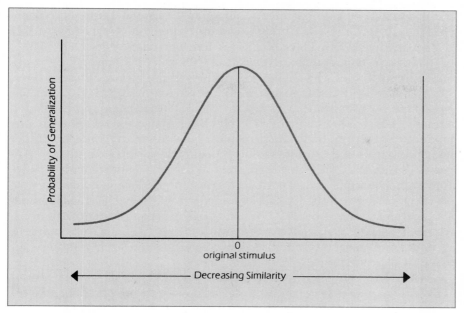

Figure 5–8.
The generalization
gradient

sponse to other cola drinks.   If they satisfy you, the tendency to generalize is reinforced and you eventually will buy any cola drink.   The more alike brands in a product category are, the more likely consumers will generalize.

Marketers must combat consumers' tendency to generalize.   Each tries to make its brand different from others in the same product category by making it distinctive in appearance and displaying its brand name prominently.   Xerox, for example, does not want people to generalize the brand name Xerox to the photocopying machines made by its rivals Savin and IBM.   We will discuss product differentiation in greater detail in Chapter 8.

Marketers try through **discrimination training** to make reinforcement dependent on the presence of their brand names.   Consumers must receive reinforcement from the marketer's brand but not when they make a generalized response to rival brands.   That part of the stimulus situation that is different is called a *cue*.   Brand names are cues.   Puritan Fashions Corporation used to market low-budget, unbranded apparel and spent nothing on advertising.   But in the late 1970s it started using Calvin Klein's label on its prestige trousers.   This gave it a name to advertise.

As we will see in Chapter 12, brand names are so valuable in helping consumers to discriminate that they can be protected by law as registered trademarks.   Advertising helps teach consumers to identify brand names. Pioneer brands often become synonymous with the product category through generalization.   Thus some people call all cola drinks Coke and use Xerox as a verb to describe making copies on photocopying machines

discrimination
training

even though both are registered trademarks. Generalization is so effective that a firm also can obtain a share of a market without expensive advertising by making its product look like the industry leader. Notice how many suntan lotions are packaged to look like Coppertone. Generalization responses by some consumers will produce some sales.

Many firms, however, use consumers' tendency to generalize to their advantage by promoting a company image rather than specific brand names. This helps consumers generalize good experiences with one product to other products the firm sells. Examples are English Leather men's toiletries and clothing sold by Levi Strauss and Hang-Ten. Anheuser-Busch says, "Good taste runs in the family." But this can backfire when a consumer's bad experience with one product is generalized to others the firm markets. Chrysler Corporation's Volare and Aspen models experienced major recalls. When Chrysler replaced them with front-wheel-drive cars, it named the Plymouth version Reliant to help give it an image of dependability and to keep consumers from generalizing their previous bad experiences.

When 3M Company, maker of Scotch-brand tape, developed Mmm! What a Tan!, it was very careful to say in its ads that the product adheres to the skin without feeling sticky. It did not want consumers to generalize the idea of "sticky" from Scotch tape to the new suntan lotion.[17]

## Oscillation

Even with repetition, the probability that a buying habit will remain completely unchanged never reaches 100 percent. (See Figure 5–6.) Normally loyal consumers sometimes buy a new brand simply because they are bored with the usual brand and want to try something new. Usually they will return to their old brands. But if they find the new brand more reinforcing, they may continue buying it.

oscillation responses

**Oscillation responses** are buying responses in which a brand other than the normally used brand is chosen. They are a problem if the consumer is a loyal buyer of the marketer's brand. They are an opportunity for the marketer of a rival brand. Attempts to switch consumers of a rival's brand are expensive. The methods often used are personal selling or advertising blitzes. A less intense, longer-lasting campaign stressing a product as something different often is better, especially if the brand is noticeably superior. Several years ago 7Up launched its "Uncola" campaign to set it apart from cola beverages. But the firm dropped the theme in 1979 because it felt it was missing the heavy users of soft drinks—the cola drinkers.

Oscillation responses are a very small percentage of a loyal brand-user's response. Thus a marketer has to keep a new brand on the market long enough for loyal users of other brands to oscillate. Generally, the greater the buying frequency, the more quickly the new brand can be evaluated. A new brand that is bought two times a year should be kept on the market longer than one that is bought weekly. The chances are good that a newly launched brand of cigarettes that does not achieve a satisfactory level of sales within six months will be withdrawn from the market. But a new brand of oil filter probably should be kept on the market longer.

### Vicarious Reinforcement and Imitation

If you observe that another person's behavior leads to reinforcement, you may try the same behavior when you are in the same situation. The receipt of reinforcement by another person appears to result in learning by the observer. This is called **vicarious reinforcement.**

vicarious
reinforcement

It would be hard for a consumer to learn through direct experience everything needed to cope in a modern economy. Imitation is an efficient method of learning because it relies on the research and experience of others. It is a key factor in the adoption of new products by consumers and their diffusion throughout the population.

When a rock star appears in a concert with a new brand of guitar, its sales will likely increase because of imitation. Many marketers use testimonials in their ads. The FTC requires that endorsers who claim to use a product regularly must actually use it. But there is no law against endorsers' switching from one brand to another. For example, Miller Lite commercials used to feature endorsements from Joe Frazier, Mickey Mantle, and Nick Buoniconti but they later switched to Anheuser-Busch's Natural Light.

Consider a family buying a new car. The satisfaction they display may lead some of their friends to buy that model. The adoption of new clothing fashions also depends heavily on imitation. It also is the method by which parents influence the consumer behavior of their children. We will discuss this in the next chapter.

### SUMMARY AND LOOK AHEAD

The intrapersonal factors that influence consumer behavior affect how consumers adjust their behavior to the marketplace. Needs result from imbalances in a person's internal and external conditions, and behavior is an attempt to maintain an optimal level of stimulation. Needs that account for behavior (physiological, safety, love, esteem, self-actualization, cognitive, and territorial) remain the same throughout a person's life, but cultural and social demands determine how they will be satisfied. These demands are called developmental tasks.

Perception is the process by which people filter out, transform, and organize data from their environment. How a person perceives something is determined by stimulus properties (color, context, location, intensity) and personal factors (motivation, previous experiences, and emotions).

Cognition is the process by which people assign meaning to their experiences and solve problems. Two types of meanings are assigned to products: functional and subjective. Functional meanings deal with how well the product does what it was designed to do. Subjective mean-

Chapter 5   INTRAPERSONAL INFLUENCES ON CONSUMER BEHAVIOR          137

ings may be either social or symbolic. Social meanings are determined by the reactions of others. Symbolic meanings result from product qualities, such as activity, form, color, and shape.

Learning is how people adjust their behavior in the light of its results. Generalization, discrimination, oscillation, imitation, and extinction are parts of learning that are important to marketers. They affect brand loyalty, marketing research, and promotional efforts.

In the next chapter we will discuss how other people influence a consumer's behavior. Family, social, and cultural influences together form the background in which the intrapersonal factors discussed in this chapter operate.

## REVIEW QUESTIONS

**1.** Identify several safety needs and give examples of products that satisfy them.

**2.** Give an example of multiple determination of behavior.

**3.** Why do some people take vacations in the country and others in the city?

**4.** Identify the developmental tasks of early adolescence. Give examples of products that are related to these tasks.

**5.** Why would a marketer use color ads rather than black-and-white ads?

**6.** Identify and discuss the stimulus factors that affect perception.

**7.** Identify and discuss the personal factors that affect perception.

**8.** Is a candy bar with 34g of sugar noticeably

sweeter than one with 30g? (Assume a K value of 20 percent.) Explain your answer.

**9.** Identify four types of symbolic meanings. Why do marketers want to know the symbolic meanings of their products?

**10.** Why is quality control so important in marketing new products?

**11.** How are semantic differential scales used in marketing?

**12.** Why would Coca-Cola use the theme "It's the real thing" in its advertising?

**13.** Why might a marketer not want to use similar packages for different products so buyers could tell the firm makes all of them?

**14.** How can oscillation responses be a problem for a marketer?

## DISCUSSION QUESTIONS

**1.** Is it ethical for marketers to attempt subliminal stimulation in promoting their products?

**2.** Have you ever purchased a product on the basis of "emotional" motives? If so, give some examples.

**3.** Why is perception a selective process?

**4.** Why do so many people say "make a Xerox copy" even when the photocopying machine is not manufactured by Xerox? Is this good for the Xerox Corporation?

**5.** Why do manufacturers of margarine add yellow coloring to their product?

## NOTES

1. See R. A. Mittelstaedt, S. L. Grossbart, W. W. Curtis, and S. P. DeVere, "Optimal Stimulation Level and the Adoption Decision Process," *Journal of Consumer Research*, September, 1976, pp. 84–94.
2. See Samuel B. Cousley, Jr., "The Impact of

Color Contrast on Advertising Effectiveness," *Proceedings: Southern Marketing Association*, 1976 Conference (Starkville, Miss.: Mississippi State University, 1976), pp. 249–251.
3. This is called *advertising wearout.* See C. Sam-

uel Craig, Brian Sternthal, and Clark Leavitt, "Advertising Wearout: An Experimental Analysis," *Journal of Marketing Research*, November, 1976, pp. 365–372.

4. See Steuart Henderson Britt, "How Weber's Law Can Be Applied to Marketing," *Business Horizons*, February, 1975, pp. 21–29.

5. "Marketing Briefs," *Marketing News*, January 25, 1980, p. 16.

6. For further discussion of subliminal perception, see James F. Engel, David T. Kollat, and Roger D. Blackwell, *Consumer Behavior*, 2d ed. (New York: Holt, Rinehart and Winston, 1973), pp. 223–224. During the 1970s the issue of subliminal perception was raised again. In *Subliminal Seduction*, Wilson Bryan Key suggests that consumers are being manipulated by advertisers who hide messages in print ads and television commercials. The letters *s-e-x*, for example, are said to be hidden in many ads. See Lynn Sharpe, "Subliminal Communication: Insidious Advertising," *Encore*, December, 1974, pp. 39–40. Also see Joel L. Saegert, "Another Look at Subliminal Perception," *Journal of Advertising Research*, February, 1979, pp. 55–57; and J. Steven Kelly, "Subliminal Embeds in Print Advertising: A Challenge to Advertising Ethics, *Journal of Advertising*, Summer, 1979, pp. 20–24.

7. See Wolfgang Schaefer, "Selective Perception in Operation," *Journal of Advertising Research.* February, 1979, pp. 59–60.

8. See Rom J. Markin, Jr., *Consumer Behavior: A Cognitive Orientation* (New York: Macmillan Publishing Company, 1974). Also see Richard J. Lutz, "Changing Brand Attitudes through Modification of Cognitive Structure," *Journal of Consumer Research*, March, 1975, pp. 49–59.

9. "Tobacco Marketers' Success Formula: Make Cigarets in Smoker's Own Image," *Wall Street Journal*, February 29, 1980, p. 10.

10. Bernard F. Whalen, "Marketer Designs Permanent Media to Position Firms," *Marketing News*, November 2, 1979, p. 8.

11. Mason Haire, "Projective Techniques in Marketing Research," *Journal of Marketing*, April, 1950, pp. 649–656.

12. Frederick E. Webster, Jr. and Frederick Von Pechmann, "A Replication of the 'Shopping List' Study," *Journal of Marketing*, April, 1970, pp. 61–63. Also see James C. Anderson, "The Validity of Haire's Shopping List Projective Technique," *Journal of Marketing Research*, November, 1978, pp. 644–649.

13. See Darego W. MacLayton and Joseph F. Hair, "The Semantic Differential: An Information Source for Measuring Pharmaceutical Corporate Image," *Journal of Medical and Pharmaceutical Marketing*, November–December, 1975, pp. 9–12. Also see John Dickson and Gerald Albaum, "A Method for Developing Tailor-made Semantic Differentials for Specific Marketing Content Areas," *Journal of Marketing Research*, February, 1977, pp. 87–91.

14. For discussion of learning concepts that are helpful in marketing communications, see Steuart Henderson Britt, "Applying Learning Principles to Marketing," *MSU Business Topics*, Spring, 1975, pp. 5–12.

15. "There's No Way to Tell If a New Food Product Will Please the Public," *Wall Street Journal*, February 26, 1980, p. 1.

16. Brand switching is the least troublesome approach consumers have to register dissatisfaction. See Betty J. Diener and Stephen A. Greyser, "Consumer Views of Redress Needs," *Journal of Marketing*, October, 1978, pp. 21–27.

17. "3M Will Market Adhesive Concoction for Sun Worshipers," *Wall Street Journal*, March 25, 1980, p. 31.

# Chapter 6

# Interpersonal Influences On Consumer Behavior

## OBJECTIVES

*After reading this chapter you should be able to*

1. identify the effects of the nuclear family unit on marketing decisions.

2. tell why marketers should understand how the family unit operates.

3. identify the stages of the family life cycle and the buying patterns at each stage.

4. discuss the relative roles played by spouses in purchase decisions.

5. explain the effects on marketing of the increasing number of nonfamily households.

6. give examples of products that have social value and those that do not.

7. explain how reference groups and social class influence buying decisions.

8. explain how innovation in buying behavior takes place.

9. define culture and identify the major values of the dominant culture in the United States.

10. identify rites of passage and explain how products can be marketed using them.

11. identify three major subcultures and discuss their buying patterns.

## KEY CONCEPTS

*Look for these terms as you read the chapter:*

Nuclear Family Unit
Extended Family Unit
Family Life Cycle
Joint Decisions
Roles
Reference Groups
Range of Acceptable Behavior
Self-Concept
Psychosocial Risk
High-Risk Perceivers
Social Classes
Culture
Cultural Values
Rites of Passage
Subculture

*Your buying behavior is influenced by your membership in a family and a social system and by cultural values. Marketers must be aware of these continuously changing interpersonal influences on buyer behavior.*

*Consider changes in the make-up of the family unit. Life insurance companies are having to cope with young adults postponing marriage and children. Sales of some types of life insurance policies are down because single people typically do not buy as much life insurance as married people with children do. The increase in the number of divorced working women who head households is affecting marketers of clothing, food, and financial services.*

*What about a person's membership in the larger society? In the early 1970s many people were caught up in the back-to-nature movement. They wanted to lead simpler and more healthy lives. Consider how this affected breakfast cereal marketers. Natural foods became very popular, such as breakfast cereals containing nuts and oats. But the popularity of natural foods declined when nutritionists pointed out that some natural foods were full of sugar and were not very nutritious. They favored high-fiber diets and this started a trend to bran-based cereals fortified with vitamins. Many of these products were targeted to adults. Traditionally, cereals have been targeted primarily to children.*

*The do-it-yourself trend also has become popular in recent years. Valvoline ads tell us how easy it is to save money by changing our motor oil ourselves, numerous toolmakers tell us how much money we can save by doing home repairs ourselves, and building supply dealers are sponsoring clinics to teach us how to save money by doing basic home remodeling and repair jobs ourselves.*

Interactions with other people influence a consumer's behavior. The interpersonal factors that affect consumer behavior are family, social, and cultural. The family is one of the social groups that operates within the culture. The decision to buy a tube of toothpaste is influenced by interpersonal factors. Using toothpaste to clean teeth is culturally determined, while the desire for cleaner teeth may be the result of social influences. The brand bought may be the result of a family decision based on how well the different brands clean and prevent cavities.

## FAMILY INFLUENCES

Marketers must understand the family unit to make good marketing decisions for the following reasons:

1. Many buying decisions are made in the family unit. It is considered the basic economic unit in our country.[1]
2. Consumer behavior starts in the family unit.[2] Children learn from

parents patterns of marketplace behavior. By nine years of age the child is an active consumer.

3.  The family roles and product preferences children observe are the models they imitate, alter, or reject in establishing their own families. Transmitting brand preferences from one generation to the next is an important part of the marketer's effort to maintain brand loyalty.

4.  Family buying decisions are a mixture of family interaction and individual decisions. Products bought on the basis of family interaction must be marketed differently from those bought on the basis of individual decisions. The type of buying decision a product represents is an important concern of marketers.

5.  The family acts as an interpreter of cultural and social forces for the individual.[3]

The following discussion of the family influences on consumer behavior centers on (1) family structure, (2) family life cycle, and (3) family interactions and role differentiation.

### Family Structure

**nuclear family unit**
**extended family unit**

The American family structure is changing continuously. Unlike the family structure in many other countries, ours has shifted from an extended family unit to a nuclear family unit. **A nuclear family unit** is composed of a mother, father, and their children.

Nuclear family units are smaller than extended family units. **Extended family units** also include grandparents, unmarried aunts and uncles, cousins, married children, and divorced children and their offspring. Such consumer durables as furniture, home appliances, and cars, therefore, must reflect the declining size of the basic family unit. Dining room furniture of the early 1900s was designed for eight people. Now it is designed for four or six.

Marriages of children from nuclear family units create separate economic units that must buy products such as housing, furniture, and appliances to set up their new households. As we saw in Chapter 3, the marriage rate has a big effect on the demand for consumer durables. Newly married couples must make decisions about many products they have never bought. They turn to other young married couples, sales personnel, brochures, and institutional advice such as *Consumer Reports* to get information. The least-used source of information often is the couple's parents. Their desire to make their own decisions must be reflected in ads targeted to them.

Because they do not carry their parents' status with them, the new family unit lacks an established status. They must communicate their status aspirations to other people. The types of home, clothes, and car they buy tell other people the position they want to occupy in the community. These purchases also tell other people who are acceptable as friends. The symbolic meanings of products, therefore, are important factors in determining consumer behavior. They are status symbols.

The marriage of children leaves parents alone and they alter their living and spending patterns considerably. Many products that used to be irrelevant to these empty nesters become important. They have more buying power and can buy products—for example, extended vacations and recreational vehicles—that used to be beyond their means.[4]

### Family Life Cycle

The family unit's structure goes through a series of changes. Each developmental stage in this **family life cycle** can be identified by the number and characteristics of the family members.

family life cycle

Table 6–1 shows that the family unit's developmental stage affects its consumption patterns. Family spending by product categories varies with life cycle stages.[5] Young married couples with children under six years of age may pass up vacations to spend more on the children. Pur-

**Table 6–1.** *Stages of the family life cycle*

| Stage | Purchase Characteristics |
|---|---|
| Young single (not living at home) | Few financial commitments. Major expenses are for fashionable clothes, cars, basic furniture, kitchen utensils, travel, and entertainment. |
| Young married without children | Both spouses work. Purchase major consumer durables, entertainment, travel, multifamily dwellings, and more expensive furnishings. |
| Young married with children under six years | Commitment to the home. One spouse leaves labor force. Little discretionary income. Buy necessities and toys for children and more food. Defer major consumer durable expenditures or purchase lower-priced lines. |
| Married with children over six years | Previously unemployed spouses may reenter labor force. Quantity purchases of consumables, medical and dental service, and instruction for children. |
| Older married with dependent children | Financial position better with both spouses working. More purchases of nonessentials and expensive consumer durables. |
| Older married with no children | Financial position best. Travel, recreation, self-improvement, luxury, home improvements, and medical expenses high. Investments and leisure-time activities are expensive. Drastic cut in income and living standards if retired. |
| Older single and surviving spouse | Changes living situation, sells home, income good if working, purchasing power high for some even if retired because of investments, savings, retirement funds, and Social Security. Others have little purchasing power. |
| Others | Less discretionary income. Purchases much like young families with children. Not as likely to own home. |

Source: *Journal of Marketing Research.*

chases of consumer durables in the same product categories also vary in different stages. A young couple with children may buy a middle-of-the-line sedan, while those without children at home might buy a sports car.

The family life cycle concept helps marketers develop products and ads that fit the consumption patterns in each stage. An expensive but smaller version of a washing machine would appeal to young singles, young marrieds without children, older singles, and older marrieds without children. An inexpensive but larger version would appeal to young couples with children under six years. A more expensive larger version would appeal to young marrieds with children over six and older marrieds with children.

Merrill Lynch, recognizing the growing number of divorced or widowed employed women who head households, put together a package of services and an ad campaign to attract them as clients. "Merrill Lynch has special help for women with special money problems." Older, affluent women who are divorced or widowed are appealed to with "11 ways Merrill Lynch helps women manage money better."

### Family Interactions and Role Differentiation

Traditionally, the father was perceived to be the family unit's task leader. He was assumed to be more interested in functional values, such as cost, construction, and technical aspects of products. The mother, on the other hand, was perceived as the family unit's social leader. Expressive values, such as color, design, and style, were assumed to be more important to her in choosing products. The father based buying decisions on functional values and the mother based buying decisions on expressive values. The father was oriented to the family's relationship with the outside world, while the mother was oriented to the family's internal functioning.

Given these traditional mother-father roles, a decision matrix could be developed to show who had primary responsibility for different kinds

**Table 6–2.** *Role differentiation in family purchases*

|  | *External* | *Internal* |
|---|---|---|
| Functional values | Decisions made primarily by father. Life insurance, bank, legal services. | Joint decisions. Washing machines, vacuum cleaners, mattresses, refrigerators. |
| Expressive values | Joint decisions. Vacations, country club membership, entertainment. | Decisions made primarily by mother. Color of carpet and drapes, style of living room furniture, piano, china. |

Adapted from Myers and Reynolds, *Consumer Behavior and Marketing Management.*

of product decisions.   (See Table 6-2.)   **Joint decisions** typically were   joint decisions
the results of the husband's concern for functional aspects and the wife's
for the expressive aspects of products.   Products like cars that involved
a joint buying decision could be advertised in both a man's and a woman's
magazine by using different ads that featured different aspects of the
product.   The ad for the male might feature compression ratio and other
mechanical features; the woman's ad might stress color and upholstery
options.   These traditional decision patterns, however, are changing rapidly because of a number of factors, especially the women's rights movement and dual-income families.[6]

For many years, marketers operated under the assumption that
women, mostly "housewives," make about 80 percent of all consumer
purchases because they enjoyed the social pleasures of shopping.   The
typical employed woman in past years was either (1) young and single,
(2) a married woman who had to work to supplement her husband's
income, or (3) a married woman whose husband had died or left home.
Women who held jobs outside the home were in the minority.[7]

Today, however, almost half of all women over age sixteen are in the
labor force.   The typical modern working woman is married, older, and
has one or more children under age eighteen living at home.   She combines two societal roles: (1) homemaker and mother and (2) worker employed outside the home.   This modern "workwife" has less time for
shopping, and her consumer behavior differs significantly from the traditional "housewife" stereotype.

Figure 6–1 shows a more complete view of all decisions made by a
family.   Husband-dominant, wife-dominant, and syncratic (true joint)
decisions fit the traditional concept of family decisions.   This model,
however, also includes autonomic decisions—those made by an individual member either because the product is for his or her own use or that
person has superior knowledge.

Complex and especially important buying decisions usually are joint
decisions.[8]   The redefinition of traditional sex roles has led to more joint
decision making.[9]   Women have become more interested in functional
aspects of products and men have become more interested in expressive
aspects.

In some families one spouse may dominate buying decisions.   The
dominant spouse has more influence in joint decisions but tends to spend
less on his or her personal needs.   When neither spouse is dominant,
children have more influence, especially when neither spouse has a strong
preference for any of the products being considered.[10]

As children get older their opinions about products become more
important in family buying decisions.   Some family purchase decisions
may be made solely by teen-age children.   A teen-ager who cooks and
cleans house may decide which foods and cleaning products to buy.   In
families where both spouses work, teen-age children often do the family
shopping with little supervision from parents, especially when parents

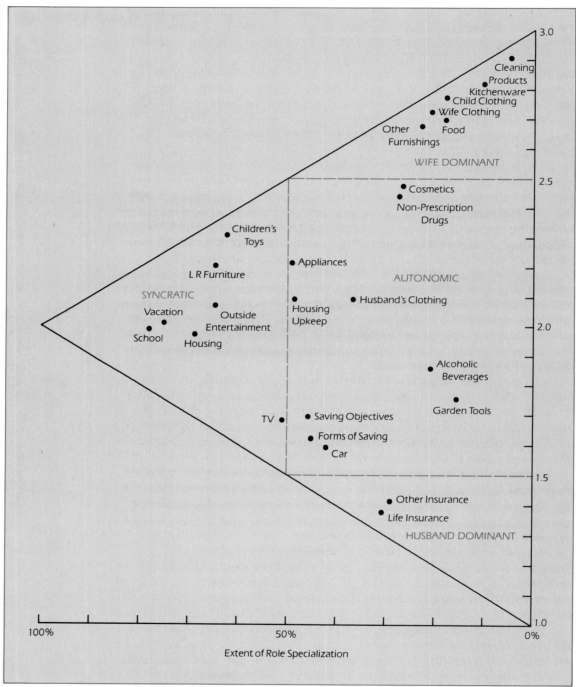

**Figure 6–1. Relative influence of husbands and wives**
Source: *Journal of Consumer Research.*

commute to work.[11]    Thus ads for Stove Top Dressing sometimes feature teen-agers preparing a meal.

## Nonfamily Economic Units

More than half of America's households no longer fit the nuclear family unit stereotype.    Three factors help explain the growing importance of nonfamily economic units: (1) longer life expectancy increases the period a household exists after children leave, (2) the divorce rate is going up, and (3) more people are staying single.

Demands on family income decrease as children leave home and discretionary income increases.    Family income also may increase because of more earning power or the return of a previously unemployed spouse to the labor force.    The family can afford to buy products that used to be considered too expensive.    Although households headed by persons forty-five to sixty-four years of age account for only one-third of the total number of households, they account for more than 40 percent of total spending power.    These households have the highest average income.

After retirement, the family's ability to sustain its spending patterns depends on its assets and retirement income.    Elderly couples living on fixed incomes have more trouble coping with inflation than those who have investments and other assets.

As we saw in Chapter 3, divorce produces, at least for a while, increased demand for some products by creating two economic units in place of one.    Newly divorced persons must reestablish the social aspects of their lives.    New clothes, physical fitness, housing, and leisure-time activities are important.    Divorce also may result in a formerly nonemployed spouse's entering the labor force or entering school to upgrade job skills.    If children are present, child day-care services, professional cleaning services, and convenience foods become necessities instead of luxuries.    Most divorced people eventually remarry but the time between marriages is growing.    Divorced people, therefore, are an important market segment.    Many who choose not to remarry establish satisfying lives outside of marriage.

An increase in the number of people who elect a single lifestyle is important to marketers.    The age at first marriage is increasing for both men and women in the United States.    The singles market demands apartments, condominiums, and townhouses designed to meet their needs for mobility, investment advantages, and low maintenance.    Single-serving food packages also are becoming more common in supermarkets. Many nightclubs identify themselves as singles bars, many churches have singles programs, and several magazines such as *Apartment Life* and *New Woman* cater to the single adult.[12]

The singles market, of course, is less important for marketers of life insurance, station wagons, and top-of-the-line appliances.    Many singles do not buy single-family homes.    But some who are committed to a permanent singles lifestyle are leaving multiple-unit housing for single-family houses.

## SOCIAL INFLUENCES

The demands of others create social influences on consumer behavior. By age seven a child knows the social value of products.

Laws, which define what is acceptable and unacceptable behavior, are formal social influences. Products like marijuana, pornography, and amphetamines are illegal or controlled because they are considered dangerous to society. What others expect of a person are informal social influences (**roles**). Role conflict results when the demands of one role are unacceptable to another role.

roles

Four factors influence the roles you are expected to fulfill: (1) reference groups, (2) your status in reference groups, (3) social class, and (4) your perceptions of these demands on behaviors.

### Reference Groups

reference groups

Groups to which you belong or aspire to belong are **reference groups**. They may be organized, with stated goals, or unstructured, like children's play groups. A number of reference groups are organized around work, religion, and social activities. The only requirement is that you see yourself as a member of that group (membership reference group) or at least want to belong to it (aspirational reference group).

*limited to conspicuous consumsion*

Reference groups have certain requirements for membership. These are formalized and related to group goals in structured groups. In unstructured groups they often are defined vaguely and are based mainly on personal characteristics. Education, special skills, or being a parent may be necessary for membership in structured groups. Appearance, dress, and owning a home in the same neighborhood may satisfy membership requirements in unstructured groups.

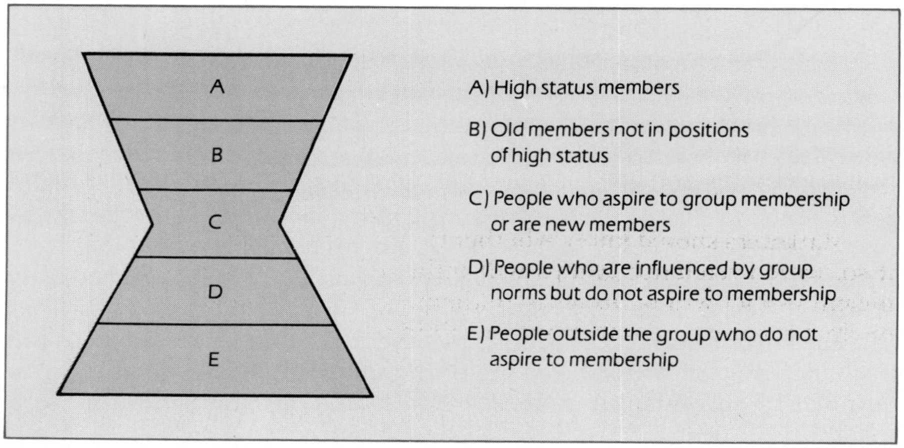

Figure 6–2.
**The relationship between range of acceptable behavior and status position in the group**

A) High status members

B) Old members not in positions of high status

C) People who aspire to group membership or are new members

D) People who are influenced by group norms but do not aspire to membership

E) People outside the group who do not aspire to membership

**Acceptable behavior.** The survival of any group depends on its ability to define and enforce a **range of acceptable behavior**, or group norms. Members must conform to group values, beliefs, and behavior within established limits. The range varies according to your status position in the group. (See Figure 6–2.)

range of accept-
able behavior

The longer you have been a member, or the higher your status in the group, the wider your range of acceptable behavior. New and prospective members have the smallest ranges and they must conform closely to group norms. Behavior that falls outside the limits set by the group are punished. Buying an inappropriate product, for example, may lead to a loss of membership in the group.

Most of us try to play roles in many reference groups and sometimes we do not see clearly what others expect of us. Sanctions help in defining acceptable behavior when group norms are unclear. As you learn the limits on your behavior in different reference groups, they become a part of your self-concept—how you see what you are.

Your **self-concept** is the filter by which your behavior is tested. Products covered by group norms are not bought if you believe they are "not me." They do not fit your view of yourself and your roles in reference groups.[13]

self-concept

The self-concept includes (1) how you see yourself (real self), (2) how you would like to be (ideal self), and (3) how you would like others to see you (public self).

The public and ideal selves may be different from your real self. These aspects of the self-concept come from new reference groups to which you want to belong. Buying products that are outside your present range of acceptable behavior may be based on these aspects of the self-concept. An older woman may buy a very modish dress because she wants to look younger (ideal self). A couple may buy an expensive home they really cannot afford because they want others to see them as being richer than they are (public self).

Purchases of products that are influenced by reference groups have social value. They must be visible and different from other products in the same product category to give them social meaning that others can interpret readily. Cars are an example. Different characteristics are attached to Honda, Buick, and Cadillac owners. Houses, clothes, jewelry, beer, colleges, entertainment, and luggage are other examples. Antifreeze, sugar, light bulbs, and sheets, on the other hand, have little or no social value and their purchase is not influenced much by reference group pressures.

Marketers should know whether their products have social value, and if so, which reference groups will influence purchase decisions and the meanings that will be attached to them. This helps to determine which product features are important in gaining customer acceptance.

Tailoring a product or its advertising to a specific market segment may increase its appeal to other segments. Designer label jeans, Honda motorcycles, and herbal colognes are youth-oriented products whose appeal to other market segments has increased. The ad "Should a gentleman offer a lady a Tiparillo?" broadened the product's market without destroying its primary target. The same is true of Irish Spring's "Manly yes! But gentle enough for a woman." In other cases, appealing to a specific segment may lead to a product's rejection by other groups. Consider the effects of identifying a product as primarily for the balding male.

**psychosocial risk**

**Psychosocial Risk.** Buying decisions for products with social value are risky for consumers when reference groups lack well-defined norms. The degree of **psychosocial risk** is determined by the possible consequences of the purchase decision and the probability of their occurrence. Buying a dress for a Christmas party may involve severe risk. Buying peanut butter may involve little or none.

**high-risk perceivers**

People perceive risk differently.[14] **High-risk perceivers** lack confidence in themselves and perceive more risk than do other consumers in the same situation. If they have low status in reference groups, their perceptions of higher risk may be accurate. Their range of acceptable behavior is more restricted. Marketers can try to reduce the consumer's perceived risk. Ads that offer social support through phrases like "the typical working-class male" for beer and "the typical family" for car purchases are examples. Women who wanted to wear their leotards with a skirt but were skeptical probably were helped by the ad slogan "Danskins are not just for dancing."

**Opinion Leadership.** The values of social groups change. Change usually is introduced by persons who have freedom to behave differently because of their high status, specialized skills, or knowledge. In many cases other members look to these innovators, or opinion leaders, to define what is acceptable behavior. Often this includes advice and information about new products.

Opinion leadership is a shared task. A person with multiple reference groups may turn to several opinion leaders in different groups for advice and information about new products. That person's buying behavior, therefore, cannot be predicted simply on the basis of one opinion leader or one reference group. He or she may look to a work associate for advice about life insurance, a friend for advice about clothes, and a neighbor for advice about lawn-care products.

Figure 6–2 suggests that innovation is more likely to occur outside reference groups than in them because group membership restricts behavior. Innovation here means generating new products or new uses for existing products.

Some male fashions, for example, can be traced to three groups: (1) the black male, (2) the teen-age male, and (3) the homosexual. Large segments of these three groups typically have been disenfranchised in our society. Casual denims, disco, shoes with high heels, pants with flared legs, boldly printed nylon tricot underwear, pocketless pants, and male jewelry had their origins in one or more of these groups. Some record companies also hire gay executives because of their knowledge of music trends.

Reference group influence, however, is not dictatorial. A suburban couple whose friends have all bought hot tubs may be under pressure to buy one. The brand, size, style, when and where they will buy it, and how much they will spend are individual decisions.

## Social Class

As we saw in Chapter 3, the United States is not a big melting pot. Furthermore, it is not a classless society. There is a social class structure. **Social classes** are the divisions in society into which individuals, families, or groups that share similar values, lifestyles, interests, and behavior can be placed. The social class structure is a larger grouping of reference groups: (1) people are conscious of it, (2) social interactions generally occur between people on the same class level, and (3) people within a social class are very much alike in terms of values, interests, and behavior.

social classes

A combination of the following factors, in order of importance, can be used to measure a family's social class in the United States: (1) occupation, (2) source of income, (3) type of house, (4) dwelling area, (5) education, (6) interaction patterns, (7) kinship, and (8) family ancestry.

Members of a lower social class who share some characteristics (income, education) with a higher social class are overprivileged members of the lower class. Those in a higher social class who share income and possession characteristics with a lower social class are underprivileged members of the higher class. Both lack clearly identified social positions and are not totally acceptable to either social class.

Often overprivileged and underprivileged members of a social class are in the process of moving to new social classes. Social mobility, especially upward, is an important part of the folklore of the United States. But it is more limited than is commonly thought. Movement usually is limited to one class level for a generation. The children of a highly successful plumber may move to the middle class if the family's values, home, and behaviors change. A salesman who wins a million-dollar lottery will still likely remain a member of the same social class. His values, behavior patterns, and interests probably will not change enough to make him feel comfortable in a higher class. Money alone does not change a family's social class.

**Social Class Characteristics.** Characteristics of the five social classes are summarized in Table 6–3. Although the percentages suggest the relative importance of each as a potential market, there is a disproportionate amount of discretionary income in the upper-level classes.

Your social class limits the reference groups to which you can belong and determines future opportunities by the values placed on education and vocational goals. It is the background in which the family unit and a person's reference groups function.

**Social Class and Marketing.** Several important implications of social class for marketing are: (1) consumer behavior varies more between social classes than within a social class, (2) social class measures can help in segmenting markets, (3) social class affects the product diffusion process,

**Table 6–3.**  *Summary of social class characteristics*

| | |
|---|---|
| Upper class 3% | Wealth inherited or received from high-income professions, managerial positions with major corporations, or entrepreneurship; live in a large home in best suburbs; often maintain a second home in metropolitan or resort areas; relatively conservative in tastes and do not spend money for display; children educated at best private schools and are often symbols of parents' wealth and status. |
| Upper middle class 12% | Successful professionals and business people; education their major asset for maintaining their position and for their children's future; demand good performance from children; consumption "fashionable" and "high quality"; wife considered a major asset if she can maintain a "gracious" household, entertain, and care for children; homes in better areas but not extremely large. |
| Lower middle class 30% | Small business owners, white-collar salaried workers, ministers, teachers, salespeople; good, respectable, hard-working, common people with typical American values and standards of behavior; homes neat, up-to-date, clean, small and in good areas; much of the maintenance and decoration done by husband and wife; centered on family and children; wives price-conscious shoppers; stress control and conformity in children; future oriented. |
| Upper lower class 35% | Semiskilled workers; live in less desirable homes or apartments; life characterized as routine for both male and female; wife primarily mother to children as reason for existence; purchase decisions characterized by impulsiveness and brand loyalty; wife's contacts outside home primarily with family and close neighbors and mother-related, such as P.T.A. or church; if available, money spent on elaborate appliances; many have some high school but did not graduate. |
| Lower lower class 20% | Poorly educated; low income; work history shows numerous changes; relaxed attitudes about childrearing; subsidized housing or lowest residential areas; lower impulse control reflected in buying habits that result in paying too much for inferior quality; generally hold no hope of social mobility; little or no savings; present oriented. |

Source: Warner, Meeker, and Eeles, *Social Class in America:* and Engel, Kollat, and Blackwell, *Consumer Behavior,* 2nd ed.

(4) social class affects the choice of advertising media, and (5) social class is a good indicator of shopping behavior.

Buying patterns, decision processes, and the use of products are different in each social class. Although behavior within social classes varies, the variance is not as great as that between social classes. For example, upper lower-class families will visit distant relatives, go hunting and fishing, or stay at home and watch TV for a vacation because they feel uncomfortable out of their immediate surroundings; middle-class families travel by car to the beach or mountains; and upper-class families spend vacations in fashionable resorts, such as Aspen, Colorado, at second homes, or in foreign resorts.

The similarities in selecting and using products and the goals of each class suggest that social-class measures can be used to segment markets. For example, different market segments buy different price lines of household appliances. Upper lower-class consumers are more likely to buy more expensive models than middle- or upper-class consumers.

Social class data also help in understanding product diffusion. Persons within a social class are much more likely to interact than people in different classes. The greater the social distance between the classes, the less likely direct interaction or influence will occur. A marketer, therefore, cannot depend on a simple trickle-down approach in which a new product is adopted first in the higher classes and then trickles down to the lower classes. Instead, an effort must be made to introduce new products appropriate for each social class level.

Some products work their way up from the lower classes to higher classes without adoption in the intermediate social classes. An example is the turquoise jewelry of the southwestern Indians, a low-class product that became popular with the upper class. Other examples might include four-wheel-drive vehicles, pickup trucks, and the cornrow hairstyle.

Understanding social class also helps in making media decisions, such as the choice of radio, television, or magazines for advertising. A country-and-western station, for example, draws its audience from a different social class than an easy-listening or hard-rock station.

Finally, a person's social class is a good indicator of shopping behavior. Lower-class persons tend to shop closer to home, do not use disclosure of interest rate information as much,[15] do not engage in much prepurchase information gathering,[16] and have less knowledge of shopping alternatives.

Stores project definite class images. Personnel in higher-status stores like Neiman-Marcus behave and look differently from those in middle- or lower-class stores. Higher-class stores smell different and have less merchandise in the display windows. Width of aisles, lighting, and choice of materials and fixtures also affect consumers' perceptions of store status.

Consumers can rate the relative social class of stores and this influences their shopping behavior. Whether they patronize a store depends partly on the matching of the class elements of the store's image with perceptions of their social class. Their patronage may also represent their aspirations for future status (the ideal self). The shopping behavior of the lower middle class, however, seems to be determined more by price than that of other social classes.

## CULTURAL INFLUENCES

**Culture** is the sum total of knowledge, beliefs, values, customs, and artifacts that we use to adapt to our environment and that we hand down to succeeding generations. The intrapersonal and interpersonal factors that influence consumer behavior operate within the culture.[17] Consumer behavior is the individual's attempt to obtain satisfactions for needs. Culture determines the products available for satisfying those

culture

needs and the behaviors used to obtain these satisfactions. The cultural influences on consumer behavior center on cultural values, customs, and cultural change.

## Cultural Values

cultural values

**Cultural values** are the most effective ways previous generations have found to satisfy basic needs. Objects that satisfy needs are valued by a culture. Valued objects in primitive cultures are related directly to the physiological and safety needs in Maslow's hierarchy. Camels, goats, and yaks are the unit of wealth, status, and exchange. By contributing meat, milk, hides, and hair they are crucial to the continued existence of people. Valued objects in more industrialized cultures often are satisfactions for higher-order needs, such as continuing education programs, travel, and vacation homes.

Valued objects sometimes are quite removed from the direct satisfaction of needs. They have expressive value. Silver flatware once was valued for its function. It was the only metal for making knives and forks that did not rust or change the taste of food. This functional value decreased with the invention of stainless steel. Other than the value of the silver, the primary reason for buying silver flatware today is expressive. Antique furniture and candles are other examples of expressive value. Perhaps wood-burning fireplaces once again are becoming functional, as well as expressive, because of skyrocketing energy costs.

Behaviors that satisfy needs are highly valued and are transmitted to succeeding generations. Those that are inappropriate for foreseeable future circumstances are not. Some behaviors, however, become so highly valued that they are transmitted to succeeding generations even though they are no longer functional. Hunting was a necessary skill for survival during the frontier period. It no longer serves a survival function but is a major sport supporting several major industries, including camping equipment, firearms, and outdoor clothing.

Behaviors passed down but no longer functional often become cultural myths. The young are taught to believe in and strive for the attainment of these behaviors. They can be used to market many products. By developing products that incorporate these myths into their design, the expense and time necessary to build product acceptance may be shortened. Tying products to cultural myths through ad campaigns also can create customer loyalty or develop new markets for existing products. The "Marlboro man" is a variation of the rugged individualist ideal of masculinity. The sale of diamonds, china, and silver is tied to the concept of eternal love, a variation of the "till death do us part" myth.

Several important values in the American culture relate to (1) science and technology, (2) youth, (3) work and leisure, (4) change, (5) religion and sensuality, (6) education, (7) rejection of complexity, and (8) rites of passage.

**Science and Technology.** As we saw in Chapter 2, our culture places great importance on science and technology. The desire to control pop-

*An ad appealing to the concept of eternal love*

ulation growth led to the birth control pill rather than to changes in attitudes. Pollution has been attacked by emissions control devices for factories and cars rather than by reduced use of products that pollute. The large number of deaths on the highway led to the use of seat belts and air bags rather than to more restrictive practices in issuing driver's licenses. This high regard for science has decreased the importance of experience. Many modern homemakers use products, such as trash compactors, food processors, and microwave ovens, that were unheard of by their mothers. This rapid rate of new product development makes the opinions of older people outdated.

**Youth.** Youth is highly prized in our culture. The young adult is considered the ideal in physical appearance, sexual appeal, health, and attitudes toward living. Many of us fear aging—baldness, wrinkles, and gray hair. Middle-aged adults are attracted to leisure activities, exercise aids, clothing, hair pieces, face lifts, and other products that help them create an image of youthfulness. Increased consciousness of weight probably is due in part to this cultural value. This probably played a part in H.J. Heinz Company's decision to acquire control of the Weight Watchers food label several years ago.

**Work and Leisure.** An important aspect of our cultural values is reflected in our awareness of time and how we use it. A trend toward adopting a leisure ethic in place of a work ethic may be occurring. The work ethic reflects a belief in the value of hard work and accumulating wealth; idleness is undesirable. But today the purchase of many products represents attempts to buy leisure time. Fast-food restaurants, microwave ovens, food blenders and processors, automated bank tellers, dishwashers, power mowers, lawn-care services, and home computers are examples of the new leisure ethic.

**Change.** Change, another cultural value, has two elements. First, we place a high value on the new and unique. Older models of products that are still serviceable are traded in and replaced by new models. Yearly model changes are common for cars, household appliances, stereo equipment, and many other products. Some consumers buy new models to avoid costly repair bills, but many just want change. Owning the newest also may communicate social status.

The second element is the emphasis placed on mobility. We mentioned a decline in the willingness of some Americans to move to new cities for job promotions in Chapter 3. But there still is some tendency for mobile Americans not to become involved in their communities or with their acquaintances. Some suburbanites, for example, consider their homes temporary even though they own them. Job transfers, changing economic conditions, and the desire to live in a different part of the country are factors. Mobility influences buying patterns. More money is invested in products that can be moved easily. Mobile families have a core of such products (core possessions), which are augmented by others that are sold or discarded before each move. Thus sales of customer-assembled furniture are increasing partly because it is more portable than traditional furniture.

The leasing and renting of products, including furniture, appliances, videocassettes, and cars, are growing. Video Corporation of America started Vid America, the first videocassette rental club in the United States. The big decline in new car sales during the onset of recession in early 1980 lured some new car dealers into the car rental business. Hertz, Avis, and National's business is mainly related to air travel. But car dealer rentals basically are local in nature. One market segment they seek to reach is families who buy small cars for fuel economy but rent larger cars for vacation travel.[18]

Whether a product is a core long-term possession or one that will be exchanged for a new model or discarded upon moving must be considered in product design, promotional appeals, and pricing decisions. The added costs of making products more durable may not be justified in some cases. Research can help determine what consumers expect regarding product life.

**Religion and Sensuality.** The sanctity of the family, delay of need satisfaction, expectations of a better future, and the intervention of a higher power in human events are basic elements of American culture. But many quasi-religious groups that emphasize mysticism, humanism, and the occult are challenging established religions, of which many of these elements are a part, as modes of spiritual expression. Newer practices of the "me" generation focus on immediate need satisfaction, increased sensitivity to one's own body, and sexual behavior as fun. Although some of these values are extensions of traditional religious beliefs, some are not. The phrase "Do your own thing" describes current religious expression for many people. Some marketers recognize this newer style of religious expression and supply products that suit it. Consider the ready availability of incense, sex-related products, and horoscopes; the emphasis on bright colors, soft textures, and natural lines in fashion; and the mass marketing of biofeedback equipment.

**Education.** Education traditionally has been the surest road to social mobility and higher-income occupations. For many students the major emphasis in education has shifted from pure knowledge to career education. This affects what and how all subjects are taught. English and math, for example, are tied to their uses in jobs and everyday life. These changes will have far-reaching effects on how consumers view products and the criteria by which they make purchase decisions.

**Rejection of Complexity.** Many people are unprepared for the complexities of urban life, which create interdependence and less personal freedom and privacy. Some consumers feel that the growth of large, multiproduct firms has resulted in a loss in product quality. Bigness in many instances is becoming synonymous with lower quality. The replacement of locally owned grocery and department stores by national chains reduces the chances of personalized service. The addition of flavor enhancers and preservatives to foodstuffs causes consumer concern about the effects on health.

These and many other aspects of modern life have created a trend toward a simpler lifestyle. Complicated, mass-produced products sometimes are valued less than simpler, handmade, and more natural products. The upsurge in denim and leather clothing, flea markets, home gardening and canning, camping equipment, natural foods, and smaller cars is due partly to a rejection of complexity. The migration of industry from metropolitan areas to small towns is partially due to this trend also.

The trend toward a simpler lifestyle affects marketing activities. For example, the marketing of legal services has changed drastically in some areas since lawyers began to advertise and set up retail store-type law offices. Fashion, yearly model changes, and elaborate appliances may become less important than utility and function. There are some estimated twenty million consumers, described as "voluntary simplifiers," including "neo-econo-sapiens, conspicuous conservers, and the middle-

**Table 6–4.** *Differences between voluntary simplifiers and nonsimplifiers*

| Simplifiers | Nonsimplifiers |
|---|---|
| *Value Premises* | *Value Premises* |
| Material sufficiency coupled with psychospiritual growth | Material growth |
| People within nature, equilibrium | Man over nature |
| Enlightened self-interest | Competitive self-interest |
| Cooperative individualism | Rugged individualism |
| Rational and intuitive | Rationalism |
| *Social Characteristics* | *Social Characteristics* |
| Smaller, less complex living and working environments | Large, complex living and working environments |
| Reduction of material complexity | Growth of material complexity |
| Appropriate technology | Space age technology |
| Identity found through inner and interpersonal discovery | Identity defined by patterns of consumption |
| Greater local self-determination coupled with emerging global institutions | Centralization of regulation & control at nation/state level |
| More integrated work roles (e.g., team assembly, multiple roles) | Specialized work roles—through division of labor |
| Balance of secular and spiritual | Secular |
| Hand-crafted, durable, unique products | Mass-produced, quickly obsolete, standardized products |
| "Spaceship Earth" ethic | Lifeboat ethic in foreign relations |

class poor," who have decided voluntarily to simplify their lifestyles and consumption patterns.[19]   (See Table 6–4.)

**Rites of Passage.**   All cultures observe valued changes in status and life situation with **rites of passage.** Three phases of rites of passage are (1) the separation from old status groups or life situation, (2) transition period when one is a member of neither the old nor the new group, and (3) incorporation into the new status group or life situation.

*rites of passage*

Marketers should be aware of the rites of passage of our culture. These include going off to college, motherhood, buying a first home, getting married, graduation, fraternity initiations, ordinations, christenings, oaths of office, and baptisms.   Ad appeals that tie products to these rites may help in developing new markets.   Consider the transition from single to married status.   The separation phase is the dating period, when the young man or woman begins to spend less time with same-sex peer groups.   Expenditures center around entertainment, food, clothes, transportation, and impersonal and inexpensive gifts.   Beginning with the

**Table 6–4.**   *Cont.*

| *Simplifiers* | *Nonsimplifiers* |
| --- | --- |
| *Social Characteristics* | *Social Characteristics* |
| Cultural heterogeneity, eager acceptance of diversity | Cultural homogeneity, partial acceptance of diversity |
| Laid-back, relaxed existence | High-pressure, rat-race existence |
| *Consumer Behavior* | *Consumer Behavior* |
| Conservation society | Consumption society |
| Quality of life | Hedonistic life |
| Small is better | Big is beautiful |
| Preference for quality | Preference for quantity |
| Essential products | Luxury products |
| More emphasis on durability | Less emphasis on durability |
| Ecologically and environmentally more responsible | Ecologically and environmentally less responsible |
| Preference for small, personal outlets (stores) | Preference for big outlets (stores) |
| More receptivity to innovative outlets (e.g., flea markets, street vendors) | Less receptivity to innovative outlets |
| More do-it-yourself orientation | Less do-it-yourself orientation |
| More co-op buying | Less co-op buying |
| Print, radio orientation | Television orientation |

Source: *Marketing News.*

**Table 6–5.** *Selected rites of passage of the United States and related products*

| | |
|---|---|
| Graduation | Robe rentals, corsages, luggage, travel alarm clocks, writing instruments, cars, shirts, and colognes |
| Retirement | Golf clubs, power tools, fishing and camping equipment, jewelry |
| Baby arrival | Products related to care, feeding, clothing the newborn baby, lingerie for the mother, kitchen timers, silver and food preparation utensils |
| Funerals | Flowers, foodstuffs, caskets, gravesites, clothing, tombstones, and transportation |

diamond engagement ring, the expenditures involve more money and are more personal in nature. Investments often are made in items to be used in the future home. The incorporation phase is marked by showers, receptions, and the marriage ceremony. Expenditures by the couple, their families, relatives, and friends are considerable. Table 6–5 lists some American rites of passage and the products associated with them.

In some instances, marketers should revive or strengthen declining rites of passage because of their profit potential. Housewarmings used to be common but have declined. The economic potential of this rite of passage is staggering in a mobile society. Maxwell House coffee uses it in its ads. A woman is anxious to serve good coffee so she serves Maxwell House when neighbors drop by. Because of declining high school enrollments, Jostens, Inc. is trying to encourage the graduation rite of passage in junior high and elementary schools to increase sales of yearbooks. The greeting card industry, which seems to have developed some occasion for practically every day of the year, has been energetic in exploring the potential of the rites of passage market.

### Subcultures

subculture

There are many subcultures in addition to the dominant American culture. A **subculture** is a group that shares values and behavior patterns that differ in important ways from those of the dominant culture.

We must use a combination of such factors as age, social class, religion, geographic location, family size, and national origin to identify a subculture. Among the many subcultures in the United States are Hispanic, teen-age, elderly, and American Indian. Although members of a particular subculture tend to share many of the values held by people in the dominant culture, they also share their own specific values.

The people within a particular subculture, therefore, tend to be very similar with respect to certain characteristics, such as attitudes and values. By studying subcultures that exist within the larger, dominant culture, marketers can develop marketing mixes that are more specifically tailored to a subculture's needs.

There always have been groups whose values and behavior differed significantly from those of the prevailing culture. The counterculture, as a strong subculture, arose in the 1960s in the United States. Disillusioned with materialism, affluence, the work ethic, status seeking, political processes, and traditional religions, the counterculture is a mixture of people from all age groups, social classes, and ethnic groups.

Although the values and customs of different elements of the counterculture differ, they share some values and behaviors. They are antagonistic toward dominant American values and traditions and toward the traditions of existing American subcultures as well. Natural foods and vegetarian diets, self-exploration and meditation, utility rather than fashion in clothing, communal extended-family living, the use of drugs, and the radical change of political institutions are among the values and behaviors of various elements of the counterculture.

Marketers must be aware of counterculture groups because their members often are innovators in the use of existing products and demand new products that may appeal to broader markets. For example, organic gardening and natural foods were "in" with elements of the counterculture long before they were adopted by elements of the prevailing culture. Thus change in the dominant culture can be the result of a strong counterculture.

## SUMMARY AND LOOK AHEAD

The interpersonal influences on consumer behavior are family, social, and cultural. They provide the context within which the individual factors we discussed in Chapter 5 function.

Role differentiation, interaction patterns, and stage of the family life cycle of the nuclear family unit determine to a large extent how consumer decisions are made. Within the family unit the trend is toward more joint decisions and increased influence by teen-age children on family purchases. The increasing number of nonfamily households has reduced the importance of the family unit and has created opportunities for new products.

Social class and reference groups become part of the consumer's view of himself or herself. Our purchase behavior reflects the behaviors that are appropriate for our reference groups and social class. These behavioral norms may be either formal or informal. Opinion leaders are members to whom others turn for advice about purchase decisions. Opinion leadership is a shared task and often results from these consumers' being better informed.

Culture affects the products available to satisfy basic needs and the behaviors used to obtain these satisfactions. Cultural values reflect how adaptive and desirable products and behaviors are. Subcultures are groups within the prevailing culture that have significantly different values and behavior patterns.

As we said in Chapter 3, there are ultimate consumers and industrial users. Up to now, our primary focus has been ultimate consumers. The next chapter discusses industrial users and their behavior.

## REVIEW QUESTIONS

**1.** Why is the family unit an important influence on marketing decisions?

**2.** How do products become status symbols?

**3.** What are the stages in the family life cycle? How is this concept useful to marketers?

**4.** Contrast the functional and expressive values of products.

**5.** What factors account for the growth of non-family economic units in the United States?

**6.** Contrast formal and informal social influences on buying behavior. Give two examples of each.

**7.** What are reference groups?

**8.** Discuss the concept of range of acceptable behavior.

**9.** What factors determine a person's social class?

**10.** Identify five important implications of social class for marketers.

**11.** Would a new product's acceptance within a social class happen faster than its movement from one social class to another? Why or why not?

**12.** How do upper-class stores differ in appearance from lower-class stores?

**13.** What are cultural myths? Give an example.

**14.** What determines the degree of psychosocial risk in buying decisions?

**15.** Why do many Americans trade in their cars when they are still serviceable?

**16.** What is a core possession?

**17.** Give an example of a rite of passage in our culture and identify a product that is related to it.

**18.** What are the relative advantages and disadvantages of identifying a product with a subculture?

**19.** Why are subcultures often sources of consumer innovations?

## DISCUSSION QUESTIONS

**1.** Is the concept of the extended family still useful in American marketing?

**2.** Is the high divorce rate in the United States "good" for marketers?

**3.** What benefits do people derive from membership in reference groups? What about aspirational reference groups?

**4.** What types of products have social value?

**5.** Why is there a social class structure in the United States?

**6.** How have American cultural values changed over the last two decades?

## NOTES

1. See Yoram Wind, "Preference of Relevant Others and Individual Choice Models," *Journal of Consumer Research*, June, 1976, pp. 50–57.
2. See Roy L. Moore and Lowndes F. Stevens, "Some Communication and Demographic Determinants of Adolescent Consumer Learning," *Journal of Consumer Research*, September, 1975, pp. 80–92; and George P. Moschis and Roy L. Moore, "Decision Making among the Young: A Socialization Perspective," *Journal of Consumer Research*, September, 1979, pp. 101–112.
3. In one study it was found that buying behavior may be related very closely to general household char-

acteristics. See Robert C. Blattberg, Peter Peacock, and Subrata K. Sen, "Purchase Strategies across Product Categories," *Journal of Consumer Research*, December, 1976, pp. 143–154.
4. How people use their time is significant in helping to explain their purchases of durables, ownership of credit cards, and the amount of insurance they have. See Lucy Chao Lee and Robert Ferber, "Use of Time as a Determinant of Family Market Behavior," *Journal of Business Research*, March, 1977, pp. 75–91.
5. The family life cycle was found to be a better explanatory variable than length of marriage in prefer-

ences of husbands and wives for automobiles. See Eli P. Cox, III, "Family Purchase Decision Making and the Process of Adjustment," *Journal of Marketing Research*, May, 1975, pp. 189–195. Also see Patrick E. Murphy and William A. Staples, "A Modernized Family Life Cycle," *Journal of Consumer Research*, June, 1979, pp. 12–22.

6. One study of American women's sex-role attitudes indicated a considerable shift toward more egalitarian role definitions. The change has occurred equally among higher- and lower-status women. See Karen Oppenherm Mason, John L. Czajka, and Sara Arber, "Change in U. S. Women's Sex-Role Attitudes, 1964–1974," *American Sociological Review*, August, 1976, pp. 573–596.

7. This and the following paragraph are adapted from Suzanne H. McCall, "Meet the 'Workwife'," *Journal of Marketing*, July, 1977, pp. 55–65.

8. See Gary M. Munsinger, Jean E. Weber, and Richard W. Hansen, "Joint Home Purchasing Decisions by Husbands and Wives," *Journal of Consumer Research*, March, 1975, pp. 60–66; and Harry L. Davis, "Decision Making within the Household," *Journal of Consumer Research*, March, 1976, pp. 241–260.

9. See Robert T. Green and Isabella C. M. Cunningham, "Feminine Role Perception and Family Purchasing Decisions," *Journal of Marketing Research*, August, 1975, pp. 325–332; and Alvin C. Burns and Donald H. Granbois, "Factors Moderating the Resolution of Preference Conflict in Family Automobile Purchasing," *Journal of Marketing Research*, February, 1977, pp. 77–86.

10. See George P. Moschis, Roy L. Moore, and Lowndes F. Stephens, "Purchasing Patterns of Adolescent Consumers," *Journal of Retailing*, Spring, 1977, pp. 17–27.

11. In one study, 17 percent of the employed married females delegated major food-shopping duties to another person in the household, predominantly the husband. This compares to 6 percent for nonemployed married females. See Suzanne H. McCall, "Meet the 'Workwife'," *Journal of Marketing*, July, 1977, pp. 57, 63.

12. For discussion of spending patterns of single young adults, see Fabian Linden, "Singular Spending Patterns," *Across the Board*, July, 1979, pp. 31–34.

13. See George P. Moschis, "Social Comparison and Informal Group Influence," *Journal of Marketing Research*, August, 1976, pp. 237–244.

14. See Raymond A. Bauer, "Consumer Behavior as Risk Taking," in *Dynamic Marketing for a Changing World*, ed. Robert S. Hancock (Chicago:American Marketing Association, 1960), pp. 389–398; Jeffrey A. Barach, "Advertising Effectiveness and Risk in the Consumer Decision Process," *Journal of Marketing Research*, August, 1969, pp. 314–320; and Ted Roselius, "Consumer Rankings of Risk Reduction Methods," *Journal of Marketing*, January,1971, pp. 55–61.

15. George S. Day and William Brandt, "Consumer Research and the Evaluation of Information Disclosure Requirements: The Case of Truth in Lending," *Journal of Consumer Research*, June, 1974, pp. 21–32.

16. John D. Claxton, Joseph N. Fry, and Bernard Portis, "A Taxonomy of Prepurchase Information Gathering Patterns," *Journal of Consumer Research*, December, 1974, pp. 35-42.

17. For discussion of culture as an underlying determinant of buyer behavior, see Walter A. Henry, "Cultural Values Do Correlate with Consumer Behavior," *Journal of Marketing Research*, May, 1976, pp. 121–127.

18. "Car Rentals Ease Dealer Pains," *Business Week*, May 12, 1980, pp. 126–127.

19. "How Marketers Can Cater to 'Voluntary Simplicity' Segment," *Marketing News*, March 21, 1980, p. 1.

# Chapter 7

# The Industrial Market and Buying Behavior

**OBJECTIVES**

*After reading this chapter you should be able to*

1. classify industrial buyer needs into three product types.

2. identify and discuss several important characteristics that distinguish the industrial market from the consumer market.

3. discuss the factors that influence a firm's make-or-buy decision.

4. identify and discuss the three basic types of buyclasses.

5. identify and discuss the buyphases in the procurement function.

6. identify and discuss the five types of actors who might participate in an industrial buying decision.

7. compare value analysis and vendor analysis.

8. identify the major factors industrial buyers consider in making buying decisions.

9. identify and discuss five major types of industrial markets.

10. explain how the Standard Industrial Classification (SIC) system can help industrial marketers select, locate, and evaluate market targets.

11. cite several specific marketing mix considerations for industrial marketers.

**KEY CONCEPTS**

*Look for these terms as you read the chapter:*

Standard Industrial Classification (SIC) System
Derived Demand
Make-or-Buy Decision
Buyclasses
New Task Buying
Modified Rebuy Buying
Straight Rebuy Buying
Buyphases
Multiple Buying Influence
Buying Center
Value Analysis
Vendor Analysis
Systems Selling
Multiple Sourcing
Reciprocity
Value Added by Manufacturing
Agribusiness
Institutional Market

*Skyrocketing oil prices have helped to stimulate demand for coal during recent years. This, in turn, has stimulated the demand for more efficient coal mining equipment. In the western United States, for example, strip coal mining companies are using multimillion dollar mechanical shovels and draglines that can move well over 200 tons of earth in a single scoop. Buying decisions and processes in this industrial market are different in important ways from those in the consumer market. In fact, the same is true of all industrial markets, whether a prospective customer is thinking about buying a multimillion dollar data processing system from a computer maker, the Navy is discussing the design of a new type of ship with a shipbuilder, or your school is requesting suppliers to submit bids for a new garbage truck.*

*The professionals who handle the buying for their organizations are called purchasing agents, or purchasing managers. The National Association of Purchasing Management, a professional organization, awards purchasing managers who meet its certification requirements the CPM (Certified Purchasing Manager) designation.*

*It is likely that organizational buyers will focus even more carefully on purchasing management during coming years in their efforts to enhance productivity. By working closely with their purchasing departments, for example, many business firms have been able to save money on the products they buy by eliminating unnecessary frills. By dealing ethically and honestly with suppliers during periods of adequate supplies, many purchasing managers have found that they can be accommodated during periods of short supply.*

As we saw in Chapter 3, industrial users do not buy for their personal and/or household consumption. They buy products to satisfy the needs of the organizations to which they belong. These needs can be classified into three product types:

1. products needed to make other products, such as machinery bought by General Motors to make cars
2. products needed to carry on the organization's operations, such as data processing equipment bought by Sears, Roebuck and Company to keep inventory records
3. products bought for resale, such as plumbing supplies bought by a wholesaler for resale to plumbing contractors

All business and nonprofit organizations are industrial users. This includes wholesaling establishments, retailers, manufacturers, farmers, governments, churches, hospitals, charities, and colleges. Together they make up the industrial market. Sometimes it is called the organizational market.

The industrial market is very different in many ways from the consumer market. We will look at these differences and examine industrial buyer behavior. We also will consider important decisions industrial marketers face in marketing to industrial users.

**Table 7–1.**  *Standard Industrial Classification (SIC) divisions and code numbers*

| | |
|---|---|
| Agriculture, forestry, and fisheries | (01–09) |
| Mining | (10–14) |
| Contract construction | (15–18) |
| Manufacturing | (19–39) |
| Transportation, communication, electric, gas, and sanitary services | (40–49) |
| Wholesale and retail trade | (50–59) |
| Finance, insurance, and real estate | (60–69) |
| Services | (70–89) |
| Government | (90–98) |
| Nonclassified establishments | (99) |

## THE STANDARD INDUSTRIAL CLASSIFICATION (SIC) SYSTEM

standard indus-
trial classi-
fication (SIC)
system

All business and nonprofit organizations are industrial users.  The U. S. Bureau of the Census breaks down industrial users according to the **Standard Industrial Classification (SIC) system** into ten major divisions as shown in Table 7–1.

For example, code 10 means metal mining; code 11 means anthracite mining; and code 12 means bituminous coal and lignite mining.  Code 20 means food and kindred products; code 21 means tobacco manufacturers; and code 28 means chemical and allied products.  The two-digit code identifies the major industry.

More detailed data are available for subindustries within each of the two-digit industry classifications.  For example, 23 is apparel and other finished products made from fabrics and similar materials; 232 is men's, youths', and boys' furnishings, work clothing, and allied garments; and 2321 is shirts, collars, and nightwear.  In some cases the SIC system is broken down into seven-digit product codes.  The government uses the SIC system in reporting detailed data, such as the number of establishments and their sales volume by county and SMSA.  This is useful to marketers in selecting market targets.[1]

Before we discuss specific groups of industrial buyers we will focus on some of the major characteristics of the industrial market.

## CHARACTERISTICS OF THE INDUSTRIAL MARKET

As we will see in Chapter 10, industrial products range from simple items like paperclips and wiping cloths to costly buildings and heavy equipment.  The demand for these products varies, as do selling and buying practices.  For example, there is a world of difference between General

Electric's marketing of light bulbs to an industrial buyer on a routine basis and its marketing of a new aircraft engine to an airplane manufacturer. Nevertheless, the following are some of the more important characteristics that, in general, distinguish the industrial market from the consumer market: (1) derived demand, (2) greater total sales volume, (3) smaller numbers of buyers, (4) larger volume of purchases, (5) geographical concentration of customers, (6) greater demand inelasticity, (7) professional buying, (8) direct buying, (9) more specification buying, (10) complex negotiation, (11) infrequent negotiation, (12) reciprocal buying, (13) greater use of leasing, and (14) more make-or-buy decisions.

## Derived Demand

Shoemakers buy shoemaking machinery because ultimate consumers demand shoes. Supermarkets buy modern cash registers because ultimate consumers demand speedy service at checkout aisles. Thus the demand for industrial products is a **derived demand.** It arises from the demand for consumer products. Derived demand is a factor in the business cycle. A sharp drop in ultimate consumer demand for new American-made cars, as occurred in 1980, leads automakers to cut back on employment and output. They will buy less steel, and steel producers will buy less coal to fire their blast furnaces. Coal mining firms will lay off workers and this leads to reduced buying of all types of consumer products. Manufacturers of auto components, such as batteries and tires, will also cut production.

*derived demand*

These examples illustrate the interdependence of American industry. The cutback in coal production, for example, was caused by an event far removed from the coal industry—a decline in the demand for cars. Fluctuations in consumer demand send out shock waves in the industrial market that tend to magnify the further back we get from the ultimate consumer. Consumer confidence in the economy can produce extreme optimism among businesspeople, while the lack of it can lead to extreme pessimism. Thus we often refer to the industrial market as a "boom-or-bust" industry. Figure 7–1 shows that a mild increase in consumer demand is magnified into a steep increase in demand in the industrial market. Notice also that a mild decrease in consumer demand leads to a much steeper decrease in demand in the industrial market.

Sometimes industrial marketers try to increase demand in the consumer market in order to increase sales of their industrial products. For example, General Tire and Rubber Company sold fewer tires to American automakers because of the sharp drop in demand in 1980. To help stimulate sales of American-made cars, the firm announced that beginning on June 15, 1980 it would offer a $100 rebate to any of its employees who bought a new American-made car within thirty days.[2]

## Greater Total Sales Volume

Total dollar sales in the industrial market are greater than total dollar sales in the consumer market even though there are far fewer industrial

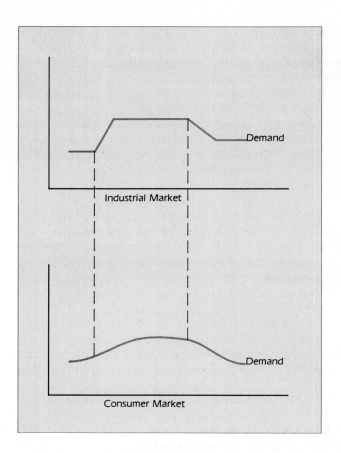

Demand

Industrial Market

Demand

Consumer Market

*Figure 7–1.*
*Derived demand*

users than ultimate consumers. A car bought by an ultimate consumer counts as one sale in the consumer market. But many sales transactions occurred in the process of manufacturing that car. Iron ore was mined and sold to a steel producer who, in turn, sold steel to the automaker. Hundreds of other industrial transactions also occurred before the car rolled off the assembly line.

### Smaller Numbers of Buyers

A typical industrial marketer sells to a much smaller number of buyers than a typical consumer products marketer. Firms that sell to manufacturers usually have less trouble identifying potential customers than do firms that sell to ultimate consumers. General Electric sells its jet engines to a handful of airplane manufacturers, but when it sells to ultimate consumers its potential market includes millions of people.

### Larger Volume Purchases

Industrial marketers also sell to customers who buy in larger quantities than ultimate consumers do. While a consumer may buy home heating oil by the gallon, a large electric utility may buy thousands of barrels under a long-term contract with its supplier. Also, in many industries there is a high degree of concentration. A few firms may account for the bulk of the industry's sales and purchases.

## Geographical Concentration of Customers

Industrial buyers are geographically concentrated. Manufacturers are concentrated in the SMSAs of big industrial East–North Central states, Middle Atlantic states, and California. Over half are located in seven states: New York, California, Pennsylvania, Illinois, Ohio, New Jersey, and Michigan. There is also considerable geographical concentration in some industries. The steel industry, for example, is concentrated in Chicago, Pittsburgh, and Birmingham, Alabama. These areas are favorably situated for labor supply, energy, raw materials, and transportation, which reduces production and marketing costs. The aircraft and microelectronics industries are concentrated on the West Coast, and many firms that supply the automakers are concentrated near Detroit.

## Greater Demand Inelasticity

As we will see in greater detail in the discussion in Chapter 20 of price elasticity of demand, changes in a product's price may cause sales to go up or down. But there is less opportunity for industrial marketers as a whole to stimulate sales through price cuts than there is for consumer products marketers.

Book publishers buy glue to bind pages in a book. If the price of glue goes down, book publishers are unlikely to increase greatly their purchases of glue. If they expect the price cut to be temporary, however, they may stockpile some, but this merely amounts to a change in the timing of orders, not an overall increase in the long-run volume of purchases. The cost of glue accounts for a very small part of the total cost of producing a book, and a reduction of a few cents in the selling price of books is unlikely to stimulate book sales. Furthermore, the price of glue could go up considerably before it would have much effect on sales of glue.

The price of an industrial product ordinarily does not have much effect on its sales volume, largely because of the derived nature of its demand. But when substitutes are available for a particular product, increases in price often will lead to reduced sales as buyers switch to the substitutes. Also, price can play a very crucial role in selecting suppliers. Thus a glue supplier whose price is a few cents less than that of rival producers who offer comparable quality and service is likely to make more sales.

## Professional Buying

As we will see later in this chapter, industrial buyers generally take a more formalized approach to buying than ultimate consumers do. A salesperson who is selling portable typewriters at Sears deals with only one prospect. But an IBM typewriter salesperson may have to give product demonstrations to a firm's secretaries, office manager, and purchasing agent. Industrial buyers are professional buyers and selling to them requires professional salespersons. We will discuss professional selling in Chapter 18.

### Direct Buying

Most ultimate consumers buy products from retailers instead of buying them directly from producers. But many industrial products are sold by manufacturers directly to industrial buyers. A consumer may buy car tires in a retail store but the automakers will buy them directly from tire manufacturers. The more complex and costly the industrial product is and the more after-sale service it requires, the more likely the buyer will buy it directly from the manufacturer.

### More Specification Buying

Industrial marketers also engage in more production to order than consumer products marketers. We suggested this in the discussion in Chapter 1 of the made-to-order era. A firm that manufactures products for Sears, for example, will follow Sears' specifications in producing the product. This type of purchasing often is called *contract buying.*

### Complex Negotiation

Considerable buyer-seller negotiation exists in the purchase and sale of more expensive industrial products. In addition to product specifications, delivery dates, payment terms, and price may be subject to negotiation. In many cases buyer representatives will meet with seller representatives to negotiate sales contracts. This may continue over several months.

### Infrequent Negotiation

An industrial buyer of an expensive piece of machinery may expect it to last several years. Once the sale is made, it may be years before the buyer and the seller negotiate another sale. If IBM installs a computer system in an oil refinery, it may be a long time before IBM negotiates another sale with that firm. But after-the-sale service is extremely important. Industrial marketers must maintain such a customer's goodwill to increase the probability of further negotiation with that customer.

### Reciprocal Buying

As we will see later in this chapter, there is a good deal of reciprocal buying in industrial marketing. A marketer may buy from its supplier mainly because that supplier also buys from the marketer.

### Greater Use of Leasing

Although ultimate consumers also lease products, the practice is more widespread among industrial buyers. Computers, trucks, heavy equipment, and cars often are leased rather than purchased outright. A firm that leases a product (lessee) from a supplier (lessor) rents rather than purchases it. Leasing is discussed in greater detail in Chapter 22.[3]

### More Make-or-Buy Decisions

Many industrial buyers make the component parts needed in manufacturing their main product rather than buy them from outside suppliers. Thus General Motors makes its own Delco batteries rather than buy them from another company.

### THE MAKE-OR-BUY DECISION

Industrial buyers, especially manufacturers, often face a **make-or-buy decision.** Instead of buying component parts or equipment from vendors, for example, a manufacturer might decide to make the part for itself if the results of a cost-benefit analysis indicate that this would be the more profitable alternative. The manufacturer fills some of its own product requirements.

make-or-buy
decision

**Table 7–2.** *The make-or-buy decision*

---

*A firm might favor making rather than buying some of its requirements when:*

1. no suitable vendors exist
2. the firm requires such small quantities that no vendor is interested in supplying the firm
3. the product is so specialized that vendors cannot, or do not want to, meet the potential buyer's specifications
4. the product was designed by the using firm and it wants to protect its design and manufacturing process from other firms
5. the user can produce the product more cheaply than vendors
6. the user wants to demonstrate its ability to produce part of its requirements to gain bargaining leverage in negotiating with vendors who fill its other requirements
7. producing some of its requirements may utilize excess manufacturing capacity
8. the amount used is sufficient for the firm to realize economies of scale in producing the product (backward vertical integration)

---

*Some of the potential drawbacks to making rather than buying are:*

1. new equipment and skills may be needed and the firm may be entering a new line of business
2. demand for the end product (the product the part is used to make) is questionable or marginal
3. existing producers may control patents and/or sources of materials
4. production scheduling may be upset
5. the firm has to keep up with the latest technology in producing the part or the end product will deteriorate relative to its competitors
6. there is reduced chance for reciprocal buying arrangements
7. alienated vendors can be a source of adverse word-of-mouth advertising and the firm loses goodwill
8. the firm locks itself into one supplier—itself

---

For example, canmakers have been hurt in recent years by a trend among some of their largest beverage-making customers, especially the major beer companies, to make their own cans to cut costs. Canmakers also have been hurt in recent years by some basic aluminum producers like Reynolds Metal Company who have started making cans for sale.

The make-or-buy decision is complex, especially when a "make" decision requires expanding the firm's production system or buying another firm. Electrolux decided to try buying out a manufacturer of aluminum, copper, and other materials it uses in making its products. Table 7–2 lists several factors that might favor making rather than buying and also some of the potential drawbacks.

Modern firms recognize the important role the purchasing department can play in make-or-buy planning.[4] The following discussion of the procurement function assumes the firm "buys" rather than "makes."

## THE PROCUREMENT FUNCTION

Industrial buyers are professionals who approach the buying process in a logical manner.[5] The major types of industrial buying situations will be discussed first.

### Types of Industrial Buying

Industrial buying can be divided into three basic types: (1) new task buying, (2) modified rebuy buying, and (3) straight rebuy buying. These also are called **buyclasses.**[6]

**New Task Buying.** In **new task buying** the firm faces a new need or problem and the buyer gathers information from vendors who can offer products to satisfy the need or solve the problem. This type of buying decision is nonprogramed and involves extensive problem solving. For example, the federal government's requirements for greater fuel efficiency led automakers to search for vendors and products that could help them meet the more-miles-per-gallon requirements. This created opportunity for firms like PPG Industries, Inc. (formerly Pittsburgh Plate Glass Company) to sell automakers on the benefits of fiberglass-reinforced plastic in reducing car weight by replacing component parts made of steel.

New task buying is common when a firm begins production of a new product. In cases like this, the reputations of potential suppliers are the major factor in choosing suppliers. Those with problem-solving sales personnel have the upper hand, as we will see in Chapter 18. New task buying involves more time than the other two buying processes and more people usually participate in the buying decision.

**Modified Rebuy Buying.** In **modified rebuy buying** the buyer seeks to modify product specifications, delivery schedules, prices, or suppliers. Because of soaring energy costs in recent years, for example, firms in the construction industry have been shifting from ordinary flat glass to in-

*(margin notes)*
buyclasses
new task buying

modified rebuy
buying

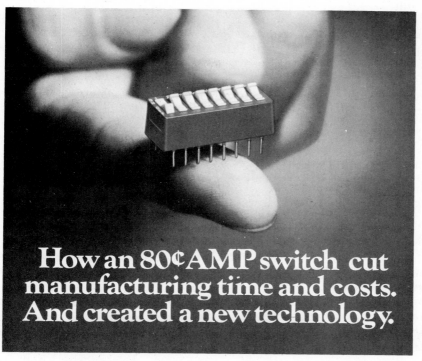

## How an 80¢ AMP switch cut manufacturing time and costs. And created a new technology.

Many companies don't call AMP until they need electrical connectors or switches. But why wait till then? If you involve us early enough, we can help you save money. A lot of money.

**Here's an example:**
Programming printed circuit boards used to involve installing an intricate network of jumper wires and plugs.

Until a customer asked us to find a better way.

We invented the DIP switch, which made programming p-c boards as easy as pushing number-coded actuators.

As a result, our customer was able to produce standardized boards that they could easily and quickly customize according to orders.

They saved hundreds of thousands of dollars in manufacturing and inventory costs. And a whole new technology was born.

**Can we produce the same kind of savings for you?**
If your company manufactures electrical/electronic products, the answer is probably yes. But it's important for you to call us in early.

That's when our experience in developing connectors, switches and application equipment for hundreds of industries worldwide can help you the most.

**Early Involvement.**
At AMP, we call this approach to solving our customers' problems "Early Involvement." It's our better way. And it's what makes an 80¢ AMP switch worth so much more than 80¢.

Ask for a copy of our brochure, "AMP Has a Better Way."

Call Cupertino, CA (408) 255-3830, Ext. 35, or Compton, CA (213) 537-4490, Ext. 315.

Or write to AMP Incorporated, Dept. W, Harrisburg, PA 17105.

## AMP
INCORPORATED

**AMP has a better way.**

Barcelona • Brussels • Buenos Aires • Frankfurt • Harrisburg • Helsinki • s-Hertogenbosch • London • Luzern • Mexico City • Montreal
Paris • San Juan • Sao Paulo • Stockholm • Sydney • Turin • Toronto • Tokyo

8027-W

*An ad that focuses on new task buying*

Source: AMP Incorporated.

sulating glass. Like new task buying, modified rebuy buying decisions are nonprogramed and several people may participate in decision making. Rival suppliers who can offer products that better match the buyer's needs can take business from the present supplier. These buying situations

**Table 7–3.** *Characteristics of industrial buyclasses*

| Buyclasses | Problem Solving | Decison Type | Extent of Multiple Buying Influence | Time Required for Decision |
|---|---|---|---|---|
| New task buying | Extensive | Nonprogramed | Maximally present | Maximum |
| Modified rebuy buying | Limited | Nonprogramed | Somewhat present | Somewhat lengthy |
| Straight rebuy buying | Routine response (often automated) | Programed | None | Least |

cause the present vendor to be concerned about losing the customer. Potential vendors consider it an opportunity to win new business.

**straight rebuy buying**

**Straight Rebuy Buying.** **Straight rebuy buying** means buying a product that has been purchased before with satisfactory results from an established vendor. Rival suppliers have a tough time taking business from such an entrenched supplier. This is a programed buying decision. Such order-reorder buying requires less time than new task or modified rebuy buying and, as we will see in Chapter 16, often is automated because of its repetitive and routine nature.[7] (See Table 7–3.)

### The Industrial Buying Process

The industrial buying process we will describe applies basically to new task buying. It is similar to our discussion of nonprogramed decisions in Chapter 4. Modified and straight rebuys generally do not involve all these steps because they require less extensive problem solving. The

**buyphases**

steps, which are called **buyphases,** are (1) recognizing a need, (2) specifying the need, (3) searching for potential suppliers, (4) inviting, acquiring, and analyzing vendor proposals, (5) selecting the vendor and placing the order, and (6) following up.[8] The buyer's commitment to a particular vendor increases in successive buyphase stages and there is less opportunity for other vendors to make proposals.

**Recognizing a Need.** Need recognition is the starting place in the procurement process. It can result from internal or external developments. Internal developments include: (1) the user of a piece of machinery demonstrates its inefficiency to a supervisor, (2) the purchasing agent believes the firm is receiving poor after-sale service from its present supplier and wants to seek a new one, (3) a major piece of equipment becomes obsolete and must be replaced, (4) inventory reaches the reorder point, and (5) the firm wants to market a new product and needs new equipment to produce it.

External developments include: (1) a vendor's salesperson calls on the purchasing agent to demonstrate a product that will save the firm money,

# "A RYDER TRUCK LEASE SAVES US $250,000 A YEAR. AND WE'RE MORE LIQUID THAN EVER."

On December 13 Ryder received an unsolicited letter from Kurfees Coatings, Inc. out of Louisville, Ky.:

"We are an architectural paint manufacturer, marketing to retailers in sixteen states. In early 1977, we leased Ryder tractor/trailer units to replace regional warehouses using common carrier to serve our customers. Through a series of dedicated route 'peddle runs' weekly, our service to customers has significantly improved. Orders are received more timely; products are fresher due to increased turns of fewer inventories; less damage and no more hassle over claims.

"As for cost reduction, we experienced an immediate reduction of over $150,000 in inventory. In the first fully operational year, distribution expense dropped in excess of $100,000."

When our customers can write ads for us, we must be doing something right. Like maintaining trucks better than anybody in the business. With a coast-to-coast network of company-owned truck service centers to handle repairs, 24 hours a day, 7 days a week. With a large inventory of substitute trucks. With fuel provided by Ryder at a low rate with no retail markup. And with everything included in the lease rate so there are no expensive surprises. *Ryder rents and leases trucks in the U.S. and Canada. In the U.S. call toll-free 800-327-1575. Or mail coupon now.*

## TRY A RYDER TRUCK LEASE FOR 90 DAYS WITH NO RISK.

Ryder has a way you can arrange for a 90-day trial truck lease. If you take advantage of this offer, and you're not completely happy with Ryder service, you just pay for the time you used the truck and you walk away clean.

Ryder, I'm not signing up for anything yet, but I certainly want to know more.

_____
Name/Title

_____
Company Name

_____
Address

_____
City/State/Zip

_____
Phone

**RYDER**  Mail to: Ryder Truck Rental, Inc.
Harmon Hoffmann, President
P.O. Box 520816
Miami, Florida 33152                BW26

*This ad may help prospective customers recognize the attractiveness of leasing Ryder trucks*
Source: Ryder Truck Rental.

(2) a vendor sends a brochure to the production manager explaining how its equipment can reduce maintenance costs, (3) attendance at a trade association meeting convinces top managers that the firm's equipment is obsolete, and (4) an article in a trade journal discusses a new data processing system that will cut costs and make information available to decision makers faster.

Industrial marketers must capitalize on every opportunity to convert these developments to sales.[9]   They do this by developing effective ad campaigns and professional salesforces to reach these people and help them recognize their needs.   The Ryder ad explains how leasing helped one of its customers.   That information may be very helpful to another prospect who faces a similar need.   The coupon helps to stimulate the reader's response.

**Specifying the Need.**   In specifying its need the buyer identifies and describes in detail the quantity and quality of the needed product.   It develops the specifications of what it needs to buy.   We will discuss value analysis, a tool that helps buyers do this, later in the chapter.

**Searching for Potential Suppliers.**   In searching for potential suppliers the buyer will identify vendors that are likely to be able to supply the needed product.[10]   Industrial marketers place great value on a good reputation to help create word-of-mouth advertising so that their names will get around.   They also make sure they are listed in appropriate trade directories.   If they are unknown they cannot be included on a list of qualified potential suppliers.

**Inviting, Acquiring, and Analyzing Vendor Proposals.**   Buyers invite qualified vendors to submit proposals for evaluation.   Perhaps the vendor will respond by mailing a catalogue or sending a sales representative to make a call.   In seeking proposals for complex equipment the buyer may request vendors to submit detailed specifications and make a personal presentation to the buyer.   Industrial marketers must be skilled in preparing written and oral presentations and should receive assistance from technical people, such as engineers, in preparing them.   They need to find some edge over their competitors to create a differential advantage for their product.

**Selecting the Vendor and Placing the Order.**   Choosing the vendor that best satisfies the firm's needs and placing the order require the buyer to prepare a list of desired vendor attributes.   Examples are ability to provide (1) technical support services, (2) dependable delivery, (3) reasonable credit terms, and (4) adequate product warranty.   Each vendor is rated in terms of these criteria and one (or several) selected.   But prior to actually placing the order, there may be some further negotiation on the product's specifications, price, delivery date, and so on.   In the end, however, the final order is written.

**Following Up.**   The follow-up involves an evaluation of product and vendor performance.   Again, value and vendor analysis can help in this stage.   They are discussed later in the chapter.

## Participants in Industrial Buying Decisions

As we saw in Chapter 6, all household members might participate in some consumer purchase decisions. These are called joint decisions. For example, spouses may jointly decide on the purchase of a new car. In industrial marketing we call this **multiple buying influence.**[11] It is very common in new task buying.

A **buying center** is made up of people who determine what will be purchased to fill the organization's needs and from whom the products will be purchased. Industrial buyers of more expensive products want facts from potential vendors regarding their products' operating costs, maintenance costs, expected useful life, and vendor service capability.

Five different types of actors can play a role in industrial buying decisions: (1) users, (2) influencers, (3) gatekeepers, (4) deciders, and (5) buyers.[12] Only users and buyers might be involved in purchases of routinely bought supplies like paperclips, light bulbs, and other relatively inexpensive products. At the other extreme, all five actors may participate in buying long-lived, costly products like heavy equipment and buildings. In either case, a person may play more than one role.

Industrial salespersons must recognize the different roles these participants play and be able to identify the persons playing them.[13] This helps them to tailor buying appeals to the different actors.[14] An industrial salesperson is selling to an organization *and* the individuals who participate in buying decisions. The intrapersonal and interpersonal influences we discussed in Chapters 5 and 6 are relevant in selling to people in buying centers. In addition, the salesperson must understand the nature of the organization's formal buying process.[15] We will discuss this after elaborating on the five actors in industrial buying decisions.

**Users.** Users are the people who will use the product. Secretaries use typewriters, factory workers use machine tools, and warehouse personnel use forklift trucks. They often exert considerable buying influ-

multiple buying
influence

buying center

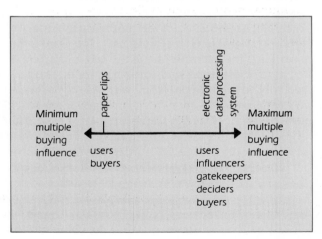

*Figure 7–2.*
*A continuum of*
*multiple buying*
*influence*

ence and salespersons must recognize this, perhaps by talking with them to learn about their needs.

**Influencers.** Influencers are people inside and outside the organization who help to shape buying decision criteria. They have some voice in setting product specifications or evaluating vendor offerings. Finance personnel may set maximum price limits on buying alternatives, engineering personnel may set tolerance limits for precision equipment, and an outside consulting engineer may be called upon to evaluate the merits of several vendors' product designs. These people cannot be ignored by salespersons.

**Gatekeepers.** Gatekeepers control the flow of information into, within, and out of the buying organization. Secretaries can turn away vendor salespersons, and a production manager can establish policies preventing vendor salespersons from talking to assembly line workers. A salesperson may never get to the other participants if he or she cannot deal effectively with gatekeepers. This often requires considerable human relations skills.

**Deciders.** Deciders are the persons authorized to make the final choice of what will be bought. When very costly products are involved, the deciders may be members of top management. For less expensive, routinely purchased products the decider is also the buyer.

**Buyers.** Buyers are the persons authorized to handle the details of contracting with suppliers. A buyer often is called a purchasing agent. But if the contract is a long-term one involving considerable purchase commitments, members of top management actually may participate as buyers. (See Figure 7–2.)

## Purchasing Departments

Large industrial buyers increasingly are practicing centralized buying instead of allowing individual departments or divisions to make their own purchases. Their purchasing departments handle the procurement function. The importance of purchasing has increased greatly in recent years, in large part because of the energy problem, inflation, and shortages of some key productive resources. Du Pont's Energy and Materials Department, for example, buys all raw materials, supplies, and equipment for all the domestic and foreign branches and subsidiaries of the firm in addition to planning for long-term energy procurement. Purchasing jobs in many firms now are at the vice-president level. Many firms have also developed incentive systems to reward exceptional performance in handling the procurement function, very much like the bonuses salespersons receive for exceeding their sales quotas.[16]

Depending on the product, the purchasing department may provide different types of advice and perform different types of services in the buying process. It usually makes the price and quality decision on its own when buying routinely purchased items. But it works much more closely with executives in other departments in buying expensive, long-lived products.[17]   Value and vendor analysis are important tasks of the purchasing department.

**Value analysis** involves reviewing existing product specifications as set by user departments to identify and eliminate inessential cost factors. A committee of engineers, cost accountants, and production and finance personnel may be set up to work with the purchasing department in reviewing the specifications set by the user department.   If the production department has been using costly brass nuts and bolts to make wooden swings that retail for $25, the product may be overdesigned. Value analysis might indicate that less costly steel nuts and bolts could be substituted without sacrificing product quality and customer satisfaction.

**Vendor analysis** is an approach to evaluating the performance capability of potential suppliers.   Vendors are rated on their past performance in the areas of technical, financial, and managerial abilities.   It is a method by which facts can be substituted for feelings in selecting suppliers.   Value and vendor analysis also are integral parts of the follow-up step in the industrial buying process.

value analysis

vendor analysis

## Purchasing Decision Criteria

Industrial buyers consider many factors in their purchasing decisions. Most are economic, or rational, factors but emotional factors also are present.[18]   An industrial marketer must analyze the prospective buyer's situation and develop a total product for solving the problem or capitalizing on an opportunity.

In recent years, a great deal of attention has been given to **systems selling.**   This involves development of a total product offering that will provide a total solution to a customer's problem.   The concept began in the military as systems buying.   Military procurement offices used to buy different components for a total weapons system from different vendors.   The military would put the system together itself.   During the 1960s, the emphasis shifted to dealing with a prime contractor who would deliver the total system.   The prime contractor would handle all the details of subcontracting with suppliers of system components.

systems selling

An industrial buyer who wants to buy a data processing system and a word processing system could negotiate with data processing vendors and word processing vendors.   But this might involve problems related to the compatability of the systems, and the buyer might have to anticipate and solve these problems for itself.   Exxon Information Systems has been working on combining data processing and word processing in one office system.   Thus the buyer could deal with only one vendor who could offer a total system.

Among the more important purchasing decision criteria are (1) dependability, (2) product quality, (3) cost, (4) vendor production capacity, (5) after-sale service, (6) vendor reliability and integrity, (7) reciprocity, and (8) emotional factors.

**Dependability.** A major concern in selecting suppliers is their dependability, such as meeting promised delivery dates. Late deliveries can cause production scheduling problems and downtime in production operations. Early deliveries can cause storage and inventory problems. Marketers who provide consistent and dependable delivery help to create a differential advantage for their firms.[19]

**Product Quality.** Product quality is another crucial factor. Faulty nuts and bolts can cause problems in the industrial buyer's finished product. Many automakers have spent millions of dollars on product recalls to replace minor parts that caused or could cause problems for car owners. Some dramatic failures in our nation's space missions have been due to failures of minor and inexpensive parts in multimillion-dollar spacecraft. Industrial marketers tend to insist on strict quality control procedures to minimize this type of problem.

**Cost.** Industrial buyers set quality standards for the parts they buy and try to buy parts that meet them at the least cost. Value analysis helps to avoid setting quality standards that are too high or too low. Because the cost of component parts must be included in the finished product's price, industrial buyers want to avoid buying over-designed parts. They also want to avoid under-designed parts that will lower the finished product's quality.

**Vendor Production Capacity.** A vendor's production capacity is another important consideration. Buyers want assurances that suppliers can meet their present and forecasted volume requirements.[20] Otherwise, orders will back up. This is one reason many buyers buy from
multiple sourcing more than one supplier. This is called **multiple sourcing**—establishing a buying relationship with two or more vendors. Figure 7–3 shows how multiple sources could fulfill a buyer's fuel oil needs. While buying from more than one source ensures that a strike, major accident, or natural catastrophe at A's plant(s) will not completely shut off supplies, buying a relatively large share of total requirements from A may help the buyer negotiate favorable purchase terms with that supplier. Multiple sourcing is especially important in industries subject to supply shortages. For

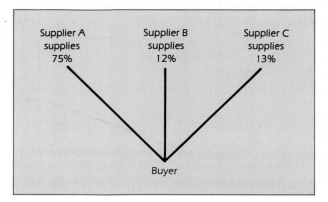

**Figure 7–3.**
*Multiple sourcing of fuel oil*

example, Loctite holds an 85 percent market share in anaerobic adhesives. Some other firms have entered the industry mainly by capitalizing on the hesitancy of some of Loctite's customers to depend on a single source.[21]

**After-Sale Service.** Industrial marketers' ability to provide service on the products they lease or sell to their customers is a very important consideration. For example, breakdowns in equipment can cause expensive downtime in production operations if the equipment is not repaired promptly. Notice in the Ryder ad earlier in the chapter the reference to Ryder's coast-to-coast network of company-owned truck service centers that provides service twenty-four hours a day, seven days a week.

**Vendor Reliability and Integrity.** Industrial buyers also want assurance that vendors can meet the buyer's product specifications and deliver on time. This concern extends to the vendor's production, service, engineering, and sales personnel. The vendor's integrity in living up to service and warranty commitments also is important.[22]

**Reciprocity.** **Reciprocity** is common in industrial marketing.[23] This means buying from a supplier if that supplier also buys from its customer. Reciprocal buying arrangements can take many forms and might involve several firms. Company A might try to influence B to buy from C, which is A's customer. Reciprocity's importance as a buying strategy depends a lot on environmental variables. For example, it can help offset declining sales during a recession without costly advertising.

reciprocity

Reciprocity among small firms often is based on friendship. But it goes way beyond friendship in some larger firms. Some have trade relations departments that use computers to analyze their purchases and sales by supplier and customer. This helps identify opportunities for reciprocal dealings with suppliers and customers.

Reciprocity, of course, can be used to restrain trade. Thus the Federal Trade Commission and the antitrust division of the Justice Department sometimes take a close look at reciprocal dealings.[24] Another risk is that reciprocal buying and selling deals negotiated by upper-level managers will demoralize purchasing and sales personnel.

**Emotional Factors.** Industrial buyers are professionals but they are also influenced by emotional factors in their buying behavior. Marketers of office furniture appeal to the buyer's desire for attractive as well as functional furniture. Ads for business jets explain how the planes can save executives time but also feature attractive interiors to reinforce their status needs. Industrial trade shows often feature attractive female models to draw attention to products.

Emotional factors are most likely to enter into buying decisions when rival vendors offer essentially the same total product. Friendship with the vendor or vendor salespersons takes on more importance when rival offerings are practically identical.

Now that we have a basic understanding of the procurement process we can turn to a discussion of several specific types of industrial buyers.

## INDUSTRIAL MARKETS

As pointed out earlier in this chapter, a wide variety of types of buyers are industrial buyers—producers, resellers, and governments. Refer back to Table 7–1. All except wholesale and retail trade, government, and nonclassified establishments are included in the producer market. The following discussion gives a brief overview of several industrial markets: (1) manufacturers, (2) retailers and wholesaling establishments, (3) farmers, (4) government, and (5) institutions.

### Manufacturers

value added by
manufacturing

There are more than 300,000 manufacturing plants in the United States. Many are small enough to be owned by one or two people and operated by a handful of employees. But the relatively few large plants account for a big proportion of the **value added by manufacturing.**[25] When processing or manufacturing operations cause a change in a product's form utility, value has been added by manufacturing. Roughly 5 percent of all manufacturers have 250 or more employees but they account for about 65 percent of total value added by manufacturing. Thus there is a lot of concentration in manufacturing in terms of value added by manufacturing.

### Retailers and Wholesaling Establishments

Retailers and wholesaling establishments buy products from their suppliers and resell them to their customers. They are resellers of these products. But they also buy products necessary to conduct their business operations. These include light bulbs, floor cleaners, data processing equipment, and buildings. Buying procedures for these products generally are similar to those discussed earlier. We will discuss retailer and wholesaling establishment purchasing of products for resale in Chapters 14 and 15. Except for products that manufacturers sell directly to their final buyers, all products are sold through these resellers.

**Retailers.** Retail trade includes firms engaged primarily in selling merchandise to customers for personal and/or household use. Service establishments, on the other hand, are engaged primarily in rendering a wide variety of services to customers. The main difference between retailers of merchandise and retailers of services is that service retailers cannot be separated from their "products." Hair stylists, for example, cannot be separated from the hair styles they produce. Service retailing, therefore, tends to be very localized.

There are over one million firms in the following kinds of service business: hotels, motels, camps, personal service, auto repair, garages, miscellaneous repair services, motion pictures, and amusement and recreation (excluding motion pictures). The number of service establishments is growing rapidly. This is an area of growing opportunity for marketers.

Only about 3 percent of the retailers in the United States have sales of $1 million or more, but they account for about 45 percent of total retail sales. Thus there are many small retailers. A little over 70 percent of retail sales are concentrated in SMSAs. Within the SMSAs, about 60 percent of retail sales are made in the suburbs.

**Wholesaling Establishments.** About 10 percent of the roughly 310,000 wholesaling establishments have annual sales of $2 million or more, but they account for close to 70 percent of total wholesale sales. A lot of these sales are made by wholesaling establishments owned and operated by the manufacturer. Wholesaling, therefore, also is a concentrated business. Wholesaling activity is greatest in the industrialized northeastern states. The greatest volume of wholesale sales and the greatest number of wholesaling establishments are in our SMSAs. The New York City SMSA, for example, accounts for about 18 percent of all wholesale sales.

### Farmers

The number of farms in America continues to decline but the ones that remain (roughly three million) tend to be much larger than the typical farm of the past. Large farmers are in **agribusiness**—large-scale farming enterprises that are managed as a business to make a profit. Roughly 90 percent of total farm output is produced by half of the farms.

agribusiness

Many farmers specialize in producing only one or two products. Poultry farmers may raise only poultry but some specialize even further—broilers, turkeys, or eggs. They are production specialists and firms that market to them must offer specialized products. Poultry feed marketers, for example, market various types of poultry feed for sale to different types of poultry farmers.

Many farmers also engage in contract farming. Some poultry growers receive baby chicks and feed from big poultry packers. The packer tells the grower how to raise the chickens. This helps ensure consistency of quality for the packer while giving the grower a guaranteed buyer. It also means that chicken feed marketers may be selling to packers as well as to growers.

### The Government Market

The biggest customer in the United States is government—1 federal government, 50 state governments, over 3,000 county governments, and over 18,000 city governments. They buy thousands of products, from nuclear submarines to floor cleaners, sold by thousands of vendors. Roughly 20 percent of our gross national product (GNP) is bought by government.

Government purchases are affected by our social, political, and economic goals. Some, for example, are reserved for minority-owned small businesses. Another goal is evident in the provisions of the Buy American Act. This act specifies that foreign suppliers must meet one of two conditions to compete with American suppliers for government contracts: (1) the foreign product must use 50 percent American-made parts and (2) the foreign product must be priced more than 6 percent below the closest comparable American-made product. Still another example of how the political environment affects the industrial market is what happened when relations between the United States and the Soviet Union began to cool in 1980. This led to stepped-up defense spending and potential sales for firms in the defense industry, such as Rockwell International, Raytheon, General Dynamics, Litton, Lockheed, Boeing, McDonnell Douglas, and Martin Marietta Corporation.

The federal government engages in two major types of buying: civilian and military. Each government agency does some of its own purchasing but the General Services Administration (GSA) does a lot of centralized buying of branded products and highly standardized products for the civilian sector. Military buying is done by the Department of Defense.[26] The Defense Supply Agency buys products that the Army, Navy, and Air Force use in common. Each service buys for itself products for which it is the only user. Many state and local governments have an agency similar to the GSA, but independent agencies like school districts and highway departments also are buyers.

There is a lot of red tape in selling to government because taxpayers want assurance that government gets what it pays for and that there is no favoritism in selecting suppliers. The federal government encourages potential suppliers to get involved in government marketing. The Small Business Administration (SBA), for example, prints the booklet *U.S. Government Purchasing, Specifications, and Sales Directory* that lists thousands of products the government buys and cross-references them to the agencies that are the heaviest users. The SBA is especially active in helping small firms to get military and civilian government contracts. The SBA can act as a prime contractor for certain types of products and can subcontract the work to small firms, many of which are owned by members of minority groups. Roughly one-third of all federal government buying is from small firms.

Government units buy on either a bid basis or a negotiated basis. The objective of both types of buying procedures is competitive procurement.

**Bids.** Suppliers who want to sell to a government agency must request placement on its list of qualified bidders. The agency draws up a complete description of what it wants to buy (the specifications, or "specs") and mails invitations to bid to firms on that list. If any bid is accepted it usually must be the one that meets the "specs" at the lowest price. Allowance, however, is made in some cases for a bidder's past adherence to the terms of bidding contracts, such as timely delivery, superior product performance, and fast, efficient after-sale service. In purchases of equipment the agency may request bids that also include maintenance on the equipment over its useful life.

Bidders must pay close attention to the buying agency's specifications. This is not a major problem in the case of fairly standardized products. But great care is required in deciding if the firm has the resources and capability to meet the "specs" for nonstandardized products. Government agencies, of course, are prohibited from rigging them so that only one preferred supplier is qualified to bid.

**Negotiated Contracts.** A government agency that wants to buy a product it cannot describe in precise detail will negotiate a contract directly with a prospective supplier. This is the usual procedure in buying complex military hardware like the Army's XM1 tank. Development work on the new tank began in 1973 but it was February 1980 before it was delivered to the Army. The agency negotiates with firms that have the resources and capability to provide the product. The firm that can provide it at the best price will be awarded the contract.

Negotiated contracts can take many forms. Price can be based on cost plus an agreed upon percentage for profit, or a fixed price can be set. Critics of cost-plus pricing argue that suppliers have no incentive to hold costs down. A fixed-price-and-incentive contract enables the firm to earn more profit by decreasing costs. There also may be provisions for renegotiating contracts if it appears that the supplier will make more than a reasonable profit.

**Customer-Oriented Government Marketers.** Government marketers often have tended to be production oriented, especially when the government buys on a bid basis. A firm simply requests listing on a bidder's list and the government buying unit tells the firm what it wants, down to the most minute specification. Little opportunity exists for competing on any basis other than price. There is more opportunity to stress product design and personal selling in negotiated contracts. A growing number of government marketers are setting up marketing departments. Some also are taking the initiative in developing offerings that match specific agency needs rather than waiting for the agency to send out invitations to bid.

## The Institutional Market

Churches, museums, fraternal organizations, labor unions, private hospitals, schools and colleges, charities, civic clubs, political parties, and many other organizations have objectives that differ basically from those of traditional business organizations. Organizations in this **institutional market** often are called nonprofit organizations because their major goals are not tied to profit, market share, and return on investment. They are not government organizations nor are they traditional types of business firms. But they buy billions of dollars of products from other nonprofit and business organizations. They are an important part of the industrial market and an important source of opportunity for their suppliers because of their growing demand for products. This demand is growing at a faster rate than our population.

Inflation, recession, shortages, and rising costs are causing organizations in the institutional market to approach the procurement function more as business firms do. They want to maximize purchasing efficiency to stretch their increasingly scarce funds. Marketers who sell to them must recognize this and present rational reasons for buying. Thus a

institutional
market

food-service marketer is likely to use a cost-benefit study to demonstrate the advantages to a small, private college of buying student meals from the vendor rather than having college employees prepare them. Likewise, a museum considering the purchase of a new security system will engage in a buying process very similar to the one we described earlier.

## INDUSTRIAL MARKETING MANAGEMENT

As we said in Chapter 1, a firm must select its market target and develop a marketing mix to satisfy it. This is true for both industrial and consumer products marketers.

### Selecting, Locating, and Evaluating the Market Target

The SIC system we discussed earlier can help industrial marketers select market targets. For example, a firm that sells equipment to produce shirts is interested in SIC code 2321. From government statistics in such sources as *Census of Business, County Business Patterns*, and *Census of Manufactures*, it could tell how many establishments produce shirts. They are prospects to buy the marketer's equipment. Next, the marketer could go to various state and commercial industrial directories, which list names, addresses, phone numbers, and other data about specific firms that have code number 2321. Or the marketer could save time and pay Dun & Bradstreet or another seller of commercial data to do it.

The next step is to estimate potential sales revenue for each of the prospects. This can be done by sampling a group of them to determine if there is a relationship between their purchase potential and one or more variables reported in SIC statistics. Perhaps the sampling will suggest a relationship between a prospect's annual sales volume and its purchase potential for the marketer's product. Then the marketer can estimate potential sales to each firm and select those that offer the most revenue potential, given the marketer's resources and capabilities to reach them with a satisfying marketing mix.

### Marketing Mix Considerations

Marketing mixes for industrial products and consumer products often differ because industrial buyers and ultimate consumers buy for different reasons.[27] Industrial buyers purchase products to satisfy their organizations' needs. Consumers buy products for their personal and/or household use. The following discussion shows the importance of this difference in buying motives.

**Product.** As we saw in Chapter 1, consumer products often were made to individual customer specification during the made-to-order era. This is uncommon today except for some major consumer products, such as custom-built homes. But many industrial products are built to individual customer specifications. An industrial marketer's engineering, production, finance, and marketing personnel may spend weeks or months developing a proposal for a data processing or in-plant materials handling system that fits a specific customer's needs. Thus a long period of time can pass between the time the marketer starts to learn about the potential customer's needs and delivery of the product to satisfy those needs. In the interim, the marketer has to draw up specifications for the product, submit design and cost proposals, and secure a purchase contract.[28]

A major consideration for many industrial buyers is the seller's ability to provide after-sale service. A well-designed data processing or word processing system, for example, may not sell if the marketer cannot provide adequate after-sale service.

**Place.** Consumers typically go to retail stores to buy consumer products. They seldom buy directly from manufacturers. But in industrial marketing the seller typically goes to the buyer, and this seller often is the manufacturer. Buyers of very expensive equipment and some other types of products want to buy directly from manufacturers.

This direct buying is much more common in industrial marketing because there are few potential buyers in comparison to the consumer market. As we saw earlier, industrial buyers also buy in larger quantities and are geographically concentrated. Of course, many low-cost industrial products like everyday supplies and some small equipment often are sold nationwide through wholesalers. Some larger items also are sold this way when the seller cannot afford its own direct salesforce to call on potential customers.

**Promotion.** Consumer product marketers like Procter & Gamble and Gillette rely heavily on advertising in mass media—TV, radio, and mass circulation magazines like *Reader's Digest*. Industrial marketers rely more on professional selling by their own salesforces, industrial trade shows, and advertising in specialized media like *Hardware Age* to promote their products. This promotion is targeted to users, influencers, deciders, buyers, and gatekeepers.

Many types of industrial products are bought infrequently. A bank, for example, does not buy a heating and air conditioning system very often. Even many small items that are used daily are bought under supply contracts negotiated between the buyer and the seller. But the marketer cannot ignore these customers. Sales calls are still needed. This keeps customers informed of new product developments and keeps salespersons up-to-date on potential buyers and their needs.

As we said earlier, many firms are centralizing the purchasing function. This has led some industrial marketers to reorganize their sales organizations. Instead of regional or district salespersons calling on a firm's various plants, the central buying unit is serviced by a national account salesperson. Because the volume involved in such an account is much larger than that of a regional account, the national account salesperson must be a dedicated professional.

**Price.**   In many countries consumers haggle over the selling prices of the products they buy.   This is much less common in consumer products marketing in the United States.   But seller-buyer negotiation of prices in industrial marketing is very common.   Just as the product often is tailored to the individual industrial buyer, so is the price.   This may help the salesperson create a differential advantage for the firm's total offering to the buyer.   As we said earlier, leasing also is more common in industrial marketing.[29]

## SUMMARY AND LOOK AHEAD

Industrial buyers buy products to satisfy their organizations' needs. These products are (1) needed to make other products, (2) needed to carry on the organization's operations, or (3) bought for resale.   All business and nonprofit organizations are industrial users.   Total dollar sales in the industrial market are much greater than those in the consumer market.

Among the major characteristics of the industrial market that distinguish it from the market for consumer products are (1) derived demand, (2) greater total sales volume, (3) smaller numbers of buyers, (4) larger volume of purchases, (5) geographical concentration of customers, (6) greater demand inelasticity, (7) professional buying, (8) direct buying, (9) more specification buying, (10) complex negotiation, (11) infrequent negotiation, (12) reciprocal buying, (13) greater use of leasing, and (14) more make-or-buy decisions.

Industrial buying can be divided into three basic types: (1) new task, (2) modified rebuy, and (3) straight rebuy.   These are called buyclasses. New task buying decisions are nonprogramed and involve extensive problem solving.   Straight rebuy decisions are programed.

The industrial buying process consists of six buyphases: (1) recognizing a need, (2) specifying the need, (3) searching for potential suppliers, (4) inviting, acquiring, and analyzing vendor proposals, (5) selecting the vendor and placing the order, and (6) following up.   This process applies mainly to new task buying.   Fewer buyphases are involved in modified and straight rebuys.

Participants in industrial buying decisions may include (1) users, (2) influencers, (3) gatekeepers, (4) deciders, and (5) buyers.   The more complex the decision, the greater the likelihood and extent of multiple buying influence.

Large industrial buyers increasingly are practicing centralized purchasing.   Value and vendor analysis are important tasks of purchasing departments.

Industrial purchasing criteria include (1) dependability, (2) product quality, (3) cost, (4) vendor production capacity, (5) after-sale service, (6) vendor reliability and integrity, (7) reciprocity, and (8) emotional factors.

Manufacturing is very concentrated in terms of value added by manufacturing. Manufacturers also are concentrated in our SMSAs. Retailing and wholesaling activities involve buying products for resale. These industries also are concentrated. Retail trade includes retailers of merchandise and retailers of services. Modern farmers are in agribusiness and contract farming is growing in importance. Government is the biggest customer in the United States. The federal government's buying can be broken down into two major types, civilian and military. Government purchases may be on a bid basis or a negotiated basis. Nonprofit organizations such as churches, charities, and civic organizations make up the institutional market. They are a very important source of market opportunity for industrial marketers.

The Standard Industrial Classification system can help industrial marketers in selecting market targets. Developing effective industrial marketing mixes requires an understanding of the nature of the industrial market and the specific market target.

The next section of the text focuses on targeted marketing and marketing research. We will see how marketing organizations go about matching their capabilities and resources with market targets.

## REVIEW QUESTIONS

1. Industrial buyers buy products to satisfy three types of needs. Identify them and give an example of each.

2. Identify and discuss briefly several characteristics that distinguish the industrial market from the consumer market.

3. Explain why the demand for industrial products is a derived demand.

4. Why is the industrial market often referred to as a "boom-or-bust" industry?

5. What are the relative advantages and disadvantages of an industrial marketer's decision to produce some of its own requirements rather than buy them from vendors (the make-or-buy decision)?

6. Identify and discuss the three buyclasses.

7. Identify and discuss the six buyphases in the procurement function.

8. What is multiple buying influence in industrial marketing? Give an example.

9. Identify and discuss the five different types of actors who can play a role in industrial buying decisions.

10. Why is the procurement function growing in importance?

11. What is value analysis?

12. What is vendor analysis?

13. What is systems selling?

14. Identify and discuss eight important purchasing decision criteria for industrial buyers.

15. "Manufacturing activity in the United States is concentrated in terms of geography and in terms of value added by manufacturing." Explain.

16. Recalling what you learned about SMSAs in Chapter 3, explain why more than half of total retail sales in our SMSAs are made in the suburbs.

17. What is contract farming?

18. How does the bid basis for buying differ from the negotiated basis in government marketing?

19. What is the institutional market?

20. What is the SIC system? How can industrial marketers use it in selecting, locating, and evaluating market targets?

## DISCUSSION QUESTIONS

**1.** What are the implications for industrial marketers of our discussion in Chapter 3 of the Sunbelt?

**2.** Manufacturing, wholesaling, and retailing are concentrated industries. Does this mean our macromarketing system is less competitive than it should be?

**3.** What implications do you see for the small family farmer in the growth of agribusiness and contract farming?

**4.** Do you think such social problems as pollution and urban decay might be solved more readily if more government marketers took the initiative in developing offerings for government agencies rather than waiting for them to send out invitations to bid?

**5.** In your opinion is reciprocity good for industrial marketers? Is it good for consumers?

## NOTES

1. See Robert F. Hartley, "Use of Customer Analysis for Better Market Penetration," *Industrial Marketing Management*, March, 1976, pp. 57–62.

2. "Firm's Workers Can Get $100 for Buying U.S. Car," *Wall Street Journal*, June 4, 1980, p. 33.

3. See Paul F. Anderson, "Industrial Equipment Leasing Offers Economic and Competitive Edge," *Marketing News*, April 4, 1980, p. 20.

4. See Wayne E. Buckhout, "Chemical Firms Mull Make-Buy Decisions," *Chemical Marketing Reporter*, May 3, 1976, pp. 11–16.

5. See David Lambert and Bruce H. Allen, "The Buyer as Marketing Practitioner," *Journal of Purchasing and Materials Management*, Fall, 1976, pp. 19–23.

6. Patrick J. Robinson, Charles W. Faris, and Yoram Wind, *Industrial Buying and Creative Marketing* (Boston: Allyn and Bacon, Inc., 1967), p. 14.

7. See H. L. Mathews and D. T. Wilson, "Industrial Marketing's New Challenge: The Computerized Buyer," *Journal of the Academy of Marketing Science*, Spring, 1974, pp. 367–373.

8. Adapted from Patrick J. Robinson, Charles W. Faris, and Yoram Wind, *Industrial Buying and Creative Marketing* (Boston: Allyn and Bacon, Inc., 1967), p. 14.

9. See Michael A. Belch and Robert W. Haas, "Using the Buyer's Needs to Improve Industrial Sales," *Business*, September–October, 1979, pp. 8–14.

10. See Alan J. Brokaw and Charles N. Davidson, "Positioning a Company as a Preferred Customer," *Journal of Purchasing and Materials Management*, Spring, 1978, pp. 9–11.

11. See Kjell Gronhaug, "Autonomous vs. Joint Decisions in Organizational Buying," *Industrial Marketing Management*, October, 1975, pp. 265–272.

12. Frederick E. Webster, Jr. and Yoram Wind, "A General Model for Understanding Organizational Buying Behavior," *Journal of Marketing*, April, 1972, pp. 17–18. Also see Jagdish Sheth, "A Model of Industrial Buyer Behavior," *Journal of Marketing*, October, 1973, pp. 50–56.

13. See James R. Cooley, Donald W. Jackson, Jr., and Lonnie L. Ostrom, "Relative Power in Industrial Buying Decisions," *Journal of Purchasing and Materials*

*Management*, Spring, 1978, pp. 18–20; and Robert E. Spekman and Louis W. Stern, "Environmental Uncertainty and Buying Group Structure: An Empirical Investigation," *Journal of Marketing*, Spring, 1979, pp. 54–64.

14. See R. Karl van Leer, "Industrial Marketing with a Flair," *Harvard Business Review*, November–December, 1976, pp. 117–124.

15. See David W. Cravens, "Supplier Marketing Strategies and Their Impact on Purchasing Decisions," *Atlanta Economic Review*, January–February, 1977, pp. 18–23.

16. "The Purchasing Agent Gains More Clout," *Business Week*, January 13, 1975, pp. 62–63.

17. See Monroe Murphy Bird, Jr. and Edward M. Mazze, "Measuring the Efficiency of the Industrial Purchasing Department," *Industrial Marketing Management*, March, 1976, pp. 17–22; and G. E. Kiser, "Elements of Purchasing Strategy," *Journal of Purchasing and Materials Management*, Fall, 1976, pp. 3–7.

18. See W. S. Penn, Jr. and Mark Mougel, "Industrial Marketing Myths," *Industrial Marketing Management*, April, 1978, pp. 133–138.

19. See William D. Perreault, Jr. and Frederick A. Russ, "Physical Distribution Service in Industrial Purchase Decisions," *Journal of Marketing*, April, 1976, pp. 3–10; J. Patrick Kelly and James W. Coaker, "The Importance of Price as a Choice Criterion for Industrial Purchasing Decisions," *Industrial Marketing Management*, October, 1976, pp. 281–292; and Monroe Murphy Bird, Jr., "Small Industrial Buyers Call Late Delivery Worst Problem," *Marketing News*, April 4, 1980, p. 24.

20. See Richard M. Hill, "Suppliers Need to Supply Reliably, in Volume, with Value Engineering Analysis, Market Data," *Marketing News*, April 4, 1980, p. 7.

21. "Loctite: Ready to Fend Off a Flock of New Competitors," *Business Week*, June 19, 1978, pp. 116, 118.

22. See Dillard B. Tinsley and John H. Lewis, "Evaluating Industrial Services," *Journal of Purchasing and Materials Management*, Winter, 1978, pp. 29–31.

23. See Reed Moyer, "Reciprocity: Retrospect

and Prospect," *Journal of Marketing*, October, 1970, pp. 47–54, and Robert E. Weigand, "The Problems of Managing Reciprocity," *California Management Review*, Fall, 1973, pp. 40–48.

24.   See F. Robert Finney, "Reciprocity: Gone But Not Forgotten," *Journal of Marketing*, January, 1978, pp. 54–59.

25.   Value added by marketing is sales revenues minus the sum of cost of goods sold and the cost of purchased services.

26.   See Jacques S. Gansler, "Let's Change the Way the Pentagon Does Business," *Harvard Business Review*, May–June, 1977, pp. 109–119.

27.   See William Copulsky, "Strategies in Industrial Marketing," *Industrial Marketing Management*, March, 1976, pp. 23–27.

28.   See Benson P. Shapiro and Ronald S. Posner, "Making the Major Sale," *Harvard Business Review*, March–April, 1976, pp. 68–78.

29.   See Paul F. Anderson and William Lazer, "Industrial Lease Marketing," *Journal of Marketing*, January, 1978, pp. 71–79.

# Section III

# Matching Market Targets with Capabilities and Resources

Section II introduced consumer and industrial markets and buyer behavior. This section examines how a marketer goes about matching the organization's capabilities and resources with target-customer wants.

Chapter 8 discusses targeted marketing. We will see how marketers select their market targets. Some marketers take very broad aim at the market and try to sell to a mass market. Others select a very small segment of that mass market as the focus for their marketing effort.

Chapter 9 brings us to a discussion of marketing research. We will look at how marketers study their markets and use the information they gather to do a better job of satisfying their market targets.

# Chapter 8

# Targeted Marketing

## OBJECTIVES
*After reading this chapter you should be able to*

1. compare the two general strategies for identifying market targets.

2. give examples of product differentiation.

3. identify and discuss the two types of segmentation strategies.

4. identify the two major segmentation variable decisions.

5. state the three major guidelines for selecting segmentation variables.

6. give examples of demographic, psychological, and product-related consumer characteristics segmentation variables.

7. identify and discuss four bases for segmenting industrial markets.

8. identify and discuss the two basic tasks in evaluating market targets.

9. compare economic, market, and sales forecasting.

10. give an example that illustrates the concept of marketing effort response elasticity.

11. discuss several approaches to sales forecasting for established and new products.

12. identify three key characteristics of an ideal market segment.

## KEY CONCEPTS
*Look for these terms as you read the chapter:*

Mass Market Strategy
Product Differentiation
Market Segmentation
Concentration Strategy
Multisegment Strategy
Segmentation Variable
Demographic Segmentation
Psychographic Segmentation
Product-Related Consumer Characteristics
    Segmentation
Brand Loyalty
Benefit Segmentation
Economic Forecasting
Market Potential
Market Forecast
Sales Potential
Sales Forecast
Marketing Effort Response Elasticity
Trend Extension Technique
Regression Analysis
Jury-of-Executive-Opinion
Market Test

*Why does Anheuser-Busch market so many brands of beer, including Busch, Budweiser, Natural Light, Michelob, and Michelob Light?  Why does Procter & Gamble market so many brands of soap, including Camay, Coast, Ivory, Safeguard, Zest, and Lava?*

*Anheuser-Busch and Procter & Gamble, like firms in the auto, sporting goods, cigarette, and many other industries, know they cannot expect to please everybody with only one market offering.  The people who drink Michelob Light have different characteristics and wants from people who drink Busch.  Similarly, people who use Camay are different from those who use Safeguard.  Instead of looking at beer drinkers as a homogeneous group of people, Anheuser-Busch researches them carefully to detect differences that can help the firm to tailor more satisfying market offerings for them.  The same is true of Procter & Gamble.*

*What about dog food?  Some dog owners (buyers of dog food) feed their dogs (consumers of dog food) table scraps, some feed them canned food, some feed them dry, packaged foods that are mixed with water, and so on.  But General Foods found a segment of buyers that probably considers their dogs to be pretty much like people.  It targets Cycle dog food to them.  Cycle 1 is for puppies up to eighteen months old, Cycle 2 is for active adult dogs one to seven years old, Cycle 3 is for less active dogs who get too many calories, and Cycle 4 is for dogs over seven years old.*

*As we saw in Chapter 1, marketing strategy planning consists of two interrelated tasks: (1) selecting the market target and (2) developing the marketing mix.*

*This chapter discusses the selection and evaluation of market targets. Customer-oriented firms practice targeted marketing by focusing their effort on creating satisfying market offerings for their target customers.*

*Two general strategies for identifying market targets are (1) the mass market strategy and (2) the market segmentation strategy.*

## THE MASS MARKET STRATEGY

mass market strategy

The **mass market strategy** (or total market strategy) assumes people in the mass market for a product category have very similar characteristics and wants.  The market is assumed to be homogeneous, and one market offering (one marketing mix) will satisfy everybody.

Some common characteristics and wants do exist among Americans. Our common language enables us to communicate effectively with each other, and mass media, such as TV and magazines, reach all of us.  Modern communications and transportation help overcome distance gaps and diminish regional differences in tastes and attitudes by bringing us into closer contact.  Increasing urbanization makes us more similar because we live and work close together.  Our political-legal system also plays a part.  Antidiscrimination laws, for example, reduce social and economic distance between races and sexes.

A firm that uses the mass market strategy defines its market target as all potential buyers of brands in a product category. The product is designed to appeal to the entire mass market and is advertised in mass media. Henry Ford, Sr. used this approach when he offered only the black Model-T to the mass market. This enabled him to schedule long production runs and hold inventory costs, distribution costs, and marketing research costs to a minimum.

The mass market strategy often is accompanied by a strategy of **product differentiation.**[1] This involves creating a difference between the marketer's brand and rival brands that seek to serve the same mass market target. Advertising, packaging, and/or minor physical changes in the product are used to broaden the brand's appeal to a greater number of potential buyers. Perrier water, for example, is naturally carbonated while most of its rival spring waters are injected with carbon dioxide.

product
differentiation

Many products have a general appeal and it is hard to create physical differences among them. Such products often are marketed to the mass market by differentiating them in some other way from their rivals. "Coke adds life" and "America's turning 7Up" are examples of differentiating through psychological appeal. On the other hand, Morton salt is differentiated by its shaker spout and the ad slogan "When it rains, it pours." Ivory soap floats in the bathtub. Procter & Gamble's Bounce is differentiated from liquid fabric softeners that are poured into the washing machine during the rinse cycle. Bounce is a nonwoven rayon sheet with a softener in it that is used in the dryer.

Marketers sometimes search for consumer characteristics and wants that are common among people of different ages, races, sexes, and incomes. A good-tasting, nutritious cereal may be a common want among people of all ages. Using different ad appeals may enable a cereal marketer to combine these different age groups into one mass market that can be served with one basic product. This is called *market aggregation*.

In some cases, however, product differentiation may not lead to a larger market for the product. Differentiating the product may, in fact, reduce the number of potential buyers and, at the same time, increase the probability of purchase by some target customers. Product differentiation, therefore, sometimes is used along with a strategy of market segmentation.

## THE MARKET SEGMENTATION STRATEGY

Although some factors tend to make Americans more similar, others tend to make us more dissimilar, or heterogeneous. A heterogeneous market is made up of people whose characteristics and wants are different. There are good reasons why marketers should not assume all people want the same kind of car, food processor, or clothing. The forces that tend to make us more similar probably have led to a reaction against sameness. New Yorkers still call their long sandwiches hero sandwiches, Pennsyl-

**Table 8–1.** *Market segmentation and product differentiation*

| Strategy | Goal |
|---|---|
| Market segmentation | Start with a heterogeneous mass market and divide it into two or more segments. Each segment has fewer people than the mass market but they are more homogeneous in their wants and characteristics. This helps the marketer select one or more segments for which market offerings can be developed. It narrows a marketing offering's appeal to the people in the segment for which it is designed. |
| Product differentiation | Create a difference between our brand and rival brands through advertising, packaging, and/or minor physical changes in the product. The intended effect is to broaden the brand's appeal to a greater number of potential buyers. |
| Combination strategy | When the number of people in a market segment is very small, the marketer can broaden the brand's appeal to people outside the segment through product differentiation. |
| | When a successful segmentation strategy attracts rival firms to compete for customers in that segment, each firm may compete for customers in this segment by differentiating its products. |

vanians call them hoagies, and Louisianans call them poor boys. Many people want products that help to express their individuality. Camel filtered cigarettes uses the slogan "Camel filters, they're not for everybody."

Our society has become more tolerant of people whose lifestyles do not fit neatly stereotyped roles. Unmarried couples living together, childless couples, spouses who take separate vacations, and households headed by women are a few examples. As we saw in Chapter 6, many subcultures exist within our culture. Their product wants and buying behavior differ from those of the dominant culture and from each other.

In a heterogeneous market marketers must identify the characteristics and wants of people in the different market segments because one market offering will not satisfy all of them.[2] **Market segmentation** is the process of finding smaller markets (segments) that exist within a larger mass market. People in a market segment are supposed to be similar in terms of the criteria, or variables, by which they were segmented. People in different segments are supposed to be different in terms of those variables. Segmentation helps marketers develop marketing mixes that satisfy people in their market targets. (See Table 8–1.) There are two segmentation strategies: (1) the concentration strategy and (2) the multisegment strategy.

### The Concentration Strategy

A **concentration strategy** involves developing one market offering for one market segment. One segment of the mass market is selected to be the firm's market target. If that segment is very large, the concentration strategy is similar to the mass market strategy. (See Figure 8–1.)

**Advantages of Concentration.** Because the firm's effort focuses on a single segment of the total market, it can research target customer

*market segmentation*

*concentration strategy*

MASS MARKET STRATEGY: Assumes people in the mass market for a product category are highly homogeneous in their wants and characteristics. Thus one market offering is targeted to them.

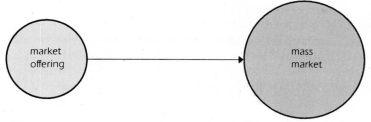

MARKET SEGMENTATION STRATEGY: Assumes people in the mass market for a product category are highly heterogeneous in their wants and characteristics.

CONCENTRATION STRATEGY: The marketer focuses on a single segment of the mass market.

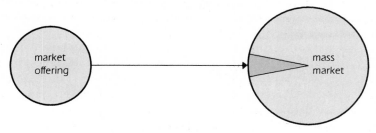

MULTISEGMENT STRATEGY: The marketer focuses on two or more segments of the mass market.

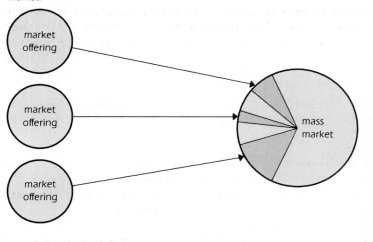

*Figure 8–1.*
*Strategies for*
*identifying market*
*targets*

wants in great detail. Long production runs are possible and advertising and distribution can be keyed to satisfying one target segment. Rolls-Royce concentrates on the luxury-car buyer segment; Curtis-Mathes concentrates on the very high-quality TV buyer segment; and Fisher-Price concentrates on toys for preschool children. Volkswagen used to concentrate on the economy-minded segment of the car market with its "Beetle." Lane Bryant concentrates on clothing for larger-sized women, while Bobbie Brooks concentrates on sportswear for junior women. Many auto tune-up franchises concentrate on minor tune-ups, such as changing points and spark plugs.

A small firm trying to enter a market dominated by a few large firms may gain easier entry by concentrating on a small segment the big firms are ignoring. If the segment is so small that only one firm can make a satisfactory profit, potential rivals may continue to ignore it. Picayune cigarettes appeal to smokers who want a very strong cigarette. Since this segment is relatively small, rivals tend to ignore it. Some small airlines like Mohawk and Shawnee concentrate on serving customers who make short trips between nearby cities. Small planes help make these operations profitable, and major airlines are willing to let the small airlines have this segment.

Many firms, however, often want to concentrate on the segment of the mass market that has the most people. This sometimes is referred to as the *majority fallacy*.[3] Stiff competition among rivals for the big segment occurs while smaller segments are left untouched. This provides opportunity for smaller firms to position themselves in these smaller segments. Iroquois Brands, Ltd. markets Champale, Black Horse Ale, Yoo-Hoo chocolate-flavored drink, Angostura bitters, and Raffeto condiments and delicacies. These low-frequency purchase products are targeted to small segments, ones that volume-oriented large firms tend to avoid.

**Disadvantages of Concentration.** The big disadvantage of the concentration strategy is that a firm cannot spread its marketing risk. A decline in the selected segment's buying power, a change in tastes, or the entry of rivals can have a bad effect on the firm. It may have a hard time redirecting its efforts to other segments. The growing popularity of 35mm photography caused problems for Fotomat Corporation's photofinishing huts, which at one time did not accept 35mm film. The declining birthrate played a big part in Hasbro Industries' decision to diversify into segments other than children's toys—family games, arts, and crafts.

Volkswagen Beetle's established niche in the American market finally was eroded by the entry of Datsun, Toyota, and Honda. Volkswagen has had to shift into other segments with models like the Rabbit, a car that appeals to a more affluent buyer. The firm has diversified even further by entering the electronic office-of-the-future market.

Xerox used to concentrate on high-priced, sophisticated copying machines for firms with high-volume copying requirements. It dominated this segment but it did not offer low-speed, low-priced models for smaller firms with low-volume copying requirements. Japanese competitors entered the American market to fill this void. In more recent years, Xerox has marketed products that compete with the Japanese copiers.

## The Multisegment Strategy

Instead of concentrating on one segment with one marketing mix, the **multisegment strategy** involves developing two or more market offerings for two or more market segments. Some firms start out with a concentration strategy and their success may lead them to expand into other segments. Billy the Kid, an apparel firm, used to concentrate on boys' wear but expanded to girls' wear. International Playtex used to concentrate on bras and girdles but now markets pantyhose, tampons, and toiletries. In 1980 it acquired Danskin, Inc., a marketer of leotards, warm-up suits, tights, and swimsuits. Burger King and McDonald's used to focus mainly on children but have expanded their menus to improve their position in the family dining market. In fact, a firm may aim at practically every segment. Revlon, Inc. offers cosmetics, toiletries, and fragrances in all price ranges through a broad variety of outlets, such as exclusive department stores, beauty salons, and discount stores.

multisegment
strategy

**Advantages of the Multisegment Strategy.** Procter & Gamble can satisfy nearly every segment of the detergent market with its many brands, which include Tide, Bold 3, Gain, Dash, Cheer, Oxydol, and Duz. Lever Brothers Company targets Pepsodent toothpaste to families whose children have grown and left home, Close-Up to teen-agers and young adults, and Aim to younger, cavity-prone children.

Several decades ago Coca-Cola probably used the mass market strategy. There was one drink, one container size and type, and fairly standardized advertising throughout the world. In more recent years Coca-Cola has given up this strategy. Diet colas like Tab and other brands like Mr. Pibb are marketed along with many types and sizes of containers for the firm's different drinks. Coca-Cola is also pushing its overseas sales effort.

A market segmentation strategy does not mean a marketer has to settle for a smaller sales volume than one who uses the mass market strategy. Segmenters aim at a smaller market(s) but they expect to penetrate it in much greater depth than they could penetrate the mass market. The multisegment strategy gives a firm an opportunity to serve a greater number of potential customers. This is a big advantage to volume-oriented firms. Firms with excess production capacity may try to use it by appealing to new segments.

**Disadvantages of the Multisegment Strategy.** The big disadvantage of the multisegment strategy is that a firm may spread itself too thinly. It may focus on too many segments with too many offerings. Marketing costs tend to go up because new marketing channels and promotional programs may be needed.

*- greater depth*
*" # of potential customers*

*Disadvantage*
*- spreading out too thinly*
*- costs of advertising & promotion*

Some consumerists argue that marketers sometimes segment markets too much. They say that dividing up the detergent and car markets into so many segments, for example, causes higher prices for consumers in all the segments and wastes natural resources. The goal of market segmentation is to satisfy more precisely the wants of consumers in target segments. The societal marketing concept suggests that perhaps there should be limits to conserve productive resources and reduce marketing costs.

### To Segment—Or Not to Segment

Segmentation may be desirable when a firm has the capability to develop marketing mixes that satisfy selected segments at an acceptable rate of return on investment.[4] Research on present and potential customers is the best place to start in deciding whether to segment. Budget Rent-A-Car Corporation's research helped it to focus on a niche in the rental car market, the "professional care segment," that the "big three"—Hertz, Avis, and National—had not identified. This segment is made up of people who consider travel directions a very important part of renting a car. Budget, therefore, developed a program that gives its customers very specific preprinted directions.[5]

If all present and potential customers want the same offering, the mass market is homogeneous and segmentation is unnecessary. If their wants are only slightly different, the differentiated mass market strategy may work. But the more heterogeneous their wants are, the more attractive a segmentation strategy becomes.

The American motorcycle market prior to the 1960s was fairly homogeneous. But during the 1960s the market became heterogeneous, and Japanese-made Hondas, Kawasakis, Suzukis, and Yamahas took sales from such American firms as Harley-Davidson. By the early 1970s Honda offered twenty-six models, Yamaha offered twenty, Kawasaki offered thirteen, and Harley-Davidson offered ten. Engine sizes ranged from 50cc to 1200cc and minicycles and dirt bikes were introduced. Females and older adults also were recognized as important new segments.[6]

### Segmentation Variables

segmentation
variable

To segment a mass market we need some basis for dividing it. **A segmentation variable** is some characteristic of people in the mass market that aids in dividing it. Examples are age, race, sex, income, psychological attributes like compulsiveness and aggressiveness, and social class. Suppose we want to segment a market on the basis of social class. The segmentation variable is social class and the mass market might be divided into lower- , middle- , and upper-class people. Marketers must make two major decisions about segmentation variables: (1) which type to use and (2) how many to use.

The types of variables selected should help to identify segments the firm can satisfy at a satisfactory return on investment. The goal is to help develop more satisfying marketing mixes. Segmentation is not an exercise in developing elaborate segmentation schemes that are unrelated to company capabilities and market requirements.

Marketers also must decide how many segmentation variables to use. One-variable segmentation means that only one characteristic is used to divide the mass market. Multivariate segmentation means that more than one characteristic is used. The more variables we use, the more segments we create and the more detailed the description is of people in each segment. Using only age places more people in a segment than if we use age, race, income, and sex. There are fewer people in each segment with multivariate segmentation and the possible sales in each segment are less. Additional variables should be used only if they will help in developing better marketing mixes. Marginal analysis is needed to determine if the use of additional variables is worth the extra cost.

The segmentation variables a firm uses should help it to

1. develop marketing mixes for the selected segments. Do not use age if age is unimportant in developing the marketing mix.
2. identify segments that are large enough to serve profitably. Do not misdirect marketing effort to segments that are too small to serve profitably, especially when using a multisegment strategy. Carried to its extreme, each person in the mass market would be an individual segment. Very rarely could this be profitable for a firm.
3. identify segments that can be reached. Do not use variables that do not help in developing ad campaigns to reach people in those segments.

There is no limit to the number of variables that can be used to segment a market. The one(s) chosen depends partly on whether the firm is marketing to ultimate consumers or to industrial users.

## SEGMENTING ULTIMATE CONSUMER MARKETS

Three categories of variables generally used for segmenting ultimate consumer markets are (1) demographic variables, (2) psychological variables, and (3) product-related consumer characteristics. (See Figure 8–2.)

### Demographic Variables

In **demographic segmentation,** market targets are selected on the basis of statistical data, such as age, sex, marital status, race, income, geographic location, education, and occupation. This approach is used most because these variables are easy to measure through observation and surveys. Census data can also be used.[7]

**Age.** Marketers of products like clothing and cars know that people of different ages have different wants. Sporty cars may be targeted to younger people and luxury cars may be targeted to older people. Of course, the markets for different products can be divided into varying numbers of age segments. The clothing market might be segmented

demographic segmentation

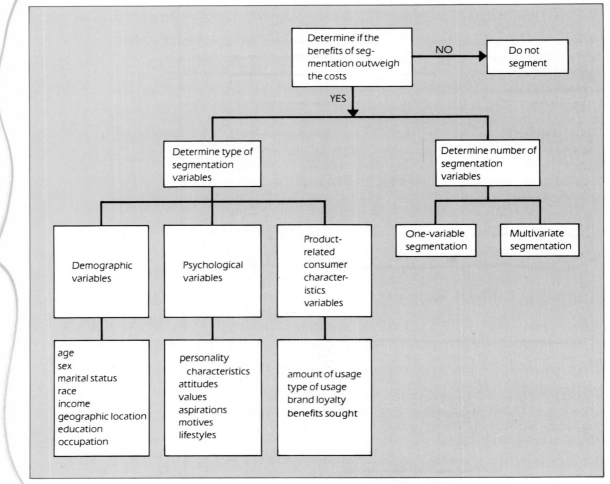

*Figure 8–2. Ways to segment an ultimate consumer market*

into infant, toddler, junior, preschool, and so forth, whereas the deodorant market may have only two or three age segments.

**Sex.** Sex is an important segmentation variable for products like magazines, deodorants, bath soaps, soft drinks, and sporting goods.[8] Furniture marketers are more likely to advertise in women's magazines than in men's magazines because women play the dominant role in buying furniture. Segmentation research, however, can yield some interesting results. Homelite, a division of Textron, found that 25 percent of its buyers of chain saws are women who buy them as gifts.[9]

**Marital Status.** A person's marital status and the presence of children affect buying patterns. Unmarried people tend to be less interested in life insurance and station wagons than are married people with young children. We discussed unmarried couples earlier in the text. It would

**An ad targeted to the female segment of the deodorant market**
Source: Procter & Gamble.

be a mistake, however, to consider all unmarried couples who live to-gether as one market segment.

One researcher has identified five types of cohabiting relationships: (1) casual, partners date others; (2) transitory, exclusive relationship but the future is uncertain; (3) stable, partners plan to stay together for some time; (4) trial marriage, partners will marry if cohabitation works out; and (5) permanent alternative, partners will cohabit for life, but not marry.[10] In the less-committed types of relationship each person buys his or her own nondurables, and durables belong to either one or the other partner. There is little mixing of funds, and they spend less on durables than married couples because of the problems they foresee in dividing up the property when the relationship ends. In the more-committed types of relationship the partners mix their funds, and there is less identification of durable products as belonging to one or the other partner. They tend to spend as much as married couples.

**Race.** Race also affects what products people buy. Blacks and whites, for example, differ in some buying patterns. For many years, many cosmetics makers failed to recognize that black females were an important market segment. Cosmetics and hair care products designed mainly for white women simply do not appeal to black women.

**Income.** Income affects the types of products people buy, the quality of what they buy, and where they buy it. But using income by itself as a segmentation variable can be dangerous. A plumber and a junior ex-ecutive may have the same income, but they tend to spend it in different ways. The plumber is more likely to join a bowling team, whereas the executive is more likely to play golf.

**Geographic Location.** Where people live plays a big role in the de-mand for many types of products. Climate, for example, affects the demand for sports equipment, clothing, gardening supplies, and building supplies. Population density is another factor to consider. People in rural areas spend less on entertainment away from home than do people in large cities.

**Education.** The type and extent of a person's education affect buying patterns. College graduates are more likely to buy *The New Yorker* and *National Geographic* than noncollege graduates, who probably are more likely to buy magazines like *National Enquirer* and *True Confessions*. This is important in placing ads for products.

**Occupation.** Occupation also affects buying patterns. Executives buy some products that do not appeal to blue-collar workers, and blue-collar workers buy some products that do not appeal to executives. A young executive may prefer renting an apartment to buying a house in order to remain mobile. Turning down a transfer to another city because of the problems in selling a house may cost the executive a promotion.

## Psychological Variables

Demographic segmentation, however, does not shed much light on the psychological attributes of target customers. In fact, a market segment may be made up of people who are very similar in demographic characteristics but very different in their social class, personalities, and lifestyles.

We discussed social class in Chapter 6. Some products, like cars and wines, are targeted to specific social classes. Their marketers build in product features and design ads that appeal to people in selected social classes.

When marketers try to segment markets by personality variables, they try to offer brands whose images will appeal to the consumer personalities they identify. Some marketers, therefore, use personality inventories to gain insight into the psychological make-up of target customers. But there are problems with using personality inventories in segmentation. A big problem is accuracy of measurement. A retail store manager may suspect that compulsiveness is an important characteristic of the store's best customers. But how can customers who have this trait be identified? The retailer cannot administer a personality inventory to each customer. Furthermore, most personality inventories are for clinical use and are not suitable for the general population. Another problem is the "reachability" of the segments. Suppose mentally depressed people are good prospects to buy a certain brand of mouthwash. How could the firm direct its ads at this segment? There are no magazines or TV programs that reach this segment exclusively.

Psychographics, on the other hand, is a more recent method of attempting to identify the lifestyle characteristics that affect people's buying behavior. **Psychographic segmentation** has become increasingly popular in recent years. By asking people to indicate activities, interests, and opinions that are characteristic of them, marketers can identify how the purchase of a product fits in their lifestyle and what other products they might buy.[11] Although psychographics is not an exact science, the people in a given segment will tend to be similar in attitudes, values, aspirations, motives, personality characteristics, and habit patterns.

psychographic
segmentation

*activities*
*interests*
*opinions*

*must be
researched—
not written
exactly*

Psychographic research helped Warner's Slimwear, a division of Warnaco, Inc. to develop a lifestyle segmentation scheme of bra buyers. The consumer segments identified were (1) conservative, (2) fashionable, (3) brand-conscious, (4) outgoing, and (5) home/price-oriented. This helped the firm to develop products, advertising, and sales promotions tailored to its selected segments.[12]

Demographic data like age, sex, and race are reported in many published sources, including government census data. But psychographic data that may be useful to a marketer usually are not found in libraries. The data have to be collected through primary research. We will discuss this in Chapter 9.

Psychographic data can be useful in segmentation because they deal with observable behavior. A marketer chooses one or more observable behaviors closely related to the product's purchase and advertises the product as one that is suited to people who have, or want to have, that characteristic. A maker of women's perfume who finds that career-

Fleischmann's.
The margarine for people who
don't take life lying down.

This is Marty. He's one of
five million Martys who share
what Fleischmann's calls an
appetite for life.
In other words, they don't
sit it out.
Another thing they share is
an appetite for the foods we
make. Like our 100% Corn Oil
Margarine.
It's high in polyunsaturates,
has no cholesterol, and it's a
delicious part of a low cholesterol,
modified fat diet.
No wonder so many people
ask for Fleischmann's by name.
They're demanding more than
ever from their lives.
Why shouldn't they
expect the same from
their margarine?

# Fleischmann's Margarine.
# Because you have
# an appetite for life.

Another fine product of ℬ Standard Brands INCORPORATED

*An ad targeted to people who share an active lifestyle*

Source: Standard Brands, Inc.

oriented women use more perfume than others might advertise its brand
as one that is not for the "ordinary housewife" but for the "independent
woman who knows who she is and what she wants."

All segmentation decisions raise the issue of how to reach target
segments. One approach is controlled market coverage. The firm defines its target segments and tries to reach them exclusively. A marketer

of hiking equipment may define its target segment as serious hikers and advertise in a magazine that appeals only to them. The firm also sells only through hiking equipment shops to avoid wasted coverage—reaching people who are not in the target segment.

Another approach is to practice less controlled coverage. The hiking equipment is advertised in magazines of general appeal and sold through mass outlets like department stores and discount stores, even though it is designed for the serious hiker segment. Serious hikers who do not read the specialized hiking magazine nor shop at the hiking equipment shop, therefore, may be reached.

## Product-Related Consumer Characteristics

Another approach to market segmentation is to divide the mass market on the basis of one or more characteristics of the consumer's relationship to the product. This is **product-related consumer characteristics segmentation.**

product-related consumer characteristics segmentation

**Amount of Usage.** One element in a consumer's relationship to a product is the amount of usage. For any product there are users and nonusers. Users often can be divided into heavy users, moderate users, and light users. This is a type of volume segmentation. Nonusers often can be divided into two subsegments: (1) those having strong negative attitudes about the product and (2) those having neutral attitudes about the product.

Research into usage rates can yield useful insights for marketing strategy. It may suggest ways to approach nonusers, increase usage among light users, reinforce heavy usage, and so on. Pet Evaporated Milk's research showed that 17 percent of its customers accounted for 87 percent of its sales. Thus it focused its ads on the heavy users: blacks, Mexican-Americans, and rural whites.[13] When Philip Morris, Inc. acquired 7Up it abandoned the "Uncola" campaign because the heavy users of soft drinks are cola drinkers. The "Uncola" campaign was replaced with "America's turning 7Up."

**Type of Usage.** Some markets can be segmented on the basis of how the user uses the product. During the 1960s, for example, Procter & Gamble's research showed that the number of weekly laundry loads in the average household went from 6.4 to 7.6, while the average wash temperature dropped fifteen degrees. Further research indicated that some clothes made from synthetics and other new kinds of fabrics had to be washed separately in cold or lukewarm water. Procter & Gamble, therefore, developed Cheer, an all-temperature detergent, and targeted it to people who wanted one detergent that could be used to wash all types of clothes.[14]

Some users may use a multipurpose household cleaner only for cleaning woodwork. Others may use it for cleaning bathtubs, floors, and windows. The multiuse segment might be offered an industrial-strength, gallon-sized container, while the single-use segment might be offered a milder version in a smaller container. One way to increase usage is to advertise a product as a multipurpose product. Spic and Span and Glass Plus are examples.

**Brand Loyalty.** The degree to which a buying unit, such as a household, concentrates its purchases over time on a particular brand within a product category is called **brand loyalty.** It can be used as a segmentation variable.[15]

brand loyalty

Suppose the users of a particular brand of soap can be divided into loyal and nonloyal buyers. By studying the demographic and psychographic characteristics of its most loyal users, the marketer may get a better understanding of the brand's market target. Likewise, by studying its less loyal buyers the marketer may get a better understanding of its major rivals. Persuading nonloyal users to become loyal requires a different type of effort than what is needed to keep presently loyal users. Perhaps cents-off coupons are needed to increase loyalty among nonloyal users.

The brand's nonusers can be divided into those who are loyal to other brands and those who are not. The marketer must decide whether to try to attract them as users. Ads that attempt to switch nonusers who are loyal to other brands may have to feature comparisons between the marketer's brand and the brands to which they are loyal. Effort to build loyalty among nonusers who are not loyal to rival brands may have to focus on price and/or offer them unique product benefits. (See Figure 8–3.)

The concept of brand loyalty is not all that exact and it can be misunderstood. For example, some consumers who habitually buy a particular brand may be doing so because of their indifference to other brands in a product category. If the marketer of that brand assumes that consumers are "loyal" to it, he or she may be in for a surprise from a rival who introduces a brand that focuses more exactly on their wants. Brand loyalty is a useful concept but it is not entitlement—it does not guarantee market share over time.

**Benefits Sought.** Dividing the market on the basis of benefits consumers expect from using the product is called **benefit segmentation.** The marketer tries to identify benefits consumers may be seeking in the product category, consumer segments that might be seeking each benefit, and the brands on the market that appear to offer each benefit. Ideally,

benefit
segmentation

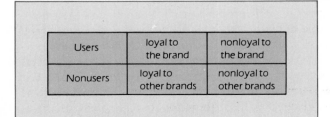

|  | loyal to the brand | nonloyal to the brand |
|---|---|---|
| Users | loyal to the brand | nonloyal to the brand |
| Nonusers | loyal to other brands | nonloyal to other brands |

*Figure 8–3.*
*Types of users and*
*nonusers*

**Table 8–2.** *Toothpaste market segment description*

| Segments: | Sensories | Sociables | Worriers | Independents |
|---|---|---|---|---|
| Principal benefit sought | flavor, product appearance | brightness of teeth | decay prevention | price |
| Demographic strengths | children | teens, young people | large families | men |
| Special behavioral characteristics | users of spearmint-flavored toothpaste | smokers | heavy users | heavy users |
| Brands disproportionately favored | Colgate Stripe | Macleans Plus White Ultra Brite | Crest | brands on sale |
| Personality characteristics | high self-involvement | high sociability | high hypochondriasis | high autonomy |
| Lifestyle characteristics | hedonistic | active | conservative | value-oriented |

Source: *Journal of Marketing.*

the marketer will be able to focus on a new benefit that is not being offered and introduce a brand that offers this benefit. Table 8–2 shows the use of benefit segmentation in segmenting the toothpaste market. The segments identified were the sensories, the sociables, the worriers, and the independents.[16]

## SEGMENTING INDUSTRIAL MARKETS

Usually, industrial marketers have fewer customers than do consumer marketers. A firm that sells component parts to automakers sells to a handful of customers, whereas Procter & Gamble's customers number in the millions. The chances that one customer could comprise a market segment are much greater in industrial marketing.

### Bases for Segmentation

In segmenting consumer markets we are segmenting ultimate consumers. In segmenting industrial markets we are segmenting organizations *and* the people in them who make and/or influence buying decisions. (See Figure 8–4.) Ads for office equipment directed at large banks and small colleges may differ. Furthermore, ads aimed at secretaries may differ from those aimed at office managers and purchasing agents. Thus segmentation variables like age and sex also are important in segmenting the people who make and/or influence industrial buying decisions. Industrial markets can be segmented by (1) type of organization, (2) size of organization, (3) product usage, (4) geographic location, and (5) structure of organization.

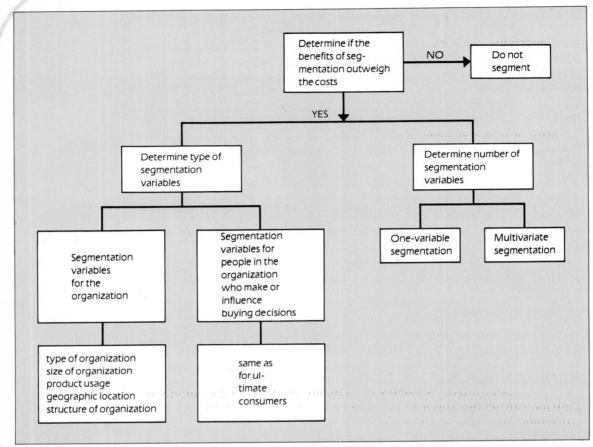

*Figure 8–4.  Ways to segment the industrial market*

**Type of Organization.**   The market for tires includes airplane, farm equipment, truck, trailer, mobile home, and car manufacturers.   Each segment has different marketing mix requirements and each could be divided further.   They could, for example, be divided into an original equipment market (selling tires to Ford Motor Company) and a replacement market (selling tires to retailers).   One tire manufacturer might concentrate on the original equipment segment in the auto industry, while another may focus on multiple segments with multiple mixes. The SIC code that we discussed in Chapter 7 is useful in segmenting industrial markets.

**Size of Organization.**   Some firms segment customers by order size because large buyers usually require a different marketing mix than small buyers.   The salesforce may have to make regular calls on big buyers, whereas small buyers may be expected to call in their orders.

**Product Usage.**   Industrial markets also can be divided on the basis of the buyer's use of the product.   Steel is used for making a wide variety of products and as a construction material. These different types of applications often call for different types of marketing mixes.

**Geographic Location.** Some industries, such as textile and furniture manufacturing, are concentrated geographically. Firms in the areas of concentration can be treated as one segment, while those outside may be treated as one or more other segments. Garment makers in New York City might be lumped into one segment, while those in other cities might be separate segments.

**Structure of Organization.** The degree to which decision-making power is concentrated in a firm is another basis for dividing industrial markets. A firm that sells to supermarkets may segment on the basis of centralized vs. decentralized buying authority. Getting a new product on the shelves of A&P's supermarkets may involve one sales presentation before A&P's central buying committee. Getting it on the shelves of independently owned grocery stores requires calls on each of the stores.

## EVALUATING MARKET TARGETS

Serving a market target profitably requires the cost of the marketing effort to be less than the sales revenues realized from serving it. In evaluating potential targets we must estimate sales revenue potential and the cost of developing the effort needed to make the desired market impact.

### Estimating Revenue Potential

Estimating revenue potential in one or more market segments involves preparing quantitative estimates of demand, or demand measurement. Demand can be measured by (1) product level, (2) competitive level, (3) geographic area, and (4) time frame.

On the product level we can measure demand for a specific product (frozen spinach) or for a product line (frozen vegetables). On the competitive level demand can be measured from the firm's perspective or that of the industry in which it operates. Demand estimation also requires the marketer to specify the geographic area included, such as a particular sales territory or an entire nation. Finally, the marketer also must specify the estimate's time frame—long, intermediate, or short range.

The purpose of measuring demand influences the approach to be taken. Consider the time frame. Consolidated Edison wants to estimate demand for electricity over the next thirty or forty years if it is considering building new generating stations. Marketers of high-fashion clothing usually estimate demand over a much shorter period.

When estimating revenue potential in one or more market segments, marketers engage in three levels of estimation: (1) economic forecasting (economic potential and economic forecast), (2) market forecasting (market potential and market forecast), and (3) sales forecasting (sales potential and sales forecast). (See Table 8–3.)

**Economic Forecasting.** The economic potential of the overall economy is the total possible GNP. This is tough to estimate and concerns

**Table 18–3.** *Economic, market, and sales forecasting*

| | |
|---|---|
| *Economic Forecasting:* | |
| Economic potential: | the total possible GNP |
| Economic forecast: | a forecast of GNP |
| *Market Forecasting:* | |
| Market potential: | the highest level of demand possible in a given marketing environment |
| Market forecast: | the estimated market demand that will exist in an industry given an estimated level of marketing effort by all firms in that industry |
| *Sales Forecasting:* | |
| Sales potential: | the highest level of sales a firm might reach with a given level of marketing effort |
| Sales forecast: | the number of units or dollar sales volume of a product the firm expects to sell during a certain time period with a given level of marketing effort |

**economic forecasting**

economists more than marketers. Marketers are more interested in **economic forecasting,** which involves analyzing government monetary and fiscal policies, the volume of consumer spending and business investment, the consumer price index, railcar loadings, and so on to help in estimating overall future business activity.

Manufacturers of car batteries and tires know their sales in the original equipment market depend heavily on the level of economic activity. As we saw in Chapter 7, the demand for these products is derived from the demand for new cars, which is affected by the overall level of business activity. Battery and tire manufacturers, therefore, are interested in a forecast of overall business activity. In the replacement market, battery and tire sales are related mainly to the number and ages of cars on the road.

**market potential**

**Market Forecasting.** The highest level of demand possible in a given marketing environment is **market potential.** Additional marketing effort by marketers would have little or no effect in stimulating more demand. The market potential for a product is the unit or dollar volume an entire market or a market segment might buy from all sellers during a period of time if all sellers were putting forth their maximum marketing effort.

**market forecast**

The **market forecast** shows the estimated market demand that will exist, given an estimated level of marketing effort by all firms in the industry. Because the marketing efforts of individual firms vary, a marketer has to consider how the level of industry efforts will change in the future. The economic forecast may help here.

**sales potential**

**Sales Forecasting.** The highest level of sales a firm might reach with a given level of marketing effort is **sales potential.** A firm's sales po-

# ONE OF THE GREAT MISCALCULATIONS IN IBM HISTORY.

In the early 1950's, we took a hard look at the future for business computer systems.

Our best estimate, at the time, was a potential of 50 new customers.

But in a relatively short time, we'd built and installed 75 systems.

And by the time the dust had settled, we'd sold 1500 of them.

It's hard to believe that a forecast could have been so wide of the mark.

But then, as now, this industry continues to surprise nearly everyone.

Who would have dreamed, back in the '50s, that in less than 30 years this would be an industry that has installed more than 500,000 computer systems in the U.S. alone.

Who could have guessed that a business started by a few dozen scientists, inventors, and engineers would become a multibillion dollar industry employing more than three-quarters of a million people here in the United States.

For the past 30 years computer technology has been exploding, and even today demand continues to exceed the most optimistic forecasts.

There is one forecast, however, we feel confident in making.

As long as we can keep driving the cost of using a computer down, this looks like an industry with nowhere to go but up. IBM

*Forecasting is not always easy*

Source: IBM Corporation.

tential is limited by the product's market potential and rivals' activities. Primary demand for a product is the total market demand for it. Selective demand is the demand for a particular brand. Marketing effort of rivals can affect primary demand and, therefore, market potential. Cobra's advertising during the height of the CB craze, for example, probably increased the primary demand for CBs, not just the demand for Cobra CBs.

Two basic ways to estimate sales potential are the breakdown approach and the build-up approach. The breakdown approach assumes a product's sales potential varies with the country's general level of business activity. Starting with a forecast of GNP, we break GNP down to forecasts of (1) industry sales, (2) company sales, and (3) brand sales. This is not too hard to do if the firm has kept accurate sales records. The library has government forecasts of GNP, and industry trade associations have specific industry forecasts. Hereafter, the going gets tougher because the marketer is forecasting sales for the firm and its brands. We will discuss this again later in this chapter.

The build-up approach starts with an estimate of the number of units of the product category a typical buyer in a typical sales territory will buy during a given time. We multiply this by the number of potential buyers in that territory and follow the same procedure for all the other territories. We add the figures for an estimate of market potential. Then the marketer makes several estimates of the share of that market potential the firm will get based on different levels of marketing effort.

sales forecast

Finally, in sales forecasting we estimate the sales volume our firm actually will achieve at a given level of marketing effort. **A sales forecast** is the number of units or dollar sales volume of a product the firm expects to sell during a certain time period with a given level of marketing effort.

### Estimating the Cost of Marketing Effort

The marketer also has to estimate the cost of the effort needed to make the desired market impact on the various potential targets. We can rank targets in terms of their relative attractiveness by comparing cost estimates to sales potential in the various targets.

What we expect rivals to do affects our estimates of the effort needed to serve a target. A more costly effort is needed if rivals are expected to enter the market quickly, because we will want to gain a solid foothold as soon as possible. The longer rivals stay out, the more time available to phase the marketing effort in gradually.

Overestimating is usually better than underestimating the cost of the needed effort. Underestimating may force us to give up the effort to penetrate a target after having committed resources to it. Those resources ordinarily are not recoverable. Of course, it also is wise to avoid an overcommitment to any one target. That could result in putting too many eggs in one basket. Personnel in different departments should cooperate in making the estimates. This helps ensure better estimation and increases their commitment to making the desired market impact.

### SALES FORECASTING

In estimating sales potential we seek insight into the market's responsiveness to different levels of marketing effort. Increases in spending on effort, however, may not return proportional increases in sales revenues. The concept of **marketing effort response elasticity** is useful here.[17]

By the late 1970s steel-belted radial tires accounted for about 80 percent of original-equipment tire sales. Sales in the replacement market had stabilized at about 26 percent.[18] Increasing that 26 percent share would be tough. Many buyers trade new cars in before the radials wear out, and used-car buyers tend not to replace worn-out radials with new radials. Thus some tire manufacturers focus on other segments where the marketing effort response elasticity is greater, such as making rear radials for farm tractors.

A firm also may derive less return (sales revenues) for each dollar it spends on its effort than a rival. The rival, for example, may create better ads or have a better sales training program that generates more sales revenue per dollar spent. The rival is more effective in using its available resources.

It is also possible that there will be diminishing returns to spending on marketing effort. A firm that spends $1 million on advertising may switch some buyers of rival brands to its brand. But spending $3 million on advertising may not produce three times as much brand switching. The first $1 million may cause many nonloyal buyers of rival brands to switch but eventually the advertiser will encounter the problem of switching loyal buyers of rival brands. This may take a much more costly advertising effort.

As we said earlier, a sales forecast is an estimate of the sales volume we will achieve at a given level of effort. It is a tool for planning and controlling. How much inventory of raw materials is needed depends on how many units of the finished product we expect to sell. Production scheduling, financial requirements, and personnel requirements also are related closely to the sales forecast. It also sets a sales performance standard against which actual sales results can be compared for control purposes.

Many methods and techniques exist for developing sales forecasts.[19] None is perfect. We will look at (1) sales forecasting for established products and (2) sales forecasting for products that are new to the firm.

### Sales Forecasting for Established Products

Sales forecasting depends partly on past sales data—knowing who our customers are, where they are located, their types of business, the typical size of their orders, and so on. Electronic data processing helps increase the efficiency and reduces the cost of collecting relevant sales data for use in sales forecasting.

**Trend Extension.** One approach to sales forecasting is extrapolation, also referred to as the historical approach, or the **trend extension technique.** We plot sales figures for past years on a graph and draw a straight line to fit the data. Extending the line forward gives us a sales forecast. (See Figure 8–5.) We assume that future sales will be determined by the

*marketing effort response elasticity*

*trend extension technique*

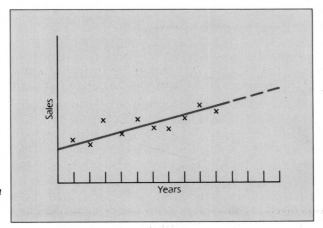

**Figure 8–5.
The trend extension
method of sales
forecasting**

*The Xs represent
sales for past years.
The dashed portion
of the line shows
the extension of the
trend. This
provides a sales
forecast.*

same variables that caused past sales and that the relationships among
those variables will remain the same. This approach is more realistic
for products with a history of stable demand than for products with erratic
sales. In general, trend extension is more accurate for short-term than
for long-term forecasts. There are many complex statistical techniques
for refining this approach.

**Correlation.** Correlation methods also are based on historical sales
data. The forecaster might observe a relationship between past sales
and one or more variables, such as GNP, the birthrate, population, or
personal bankruptcies. Past sales are the dependent variable and the
other variable(s) is the independent variable.

For example, a small retail appliance dealer's analysis of past sales
data suggests a correlation between sales and the number of marriage
licenses and building permits issued in the county. **Regression analysis**
can be used to analyze the statistical relationships among changes in past
sales and changes in these variables. The aim is to develop a mathematical formula that describes the relationship among the dependent and
independent variables. Although the formula cannot prove that changes
in the number of marriage licenses and building permits caused sales to
go up or down, the correlation method may still be very useful. The
retailer does not care whether these variables cause sales as long as they
continue to predict sales in a reasonably accurate way.

**Executive Judgment.** Marketers often supplement forecasts with
judgment. The **jury-of-executive-opinion** approach involves asking executives in different departments their opinions about future sales. If
they have had a lot of experience with the product and if demand has
been fairly stable, this approach can work because extreme pessimism
and optimism tend to balance out. The big problem is that more recent
experiences weigh more heavily than more distant ones. The "Delphi
Technique," a more sophisticated and objective approach, is better suited
to long-range forecasts than the jury-of-executive-opinion approach.[20]

**regression
analysis**

**jury-of-executive-
opinion**

**Salesforce Estimates.**   Marketing managers often ask each salesperson to forecast attainable sales volume in their territories for a given period.[21]   Then these forecasts are combined into a total forecast, which for a number of reasons often requires some adjustment.

First, salespersons may not be very objective in preparing their estimates.   They tend to be swayed too much by their most recent sales performance, which may result in estimates that are biased either upward or downward.   If they believe they are expected to turn in high forecasts, they may do so even though they know the estimates are unattainable. They also may do this if they believe promotional funds will be distributed among territories on the basis of territorial sales estimates.   At the other extreme, they may turn in very low estimates when the estimates alone are used to set sales quotas.

Second, salespersons often are unaware of company marketing plans that will affect the sales outlook in their territories.   A salesperson may be unaware that the firm is planning to launch a new ad campaign during the period covered by the forecast.

Third, salespersons do not always have the marketing manager's broader perspective on developments in the economy and the industry. They do not have as much access to market research studies and other internal company data.   Also their estimates often are way off during swings in the business cycle.

Finally, salespersons have a natural tendency to concern themselves more with making sales than with forecasting sales.   Preparing these estimates may seem like needless paperwork.

Marketing managers are responsible for improving the salesforce's willingness and ability to make accurate sales forecasts.   An incentive system might motivate them to take forecasting more seriously, and aids, such as a sales recording and reporting system that minimizes the time needed to prepare estimates, can help.   Some firms use pamphlets to inform salespersons of management's forecasts about the economy and the industry along with information about company plans for the future. Giving each salesperson his or her past sales estimates along with individual performance records on actual sales also can help.

These efforts show that management considers the salesforce to be a resource in preparing sales forecasts.   Salespersons are closest to the customers and often can spot developing trends before people in the office. They also are in direct touch with their customers' future product needs, which is especially important in industrial marketing.   This bottom-up approach can provide sales estimates broken down by salesperson, customer, product, and territory.

**Surveys of Buyer Intentions.**   Forecasting attempts to predict what potential buyers will buy under stated conditions during a future time period.   Another approach to preparing a forecast is to survey buying intentions—ask potential buyers if they will buy and, if so, how many units and from whom they will buy.   But to do such a survey the surveyor has to identify potential buyers, potential buyers must be able and willing to give accurate and honest information about their buying intentions, and the surveyor has to be willing to pay the frequently high cost of the survey.

Surveys of this type are used mainly for consumer durables and industrial products, such as installations and accessory equipment. As we saw in Chapter 3, the Survey Research Center interviews consumers in a carefully drawn sample of potential buyers of consumer durables. Industrial marketers often use their marketing research people to conduct these surveys. The U.S. Department of Commerce also conducts surveys of industrial buyers.

**market test**

**Market Tests.** The firm distributes the product in one or more test markets to test customer response to the marketing mix in a **market test.** The market test measures actual sales rather than intentions to buy and is very useful when opinion surveys are too costly or the information may be of questionable value. If test markets are selected wisely and the test is conducted properly, the marketer can generalize test experience to the entire market. This helps in sales forecasting and in ironing out bugs in the marketing mix while the product still is in the test market. Test marketing is discussed again in Chapter 11.

## Sales Forecasting for New Products

It is tougher and more risky to forecast sales for new products because of the absence of past sales data. Texas Instruments is one firm that knows being the first on the market with a new product is not always desirable. "At Texas Instruments, marketers consider three acronyms—PAM, TAM, and SAM. They stand for potential available market, total available market, and served available market. The company goes ahead with a new product only when the potential is assured, competitors assessed, and the company's service capabilities analyzed."[22]

**Substitute Method.** As we will see in Chapter 10, marketers like Polaroid and Kodak often introduce new products to replace older ones with declining profit potential. Gillette introduced ATRA (Automatic Tracking Razor Action) to replace its Trac II and by the time you read this ATRA may have been replaced by a newer shaving system. One way to forecast sales for a new product that is replacing an older one is to analyze sales of the old product. This is the substitute method.

**Market Tests.** Some products are so totally new that there are no substitutes available for comparison. One way to forecast their sales is to test them in one or more test markets. This approach is similar to the one we discussed for established products. One problem, however, is that the product's newness may lead some people to buy it simply because it is new. This novelty buying tends to die out as the product's newness wears off.

**Survey Method.** Another approach is to survey potential buyers. People who may have a need for the product are asked if they would buy it. These surveys often are conducted before the product is produced in volume quantities to determine if the marketer really has a marketable

**Table 8–4.** *Information bases for sales forecasting*

| Information Base* | Forecasting Approaches |
|---|---|
| What people say | Executive judgment |
| | Salesforce estimates |
| | Surveys of buyer intentions |
| What people do | Market tests |
| What people have done | Trend extension |
| | Correlation |
| | Substitute method |

*See Philip Kotler, *Marketing Management: Analysis, Planning, and Control*, 3d ed. (Englewood Cliffs, N.J.: Prentice-Hall, Inc., 1976), p. 129.

product.   The potential buyer may be shown a prototype, or mock-up, of the product and perhaps the product's benefits are described.   In recent years some potential marketers of battery-powered cars have done this.

Often, the surveys also include retailers and wholesalers.   Many consumer products will either succeed or fail depending on how much selling effort retailers give the product.   Furthermore, the willingness of wholesalers and retailers to stock a new product often hinges on their feelings about its marketability.   Retailers are closer to ultimate consumers than most manufacturers, so they can be a good source of information in gauging a new product's marketability.

Finally, the salesforce can help in sales forecasting for new products, especially in industrial marketing.   Computer salespersons, for example, often serve as consultants to their present and potential customers. Their knowledge of customers' operations and product needs can help in forecasting sales for new products and in suggesting new product ideas to their employers.   (See Table 8–4.)

## SELECTING MARKET TARGETS

After identifying potential market targets, estimating their revenue potential, and estimating the effort needed to make the desired market impact, the marketer is ready to select specific targets.   This selection is guided by several key characteristics of an ideal market segment:

1. Its unique requirements can be satisfied with the firm's resources and capabilities at a satisfactory rate of return on investment.
2. It represents opportunity that potential rivals have not recognized.
3. It has the capacity to grow in size.

Although there may be few actual cases where all three characteristics are present, they can be useful in assessing opportunities.

Seven potential market targets are ranked in terms of their sales revenue potential in Table 8–5.   The table also shows the cost of the effort needed to make the desired market impact on the target, the speed of competitive reaction, and the marketer's confidence in these estimates.

**Table 8–5.** *Market target selection*

| Potential Target | Ranking of Sales Revenue Potential | Estimated Competitive Reaction* | Confidence in Estimates** | Estimated Effort in Dollars |
|---|---|---|---|---|
| A | 3 | I | M | $ 800,000 |
| B | 5 | I | V | 900,000 |
| C | 1 | S | M | 900,000 |
| D | 6 | L | C | 200,000 |
| E | 2 | L | M | 1,000,000 |
| F | 4 | S | V | 300,000 |
| G | 7 | I | C | 500,000 |

*L = long-range       **V = very little
I = intermediate-range    C = considerable
S = short-range       M = much

Suppose the firm is willing to invest $1 million in its marketing effort but does not want to commit all its resources to any one target. It also wants to avoid targets that rivals are expected to go after quickly. Given these constraints, we can eliminate target E because it alone requires an effort of $1 million. We also can eliminate targets C and F because we expect competition to develop quickly.

Targets A, B, D, and G remain. Target B is not promising because of low confidence in the estimates. Selecting B also would leave no other targets since it requires an effort of $900,000, which would leave only $100,000—too little to make an impact on any other target. Still remaining are targets A, D, and G. Since we do not want to commit all our resources to any one target, the choice is between A and D or D and G. Targets A and D would exhaust the entire $1,000,000, whereas targets D and G would require only $700,000. If we wished to be conservative we might select targets D and G. Target A, however, is ranked third in revenue potential, whereas G is ranked seventh. We also have more confidence in estimates for A than for G.

Given these constraints, targets A and D probably would be selected. The marketing effort for D could be phased in gradually since we are confident that competition will not develop in the short run nor in the intermediate run.

## Developing the Marketing Mix

Now we can proceed with developing specific marketing mixes for the selected targets. This involves writing up a formal marketing program for delivering the desired impact to the targets. We may put the program through a trial run in one or more test markets.

If the test is successful we are ready to sell the program to top management by showing them how it fits into the firm's mission. Providing evidence that several targets were identified along with cost data relating to the effort needed to reach them is helpful. We should also explain our reasons for selecting the chosen targets and back them up with evidence of successful test marketing.

Next we put the approved plan into action. This requires selling the plan to the people who carry it out.

Finally, we monitor the results of implementation for control purposes. A close check helps to ensure the marketing effort is making the desired impact. If it is not doing this, the program needs revision.

## SUMMARY AND LOOK AHEAD

All customer-oriented firms seek to create satisfying marketing mixes for their market targets. They practice targeted marketing. Two general strategies for identifying market targets are the mass market strategy and the market segmentation strategy.

The mass market strategy assumes people in the market for products in a particular category are very much alike in their characteristics and wants. Thus it is assumed that one product offering will satisfy everyone. In some cases product differentiation accompanies this strategy to differentiate the firm's product from rival offerings.

The market segmentation strategy, on the other hand, assumes that people in the market for products in a particular category are heterogeneous in their characteristics and wants. The concentration strategy focuses on developing one offering for one segment of the mass market. The multisegment strategy focuses on two or more segments.

A mass market is segmented by using one or more segmentation variables. Which type and how many to use are two big decisions. Variables selected should help in (1) developing good marketing programs, (2) identifying segments large enough to serve profitably, and (3) identifying segments that can be reached.

Ultimate consumer markets can be segmented by using demographic variables, psychological variables, or product-related consumer characteristics. The most frequently used approach is demographic segmentation.

Industrial markets can be segmented on the basis of the type of organization, the size of the organization, product usage, geographic location, SIC codes, and the structure of the organization.

Evaluating market targets requires estimation of sales revenue potential and of the cost of developing the effort needed to make the desired market impact. Three levels of estimation often are involved in estimating revenue potential: economic, market, and sales forecasting. Cost estimation requires interdepartmental coordination.

Several approaches can be taken to sales forecasting for both established and new products. They include executive judgment, salesforce estimates, surveys of buyer intentions, market tests, trend extension, correlation, and the substitute method.

Company objectives must be kept in mind when selecting market targets. After selecting targets the marketer develops specific marketing mixes for them in order to achieve the desired market impact.

In the next chapter, we will study marketing research. Much of the information needed for good segmentation decisions is generated by marketing research.

## REVIEW QUESTIONS

1. Is it unreasonable to assume there are some common characteristics and wants among Americans? Explain.

2. What factors contribute to the existence of a heterogeneous American market?

3. What is the mass market strategy?

4. What is product differentiation and how does it help in the market aggregation process?

5. Compare the concentration and the multisegment approaches to market segmentation and discuss the relative advantages of each.

6. What is meant by "segmentation variable"?

7. What factors influence the choice between one variable and multivariate segmentation?

8. Identify and discuss three guidelines to follow in selecting segmentation variables.

9. Identify and discuss five important variables that can be used in demographic segmentation.

10. Why is demographic segmentation the most frequently used approach to segmenting ultimate consumer markets?

11. What is meant by the "reachability" of a market segment?

12. What is psychographic segmentation?

13. Identify and discuss three product-related consumer characteristics that can be used as segmentation variables.

14. Identify and discuss four bases for segmenting industrial markets.

15. Identify and discuss the three levels of estimation in estimating the revenue potential in one or more market segments.

16. Compare the breakdown and the build-up approaches to estimating sales potential.

17. Why is it usually better to overestimate than underestimate the cost of the marketing effort needed to make the desired market impact on the market target?

18. Discuss the concept of marketing effort response elasticity.

19. Identify and discuss three approaches to sales forecasting for established products.

20. Identify and discuss three approaches to sales forecasting for new products.

21. What are the characteristics of an ideal market segment?

## DISCUSSION QUESTIONS

1. In Chapter 1 we discussed the made-to-order era in the evolution of the marketing concept. Do you see any parallels between that type of marketing and market segmentation?

2. Why do some marketers insist on practicing market segmentation when it probably adds to the cost of marketing products?

3. Would a firm that practices market segmentation ever advertise its product in a mass circulation magazine such as *Time* or *Reader's Digest?*

4. Why are there so many brands of cereal, toothpaste, bath soap, and deodorant on the market?

5. There are three information bases for sales forecasting: (a) what people say, (b) what people do, and (c) what people have done. Which is most reliable?

**6.** How might the societal marketing concept influence a firm's selection of its market target(s)?

**7.** Is the practice of market segmentation the result of differences in wants among consumers, or are those differences the result of market segmentation?

## NOTES

1. See Wendell R. Smith, "Product Differentiation and Market Segmentation as Alternative Marketing Strategies," *Journal of Marketing*, July, 1956, pp. 3–8; and Theodore Levitt, "Marketing Success through Differentiation—of Anything!" *Harvard Business Review*, January–February, 1980, pp. 83–91.

2. For discussion of two major segments for banks, see W. Thomas Anderson, Jr., Eli P. Cox, III, and David G. Fulcher, "Bank Selection Decisions and Market Segmentation," *Journal of Marketing*, January, 1976, pp. 40–45.

3. Alfred A. Kuehn and Ralph L. Day, "Strategy of Product Quality," *Harvard Business Review*, November–December, 1962, pp. 101–102.

4. See Frederick W. Winter, "A Cost-Benefit Approach to Market Segmentation," *Journal of Marketing*, Fall, 1979, pp. 103–111.

5. "Budget 'attacks' Hertz with Military Marketing Strategy," *Marketing News*, January 25, 1980, pp. 7–8.

6. Kathleen Crighton, "Cycle Market Revs Up Again after Slump," *Advertising Age*, September 4, 1972, pp. 2, 57.

7. See Ed Spear, "Using Census Bureau Publications to Estimate Segments of the Total Population," *Sales & Marketing Management*, March 14, 1977, pp. 68–70.

8. For discussion of the changing position of women in the United States and the implications for marketers, see William Lazer and John E. Smallwood, "The Changing Demographics of Women," *Journal of Marketing*, July, 1977, pp. 14–22. Also see Fred D. Reynolds, Melvin R. Crask, and William D. Welles, "The Modern Feminine Life Style," *Journal of Marketing*, July, 1977, pp. 38–45.

9. "Market Research Shows Company That Women Buy 25% of Chain Saws," *Marketing News*, January 27, 1978, p. 10.

10. The researcher is Professor Lawrence H. Wortzel. This paragraph is based on "Relationship's Durability Affects Spending of Cohabiting Couples," *Marketing News*, December 31, 1976, p. 9.

11. See Joseph T. Plummer, "The Concept and Application of Life Style Segmentation," *Journal of Marketing*, January, 1974, pp. 33–37; Douglass K. Hanes, "Psychographics Are Meaningful . . . Not Merely Interesting," *Journal of Travel Research*, Spring, 1977, pp. 1–7; Stuart Van Auken, "General versus Product-Specific Life-Cycle Segmentations," *Journal of Advertising*, Fall, 1978, pp. 31–35; and Mary Lou Roberts and Lawrence H. Wortzel, "New Life-Style Determinants of Women's Food Shopping Behavior," *Journal of Marketing*, Summer, 1979, pp. 28–39.

12. Elizabeth A. Richards and Stephen S. Sturman, "Life-Style Segmentation in Apparel Marketing," *Journal of Marketing*, October, 1977, pp. 89–91.

13. "Jell-O's Revival Shows Sales Can Grow with Older Products," *Wall Street Journal*, September 11, 1980, p. 25.

14. "At Procter & Gamble, Success Is Largely Due to Heeding Consumer," *Wall Street Journal*, April 29, 1980, p. 24.

15. See Robert C. Blattberg, Thomas Buesing, and Subrata K. Sen, "Segmentation Strategies for New National Brands," *Journal of Marketing*, Fall, 1980, pp. 59–67.

16. Russell I. Haley, "Benefit Segmentation: A Decision-Oriented Research Tool," *Journal of Marketing*, July, 1968, pp. 30–35. Also see Russell I. Haley, "Beyond Benefit Segmentation," *Journal of Advertising Research*, August, 1971, pp. 3–8; and Kenneth E. Miller and Kent L. Granzin, "Simultaneous Loyalty and Benefit Segmentation of Retail Store Customers," *Journal of Retailing*, Spring, 1979, pp. 47–60.

17. See Nariman K. Dhalla and Winston H. Mahatoo, "Expanding the Scope of Segmentation Research," *Journal of Marketing*, April, 1976, pp. 38–41; Henry Assael, "Segmenting Markets by Response Elasticity," *Journal of Advertising Research*, April, 1976, pp. 27–35; and Henry Assael and Marvin Roscoe, Jr., "Approaches to Market Segmentation Analysis," *Journal of Marketing*, October, 1976, pp. 67–76.

18. "Goodyear's Solo Strategy: Growth Where Nobody Else Sees It," *Business Week*, August 28, 1978, p. 68.

19. See C. Mike Merz, "Measuring Sales Forecast Accuracy," *Management Accounting*, July, 1975, pp. 53–54; Douglas J. Dalrymple, "Sales Forecasting Methods and Accuracy," *Business Horizons*, December, 1975, pp. 69–73; N. Carroll Mohn, W. A. Schaffer, and L. C. Sartorius, "Input-Output Modeling: New Sales Forecasting Tool," *University of Michigan Business Review*, July, 1976, pp. 7–15; Spyros Makridakis and Steven C. Wheelwright, "Forecasting: Issues and Challenges for Marketing Management," *Journal of Marketing*, October, 1977, pp. 24–38; Robert Saveski, "Appraising the Sales Forecast," *Managerial Planning*, November–December, 1977, pp. 15–20; Kevin McCrohan, "Forecasting Business Needs in the Telephone Market," *Industrial Marketing Management*, April, 1978, pp. 109–113; and John Wacker and Jane Cromartie, "Adapting Forecasting Methods to the Small Firm," *Journal of Small Business Management*, July, 1979, pp. 1–7.

20. See Jeffrey L. Johnson, "A Ten-Year Delphi Forecast in the Electronics Industry," *Industrial Mar-*

*keting Management*, March, 1976, pp. 45–55; and Neil C. Macpherson, "Future Research: Using Delphi as a Technique," *Quarterly Review of Marketing*, Autumn, 1978, pp. 1–8.

21. See Thomas R. Wotruba and Michael L. Thurlow, "Sales Force Participation in Quota Setting and Sales Forecasting," *Journal of Marketing*, April, 1976, pp. 11–16.

22. Statements by Dan Carter, manager of advanced planning, Digital Systems Division, Texas Instruments in "Too-early Product Debut Can Mean Failure," *Marketing News*, January 25, 1980, p. 11.

# Marketing Research

## OBJECTIVES

*After reading this chapter you should be able to*

1. distinguish between informal and formal marketing research.

2. explain the use of the scientific method in marketing research.

3. distinguish between data and information.

4. classify data as internal or external, recurrent or nonrecurrent, and primary or secondary.

5. describe the basic purpose and nature of a marketing information system.

6. compare marketing research and the marketing information system.

7. identify and discuss the stages in a typical marketing research project.

8. classify marketing research according to function and methodology.

9. compare mail, telephone, and personal interview surveys.

10. critically analyze a questionnaire.

11. identify and discuss several interviewing techniques.

12. distinguish between probability and nonprobability samples.

## KEY CONCEPTS

*Look for these terms as you read the chapter:*

Marketing Research
Marketing Information System
Recurrent Data Subsystem
Nonrecurrent Data Subsystem
Hypotheses
Primary Data
Secondary Data
Research Design
Exploratory Research
Focus Group Interview
Descriptive Research
Causal Research
Predictive Research
Historical Research
Survey Research
Experimental Research
Motivational Research
Observational Method
Inquiry Method
Factual Survey
Opinion Survey
Motivational Survey
Direct Interviewing
Depth Interviewing
Projective Techniques
Sample
Probability, or Random, Sample
Nonprobability, or Nonrandom, Sample

*The beginnings of modern marketing research can be traced back to Charles Coolidge Parlin at Curtis Publishing Company, publisher of* The Saturday Evening Post. *Mr. Parlin established a Division of Commercial Research in the firm's advertising department in 1911.* The Saturday Evening Post, *the major mass medium at the time, wanted to demonstrate to a potential advertiser, Campbell Soup Company, that blue-collar workers' wives bought soup in cans. Campbell executives believed the majority of the readers of the magazine were blue-collar workers, whose wives were thought to make soup from scratch.*

*Mr. Parlin selected a scientific sample of garbage routes in Philadelphia and rented a national guard armory in the city. Then he had the contents of the carts emptied on the armory floor and counted the number of soup cans in each pile of garbage. Very few soup cans were found in the garbage from affluent neighborhoods. It was hypothesized that servants in those homes made soup from scratch. Although wives of blue-collar workers sometimes made soup from scratch, they more often made clothes from scratch. They could buy Campbell soup for ten cents a can and spend the time they saved making clothes.\* Thus Campbell Soup Company became a regular advertiser in* The Saturday Evening Post.

The research provided Campbell's executives with information they could use in decision making. Without it they might have continued to assume incorrectly that blue-collar families were not good prospects to buy canned soup. As we will see, good marketing research can help marketers make better decisions.

Creating and delivering customer satisfactions requires marketing managers to make many decisions. They need relevant information about customers, competitors, costs, and many other internal and external factors. This information is an input to the decision-making process.

Information is born out of data relating to a firm's internal and external operations. Internal and external data must be converted to meaningful information for marketing decision makers. In some cases they lack data, and in other cases they have too much. Both situations can be corrected by setting up a marketing intelligence function within the firm. This is called a marketing information system.

A marketing information system supplies relevant information to marketing managers. Some of the data fed into such a system are routinely collected. Gathering other data requires special marketing research projects. Information is a resource that requires effective management. This chapter deals with marketing intelligence, or information management.

\*Kenneth A. Hollander, "Audacious Audi Ad Echoes Parlin's Iconoclasm," *Marketing News,* January 27, 1978, p. 17.

## MARKETING RESEARCH

Although informal marketing reseach has been practiced ever since firms began to market their products, formal marketing research has developed during the past six or seven decades.[1] The key distinction is that the formal approach is systematic. As we will see later in the chapter, formal marketing research follows an orderly sequence in which each step is subordinated to a larger systematic whole. The purpose is to provide reliable information for decision making. Thus the American Marketing Association defines **marketing research** as "the systematic gathering, recording, and analyzing of data about problems relating to the marketing of goods and services."[2]

**marketing research**

Marketing research activities lend themselves to concentration in a marketing research department. Although company size and the need for research largely determine how the department is organized, it usually is wise to centralize research activity. The head of the research department should report to the marketing manager, who should provide for coordination between marketing research and technical research and development.

Good communication and coordination are essential if research objectives are to be stated clearly, the project is to be carried out efficiently, and the findings are to be used in decision making.[3] If help from outside specialists is needed, their efforts must be coordinated with those of internal company personnel.

### The Need for Marketing Research

Marketing research helps a firm to identify and evaluate market opportunity and to develop the effort needed to exploit it. It also helps to identify and solve problems. Marketing research is useful in a wide variety of activities, such as economic forecasting and sales forecasting, measuring market share, identifying market trends, measuring company and brand images, developing customer profiles, designing products and packages, locating warehouses and stores, processing orders, managing inventory, analyzing demand, measuring price perception and advertising effectiveness, analyzing audience characteristics, and scheduling advertisements.

Developing customer-oriented market offerings requires a firm to know who its present and potential customers are and what they want. The owner-operator of a small business deals face-to-face with customers and knows their wants. A more formalized approach to marketing research is needed in larger firms.

For example, the owner of a small neighborhood grocery store probably knows most of the store's customers personally. But large supermarket chain store managers often do not, even though information about their customers is just as important. Jewel Companies recently compiled the license numbers of cars in the parking lot at one of its food stores in Chicago and got a list of names and addresses of their owners from the Illinois secretary of state's office. A computer program identified the census tracts those customers lived in, thereby enabling Jewel to determine how far its customers traveled to the store and the type of neighborhoods they lived in.[4]

Although the need for marketing research is clear, ethical issues associated with it have received a lot of attention in recent years.[5] For example, have you ever been interviewed on the phone concerning your brand preferences for a certain type of product and suspected that the "researcher" was really trying to sell you something? Another major issue is the right to privacy. Some states are outlawing door-to-door surveys. Some people oppose the practice of companies that compile and sell mailing lists. If it is to fulfill its legitimate role, marketing research must be conducted ethically, especially in gathering data on competitors. For example, some firms have been known to bribe catalogue printers to get a sneak preview of their rivals' new products.

### Scientific Marketing Research

Marketing research is not a science in the sense that it seeks to develop ironclad laws. Chemists know the formula for water is $H_2O$. Every time two parts of hydrogen are mixed with one part oxygen, the result is water. But marketers deal with people and their behavior cannot be controlled.

If their research is to provide accurate and objective information to decision makers, marketing researchers must apply the scientific method in conducting their research. They should be orderly and rational in their approach, be objective and avoid interjecting personal bias into their work, be thorough and precise, and interpret their findings honestly. The scientific method is in evidence when researchers follow those principles in (1) identifying and defining problems, (2) formulating hypotheses, (3) testing hypotheses, (4) interpreting research findings, and (5) communicating their findings to decision makers.

### INFORMATION MANAGEMENT

Consider the problems three marketing managers face in deciding whether to go ahead with development of a new product. The first manager's desk is cluttered with pages of opinions, forecasts, and recommendations from the salesforce, finance and production personnel, and potential customers. Also included are detailed statistics on market test results. The second manager's desk top has only a pen and several pieces of paper, while the third manager has several reports summarizing the same type of data the first manager has in raw form. The first manager has too much data, the second has too little, and the third has relevant information. The third manager is benefiting from a systematic approach whereby the information needed for decision making has been pulled together.

Source: Xerox Corporation.

*An ad focusing on the crucial role of information management*

## Data and Information

Data and information, therefore, are not the same.[6]   Information is data that have been converted to a useful form for decision making—for solving a problem.   It is pertinent, relevant, timely, and it reduces risk in decision making.

Marketing managers face an immense volume of raw data coming from many sources, such as accounting records, reports from the sales-force, and so on.   The information explosion in marketing is the result of marketing managers' interacting with many kinds of internal and external creators and sources of data. Although computers can help in collecting and processing vast quantities of data with great speed and detail, the data flow must be managed to be useful to marketing managers.

New approaches to data presentation can help increase its usefulness. Computer graphics, a relatively new technique, converts numbers on computer printouts to charts, graphs, and three-dimensional images.[7] It helps convert data to information. The Cadillac division of General Motors puts geographic data and car registrations into a computer that develops a map showing where Cadillac owners live. Such a map could help in selecting locations for new dealerships and evaluating sales performance.[8]

Data can be classified as external or internal. External data are generated outside the firm. Examples are data on competitors' sales, customer buying habits, media rates, middlemen in the distribution channels, and government statistics. Internal data are generated within the firm. Examples are call reports by the company's salesforce, ad expenditures, credit records, and sales data.

Data also can be classified as recurrent and nonrecurrent. Recurrent data are collected routinely in everyday operations. Examples are sales data by salesperson, by sales territory, by brand, and by type of retail store. Nonrecurrent data are not collected routinely but may be collected to deal with a special problem.

Whether data are recurrent or nonrecurrent depends on the firm's data collection routine. Firms with computerized data collection systems routinely might break down aggregate sales data by individual retail outlet and by individual customer. A less sophisticated system might report sales data on individual salespersons and for the total company. Sales data for specific retail stores and individual customers are nonrecurrent data to that firm.

### Cost and Value of Information

Decision makers must consider the cost of collecting and converting data to information when specifying their informational needs. Seldom will they have all the information they want. Thus the cost of additional information must be weighed against its value for planning, implementing, and controlling marketing operations.[9]

Managers who fear decision making under risk want "all the information" before making decisions. At the other extreme are managers who want to make decisions without taking time to get information. In the middle are managers who weigh the value of additional information against its cost to improve the probability of making better decisions.

Determining the actual value of additional information is tough. Most managers estimate the cost and time needed to get it and judge whether it should be sought. Expected costs and expected value of additional information are compared with funds available for getting it.

In general, information should be sought if the expected value exceeds expected costs and the firm has no better use for the funds.[10]

## Information and the "Make-or-Buy" Decision

The discussion in this chapter assumes marketing managers generate their information internally. But many also buy it from commercial

*An ad that discusses a service offered by a supplier of marketing information*

Source: Donnelley Marketing.

suppliers. The A.C. Nielsen Company, for example, sells information about TV viewing habits of households in syndicated form. Donnelley Marketing is another commercial supplier that sells demographic data by zip code. (See Donnelley's marketing letter on page 233.) An information supplier might also be hired to collect information for a marketer's specific purposes.

Investment in marketing intelligence activities should never exceed its value to the marketer. If an information specialist can provide information more efficiently than the user, the specialist should be used. Outsiders often bring fresh insight into problems and may approach the task more objectively than company marketing or information managers.

The firm's salesforce also should be trained in intelligence gathering.[11] Their close contact with the market can make them a useful data source for manufacturers, retailers, and wholesalers. Too often, however, salespersons are trained only in selling techniques. We will return to this in Chapter 18.

## THE MARKETING INFORMATION SYSTEM

marketing information system

As we said earlier, the main distinction between informal and formal marketing research is that formal research is more systematic. In recent years, many firms have begun to view their overall marketing information management from a systems perspective. A **marketing information system** is "a structured, interacting complex of persons, machines, and procedures designed to generate an orderly flow of pertinent information collected from intra- and extra-firm sources, for use as the bases for decision making in specific responsibility areas of marketing management."[12] In this chapter we will refer to it as an MIS.[13]

An MIS gives marketing managers timely and relevant information to make better decisions. An MIS, however, cannot reduce decision making to an exact science. Experience, intuition, judgment, and information are brought together by marketing managers in their decision making. But relevant, timely, and accurate information is the key to good decisions. This includes monitoring the key environmental variables discussed in Chapter 2. Information managers (information suppliers) must understand the decisions marketing managers face and the information they need to make better decisions.[14] Good communication between them is necessary to reduce risk in decision making. It also helps the marketing manager (the information user) develop and implement good plans.

In the past, large firms with computers were the main users of the MIS concept. Computers have a superhuman ability to assemble, process, analyze, store, retrieve, evaluate, and disseminate data. They highlight the need for a system to convert data to information and manage its flow. More recently, the availability of small-scale, relatively inexpensive computers and time-sharing arrangements are making their use practical for smaller firms. Small firms also need a systematic approach to information management.

The relative importance of marketing research and the MIS depends on the scope of marketing information needs and the marketing research department's ability to meet them. Nonrecurrent information could not be supplied to decision makers without marketing research. Actually, the MIS and marketing research are interdependent. Information from a firm's MIS and information from marketing research projects are included in a firm's information bank. The trend among large firms, however, is to view overall marketing intelligence activities from the MIS perspective.

## MIS Design and Organization

The objectives information managers and information users set for a firm's MIS influence its design and how its functions will be performed. Although there is no one best model, the following functions are always performed by an MIS: (1) gathering data, (2) processing data, (3) analyzing data, (4) storing and retrieving data, (5) evaluating information, and (6) disseminating information to marketing managers.

The input is raw data. The output is relevant information. An MIS is a firm's master plan for developing and maintaining a flow of relevant marketing information to decision makers.

An MIS is a valuable tool for planning, implementing, and controlling marketing effort. Figure 9–1 brings together the important underlying concepts of an MIS.

We begin by defining the problem or opportunity and checking the availability of information in the information bank. If additional information is needed, we must decide if it is worth the cost. If it is not worth the cost, the decision is made without acquiring additional information. If we decide to acquire additional information, we gather, store, and retrieve external and internal data. These data are processed and analyzed and placed in the information bank for evaluation and dissemination.

In highly centralized firms the MIS usually is located at company headquarters. Highly decentralized firms usually have several independent divisional information systems. Decisions about their number and location should be guided by three basic goals: (1) minimizing duplication, (2) using information specialists to best advantage, and (3) maximizing the system's contribution to company-wide information requirements.

A firm that has a company-wide management information system should have its marketing information system integrated into it. The company-wide system provides information to all functional areas in the firm. Top management might appoint a director of intelligence services for the firm and place the entire information system under that person's control. Previously specialized areas like marketing research, sales fore-

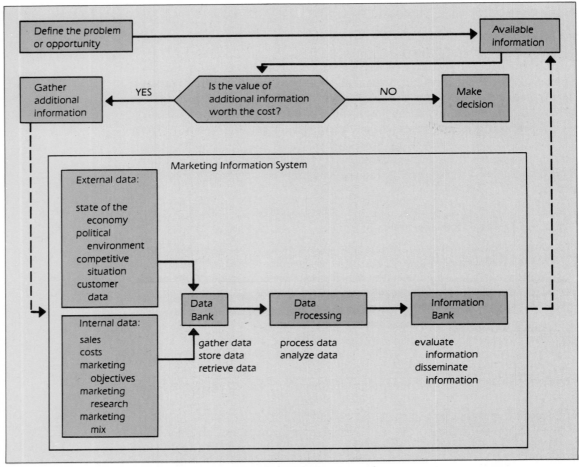

**Figure 9–1.  A marketing information system**

casting, and economic analysis would come under the intelligence director's control.[15]   Often, however, a firm's MIS is not integrated into a company-wide system because the heads of different departments often are reluctant to give up control over their respective information systems. Thus the MIS most often comes under the marketing manager's control.

An MIS can be divided into its recurrent and nonrecurrent data subsystems.   Doing this will help us to understand how an MIS works.

**recurrent data subsystem**

**The Recurrent Data Subsystem.**   The **recurrent data subsystem** (RDS) routinely performs all MIS functions on useful, recurrent internal and external data.   (See Table 9–1.)   This provides a continuous flow of data into the system for conversion to relevant information.   The RDS usually is computerized and has access to many sources of data.   Information users can directly interrogate the RDS when they understand its capacities and can use remote computer terminals to communicate with it.   Otherwise, they must go through information managers to get needed information.   A salesperson who wants a breakdown of his or her total sales by individual customer could get it from the RDS.   So could a sales

**Table 9–1.** *Major components of a recurrent data subsystem*

| | |
|---|---|
| Internal marketing data | Data on sales, inventories, product costs, accounts payable, and accounts receivable are supplied by the accounting department for use by marketers in planning, implementing, and controlling marketing operations. |
| External marketing data | Population projections, surveys of buying power, and trade association statistics help marketers keep up with developments in the marketing environment. |
| Data processing systems | The RDS requires data processing systems to gather, process, analyze, store, retrieve, evaluate, and disseminate information to marketing decision makers. |
| Analytical systems | In complex MISs mathematical models simulate the real world. Through simulation a marketer may be able to make better media-selection decisions and decide which price to use to accomplish advertising and pricing objectives. These models enable marketers to try out their decisions before implementing them in the real world. |

manager who wants total sales by individual salesperson or by sales territory.

**The Nonrecurrent Data Subsystem.** The **nonrecurrent data subsystem** (NDS) handles nonrecurring internal and external data generated because of special problems or to assess market opportunity. For example, the RDS might indicate the firm's average investment in inventory is increasing. This might lead to a research study of the causes so that corrective measures could be undertaken. Unlike the RDS, the NDS is not routinized. Marketing research, for all practical purposes, is synonymous with the NDS.

*nonrecurrent data sub-system*

## THE MARKETING RESEARCH PROCESS

A marketing manager must communicate his or her informational needs to the firm's director of marketing research, who, perhaps with assistance from outside research specialists, conducts the research project. The marketing manager does not have to be an expert on research techniques but must be able to state informational needs and assess the research findings. The researcher must be an expert on research techniques and be able to understand and satisfy the marketing manager's informational needs. Their relationship is complementary, but it is the marketing manager's job to solve the problem for which research is needed.

The nature of a given research project depends on the problem or opportunity being researched. In the following discussion we present a logical approach to the marketing research process. (See Figure 9–2.) We will discuss each of the steps outlined in Figure 9–2 in order to get an overall understanding of the process. Following that discussion we will elaborate on several aspects of the research process to gain deeper

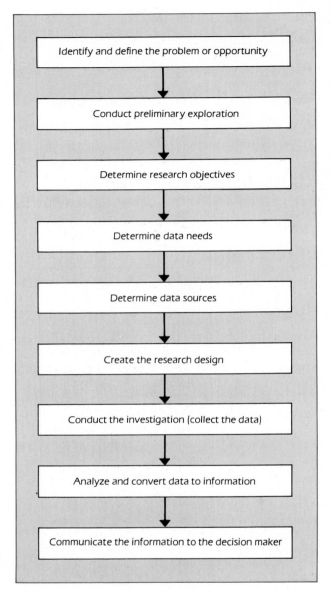

```
┌─────────────────────────────────────────────┐
│  Identify and define the problem or opportunity │
└─────────────────────────────────────────────┘
                      ↓
┌─────────────────────────────────────────────┐
│          Conduct preliminary exploration        │
└─────────────────────────────────────────────┘
                      ↓
┌─────────────────────────────────────────────┐
│          Determine research objectives          │
└─────────────────────────────────────────────┘
                      ↓
┌─────────────────────────────────────────────┐
│             Determine data needs                │
└─────────────────────────────────────────────┘
                      ↓
┌─────────────────────────────────────────────┐
│             Determine data sources              │
└─────────────────────────────────────────────┘
                      ↓
┌─────────────────────────────────────────────┐
│            Create the research design           │
└─────────────────────────────────────────────┘
                      ↓
┌─────────────────────────────────────────────┐
│   Conduct the investigation (collect the data)  │
└─────────────────────────────────────────────┘
                      ↓
┌─────────────────────────────────────────────┐
│       Analyze and convert data to information    │
└─────────────────────────────────────────────┘
                      ↓
┌─────────────────────────────────────────────┐
│ Communicate the information to the decision maker │
└─────────────────────────────────────────────┘
```

*Figure 9–2.*
*The nine steps in a*
*marketing research*
*project*

insight into the nature and practice of marketing research. We will elaborate on experimentation, survey methods, research instruments, and sampling.

### Identify and Define the Problem or Opportunity

No research project should begin until the marketing manager has communicated clearly to the researcher the nature of the problem or opportunity. A physician who defines a patient's problem as "you are not feeling well" is not helping the patient. Doctors are expected to take this general problem and work toward diagnosing more specific problems that lend themselves to solution. Care also is needed to avoid identifying only symptoms of deep-seated problems. A doctor who identifies a patient's problem as headaches and prescribes aspirin is relieving only a symptom if the root problem is a brain tumor.

Identifying and defining the problem is the first step in the process of finding a solution. Failure to meet sales objectives, an excessive increase in uncollectible accounts, and abnormal turnover of salespersons are signals, or symptoms, of deeper problems. Marketers want to identify and define the problem(s) that is causing these symptoms to appear. Marketers, like physicians, will find that a poor diagnosis leads to an ineffective solution of the problem.

For example, a marketer who defines the problem as "declining sales" is only tipping the researcher off to the general nature of the problem. This is only a symptom and the researcher must probe deeper to identify the problem. The researcher can then develop a clearly defined and researchable problem. Doing this requires the researcher to conduct a preliminary exploration of the problem situation.

## Conduct a Preliminary Exploration

After the decision maker states what he or she feels is the problem, the researcher begins a preliminary exploration of the problem situation. Confirming or rejecting the problem as stated by the decision maker is a crucial phase of the research project.

Talking to knowledgeable persons in the firm helps the researcher develop familiarity with the problem. It also may shed insight into the manager's reasons for believing the problem is as he or she stated it. This is very important when the researcher is an outside consultant.

For example, a sales manager who notices sales are declining might identify the problem as ineffective advertising. The researcher, therefore, is asked to investigate the effectiveness of the firm's advertising. In talking with salespersons, wholesalers, and retailers of the firm's products, however, the researcher discovers that middleman support began declining when a rival firm introduced a new product that gives them a bigger margin on sales. They make more profit by selling the rival's product. This gives the researcher a new perspective on the problem. It also makes it clear that an investigation of advertising effectiveness will not solve the problem. A different type of research project is needed.

Some researchers distinguish between a situation analysis and an informal investigation. An investigation limited to discussions with company personnel and research of company records and library materials is called a *situation analysis.* When the investigation is broadened to include persons outside the firm, such as suppliers, wholesalers, retailers, the firm's customers, and rival firms' employees and customers, it is called an *informal investigation.*

### Determine Research Objectives

hypotheses

The researcher now has a better feel for the problem. The earlier steps help in formulating hypotheses that fit the problem. **Hypotheses** are tentative explanations of the problem formulated on the basis of insight and knowledge about the problem. The hypotheses may be right or wrong. The research objectives can be stated as hypotheses to test. This requires the researcher to collect data. The data may lead to acceptance of some hypotheses and rejection of others. In either case, they become conclusions that the researcher draws from the research and presents to the marketing manager.

In our example the preliminary exploration might lead the researcher to reason that sales are declining because (1) product quality and price are too high and/or (2) middlemen do not earn an adequate margin and/or (3) the product is becoming obsolete. If the test of the first hypothesis leads to its acceptance, one conclusion is that product quality and price are too high. If it is rejected, we can conclude that quality and price are not too high and proceed to test the other hypotheses.

Thus the hypotheses guide the research effort and suggest what data are needed. In real-world marketing research projects the number of hypotheses formulated for testing is limited because of time and budget constraints.

### Determine Data Needs

The researcher's hypotheses guide the data collection effort. To test the hypothesis "sales are declining because product quality and price are too high" the researcher would want to know (1) customer expectations about product quality and price, (2) what products customers consider to be substitutes, and (3) the prices of competing products.

primary data

Researchers use primary and secondary data. **Primary data** are originated and collected for a specific problem. The data have not been collected previously and must be generated by original research through observation and/or inquiry. A big advantage is that the data relate specifically to the problem at hand. In gathering them the researcher may sharpen the research project's focus and uncover new problems. The main disadvantages are the cost and time required to collect primary data.

secondary data

**Secondary data** already exist; they are historical data gathered by people either inside or outside the firm to meet their needs. If those needs are similar to the researcher's needs, secondary data can be useful. Although usually cheaper and faster to collect than primary data, researchers must consider the relevance, accuracy, credibility, and timeliness of secondary data.

Data on customer expectations about the firm's product and price are primary data if they have not been collected previously by the firm. To gather these data the researcher may actually have to observe customer behavior or question customers by mail, telephone, or in person. Sales data obtained from accounting records are secondary data.

**Table 9–2.** *Illustrative sources of marketing information*

---
### General Sources
---

Public libraries
Bureaus of business research in colleges and universities
Government agencies
Trade associations
Chambers of Commerce

---
### Specialized Sources for Client Subscribers
---

A. C. Nielsen Company
Pulse, Inc.
Opinion Research Corporation
Market Facts, Inc.
Market Research Corporation of America
Donnelley Marketing

---
### Specific Publications
---

*Statistical Abstract of the United States*
*Sales Management Magazine: Annual Survey of Buying Power*
*Monthly Catalog of U.S. Government Publications*
*The Wall Street Journal Index*
*Index of Publications of Bureaus of Business and Economic Research*
*Measuring Markets: A Guide to the Use of Federal and State Statistical Data*
*Marketing Information Guide*
*Census of Population, Current Population Reports*
*Census of Manufactures*
*Census of Business*
*Census of Housing*
*Survey of Current Business*
*Economic Indicators*
*Facts for Marketers*
*County and City Data Book*

---

## Determine Data Sources

Research data can be derived from either a secondary source or a primary source. Both sources can be either internal or external to a firm. The major internal secondary source is company records. Major external secondary sources include libraries, trade associations, and government publications. Using secondary sources can save time and money in the preliminary exploration stage. It may eliminate the need to tap primary sources. Cost savings are possible when such data are used wisely, but historical data should be used only when historical facts can legitimately be projected into the future.

It is important to understand that secondary data can be collected from an originating source or a nonoriginating source. Population data for Minnesota can be secured from detailed census publications (the originating source) or from the *Statistical Abstract of the United States* (nonoriginating source), which takes its data from the detailed census publications. Using the originating source usually is better because the data are more complete and often more accurate. It also provides more explanation of definitions and the research methodology used in collecting the data. This helps researchers to evaluate the usefulness of the data for their needs.

Primary sources of data are hard to classify. Knowing what primary data are needed gives the researcher a hint about who might have it. The major internal source is company personnel. Important external sources are retailers, wholesalers, customers, and competitors.[16]

### Create the Research Design

research design

The **research design** is the grand plan for conducting the research investigation. This probably is the single most important step in the research process and the one in which terminology is most confusing. In the following discussion we will classify marketing research by function and by methodology.[17]

**Functional Categories.** Four major functional categories of marketing research are (1) exploratory, (2) descriptive, (3) causal, and (4) predictive.

exploratory research

**Exploratory research** is conducted when more information about the problem or opportunity is needed, tentative hypotheses need to be formulated more specifically, or new hypotheses are needed. Examples of this type of research are the situation analysis, the informal investigation, and the case study. The purpose is to gather data that suggest meaningful research questions. Exploratory research may generate hypotheses but it does not test them. The researcher is exploring the problem or opportunity's background to gain familiarity and insight. A firm considering diversifying into new lines of business may use exploratory research to learn more about opportunities outside its traditional line of business.

focus group interview

Researchers often use the **focus group interview** technique in exploratory research.[18] A moderator leads eight to twelve people through unstructured discussion on a given topic to develop hypotheses that might lead to more specific research projects. A firm that developed a new filter for auto air-conditioning systems used the technique to help formulate hypotheses for identifying potential market targets, to determine the product's advantages and disadvantages from the consumer viewpoint, and to identify specific questions to include in a questionnaire. The

# We never tailor your problem to fit our solution.

We have no allegiance to any standardized methodology because we approach every problem as unique, deserving its own solution. National Analysts offers you custom research—a solution to your problem, not someone else's.

It starts with our people: as a group, the most highly trained and experienced professionals available today. They have no methodological axes to grind, because they are familiar with all methods of data collection, at any level of depth, and any level of sampling precision.

Our people also analyze data in the way that is most appropriate for your problem. We cover the spectrum from pure qualitative analysis, through standard cross-tabs, to the most sophisticated multivariate statistical analyses.

In addition, our people interpret the data. Our final presentations run a high proportion of text to tables, representing not only findings, but actionable conclusions.

Because we understand the importance of the decisions you will make based on research, we believe in a quality, custom approach to your research problem. You can believe in it, too.

**National Analysts**

Offices in: Philadelphia (215) 627-8110,
Chicago (312) 346-1900, New York (212) 697-1900

*An ad underscoring the importance of fitting research methodology to the client's needs*

Source: Booz, Allen and Hamilton, Inc.

interviews identified families in which one or more members had allergy or respiratory problems and persons seriously concerned about air pollution as good potential targets.[19]

**descriptive research**

**Descriptive research** assumes the problem or opportunity has been defined clearly. The purpose of this type of research is to describe some market segment or other group of people by developing summary measures or statistics on it. The marketer's job is to find adequate methods for collecting and measuring data. A firm that wants to break down total industry sales into market shares for individual firms in the industry would conduct a descriptive investigation. A brewery that wants to know how many females between eighteen and twenty-five years of age drink beer at least once a week also would conduct a descriptive investigation.

**causal research**

**Causal research** is conducted to test hypotheses about causal relationships between an independent and a dependent variable. A descriptive investigation may suggest that a cut in price leads to increased sales of a product. The investigation, however, cannot tell us definitely if the price cut was the actual cause of the sales increase. Sales may have increased because of other factors, such as an increase in customer buying power or a decline in competitors' marketing efforts. The causal investigation would try to show that the independent variable (price cut) is the cause of the dependent variable (increased sales) or that the price cut is not the cause of increased sales. This requires the marketer to keep all variables except price and sales constant. This, at best, is hard to do.

**predictive research**

**Predictive research** is used to forecast future values. Sales forecast-

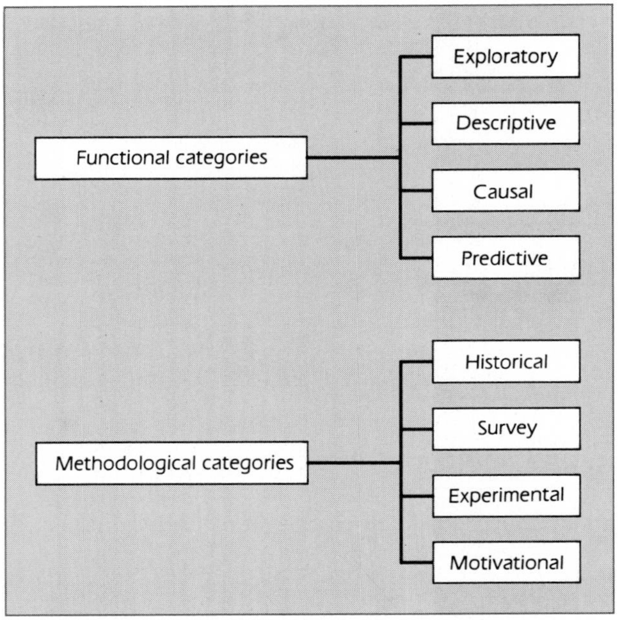

*Figure 9–3.*
*Classifying*
*marketing research*
*projects*

ing, as we saw in Chapter 8, may involve sampling, questionnaire design, computer analysis of data, error estimation, and so on to predict sales. Political pollsters use predictive research to predict how many voters will vote for a particular candidate in an upcoming election.

**Methodological Categories.** Four methodological categories of marketing research are (1) historical, (2) survey, (3) experimental, and (4) motivational.

**Historical research** involves using past experiences in finding solutions to marketing problems. For example, in projecting future population and GNP, marketers often engage in historical research. The preliminary exploration stage in most marketing research projects involves historical research.

**historical research**

**Survey research** is the type of research with which most of us are familiar. Surveys usually are done in person, by telephone, or by mail.

**survey research**

**Experimental research** involves observing the effect on a dependent variable (usually sales) of manipulating independent variables like advertising and price. A researcher who wants to estimate how many units of a product would be demanded at different possible prices could manipulate price while attempting to hold all other variables constant.

**experimental research**

**Motivational research** is based on the theories and techniques of the behavioral sciences, especially psychology. It is an attempt to discover the "whys" of consumer behavior.

**motivational research**

## Conduct the Investigation

If the researcher can get the needed data from secondary sources, the problem becomes one of searching for and securing the data. This requires a good knowledge of secondary data and sources. Good researchers always consult others who may have faced a similar problem to benefit from their knowledge. But when primary data are needed, the researcher must collect them through observation and/or inquiry. In collecting data, the researcher implements the research design. Even large firms

**Table 9–3.** *Primary and secondary data sources and data collection methods*

| Type of Data | Examples of Sources | Data Collection Methods |
|---|---|---|
| Primary data | Internal: company personnel | Observation: personal |
| | | mechanical |
| | External: retailers | Inquiry: mail survey |
| |       wholesalers |       telephone survey |
| |       customers |       personal interview |
| |       competitors |       survey |
| Secondary data | Internal: company records | Search for and secure data |
| |       marketing data bank | previously collected |
| | External: general sources | |
| |       specialized sources | |
| |       (by subscription) | |
| |       specific publications | |

with their own marketing research departments sometimes use outside specialists to help in gathering and analyzing data. (See Table 9–3.)

**Observational Method of Data Collection.** The **observational method** involves gathering data by observing and recording. Most of this research is conducted by trained observers (personal observation), but some is done by mechanical and electronic devices (mechanical observation). In some cases both methods are combined. A retailer who wants to study the effectiveness of a new merchandise display might station an observer nearby to record the number of people who pass the display, stop to examine the merchandise, and purchase the displayed products. A manufacturer of breakfast cereals who wants to study the attention-producing value of a new package might station observers equipped with cameras and tape recorders behind the supermarket aisles where the cereal is shelved.

Observation may be more objective than interviewing because no questions are asked. Observers, however, interpret the behavior they witness. This interpretation may be inaccurate and/or biased. A shopper may pick up a package of cereal, examine it, and walk away without buying it. Maybe the shopper wanted it but did not have enough money to buy it. An observer, however, might interpret this behavior as lack of interest in the product.

Mechanical observational devices include Disney World's turnstile counters that monitor visitor traffic flow, jukebox counters that keep track of the number of times a record is played, and the mechanical device that counts the cars that pass through a major highway intersection. A. C. Neilsen Company uses an Audimeter in developing rating points for TV shows. It records when the TV set is on and to which channel it is tuned. This is more practical than stationing human observers in the sample households, but even the Audimeter has its limitations. It does not record how many (if any) persons are viewing a program to which the TV set is tuned.

We discussed the Universal Product Code (UPC) in Chapter 2. (Figure 9–4 is a UPC symbol.) One research firm made use of the UPC as

observational method

*Figure 9–4.*
*A Universal Product Code (UPC) symbol*

Section III  MATCHING MARKET TARGETS WITH CAPABILITIES AND RESOURCES

a data collection device. The firm gave selected households in test markets identification cards to use in supermarkets it had supplied with scanning equipment. The scanner signaled the computer not only to display the product's name and price on a display screen at the checkout, print that information on an itemized receipt for the customer, and deduct from inventory each item sold, but also to send a list of items each customer bought to the firm's central computer. Customers' purchases, therefore, could be identified by price, brand, and size without customers' having to keep written diaries.[20]

**Inquiry Method of Data Collection.** In the **inquiry method** data are gathered through asking people questions by mail, phone, or in person. We will discuss this method in greater detail later, in the section on survey methods.

inquiry method

Often, the inquiry method is used together with observation. In a personal interview survey, for example, the interviewer will ask the respondent questions but also jot down notes regarding his or her sex, race, apparent social class, and so on based on observation.

Good research design, however, helps in conducting the investigation. A good design reduces the problem of supervising and controlling the investigation. Although detailed discussion of the problems in conducting the investigation is beyond our scope we can give an example. It illustrates the problem of interviewer bias when data are collected through inquiry.[21]

Suppose a magazine publisher wants to research readership habits of young men. An interviewer's style of dress, sex, age, and race might have some effect on the respondent. Thus the responses different interviewers get may vary because of differences in these characteristics among them. The researcher could attempt to gauge the extent of this interviewer bias by comparing responses received by different interviewers.

Interviewer bias also results when interviewers are inexperienced and/or do not understand their job. Extreme efforts to reduce costs may lead to hiring poorly trained interviewers. The result will be a poor survey and poor survey results mean a poor research project. The adage "garbage in, garbage out" applies here.

## Analyze and Convert Data to Information

After the investigation the data collected must be analyzed and interpreted. This may lead to acceptance or rejection of the research hypothesis. Data analysis techniques should be planned in advance of data collection as part of the research design. For example, more data might be collected if computers are used than if the analysis is to be done by hand. Evaluating data as it becomes available during the investigation also helps the researcher gain insight into areas that perhaps should be examined in greater depth during analysis and interpretation. It may help in identifying other techniques for data analysis. These techniques range from the very simple to the very complex, and in some cases outside specialists are used. Nevertheless, the researcher's job in this step is to

Chapter 9  MARKETING RESEARCH      247

**Table 9–4.** *A hypothetical cross-tabulation example: most important cigarette selection factors for respondents cross-tabulated by amount of usage*

| Selection Factors | Light Smokers | Heavy Smokers | Total |
|---|---|---|---|
| Taste | 30% | 80% | 55.0% |
| Length | 10 | 15 | 12.5 |
| Tar and nicotine content | 60 | 5 | 32.5 |
| Totals | 100% | 100% | 100% |

study the data to determine its meaning in order to convert it to relevant information for decision makers.

Collected data must be edited, coded, and tabulated. Editing helps eliminate errors in the data before coding and tabulating. Editors go through completed questionnaires to eliminate those completed by the wrong respondent and those that are illegible. They also may contact interviewers who submitted questionnaires with unanswered questions to determine why they were unanswered. Editing also involves setting up categories for the data in accordance with the research design. In a survey of cigarette smokers to determine brand usage, these categories might consist of brands, types of cigarettes (filtered, unfiltered, menthol, etc.) city size, household income, and so on.

Coding assigns the data to proper categories. For example, Carlton 100s might be coded brand number 1 and Salem, brand 2, while cities of 20,000 population or less might be coded city size number 1, those with one million or more people, number 5, and so on. Sometimes questionnaires are precoded (the code is printed on the questionnaires themselves) to permit key-punch operators to key-punch responses directly from the questionnaire.

Tabulating involves counting the numbers of items that fall into established categories. Cross-tabulations also are used. Table 9–4 is a hypothetical table that cross-tabulates amount of usage of cigarettes with taste, size, and tar and nicotine content.

## Communicate the Information

A communication problem often exists between line managers and staff personnel. The director of marketing research is a staff specialist who is familiar with the technical jargon of marketing research. The marketing manager is a line executive who often lacks familiarity with this jargon. After converting data to information the research director must communicate it to the marketing manager.[22]

Reporting research findings involves preparing a concise report that outlines in an understandable and interesting manner the researcher's findings and recommendations. It should be supplemented by appendixes that discuss research design, technical aspects of the investigation, and data analysis. Finally, an oral presentation helps in selling the research results to the decision maker. This gives the decision maker a chance to ask questions and helps him or her to use the findings in developing marketing strategy.

Now that we have completed the outline of the steps in the marketing research process, we will examine several aspects in greater depth: experimentation, survey methods, research instruments, and sampling.

Experimentation, as suggested earlier, is concerned with observing the effect on a dependent variable of manipulating independent variables. We are discussing it in greater detail primarily because of its importance in test marketing. As we will see in Chapter 11, many firms test new products in test markets before deciding whether to introduce them to the entire market. The purpose is to shed light on a product's chances for success.

Survey methods are concerned with getting primary data through inquiry. You may recall from our earlier discussion of step 7 in a marketing research project (conduct the investigation) that primary data can be collected through observation and/or inquiry. We discussed the observational method in some detail but deferred discussion of the inquiry method.

Marketing researchers use research instruments to gather data. The inquiry method requires the use of questionnaires. Thus we will discuss questionnaire design and interviewing techniques in some detail.

Finally, most marketing research is based on sampling. We will discuss how researchers go about selecting sampling units. This is an important consideration in creating the research design, step 6 in a marketing research project.

## EXPERIMENTATION

Experimental research can be conducted in a laboratory or a field setting. Respondents could be asked to come to a lab where a researcher is testing several types of packages for potato chips before introducing them on the market. Respondents give their reactions to the different packages. The only independent variable operating is package size. Thus the lab setting is unlike the real world where other variables might influence consumer reaction. For example, a lower-priced rival brand is not in the lab, but may be on the supermarket shelf.

Researchers conduct experimentation in the real world when they use a field setting. The setting is more realistic but harder to control. Field research involves conducting a small-scale trial of a solution to a problem. For example, an advertising manager who wants to test a proposed newspaper ad's effectiveness would select two cities similar in population characteristics, income distribution, and so on. One is the control city and the other is the test city. The manager formulates a null hypothesis: "sales will be the same in both cities." The ad appears in the test city's newspaper but not in the control city's newspaper. After the ad appears sales of the product are recorded. Any difference in sales in the two cities is attributed to the ad.

Three assumptions are made: (1) two or more similar cities can be found, (2) the control city's environment can be controlled, and (3) test conditions are the same as those that will exist when the ad is run in the real market. But locating two fairly identical cities for testing is not always easy. Also, if a rival withdraws its product in the control city, sales of the researcher's product might increase. If test city sales are lower than those in the control city, the researcher might incorrectly conclude the ad is ineffective. Thus it is practically impossible to ensure that test conditions are the same as those that will exist in the real market. A major use of experimentation is in test marketing, as we will see in Chapter 11.

## SURVEY METHODS

Survey methods deal with obtaining data from respondents by mail, telephone, or personal interview. Three types of data that might be sought are facts, opinions, and motives.

factual survey

In a **factual survey** respondents are asked questions like "What brand of toothpaste do you use?" The purpose is to gather facts unavailable from secondary sources. The main problems are the respondent's inability to remember, unwillingness to answer, giving untrue answers to "help" or "mess up" the researcher, or inability to give a specific answer to a specific question—a price shopper regularly might buy the cheapest brand available, so the brand might vary from purchase to purchase.

opinion survey

In an **opinion survey** respondents are asked to give opinions, although they believe they are reporting facts. For example, "Which department store carries the highest quality merchandise?" This type of survey has the same problems as the factual survey. It also may require respondents to form opinions hastily. Their answers might be different if they were given more time to think about them.

motivational survey

In a **motivational survey** respondents are asked to interpret and report their motives. These are "why" questions—"Why do you buy Colgate toothpaste?" The same problems are present here as in factual and opinion surveys. But there are others. Respondents may not know why they do what they do, may know why but are unable to explain it, or may know why but do not want to tell the truth, so they refuse to answer or they make up an answer that will be socially acceptable. In many cases potential respondents consider all types of surveys to be an invasion of their privacy.

## Mail Survey

The mail survey is favored when the geographical area to be covered is large, the questions are simple, time is not a major factor, and the questionnaire is relatively short.[23]   Respondents can answer at their convenience and there are no interviewers to bias the results.

Among the major problems are low response rates, often less than 10 percent, because some recipients put the questionnaire aside and forget it or they discard it as junk mail; misunderstanding of difficult questions because there is no interviewer to clarify them; the difficulty of compiling or the high cost of acquiring an up-to-date and accurate mailing list; the difficulty of getting in-depth information about respondents and their answers because no interviewer is present; respondents' reluctance to give written answers to some types of questions; the high cost per returned questionnaire when only a few are returned.   Also, returned questionnaires may be answered by the wrong family member, such as a child who answers a questionnaire about household buying intentions; trickle in at different times, which may mean they are not comparable to each other—some respondents, for example, may answer a survey about car preferences before the start of the new model year and some may answer after; be answered by people who are not representative of the group to whom the questionnaire was sent, such as people who especially enjoy answering them and who respond very heavily while others simply do not respond; and be filled in by people who supply "joke" answers because the survey is so impersonal.

## Telephone Survey

The telephone survey is favored when the questionnaire is short, time is limited, and research funds are scarce.[24]   The response rate usually is higher than for mail surveys because it is more convenient for respondents to cooperate.   Well-trained interviewers can establish rapport quickly and ask respondents probing questions.   Coincidental measurement also is possible.   For example, interviewers can ask people questions about which TV programs or ads they are watching while the programs or ads actually are on the air.   Reactions to a televised political debate can be surveyed while the debate is being telecast or immediately after.

But the telephone survey has its limitations also.   These include people's reluctance to talk to strangers on the phone, the timing of the call when people are too busy or are not at home, getting an up-to-date and accurate list of telephone subscribers, the lack of rapport between respondent and interviewer due to such factors as voice inflection, the fact that the questionnaire must be short and simple because people may become bored and hang up or supply inaccurate answers, the inability to use visual aids in conducting the survey, and the fact that not all households have phones or listed phone numbers.

In recent years new techniques have been developed to draw telephone samples without having to rely on phone directories that do not list all phone subscribers. One type of nondirectory telephone sample is generated by random-digit dialing.[25] With this procedure at least some digits of each sample telephone number are generated randomly. Thus the sample will include both listed and unlisted numbers. One potential disadvantage, however, is that some unassigned telephone numbers (not actual working phone numbers) will be drawn and must be called.

### Personal Interview Survey

The personal interview survey is the most direct type of survey because respondent and intevviewer are in face-to-face contact. The interviewer can make observations about the respondent's social class and answer questions about the questionnaire. Audiovisual aids can be used and rapport can be built, which may make it possible to conduct longer interviews. Whenever a survey requires respondents to do something they cannot do by mail or phone—taste a new flavor of soft drink, for example, or smell a new brand of air freshener—a personal interview survey is necessary.

Some limitations of personal interview surveys are respondents' refusal to talk to strangers, especially those they suspect will try to sell them something; the not-at-home problem, which often results in expensive call-backs or attempts to reach respondents by phone or mail, or

**Table 9–5.** *Comparison of mail, telephone, and personal interview surveys*

|  | *Mail Survey* | *Telephone Survey* | *Personal Interview Survey* |
|---|---|---|---|
| Cost (assuming a good response rate) | often lowest | usually in-between | usually highest |
| Ability to probe | no personal contact or observation | some chance for gathering additional data through elaboration on questions, but no personal observation | greatest opportunity for observation, building rapport, and additional probing |
| Respondent ability to complete at own convenience | yes | no | perhaps, if interview time is prearranged with respondent |
| Interviewer bias | no chance | some, perhaps due to voice inflection, etc. | greatest chance |
| Ability to decide who actually responds to the questionnaire within a household | least | some | greatest |
| Sampling problems | up-to-date, accurate mailing list and low response rates | up-to-date, accurate phone subscriber list, unlisted numbers, no phones, refusals | not-at-homes and refusals |

possibly deleting them from the survey, which may bias the results; interviewer bias from interpreting the same question in different ways for different respondents or from the effect the demographic characteristics of the interviewer has on the answers and on the number and types of respondents who will participate; the high cost of hiring and supervising personal interviewers; and the lack of skillful interviewers and the high cost of training them.   (See Table 9–5.)

TELLUS is an electronic push-button questionnaire developed in recent years for use in conducting interviews in retail stores.   Instead of personal interviewers asking shoppers questions, a computer asks the questions.   A TELLUS unit is placed in a store and a large display sign invites shoppers to answer the questions by choosing from among the answers provided and pushing buttons.[26]   The research is therefore cheaper to conduct and the data are collected faster than when personal interviews are used.

Regardless of the survey method, the researcher must develop a questionnaire.   This requires planning and skill.

## THE RESEARCH INSTRUMENT

Marketing researchers use research instruments to collect data (step 7 in the marketing research process).   As we saw earlier, primary data can

**Table 9–5.**   *cont.*

|  | Mail Survey | Telephone Survey | Personal Interview Survey |
|---|---|---|---|
| Impersonality | greatest | some due to lack of face-to-face contact | least |
| Complex questions | least suitable | somewhat suitable | most suitable |
| Visual aids in survey | little opportunity | no opportunity | greatest opportunity |
| Opportunity for building rapport | least | some | greatest |
| Potential negative respondent reaction | "junk mail" | "junk calls" | invasion of privacy |
| Interviewer control over interview environment | least | some in selection of time to call | greatest |
| Time lag between soliciting and receiving response | greatest | least | may be considerable if a large area is involved |
| Suitable types of questions | simple, mostly dichotomous (yes–no) and multiple-choice questions | some opportunity for open-ended questions, especially if interview is recorded | greatest opportunity for open-ended questions |
| Requirement for technical skills in conducting interview | least | medium | greatest |

be collected through observation and/or inquiry. Examples of research instruments include tally sheets, questionnaires, and mechanical instruments, such as tape recorders and cameras. These instruments are chosen and developed to get the data needed to satisfy the research project's data needs. Thus the selection of research instruments also is related to determining data needs and sources and creating the research design. The discussion that follows focuses on questionnaire design because questionnaires are the research instrument most often used to collect primary data.

### Questionnaire Design

Regardless of the type of survey, questions should be worded properly, should be realistic, and should be asked in the proper sequence. Questionnaire design is an art. Care is needed to avoid asking questions that

**Figure 9–5.** *A poorly designed questionnaire*

| Questions | Potential Respondent Reaction |
|---|---|
| 1. Please state your exact income. $ _____ | Do you mean take-home pay? Annual or monthly? Should I include interest on my savings account? What business of yours is my exact income? |
| 2. Kindly check your marital status.<br>single _____ married _____ | Really, I'm not either. I'm legally separated from my spouse. |
| 3. Kindly check the region of the United States in which you live.<br>south _____ west _____<br>east _____ north _____ | I live in Chicago. I'm not sure which I should check. |
| 4. Kindly check your age group.<br>young _____<br>middle-aged _____<br>elderly _____ | I'm 32. I'm not sure if that is young or middle-aged. |
| 5. Kindly check your social class.<br>upper _____<br>middle _____<br>lower _____ | I'm not rich but I'm not poor either. I guess I'm in the middle class. |
| 6. Do you think transverse-mounted motors in cars help to promote fuel efficiency?<br>yes _____<br>no _____ | What is a transverse-mounted motor? |
| 7. Does your present car have any foreign-made components?<br>yes _____<br>no _____ | Which car do you mean? I own two. I don't know if either has any foreign-made parts. Both are Fords but maybe some parts were imported. |

require information not readily available to respondents—asking a father what brand of tennis shoes his teen-age daughter buys, for example; that create suspicion or antagonism—asking what the family income is (if this is needed, ask at the end of the questionnaire and provide income ranges); that lead the respondent—"Do you use Safeguard soap?"; and that create misunderstanding—"What brand of tomato paste do you regularly use?" (what does "regularly" mean?).

The choice of words can make the difference between a good and a poor questionnaire. They should be simple and unambiguous so that they will mean the same thing to all respondents. Pretesting a questionnaire on a sample of respondents before using it in the full survey is advisable. Figure 9–5 is a hypothetical questionnaire prepared by a novice researcher to test consumer feelings about foreign-made cars. What do you think of the questionnaire?

**Figure 9–5.** *cont.*

| Questions | Potential Respondent Reaction |
|---|---|
| 8. If you were to be involved in a collision with another car would you rather be in a heavy car than in a small unsafe car? <br><br> yes _____ <br> no _____ | What a leading question! I'd be a fool to say no the way this question is stated. |
| 9. Don't you think air bags should be required equipment on all new cars since they make for safer cars and save lives? <br><br> yes _____ <br> no _____ | Again, how could I possibly say no? |
| 10. Would you buy a car made in a foreign country if it meant a layoff for another American autoworker? <br><br> yes _____ <br> no _____ | Here's another leading question. I don't want to be the cause of somebody's losing a job. |
| 11. Next time you buy a car will you buy for mileage, safety, or appearance? (check one) <br><br> mileage _____ <br> safety _____ <br> appearance _____ | I just bought a new car last month. I have no idea what I'll be looking for when I buy a new one perhaps two years from now. I'll probably consider all three factors, plus price. |
| 12. Would you buy a cheap American-made car? <br><br> yes _____ <br> no _____ | What does "cheap" mean? A low-priced or a poorly made car? |

### Interviewing Techniques

Researchers use several interviewing techniques. These include direct, depth, and projective interviewing.

**direct interviewing**

**Direct Interviewing.** In **direct interviewing** questions are designed to get specific responses to direct questions. An example is "How many miles per gallon of gasoline do you get with your present car?" The interviewer jots down specific answers by checking the correct response:

——1–16 miles
——17–25 miles
——26–34 miles
——over 34 miles

Direct questions elicit direct responses and are used when survey results are to be analyzed quantitatively. For example, the researcher can determine very quickly the percentages of all respondents who selected each of the four possible responses.

**depth interviewing**

**Depth Interviewing.** A researcher who wants more in-depth responses might use **depth interviewing.** "What do you think about your car's fuel economy?" This open-ended question permits respondents to talk and interact with the interviewer, who might interject responses such as "Why?" and "Tell me more."

Skilled interviewers can use open-ended questions to elicit more qualitative information. Respondents who say they get seventeen to twenty-five miles per gallon do not provide much information about whether they consider that satisfactory, or if better mileage might be an effective feature to use in advertising a new car. When open-ended questions are used the number of people interviewed usually is smaller than in the direct-question surveys. Also, responses to open-ended questions are harder to tabulate because they are not as clear-cut.

**projective techniques**

**Projective Interviewing.** **Projective techniques** may be used if the researcher believes the respondent will refuse or be unable to provide needed information.[27] The technique is to make respondents believe they are answering the questions for somebody else, not themselves. If the technique is successful, the respondents project their own feelings and opinions into the situation.

In a word-association test the respondent is asked to say the first word that comes to mind when given a stimulus word by the interviewer. This can be useful in studying ad appeals and brand and company images. If respondents tend to respond to the company's name or to one of its brands as "cheap," or "inferior," an image problem exists.

In the psychodrama and in the cartoon test respondents are asked to project themselves into a marketing situation. In a cartoon test a character might be drawn sitting in a car talking to a service station attendant. A balloon (like those in the comic strips) over the attendant's head might say, "Can I fill it up?" The balloon over the motorist's head contains no words.   Respondents provide the answer by projecting themselves into the motorist's situation.

Depth and projective interviewing are techniques of motivational research.   Although part of marketing research, motivational research, as we saw earlier, seeks to develop deeper insight into the "whys" of consumer behavior.   Traditional marketing research focuses on overt aspects of consumer behavior—who buys, where they buy, when they buy, and so on.   Motivational research studies involve fewer respondents who are studied in greater depth.   Trained psychologists often are used in conducting motivational research studies.

Marketing researchers ordinarily select only a few people from the group whose behavior they want to study.   How they go about deciding which ones to include is a very important aspect of marketing research. The final section of this chapter looks at sampling.   Most marketing research is based on sampling.

## THE SAMPLING PLAN

The sampling plan is relevant to determining data sources, creating the research design, and conducting the investigation.   Suppose a department store manager wants to survey credit customers' attitudes about the store. The manager could get a list of credit customers from the accounting department and interview each customer.   The list of all credit customers is the relevant population, or universe.   Since the survey includes all persons in the population, it is a complete enumeration, or a census, of the population.

A toothpaste manufacturer who wants to survey users faces a tougher problem because the firm does not have a list of their names.   The population is not as well defined as in the department store example. Sampling, therefore, is necessary.

A population, or universe, is the frame from which sample items are selected.   The entire population is selected in a complete enumeration. Otherwise, only part of the population is selected.   Items (persons, stores, cars, etc.) selected from their relevant populations are called *sampling units*.   The whole set of selected units is the **sample.**                                  sample

Most marketing research is based on sampling.   Although marketing managers are not expected to be experts in sampling techniques and procedures, they must know enough about the basics to communicate with researchers and determine whether information collected by sampling is valid.

### Types of Samples

A good sampling plan will produce a sample that is representative of the characteristics of the population from which it is drawn.   Two basic types of samples are probability (random) and nonprobability samples.

| probability, or random sample | In a **probability, or random, sample** each item in the population has a known chance of being included in the sample. Strict statistical rules and procedures must be followed in selecting items for inclusion in the sample. The selection process cannot be arbitrary or based on judgment. A random sample's probability of representativeness can be mathematically appraised, as we will see later in our discussion of sampling theory. |

Suppose the student government at State College will hold an election next week and one of the candidates wants to take a random sample to determine the probable outcome. The candidate gets a list of all eligible voters. Assume there are 10,000 eligible voters and 100 people will be included in the sample. To qualify as a random sample, each student must have a probability of 1 in 100 of being included in the sample. Three types of probability samples are discussed in Table 9–6.

**nonprobability, or nonrandom, sample**

A **nonprobability, or nonrandom, sample** does not give every item in the population a known chance of being included. The researcher's judgment enters into the selection of items for inclusion in the sample. A nonprobability sample's probability of representativeness cannot be mathematically appraised. Its representativeness depends on how good the researcher's judgment is.

Perhaps the candidate discussed above would select a quota sample, a type of nonprobability sample. Suppose the candidate knows the percentages of students in the population that fall into various categories based on age, sex, and race. Interviewers might be told to interview a given number of students in these categories so that the percentages interviewed are in direct proportion to those of the universe.

If 24 percent of the students eligible to vote are twenty-year-old white females, the quota sample would be selected so that 24 percent of the sampled units are twenty-year-old white females. The interviewers would be told to fill their quotas on the basis of convenience. Perhaps they would go directly to a sorority house to fill this quota. Thus the quota sample's proportionality is forced and every student does not have a known chance of being selected for the quota sample. In this case, a white twenty-year-old female who is not a member of this sorority does not have a chance of being included in the sample. Furthermore, if one of the candidates is a member of that sorority, the results very likely will be biased in her favor. Table 9–7 discusses two other types of nonprobability sampling techniques.

**Sampling Error**

Both complete censuses and samples can contain errors. Two types of error are nonsampling error and sampling error.

The only error possible in a complete census is nonsampling error because there is no sampling. Incorrect recording of respondent answers and incorrect transferring of data from questionnaires to punched cards by key-punch operators are examples of nonsampling error. Nonsam-

**Table 9–6.** *Three types of probability (random) sampling techniques*

| | |
|---|---|
| *Simple Random Sampling* | This requires the researcher to have a list of all items in the population. Sampling units are selected in a random fashion. For example, assume each student in your class is assigned a sequential number written on a card and all students' cards are put in a container and mixed up. A blindfolded person could choose sampling units from the population by picking out cards. Each card has an equal chance of being chosen for the sample. |
| *Stratified Sampling* | This requires the researcher to divide the population into mutually exclusive subgroups (strata) based on a common characteristic. The basis for stratification (age, income, occupation, sex, etc.) should be characteristics that are relevant to the research project. In studying leisure activities of people in the population the researcher may believe that age is relevant. Thus the population is stratified by age. People in a particular stratum are of similar age but each stratum differs from others with respect to age. Simple random sampling could be used to select sampling units from each stratum. A researcher needs more information on the population to select a stratified sample than to select a simple random sample and he or she must be able to place each item in the population in the proper stratum. |
| *Area (Cluster) Sampling* | This requires the researcher to select a random sample of geographic areas, such as blocks or census tracts in the area to be studied, and to select households in these areas randomly for inclusion in the sample. The geographic areas are the primary units in selecting the sampling units, and the selection of households within each area can be accomplished by selecting every $n$th house. Census Bureau data are very useful in selecting random samples when the researcher does not have a complete list of households in the population. |

pling error cannot be measured but it can be minimized through careful planning and control of the research project.

A sample can contain both types of error. Because a sample is only part of the population from which it is drawn, it is possible that a complete enumeration would produce different results. Suppose the instructor wants to determine the average age of students in your class. A complete census would require asking each student his or her age, totaling them, and dividing by the number of students. This gives the true universe mean, or the true value of the population. Assume, instead, that the instructor selects a sample from the class and follows the same procedure. If the sample estimate and the true universe mean are not identical, the sample estimate contains sampling error.

A sample, however, may contain fewer errors than a complete census. Marketing researchers usually work under time and budget constraints. Doing a complete census of a large population may necessitate using

**Table 9–7.** *Two types of nonprobability sampling techniques*

| | |
|---|---|
| *Convenience Sampling* | Sampling units are chosen by the researcher simply on the basis of convenience. Examples include "on the street" interviews by television reporters, asking people in a supermarket their opinions about a new brand of detergent, and conducting taste tests with supermarket customers. People not at the same place on the street on the same date and time that the TV reporter is there clearly do not have a chance of being included in the sample, nor do people who are not in that particular supermarket at the date and time opinions or taste reactions are being sought. |
| *Judgment Sampling* | Sampling units are chosen by the researcher based on his or her opinion as to their representativeness. Examples include selecting a sample of salespersons for their opinions as input in preparing a sales forecast, the selection of cities to test market new products, and a TV reporter's selection of people to interview to get an informed view of the likely outcome of an upcoming election. The representativeness of these samples depends on the judgment of the person doing the selecting. |

poorly trained interviewers. More qualified interviewers can be hired if a sample is selected.

In marketing research projects the true value of a population ordinarily is not known. Probability theory, however, allows us to measure the sampling error, but only when the sample is a probability sample.

Consider the following example. There are ten supermarkets in a city of 125,000 people. None is open on Sunday because the managers believe citizens are opposed to Sunday shopping. One store manager, however, is considering opening on Sunday and takes a survey to determine if people really are opposed to Sunday shopping. A probability sample of 100 persons from the city's population indicates that 10 percent favor Sunday openings. Suppose, however, that another sample using the same procedures is drawn and it indicates that 12 percent favor Sunday openings. How can we have faith in sampling when "different samples tell different things?"

The true percentage in favor of Sunday shopping is unknown because the store manager did not do a complete enumeration. To overcome this problem marketing researchers use confidence intervals when dealing with probability samples. This technique allows them to be confident that if they draw repeated samples, the true population percentage would lie within a certain interval, for example, 95 out of 100 times. As the concept is used in practice, however, the person who conducted the first survey is likely to feel 95 percent confident that the interval from 4 percent to 16 percent contains the true percentage of the population that favors Sunday openings. As we said earlier, however, the use of confidence intervals is legitimate only for probability samples.[28]

## Sample Size

The adequacy of sample size can be measured statistically only for probability samples.[29]   Common sense, however, suggests that a researcher can narrow the confidence interval by using a larger sample.   But increasing the sample size can reduce only the sampling error; nonsampling errors can still affect the results.   Although determining sample size requires using statistical procedures beyond our scope, a few guidelines can be provided.

First, if the researcher expects considerable variance among responses, the sample size should be larger than if little variance were expected. Second, the greater the amount of permissible sampling error, the smaller the sample size needed.   This is why drug manufacturers sample more items in their quality control efforts than do trash can manufacturers. Third, available research funds often affect sample size decisions.   The budget constraint sometimes results in grossly inadequate sample sizes.

## Sampling and Marketing Research

Both probability and nonprobability samples have their place in marketing research.   The major advantages of a probability sample are that sampling error can be measured and that the sample size needed can be determined in advance.   Its major practical drawbacks are that probability techniques must be used to select sample items and that much time and cost and knowledge of statistics are needed to develop a probability sample.

Sampling error cannot be statistically measured for a nonprobability sample.   Its presence and extent must be judged subjectively.   The sample size also is based on judgment.   Since the cost, time, and statistical expertise required are much less, however, most marketing research projects are based on nonprobability samples.[30]

## SUMMARY AND LOOK AHEAD

Marketing managers need information to make good decisions.   Information management converts data to information to help reduce the risk in decision making.   It helps marketing managers identify market opportunities and solve marketing problems.

Marketing research is a systematic process by which data about problems are gathered, recorded, and analyzed.   It follows the scientific method when the researcher proceeds in an orderly and rational manner, is objective, thorough, and precise, and interprets the research findings honestly.

Data and information are not synonymous terms.   Data must be converted to a useful form for decision making before it becomes information.   The value of information must be weighed against its cost.

Expected costs must be compared to expected value of information in the light of funds available for getting more information. Marketing managers can generate their information internally and/or buy it from commercial suppliers such as Donnelley Marketing.

A marketing information system (MIS) collects and converts data to timely and relevant information for decision making. This includes external and internal, recurrent and nonrecurrent, and primary and secondary data. An MIS gathers, processes, analyzes, stores, and retrieves data and evaluates and disseminates information to marketing managers. It has a recurrent data subsystem and a nonrecurrent data subsystem. Marketing research supplies an MIS with nonrecurrent data to help identify market opportunities and solve marketing problems. In some firms the MIS is integrated into the company-wide management information system.

Marketing managers must communicate their information needs to marketing research directors. The director carries out the research project but solving the problem for which the research is needed is the marketing manager's job. Good communication between marketing researchers (information suppliers) and marketing managers (information users) is crucial. Their relationship is complementary.

The basic steps in the systematic marketing research process are the following: (1) identify and define the problem or opportunity, (2) conduct a preliminary exploration, (3) determine research objectives, (4) determine data needs, (5) determine data sources, (6) create the research design, (7) conduct the investigation, (8) analyze and convert data to information, and (9) communicate the information.

Most marketing research projects are based on sampling instead of complete enumerations. Two types of samples are probability (random) samples and nonprobability (nonrandom) samples. Two types of error are nonsampling and sampling error. The only error possible in a complete enumeration is nonsampling error. Both types can be present in a sample. Sampling error and the adequacy of sample size can be measured statistically only for probability samples. Nonprobability sampling, however, is used more often in marketing research projects.

The next section of the text discusses the product element in the marketing mix.

## REVIEW QUESTIONS

**1.** What is the key distinction between informal and formal marketing research?

**2.** Explain how marketing research uses the scientific method.

**3.** Are data and information the same thing? Explain.

**4.** Give two examples of internal data and two examples of external data.

**5.** How do recurrent data differ from nonrecurrent data?

**6.** Why would a marketing manager want to

compare the expected cost of information to its expected value?

**7.** Why might a marketer buy information from an outside commercial supplier?

**8.** Why is communication between information suppliers and information users so important?

**9.** What are the six functions of a marketing information system?

**10.** What three basic goals should guide decisions about the number and location of marketing information systems?

**11.** What are the nine steps in a marketing research project?

**12.** What is the relationship between hypotheses and research objectives?

**13.** Contrast primary data and secondary data.

**14.** Identify and discuss briefly four functional categories of marketing research.

**15.** Identify and discuss briefly four methodological categories of marketing research.

**16.** Contrast the observational and inquiry methods of data collection.

**17.** Discuss the relative advantages and disadvantges of mail, telephone, and personal interview surveys.

**18.** What is a research instrument?

**19.** Contrast direct interviewing and depth interviewing.

**20.** Why might a marketing researcher want to use projective techniques in interviewing respondents?

**21.** What is a complete enumeration, or census?

**22.** Contrast probability samples and nonprobability samples.

**23.** Give an example of nonsampling error and an example of sampling error.

## DISCUSSION QUESTIONS

**1.** What do you think of marketing managers who always put off making decisions until they have "all the information"?

**2.** Does the presence of a marketing information system in a firm mean the marketing manager can stop using judgment and experience in decision making?

**3.** Is it desirable that nonprobability samples are used more often in marketing research than probability samples?

**4.** How do information suppliers differ from information users?

**5.** "When a firm installs a marketing information system it can forget about marketing research." Do you agree?

**6.** Are governmental restraints needed to ensure that marketing researchers do not invade our privacy?

## NOTES

1. See Victor P. Buell, "60 Years of Progress in Marketing Research, But Will It Meet New Opportunities, Problems?" *Marketing News*, March 14, 1975, pp. 1, 5, 8, 13.

2. Committee on Definitions, *Marketing Definitions: A Glossary of Marketing Terms* (Chicago: American Marketing Association, 1960), p. 17.

3. See James R. Krum, "B for Marketing Research Departments," *Journal of Marketing*, October, 1978, pp. 8–12.

4. "Census Is Eagerly Awaited by Marketers; Strategies and Tactics Hinge on Findings," *Wall Street Journal*, March 26, 1980, p. 42.

5. See Kenneth C. Schneider, "Subject and Respondent Abuse in Marketing Research," *MSU Business Topics*, Spring, 1977, pp. 13–19; and Marilyn Landis Hauser, " 'Gutsy' Ethics Code Stressing 'Thou Shalt Not's' Is Drafted by Committee of AMA's N.Y. Chapter," *Marketing News*, January 27, 1978, p. 5. The code of ethics endorsed by the New York Chapter of the American Marketing Association is reproduced in *Marketing News*, September 19, 1980, p. 24.

6. See Jack D. Sparks, "Taming the 'Paper Elephant' in Marketing Information Systems," *Journal of Marketing*, July, 1976, pp. 83–86.

7. See Ira Alterman, " 'Computer Graphics' Maps

Help Executives Quickly Understand Voluminous Data," *Marketing News*, January 27, 1978, pp. 1, 14; and Hirotaka Takeuchi and Allan H. Schmidt, "New Promise of Computer Graphics," *Harvard Business Review*, January–February, 1980, pp. 122–131.

8. "Computers, Linked to TV-Like Screens, Are Drawing Graphs, Blueprints, Maps," *Wall Street Journal*, March 5, 1980, p. 40.

9. See James H. Myers and A. Coskun Samli, "Management Control of Marketing Research," *Journal of Marketing Research*, August, 1969, pp. 267–277.

10. Bayesian analysis is the primary tool for making this decision. It enables marketers to blend objective information with executive judgment. See Harry V. Roberts, "Bayesian Statistics in Marketing," *Journal of Marketing*, January, 1963, pp. 1–4; and Lee Adler, "How to Hold Market Research Accountable," *Sales & Marketing Management*, March 8, 1976, pp. 74–76.

11. See Dan H. Robertson, "Sales Force Feedback on Competitors' Activities," *Journal of Marketing*, April, 1974, pp. 69–71.

12. Richard H. Brien and James E. Stafford, "Marketing Information Systems: A New Dimension for Marketing Research," *Journal of Marketing*, July, 1968, p. 21.

13. Management information systems are also sometimes referred to by the acronym MIS.

14. See Lee Adler, "Working with Researchers," *Sales & Marketing Management*, November 8, 1976, pp. 116–120; and William B. Locander and Richard W. Scamell, "A Team Approach to Managing the Market Research Process," *MSU Business Topics*, Winter, 1977, pp. 15–26.

15. See John T. Small and William B. Lee, "In Search of an MIS," *MSU Business Topics*, Autumn, 1975, pp. 47–55; and Phillip Ein-Dor and Eli Segev, "Information-System Responsibility," *MSU Business Topics*, Autumn, 1977, pp. 33–40.

16. For discussion of sources of primary data, statistical information, and general reference sources of business information and ideas, see Charles R. Goeldner and Laura M. Dirks, "Business Facts: Where to Find Them," *MSU Business Topics*, Summer, 1976, pp. 23–36.

17. The division of marketing research into functional and methodological categories appears in Walter B. Wentz and Gerald I. Eyrich, *Marketing Theory and Application* (New York: Harcourt, Brace & World, Inc., 1970), pp. 475–478.

18. See Roger E. Bengston, "Despite Controversy, Focus Groups Are Used to Examine Wide Range of Marketing Questions," *Marketing News*, September 19, 1980, pp. 18, 25.

19. Keith K. Cox, James B. Higginbotham, and John Burton, "Applications of Focus Group Interviews in Marketing," *Journal of Marketing*, January, 1976, pp. 78–79.

20. "Market Research by Scanner," *Business Week*, May 5, 1980, p. 113.

21. See John Freeman and Edgar Butler, "Some Sources of Interviewer Variances in Surveys," *Public Opinion Quarterly*, Spring, 1976, pp. 79–81.

22. See Bruce J. Walker and Michael J. Etzel, "Communicating Research Results: Bridging the Gap," *Arizona Business*, March, 1975, pp. 26–32.

23. For further discussion of mail surveys, especially relating to the response rate, see Richard T. Hise and Michael A. McGinnis, "Evaluating the Effect of a Follow-up Request on Mail Survey Results," *Akron Business and Economic Review*, Winter, 1974, pp. 19–21; Marvin Roscoe, Dorothy Lang, and Jagdish N. Sheth, "Follow-up Methods, Questionnaire Length, and Market Differences in Mail Surveys," *Journal of Marketing*, April, 1975, pp. 20–27; Leslie Kanuk and Conrad Berenson, "Mail Surveys and Response Rates: A Literature Survey," *Journal of Marketing Research*, November, 1975, pp. 440–453; Douglas R. Berdie and John F. Anderson, "Mail Questionnaire Response Rates: Updating Outmoded Thinking," *Journal of Marketing*, January, 1976, pp. 71–73; William J. Whitmore, "Mail Survey Premiums and Response Bias," *Journal of Marketing Research*, February, 1976, pp. 46–50; Eli P. Cox, III, "A Cost/Benefit View of Prepaid Monetary Incentives in Mail Questionnaires," *Public Opinion Quarterly*, Spring, 1976, pp. 101–104; Roger A. Kerin and Michael G. Harvey, "Methodological Considerations in Corporate Mail Surveys: A Research Note," *Journal of Business Research*, August, 1976, pp. 277–281; Christopher H. Lovelock, Ronald Stiff, David Cullwick, and Ira M. Kaufman, "An Evaluation of the Effectiveness of Drop-off Questionnaire Delivery," *Journal of Marketing Research*, November, 1976, pp. 358–364; Thomas Vocino, "Three Variables in Stimulating Responses to Mailed Questionnaires," *Journal of Marketing*, October, 1977, pp. 76–77; Marvin A. Jolson, "How to Double or Triple Mail-Survey Response Rates," *Journal of Marketing*, October, 1977, pp. 78–81; Dan H. Robertson and Danny N. Bellinger, "A New Method of Increasing Mail Survey Response: Contributions to Charity," *Journal of Marketing Research*, November, 1978, pp. 632–633; and Arthur C. Wolfe and Beatrice R. Treiman, "Postage Types and Response Rates in Mail Surveys," *Journal of Advertising Research*, February, 1979, pp. 43–48.

24. For further discussion of telephone surveys, see Theresa F. Rogers, "Interviews by Telephone and in Person: Quality of Response and Field Performance," *Public Opinion Quarterly*, Spring, 1976, pp. 51–65; Don A. Dillman, Jean G. Gallegos, and James H. Frey, "Reducing Refusal Rates for Telephone Interviews," *Public Opinion Quarterly*, Spring, 1976, pp. 66–78; Robert M. Groves, "Comparing Telephone and Personal Interview Surveys," *Economic Outlook USA*, Summer, 1978, pp. 49–51; and Tyzoon T. Tyebjee, "Telephone Survey Methods: The State of the Art," *Journal of Marketing*, Summer, 1979, pp. 68–78.

25. See Gerald J. Glasser and Gale D. Metzger, "Random-Digit Dialing as a Method of Telephone Sampling," *Journal of Marketing Research*, February, 1972, pp. 59–64; J. Taylor Sims and John F. Willenborg, "Random-Digit Dialing: A Practical Application," *Journal of Business Research*, November, 1976, pp. 371–381; A. B. Blankenship, "Listed versus Unlisted Numbers in Telephone-Survey Samples," *Journal of Advertising Research*, January, 1977, pp. 39–42; Martin R. Frankel

and Lester R. Frankel, "Some Recent Developments in Sample Survey Design," *Journal of Marketing Research*, August, 1977, pp. 280–293; Randolph Grossman and Douglas Weiland, "The Use of Telephone Directories as a Sample Frame: Patterns of Bias Revisited," *Journal of Advertising*, Summer, 1978, pp. 31–35; and Peter C. Ellison, "Phone Directory Samples Just as Balanced as Samples from Computer Random Digit Dialing," *Marketing News*, January 11, 1980, p. 8.

26. Ernest R. Cadotte, "TELLUS Computer Lets Retailers Conduct In-Store Market Research," *Marketing News*, December 12, 1980, p. 17.

27. You may want to review the discussion of projective techniques in Chapter 5.

28. For discussion of confidence intervals, see F. E. Brown, *Marketing Research: A Structure for Decision Making* (Reading, Mass.: Addison-Wesley Publishing Company, 1980), pp. 173–183.

29. Ibid., pp. 195–223, for discussion of determining sample size.

30. For discussion of marketing research techniques used in modern business firms, see Barnett A. Greenberg, Jac L. Goldstucker, and Danny N. Bellenger, "What Techniques Are Used by Marketing Researchers in Business?" *Journal of Marketing*, April, 1977, pp. 62–68.

# Section IV
# The Product

The product is a marketer's major vehicle for delivering customer satisfactions. It can be a physical product, an intangible service, or a combination of them. The total product is a product item that has been augmented to meet customer requirements.

Chapter 10 discusses consumer and industrial products and presents a system for classifying them. The product life cycle concept is introduced as a basic planning tool for marketing managers. Other topics include the adoption and diffusion processes. These refer to the stages buyers go through in deciding to adopt a new product and the spread of the product's acceptance in the marketplace.

Chapter 11 takes the concepts developed in Chapter 10 and examines their use in product management. Product objectives, product positioning, and product meanings are discussed along with product innovation. We will see how new products are developed and managed from the idea stage to their eventual withdrawal from the market.

Branding, labeling, and packaging are major product decisions. They are discussed in Chapter 12.

# Chapter 10

# The Product Offering

## OBJECTIVES

*After reading this chapter you should be able to*

1. contrast product items and total products.

2. distinguish between consumer and industrial products.

3. explain why and how consumer products are classified.

4. identify important reasons for the growth in services and important characteristics of services.

5. explain the basis upon which industrial products are classified and identify the classes of industrial products.

6. draw a figure illustrating the product life cycle and discuss each stage.

7. relate the adoption and diffusion processes to the product life cycle.

8. identify the stages in the adoption process and the five categories of adopters.

9. identify five important product characteristics that affect the adoption rate.

10. discuss the fashion cycle.

11. discuss the product mix and product lines in multiproduct firms.

## KEY CONCEPTS

*Look for these terms as you read the chapter:*

Product
Consumer Products
Industrial Products
Convenience Products
Staple Products
Impulse Products
Emergency Products
Shopping Products
Homogeneous Shopping Products
Heterogeneous Shopping Products
Specialty Products
Regularly Unsought Products
New Unsought Products
Raw Materials
Forward Buying
Component Parts
Component Materials
Installations
Accessory Equipment
MRO Items
Business Services
Product Life Cycle
Adoption Process
Product Mix
Product Line
Cannibalization

*Disco and hula hoops have come and gone. A few years ago it seemed that practically everyone was into tennis but its popularity has declined. Fads come and go. Marketers also are continually adding new products and dropping old ones. 3M Company expects each of its divisions to get 25 percent of its sales each year from products that did not exist five years earlier.\* SCM announced in 1980 that it was getting out of the copier business. Honeywell stopped making residential smoke detectors in 1981 because they had become unprofitable due to market saturation.*

In a buyer-seller transaction the buyer exchanges purchasing power for something bought from the seller. This something is a product. In marketing, the term *product* means commodities, physical products, and intangible services. Raw cotton, a quart of milk, and a hairstyle are products. Tangible products such as cars and TVs usually are called products, whereas intangible products such as haircuts and psychiatric counseling usually are called services. Most products, however, have both tangible and intangible features.

This chapter begins with a discussion of the product. Next we discuss a product classification system for consumer products and one for industrial products. The product life cycle also is discussed. We shall see how new products become old products: wringer washers, cream deodorants, straight-edge razors, 78-r.p.m. records, and "number please" telephones are almost gone from the market, although at one time they were new products. Black-and-white TVs, dial telephones, operator-assisted long distance phone calls, unfiltered cigarettes, tooth powder, live-in household servants, ceramic tile bathrooms, bias-ply tires, and cars with eight-cylinder motors are examples of other declining products.

To help us understand why products go through a life cycle, we will discuss how consumers adopt new products and how a new product becomes generally accepted on the market. Then we will devote some time to the fashion cycle and the factors that affect a firm's decision to add new products and drop old ones.

## WHAT IS A PRODUCT?

Production-oriented firms view a product from the firm's perspective—as a manifestation of the resources used to produce it. Customer-oriented firms view a product from the target customer's perspective—as a bundle of satisfactions, benefits, or utilities that will satisfy the target's wants. They take physical product items and enhance them for target customers. The result is the total product.

---

\*"How Four Companies Spawn New Products by Encouraging Risks," *Wall Street Journal*, September 18, 1980, p. 1.

## The Total Product

Product items are "things" produced in factories. Record companies produce black discs with a hole and grooves, cosmetics companies combine chemicals to make lipstick, camera makers produce mechanical devices that take pictures, and vitamin manufacturers produce little pills. Marketing's task is to take these product items and enhance them for the market target. A total product incorporates the utilities or benefits that its target customers want. Records become a source of listening satisfaction, lipstick becomes beauty and hope, cameras become tools for capturing and preserving the present, and vitamins become hope for a healthier and fuller life. Thus a total product is what marketers have in mind when they talk about products. A total product is much more than the physical product item.

We discussed form, time, place, possession, and ownership utilities in Chapter 1. We could add image, or psychological, utility to reflect a total product's ability to provide satisfactions through the user's perception of its personal and social satisfactions.[1] For example, a serious runner may derive more psychological utility from wearing Adidas running shoes than from wearing a lesser-known, cheaper brand.

It is a consumer's expectation of benefits that makes a "something" a product, and those expectations are dynamic. The Model T's major benefit was low-cost transportation, but through the years consumers have expected cars to provide other benefits, such as prestige, glamour, easy maintenance, roominess, and so on. Although American automakers still mass produce plain, basic models, potential customers are encouraged to have them "custom built" by ordering optional equipment that is installed as cars are being assembled. Oldsmobile's "Can we have one built for you?" ad theme is an example.

## Perspectives on the Product

The product is a firm's major vehicle for delivering customer satisfactions. There is no need to promote, price, and distribute a product that offers no customer benefits. Thus product decisions play a key role in defining a company's mission. Its products must fit its concept of its proper line of business.

But marketers and consumers (or users) often perceive products differently. A firm whose business is selling transportation might consider private cars and buses to be close substitutes, but many consumers do not. To them, the car's benefits are privacy and independence, which they do not enjoy when riding a bus. On the other hand, some home builders have considered mobile homes and permanent housing as nonsubstitutes. Many consumers, however, think of them as substitutes.

A dishwasher's benefits to the buyer may include freedom, germ-free dishes, confidence that the manufacturer will stand behind the product, installation, and opportunity to buy on credit. Clearly, the retailer's services also are part of the total bundle of satisfactions.[2] Likewise, the

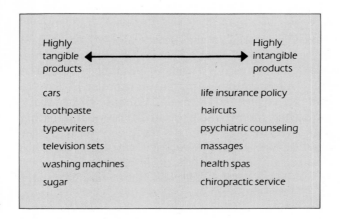

**Figure 10–1.**
*A continuum of*
*product tangibility*

wholesaler's services are part of the bundle of satisfactions the retailer buys, and the manufacturer's services are part of the bundle of satisfactions the wholesaler buys. Ultimate consumers and middlemen buy consumer products to satisfy their wants. A consumer's satisfactions relate to use, whereas those of middlemen relate to profit.[3] As we saw in Chapter 7, industrial users buy industrial products to satisfy their organizations' objectives.

Thus a dishwasher in the manufacturer's factory, in the wholesaler's warehouse, on the retailer's display floor, or in the consumer's home is not the same bundle of satisfactions. Five years after buying it the consumer may view its bundle of satisfactions differently and may be ready to replace it.

product

A **product,** therefore, is a bundle of physical, chemical, and/or intangible features that has the potential to satisfy customer wants. (See Figure 10–1.)

## PRODUCT CLASSIFICATION SYSTEMS

Scientists classify similar plants and animals into groups to study them. Marketers also classify products into groups to develop generalizations about desirable marketing mixes for the different groups.

In Chapter 3 we classified buyers as ultimate consumers or industrial users. Products also can be classified as consumer or industrial.

consumer
products

**Consumer products** are "destined for use by ultimate consumers or households and in such form that they can be used without commercial processing."[4]

industrial
products

**Industrial products** are "destined to be sold primarily for use in producing other goods or rendering services as contrasted with goods destined to be sold primarily to the ultimate consumer."[5]

Some products, such as lipstick and toothpaste, are destined exclusively for use by ultimate consumers. Others, like railroad box cars, jet engines, and gantry cranes are destined exclusively for use by industrial users. But many products can be used by both ultimate consumers and industrial users. For example, the car a family buys for family use is a consumer product. That same make and model is an industrial product if a firm buys it for a salesperson's use.

## CLASSIFYING CONSUMER PRODUCTS

Several bases could be used to classify consumer products, but the one used most is buyer behavior. This classification system is based on differences in the buying behavior of the people who buy the products—not on differences in the products themselves. Any product, therefore, could be classified differently depending on the buyer's behavior. The system works because many consumers behave alike in buying a given type of product. This helps marketers in making generalizations to guide development of a product's marketing mix. Four classes of consumer products are (1) convenience products, (2) shopping products, (3) specialty products, and (4) unsought products.[6]

### Convenience Products

**Convenience products** are low-priced and nationally advertised items like cigarettes, chewing gum, candy, and razor blades. They are bought frequently but buyers are unwilling to shop actively for them because consumers do not think it is worth the effort to compare price and quality. Thus convenience products are available in many outlets, often including vending machines. Three subclasses are (1) staple products, (2) impulse products, and (3) emergency products.

| convenience products

**Staple products** like bread and milk are bought regularly and routinely. The household buyer routinely buys these items from a convenient source because the family routinely consumes them. The only real thinking involved in buying a staple product occurred when the buyer initially added it to the list of regularly consumed products. Thereafter it is bought routinely because the decision is programed. Grocery shoppers who do not use a written shopping list rely on the store's display of products to remind them of what they need. This in-store cue reminds the shopper that the staple is almost depleted at home. This is why complementary products such as snacks and snack spreads are located close together.

| staple products

Purchases of **impulse products** are completely unplanned. Exposure to the product triggers the want. Before going shopping you could prepare a list of the staple products, but not the impulse products, you would buy. The desire to buy staple products may cause you to go shopping. The desire to buy impulse products is a result of your shopping. This is why impulse products are located where they will be noticed. *People* and *Us* magazines, Tic-Tac mints, and chewing gum are impulse products for many consumers. These products are displayed in heavy traffic areas, such as checkout aisles in supermarkets. Home economists often urge

| impulse products

consumers to use shopping lists to avoid impulse purchases. Department stores also feature products in window displays to draw people into the stores.[7]

**emergency products**

Purchases of **emergency products** result from urgent and compelling needs. If your windshield wiper blades fail during an unexpected rainstorm you will drive into the nearest service station to replace them. You are not interested in comparison shopping for replacement blades. You also will pay more than if you had anticipated this need and bought them at a discount store. But you are not concerned with price or quality comparisons this time. Hotels, motels, and airports use vending machines to sell products such as handkerchiefs and toothbrushes, which are emergency products for travelers who left theirs at home. Ambulance and wrecker services also are emergency products.

**Summary Comments on Convenience Products.** As discretionary incomes go up there is less price and quality comparison shopping for many types of products that become staples or impulse products. Some car dealers even offer on-the-spot credit approval to discourage prospects from going home to rethink the decision to buy. Inflation, shortages of some products, and recession, however, make some shoppers more careful buyers. Expected shortages or rapid price changes of some products sometimes lead to panic buying and, whenever feasible, hoarding. These changes in buying behavior cause some products to shift from one class to another. Gasoline ordinarily is a staple product for most consumers. But long lines at gasoline stations mean they are buying an emergency product. Many will be trying to top off their tanks.

## Shopping Products

**shopping products**

Unlike convenience products, **shopping products** involve price and quality comparisons. Shoppers think it is worth the time, cost, and effort to compare because they perceive more risk in buying these products. Shopping products can be homogeneous or heterogeneous.

**homogeneous shopping products**

Consumers consider **homogeneous shopping products** to be alike. A person who thinks all top-of-the-line 17-cubic-foot refrigerators are very similar will limit shopping effort to making price comparisons. Thus sellers tend to engage in price competition. Manufacturers also may stress differences in design and try to distinguish between the physical product and its product-related services. One might set up service centers to differentiate its product from rivals. A retailer might advertise that the refrigerator's price includes ninety days of interest-free financing. Consumers who want to stretch their disposable incomes are more likely to consider a product as a homogeneous shopping product than as a convenience product.

**heterogeneous shopping products**

Consumers consider **heterogeneous shopping products** to be unalike, or nonstandardized. They shop for the best price-quality combination. Price often is secondary to style and quality when price comparisons are hard to make. Using price to compare clothing, jewelry, cars, furniture, and apartments is tough, for example, because quality and style vary within each product class. A couple searching for an apartment may spend a lot of time comparing decor, floor plans, distance from bus lines, and so on. Once they find the "right" one they consider price. If the rent is reasonable compared to the alternatives, they probably will lease it.

**Summary Comments on Shopping Products.** The percentage of women in the labor force is increasing. Women who work outside the home tend to have less time for shopping.[8] Leisure time, however, is also increasing but there are many ways to spend it. Shopping has to compete for a consumer's time.[9] As we will see in Chapter 14, the growth in mail order and telephone retailing suggests that some people prefer a more passive type of shopping. Stores are located close together in planned shopping centers to help reduce the effort required for making price and quality comparisons.

## Specialty Products

Consumers will make a special effort to buy **specialty products.** These are products for which the buyer has a strong conviction as to brand, style, or type. Steinway pianos, Leica cameras, Steuben glassware, and a Rolls-Royce are examples. Consumers will go out of their way to locate and buy these products because they perceive quality and other benefits in owning them. A person may willingly travel 200 miles to the nearest dealer who sells the Rolls-Royce.

specialty products

There is no comparison shopping. The consumer shops only to locate a specialty product. Physicians, attorneys, and tax consultants who enjoy a loyal following of patients and clients are selling specialty products.[10] Marketers try to create specialty status for their products with advertising phrases like "accept no substitutes," "insist on the real thing," and "it's worth the trip from anywhere." They build customer loyalty when consumers consider their brands to be specialty products. A specialty product can be less intensively distributed than a convenience or shopping product because buyers will search to find it. If you believe that "when you're out of Schlitz, you're out of beer," Schlitz beer is a specialty product to you. Figure 10–2 outlines the major characteristics of the four major types of consumer products.

## Unsought Products

Unsought products are products potential buyers do not know exist or do not yet want. There are two types, regularly unsought products and new unsought products.

Caskets, life insurance, a lawyer's services in preparing a will, and a physician's services in giving a cancer checkup are **regularly unsought products.** These are existing products that consumers do not want now, although they may eventually purchase them. Marketers face a tough

regularly unsought products

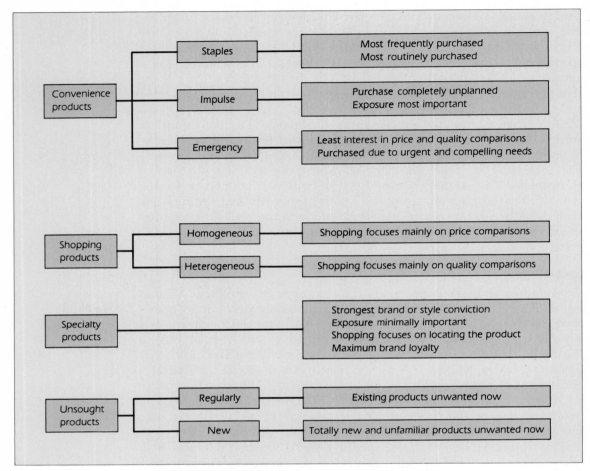

*Figure 10–2. Classification of consumer products*

challenge in persuading consumers to buy them. The American Cancer Society tries to motivate people to have a checkup and to learn to recognize cancer's symptoms. Many people also lack the motivation to visit a lawyer to prepare a will. Some cemeteries and marketers of granite grave markers have promoted their products in recent years as a hedge against inflation to stimulate sales to the value-conscious segment of the market.

**new unsought products**

Products that are totally new and unfamiliar to consumers are **new unsought products.** The marketer's task here is to inform target customers of the product's existence and lift it out of the new unsought category by stimulating demand for it. Oral polio vaccine at one time was a new unsought product. But heavy promotion and acceptance of the product practically eradicated polio. More recently, many parents apparently have forgotten about the dreaded disease. Thus we see ads on TV urging parents to have their children take the vaccine. Efforts to overcome a new product's unsought status may have to be renewed with new prospective users, in this case parents who grew up without fear of polio because their parents had them immunized.

## SERVICES

During the 1950s and the 1960s, our economy began changing from an industrial economy based on manufacturing tangible products to a post-industrial economy based on creating intangible services.[11] High economic growth contributed to record high levels of disposable income, and many consumers began buying huge amounts of intangible services. This trend to rely more on others to provide many of the services our parents provided for themselves has created market opportunity for many firms. The service industries now employ roughly half of our labor force, and roughly one business in three is a service business. A service business is one that provides an intangible product for its customers. Non-profit organizations, including government, also provide many services to consumers and industrial users.

Services differ from physical products in that they are intangible and production and consumption occur together. Hotels, laundries, beauty shops, movie theaters, car repair shops, airlines, banks, and real estate firms are among the many types of service firms. Most are small in comparison to manufacturers of physical products, and they have greater difficulty in reducing costs and increasing productivity through mecha-

*Table 10–1.* *Reasons for the growth in service industries*

| | |
|---|---|
| 1. Increasing affluence | Greater demand for lawn care, carpet cleaning, and other services that consumers used to provide for themselves. |
| 2. More leisure time | Greater demand for travel agencies, travel resorts, adult education courses. |
| 3. Higher percentage of women in the labor force | Greater demand for day care nurseries, maid service, away-from-home meals. |
| 4. Greater life expectancy | Greater demand for nursing homes and health care services. |
| 5. Greater complexity of products | Greater demand for skilled specialists to provide maintenance for such complex products as cars and home computers. |
| 6. Increasing complexity of life | Greater demand for income tax preparers, marriage counselors, legal advisers, employment services. |
| 7. Greater concern about ecology and resource scarcity | Greater demand for purchased or leased services, such as door-to-door bus service and car rental instead of car ownership. |
| 8. Increasing number of new products | The computer sparked development of such service industries as programing, repair, and time sharing. |

"I think the warranty program on our new GM car is fine. But just as a hedge against inflation, we got GM's Continuous Protection Plan, too."

*The GM Continuous Protection Plan enhances the total product and makes car repair a specialty service for people who purchase the plan.*

nization.   Rising labor costs and small productivity increases lead to higher prices for services.[12]   Table 10–1 discusses several reasons for the growth in services.

Services also can be classified on the basis of buyer behavior.   Many consumers consider automatic car washing outlets to be a convenience service.   Many also probably consider car repair service to be a shopping service.   Most consumer services that involve a lot of skill probably

Source: Reprinted with permission of General Motors Corporation.

are considered specialty services. Examples are the services of physicians and dentists. Table 10–2 discusses several important characteristics of services.

In recent years, some consumers have been substituting tangible products for services purchased from service businesses. Among the reasons for this are high prices charged by some service providers, low quality of service provided, and shortages of skilled service providers. The Early

***Table 10–2.*** *Characteristics of services*

1. *Sold exclusively on the basis of benefits* since there is no physical product to sell. A car salesperson sells prospects on the car's benefits but also can take them for a test drive. A hairstylist, however, must help prospects picture themselves with a new hairstyle because they cannot test it before buying it. Thus a good reputation and word-of-mouth advertising are crucial in marketing services.
2. *Cannot be produced in anticipation of demand* because they are consumed as they are produced. Cars can be placed in inventory, or stored. Hairstyles cannot.
3. *Time utility is crucial because services cannot be stored.* A new car may remain in inventory several weeks before it is sold. A hairstylist who sits idle waiting for customers loses that time forever. This is why appointments usually are required.
4. *Cannot be produced in one location for consumption in another.* A car made in Detroit can be bought by a buyer in Houston. Hairstylists must have their customers seated in front of them. This is one reason service firms tend to be small.
5. *Perish upon offering.* A person who misses a music concert can never recapture it because it perishes as it is produced.
6. *Once consumed, a service cannot be returned to the seller.* A defective car can be returned but a bad hairstyle cannot. This is why many services are considered specialty products. Customers will go out of their way to have their hair styled by stylists who have demonstrated their skill on them. This is a type of risk-reducing behavior.
7. *Quality control is tougher than for tangible products.* Although GM can be reasonably confident that all units of a certain car model are identical in quality, a buyer who requires repair work cannot be certain that all repairpersons will produce repair services of identical quality. Even the quality of any given worker's service might vary depending on the time of the day and his or her general attitude at that time.

Pregnancy Test (EPT) is a product that can be substituted for a pregnancy test at a physician's office or clinic. Other examples are blood pressure testing kits, carpet cleaners, records, home permanents, and devices to flush radiators on cars. The important point is that potential customers are seeking satisfaction of their wants. They may not care whether those wants are satisfied by tangible products or intangible services.

In the next section we will discuss the classification of industrial products.

## CLASSIFYING INDUSTRIAL PRODUCTS

Many firms that marketed computers for home use (a consumer product) have decided to retarget their products for use in small business (an industrial product). Video discs and video disc players can be either consumer or industrial products. When sold to consumers for home entertainment, they are consumer products. When sold to business firms for use in training salespersons or to school systems for use in educational instruction, they are industrial products.

Industrial products can be classified according to the uses to which they are put. The two categories are products that become part of the product they are used to produce and products that do not become part of the product they are used to produce but are needed to conduct the organization's operations. Tires, batteries, and headlights become a part of Ford cars. The heavy equipment in Ford's assembly plants does not but is used to make the cars.

Three types of industrial products become part of the product they are used to produce: (1) raw materials, (2) component parts, and (3) component materials.

## Raw Materials

Products that have undergone only enough processing to permit convenient and economical handling, transportation, and storage are **raw materials.** Two broad subclasses are farm products, such as tobacco, wheat, and soybeans; and natural products, such as the product of mines, forests, and the sea. The eggs a farmer sells to a household are a consumer product. Those sold to a bakery are a raw material. The same is true of natural products. Fish sold to a household are a consumer product, while those sold to a canning factory are an industrial product.

Raw materials are expense items because their cost is charged off in the year they are bought. Buying procedures depend on the current and anticipated market supply, price, and the percentage of the finished product's total production cost that is due to the raw material.

When supplies are adequate, raw materials are bought routinely when inventory reaches the reorder point (straight rebuy). Purchasing is less routine and higher-level executives join in the buying decision (modified rebuy) when supplies are short. They might try to ensure adequate supplies by dealing directly with producers rather than distributors and by forward buying. **Forward buying** involves entering into contracts with suppliers to buy products that will be delivered in installments over a period of time.[13] A firm might even vertically integrate backward and produce the raw material for itself, such as Ford producing its own steel (the make-or-buy decision).

Supply problems in some industries may lead raw material users to search for new sources and substitute materials. Eastman Kodak buys fifty million ounces of silver annually for use in its photographic films and papers. When the price of silver skyrocketed to $50 per ounce in early 1980, Kodak stepped up its efforts to find a substitute for silver (new task buying).[14]

The total supply of some natural products cannot be controlled by humans, whereas the supply of farm products is more controllable. The dividing line here is often hazy, however. Producers who "farm" fish and trees and "plant" oyster beds are producing farm products.

Raw materials often are bulky, low in value, and found at locations far removed from where they are needed. Thus transportation cost is very important. In an effort to hold these costs down, some firms, such as large grain marketers and oil companies, own their own transportation equipment. We will discuss this in greater detail in Chapter 16.

raw materials

forward buying

## Component Parts and Materials

component parts

**Component parts** either are ready for direct assembly into the finished product or require only a minor amount of further processing. Examples are motors for lawnmowers and headlights for cars. Standardized parts are available ready-made from many suppliers. Specialized parts are made to order.

component materials

**Component materials** (semimanufactured or semiprocessed materials) require further processing before becoming a part of the finished product. Examples are paper, textiles, cement, and leather.

Component parts and materials become part of the finished product and are expense items. The buyer is interested in quality, price, and the seller's delivery capability since an out-of-stock situation might force the buyer to shut down operations. When the buyer needs a large, continuous supply, top-level executives in both the buying and selling firms may negotiate a long-term contract, especially when consistency of quality is important and quality varies among suppliers. During recent years, some Japanese makers of component parts for cars have set up manufacturing operations in the United States. They have more experience in producing components for small cars, the type of cars American automakers have been switching to.

Some manufacturers of component parts brand and advertise their parts to ultimate consumers. Goodyear might advertise that its tires are standard equipment on new Chevrolets. This might cause some new-car buyers to prefer Chevrolets and result in more sales for Goodyear. Because many car owners replace worn-out tires with the same brand, Goodyear's sales may increase in the replacement tire market, where profit margins are higher than in the original equipment market.

Sometimes firms that develop components for their products find users for the components in other industries. Polaroid developed the sonar transducer, which sends out a sound wave that bounces off the subject and gives a distance reading to Polaroid's SX-70 OneStep Camera. Polaroid began marketing the device to other firms for nonphotographic applications in robotics, instrumentation, machinery control, and fluid and bulk inventory control.

Four types of industrial products do not become part of the product they are used to produce: (1) installations, (2) accessory equipment, (3) supplies, and (4) business services.

## Installations

installations

Land, land rights, plants, and buildings are one subclass of **installations.** Another subclass is major equipment. The first subclass includes such assets as plant sites, mineral rights, factories, warehouses, stores, and office buildings. The second subclass includes such assets as blast furnaces, drill presses, printing presses, and elevators. Major equipment is either standard or custom-made. Lathes typically are standardized to suit many types of buyers. Custom-made major equipment, such as many kinds of packaging machinery, is built to individual customer specifications.

Installations, which do not become part of the finished product, are capital items. They last for many years and, except for land, depreciate over time. Because of the high cost involved, high-level executives from different departments often participate in the buying decision (multiple-buying influence). As we saw in Chapter 7, the high cost of buying may favor leasing, especially when the lessor includes service in the lease price. For example, a retailer who leases a store from a shopping center owner may receive on-going maintenance services.

### Accessory Equipment

Products similar to some of the smaller standardized major equipment are **accessory equipment.** Examples are typewriters, office copying machines, cash registers, store fixtures, and forklift trucks. It does not become part of the finished product and is a capital item. Compared to major equipment, accessory equipment has a shorter useful life, is more standardized, is less expensive, usually is smaller in size, and is bought with less executive influence.

accessory equipment

### Supplies

Three subclasses of supplies are maintenance supplies, repair supplies, and operating supplies. They often are referred to as **MRO items.**

MRO items

Maintenance supplies are used to preserve the plant and equipment in good working condition. Examples are brooms, sweeping compounds, and wiping cloths. Repair supplies are used to keep equipment in operating condition or to repair inoperable equipment. Truck mufflers, nuts and bolts, and power transmission belts are examples. Operating supplies include coal, fuel oil, natural gas, pencils, and typewriter ribbons.

Supplies do not become part of the finished product and are expense items. Most are bought routinely when needed. Janitorial supplies, for example, are bought routinely from the source that offers the best combination of price and service. Supplies are often standardized and so quality usually does not vary much among suppliers. When Liquid Paper Corporation introduced correctable typewriter ribbons in 1978, it made the ribbons compatible with several different typewriter systems so it could penetrate the replacement market.[15] Barouh-Eaton Allen Corporation competes with IBM for part of the $600 million-a-year market for ribbons that fit IBM typewriters.[16] Some operating supplies, such as coal for an electric generating station, are bought under long-term contracts with several suppliers.

### Business Services

Services provided to firms by banks, insurance companies, advertising agencies, CPA and law firms, employment agencies, and management consultants are **business services.** Other examples are purchased main-

business services

| Industrial product | Product becomes part of the product it is used to make | Product is used to conduct the organization's operations | Expense item | Capital item |
|---|:---:|:---:|:---:|:---:|
| Raw materials | ✓ | | ✓ | |
| Component parts | ✓ | | ✓ | |
| Component materials | ✓ | | ✓ | |
| Installations | | ✓ | | ✓ |
| Accessory equipment | | ✓ | | ✓ |
| Supplies | | ✓ | ✓ | |
| Business services | | ✓ | ✓ | |

*Figure 10–3.
Use and expense
classification of
industrial products*

tenance services (landscaping and window washing), purchased repair services (those bought from mechanical, plumbing, and electrical contractors), and operating services (in-plant lunches and uniform rental).

Business services are expense items that do not become part of the finished product. The buyer has decided that buying the service from outside specialists is less costly than having company employees perform it. Multiple-buying influence may be present when the cost of the service exceeds a set amount. (See Figure 10–3.)

Consumer and industrial products both have life cycles. We will discuss this in the next section.

## THE PRODUCT LIFE CYCLE

product life cycle

Products, like people, have life cycles. The **product life cycle** (PLC) depicts a product's sales history through four stages: (1) introduction, (2) growth, (3) maturity, and (4) decline.[17] (See Figure 10–4.) A product's marketing mix changes as it moves through the life cycle because of changes in the competitive environment, buyer behavior, and the composition of its market.[18]

The PLC concept can apply to a product category (deodorant); to a particular product form (roll-on and sprays); or to a particular brand (Ban or Sure). The life cycle of the product category is the longest, whereas

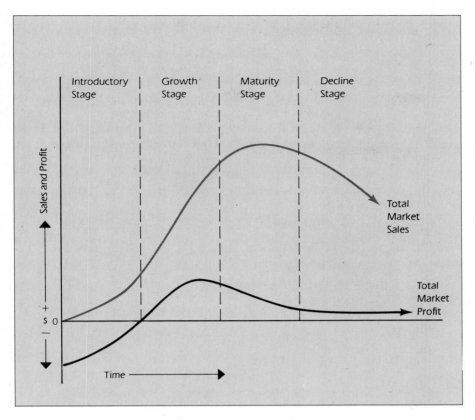

Figure 10–4.
The product life cycle

that of the brand typically is the shortest. People still use deodorant but cream deodorant (product form) practically has disappeared. Ban deodorant (brand) has changed forms over the years and presently is available in several forms. Some brands like Stopette are no longer marketed.

**Introductory Stage**

The launching of a new product (category, form, or brand) is called the introductory stage. A new product category requires a longer introductory period because primary demand (demand for the product category as opposed to the demand for a specific brand) must be stimulated. Even a brand that has achieved acceptance in other markets will require introduction in new markets. The demand for a specific brand within a product category is called selective demand.

The basic goals in the introductory stage are to pioneer acceptance and to gain initial distribution. Promotion is needed to inform potential buyers of the product's availability, nature, and uses, and to encourage wholesalers and retailers to stock it. Funds are invested in promotion on the expectation of future profits. Profits, however, are negative in the introductory stage because sales volume is low, distribution is limited, and promotional expenses are high.

### Growth Stage

If a product has been launched successfully, the major thrust in the growth stage is to keep the ball rolling. Sales begin to increase rapidly as new customers enter the market and old customers make repeat purchases. New wholesalers and retailers, new package sizes, and so on may be needed. This is the stage of peak profits. Just as new customers are attracted, so are rivals who copy and improve on the innovative product's features. New product forms and brands enter. Competition intensifies and industry profits start to decline near the end of the growth stage. But total industry sales are still rising.

### Maturity Stage

The greatest number of competitors, competitive product forms, and brands exists in the maturity stage. Rivals copy product features of successful brands and they become more alike. Thus price competition develops along with heavy promotion of whatever unique brand features still exist.

Industry sales peak and decline as fewer customers remain to be cultivated and wholesaler and retailer support dwindles because of shrinking profit margins on the product. Middlemen often introduce their own brands, which makes competition even tougher. The decline in industry profits that began in the growth stage accelerates.

Once the market for a product is saturated, most of its sales are repeat sales to earlier buyers. There is little growth potential for the product, which leads to a further lack of support by middlemen.

### Decline Stage

The decline stage is the final stage in the life cycle. Product forms and brands, like the soft-top convertible and the De Soto car, typically enter into decline stages. Product categories last longer. Competition is the reason products enter the decline stage. As we will see in Chapter 11, marketers often focus effort on extending the lives of their existing brands.

Sales and profits fall off rapidly and competitors become more cost conscious in the decline stage. But brands with strong acceptance by some customer segments may continue to produce profits. Thus Spic and Span still is a leading household cleaner even though its powdered form is less popular than liquids and sprays.

Sick (declining) products drain company resources and effort from healthy products. Some firms conduct product audits to identify declining products. Often they are dropped. Sometimes, however, a careful study of the product may lead to changes in manufacturing and/ or marketing methods that permit the firm to reduce costs and increase profit. In the next chapter we will discuss in greater detail how marketers use the PLC concept.

# THE ADOPTION AND DIFFUSION PROCESSES

The PLC concept is related to the adoption and diffusion processes that we discussed briefly in Chapters 4 and 6. The **adoption process** is the series of stages potential buyers of a product go through in deciding whether to buy it. Some actually must buy the product or else it will have no life cycle. Thus the adoption process gives rise to the product life cycle. The PLC concept also is related to the diffusion process, or the spread of acceptance of a new product among potential buyers. It affects the length of a product's life cycle.

adoption process

## The Adoption Process

No product will survive the introductory stage unless some potential buyers (prospects) actually buy it. Several stages in the adoption process are shown in Figure 10–5.[19] You may want to review the discussion of nonprogramed decisions in Chapter 4. The decision to adopt or reject a new product is a nonprogramed decision.

Marketing effort seeks to move potential customers rapidly to the adoption stage. Marketers hope that promotion in the introductory stage will create awareness of the product and whet potential buyers' appetites for more information (interest) about it so they will evaluate it. Notice that a trial purchase is not made until rather late in the adoption process. If the product is expensive, radically new, and complex, prospects may perceive the risk of a trial purchase to be greater than its perceived benefits. Less expensive and less complex products often are distributed as free samples. The goal is to induce prospects to try them by reducing perceived risk.

Customers who make a trial purchase make a monetary commitment to the product and then carefully evaluate the "rightness" of the decision.

*Figure 10–5.* **Stages in the adoption process**

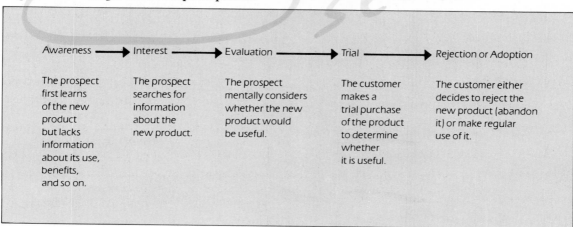

Awareness → Interest → Evaluation → Trial → Rejection or Adoption

The prospect first learns of the new product but lacks information about its use, benefits, and so on.

The prospect searches for information about the new product.

The prospect mentally considers whether the new product would be useful.

The customer makes a trial purchase of the product to determine whether it is useful.

The customer either decides to reject the new product (abandon it) or make regular use of it.

Rivals may attempt to switch them to their brands. There is no assurance customers will remain committed even after adoption. As we saw in Chapter 4, they may experience dissonance, which may lead them to a search for additional information to confirm the wisdom of the decision. Providing this information may help the marketer to reduce dissonance and raise buyer commitment, or loyalty, to the brand.

### The Diffusion Process

The speed with which a new product is diffused affects the length of its life cycle. A slowly diffused product will have only a few customers in the introductory stage and pioneering acceptance will require a lot of time.

As we saw in Chapter 4, there is no general personality pattern for the five traditionally recognized categories of adopters: (1) innovators, (2) early adopters, (3) early majority, (4) late majority, and (5) laggards. A new product that has been adopted by innovators and early adopters still has 84 percent of its potential customers in the nonadopter category. (See Chapter 4, Figure 4–7.) But if innovators and early adopters do not adopt, the product is doomed to failure.[20]

### Adoption Rate

Five product characteristics affect the rate of speed with which a new product is adopted: (1) relative advantage, (2) compatibility, (3) complexity, (4) divisibility, and (5) communicability.[21]

**Relative Advantage.** The greater a product's perceived degree of superiority over previous products in terms of lower price, greater convenience, ease of use, and so on, the faster the adoption rate. Examples are cartridge typewriter ribbons, boil-in-the-bag vegetables, Teflon-coated cookware, and disposable diapers.

**Compatibility.** Compatibility refers to the product's consistency with prospects' cultural values and habitual ways of doing things. It includes the perceived risk (personal and social consequences) of using the products. Low-sudsing detergents diffused slowly because consumers associated plenty of suds with cleaning power. Directions on the labels recommending one-half cup of detergent were contradictory to what consumers expected, a full cup. Toothpaste in aerosol cans failed because consumers were used to squeezing it from a tube. But Sizzlean, a breakfast strip that is leaner than bacon, offers this benefit while also being compatible with traditional ways of preparing breakfast.

**Complexity.** Complexity means the relative difficulty in understanding or using the product. Highly complex products require more time to diffuse. Examples include heat pumps, very sophisticated microwave ovens, food processors, and home computers.

**Divisibility.** Divisibility is the degree to which the product can be used on a trial basis.[22] Free samples and small-sized introductory packages often are used in marketing such products as cosmetics, household cleaners, and razor blades to help speed the adoption rate. When Mattel introduced Intellivision, it attempted to straddle two markets, video-games that hook up to TV sets and home computers. Mattel executives believed the word "computer" scares people, so they decided to market the product in two parts. The first part, the master component, performs functions like other programable video games. The second part, a sep-arate keyboard, attaches to the first unit and adds computer capabilities.[23]

**Communicability.** Communicability is the degree to which product results can be observed by others or described to them. The greater the communicability, the faster the adoption rate because people will talk it up and perhaps give it word-of-mouth advertising.[24] Examples include pantyhose, the Weed Eater, automated bank tellers, Home Box Office, hot tubs, and suntanning booths.

Although the PLC concept and the adoption and diffusion processes apply generally to most products, fashion products present a special case.

## FASHION CYCLES

Three terms are important in understanding fashion cycles: *style, fashion,* and *fad*. A style is a distinctive mode of presenting a product. Bikinis, maillots, and swimdresses are styles of bathing suits. A fashion is a style that currently is popular. During recent years, for example, mail-lots probably have been more fashionable than bikinis. A fad is a fashion that is popular for a very short time. Examples from recent years include the Gatsby look, lemon-scented cosmetics and household cleaners, leisure suits, and Pet Rocks.[25] Most fads die out in a matter of months, but it is hard to tell beforehand whether a new fashion will be a fad or a longer-lived fashion.[26] Many people probably expected water beds, miniskirts, jeans, disco, and Frisbees to die out very quickly, but they were wrong. Some fads also have a recurring cycle. Hula hoops, yo-yos, and some dance fads reappear every few years.

Product design changes not due to technological advances are made for fashion's sake. Fashion exists because people tend to dislike com-plete uniformity even though most of us do conform to established fash-ions to varying degrees.[27] In fact, the heterogeneous shopping products category exists because of fashion.

### Fashion Adoption and Diffusion

The trickle-down theory emphasizes the vertical flow of adoption from innovators to laggards. Thus a designer of women's apparel might seek to induce the "jet set" to adopt a new design and hope it will catch on with early adopters and move on down to the other classes of adopters (emulators). But by the time emulators have adopted, the fashion's dis-tinctiveness is eroded and innovators have already begun to accept a new style and make it fashionable.

As we said in Chapter 6, the lateral diffusion process involves the

spread of a new product or fashion across a particular social class. This diffusion generally occurs at a faster rate than the vertical diffusion from the upper to the lower social classes. Thus a new fashion concept introduced in fashion capitals is copied quickly, but with cheaper and lower-quality materials. Modern production technology permits mass production of cheaper versions, and efficient physical distribution systems deliver them to resellers while they still are new fashions.

Within each social class innovators buy the new fashion first. If it catches on with the early and later adopters, it becomes widely diffused within each social class. TV and magazines help to speed the diffusion process among all social classes.

It is doubtful, however, that fashion can be forced. Retailers who stocked midiskirts, baggy jeans, granny dresses, and Nehru jackets discovered this several years ago. Women can be observed at parties in dresses of varying lengths, pant suits, and so on, and they all feel dressed for the occasion. But fashions can be controlled to the extent that once a trend is under way promoting it may speed its diffusion. This shortens the fashion's life cycle and prepares the way for a replacement. This assumes, however, that the trend already is under way.

The significance of fashion is not limited to clothing. It is important for many other consumer and industrial products. Wristwatches, home appliances, and office furniture and equipment are a few examples. Firms that used to be unconcerned with fashion are now concerned with product design and fashion obsolescence. Consider the fashion element in eyeglasses, men's underwear, and office furniture today. Marketers must forecast the fashion cycle for their products. If they wait too long to produce and stock fashion products that catch on, they may enter the market on the fashion's downswing.

## Societal Considerations

Fashion's key element is newness, or novelty. As fashions are diffused more rapidly, the fashion cycle becomes shorter and effort focuses on finding new fashions. Firms often use trial-and-error procedures to come up with fashionable products; some will always be losers.[28] Inevitably, this increases the cost of producing and marketing products.

Some conservationists say marketers waste natural resources when they devote too much effort to developing new products when existing

---

*Table 10–3.* *Reasons many firms do not want to limit themselves to one product*

1. to counteract the effects of the product life cycle on a one-product firm
2. to even out seasonal sales patterns
3. to use company resources and capabilities more effectively
4. to capitalize on middlemen and consumer acceptance of established products
5. to spread production and marketing costs over a wider product mix
6. to become better known and respected by middlemen and consumers

ones are satisfactory. Some consumerists say marketers are too concerned with creating a never-ending desire for newness.[29] Some ecologists say too many products are designed to be short-lived and that this creates a big waste-disposal problem as old models are discarded for new models. We will discuss the issue of planned obsolescence in the next chapter.

The following discussion focuses on product considerations in multiproduct companies. Such firms market more than one product.

## PRODUCT MIX AND PRODUCT LINE

A firm's **product mix** includes all product items it offers. Procter & Gamble's product mix includes toothpaste, soap, detergent, deodorant, and cake mixes.

product mix

A **product line** is a group of products that are related because of customer, marketing, and/or production considerations. Crisco, Crisco Oil, and Duncan Hines are part of Procter & Gamble's food line and Cheer, Dash, Duz, and Gain are part of its detergent line.

product line

Table 10–3 lists several reasons many firms choose not to limit themselves to one product. A typical large multiproduct firm's product mix includes new, growing, maturing, and declining products. They hope that the new products will be the profit makers in the future. Growing products are the major profit contributors today ("cash cows") and maturing products also return some profits. Declining products were the firm's major profit contributors in past years. One author divides a firm's products into six categories: (1) tomorrow's breadwinners, (2) today's breadwinners, (3) products capable of becoming net contributors if something drastic is done, (4) yesterday's breadwinners, (5) also-rans, and (6) failures.[30]

### Breadth and Depth

A product mix has the structural dimensions of breadth (or width) and depth. Breadth refers to the number of different product lines. Depth refers to the number of product items within each line. (See Figure 10–6.)

A firm can expand its product mix by increasing the number of product lines or the depth within one or more lines. Procter & Gamble expanded in breadth when it bought the non-Canadian business of Crush International Ltd. It expanded in depth when it added Puritan Oil.

A firm can contract its product mix (product mix simplification) by reducing the number of product lines or the depth within one or more lines (product line simplification). RCA reduced breadth when it dropped computers. SCM Corporation reduced the depth of its electric typewriter line when it dropped large-size typewriters.

### Drop-Add Decisions

A firm's product-market matching strategy depends mainly on its philosophy of growth. It can seek growth by (1) increasing market share of

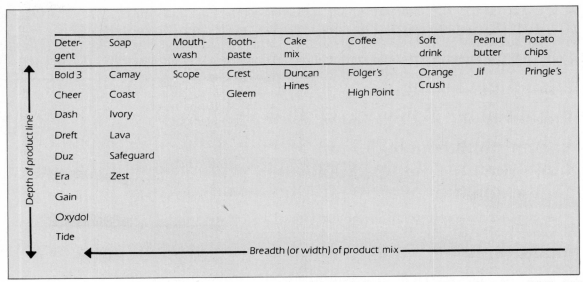

| Detergent | Soap | Mouthwash | Toothpaste | Cake mix | Coffee | Soft drink | Peanut butter | Potato chips |
|---|---|---|---|---|---|---|---|---|
| Bold 3 | Camay | Scope | Crest | Duncan Hines | Folger's | Orange Crush | Jif | Pringle's |
| Cheer | Coast | | Gleem | | High Point | | | |
| Dash | Ivory | | | | | | | |
| Dreft | Lava | | | | | | | |
| Duz | Safeguard | | | | | | | |
| Era | Zest | | | | | | | |
| Gain | | | | | | | | |
| Oxydol | | | | | | | | |
| Tide | | | | | | | | |

Depth of product line ↑

← Breadth (or width) of product mix →

*Figure 10–6.  Procter & Gamble's product mix and product lines (partial listing)*

existing products in present markets, (2) penetrating new markets with existing products, (3) developing new products to sell in present markets, or (4) developing new products to sell in new markets.   External and internal factors affect a firm's decision to add or drop products from its product mix.

**External Factors.**  Demographic change, such as a declining birthrate, has led some toy makers to add adult games to their product lines. Rising discretionary incomes led Timex to add higher-priced watches.

Changes in the economic and competitive environment also are important.   One of the reasons Kodak entered the instant photography market and also introduced its Ektaprint copier-duplicator was its expectation of greater competition in the film market.

Developments in the legal environment are another factor.   Several years after Procter & Gamble acquired the Clorox Company, the Federal Trade Commission required Procter & Gamble to sell it.   The FTC feared the acquisition would lessen competition.   Thereafter, Clorox started adding new products.   It did not want to limit its product mix to bleach products, which were in the maturity stage of their life cycles.

Changes in consumer behavior influenced supermarkets to add non-food items to satisfy increased customer preference for one-stop shopping. The consumerism movement played a big part in Chevrolet's decision to drop the Corvair.   The big increase in popularity of rum was a factor in National Distillers Products Company's decision to add CocoRibe.

**Internal Factors.**  A firm's mission, resources and capabilities, product characteristics, perceived profit potential, and perceived risk influence its decisions to add or drop products.   Hane's success with L'eggs led the

| Deodo-rant | Shampoo | Toilet tissue | Diapers | Cooking prep-arations | Cleansing products | Laundry prep-arations | Hand lotion | Tissues |
|---|---|---|---|---|---|---|---|---|
| Secret | Prell | Charmin | Pampers | Crisco | Comet | Bounce | Wondra | Puffs |
| Sure | Head & Should-ers | White Cloud | Luvs | Crisco Oil | Comet Liquid | Downy | | |
| | Agree | | | Puritan Oil | Mr. Clean | | | |
| | Pert | | | | Spic & Span | | | |
| | | | | | Top Job | | | |

Figure 10–6. Cont.

firm to try its skills at marketing socks, men's underwear, and cosmetics through supermarkets, drugstores, and discount stores. Financial considerations often favor product additions to spread risk, reduce seasonal fluctuations in sales volume, and to spread the cost of maintaining a product-servicing operation.

Dropping slow-moving products may reduce a firm's total sales but it may cut total costs even more and lead to greater overall profit. Production factors may favor adding new products to use excess capacity or waste materials. Similarly, production factors may lead to the dropping of a product because of the rapidly rising cost of a key raw material. Marketing factors may favor adding new products to give the salesforce a fuller line. Marketing factors may also favor dropping a slow-moving product so that the salesforce can concentrate its efforts on more profitable products.

**Cannibalization.** When increasing sales of a firm's new product are due mainly to decreasing sales of its established product or products, **cannibalization** has occurred. To avoid this, the new product should not be identified too closely with established products. It should be targeted with new appeals to different market segments. Estimates are that as much as one-half the sales of a newly introduced low-tar version of an established brand of cigarettes comes from that established brand's sales.[31]

cannibalization

McDonald's and other fast-food restaurants want to introduce new products that bring in new business. McDonald's test marketed McFeast for two years to gauge its potential for cannibalizing the Big Mac. When Ford introduced the Falcon it promoted the car as a "new-sized Ford."

Chevrolet introduced the Corvair the same year but did not associate it with the standard-size Chevrolet. The Falcon cannibalized the standard-size Ford because Falcon's sales increased while sales of standard-size Fords decreased. Corvair sales increased but so did sales of standard-size Chevrolets.[32] Cannibalization is especially undesirable when a lower-profit product cuts into the sales of higher-margin products.

## SUMMARY AND LOOK AHEAD

Production-oriented firms view products as a manifestation of the resources used to produce them. Customer-oriented firms view products from the customer's perspective—as a bundle of satisfactions, benefits, or utilities. They think in terms of the total product.

Two broad categories of products are consumer and industrial products. Consumer products are used by ultimate consumers or households. Industrial products are used to produce other products or to conduct the buying organization's operations.

One basis for classifying consumer products is buyer behavior. The four classes of products are (1) convenience products, (2) shopping products, (3) specialty products, and (4) unsought products.

Convenience products are relatively inexpensive, frequently purchased items that do not involve much shopping effort. Staple products, impulse products, and emergency products are the three subclasses. Purchases of shopping products involve price and quality comparisons because consumers perceive more risk in buying them. Price comparisons are most important for homogeneous shopping products. Consumers shop for the best price-quality combination when buying heterogeneous shopping products. Specialty products are those for which strong conviction as to brand or style already exists in the buyer's mind. Consumers will make a determined effort to locate these products. Regularly unsought products are those the consumer avoids. New unsought products are totally new and unfamiliar to the consumer.

Our economy is becoming more service oriented. Hotels, laundries, and airlines are examples of service firms. Like physical products, services are classified on the basis of buyer behavior.

Industrial products are classified according to the uses to which they are put. Raw materials, component parts, and component materials become part of the product they are used to produce. Installations, accessory equipment, supplies, and business services do not.

All products have a life cycle. The stages are (1) introduction, (2) growth, (3) maturity, and (4) decline. The product life cycle concept applies to a product category, a particular product form, or to a particular brand. A product's marketing mix ordinarily changes as it moves through its life cycle.

The consumer adoption process consists of five stages: (1) awareness, (2) interest, (3) evaluation, (4) trial, and (5) rejection or adoption. The spread of a new product idea throughout the market is called the diffusion process. The categories of adopters for a new product are innovators, early adopters, early majority, late majority, and laggards. The rate of speed with which a new product is adopted is affected by its relative advantage, compatibility, complexity, divisibility, and communicability.

The fashion cycle is important to marketers of products that have a high element of fashion. These products range from clothing to office furniture.

A multiproduct firm's product mix is made up of all the products it offers. A product line is a group of products that are related because of customer, marketing, and/or production considerations. Internal and external factors affect a firm's decision on adding new products and dropping old products. The potential for cannibalization of older products must be considered when adding new products.

In the next chapter we will expand the discussion of the product life cycle; we will also discuss product management.

## REVIEW QUESTIONS

1. Contrast a production-oriented and a customer-oriented view of the product.

2. How does the total product differ from the product item?

3. How does classifying consumer products on the basis of buyer behavior help marketers?

4. Identify, define, and give the subclasses under each of the four major classes of consumer products.

5. Identify and discuss five reasons for the growth in the marketing of services in the United States.

6. In what two basic ways do services differ from physical products?

7. Identify and discuss the types of industrial products that become part of the product they are used to produce.

8. Identify and discuss the types of industrial products that do not become part of the product they are used to produce.

9. Draw a graph that illustrates the product life cycle concept. Include a total market sales curve and a total market profit curve.

10. In which stage of the product life cycle is pioneering acceptance, or stimulating primary demand, most crucial? Explain.

11. Why are profits negative in the introductory stage of the product life cycle?

12. Why does the total market profit curve turn down before the total market sales curve in the product life cycle?

13. Why should multiproduct firms conduct product audits?

14. How does the diffusion process affect the product life cycle concept?

15. Identify and discuss the five stages in the consumer adoption process.

16. Identify and discuss five general product characteristics that affect the rate of speed with which a new product will be adopted.

17. How does a fad differ from a fashion?

18. What is meant by product mix and product line?

19. Identify and discuss the two structural dimensions of a product mix.

20. What is product mix simplification and product line simplification?

21. What does cannibalization mean in the context of product management?

## DISCUSSION QUESTIONS

**1.** Why do consumers not think it is worth the effort to compare price and quality for convenience products?

**2.** An exclusive restaurant in a large city may have only one outlet, whereas McDonald's and Burger King each may have ten or more outlets. Explain this in terms of the classification system for consumer products.

**3.** Is the total product a highly individualized concept? In other words, do different people perceive products differently?

**4.** Why is quality control tougher for services than for tangible products?

**5.** Why do some consumer products companies like Procter & Gamble give away free samples when introducing new products?

**6.** How do fads get started?

**7.** In launching a new brand, what can a firm do to minimize the chances it will cannibalize the firm's already existing brand in the same product category?

## NOTES

1. See Roman R. Andrus, "Marketing's Other Function," *Business Quarterly*, Winter, 1968, pp. 34–38.
2. For example, one study found that many consumers turn to nearby retailers in preference to distant manufacturers in remedying warranty problems. See Robert E. Wilkes and James B. Wilcox, "Consumer Perceptions of Product Warranties and Their Implications for Retail Strategy," *Journal of Business Research*, February, 1976, pp. 35–43.
3. For a discussion of the factors and characteristics of new products that are associated with acceptance or rejection by supermarkets, see David B. Montgomery, "New Product Distribution: An Analysis of Supermarket Buyer Decisions," *Journal of Marketing Research*, August, 1975, pp. 255–264.
4. *Marketing Definitions: A Glossary of Marketing Terms* (Chicago: American Marketing Association, 1960), p. 11.
5. Ibid., p. 14.
6. The classification of consumer products into convenience, shopping, and specialty products originally was proposed by Melvin T. Copeland in "Relation of Consumers' Buying Habits to Marketing Methods," *Harvard Business Review*, April, 1923, pp. 282–289. The category of unsought products was proposed by E. Jerome McCarthy in his book *Basic Marketing: A Managerial Approach* (Homewood, Ill.: Richard D. Irwin, Inc., 1960). Also see Richard H. Holton, "The Distinction between Convenience Goods, Shopping Goods, and Specialty Goods," *Journal of Marketing*, July, 1958, pp. 55–56. For a discussion of other approaches to classifying consumer products, see Leo V. Aspinwall, "The Characteristics of Goods Theory," in *Managerial Marketing: Perspectives and Viewpoints*, eds. William Lazer and Eugene J. Kelley (Homewood, Ill.: Richard D. Irwin, Inc., 1962), pp. 633–643; and Gordon E. Miracle, "Product Characteristics and Marketing Strategy," *Journal of Marketing*, January, 1965, pp. 18–24.
7. See Steuart Henderson Britt, "A Note on the 'Unplanned' Purchase," *University of Michigan Business Review*, January, 1976, pp. 13–15. Also see Danny N. Bellenger, Dan H. Robertson, and Elizabeth C. Hirschman, "Impulse Buying Varies by Product," *Journal of Advertising Research*, December, 1978, pp. 15–18.
8. One study found that consumers will adopt more price information in shopping when their alternative uses of time are unattractive. See Frederick W. Winter, "Laboratory Measurement of Response to Consumer Information," *Journal of Marketing Research*, November, 1975, pp. 390–401. Another study investigated the effect of considering cost and time in shopping for food products. Opportunity costs of devoting time to shopping differ among individuals, such as retired persons and employed persons. See Patsy M. Crowell and Jean S. Bowers, "Impacts of Time and Transportation Costs on Food Shopping," *Journal of Consumer Affairs*, Summer, 1977, pp. 102–109.
9. For a discussion of the pleasures of shopping, see Edward M. Tauber, "Why Do People Shop?" *Journal of Marketing*, October, 1972, pp. 46–49.
10. Lack of confidence in a physician, high cost of services, and inconvenient location or office hours, however, have been identified as factors related to the tendency to shop for physicians. See Josephine Kastelei, Robert L. Kane, Donna M. Olsen, and Constance Thetford, "Issues Underlying Prevalence of 'Doctor-Shopping' Behavior," *Journal of Health and Social Behavior*, December, 1976, pp. 328–339.
11. See William J. Regan, "The Service Revolution," *Journal of Marketing*, July, 1963, pp. 57–62; Robert C. Judd, "The Case for Redefining Services," *Journal of Marketing*, January, 1964, pp. 58–59; John M. Rathmell, "What Is Meant by Services?" *Journal of Marketing*, October, 1966, pp. 32–36; Fabian Linden, "The Business of Consumer Services," *Conference Board Record*, April, 1975, pp. 13–17; W. Earl Sasser, "Match Supply and Demand in Service Industries," *Harvard Business Review*, November–December, 1976, pp. 133–140; G. Lynn Shostack, "Breaking Free from Product Marketing," *Journal of Marketing*, April, 1977, pp. 73–80; Fabian Linden, "Service, Please!" *Across the*

*Board,* August, 1978, pp. 42–45; and Stanley C. Hollander, "Is There a Generic Demand for Services?" *MSU Business Topics,* Spring, 1979, pp. 41–46.

12. For discussion of the productivity issue in services marketing, see Dan Thomas, "Strategy Is Different in Service," *Harvard Business Review,* July–August, 1978, pp. 158–165; Richard B. Chase, "Where Does the Customer Fit in a Service Organization?" *Harvard Business Review,* November–December, 1978, pp. 137–142; and Christopher H. Lovelock and Robert F. Young, "Look to Consumers to Increase Productivity," *Harvard Business Review,* May–June, 1979, pp. 168–178.

13. See J. Donald Weinrauch, "How Significant Is Industrial Marketing in Periods of Excessive Buyer Demand?" *Industrial Marketing Management,* December, 1974, pp. 355–362; and J. E. Tusing and R. E. Moll, "Forward Buying for Profit Maximization," *Business Horizons,* December, 1976, pp. 82–86.

14. "Kodak Urges Caution on Outlook, Predicts Calm in Silver Market," *Wall Street Journal,* May 8, 1980, p. 28.

15. "Paper Mate's Broader Outlook," *Business Week,* January 28, 1980, p. 69.

16. "IBM Rival Is Upheld in a Suit Concerning Typewriter Ribbons," *Wall Street Journal,* May 16, 1980, p. 39.

17. Some authors add an additional stage, *saturation,* which comes between maturity and decline. The maturity stage ends when the sales curve reaches its peak. This becomes the saturation stage, which lasts until an actual decline in sales occurs.

18. For additional discussion of the product life cycle, see Theodore Levitt, "Exploit the Product Life Cycle," *Harvard Business Review,* November–December, 1965, pp. 81–94; Philip Kotler, "Competitive Strategies for New Product Marketing over the Life Cycle," *Management Science,* December, 1965, pp. 104–119; William E. Cox, "Product Life Cycles as Marketing Models," *Journal of Business,* October, 1967, pp. 375–384; Rolando Polli and Victor J. Cook, "Validity of the Product Life Cycle," *Journal of Business,* October, 1969, pp. 385–400; Chester R. Wasson, *Product Management: Product Life Cycles and Competitive Marketing Strategy* (St. Charles, Ill.: Challenge Books, 1971); John E. Smallwood, "The Product Life Cycle: A Key to Strategic Marketing Planning," *MSU Business Topics,* Winter, 1973, pp. 29–34; Bernard Catry and Michel Chevalier, "Market Share Strategy and the Product Life Cycle," *Journal of Marketing,* October, 1974, pp. 29–34; Nariman K. Dhalla and Sonia Yuspeh, "Forget the Product Life Cycle Concept!" *Harvard Business Review,* January–February, 1976, pp. 102–112; Ben M. Enis, Raymond LaGrace, and Arthur E. Prell, "Extending the Product Life Cycle," *Business Horizons,* June, 1977, pp. 46–56; and David R. Rink and John E. Swan, "Product Life Cycle Research: A Literature Review," *Journal of Business Research,* September, 1979, pp. 219–242.

19. Everett M. Rogers, *Diffusion of Innovations* (New York: The Free Press of Glencoe, 1962), pp. 81–86. Also see Thomas S. Robertson, "The Process of Innovation and the Diffusion of Innovation," *Journal of Marketing,* January, 1967, pp. 14–19; Frederick E. Webs-

ter, Jr., "New Product Adoption in Industrial Markets: A Framework for Analysis," *Journal of Marketing,* July, 1969, pp. 35–39; James H. Donnelly, Jr. and Michael J. Etzell, "Degrees of Product Newness and Early Trial," *Journal of Marketing Research,* August, 1973, pp. 295–300; Robert W. Shoemaker and F. Robert Shoaf, "Behavioral Changes in the Trial of New Products," *Journal of Consumer Research,* September, 1975, pp. 104–109; and Everett M. Rogers, "New Product Adoption and Diffusion," *Journal of Consumer Research,* March, 1976, pp. 290–301.

20. See David W. Cravens, James C. Cotham, III, and James R. Felix, "Identifying Innovator and Non-Innovator Firms," *Journal of Business Research,* April, 1971, pp. 45–51; Lyman E. Ostland, "Identifying Early Buyers," *Journal of Advertising Research,* April, 1972, pp. 29–34; Robert A. Peterson, "Diffusion and Adoption of a Consumer Durable," *Marquette Business Review,* Spring, 1974, pp. 1–4; Steven A. Baumgarten, "The Innovative Communicator in the Diffusion Process," *Journal of Marketing Research,* February, 1975, pp. 12–18; Laurence P. Feldman and Gary M. Armstrong, "Identifying Buyers of a Major Automobile Innovation," *Journal of Marketing,* January, 1975, pp. 47–53; Edward J. Malecki and Lawrence A. Brown, "The Adoption of Credit Card Services by Banks: A Case Study of Innovation Diffusion," *Bulletin of Business Research,* August, 1975, pp. 1–4; and David F. Midgley, "A Simple Mathematical Theory of Innovative Behavior," *Journal of Consumer Research,* June, 1976, pp. 31–41.

21. Adapted from Shlomo I. Lampert, "Word-of-Mouth Activity during the Introduction of a New Food Product," in John U. Farley, John A. Howard, and L. Winston Ring, eds. *Consumer Behavior: Theory and Application* (Boston: Allyn and Bacon, Inc., 1974), p. 82; and Joseph R. Mancuso, "Why Not Create Opinion Leaders for New Product Introductions?" *Journal of Marketing,* July, 1969, pp. 20–25.

22. One study reports that an individual household, on its trial purchase of a completely new brand of product, will tend to buy a smaller quantity than it normally does on its purchase of established brands. See Robert W. Shoemaker and F. Robert Shoaf, "Behavioral Changes in the Trial of New Products," *Journal of Consumer Research,* September, 1975, pp. 104–109.

23. "Mattel Tries to Lure Skeptical Consumers by Selling Computer as High-Priced Fun," *Wall Street Journal,* March 14, 1980, p. 13.

24. See James F. Engel, Robert J. Kegerreis, and Roger D. Blackwell, "Word-of-Mouth Communication by the Innovator," *Journal of Marketing,* July, 1969, pp. 15–19.

25. For discussion of the Vitamin E fad, see Joel Saegert and Merry Mayne Saegert, "Consumer Attitudes and Food Faddism: The Case of Vitamin E," *Journal of Consumer Affairs,* Winter, 1976, pp. 156–169.

26. See Chester R. Wasson, "How Predictable Are Fashion and Other Product Life Cycles?" *Journal of Marketing,* July, 1968, pp. 36–43.

27. See Kenneth N. Dayton, "Fashion Is Change," *University of Michigan Business Review,* March, 1976, pp. 1–5.

28. For discussion of why people acquire new products when old ones are still serviceable and what they do with products that have outlived their usefulness, see Jacob Jacoby, Carol K. Berning, and Thomas F. Dietvorst, "What About Disposition?" *Journal of Marketing*, April, 1977, pp. 22–28. Also see Dean S. Roussos and Leonard J. Konopa, "Ownership Levels, Acquisition and Disposition Channels of Selected Durable Used-Goods," *Akron Business and Economic Review*, Spring, 1977, pp. 30–34; and "The New Two-Tier Market for Consumer Goods," *Business Week*, April 11, 1977, pp. 80–83.

29. See Richard J. Schonberger, "The Utility of Buying an Older Car," *Journal of Consumer Affairs*, Winter, 1976, pp. 245–250. For a discussion of the use of "new and improved" package copy claims, see Michael L. Dean, James F. Engel, and W. Wayne Talarzyk, "The Influence of Package Copy Claims on Consumer Product Evaluations," *Journal of Marketing*, April, 1972, pp. 34–39.

30. Peter Drucker, "Managing for Business Effectiveness," *Harvard Business Review*, May–June, 1963, p. 59.

31. "Cigarette Sales Up—Maybe for the Last Time," *Business Week*, December 17, 1979, p. 54.

32. William Copulsky, "Cannibalism in the Marketplace," *Journal of Marketing*, October, 1976, pp. 103–105.

# Chapter 11

# Product Management

OBJECTIVES

*After reading this chapter you should be able to*

1.   give examples of product objectives.

2.   compare market positioning to product positioning.

3.   explain the significance of product liability to marketers.

4.   identify key considerations in product design.

5.   contrast functional and planned obsolescence and give examples.

6.   give various perspectives on the meaning of a new product.

7.   identify and discuss four popular approaches to organizing for new product development.

8.   identify and discuss the six stages in the new product development process.

9.   develop examples that show how marketers use the product life cycle concept in product management.

10.   discuss mature product strategy.

11.   identify the key issues in managing declining products.

KEY CONCEPTS

*Look for these terms as you read the chapter:*

Market Positioning
Product Positioning
Functional Obsolescence
Planned Obsolescence
New Product Committee
New Product Department
Product (or Brand) Manager
Venture Team
New Product Development Process
Product Concept Test
Laboratory Tests
Brand Extensions
Extension Strategies
Product Audit

*The Edsel, Resolve analgesic, Smooth N' Easy gravy mix in the form of a margarine bar, Babyscott diapers, Glad Wags dog treats, Hunts flavored ketchups, Prime Choice steak sauce, Cooking Ease spray lubricant for frying foods, Bic pantyhose, Billy Beer, Cue toothpaste, Listerine toothpaste, Vim tablet detergent, Reef mouthwash, Chelsea (soft drink), Ensure skin care lotion, Eagle 20s cigarettes, Tramp cigarettes, Corfam synthetic leather, High Seas (after-shave lotion), quadraphonic sound equipment, the Steve Scout doll, Knorr Soups, Post cereals with freeze-dried fruit, Nine Flags men's cologne, Crazylegs (women's shaving gel), and the World Football League all have two elements in common. They were new products and product failures. Even though most were introduced by large and successful marketing organizations, they ended up as costly failures.*

*On the other hand, Church & Dwight Company has been marketing Arm & Hammer baking soda for over 130 years. But most customers no longer buy it for baking. Arm & Hammer has kept itself alive and well by finding new uses for the product, as we will see in this chapter.*

Products must be managed properly to deliver customer satisfactions. Marketers must take a dynamic view of their product offerings or else face the strong possibility that their firms eventually will die as the demand for their products dies. Product offerings must be adapted to changing customer wants, which means marketers have to develop "new" products, change "existing" products, and drop "sick" products. These are tough decisions that practically every marketer faces.

## PRODUCT OBJECTIVES AND POSITIONING

A firm's product objectives result from its effort to match present and future market requirements with its resources and capabilities. Product objectives are the "whys" of a firm's marketing effort and reflect its mission. They must be compatible and integrated with overall company objectives, the objectives of other departments in the firm, the objectives of other marketing mix elements, and societal expectations. Table 11–1 gives several examples of this.

**market positioning**

Customer-oriented firms search the market for requirements they have the resources and capability to satisfy. **Market positioning** is the strategy through which a firm identifies market targets, develops market offerings to satisfy them, and positions itself into a niche in the market. Sears, Roebuck and Company positioned itself in the financial services industry with its Allstate group and a shopping center development firm. Procter & Gamble positioned itself in the soft drink business when it acquired Crush International. H. J. Heinz Company positioned itself in the weight control industry when it acquired Weight Watchers International, Inc.

**product positioning**

**Product positioning** is a somewhat narrower concept. It is the strategy through which a firm positions its products relative to rivals—how

**Table 11–1.** *Integrating product objectives with other objectives*

| Nonproduct Objectives | Compatible Product Objectives |
|---|---|
| Overall company objective: | |
| "to survive and grow" | "to increase return on investment by introducing new products and improving established products" |
| Production department objective: | |
| "to use waste materials to maximum advantage" | "to search for new product opportunities that use waste materials from existing products" |
| "to utilize production capacity fully" | "to identify new markets and develop products for those markets" |
| Distribution objective: | |
| "to build middleman cooperation" | "to provide a line of products that helps our dealers to achieve their objectives" |
| "to increase sales by getting more shelf space in retail stores" | "to offer a full line of related products" |
| Societal objective: | |
| "to ensure the safety of consumer products" | "to offer products that have been tested thoroughly for safety" |

*product features*

it targets products to their market targets through product features and/or promotion. This strategy occurs within the firm's overall product-market matching strategy. For example, the Quaker Oats Company positioned Quaker Corn Bran as the first cereal that combined the "benefit of bran with the great taste of corn." Previously, bran cereals were made from wheat.

The goal of product positioning is to achieve a differential advantage for the product. A product might be positioned to compete directly with rivals or to fill a niche in the market that presently is unsatisfied by rival products. Product positioning is especially important for products that are physically alike.

Most products must be launched against a leader.[1] In head-on positioning the firm positions its product to compete directly with rivals. IBM and SCM copiers, for example, are positioned head-on against Xerox copiers. The Quaker Oats Company's Ken-L-Ration pet food line introduced Tender Chunks dog food and positioned it as the first dry, yet moist, dog food. Not long after, Ralston Purina introduced Moist & Chunky.

Some marketers believe head-on positioning is not the best approach and there are examples of head-on casualties, such as Xerox's computers and Bristol-Myers's Fact toothpaste. But this type of positioning has perhaps become more popular in recent years because of greater use of comparative advertising, in which one brand of product compares itself to one or more named rival brands. For example, Gillette positioned

Earth Born shampoo directly against Clairol's Herbal Essence in comparative ads.

Variations of the head-on positioning strategy might be called indirect positioning. To differentiate itself from Goodyear, B. F. Goodrich launched an extensive promotion campaign to position itself as the tire company without a blimp. Honeywell positioned itself as "the other computer company." Vick Chemical Company used "positioning with an idea" to position Nyquil as the brand that assured a good night's sleep. Avis positioned itself as the number two car rental company, after Hertz, and claimed it had to work harder to please its customers.

Product positioning requires a careful analysis of competitive offerings and market segments the marketer wants to penetrate. This helps in identifying potential customers. Customers, for example, might be attracted from rival brands, new customers might be sought for the product category, or present customers could be persuaded to use the product more often. Metrecal originally was positioned to appeal to overweight people. Carnation's Slender expanded the customer base for diet foods by appealing to people who were in shape and wanted to stay that way.

Product positioning also requires decisions about product design and promotional appeals. Virginia Slims, for example, is positioned as the cigarette that is "slimmer than the fat cigarettes men smoke." Since promotional appeals and product design should be coordinated, we chose to introduce the concept of product positioning in this chapter. Virginia Slims actually *are* slim cigarettes.

## PRODUCT MEANINGS

A product has meaning to target customers, the marketer, and society. As we saw in the previous chapter, present and potential customers view a product as a bundle of satisfactions.[2] Different people, however, expect different benefits from a product. To some people, a car's major benefit is prestige; for others, it is leg room or gas mileage.[3]

Marketers should know what their target customers expect in terms of functional qualities, such as durability, performance, and warranty, and what they expect in terms of symbolic meanings, such as prestige and sex appeal. This is the only way they can develop customer-oriented market offerings. For years, many people believed that washing their hair in beer was beneficial. Bristol-Myers Company's Body on Tap is a shampoo that has real beer in it and is advertised as such to help differentiate it from other brands.

Society's view of a product sometimes conflicts with the buyer's and/or the marketer's view. For example, the required safety equipment on cars sometimes is criticized by consumers and marketers. Societal considerations, however, are becoming more important in product decisions, especially in the areas of product safety and packaging.[4]

Product liability suits have become more common and costly in recent years. Under the old concept of product liability manufacturers and sellers were liable for damages only when they were negligent or unreasonably careless in what they made or how they made it. Under the more recent concept of strict liability the product, its packaging, and its promotion can get a marketer into trouble. "To scent a candle, a teenager poured perfume made by Faberge Inc. over a lit wick. The perfume ignited, burning a friend's neck. Claiming that Faberge had failed to warn consumers of the perfume's flammability, the friend won a $27,000 judgment. Despite its argument that there was no way to foresee that someone would pour perfume onto an open flame, Faberge lost its appeal."[5]

Because product liability laws vary from state to state, the U.S. Department of Commerce has developed a Model Uniform Product Liability Act whose adoption by the states is voluntary. It states that a product may be proven defective in one or more of the following ways: (1) it was unreasonably unsafe in construction, (2) it was unreasonably unsafe in design, (3) it failed to provide adequate warnings or instructions, or (4) it failed to conform to the seller's expressed warranty.[6]

## PRODUCT DESIGN

The first step in product design is identifying the market target and gathering information about its characteristics and product expectations.[7] This helps to avoid underdesign (omitting desired features) and overdesign (adding features target customers do not want because they do not add to the product's appeal or because they add more to the price than buyers are willing to pay).[8]

Product design also must consider the benefits middlemen expect. The benefits final customers expect relate to consumption. The benefits middlemen expect are related to resale satisfactions. Although final customers come first, middlemen should not be overlooked. Grocers, for example, do not want packages that take up too much shelf space. L'eggs pantyhose display racks were accepted by retailers because they do not require much space. When the same firm, Hanes, began test marketing socks and men's underwear, many retailers complained that the display racks required too much space to carry all the colors and sizes customers want.

People buy products to solve problems and this affects product design. For example, is a refrigerator maker trying to solve a homemaker's problem of keeping perishable foods from spoiling between weekly shopping trips, storing perishable foods for several weeks so the homemaker has a food bank in the home, or having crushed ice and ice-water readily available for parties and long-term cold storage capacity? Depending on the answer, the firm would offer either a refrigerator with a small freezer, or a side-by-side refrigerator-freezer, or a side-by-side refrigerator-freezer with crushed-ice and ice-water dispensers on the door.

Multifunction products usually have wider markets than single-function products. But if potential buyers think a product is capable of performing too many functions, they may suspect it does none of them well.  A person might not buy a side-by-side refrigerator-freezer out of fear that a breakdown will cause both refrigerated and frozen foods to spoil.

## Product Features

A product is a bundle of satisfactions because of its features—quality, styling, performance, and materials.  Each affects a product's image.

In deciding how much quality to build into a product, customer-oriented firms do not simply build the highest-quality product possible. More quality than target customers expect may price the product out of their reach.  Enough quality should be designed into a product to enable it to perform its expected functions reliably.  This is why the product lines of many calculator marketers are so broad.  A person who pays $10 for a pocket model does not expect it to perform the same operations as a $1,000 model.

The issue of product obsolescence is related to product quality.  Some products become obsolete because of technological progress.  Thus the car generator was replaced by the alternator.  This is **functional obsolescence.**

**functional obsolescence**
**planned obsolescence**

The three types of **planned obsolescence** are (1) postponed, (2) intentionally designed, and (3) fashion or style.  Postponed obsolescence means holding back on adding product improvements until present inventories run out or demand falls off sharply.  Intentionally designed obsolescence involves designing a product, or a crucial part, to wear out within a given period of time.  Fashion or style obsolescence basically is psychological—new model cars make last year's models obsolete. Planned obsolescence is the subject of a lot of controversy.[9]

A marketer may try to defend postponed obsolescence by saying a product improvement was withheld to provide more time for testing it and researching potential customer desire for and willingness to pay for the improvement, or because its premature introduction would render some inventory worthless and these losses would be offset by higher

*"Just think—you can be the last in your neighborhood to own an anachronism!"*

Source: *Pepper and Salt*, © 1980 *The Wall Street Journal* and Brenda Burbank.

prices on the improved product. Of course, the marketer always runs the risk that a rival will incorporate the improvement in its product. Likewise, a marketer might argue that intentionally designed obsolescence is risky and may cause customers to switch to other brands. Fashion or style obsolescence may result from a marketer's effort to cater to market segments that demand "newness." Obsolescence also helps to make products available for the second-hand market, and it may be a natural result of the dynamic competitive and technological environment in which modern marketers operate.

Styling (color, shape, size, and so on) is important for products ranging from tissue paper to office furniture. Styling should facilitate a product's function. The midiskirt's failure in the early 1970s was due in part to the difficulty of driving in it. One often-given reason for the Studebaker car's problems was that the cars were too advanced in styling.

Customers also expect a certain level of product performance. Automakers in the 1950s and 1960s engaged in a "horsepower derby" because people wanted high performance cars. More recently, performance for cars and many other products is measured by what it costs to use them. Winnebago has been working to produce lighter recreational vehicles and more fuel efficient motors. Outboard Marine Corporation also has made design changes that make for a better blend of fuel economy and horsepower in its Johnson and Evinrude outboard motors.

The materials that go into making a product can be very important. Materials selection decisions can affect a product's sales appeal and should not be made solely by production managers. Materials shortages in some industries and questions regarding the safety or health aspects of materials may lead firms to search for alternative materials. Many building products that used to be made of asbestos, for example, are now made with other materials.


## PRODUCT INNOVATION

Our discussion in Chapter 10 of the product life cycle suggested the need for product innovation to replace declining products. Firms spend millions of dollars on research and development (R&D) to create new products. For example, it is not unusual for a firm in the pharmaceutical industry to invest $50 million or more on a new drug. (See Table 11-2.)

### What Is a New Product?

As Figure 11-1 suggests, there are degrees of product newness.[10] At one extreme are products that previously were unthought of, such as the telephone, the car, the radio, and the birth control pill. They were new to everyone when they were introduced.

Further down the scale of newness are products that replace existing ones because of major product modifications. The ballpoint pen replaced the fountain pen and the automatic washing machine replaced the wringer-type washer.

**Table 11-2.** *Three measures of the top 10 in R&D spending*

| In Total Dollars (millions) | | In Percent of Sales | | In Dollars per Employee | |
|---|---|---|---|---|---|
| 1. General Motors | $1,950 | 1. Cray Research | 14.0% | 1. Cray Research | $11,399 |
| 2. Ford Motor | 1,720 | 2. Amdahl | 13.0 | 2. Amdahl | 10,698 |
| 3. International Business Machines | 1,360 | 3. Applied Materials | 12.9 | 3. Applied Materials | 8,059 |
| 4. General Electric | 640 | 4. Cordis | 11.2 | 4. International Flavors & Fragrances | 7,554 |
| 5. United Technologies | 545 | 5. Teradyne | 10.4 | 5. Eli Lilly | 6,602 |
| 6. Boeing | 525 | 6. Systems Engineering Laboratories | 10.3 | 6. Upjohn | 6,137 |
| 7. Eastman Kodak | 459 | 7. John Fluke Mfg. | 10.1 | 7. Shared Medical Systems | 6,131 |
| 8. International Telephone & Telegraph | 436 | 8. Intel | 10.1 | 8. Merck | 6,106 |
| 9. Du Pont | 415 | 9. Data General | 10.0 | 9. Polaroid | 5,950 |
| 10. Exxon | 381 | 10. National Semiconductor | 9.4 | 10. Lubrizol | 5,800 |

Data: Standard & Poor's Compustat Services Inc.
Source: *Business Week*

Still further down the scale are products that are not new to anyone or that are not major product modifications but are new to a particular firm. A firm that launches a new brand of toothpaste would consider it to be a new product.

Consumers and marketers often have different ideas about what *new* means. To a consumer a new product is whatever he or she thinks is new. It may not be new to a firm but it may be new to the person who buys it. Thus the Tiparillo cigar was an established product long before some women considered it to be a new product. Perhaps it is best for a marketer to consider any item that is different in any way from its previous market offering to be a new product. A firm that used to sell only roll-on deodorant should consider deodorant in a pump container to be a new product even if the only difference is a package change. Orange juice marketers began marketing a new product when they started promoting orange juice as a lunch drink as well as a breakfast drink. Procter & Gamble began marketing new products when it acquired Crush International.

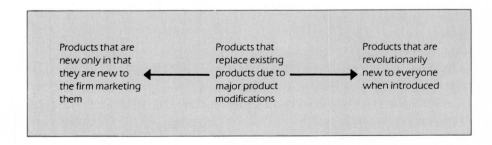

*Figure 11-1.*
*A continuum of product newness*

## New Product Development

Life cycles for many products during the 1950s, 1960s, and the early 1970s became progressively shorter and marketers turned to their R&D departments to provide a steady stream of new products. Product innovation became the "darling" of growth-oriented firms.

Increasing affluence enabled many Americans to satisfy their desire for new and improved products, and technological advances in manufacturing methods enabled firms to cater to this desire. Improved communications reduced the length of time a product would be considered new by consumers. A new product advertised on TV becomes familiar to many people rapidly. To many, new meant better. Finally, the youth orientation in our society intensified new product development because young people, and those who think young, tend to want and accept new products more readily than older people do.

Near the middle of the 1970s, materials shortages in some industries and concern about inflation, consumerism, and ecology took away some of the glamour from new product development. Many firms backed away from it and shifted their attention to extending the lives of their existing products.[11]

More recently, new product development has picked up again. Most marketers agree that a firm's long-run survival requires this effort because consumers want new products.[12] In the small appliance field, for example, new products are necessary for success.

## Sources of New Products

A firm has three basic sources of new products: innovation, modifications of existing products, and acquisition of other firms. Which approach(es) a firm takes depends largely on its mission and environment.

A firm that wants to be a trend setter in its industry will invest heavily in R&D to develop innovative products. Less aggressive firms modify their existing products. During boom periods some firms buy up other firms to get new products to broaden their market coverage. During serious recessions many shift away from innovation and acquisition and try to modify their existing products to make them new.

The rapidly increasing cost of R&D in the drug industry has tended to divide firms into two types: research-oriented firms that invest heavily in new drug development, and firms that cut R&D spending and seek less costly manufacturing methods to compete on the basis of price in the market for generic (unbranded) drugs.[13]

## Organizing for New Product Development

Top management's concept of the company's mission sets the tone for its new product development activity.[14] This activity requires cooperation and coordination among different departments, and top management must provide the framework for it. Four popular approaches to organizing for new product development are: (1) new product committees, (2) new product departments, (3) product, or brand, managers, and (4) venture teams.

new product committee

**New Product Committee.**   A **new product committee** consists of managers from different departments, such as production, marketing, finance, and R&D.   They review and act upon new product ideas generated elsewhere in the firm.   The committee brings together different types of expertise and helps build support among these managers for any ideas they accept.   The disadvantages relate to the potential for buck passing, overconservatism, too much compromise, and time-consuming committee deliberations.   Nevertheless, the committee structure is the most common approach to organizing for new product development.

new product department

**New Product Department.**   A **new product department** is accountable for all phases of the new product development process, from the idea stage to test marketing.   We will discuss this process later in the chapter.   In some cases new product ideas that are accepted by a new product committee are turned over to the new product department for development and testing.   New product development is the full-time job of the person who heads the department.   This person often reports directly to the firm's president.

product (or brand) manager

**Product, or Brand Manager.**   A **product (or brand) manager** in a manufacturing firm takes over the management of a product that has been approved for development.   His or her role in proposing and/or evaluating new product ideas may be very minor.   Product managers, however, do develop marketing strategy for their product(s).   But they almost never have line authority over people whose cooperation is vital to their effectiveness.   They select market targets and develop marketing mixes but they do not, for example, have line authority over the salesforce.   Thus they must be skilled in winning the cooperation and support of others.[15]

Many multiproduct firms like Procter & Gamble, General Foods, and Union Carbide use the product manager system.   Within each firm each brand gets individualized attention, and these brands and managers often compete for market share.   These firms believe that intrafirm competition is good.   Each brand manager, however, must be able to work effectively with the firm's research department, advertising department, and so on.   In some cases product managers handle an entire line of related products.[16]   The product manager system also is common in department stores.   Each merchandise manager manages the marketing effort for a given line of merchandise.

Those who disagree with the product manager approach argue that product managers sometimes neglect new product development because they spend too much time managing existing products.[17]   Thus in some firms there are two types of product managers: *new* product development managers handle initial development and test marketing of new products; full-scale introduction of products that pass their test marketing is the task of product managers, who manage assigned products through their life cycles.

**Venture Team.** Increasing use is being made of **venture teams,** which consist of marketing, finance, engineering, R&D, and production people who have an interest in a particular new product idea.[18] They are given free rein in developing the idea and carrying it through test marketing. The team may be separated physically from the rest of the firm and linked directly to top management. A product with demonstrated sales potential is assigned to either a division within the firm, or a new firm may be set up to market it. At that point the venture team is disbanded.

venture team

Regardless of organizational arrangement, outside specialists often are used to help firms find and/or develop new products. This often brings in new ideas and may reduce the lengthy development process. Some firms use outside specialists to help sell to other firms new ideas or products that they do not want to commit to full-scale market development.

## THE NEW PRODUCT DEVELOPMENT PROCESS

We discussed the product life cycle in Chapter 10. The **new product development process** precedes the introduction of a new product to the market. Its six stages are: (1) idea generation, (2) idea screening, (3) business analysis, (4) product development, (5) test marketing, and (6) commercialization. Before proceeding to each successive stage, management has to decide whether to proceed, seek more information, or abandon the new product development process.[19]

new product development process

### Idea Generation

The goal in the idea generation stage is to get as many new product ideas as possible because most of them will be discarded. Ideas must be received and channeled to persons or departments that have authority to act on them. Ideally, ideas are generated in a steady flow.[20]

The obvious internal source of new ideas is the R&D department, whose basic researchers study and forecast technology in order to discover new product concepts that applied researchers can use in developing products. Other internal sources are sales personnel, repair, service, and production personnel, and executives at all levels in the firm.

External sources include the "new products" section in trade journals, which may stimulate other new product ideas; observing competitors and their customers; and research done on the firm's own customers. Customers often send in letters suggesting ideas for new products.[21] Procter & Gamble receives about 4,000 ideas from consumers each year. Although the ideas are almost always politely turned down to protect against legal problems, the feedback often is useful.[22] Trade associations, private researchers, middlemen, and ad agencies are other sources. Government agencies like the Consumer Product Safety Commission can provide ideas about existing product weaknesses. Inventors who are skilled in engineering and production know-how but are lacking marketing skill some-

RON NEVISON KNOWS MORE ABOUT MUSIC
THAN 3M DOES.

THAT'S WHY WE LISTEN TO HIM.

Few people understand their jobs as well as Ron Nevison. That's why, when he talks about it, 3M listens.

In recent years, Ron has produced and engineered Led Zeppelin, Jefferson Starship and Dave Mason, among other contemporary stars.

Today, top music producers like Ron inspire exciting breakthroughs at 3M. Like 3M Digital Mastering Systems that provide greater clarity with stunning presence. And when still further advances are required, Ron Nevison will be among the first to know.

By listening to him, 3M can create more ingenious products for practical use. And that's our job. At 3M, listening is more than just good philosophy. It's vital to our future.

3M HEARS YOU

3M

*A source of new product ideas*

Source: 3M Corporation

times approach firms with new product ideas. Some firms, however, have a "not-invented-here" prejudice against outside inventors' ideas. Other firms, like 3M, welcome ideas from outside experts.

Firms also may set up teams that meet periodically to generate new ideas. To get maximum idea input in these brain-storming sessions, criticism and censorship are withheld. Table 11–3 discusses four techniques used by these teams.

**Table 11–3.** *Examples of techniques for generating new product ideas*

---

1. Listing:
   Each team member gives every new product idea he or she has.
2. Forced relationships:*
   Listing all the characteristics of an object that are markedly different from the product that is to be changed. For example, "How can you improve a chair by making it more like a car?"
3. Fantasy:
   Team members project themselves mentally into a situation. To generate new service ideas for airlines, team members could be asked to take an imaginary airplane trip. (Read the Boeing ad on page 312.)
4. Heuristic ideation technique:**
   This is a systematic method of considering all possible combinations of two variables to generate new ideas. A grid using packaging and food products could be constructed so that each type of packaging is paired with each type of food. New ideas might include grape jelly in tubes and margarine in squeezable containers.

---

*See Alex F. Osborn, *Applied Imagination*, 3rd ed. (New York: Charles Scribner, 1963), pp. 213–214.
**See Edward M. Tauber, "HIT: Heuristic Ideation Technique—A Systematic Procedure for New Product Search," *Journal of Marketing*, January, 1972, pp. 58–61.

## Idea Screening

Great care is needed to maximize creativity and minimize evaluation in the idea generation stage. The critical appraisal of those ideas occurs in the next stage, idea screening stage, because a firm can afford to undertake development of only a limited number of product ideas.[23] The less promising ones must be dropped. The two major costs here are the costs of rejecting good ideas and accepting poor ideas.

Rejecting good ideas leads to a lost opportunity. Accepting poor ideas leads to increasing costs because the costs associated with the latter stages of the development process are much higher than those in the "idea" stages. The longer it takes to scrap a poor idea, the more costly it is to the firm. Consider Ford and the Edsel, and Polaroid and Polavision.

New product ideas may be evaluated according to criteria established by management for what it thinks is an acceptable idea. Check lists may be used to rate new ideas and weights may be assigned to the various criteria to permit numerical ranking.

Column 1 in Table 11–4 lists management's requirements for a successful new product. Column 2 assigns weights to those factors in line with their relative importance. Management feels strongly that a new product should complement the existing product mix but also feels that the need to hire additional personnel is not very important in considering a new product idea. Next, management rates the product idea on a scale of 0.0 to 1.0, depending on how well the idea meets the requirements. Thus, complementing the existing product mix is rated very high (1.0), while distribution through existing channels is rated rather low (0.1). The last column is the result of multiplying the relative weight assigned

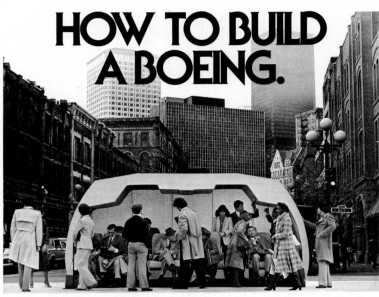

# HOW TO BUILD A BOEING.

The Boeing 767 is already a favorite way to fly even though it hasn't left the ground.

How do we know that?

A team of Boeing researchers, Kit Narodick, Karyl Landes and Dick Willy put the airplane to its ultimate consumer tests.

Actual-size passenger cabin cross sections were set up, and extensive studies were conducted among experienced passengers. They sat in actual seats and experienced an imaginary flight. Their opinions were recorded. Then they were asked to compare the 767 to other twin-aisle airplanes.

More than 7,000 people in New York, San Francisco, Hong Kong, Melbourne and lots of points in between were surveyed.

Kit, Karyl and Dick took every precaution to keep the research objective and without bias. They wanted the truth and nothing but the truth about a totally new concept in wide-body air travel.

Compared to competitive wide-body airplanes, the 767 wound up the odds-on favorite. The reasons: 1) better seating arrangements on the 767; 2) the 767 felt roomier, more comfortable.

This research team is just one of several hundred groups that worked on the development and engineering of this new generation jetliner. As a matter of fact, more than 2,500 people were involved in the project before the first sale was made.

So stand by, world. The 767 has met the test of our most severe critics — the passengers. And the verdict is: one super airplane.

**THE BOEING FAMILY**
Getting people together.

Source: The Boeing Co.

*Notice this ad's reference to the fantasy technique in new product development*

to each requirement by its rating.   The product idea scored 0.552.   On the basis of the firm's rating scale, management believes this product idea is worthy of further consideration.   It rates above the middle of the "fair" range.

Such a check list helps marketing managers to screen new product ideas systematically.   Judgment, experience, and the environment must be considered in deciding whether to proceed further with a new idea.

**Table 11-4.** *A product screening check list*

| Requirements for a Successful New Product | Relative Weight (A) | \multicolumn{11}{c}{Rating of Product Idea} | Rating (AxB) |
|---|---|---|---|---|---|---|---|---|---|---|---|---|---|

| Requirements for a Successful New Product | Relative Weight (A) | 0.0 | 0.1 | 0.2 | 0.3 | 0.4 | 0.5 (B) | 0.6 | 0.7 | 0.8 | 0.9 | 1.0 | Rating (AxB) |
|---|---|---|---|---|---|---|---|---|---|---|---|---|---|
| will complement existing product mix | 0.20 | | | | | | | | | | | ✔ | 0.200 |
| no plant expansion necessary | 0.18 | | | ✔ | | | | | | | | | 0.036 |
| protectable by patent | 0.15 | | | | | | | | | ✔ | | | 0.120 |
| can be distributed through existing channels | 0.12 | | ✔ | | | | | | | | | | 0.012 |
| development costs can be recovered rapidly | 0.12 | | | | | | ✔ | | | | | | 0.060 |
| can be promoted through currently used advertising media | 0.10 | | | | | | | | | ✔ | | | 0.080 |
| will not require extensive retraining of salesforce | 0.08 | | | | ✔ | | | | | | | | 0.024 |
| will not require hiring additional personnel | 0.05 | | | | | ✔ | | | | | | | 0.020 |
| | | | | | | | | | | | | | 0.552 |

Rating scale:
0.00–0.40 = poor
0.41–0.65 = fair
0.66–1.00 = good
A minimum rating for further consideration of a new product idea is 0.50.
(Adapted from Barry M. Richman, "A Rating Scale for Product Innovation," *Business Horizons*, Summer, 1962, pp. 37–44.)

During recessionary periods, for example, objections by finance personnel to a particular idea probably receive more attention than during boom periods.

## Business Analysis

Ideas that survive the screening stage are analyzed in the business analysis stage to determine their contribution to the firm's effort to match market requirements with company resources, capabilities, and objectives. Each idea is analyzed in terms of demand, cost, and profit potential.

We discussed demand analysis in Chapter 8. It includes forecasting market and sales potential, estimating the competitive reaction, and projecting the life cycles of the products. Cost analysis includes estimating production and marketing costs—production capacity, distribution re-

# HOW GM "PROJECT CENTERS" CREATE CARS

## FROM CONCEPT TO CUSTOMER IN THREE YEARS AND THREE BILLION DOLLARS

Throughout the history of the automobile industry, product change was almost always evolutionary. But in 1973, GM determined that the times required revolutionary changes. It started its first Project Center—which by itself heralded a revolution in the use of science and technology to meet the changing demands of the marketplace. A few months later, the Arab countries launched the oil embargo. Fortunately, machinery was already in motion in GM to create and develop new cars and components in a new way and faster than ever before.

**GM's first Project Center brought out totally new full-size cars:** smaller, yet roomier, and far more efficient than their predecessors. The advertisements said they were "designed and engineered for a changing world"—and they were. Another Project Center, begun in 1975, developed the immensely popular GM X-cars.

Led by the five car divisions, Project Centers gather people, ideas, and knowledge from all 30 divisions and staffs of General Motors. In the first stage, which we call "concepting," experimental engineers, environmental scientists, forward planners, and marketing experts pool their thinking. Their objective: what the marketplace will require. This is the most important stage. Here we must determine not only what

kind of car, but how many we might be able to build and sell years later. Economics, customer tastes, availability of various kinds of fuels must be compared with state-of-the-art technology—and what steps must be taken to advance that technology quickly yet surely.

In the "concepting" stage, a new car is conceived. If the car is to be sold to customers three years later, construction of new plants must begin and basic tooling must be ordered.

The second phase of the Project Center takes 24 to 30 months. It encompasses development, design, structural analysis, handling analysis, emissions, noise and vibration, safety, reliability, serviceability and repairability, manufacturing, assembly, marketing, financing.

Advanced product engineers and research scientists work with the one hundred fifty to two hundred people at the Project Center and thousands more in the staffs and divisions to transfer new science and technology to the new car. Components are hand-built and "cobbled" into existing models for road testing.

**Prototype cars are hand-built at a cost of more than $250,000 each.** These enable the Project Center team to determine how newly developed, pretested components operate as a unit. Then, pilot models will be built from production tooling and tested some more. New technology, such as structural analysis by computer, saves

time. Lead time has been reduced by 25% from ten years ago, when cars were far less complex.

After almost four million miles, nearly three billion dollars, and nearly three years of work, the new cars—quite unlike anything before them—start coming off the production line at a rate of better than one a minute.

**There are now eight Project Centers in General Motors.** Four are developing new cars using hydrocarbon fuels, one is creating an electric car, and others are working on computerized engines and emission controls, a new kind of automatic transmission, and the inflatable restraint system.

New and revolutionary cars can't be mass produced for the road overnight. But by putting all the parts of General Motors to work together, we found a way to speed up the process. We have integrated the creativity of thousands of human minds to make invention into reality when it's needed.

*This advertisement is part of our continuing effort to give customers useful information about their cars and trucks and the company that builds them.*

## General Motors
People building transportation to serve people

*General Motors discusses the product development process*

Source: General Motors Corporation.

quirements, promotional requirements, and so on. Demand and cost factors are brought together in the profitability analysis. Rate-of-return analysis ranks the ideas in terms of their profit potential.[24] Environmental factors also are important in this ranking process.

## Product Development

Product ideas that survive the business analysis stage are committed to technical and marketing development. Technical development involves making a product prototype that can be subjected to manufacturing methods research to determine the most efficient method of volume production. An example is the clay and wood mock-ups used for new car models.

Meanwhile, the marketing department tests the proposed product's suitability to the market target. As we said in Chapter 4, a **product concept test** may be used to learn the potential customer's feelings about it. The product is described in detail for potential customers, who give their reactions to it before it is actually produced. Both technical and marketing development must be coordinated. A product that can be produced efficiently may not sell, and a favorable product concept test may be meaningless if the product cannot be produced economically.[25]

Information gathered in this stage is the basis for deciding whether to continue, postpone, or drop further development. Although this go-or no-go decision is made at each stage in the process, once technical and marketing development begin costs increase sharply. Up to this point, the only costs incurred are research costs. A go-decision now leads to market entry costs. Often, there is a bias in favor of a go-decision. A no-go decision is very hard on the people who developed the idea.

At any rate, a go-decision requires the manufacturing department to plan for materials procurement, production facilities, and personnel. Meanwhile, the marketing department develops a final plan for introducing the product and managing it through its life cycle. Ideally, all the development work in this stage will have ironed out any bugs in the product.

## Test Marketing

If a go-decision is made, test marketing of the actual product begins under normal shopping conditions in one or more tests cities. Test cities, as we saw in Chapter 9, should be representative of the market area in which the product is intended to be sold.

The traditional market test serves as a final screening device before the decision is made to introduce the product to the entire market.[26] If test results are unfavorable, the product's introduction is postponed or the product is dropped. Ideally, however, individual product features that could be tested before the traditional market test should be pretested. Later test marketing of the product serves as a test of the new product's entire marketing program.[27]

Test marketing takes time and money and it is highly visible to rivals. The time between the test and evaluation of its results may be long enough to enable rivals to introduce competitive products. For example, Airwick Industries, Inc. developed and test marketed Carpet Fresh. A

**Table 11–5.** *Popular test markets*

| | |
|---|---|
| Albany-Schenectady-Troy | Oklahoma City |
| Atlanta | Omaha |
| Buffalo | Peoria |
| Cleveland | Phoenix |
| Columbus | Portland |
| Dallas–Fort Worth | Quad cities: |
| Dayton |    Rock Island and Moline, Illinois; Davenport and |
| Denver |     Bettendorf, Iowa |
| Des Moines | Rochester |
| Fort Wayne | Rockford |
| Fresno | Sacramento |
| Grand Rapids–Kalamazoo | St. Louis |
| Houston | Salt Lake City |
| Indianapolis | San Diego |
| Jacksonville | Seattle |
| Kansas City | Spokane |
| Milwaukee | Syracuse |
| Minneapolis–St. Paul | |

Source: *Sales Management*

rival monitored the test markets, found the product selling well, and had its brand on the market within six months.[28]

Rivals also sometimes sabotage test marketing by, for example, lowering the price of their brands in test cities or by greatly increasing spending on promotion. This is why some firms view test marketing as the first stage in expanding the product's coverage to the total market.[29] If the product performs satisfactorily in its initial distribution area, its distribution is expanded to other areas.

**laboratory tests**

**Laboratory tests** help to minimize these problems because the testing is done in a setting that conceals it from rivals. Philip Morris uses panel testing in which small groups of smokers are given new brands of cigarettes and their reactions are tested in taste tests. General Mills tests its products in its Betty Crocker test kitchens. These tests shield products being tested by limiting their exposure to a few people in a very controlled environment. But they involve fewer people and may be less reliable than test marketing in test cities.

## Commercialization

If the product's test market results are favorable, the marketer prepares to launch it into the introductory stage of its life cycle.[30] This requires finalizing the product's marketing strategy. Sometimes there may be

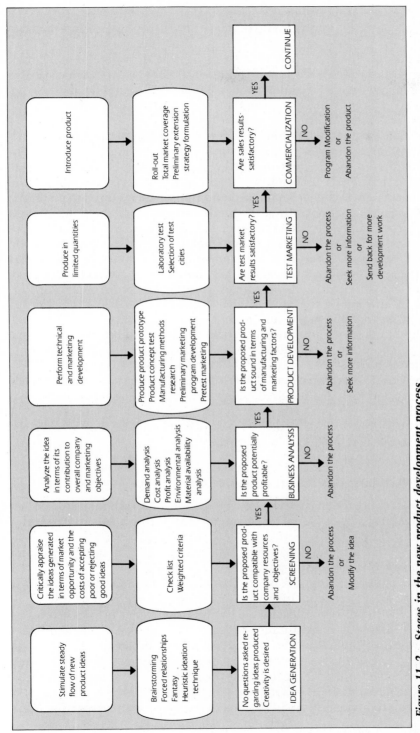

*Figure 11–2. Stages in the new product development process*

a delay between successful test marketing and full-scale marketing of the product. Green Giant tested one of its new products in San Francisco and the results were very encouraging. The product was taken off the market in San Francisco after the test to give the firm time to make final adjustments in its marketing program for national distribution. Users of the product found retailers out of stock and complained to them. Green Giant, therefore, had to explain through the newspapers why the product was unavailable.

During commercialization, therefore, the firm develops the product's marketing program over its projected life cycle. The total product, instead of simply the product item, now moves to the center of management's attention. Expenditures are greatest in this stage and interdepartmental cooperation and coordination are required in planning, implementing, and controlling the marketing effort for the new product. Among the activities that take place at this stage are the acquiring of production facilities to produce the product in volume and the preparation of final budgets. The salesforce and middlemen must be acquainted with the new product and trained and motivated to help ensure a successful introduction. The ad agency and the marketer must work together in developing the promotional program, final plans for physical distribution must be made, and so on.

The hundreds of activities involved in the commercialization stage must be coordinated carefully. Many firms use advanced scheduling techniques such as the Program Evaluation and Review Technique (PERT) and the Critical Path Method (CPM) to map out sequentially the activities necessary and the time required for each activity. The result is an elaborate flow chart that coordinates all these activities.[31] Figure 11–2 is a flow chart (not a PERT or a CPM type of diagram) that summarizes the stages in the new product development process.

## PRODUCT LIFE CYCLE MANAGEMENT

As we have said, the majority of new product ideas do not make it through the screening stage. One management consulting firm reported in a study that only about 20 percent of new product ideas survive the screening stage. Furthermore, less than 2 percent of the original new product ideas result in a successful product.[32]

The marketing literature often cites a high rate of new product failure. Some estimates range as high as 90 percent and some go as low as 20 percent.[33] In between these two extremes, there appear to be almost as many estimates as there are researchers who report on the new product failure rate. This, however, is understandable because researchers do not always agree on what constitutes a new product or a product failure.

A recent Conference Board study found that the typical failure rate for major new products is about one in three.[34] This study dealt only with new products, not modifications or improvements of existing products. It also defined a successful product as one "sent to market and meeting management's original expectations in all important respects."

Nevertheless, it is clear that the failure rate is high and considerable research supports the contention that marketing-related deficiencies contribute more to new product failures than do technical production deficiencies.[35] Even marketing powerhouses like Procter & Gamble have product failures. In 1965 it test marketed Fling, a roll of disposable, detergent-filled dishcloths made of tough flexible paper. The product failed. P&G researchers discovered that people were satisfied enough with the dishcloths they had. There was no need for Fling.[36]

In the discussion that follows we will see how marketers use the PLC concept in managing products over their life cycles.

## Introductory Stage

Suppose a firm uses test marketing as an actual test of the product's marketing mix. Then the revenues earned during the earliest part of its introductory PLC stage are due to sales made in test marketing and commercialization.[37] But, as we saw in Chapter 10, the typical product does not generate enough sales after launching to produce an immediate profit.

It is during the latter phase of the introductory stage that marketers must be especially alert in monitoring a product's market performance. The most eager buyers, the innovators, should be watched carefully to determine if any adjustments are needed in the marketing mix. This is crucial in getting the new product off to a good start in its life cycle by sustaining its demand during the critical introductory stage.

## Growth Stage

The major goal in the growth stage is to solidify the product's position relative to those of new entrants on the market. New entrants can be expected to chip away at a product's marginally satisfied customers by tailoring their offerings more closely to those customers' wants. Thus the marketer must be prepared to make adjustments in the product's marketing mix.

Perhaps the basic product may have to be modified to appeal to a wider market by introducing variations of the basic model. The Polaroid SX-70 camera, for example, was still in the growth stage when the SX-70 II was introduced.

Distribution of the product also may be expanded. Most firms tend to be conservative in launching new products and restrict distribution to prime markets. Although they may be forgoing some sales, they also are exposing themselves to less risk. Perhaps you have seen some new products advertised on TV along with a caption stating that the product is available in limited areas. But by the growth stage, the product may have proven itself worthy of wider distribution.

Price also may be adjusted. If the firm launched the product at a relatively high price in an attempt to recoup its development costs as quickly as possible, it may want to lower price to discourage new entrants. This tendency to lower the initial price is reinforced when the rapidly rising sales volume enables the firm to enjoy lower per-unit manufacturing cost (economies of scale). We will discuss this in greater detail in the chapters on pricing.

If the product is a revolutionarily new product, promotion can shift from stimulating primary demand (demand for the product category) to stimulating selective demand (demand for a particular brand), especially when rivals are entering the market rapidly. Promotional expenditures as a percentage of sales revenues also should decline as sales continue to increase. This also helps contribute to the product's profitability.

## Maturity Stage

As we saw in Chapter 10, product maturity is inevitable for many product categories, most product forms, and practically all brands. In fact, most products on the American market are mature products, but they account for far more sales and profits than new products do. For example, mature liquid and dry bleach products account for about half of Clorox Company's sales and up to 70 percent of its earnings.[38] Obviously, there is a need for mature product strategy.

Because of the risk and high cost of introducing new products, especially in recessionary periods, many firms will try to get as much mileage as possible from their established products by introducing variations, or extensions, of them. Honey Nut Cheerios, Honey and Nut Corn Flakes, and Log Cabin Pancake and Waffle Mix are some examples. **brand extensions** Often these are referred to as **brand extensions.**

Once the market for a product is saturated, however, most of its sales are due to repeat purchases and its potential for sales growth declines or disappears. This leads to a lack of middleman support. Often, a marketer must provide special promotional assistance, such as extra incentives to stock the product, to encourage middlemen. It also is likely at this stage that some retailers will desire to carry their own brand of the product. The manufacturer then has to decide whether to produce the product for the retailer to sell under the retailer's brand. We will discuss this in the next chapter.

Pricing strategy also needs adjustment in the maturity stage. Ordinarily, price becomes a more active ingredient in the marketing mix because at this point price cutting among rivals becomes more common as a basis for competition. Competitive copying of successful product

*Table 11–6.* *Extension strategies*

---
1. Increase frequency of usage among present customers.
2. Develop more varied usage among present customers.
3. Add new users by penetrating new market segments.
4. Develop entirely new uses for the product.

---

Source: Adopted from *Harvard Business Review*

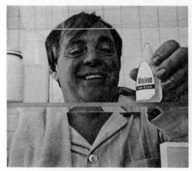

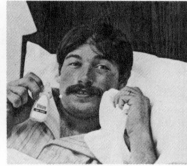

Source: Pfizer, Inc.

*Example of an ad seeking to increase usage frequency of the product*

features and the appearance of substitutes can also erode a product's uniqueness and its customer loyalty.

    **Extension Strategies.** Marketers can sometimes extend a mature product's life. These **extension strategies** should be planned before a

**extension strategies**

*Example of an ad seeking to develop more varied usage among present customers*

Source: Kraft, Inc.

product is launched. They probably are more important during recessionary periods than in more prosperous times, when marketers are more willing and able to invest more in new product development. The high failure rate of new products is reason enough for marketers seriously to consider extending the lives of their proven, but mature, products. (See Table 11–6.)

One extension strategy is to increase the frequency of present usage among present customers. Toothpaste makers promote brushing after every meal, Budweiser urges people to "pick a pair" of six-packs when they buy Bud, and Kleenex tissue is available in various package styles for different rooms in the house.

A second extension strategy is to develop more varied usage among present customers. Kraft Foods and Campbell Soup Company encourage present customers to try their recipes, which feature many uses for their products, and Lipton iced tea is promoted as a winter drink as well as a summer drink. Noxzema Skin Cream urges teen-agers to use it instead of soap every time they wash their faces. The theme "Danskins are not just for dancing" is another example of the varied usage strategy.

A third extension strategy is to add new users by penetrating new

Pure JOHNSON'S Baby Powder helps you feel good about yourself by keeping you feeling soft, and smelling clean.

It helps that come across to other people too, because it helps bring out your best. Your skin looks soft and feels silky. And you smell so clean and natural.

Now that you're older, haven't you got your own reasons for JOHNSON'S Baby Powder?

**For Older Reasons.**

*Johnson's* Baby Powder. The softness is for you. The silkiness is for him.

*Johnson & Johnson*

*Johnson's baby powder*

*Johnson & Johnson*

Source: Johnson & Johnson

*Example of an ad seeking to add new users of the product*

market segments. Johnson's baby shampoo, baby oil, and baby powder are promoted for use by adults.

A fourth extension strategy is to develop entirely new uses for the product. Arm & Hammer baking soda is advertised as a deodorant for refrigerators, sinks, and kitty litter boxes, for use in bath water and swimming pools, and as a carpet freshener.

These extension strategies help to recycle mature products. De-

Source: Church and Dwight, Inc.

*Example of an ad seeking to develop new uses for the product*

pending on the circumstances, an extension strategy might involve penetrating new market segments, product differentiation, or other changes in a product's marketing program.

Warner-Lambert's Listerine is more than 100 years old but still is the biggest seller in the mouthwash market. The firm believes in extending the lives of its successful products through advertising and product differentiation. It introduced mint-flavored Listermint in 1976 to counter Procter & Gamble's earlier introduction of Scope in 1975. It also introduced a cinnamon-flavored version in 1979.

As a product goes through its life cycle, more information is available about its buyers and rival products. This might lead a firm to reposition its product. Right-Guard deodorant, for example, originally was positioned as a man's deodorant but later was repositioned as an all-family product. Canada Dry Club Soda used to be sold solely as a mixer, but the growing popularity of wine and lighter spirits in recent years along with the successful introduction of Perrier water in the American market led Canada Dry to attempt repositioning Club Soda as a sparkling water.

In some cases, extension strategies launch a mature product into a new growth cycle. In other cases, the best that can be done is to buy additional time until a new product is ready to replace the mature one.

In case A in Figure 11–3 the extension strategy recycles the product. It starts a new life cycle before the original one runs its course. It is a break-out extension. There may be several recycles, depending on the effectiveness of the extension strategies. In case B the extension strategy lengthens the original life cycle by extending the maturity and/or decline stages. It is a stretch-out extension.

## Decline Stage

A declining product appeals primarily to the late majority and laggard segments. (See Chapters 4 and 10.) Product strategy is needed for declining products but often is overlooked. Product managers may be reluctant to consider dropping products they launched and salespersons may not want a product dropped if they still have a few buyers for it. Identifying declining products also is tough when marketers lack accurate and timely cost and profit information about their products.

A declining product ordinarily has lost its distinctiveness because of excessive copying by rivals. The appearance of these "me-too" products (parity products) leads to brand switching because there is little to hold the buyer's loyalty. Technological developments and societal or environmental considerations also may bring on a product's decline. Electronics technology, for example, practically ended the life cycle of the mechanical cash register. In 1976 the Federal Communications Commission (FCC) authorized marketers to sell forty-channel citizens band (CB) sets after January 1, 1977. To dispose of their twenty-three-channel units before that date, marketers began cutting prices on the twenty-three-channel units but discovered that most potential buyers were wait-

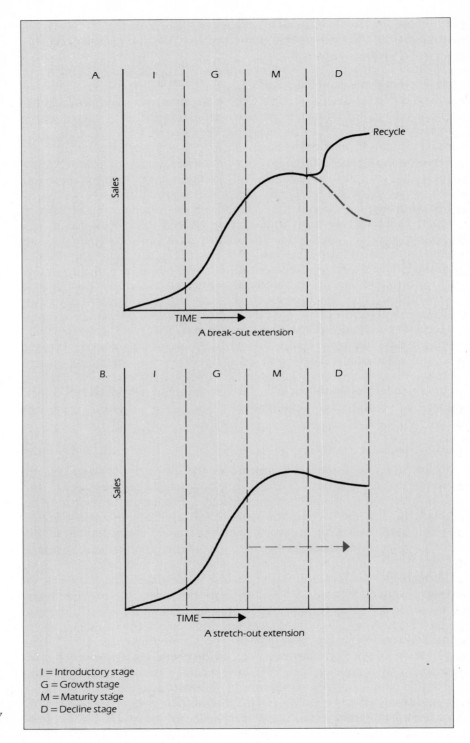

Figure 11–3.
Two types of
extension strategy
results

ing for the new forty-channel units to go on the market. Some CB marketers ended up buying back from their dealers twenty-three-channel equipment and converting it to forty channels. But by that time the market was saturated, in part because of lower-priced imports from Japan.

A declining product's price might be increased if there is a group of hard-core loyal buyers for it. Usually, however, the price will be subject to extreme downward pressure. In many cases, marketers will lower price to clear out their inventories.

Distribution strategy often focuses on removing the product from unprofitable outlets and concentrating it in outlets that service the few remaining loyal customers. Interestingly, the product probably is considered a specialty product by these buyers and they will make a concerted effort to locate and buy it.

Finally, promotional support usually is reduced, often practically to zero. The product, however, may continue to be promoted to loyal buyers and, instead of being withdrawn from the market, it may petrify at a low level of sales and remain at that level for many years.[39] Old Gold cigarettes, for example, used to be a major national seller but is now a regionally marketed brand. Bristol-Myers Company abandoned Ipana toothpaste in 1968. The next year two people reformulated the product but packaged it in essentially the same way and retained the Ipana name. Without advertising they sold $250,000 of Ipana in the first seven months they were in business.[40]

**Identifying Declining Products.** Sick (declining) products drain resources and effort from healthy products. A systematic, periodic **product audit,** or product review, helps to identify declining products. Products with declining sales, price, and profit trends become candidates for deletion in the product pruning process.[41] Other criteria include dwindling differential advantage accompanied by increase marketing costs.

product audit

Each deletion candidate should be evaluated critically to determine if its life can be extended. If the profit trend has been declining, the causes should be investigated. Perhaps a slight change in manufacturing methods or a change in the marketing program will permit a reduction in cost and higher profits.

A product that cannot be extended should at least be considered for deletion. Other factors, however, may favor its retention.[42] A declining market share may hide the fact that the product still appeals to an important market segment. Dropping it may result in lost sales of other products the firm markets. If deletion would free resources that cannot be used profitably elsewhere, the product might be carried as long as its sales revenues cover the out-of-pocket costs of making it and make some minor contribution to fixed costs. Deletion decisions require both analysis and judgment.

Products selected for deletion need not be unprofitable. Environmental factors may be as important in deletion decisions as in new product development decisions. Thus tougher Environmental Protection Agency (EPA) regulations on pesticides have led to the abandonment of some products in that industry. Many firms stopped packaging their products in aerosol containers that used fluorocarbon propellants before they were required to do so by law.

A product also may be deleted because it does not fit the company. Monsanto Chemical Company sold its All detergent to Lever Brothers because Monsanto's primary mission was selling industrial chemicals to large-volume industrial buyers. A product that requires resources that could be used more efficiently elsewhere also might be dropped. This is why General Motors sold its Frigidaire line of home appliances to White Consolidated Industries.

Despite the fact that the Volkswagen Beetle, a product launched in 1938, was at one time the leading imported car in the United States, its production ceased in West Germany in 1978. Up to that time, more than nineteen million Beetles had been sold world-wide, but sales were lagging in many markets because of such factors as tougher competition from other brands. The Beetle was not dropped completely, however. Some still are manufactured in Brazil, Mexico, and South Africa, mostly for use in those countries.

### Product Deletion

When a product is scheduled for deletion, the timing of its withdrawal and the interim commitment of resources to it become crucial decisions. Ideal timing for the firm would permit the resources freed from deleting the product to be used more profitably elsewhere—perhaps in developing a new product to replace it. During this time, finished goods, goods in process, and parts and materials inventories would be depleted. Ideal timing for customers means adequate advance warning and, in the case of durable products, the availability of replacement and repair parts. Middlemen also should be notified in advance so they can work off their inventories. Sometimes they are permitted to return product items in their inventories for credit.

If some loyal customers remain and a new product is not ready to replace the old product, distribution and some promotional support may be provided until the old product is phased out and replaced by the new product. But if a product cannot return a profit on its out-of-pocket costs and a new product is ready for immediate launching, the product should be dropped as soon as possible. Some firms are using sophisticated quantitative techniques to improve their product abandonment decisions.

## SUMMARY AND LOOK AHEAD

Product objectives are the "whys" of a firm's marketing effort. They reflect its mission and must be compatible with the objectives of the company and its various departments, other marketing mix elements, and societal expectations.

Product positioning is the strategy by which a firm positions its products relative to rivals—how it targets each product to its market through product features and/or advertising. Head-on positioning and indirect positioning are two positioning strategies. Some products have to be repositioned during their life cycles.

Customers, marketers, and society often have different perspectives on product offerings. Marketers must know the product expectations of target customers—the benefits and satisfactions they seek—to design and market customer-satisfying products.

Product design requires identifying target customers and gathering information about their characteristics and product expectations. Considering the benefits middlemen expect is also necessary. One way to approach product design is to recognize that people buy products to solve problems. A product is a bundle of satisfactions because of its features. Product obsolescence is also an important aspect of design. Some obsolescence results from technological progress. Other types—postponed, intentionally designed, and fashion or style—are planned.

Product innovation is necessary in growth-oriented firms because new products are needed to cater to ever-changing customer wants. Sometimes modifications of existing products are enough to create new products. Often, however, firms have to devote a lot of effort and resources to the new product development process. To a firm, a new product is any item that is different in any way from its previous market offering. Three basic sources of new products are (1) innovation, (2) modifications of existing products, and (3) acquisition of other firms.

Four popular approaches to organizing for new product development are (1) committee, (2) department, (3) product manager, and (4) venture team. The new product development process involves six stages: (1) idea generation, (2) idea screening, (3) business analysis, (4) product development, (5) test marketing, and (6) commercialization. Before proceeding to each successive stage, management has to decide whether to proceed, seek more information, or abandon the process.

The failure rate for new products is high and marketing-related deficiencies contribute more to new product failures than do technical production deficiencies. Products require good management over their entire life cycles.

Many internal and external factors influence decisions about adding or dropping product items in multiproduct firms. In some cases, the failure to identify declining products rules out the possibility of recycling them through extension strategies. These strategies include (1) increasing frequency of present usage among present customers, (2) developing more varied usage among present customers, (3) adding new users by penetrating new market segments, and (4) developing entirely new uses for the product. Some firms, however, neglect product deletion strategy.

The next chapter discusses other product-related decision areas—branding, packaging, and labeling.

## REVIEW QUESTIONS

**1.** Compare market positioning and product positioning.

**2.** Should marketers be concerned about the issue of product liability? Why or why not?

**3.** What is meant by product underdesign and overdesign?

**4.** Develop an example that illustrates the idea that people buy products to solve problems.

**5.** Identify and discuss the three types of planned obsolescence.

**6.** From the firm's point of view, what is a new product?

**7.** What three basic sources of new products are available to a firm?

**8.** Identify and discuss four approaches to organizing for new product development.

**9.** Identify and discuss the six stages in the new product development process.

**10.** What is the goal of the idea generation stage of the new product development process?

**11.** What two main costs are associated with idea screening?

**12.** Contrast traditional test marketing and laboratory tests.

**13.** Identify and give examples of four strategies that might extend a mature product's life.

**14.** Compare a break-out extension to a stretch-out extension.

**15.** What is the product pruning process?

**16.** Discuss the timing of a declining product's withdrawal from the market from the point of view of (a) the customer, (b) the marketer, and (c) the middleman.

## DISCUSSION QUESTIONS

**1.** Do you think a firm has an obligation to build the highest quality product possible?

**2.** Is a strategy of planned product obsolescence justifiable from a societal perspective?

**3.** Is there too much emphasis on new product development in the United States?

**4.** "Consumers would enjoy lower prices if marketers concentrated their efforts on extending the lives of their present products instead of developing new products that are only slight modifications of established products." Do you agree?

**5.** What can a marketer do to reduce risk in new product development?

**6.** Why is the new product failure rate so high?

## NOTES

1. This and the following two paragraphs borrow heavily from John P. Maggard, "Positioning Revisited," *Journal of Marketing*, January, 1976, pp. 63–66.

2. See John G. Swan and Linda Jones Coombs, "Product Performance and Consumer Satisfaction: A New Concept," *Journal of Marketing*, April, 1976, pp. 25–33.

3. One study found that consumers appear to have two types of expectations with respect to brands of cars: (1) expected performance and (2) expected congruence with the buyer's self-image and reference-group image. See J. Paul Peter and Lawrence K. Tarpey, Sr., "A Comparative Analysis of Three Consumer Decision Strategies," *Journal of Consumer Research*, June, 1975, pp. 29–37.

4. See Dale L. Varble, "Social and Environmental Considerations in New Product Development," *Journal of Marketing*, October, 1972, pp. 11–15.

5. "The Devils in the Product Liability Laws," *Business Week*, February 12, 1979, pp. 72–73.

6. Paul Busch, "Adoption of U.S. Product Liability Act Now Up to States," *Marketing News*, February 22, 1980, p. 12.

7. See Rolph E. Anderson, "Consumer Dissatisfaction: The Effect of Disconfirmed Expectancy on Perceived Product Performance," *Journal of Marketing*

*Research*, February, 1973, pp. 38–44. Also see James L. Ginter and W. Wayne Talarzyk, "Applying the Marketing Concept to Design New Products," *Journal of Business Research*, January, 1978, pp. 51–66.

8. See Peter M. Banting and Isaiah A. Litvak, "The Design Engineer and Marketing Innovation," *Business Quarterly*, Autumn, 1970, pp. 62–69. For a discussion of the use of projective methods in controlled questioning of consumers as a design input, see "Let the Buyer Be Heard," *Industrial Design*, November–December, 1976, pp. 42–44.

9. See Donald W. Jackson, Jr., "Is Planned Obsolescence Obsolete?" *Arizona Business*, November, 1976, pp. 11–17.

10. See Chester R. Wasson, "What Is 'New' about a New Product?" *Journal of Marketing*, July, 1960, pp. 52–56; and Patrick M. Dunne, "What Really Are New Products?" *Journal of Business*, December, 1974, pp. 20–25.

11. See Thomas A. Staudt, "Higher Management Risks in Product Strategy," *Journal of Marketing*, January, 1973, pp. 4–9.

12. See Paul L. Oritt, "New Product Development: Still the Key to Profitability," *Review of Business*, March–April, 1976, pp. 4–8; and Paul C. Harper, Jr., "New Product Marketing: The Cutting Edge of Corporate Policy," *Journal of Marketing*, April, 1976, pp. 76–79.

13. Eli Lilly, "New Life in the Drug Industry," *Business Week*, October 29, 1979, p. 137.

14. See Philip R. McDonald and Joseph O. Eastlack, Jr., "Top Management Involvement with New Products," *Business Horizons*, December, 1971, pp. 23–31.

15. See David J. Luck, "Interfaces of a Product Manager," *Journal of Marketing*, October, 1969, pp. 32–36; Gary R. Gemmill and David L. Wilemon, "The Product Manager as an Influence Agent," *Journal of Marketing*, January, 1972, pp. 26–30; Alladi Venkatesh and David L. Wilemon, "Interpersonal Influence in Product Management," *Journal of Marketing*, October, 1976, pp. 33–40; and Richard T. Hise and J. Patrick Kelly, "Product Management on Trial," *Journal of Marketing*, October, 1978, pp. 28–33.

16. See Richard M. Clewett and Stanley E. Stasch, "Shifting Role of the Product Manager," *Harvard Business Review*, January–February, 1975, pp. 65–73; Victor P. Buell, "The Changing Role of the Product Manager in Consumer Goods Companies," *Journal of Marketing*, July, 1975, pp. 3–11; and Joseph A. Morein, "Shift from Brand to Product Line Marketing," *Harvard Business Review*, September–October, 1975, pp. 56–64.

17. Some marketers also are critical of product positioning because they contend that it diverts time and energy from the creation of useful new products and ideas to the creation of "artificial" differences among identical product items. See Kenneth M. Warwick and Saul Sands, "Product Positioning: Problems and Promise," *University of Michigan Business Review*, November, 1975, pp. 17–20.

18. See Richard M. Hill and James D. Hlavacek, "The Venture Team: A New Concept in Marketing," *Journal of Marketing*, July, 1972, pp. 44–50; "VTA Increases New Products' Chance of Being Successful," *Marketing News*, March 15, 1973, p. 8; and James D. Hlavacek, "Toward More Successful Venture Management," *Journal of Marketing*, October, 1974, pp. 56–60.

19. See Chester R. Wasson, *Dynamic Competitive Strategy and Product Life Cycles* (St. Charles, Ill.: Challenge Books, 1974), and A. Edward Spitz, *Product Planning* (Princeton, N.J.: Auerbach Publishers, 1976.)

20. See Dik Warren Twedt, "How to Plan New Products, Improve Old Ones, and Create Better Advertising," *Journal of Marketing*, January, 1969, pp. 53–57; Tony Lantis, "How to Generate New Product Ideas," *Journal of Advertising Research*, June, 1970, pp. 31–35; Edward M. Tauber, "HIT: Heuristic Ideation Technique—A Systematic Procedure for New Product Search," *Journal of Marketing*, January, 1972, pp. 58–61; Edward M. Tauber, "Discovering New Product Opportunities with Problem Inventory Analysis," *Journal of Marketing*, January, 1975, pp. 67–70; Charles L. Alford and Joseph Barry Mason, "Generating New Product Ideas," *Journal of Advertising Research*, December, 1975, pp. 27–32; and James H. Myers, "Benefit Structure Analysis: A New Tool for Product Planning," *Journal of Marketing*, October, 1976, pp. 23–33.

21. See Eric von Hippel, "Successful Industrial Products from Customer Ideas," *Journal of Marketing*, January, 1978, pp. 39–49.

22. "At Procter & Gamble, Success Is Largely Due to Heeding Consumer," *Wall Street Journal*, April 29, 1980, pp. 1, 24.

23. See Allan D. Shocker, Dennis Gensch, and Leonard S. Simon, "Toward the Improvement of New-Product Search and Screening," in *Marketing Involvement in Society and the Economy*, ed. Philip McDonald (Chicago: American Marketing Association, 1969), pp. 168–175.

24. See Philip A. Scheuble, "ROI for New-Product Policy," *Harvard Business Review*, November–December, 1964, pp. 110–120; and Edgar A. Pessemier, *New Product Decisions: An Analytical Approach* (New York: McGraw-Hill Book Company, 1966.)

25. See Edward M. Tauber, "Reduce New Product Failures: Measure Needs as Well as Purchase Interest," *Journal of Marketing*, July, 1973, pp. 61–64; James W. Taylor, John J. Houlahan, and Alan C. Gabriel, "The Purchase Intention Question in New Product Development: A Field Test," *Journal of Marketing*, January, 1975, pp. 90–92; Edward M. Tauber, "Why Concept and Product Tests Fail to Predict New Product Results," *Journal of Marketing*, October, 1975, pp. 69–71; and Yoram Wind, Steuart Joley, and Arthur O'Conner, "Concept Testing as Input to Strategic Market Simulations," in *Combined Proceedings*, ed. Edward M. Mazze (Chicago: American Marketing Association, 1976).

26. See N. D. Cadbury, "When, Where, and How to Test Market," *Harvard Business Review*, May–June, 1975, pp. 96–105; Sally Scanlon, "Test Marketing 1976: Calling the Shots More Closely," *Sales & Marketing Management*, May 10, 1976, pp. 43–48; and Herbert

Zeltner, "When Should You Market Test? Five Guides to Help You Decide," *Advertising Age*, January 1, 1977, pp. 46–48.

27. See Jay E. Klompmaker, G. David Hughes, and Russell I. Haley, "Test Marketing in New Product Development," *Harvard Business Review*, May–June, 1976, pp. 128–138. There also is a need for coordination between technical and marketing groups in test marketing, especially in the age of consumerism. See Joseph Nemec, Jr. and Herbert Terry, "New Trends in Product Testing," *Business Horizons*, October, 1975, pp. 31–36.

28. "Some Tales of 'Copycat' Products Are Best Left Untold, Sterling Drug Learns," *Wall Street Journal*, March 11, 1980, p. 14.

29. See Linden A. Davis, "New Product Forecasting Techniques May Make Test Markets Obsolete," *Marketing News*, November 19, 1976, pp. 1, 5; Edward M. Tauber, "Forecasting Sales Prior to Test Market," *Journal of Marketing*, January, 1977, pp. 80–84; Howard N. Gundee, "Prediction Systems Really Work; Outdo Market Testing," *Marketing News*, September 9, 1977, p. 5; and Saul Sands, "Can Business Afford the Luxury of Test Marketing?" *University of Michigan Business Review*, March, 1978, pp. 19–24.

30. See William J. Constandse, "How to Launch New Products," *MSU Business Topics*, Winter, 1971, pp. 29–34.

31. See Yung Wong, "Critical Path Analysis for New Product Planning," *Journal of Marketing*, October, 1964, pp. 53–59, and Warren Dusenburg, "CPM for New Product Introduction," *Harvard Business Review*, July–August, 1967, pp. 124–139.

32. *Management of New Products* (Chicago: Booz, Allen, and Hamilton, 1968), p. 9.

33. For an excellent survey of the marketing literature on the new product failure rate, see C. Merle Crawford, "Marketing Research and the New Product Failure Rate," *Journal of Marketing*, April, 1977, pp. 51–56, at p. 51.

34. "Survey Finds 67% of New Products Succeed," *Marketing News*, February 8, 1980, p. 1.

35. See Theodore L. Angelus, "Why Do Most New Products Fail?" *Advertising Age*, March 24, 1969, pp. 85–86; William J. Constandse, "Why New Product Management Fails," *Business Management*, June, 1971, pp. 163–165; Rick W. Diehl, "Achieving Successful Innovation," *University of Michigan Business Review*, March, 1972, pp. 6–10; George J. Abrams, "Why New Products Fail," *Advertising Age*, April 22, 1974, pp. 51–52; Robert C. Cooper, "Why New Industrial Products Fail," *Industrial Marketing Management*, December, 1975, pp. 315–326; J. Hugh Davidson, "Why Most New Consumer Brands Fail," *Harvard Business Review*, March–April, 1976, pp. 117–122; Michael Paschkes,

"How to Guarantee New Product Failure," *Sales and Marketing Management*, July 12, 1976, pp. 40–42; Peter M. Banting, "Unsuccessful Innovation in the Industrial Market," *Journal of Marketing*, January, 1978, pp. 99–100; R. G. Cooper, "The Dimensions of Industrial New Product Success and Failure," *Journal of Marketing*, Summer, 1979, pp. 93–103; and David W. Nylen, "New Product Failures: Not Just a Marketing Problem," *Business*, September–October, 1979, pp. 2–7.

36. "At Procter & Gamble, Success Is Largely Due to Heeding Consumer," *Wall Street Journal*, April 29, 1980, p. 24.

37. One author suggests the term *career path* instead of life cycle. The career path more clearly identifies the precommercialization stage. See Harold W. Fox, "The Product Career Path—A Management Tool," *Quarterly Review of Marketing*, Autumn, 1976, pp. 5–12.

38. "Clorox: Picking Up the Pieces of a Diversification That Failed," *Business Week*, March 3, 1980, pp. 42–43.

39. See George C. Michael, "Product Petrification: A New Stage in the Life Cycle Theory," *California Management Review*, Fall, 1971, pp. 88–91.

40. "Abandoned Trademark Turns a Tidy Profit for Two Minnesotans," *Wall Street Journal*, October 27, 1969, p. 1.

41. See Ralph S. Alexander, "The Death and Burial of 'Sick' Products," *Journal of Marketing*, April, 1964, pp. 1–7; Philip Kotler, "Phasing Out Weak Products," *Harvard Business Review*, March–April, 1965, pp. 107–118; James T. Rothe, "The Product Elimination Decision," *MSU Business Topics*, Autumn, 1970, pp. 45–51; Paul W. Hamelman and Edward M. Mazze, "Improving Product Abandonment Decisions," *Journal of Marketing*, April, 1972, pp. 20–26; Guy R. Banville and Barbara A. Pletcher, "The Product Elimination Function," *Journal of the Academy of Marketing Science*, Summer, 1974, pp. 432–446; John A. Fiedler, "Choosing a Remedy for Sick Sales: Product Change or Advertising Change?" *Journal of Marketing*, April, 1975, pp. 67–68; Richard Hise and Michael McGinnis, "Product Elimination: Practices, Policies, and Ethics," *Business Horizons*, June, 1975, pp. 25–32; Stanley H. Kratchman, Richard T. Hise, and Thomas A. Ulrich, "Management's Decision to Discontinue a Product," *Journal of Accountancy*, June, 1975, pp. 50–54; Parker M. Worthing, "Improving Product Deletion Decision Making," *MSU Business Topics*, Summer, 1975, pp. 29–38; and "The Art of Letting Go: Product Abandonment," *Dun & Bradstreet Reports Magazine*, March–April, 1977, pp. 29–33.

42. See Walter J. Talley, Jr., "Profiting from the Declining Product," *Business Horizons*, Spring, 1964, pp. 77–84.

Chapter 12

# Branding, Packaging, and Labeling

**OBJECTIVES**
*After reading this chapter you should be able to*

1. distinguish between manufacturer and dealer brands.

2. identify and discuss the degrees of brand familiarity.

3. discuss the relative advantages of branding to buyers and sellers.

4. cite reasons for the growth in generic marketing.

5. identify the qualities of a good brand name and give examples.

6. identify the key issues in branding strategy for manufacturers and middlemen.

7. identify three branding options for multi-product marketers.

8. discuss the rivalry between manufacturer and dealer brands for market share.

9. identify several key packaging objectives and decisions.

10. discuss three types of labels.

11. identify the activities involved in a product recall.

**KEY CONCEPTS**
*Look for these terms as you read the chapter:*
- Brand
- Brand Name
- Brand Mark
- Trademark
- Manufacturer Brands
- Dealer Brands
- Brand Nonrecognition
- Brand Recognition
- Brand Rejection
- Brand Acceptance
- Brand Preference
- Brand Insistence
- Family Brand
- Individual Brand
- Packaging
- Brand Label
- Grade Label
- Informative Label

*In 1885 a druggist in Waco, Texas named Wade Morrison invented a new soft drink. He wanted to marry Ruth Pepper but her father refused to allow the marriage. The father, Charles Pepper, was a physician in Virginia. Mr. Morrison believed that if he named his new soft drink after Charles Pepper, he would allow the marriage to take place. Thus Mr. Morrison named the drink Dr Pepper.*

*Although Charles Pepper did not give his approval for the marriage, which never took place, the brand name still is in use today. Over the years, however, the company has had problems with the brand name. Some people apparently are confused by the name and think it is a type of medicine. In the early 1970s an ad campaign was built around the theme "America's Most Misunderstood Soft Drink," and in the late 1970s the "Be a Pepper" ad campaign was launched.\**

*Kraft has long been recognized as a leading brand of food products. The company merged with Dart Industries in 1980 and the name was changed to Dart & Kraft, Inc. Probably not very many users of products bearing the names Tupperware, Duracell, and West Bend could identify Dart as the manufacturer.*

*The Coca-Cola Company's Coke and Levi Strauss & Company's Levi's are two brand names that are worth millions of dollars. Their owners, like those of many other well-known and accepted brand names, go to great lengths to protect them from copiers. Today it is common for marketers to devote considerable time and effort to developing brands, packages, and labels. They can make the difference between success and failure in the marketplace.*

Beer, soft drinks, and bath soaps are product categories. Budweiser, Schlitz, Coca-Cola, Dr Pepper, Ivory, and Safeguard are brands within these product categories. In many cases, a product item's brand, package, and label are more important in marketing them than the actual contents of the package.

A brand usually appears on a label and the label usually appears on the package. Branding, packaging, and labeling can be used to identify a product item with its producer or distributor and are important in developing brand image. They are interrelated with each other and with other marketing mix elements. If the firm wants to develop a quality brand image, price should not be set low, promotion should stress the brand's exclusiveness, and distribution perhaps should be restricted to the better outlets.

Branding, packaging, and labeling decisions also require interdepartmental coordination. Quality control in production operations is nec-

---

\*Source: "Selling a Soda: Gone Slightly Flat, Dr Pepper Tries to Put Fizz Back in Its Growth," *Wall Street Journal*, June 5, 1980, pp. 1, 23.

essary when a firm brands its product and identifies it with the firm. Adequate financing is also needed to promote the brand.

## BRANDS

A **brand** is "a name, term, symbol, or design, or a combination of them, which is intended to identify the goods or services of one seller or group of sellers and to differentiate them from those of competitors."[1]

The pronounceable part of the brand is the **brand name.** Tide, Shell, and L'eggs are brand names. The part of a brand that appears as a symbol, design, or distinctive lettering or coloring is the **brand mark,** or "logo." It is recognizable by sight but is not pronounceable.

A **trademark** is "a brand or part of a brand that is given legal protection because it is capable of exclusive appropriation."[2]   On the package or label the circled "R" or "Reg. T.M." following a brand mark or brand name indicates that it is a registered trademark.   In 1980 a federal judge issued a preliminary injunction barring Montgomery Ward & Company from selling garbage disposal units called Jaws One, Jaws Two, and Jaws Power.   Universal City Studios and Merchandising Corporation of America charged in their suit that Ward had infringed on the Jaws trademark.[3] Table 12–1 lists several brand names and brand marks.

Two types of brands based on ownership are (1) manufacturer brands and (2) dealer brands.[4]  **Manufacturer brands** are owned by manufacturers.   Delco batteries (General Motors) and Frigidaire appliances (White Consolidated Industries, Inc.) are examples.   **Dealer brands** are owned by middlemen.   DieHard batteries (Sears, Roebuck and Company) and Kenmore appliances (also Sears) are examples.

*(margin notes: brand · brand name · brand mark · trademark · manufacturer brands · dealer brands)*

### Branding Objectives

The objectives of branding are to aid target customers in identifying the branded item and to familiarize them with it so they will accept it.[5]   For any given person, a particular brand may be unrecognized, recognized, rejected, accepted, preferred, or insisted upon.   These are the degrees of brand familiarity.   Brand familiarity is a major cue in consumer choice behavior.[6]   It also affects marketing mix planning.   (See Figure 12–1.)

**Table 12–1.**  *Brand names and brand marks*

| Brand Name | Brand Mark |
| --- | --- |
| Hang Ten | The distinctive feet |
| Star-Kist tuna | Charlie the tuna |
| Kellogg's Frosted Flakes | Tony the tiger |
| Morton Salt | Morton's Umbrella Girl |
| L'eggs | L'eggs egg |
| McDonald's | The McDonald's arch |

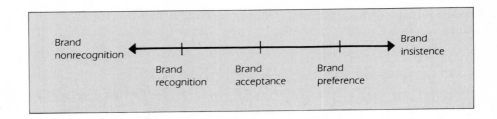

**Figure 12–1.
A continuum of
brand familiarity**

brand
   nonrecognition

**Brand nonrecognition** means a potential buyer considers a branded product to be homogeneous to other brands in the product category because he or she does not recognize it. Typical examples for many consumers are mops, paper clips, and pocket combs.

brand recognition

**Brand recognition** means potential buyers have heard or read about the brand and they remember it. They can recognize it among other brands in the product category.

brand rejection

**Brand rejection** means the brand is rejected by potential buyers. They will not buy it even though they recognize it because they have a poor image of the brand. The marketer can try to overcome this by changing the product, its other marketing mix elements, or the market target for the brand. Attempts to overcome poor brand images are costly, time consuming, and difficult.

brand acceptance

**Brand acceptance** means potential buyers accept the brand as one purchase alternative when buying a brand within the product category. The brand meets at least their minimal product expectations.

brand preference

**Brand preference** means the brand is accepted and preferred over others in the same product category. This usually occurs after satisfactory trial purchases.

brand insistence

**Brand insistence** means the customer considers only one brand in the product category acceptable. Beer drinkers who prefer Schlitz will accept another brand when their tavern is out of Schlitz. If they insist on Schlitz they will refuse to accept a substitute. To them, Schlitz is a specialty product. It is unlikely that a marketer can achieve true brand insistence for most products and customers. Instead of relying on brand insistence to make consumers search for Schlitz, for example, the brewer makes it available in many outlets and advertises it heavily.

Some marketers assume they have achieved a high degree of brand familiarity when, in fact, their brands may barely be recognized by target customers. This can lead to costly mistakes in marketing mix planning. Using marketing research to gain insight into the degree of brand familiarity a product has among target customers is wise.

**Branding and Customers**

Branding offers many advantages to customers. A brand offers customers protection when it identifies the seller.[7] Because poor product quality damages both brand and company images, the brand's owner has an in-

# 23 million people could be fooled this year.

This year, 23 million people may think they're buying a pair of Fiskars scissors and end up with an imitation.

The reason is simple. Fiskars designed the original lightweight scissors. They perfected it. They introduced it. And then, 44 other companies started copying it. Most even went so far as to use orange handles. But that wasn't quite far enough. It takes much more to make a fine pair of scissors. Like Swedish stainless steel blades that let you glide through yards of fabric without faltering. And comfort-molded handles that actually become an extension of you, offering a lifetime of effortless cutting.

So don't let the look-alikes fool you. If it doesn't say Fiskars on the blade, it's merely an imitation. And that doesn't say much for those other scissors.

**If it doesn't say Fiskars on the blade, it doesn't say much for the scissors.**

*This ad seeks to create brand insistence*

Source: Fiskars Manufacturing.

centive to maintain consistent quality. Over time, competitive pressures may also lead to improvement in quality.[8]

Brands also enable customers to make repeat purchases of branded items they have found satisfying. This makes them more confident about their buying decisions and facilitates shopping because a branded product is the same regardless of where the customer buys it. A Zenith TV is the same whether it is bought at Woolco or a prestige department store.

Finally, brands may add to the customer's psychological satisfaction.

Hallmark greeting card's slogan "When you care enough to send the very best" probably gives a lot of psychological satisfaction to the buyer, and to the receiver also.

### Branding and Sellers

Branding also offers advantages to sellers. It can help build brand and company images and develop customer loyalty. When products are branded advertising and in-store displays are meaningful, which facilitates self-service retailing. Brand promotion helps create a differential advantage for the owner and makes nonprice competition possible. Swift and Company in recent years has focused on creating branded and differentiated food products like Sizzlean and has deemphasized meat packing because branded products carry higher profit margins than fresh meat.

Although most products in the United States are branded, especially consumer products, some sellers do not brand their products. Some are unwilling or unable to maintain consistent quality and to promote their brands. Dresses and suits that do not meet quality standards, for example, are sold as rejects without the manufacturer's label.

Product items like nails and safety pins are hard to differentiate.[9] Manufacturers can use packaging to create a difference and separate brands from the product category. Lemons, bananas, and other fruits and vegetables used to be considered homogeneous product categories but branding has changed this. A satisfied buyer of Sunkist lemons or Chiquita bananas can buy that same brand next time.

Perhaps the main reason why some products are branded and others are unbranded is not due to their physical qualities. Instead, a variety of factors seem to influence the seller's decision to brand or not brand the product.

### Generic Marketing

In recent years, some consumers and marketers have taken greater interest in no-brand buying and selling. One study, for example, concluded that one effect of gasoline shortages was to alter buying patterns in favor of no-brand preference.[10] There also is more interest in no-brand (generic) grocery products: soda crackers, canned products, pasta, paper towels, and so on. These generic products usually are available in fewer package sizes, often have plain black-and-white packages and labels that indicate the generic product name, are not advertised, and are not top grade but rather are of "standard" quality that meets applicable government standards. A jar of peanut butter, for example, might contain a few specks of peanut skin. The major attraction, however, is lower prices, which may range between 10 and 35 percent lower than manufacturer brands and up to 15 percent lower than dealer brands.[11] Other generics include beer, liquor, plastic sandwich and trash bags, mouthwash, shampoo, and detergents.

Generic marketing is also growing in the drug industry. Medicare, Medicaid, and private medical insurance guidelines foster the use of lower-priced generic drugs. Some states have laws that require private druggists to use generics unless physicians who wrote the prescriptions object.

Research has suggested that some consumers tend to pick from a cluster of a few brands (sometimes including dealer brands and a generic) within a product category. Inflation, recession, and tightening family budgets tend to contribute to declining brand loyalty for certain products even within this narrow range.[12] The brand or generic product selected is the one that has the lowest price or has a coupon or some other purchase incentive. The choice of brand or generic product, therefore, may change from one purchase to the next.[13]

## Qualities of a Good Brand Name

A good brand name is necessary for successful branding and marketing. For example, a firm introduced a product very similar to Hamburger Helper one or two years prior to the launching of Hamburger Helper. The product tested well for convenience, price, and taste, and the packaging and advertising were good. But the product failed because of its brand name, Pennsylvania Dutch Casseroles. Subsequent research indicated that "Pennsylvania Dutch" was practically meaningless outside the general area of Lancaster, Pennsylvania, and "casserole" suggested a second-class meal.[14]

A good brand name should suggest the product's benefits or uses. Examples are Sundown (sunscreen), Slender (diet food), Windex and Glass Plus (window cleaners), Puppy Choice (dog food), Stir'n Frost (cake mix), Gee, Your Hair Smells Terrific (shampoo), and Softsoap (soap in a bottle).

Good brand names also should be easy to pronounce, recognize, and remember. PROPA P.H. (acne medication) and Underalls (pantyhose and panties all in one) are examples. Firms that sell in several countries have problems with brand names because of language and other cultural differences. VISA replaced BankAmericard in world-wide usage. This probably was due to the universally understood meaning of the term *visa*—a document stamped and approved by the proper officials of a country and granting entry into that country. Hershey had to change the name of its crispy bar Whatchamacallit when it introduced the product in Canada. Special Crisp was easier for French-speaking Canadians to handle.[15]

Brand names also should be short, simple, and suggest action. Examples are Purex's Toss'n Soft fabric softener and Close-Up toothpaste. This helps in advertising and displaying the product. Duz and Citgo probably are better brand names than Oxydol and Cities Service. Distinctiveness and uniqueness also are important. Ideal cement, Standard coffee, and General Tire score low on these attributes. Goodrich and Goodyear are so close that Goodrich, as we saw in the previous chapter, has tried to position itself as the tire company that does not have a blimp.

A brand name should not be generic, that is, it should not be descriptive of the product category. Aspirin, linoleum, nylon, cellophane, cola, raisin bran, elevator, and zipper once were trademarks but now are generic because the firms did not effectively establish and defend their legal claims to the names. Some trademarks are considered generic by many people although their owners have exclusive rights to them. Examples are Jell-O, Kodak, Coke, Kool-Aid, Xerox, Band-Aid, Spray Net, Jeep, Kleenex, Frisbee, and Formica. Their owners go to great lengths to inform and remind the public that they are registered trademarks. In 1978 the Federal Trade Commission asked the U.S. Patent and Trademark Office to cancel or restrict American Cyanamid Company's Formica trademark on the grounds that it had become generic.[16] But in 1980 the FTC was barred from challenging a trademark simply because it had become a common descriptive name.[17]

Avis Rent-A-Car System is owned by Norton Simon, Inc. It got into a dispute with Avis's founder, Warren Avis, over whether he could use the Avis name to establish a world-wide send-flowers-by-wire network. Xerox spends $100,000 a year on ads that explain the fact that Xerox is a registered trademark, not a synonym for photocopying. In the United States alone, the Coca-Cola Company has three lawyers to protect its trademark, Coke. Levi Strauss & Company has a security force to help prevent counterfeiters from making clothing under the Levi's brand.

Finally, brand names should be appropriate to the product and the market target. L'eggs and FemIron are appropriate for women. Cover Girl make-up and Sweet Nothings (bras and bikinis) may be appropriate for young women but perhaps not for older women.

It is hard to develop a brand name that satisfies all these requirements. Some successful brand names might score low if they were tested against them. But the rapid rate at which new brand names are appearing justifies the effort to develop good ones. Roughly one-half million brand names are in use and/or registered for use. Some firms use computer reference services in searching for these brand names and generating lists of possible new ones.[18]

## Manufacturers and Branding

Manufacturers can brand their products under their own brands, dealer brands, or a combination of both (a mixed brand approach).

Manufacturers that apply their own brand to all their products generally are large, well-financed, multiproduct firms. But this approach is becoming less popular because it precludes selling to large retailers who carry only their own brands.

Manufacturers that sell entirely under dealer brands usually are small and lack the financial and marketing resources to promote their own brands. Such a firm typically produces a few products for one or more large retailers such as Sears and J.C. Penney under their brands. The manufacturer is totally dependent on the retailer for marketing effort at the retail level.

A manufacturer's refusal to produce retailer brands will not prevent its rivals from doing so. Thus a growing number of manufacturers follow a mixed-brand approach. A mixed-brand approach enables the firm to use excess production capacity and may improve its working capital position if middlemen place large orders and pay promptly. There is no guarantee, however, that a middleman will not shift to another supplier.

Even adopting the mixed-brand approach does not completely protect the manufacturer. Suppose a supermarket chain wants to sell some bread under its own brand and it offers a baker a proposal. The bakery's capacity is 25,000 loaves per day but it sells only 18,000 under its brand. The bakery agrees to produce 7,000 loaves per day under the supermarket's brand. It makes less per loaf on the supermarket brand but the bakery does not have to promote it. The deal also permits some spreading of the bakery's overhead costs.

The bakery's brand is targeted to quality buyers, and the supermarket's brand is targeted to price buyers. But if some quality buyers switch to the dealer brand, the bakery trades off higher-profit sales for lower-profit sales. Also, the bakery becomes more dependent on this dealer brand. If enough brand switching occurs, the supermarket will want to increase its order size. This could lead the bakery to expand capacity.

The supermarket, realizing the bakery's growing dependence on the dealer brand, may negotiate for a lower price per loaf. The bakery could lose the supermarket's account if price is not lowered, which would leave it with more excess capacity than it had originally. In fact, it may have to lower price to a point where the revenue received makes only a minor contribution to fixed costs. Thus there are advantages and risks to both manufacturers and middlemen who produce and market under dealer brands. Both parties must recognize their interdependence if the relationship is to be profitable for them.

## Middlemen and Branding

Most middlemen carry only manufacturer brands because manufacturers promote the brands and they usually have a faster turnover rate. Middlemen would have to promote their own brands without help from manufacturers. Also, many middlemen do not want to risk antagonizing a multiproduct manufacturer by offering products under the dealer's brand in direct competition with products offered under the manufacturer's brand. Another concern is sustaining the quality of a dealer brand. This can be a big problem when the product is produced for the middleman by various manufacturers over a period of time.

Despite these problems, many middlemen do carry their own brands, however. Giant retailers like Sears carry their own brands almost exclusively, but most middlemen carry a much larger percentage of manufacturer brands. Middlemen carry their own brands for a variety of reasons.

An appliance store may advertise General Electric washers and convince some people to buy them, but not necessarily at that particular store. When Sears advertises its Kenmore washer, only Sears can make the sale. A satisfied Kenmore customer's goodwill goes entirely to Sears, whereas that of a GE buyer goes largely to GE. Large retailers are good promoters and they want to benefit from their promotions.

Other reasons middlemen carry their own brands include a desire to appeal to price buyers. Manufacturers can sell a dealer-branded product to a middleman at a lower price than the same product under their own brand because manufacturers do not have to promote dealer brands. Thus the middleman's profit margin usually is greater on its own brand. Middlemen also can have their brands manufactured to their specifications. Finally, manufacturers have the power to cut dealers off and open their own sales outlets. This cannot happen if the dealer carries its own brand.

## The Battle of the Brands

Manufacturer and dealer brands have competed for market share for several decades. This battle of the brands heated up when giant retail chains began promoting their own brands. Some manufacturers refuse to produce dealer brands. Some others sell more units under dealer brands than under their own brands.

Price used to be the only appeal of dealer brands. They were lower in price and lower in quality. Over the years, however, the quality gap has narrowed drastically. The price gap has not narrowed quite as much. Meanwhile, buyers have become more knowledgeable about these facts and, as a result, serious inroads have been made by dealer brands in many industries. (See Table 12–2.)

There is some question about the legality of a manufacturer's selling the identical product under dealer and manufacturer brands at different prices to competitive buyers. In 1958 the Federal Trade Commission (FTC) charged the Borden Company with violating the Robinson-Patman Act. Borden sold evaporated milk under its brand and also sold it to retailers under dealer brands. The only differences between the brands were the brand names and the prices. Borden was accused of price discrimination.

**Table 12–2.** *Percentage of sales due to dealer brands for selected product categories*

| Product Category | Percentage of Sales due to Dealer Brands |
|---|---|
| Interior wall paint | 43.7 |
| Car batteries | 42.6 |
| Frozen orange juice | 41.4 |
| Vitamins | 39.8 |
| Tires | 32.7 |
| Frozen vegetables | 31.9 |

Source: *Wall Street Journal*

Section IV THE PRODUCT

A court ruled that a manufacturer legally could sell a dealer brand at a lower price than its own brand, even though they are physically and chemically identical, as long as the price difference was not greater than the benefits consumers perceived from the manufacturer's promotion of its brand. No guidelines for measuring perceived benefits were provided, however.[19] Practically speaking, it is doubtful that a manufacturer's brand will be exactly like those sold under dealer brands because of the issue raised in the Borden case.

### Branding and the Product Mix

Multiproduct manufacturers and middlemen have three options for branding their different products: (1) family branding, (2) individual branding, and (3) combination branding.

**Family Branding.** A blanket brand, or **family brand,** can be used on an entire product mix or on all products in a particular product line. Hang Ten products are branded uner one name as are Levi's. Sears uses Allstate (insurance), Craftsman (tools), Ted Williams (sporting goods), Die Hard (batteries), and so on. Family branding may help a firm's new product introductions because goodwill on established products often spills over to new products.[20] The firm can also get more mileage from its promotion effort. But this approach is unwise when the products are different in quality, use, and price. A new product's failure also could damage established products' images.

**Individual Branding.** When products are unrelated or differ greatly in price, quality, use, and intended market segment, **individual brands** are used. General Foods, Colgate-Palmolive, and Procter & Gamble are

*family brand*

*individual brand*

**Table 12–3.** *The use of different brands to appeal to different market segments in the beer industry*

| Targeted to Drinkers of Popular-priced Beer* | Targeted to Drinkers of Premium Beer | Targeted to Drinkers of Super Premium Beer |
|---|---|---|
| Old Milwaukee (S) | Busch (A-B)** | Michelob (A-B) |
| | Budweiser (A-B) | Michelob Light (A-B) |
| | Natural Light (A-B) | Erlanger (S) |
| | Schlitz (S) | Löwenbräu (M) |
| | Schlitz Light (S) | |
| | Miller High Life (M) | |
| | Miller Lite (M) | |

*Many brewers produce beer under middlemen's brands for this market. Some regional brewers also target their brands to this market.
**Busch used to be targeted to the popular-priced drinkers but beginning in 1980 Anheuser-Busch started to reposition it in the premium category.
Key: (S) = Schlitz
(M) = Miller
(A-B) = Anheuser-Busch

**Great new ways to serve some fine old trademarks**

**Banana Delight Pie**

Prepare 1 package (6-serving size) of JELL-O® Brand Vanilla Flavor Instant Pudding and Pie Filling with 2¼ cups milk. Set aside 1 cup filling. Pour thin layer of *remaining* filling into cooled, baked 9" pie shell. Slice 1½ bananas; arrange on filling. Top with rest of filling. Blend ½ cup thawed COOL WHIP® Brand Non-Dairy Whipped Topping into measured filling. Spread over filling. Chill 3 hours. Garnish as desired.

**Lemon Chicken**

Empty 1 envelope SHAKE 'N BAKE® Brand Seasoned Coating Mix for Chicken into plastic bag. Add 2 teaspoons grated lemon rind. Moisten 2½ pounds cut-up chicken with mixture of 2 tablespoons *each* lemon juice and water. Coat and bake as directed. Makes 4 servings.

**Coffee Cordial**

Add ¼ cup rum or brandy and ¼ cup sugar to 4 cups freshly brewed SANKA® Brand 97% Caffein Free Coffee. Pour into coffee cups; add twisted orange peel strips. Makes 6 servings. A fruit-flavored liqueur may be substituted for rum; omit sugar.

**Cherry Punch**

Dissolve 4 scoops KOOL-AID® Brand Cherry Flavor Sugar-Sweetened Soft Drink Mix in 1½ quarts water with ice in nonmetal container. Add 2 cups apple juice. Makes 16 servings.

Look for these trademarks of General Foods: JELL-O,® SHAKE 'N BAKE,® SANKA,® KOOL-AID, COOL WHIP.® They're your guarantee of quality.

©GENERAL FOODS CORPORATION, 1979

*Many multiproduct firms use individual brands on their products*

Source: General Foods Corporation.

among the many firms that use this approach. Procter & Gamble's Pringles, Crisco, Tide, and Pampers are unrelated in nature. P&G's Crest and Gleem toothpastes are related in quality and nature but appeal to different market segments. P&G also markets several brands of detergent. A dissatisfied user of Tide, therefore, may try Cheer. Major brewing companies generally target different brands of beer to different market segments. This is illustrated in Table 12–3 on page 343.

Launching individual brands usually costs more and they are harder to manage. Separate divisions in the firm may be needed. On the other hand, using individual brands may stimulate competition among a firm's brands in the same product category. Many firms want this intrafirm competition, especially when they have brand managers for the different brands. An individual brand may get more management attention and aggressive promotion. The failure of one product also is less likely to injure others the firm markets.

**Combination Branding.** Some firms combine individual brands with the company name, like Kellogg's Rice Krispies.[21] Others may combine a trade name with individual brands, such as General Mills's Betty Crocker Super Moist cake mix and Betty Crocker Creamy Deluxe frosting. General Motors uses individual brands on its cars but associates them by promoting GM's "Mark of Excellence."

A firm that picks up new products through merger or acquisition may acquire a brand with strong acceptance in a certain area and retain this regional brand. When Maytag acquired a small maker of ovens several years ago it decided to continue the use of that firm's brand name rather than apply the Maytag brand to them. Notice in the Beatrice Foods Co. ad on page 346 the importance of regional brands to the firm.

**Multiple Brands.** Manufacturers and middlemen, as we have seen, often use multiple brands. Procter & Gamble markets Tide and Dreft. Each appeals to a different market segment. Tide's image is "strength," whereas Dreft's is "gentle." This enables P&G to get a larger share of the total detergent market. It also gives the firm greater pricing flexibility. It is not unusual for a rival to take direct aim at an established brand by introducing a cheaper version. The firm could react by lowering its brand's quality and price, but this might hurt the brand and company image. It might, therefore, launch a fighting brand to compete directly with the rival brand that was introduced.

Multiple brands are common in the clothing industry—shoes, shirts, and so on. A clothing store that has an exclusive franchise to sell a particular brand of shirts does not want the manufacturer to permit a rival store in the area to sell the same brand. The manufacturer could avoid a hassle by letting the rival store sell the same shirt under a different brand.

## PACKAGING

**Packaging** involves designing and producing the container or wrapper for a product. The package is an important part of many products; it may be the key factor in their market success.[22] When beer was packaged only in large kegs, consumers had to drink it in taverns or carry it home in pitchers. Women were largely excluded as customers because they were not permitted in "men only" bars. Several years ago, supermarkets tried to sell generic powdered milk but the results were disappointing. Subsequent research indicated that the product's container was respon-

**packaging**

# How the nation's leading diversified food company got that way with a lot of brands you may not recognize.

Many of Beatrice's famous products are famous in just one or more regions of the country.

At one time, however, some were famous just locally. Yet their fame has spread, and is spreading still, because of a Beatrice marketing concept that calls for the rollout of products from local to regional distribution, from regional to national, even from national to international.

It's all part of the overall Beatrice strategy for success. A strategy that also encompasses decentralized marketing and profit center management. Strong financial controls. A healthy balance between our food and non-food businesses.

And that strategy keeps right on paying off.

Our sales, earnings, and earnings per share have increased every year for the last 29 years.

That's a record of growth and performance that has impressed our peers and stockholders.

For our latest financial reports, write Investor Relations, Beatrice Foods Co., Two North LaSalle Street, Chicago, Illinois 60602.

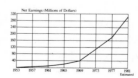

## Beatrice Foods Co.

*Regional brands are important to this company*
Source: Beatrice Foods Co.

sible. The product was packaged in a plastic bag but shoppers were used to buying it in cardboard boxes.[23]

Prepackaging improves marketing efficiency at both the macro and micro levels. In the United States most products, certainly almost all convenience products, are sold in prepackaged form. Unlike people in some other countries, we do not buy pickles, flour, sugar, and coffee in bulk from barrels and sacks. Prepackaging requires that consumers have faith in the packager's integrity and that society has control over those who violate ethical packaging standards. Self-service retailing would be less efficient, perhaps impossible, without it. Consider General Foods's marketing headaches if its products were not prepackaged.

## Packaging Objectives

Important packaging objectives are to (1) contain the contents, (2) protect the contents, (3) promote the contents, (4) differentiate the contents, and (5) increase utility to middlemen and final buyers.

**Containment.** The most obvious packaging objective is to contain the contents. A shopper who orders a half-side of beef at the supermarket will have the meat cut and wrapped by the butcher. The package probably will be freezer paper and perhaps one or more cardboard boxes. Another shopper may select three steaks from the display counter. These are packaged in a Styrofoam (another brand name) tray that is perforated with holes and enclosed in plastic film.

**Protection.** Packaging steaks helps to protect flavor. A package also can protect the contents as the product moves through its distribution channel and while it is in use. A coffee can for example, serves this function. A package also prolongs the shelf life of a product, which is important to producers, middlemen, and final buyers. It protects against spoilage, deterioration, leakage, crushing, crumbling, evaporation, dehydration, and shoplifting. One goal in designing packaging is to determine the protection needed and to minimize the cost of providing that protection.

**Promotion.** Promoting the contents is an important packaging objective, especially in self-service retailing. The package must serve as a silent salesperson and attract the shopper's attention. L'eggs's egg-shaped package played a major role in making Hanes dominant in women's hosiery. The package can also deliver promotional impact after the product is in use. Children, for example, are very responsive to illustrations of premiums that are included in the package.[24]

**Differentiation.** The package can create a differential advantage when brands in a product category are considered highly homogeneous. Morton salt's shaker spout, Pringles's crumble-proof can, and Miller beer's seven-ounce pony bottle help to differentiate their brands. Effective new packaging tends to be copied quickly by rivals. Of course, some packaging innovations are not successful. Examples include toothpaste in an aerosol can and the refrigerator-sized Tap-a-Keg beer container.

**Utility.** Increasing a product's utility to middlemen and final buyers

*An ad that emphasizes the importance of packaging*

Source: Owens-Illinois

may enhance its profit potential. Spending more on packaging can raise or lower total marketing costs, but the important consideration is customer satisfaction. Fast-food outlets are willing to pay more for sugar, pepper, coffee creamer, salt, and ketchup in small packets because it fits their requirements better. Packaging toys in plastic bubble packages with a large cardboard backing costs manufacturers more than simple cardboard boxes would. But the savings to retailers in breakage and shoplifting more than offsets the added packaging cost. Care, however, is necessary to avoid making a product's package so large in relation to the contents that it might be deceptive. Some toy makers decided to repackage their toys in smaller packages several years ago after the Federal Trade Commission complained the oversized packages deceived people about the size of the toys inside.

Attractiveness, convenience, and economy are some aspects of a product's utility to final buyers. One reason cigarette makers give so much attention to packaging is that they consider it part of a consumer's clothing. Consumers carry the package around with them.[25] Maple syrup in a reusable pitcher may be more attractive than syrup in a throw-away bottle. Pop-top cans for beer, soft drinks, peanuts, and chili are more convenient to use. Campbell's Soup for One cans are more convenient for persons who live alone. Resealable large-sized bottles of soft drinks usually are more economical per ounce, and the resealable feature retards flavor loss. Individually wrapped foil packages of Alka-Seltzer keep the product fresh and prevent crumbling. Packaging can also affect a consumer's perception of product quality. Many food product packages are hard for consumers to open, but tightly sealed packages are perceived by many consumers as a way to maintain product quality.[26] Vacuum-packed coffee and peanuts give a satisfying, reassuring "whoosh" when opened.

## Packaging Decisions

Important packaging decisions include (1) organizational responsibility, (2) package design, (3) package changes, (4) reuse packaging, (5) multiple packaging, (6) package safety, and (7) societal considerations.

**Organizational Responsibility.** Packaging used to be the job of traffic managers, who arranged transportation of products through marketing channels. Their main concern was protecting the contents. Most consumer goods companies have reassigned responsibility for packaging because of its tremendous promotional role. Many firms now have specialized packaging committees and staffs and some have vice-presidents of packaging. These committees may include packaging engineers, who test the package's ability to withstand normal handling procedures; middlemen, who appraise aesthetic and handling features; materials procurement personnel, whose advice is needed regarding costs and availability of packaging materials; and designers, who judge color and typographic styles.

**Package Design.** Consumer products marketers often have their own package design personnel but use as well outside specialists. These include design consultants from ad agencies and container makers. In-house and outside design personnel help in keeping pace with changing consumer tastes, new packaging materials, and environmental changes, all of which have a big effect on package design. During recent years, for example, makers of steel and aluminum cans and glass containers have been battling for market share. Meanwhile, the plastic bottle and

*Packaging is very important for this product*

Source: General Wine and Spirits Co.

other containers made of paper and plastic are making headway. A growing number of firms are taking a closer look at cost considerations in package design. For example, more than half the cost of making a can of beer or soft drink is accounted for by the aluminum can.[27] Thus there is greater interest in recycling packaging materials among consumers and marketers. Cost-profit squeezes in many industries are also focusing management attention on overpackaging.

**Package Changes.** Package changes may be desirable when sales are declining, promotional effectiveness is declining, new and improved packaging materials are available, the present package is defective, middlemen and final buyers want a package change, or when currently used materials are in short supply. Changing a package may create a new product. Think of all the "new products" that were created by the aerosol can and the "new products" that were created when the pump spray was introduced during the aerosol controversy. Marlboro cigarettes scored a big hit with its Marlboro box. It helped to differentiate the brand from cigarettes in soft packs. Nabisco decided to repackage its line of boxed snacks, such as Mister Salty pretzels, in foil-laminate bags. This extended the products' shelf life and helped to move them from the cookie and cracker aisles, where sales were not growing, to the rapidly growing salted-snacks section.[28]

The gradual move to the metric system in the United States is causing some package changes. Soft-drink makers were among the first to package products in metric containers. Product features have also been affected by the introduction of the metric system. Thus car engines are being designed, built, and promoted in terms of their metric size. This, in turn, affects product design for tool manufacturers.

**Reuse Packaging.** Reuse packaging means the package can serve other purposes after the contents have been consumed. Examples are coffee cans, plastic margarine containers, attractive decanters for liquor, peanuts, and mouthwash, and "collectors' editions" of jars and bottles. A major goal of reuse packaging is to stimulate repurchases.

**Multiple Packaging.** Multiple packaging means selling several units of the product in one package. The main goal is to increase total sales. A consumer who buys one bottle of a new brand of soft drink may not like the taste and never give it a second trial. A six-pack gives the person five more chances to cultivate a taste for it.

Multiple packaging is often used along with sales and promotion activities like two-for-one sales. Retailers like it because it reduces the costs of unit handling and inventory control. Products like silver polish that are used up slowly are not good candidates for multiple packaging.

**Package Safety.** Laws relating to packaging typically have resulted from misleading and deceptive packaging. Increasing attention is being focused on package safety, especially for drugs, household cleaners, insecticides, and other products that are potentially dangerous, particularly to children. Child-proof medicine bottles and tamper-proof controls on bug sprays are examples of safe packaging.

**Packaging and Societal Considerations.** In recent years, ecologists, conservationists, and consumerists have attacked some packaging practices. Ecologists are concerned about the use of nonbiodegradable beverage containers because of the solid-waste disposal problem. As a result, laws have been passed to control this type of packaging. Oregon was the first state to pass a deposit law on one-way beverage containers in 1972. Vermont, Maine, and Michigan also have passed similar laws. Washington and California have litter recycling laws that impose a tax on container makers and other firms whose products could end up as litter. The tax revenues help offset the cost of collecting and recycling the litter.

Conservationists question the wisdom of using quantities of scarce natural resources simply to make more attractive packages, for example, the use of plastic packaging in the face of dwindling petroleum supplies. A major controversy arose several years ago over the damage fluorocarbons in aerosol containers might do to the earth's ozone layer.

Consumerists often criticize packaging that adds to the cost of consumer products and deceptive packaging that makes it harder for consumers to make sound buying decisions. The Fair Packaging and Labeling Act of 1966 requires the following information on a product's package or label: (1) type of product, (2) producer or processor's name and location, (3) net quantity, and, if applicable, (4) number and size of servings. Many other similar laws cover products like foods, toys, drugs, cosmetics, furs, and textiles.[29]

## LABELING

A product's label can be a strong selling tool. The label's illustration and copy should describe adequately and fairly the contents and tell how the product should be used. At the very least the label identifies the product. Clothing labels often are tags attached to the product or the package. Sometimes the label is imprinted into the product like the label on Mason jars. Usually, however, the label is the printed material that appears on the package.

### Types of Labels

Three types of labels are (1) brand labels, (2) grade labels, and (3) informative labels.

brand label

When only the brand appears on the product item or its package, it has a **brand label.** Sunkist stamped on lemons and the Chiquita stickers on bananas are examples of brand labeling.

grade label

A **grade label** also identifies product quality by a letter, number, or word. "Choice" and "prime" stamped on beef are grade labels.[30] Supporters of compulsory grade labeling contend that (1) brand labels do not give enough information about products and this makes comparative shopping tough, (2) grade labels are simple for sellers to use and easy for consumers to understand, (3) price competition would replace a lot of nonprice competition based on alleged brand superiority if each brand in a product category carried a quality grade. Opponents say compulsory grade labeling seeks to force an objective standard rating on subjective factors like taste and fashion. How, for example, could wine be graded? They also argue that it would be hard to grade complex products like cars.

informative label

A middle position between brand and grade labeling is informative labeling.[31] An **informative label** gives written and/or illustrative objective information about the product's ingredients, use, care, performance capability, life expectancy and limitations, precautions, nutrition, and number of servings. Manufacturers of such appliances as refrigerators, refrigerator-freezers, clothes washers, room air conditioners, and furnaces are required to show on their labels the estimated cost of running each make and model for one year, based on average utility rates.

The use of confusing labels like "Giant Economy Size," "Economy Size," "King Size," "Family Size," and so on to describe package sizes contributed to passage of the Fair Packaging and Labeling Act of 1966. This law sets some mandatory labeling requirements for information about contents and encourages firms and their trade associations to set voluntary packaging and labeling standards.[32] A comparison of the label on a typical breakfast cereal package with one from several years ago would show the impact of nutritional labeling.[33] Informative labeling is beneficial, however, only if consumers read and understand the labels. Many consumers do not. Some people, therefore, favor a massive consumer education program to correct this.

### Label Design

A well-designed label can have great promotional impact and enhance brand and company images. Attention-producing graphics are important for labels that cover a large part of the package. The label on Miller Lite, for example, features a bulls-eye design that emphasizes natural ingredients by drawing attention to a picture of hops. Good label design can enhance a label's effectiveness in communicating with target customers. The label for Arrid XX, for example, features clouds to convey that it is a spray deodorant that will not damage the ozone layer. Several years ago, Foremost-McKesson introduced a new dessert topping, Magic Shell. The product forms a hard shell when it is placed on ice cream. The product's label had to communicate the product's nature to the consumer because the brand name Magic Shell was not sufficient. Thus the labels are color-coded according to flavor and include photos that show the product in use.[34]

## PRODUCT RECALLS

The Consumer Product Safety Act of 1972 makes quality control a crucial factor in product management.[35] A product that reaches the market but represents "a substantial product hazard" must be reported to the Consumer Product Safety Commission (CPSC) within twenty-four hours of discovery that it is hazardous. One study found that recalls of cars by manufacturers were not a major determinant of market share for most makes.[36] But the speed and efficiency with which a product is recalled can affect company, product, and brand images.

Total avoidance of recalls is almost impossible because that would require absolute perfection in all units. Thus manufacturers emphasize reducing the likelihood of massive recalls. Accountability for quality

"Uh, oh!"

Source: *The Wall Street Journal*

control and production should therefore be assigned to different managers. Recall authority often is delegated to another person, who can order a production halt, initiate middleman and customer notification, and co-ordinate the actual recall. Gillette, for example, has a vice-president for product integrity.

A recall involves notification, retrieval of the product from middlemen and customers (a reverse channel of distribution), distributing replacement units or repair parts along with information so that dealers can repair defective units, and communication to keep middleman support and customer loyalty. Locating owners may be tough, especially for small products, and elaborate coding systems are needed to keep track of individual units in distribution channels.[37]

## SUMMARY AND LOOK AHEAD

A product item's brand, package, and label are part of the total product. They help buyers identify products with their producers or distributors and help sellers build brand and company images. Manufacturer brands are owned by manufacturers, and dealer brands are owned by middlemen. Branding offers advantages to customers and sellers.

A good brand name suggests the product's benefits or uses in addition to being easy to pronounce, recognize, and remember. It also is short, simple, appropriate to the product and the market target, and should be capable of legal registration as a trademark.

Manufacturers can brand under their own brands and/or dealer brands but the mixed-brand approach is growing in popularity. Middlemen can carry dealer or manufacturer brands exclusively, or they can stock both. Multiproduct manufacturers and middlemen can use family brands, individual brands, or a combination of both. Multiple branding helps a firm reach different market segments. The battle of the brands, or the rivalry between manufacturer and dealer brands for market share, has intensified as dealer brands have improved in quality. Meanwhile, generic marketing has become popular for some products, especially food products.

The six degrees of brand familiarity are (1) brand nonrecognition, (2) brand recognition, (3) brand rejection, (4) brand acceptance, (5) brand preference, and (6) brand insistence. True brand insistence is very hard to achieve.

A package should contain, protect, promote, and differentiate its contents and increase the product item's utility to middlemen and final buyers. Important packaging decisions relate to organizational responsibility, design, changes, reuse, multiple packaging, safety, and societal considerations.

Three types of labels are (1) brand labels, (2) grade labels, and (3) informative labels. Good label design helps in communicating with target customers, and there is growing pressure for more informative labeling, especially for consumer products.

Managing product recalls has become a key issue in product management. A product recall requires setting up and managing a reverse channel of distribution.

The next section of this text discusses the distribution element in the marketing mix. We will start with marketing channels. Products must be available when and where buyers want them. Marketing channels help a firm match its products with its target customers.

## REVIEW QUESTIONS

**1.** Define: (a) brand, (b) brand name, (c) brand mark, and (d) trademark.

**2.** How might branding benefit an ultimate consumer?

**3.** Why might a manufacturer decide not to brand its products?

**4.** What are the qualities of a good brand name? Give an example of a brand name that satisfies each requirement you list.

**5.** Is "Coke" a generic name or a trademark? Explain.

**6.** Why might a manufacturer brand all its output under dealer brands?

**7.** What is family branding? Discuss its advantages and disadvantages.

**8.** What is the "battle of the brands"?

**9.** Identify and discuss the six degrees of brand familiarity.

**10.** Identify and discuss five objectives of packaging.

**11.** Identify several factors that might lead a firm to change a product item's package.

**12.** What is compulsory grade labeling?

**13.** What does a product recall involve?

## DISCUSSION QUESTIONS

**1.** Do you think generic marketing is good for consumers? What about marketers?

**2.** Name a brand you insist upon buying and refuse to replace with rival brands. Explain why you insist upon that brand.

**3.** Do you advocate compulsory grade labeling?

**4.** Do you think a significant number of consumers would be willing to give up attractive packages in return for lower prices on consumer products?

**5.** Give an example that illustrates the recycling of a package.

## NOTES

1. Committee on Definitions, *Marketing Definitions: A Glossary of Marketing Terms* (Chicago: American Marketing Association, 1960), p. 8.

2. Ibid., p. 10.

3. "Mobil's Wards Is Stopped from Using 'Jaws' Name," *Wall Street Journal*, May 7, 1980, p. 35.

4. Manufacturer brands are also called national brands. Dealer brands also are called distributor brands, private brands, store brands, house brands, and middleman brands. See Thomas F. Schutte, "The Semantics of Branding," *Journal of Marketing*, April, 1969, pp. 5–11.

5. See Leo Bogart and Charles Lehman, "What Makes a Brand Name Familiar," *Journal of Marketing Research*, February, 1973, pp. 17–22.

6. See Kent B. Monroe, "The Influence of Price Differences and Brand Familiarity on Brand Preferences," *Journal of Consumer Research*, June, 1976, pp. 42–49.

7. Historically, a main objective of branding is to identify the seller of a branded product. The proliferation of brand names and trademarks, however, sometimes makes it hard for consumers to identify the actual manufacturer of an advertised product when the company name is not identified in the advertising. See John M. Kuhlman, "Anonymous Offers to Sell," *Journal of Consumer Affairs*, Summer, 1977, pp. 151–157.

8. One study of nationally advertised and other brands found that the size of advertising expenditures generally seems to be a weak index of product quality. See Herbert J. Rotfeld and Kim B. Rotzoll, "Advertising and Product Quality: Are Heavily Advertised Products Better?" *Journal of Consumer Affairs*, Summer, 1976, pp. 33–47.

9. Marketers of products that are hard to differentiate in physical terms often resort to promotion as the main basis for differentiation. One author has suggested that it may be better to level with the consumer and advertise the fact that a firm's brand really is not very much different but it sells at a lower price. For example, Chesebrough-Pond's advertising for Cutex nail polish is cited: "Cutex covers as well as the high-priced spread." See E. John Kottman, "Promoting the Parity Product," *Journal of Consumer Affairs*, Summer, 1977, pp. 145–150, at p. 146.

10. See Dennis H. Tootelian and Ralph M. Gaedeke, "Impact of Supply Shortages on Consumer Buying Patterns," *Arizona Business*, August–September, 1975, pp. 22–25.

11. "No-Brand Groceries," *Time*, November 21, 1977, p. 80. Also see C. Handy and N. Seigle, "Generic Labeling," *National Food Review*, September, 1978, pp. 17–20; and Ann L. Krueger, "Retailers Expand No-Name Generic Offerings Despite Scarcity of Standard Grade Products," *Supermarketing*, April, 1979, p. 14.

12. See William J. Lundstrom, Daniel Sciglimpaglia, and William G. Zekmund, "Consumer Coping Behavior in an Inflationary Economy," *Akron Business and Economic Review*, Fall, 1978, pp. 48–52.

13. "Marketers Smart from Brand Disloyalty as Fickle Shoppers Seek Cheaper Items," *Wall Street Journal*, May 2, 1980, p. 22.

14. Willard H. Doyle, "Brand Still Crucial, But Now It's 'Manufactured,' Not Dreamed Up," *Marketing News*, February 10, 1978, p. 12.

15. "Consumer Likes Determine Hershey Bar Introduction," *Marketing News*, February 22, 1980, p. 11.

16. "Attacking a Trademark," *Business Week*, June 19, 1978, p. 40.

17. "Compromise on FTC Approved by Senate and Sent to Carter," *Wall Street Journal*, May 22, 1980, p. 5.

18. See Robert A. Peterson and Ivan Ross, "How to Name New Brands," *Journal of Advertising Research*, December, 1972, pp. 29–34.

19. See Thomas F. Schutte, Victor J. Cook, Jr., and Richard Hemsley, "What Management Can Learn from the Borden Case," *Business Horizons*, Winter, 1966, pp. 23–30.

20. You may want to refer back to the discussion of generalization and discrimination in Chapter 5.

21. See Richard Spiegelberg, "The Company behind the Brand: An Under-Exploited Commercial Asset," *Admap*, November, 1979, pp. 564–572.

22. See Donald Short, "Packaging: Marketing's Secret Weapon," *Marketing Times*, September–October, 1974, pp. 6–8.

23. "All Generic Products Losing Popularity with Public: Study," *Marketing News*, February 22, 1980, p. 7.

24. See James U. McNeal, "Packaging for the Young Consumer: A Descriptive Study," *Akron Business and Economic Review*, Winter, 1976, pp. 5–11.

25. "Tobacco Marketers' Success Formula: Make Cigarets in Smoker's Own Image," *Wall Street Journal*, February 29, 1980, p. 10.

26. Carl McDaniel and R. C. Baker, "Convenience Food Packaging and the Perception of Product Quality," *Journal of Marketing*, October, 1977, pp. 57–58.

27. "Novel Aluminum-Making Method Stirs Brewers, Can Makers to Try It Themselves," *Wall Street Journal*, April 11, 1980, p. 10.

28. "Innovators in the Salted-Snacks Market," *Business Week*, October 30, 1978, pp. 73–74.

29. See Walter McQuade, "Packagers Bear Up

under a Bundle of Regulations," *Fortune,* May 7, 1979, pp. 180–195.

30.  See John A. Miller, David G. Topel, and Robert E. Rust, "U.S.D.A. Beef Grading: A Failure in Consumer Information?" *Journal of Marketing,* January, 1976, pp. 25–31.

31.  See Warren A. French and Hiram C. Barksdale, "Food Labeling Regulations: Efforts toward Full Disclosure," *Journal of Marketing,* July, 1974, pp. 14–19; George S. Day, "Full Disclosure of Comparative Performance Information to Consumers: Problems and Prospects," *Journal of Contemporary Business,* January, 1975, pp. 53–68; and George S. Day, "Assessing the Effects of Information Disclosure Requirements," *Journal of Marketing,* April, 1976, pp. 42–52.

32.  See Warren A. French and William R. Darden, "The Fair Packaging and Labeling Act: An Assessment," *Business Ideas and Facts,* Summer, 1973, pp. 2–8.

33.  See Edward A. Asam and Louis P. Bucklin, "Nutrition Labeling for Canned Goods: A Study of Consumer Response," *Journal of Marketing,* April, 1973, pp. 32–37.  Del Monte is a pioneer in nutritional labeling; see "Living with New Labeling Rules," *Business Week,* February 3, 1974, pp. 42–45.  Del Monte, therefore, positioned itself for social accountability; see John P. Maggard, "Positioning Revisited," *Journal of Marketing,* January, 1976, pp. 63–66, at p. 65.  Also see Jacob Jacoby, Robert W. Chestnut, and William Silberman, "Consumer Use and Comprehension of Nutrition Information," *Journal of Consumer Research,* September, 1977, pp. 119–128; James U. McNeal, Donald E. Stem, Jr., and Carol S. Nelson, "Consumers' Nutritional Ratings of Fast-Food Meals," *Journal of Consumer Affairs,* Summer, 1980, pp. 165–179; and James McCullough and Roger Best, "Consumer Preferences for Food Label Information: A Basis for Segmentation," *Journal of Consumer Affairs,* Summer, 1980, pp. 180–192.

34.  "Packaging Designed for Fast Recognition of New Topping," *Marketing News,* February 22, 1980, p. 14.

35.  See Walter Jensen, Jr., Edward M. Mazze, and Duke Nordlinger Stern, "The Consumer Product Safety Act: A Special Case in Consumerism," *Journal of Marketing,* October, 1973, pp. 68–71; "Dictating Product Safety," *Business Week,* May 18, 1974, pp. 56–62; Alfred L. Edwards, "Consumer Product Safety: Challenge for Business," *University of Michigan Business Review,* March, 1975, pp. 18–22; "Consumer Product Safety Act Seen Affecting Business Actions," *Commerce Today,* June 9, 1975, pp. 7–8; Warren G. Magnuson and Edward B. Cohen, "The Role of the Consumer under the Consumer Product Safety Act," *Journal of Contemporary Business,* Winter, 1975, pp. 21–37; and Paul Busch, "A Review and Critical Evaluation of the Consumer Product Safety Commission: Marketing Management Implications," *Journal of Marketing,* October, 1976, pp. 41–49.

36.  A. James Wynne and George E. Hoffer, "Auto Recalls: Do They Affect Market Share?" *Applied Economics,* August, 1976, pp. 157–163.

37.  See "Managing the Product Recall," *Business Week,* January 26, 1974, pp. 46–48; Roger A. Kerin and Michael Harvey, "Contingency Planning for Product Recall," *MSU Business Topics,* Summer, 1975, pp. 5–12; George Fisk and Rajan Chandran, "How to Trace and Recall Products," *Harvard Business Review,* November–December, 1975, pp. 90–96; and Harland W. Warner, "Guidelines for Product Recall," *Public Relations Journal,* July, 1977, pp. 11–13.

# Section V
# **Distribution**

Products do not automatically wind up in the hands of target customers. Marketers must distribute them to their final buyers.

In Chapter 13 we look at marketing channels—what they are, the functions they perform, and how they are managed.

Chapter 14 discusses retailing—what it is, the types of retailers, and the major decisions they make.

Wholesaling is the subject of Chapter 15. We will see what wholesalers and wholesaling middlemen are, what functions they perform, and the different types that operate in modern channels.

Chapter 16 introduces physical distribution, which involves the actual movement of products through channels. Transportation, warehousing, and other physical distribution activities are necessary if products are to flow from producers to their final buyers.

# Chapter 13

# Marketing Channels

OBJECTIVES

*After reading this chapter you should be able to*

1. discuss the functions of marketing channels.

2. compare direct and indirect channels.

3. indicate the possible relationships among channel members.

4. discuss the nature of horizontal marketing systems.

5. identify important factors in channel selection decisions.

6. identify two types of channel conflict and approaches to resolving them.

7. identify important aspects of channel planning.

8. explain the role of facilitating middlemen in channels.

9. identify and compare the three degrees of market exposure.

10. discuss the concept of channels for services.

11. compare the traditional and total channel system.

12. explain the meaning and give examples of reverse channels.

KEY CONCEPTS

*Look for these terms as you read the chapter:*

Marketing Channel
Middleman
Direct Channel
Indirect Channel
Forward Vertical Integration
Backward Vertical Integration
Horizontal Channel Integration
Horizontal Marketing System
Channel Conflict
Channel Leader
Vertical Marketing System
Facilitating Middlemen
Intensive Distribution
Selective Distribution
Exclusive Distribution
Trade-Relations Department

*The channels through which products are marketed are in a constant state of change. Consider the following three examples. Many coal-burning utilities used to buy coal from independent suppliers. But many of these utilities have integrated backward and now own and operate their own coal mines. A major reason they do this is to have greater assurance of long-term supplies.*

*Poultry producers traditionally raised poultry and let others handle the marketing task. In recent years, some of these producers have started branding and advertising their poultry and are marketing it to supermarkets themselves rather than turning the job over to middlemen. They want more control over the marketing of their poultry because of the money they invest in branding and advertising it.*

*Eyeglasses and contact lenses used to be marketed mainly through the offices of ophthalmologists and optometrists. These professionals did not engage in price advertising because most states had laws that prohibited such advertising. But when the Federal Trade Commission set aside these laws in 1978, big eye-care chains got into the business through aggressive price advertising. This created problems for some manufacturers to whom ophthalmologists and optometrists complained that the big chains were at an unfair competitive advantage because their large-volume purchases and sales enabled them to undercut prices. Thus conflict soon arose between the manufacturers and the people through whom they marketed eyeglasses and contact lenses to consumers.*

The best-engineered product will not satisfy the most anxious buyer until it is available for purchase at the right place at the right time. Every year hundreds of inventors come up with new products, but many are never marketed because the inventor did not know how to get the product distributed to potential buyers. Many of these inventors, however, sell their patents to firms with established channels that reach the people the inventor wants to reach.

Products do not simply flow automatically from producers to consumers or industrial users. The flow must be induced and managed by setting up marketing channels. In this chapter we will examine what marketing channels are, what they do, and how they are managed.

## THE NATURE AND FUNCTIONS OF A MARKETING CHANNEL

marketing channel

A **marketing channel** is the series of marketing institutions that facilitates transfer of title to a product as it moves from producer to ultimate consumer or industrial user. Manufacturers, middlemen, and final buyers are participants in a channel, or channel members.

middleman

A **middleman** (marketing intermediary, or reseller) is a person or business firm, such as a wholesaler or retailer, that operates between the producer and the final buyer of a product. Middlemen specialize in buying and selling but also perform other marketing functions, such as risk taking, financing, storage, transportation, and providing information. All channels have a producer and an ultimate consumer and/or industrial buyer. But when a producer sells directly to the final buyer there are no middlemen in the channel.

Marketing channels are set up to (1) create utility, (2) improve exchange efficiency, and (3) match supply and demand.

## Creating Utility

A product that is produced to satisfy customer wants has form utility, but it must be in the right place at the right time so that the customer can take possession and ownership of it. Channels bring suppliers and buyers together by creating time, place, possession, and ownership utilities. They bridge the time and distance gaps between producers and customers. In the soft drink industry independent bottlers themselves participate in creating form utility. For example, 7Up supplies the extract to its independent bottlers, who blend, package, and distribute the soft drink. Thus middlemen also can help to create form utility.

*[handwritten margin note: time, place, possession & owner ship]*
*[handwritten margin note: middlemen can help create form utility]*

## Improving Exchange Efficiency

Specialization, or the division of labor, can occur only when there is an opportunity for exchange. But whether exchange is desirable depends a lot on how efficiently it can be conducted.

**Exchange Without Middlemen.** Suppose six people each produce a different product and they want to trade. Figure 13–1 shows that each person has to make a trip to every other person. *A* produced cotton and *B* produces wheat. When *A* goes to *B* to sell cotton, *A* accepts *B's* promise to supply wheat when it is harvested later in the year. Thus two trips are required between any two traders when the products are produced at different times and they cannot be stored. Each of the six people makes five trips for a total of thirty trips.

If, however, *A* and *B* can store their products, only one trip between them is required. Although *A* and *B*, *A* and *C*, and so on might argue about who makes the trip, only fifteen trips are needed. (See Figure 13–2.)

*Figure 13–1.* *Exchange relationships among six specialists\**
*\*Each specialist desires to exchange with each and every other specialist. Two trips are necessary between any two traders because products are produced at different times and storage is impossible.*

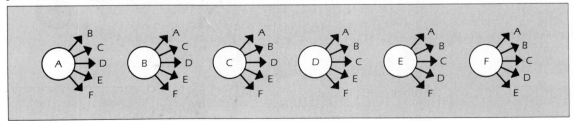

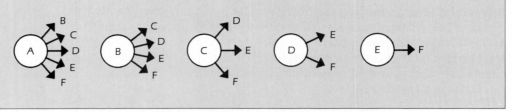

**Figure 13–2.  Exchange relationships among six specialists***
*Only one trip is required between any two traders because products are available for exchange at the same time because of storage.*

    If all traders agree to exchange in a central location on a certain date, each makes only one trip.   Each deals with the other five traders while in the central marketplace.   Thus a total of only six trips is involved. (See Figure 13–3).   Each trader, however, still has to negotiate terms with each of the other traders.

    **Exchange with Middlemen.**   Suppose a middleman bought each trader's output.   Each trader makes only one trip and deals with only one middleman, who buys and sells to them.   The traders no longer deal directly with each other.   Production specialists can spend less time exchanging and more time producing products because middlemen are exchange specialists.   Exchange is more efficient because of the middle-

**Figure 13–3.
Exchange
relationships
among six
specialists***
*All traders go to a
central market to
exchange and they
deal with each
other in that
central location.*

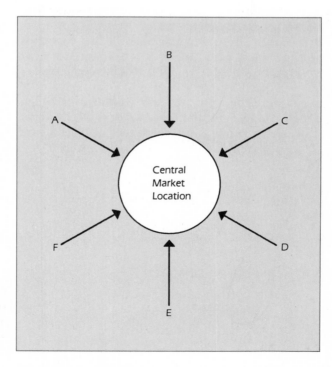

man. The early trading post in our country is an example of a middleman.

The marketing functions must be performed in all channels whether a producer distributes directly to final buyers or indirectly to them through middlemen. The functions can be shifted and shared among channel members but they cannot be eliminated.

When a supermarket ad states, "We've eliminated the middleman and we're passing the savings on to you," no marketing functions have been eliminated. The supermarket assumed functions formerly performed by the wholesaler. Distribution costs will go down if the supermarket can perform the functions more efficiently than the wholesaler. But the supermarket's inventory costs may go up because larger orders must be placed with manufacturers than with wholesalers. If inventory costs go up more than the savings realized by bypassing the wholesaler, the supermarket's operating costs will go up. There will be no savings to pass on to customers.

## Matching Supply and Demand

Channels concentrate and disperse products in response to effective demand. They help in the process of matching supply and demand.[1]

**Quantity Discrepancy.** The Green Giant Company is not interested in selling two cans of peas directly to a consumer. It wants to sell caseloads and truckloads. The quantity discrepancy between Green Giant and the household buyer is adjusted in marketing channels. Green Giant might sell a truckload of canned peas to a wholesaler, who breaks

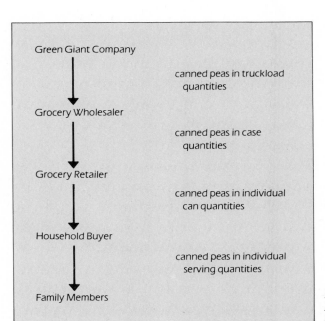

Green Giant Company

canned peas in truckload quantities

Grocery Wholesaler

canned peas in case quantities

Grocery Retailer

canned peas in individual can quantities

Household Buyer

canned peas in individual serving quantities

Family Members

*Figure 13–4.*
*Adjusting quantity*
*discrepancy*

it down into case lots for sale to grocery stores. These grocers break down the cases and stock their shelves with cans of peas. This permits the household buyer to pick two cans from the shelf. (See Figure 13–4.)

Wholesalers and retailers helped in adjusting the quantity discrepancy. But when Safeway Supermarkets buys in truckload volume from Green Giant there is no quantity discrepancy and the wholesaler is not needed. Nor are wholesalers needed when a coal producer mines coal and ships it in trainload quantities directly to an electric generating station.

**Assortment Discrepancy.** Household buyers want to buy a broad assortment of products when they go grocery shopping. Even giant firms like General Mills and General Foods do not produce the full assortment of products a household buyer wants. Thus an assortment discrepancy exists between the household buyer and the manufacturer. This also is adjusted in marketing channels. A supermarket brings together (builds up) the product assortment its customers want by buying products from many producers. It might buy directly from the producer if there is no quantity discrepancy. But this very direct buying and selling can be

*Figure 13–5. Adjusting assortment discrepancy*

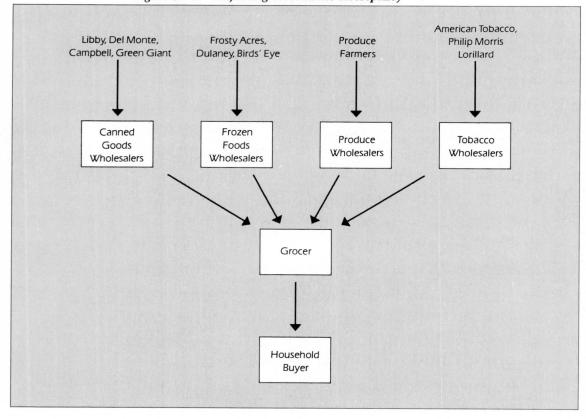

carried only so far. Because a large supermarket stocks thousands of products made by hundreds of manufacturers, the supermarket operator would have to spend too much time buying and too little time selling. Thus supermarkets buy a lot of their merchandise from wholesalers. Big chains like Safeway, A&P, and Kroger, however, buy directly from producers many of the products they sell.

Suppose a grocer buys canned goods from a canned goods wholesaler, tobacco products from a tobacco wholesaler, meat products from a meat wholesaler, and frozen foods from a frozen foods wholesaler. Each wholesaler buys products from manufacturers whose products fit the wholesaler's line of products. The canned goods wholesaler buys from Green Giant, Libby's, and Del Monte. The grocer can deal directly with one canned goods wholesaler instead of many canned goods manufacturers. The grocer does the same in buying from other wholesalers who carry other types of products. (See Figure 13–5.)

## CHANNEL CHARACTERISTICS

Figure 13–6 shows several examples of channels for consumer and industrial products, which help in understanding two important channel characteristics: (1) channel structure and (2) relationships among participants.

### Channel Structure

The different types of participants in a channel determine its vertical dimension, or length. The fewer types of participants, the more direct (shorter) the channel is. The greater the variety, the more indirect (longer) the channel is. Direct channels have fewer types of participants.

**Direct Channels.** In the most **direct channel** there are no middlemen between producer and final buyers. The producer sells directly to those final buyers. Among the reasons producers use direct channels are (1) they believe they can do a better job than available middlemen, (2) acceptable middlemen are absent, (3) acceptable middlemen are unwilling to handle the product, (4) the market is very narrow (few customers), (5) extensive training must accompany sales to customers, and (6) products are heavy or bulky.

direct channel

The producer's advantages in using direct channels include (1) greater control over the product's distribution, (2) closer contact and communication with final buyers, (3) easier marketing research, and (4) quicker marketing mix adjustments.

Channel 1 in Figure 13–6 illustrates the most direct consumer products channel: manufacturer → consumer. The most direct industrial products channel is channel 5: manufacturer → industrial user. Direct channels are much more common in industrial than in consumer products marketing because industrial buyers often are concentrated geographically, buy in large quantities, buy products with a high unit value, buy complex products that require after-sale service, and insist on dealing directly with producers.

As we will see in Chapter 14, direct channels sometimes are used for consumer products. Fuller sells brushes, Avon sells cosmetics, and Electrolux sells vacuum cleaners door-to-door to ultimate consumers. Some products like phonograph records are also sold directly by mail. Although most services are also sold directly by the producer to the consumer, agent middlemen are common in marketing airline tickets and some types of insurance.

**Indirect Channels.** One or more independent middlemen stand between producer and final buyer in an **indirect channel.** The producer entrusts some part of the distribution task to middlemen, who are not under the producer's direct control. But the producer must work closely with its middlemen to ensure final buyer satisfaction and maintain a feel for their wants.

In consumer products marketing the manufacturer → retailer → ultimate consumer channel is common for shopping products like cars, clothing, and home appliances. (See channel 2 in Figure 13–6.) The manufacturer → wholesaler → retailer → ultimate consumer channel is common for convenience products. (See channel 3 in Figure 13–6.) Channels for convenience products tend to be long because consumers want to buy them with a minimum of effort. Thus producers have to sell through a very large number of outlets. Chewing gum manufacturers would have a very tough job selling directly to the tens of thousands of retail outlets, including vending machines, that sell chewing gum.

Indirect channels also are fairly common for industrial products, except installations and products manufactured to the buyer's specifications. Generally, however, indirect channels for industrial products are shorter than consumer products channels.

**Vertical Channel Integration.** A channel's vertical structure can be altered through vertical integration. This means combining two or more stages of a channel under one participant's control. It can be accomplished in two ways. First, one participant may buy out another's operations, such as a manufacturer buying out a wholesaler. Second, one participant may assume the functions of another, such as a retailer bypassing a wholesaler and buying directly from a manufacturer.

Vertical integration can be backward or forward. In **forward vertical integration** the integrating firm's operations take it closer to the final buyer in the channel, such as when a wholesaler goes into retailing or a manufacturer goes into wholesaling.

In **backward vertical integration** the integrating firm's operations take it further away from the final buyer in the channel and closer to supply sources. Examples are a wholesaler who goes into manufacturing or a retailer who goes into wholesaling. Revco, a large drug retailer, did this when it acquired several small drug producers several years ago.

In Figure 13–7 backward vertical integration would result if the retailer in channel 2 merged with or assumed the marketing functions of

margin notes:
indirect channel

forward vertical integration

backward vertical integration

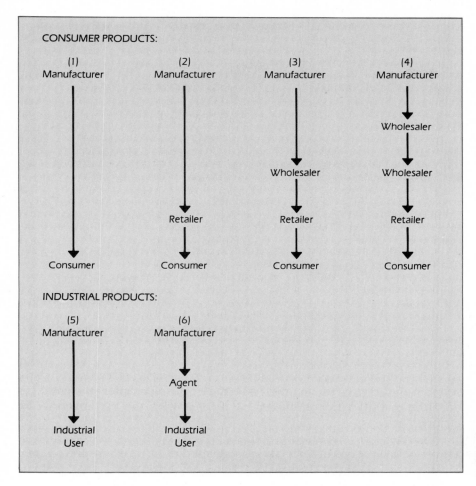

CONSUMER PRODUCTS:

| (1) | (2) | (3) | (4) |
|-----|-----|-----|-----|
| Manufacturer | Manufacturer | Manufacturer | Manufacturer |
| | | | Wholesaler |
| | | Wholesaler | Wholesaler |
| | Retailer | Retailer | Retailer |
| Consumer | Consumer | Consumer | Consumer |

INDUSTRIAL PRODUCTS:

| (5) | (6) |
|-----|-----|
| Manufacturer | Manufacturer |
| | Agent |
| Industrial User | Industrial User |

*Figure 13–6.*
*Typical channels*
*for consumer and*
*industrial products*

the second wholesaler in that channel. Total vertical integration means one firm controls all activities from production of the product to its sale to the final buyer. Oil companies that own oil wells, refineries, and retail gas stations are examples.

**Horizontal Channel Integration.** The number of participants of any one type on the same level in a channel determines its horizontal dimension, or width: the larger that number, the wider the channel; the smaller that number, the narrower the channel. The vertical and horizontal dimensions of a channel determine its structure.

**Horizontal channel integration** means that participants on the same level in the channel combine under one participant's control. It also can be accomplished in two ways. First, one participant may buy out another's operations, such as when a local wholesaler buys out other local wholesalers to build a stronger regional wholesaling operation. Second, one participant may expand the number of units it operates by opening

horizontal chan-
nel integration

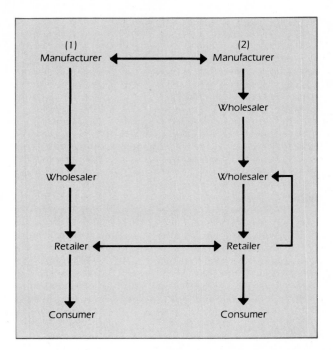

*Figure 13–7.*
*Horizontal and*
*backward vertical*
*integration*

new ones at one level in the channel, such as when a retailer opens additional retail stores. In Figure 13–7 horizontal integration would result if the retailer in channel 1 merged with the retailer in channel 2, or if the manufacturer in channel 1 merged with the manufacturer in channel 2.

Channel participants might integrate horizontally in the hope of achieving economies in their advertising, marketing research, and buying. But there are potential drawbacks—there may be problems in coordinating the operations of a greater number of units. If independent units can perform the marketing functions more efficiently, horizontal integration is not desirable.

### Relationships Among Participants

A channel is a type of social system because each member has certain roles to fulfill. Other members in the channel expect that member to behave in predictable ways.[2] Manufacturers may expect wholesalers to provide good service to retailers and keep manufacturers informed about sales at the retail level. Wholesalers, in turn, may expect manufacturers to inform them of planned new product introductions. Retailers may expect wholesalers to keep adequate inventories and provide reliable and speedy delivery. Three basic types of relationships among members in channels are (1) competitive, (2) cooperative, and (3) conflict.[3]

**Competitive Relationships.** General Motors and its dealer organization compete with the other domestic and foreign car manufacturers and their dealer organizations. These channel systems compete with each other. This is interchannel competition.

Competitive relationships also may exist within a given channel. An appliance manufacturer who sells through appliance stores and discount stores will find them competing for sales if they seek to serve the same market target.

**Cooperative Relationships.** Cooperative relationships among members in a vertical channel are necessary for it to function as an integrated system of effort for creating and delivering customer satisfactions. It will remain a viable structure only if each member perceives some benefit from being on the team. Each expects to gain something from others in the channel, which requires cooperation. When Kraft undertakes massive couponing for one of its food products, it expects retailers to accept the coupons from consumers. Otherwise, the effort is wasted. Point-of-purchase displays supplied by Colgate-Palmolive, Gillette, and Schlitz also must be put in place by retailers if they are to be effective.

Cooperation, however, is not restricted to the vertical dimension of a particular channel. In a **horizontal marketing system** (HMS) two or more firms on the same level of distribution cooperate to accomplish a common goal. HMSs take many forms. American Motors Corporation (AMC) and Renault reached an agreement to produce and market front-wheel drive cars designed by Renault and manufactured by AMC. This saved AMC development costs and provided a dealer organization in the United States for Renault.

Downtown merchants' associations also are HMSs. Individual merchants may get together to set up a joint promotion fund to promote downtown shopping. Trade associations like the Florida Orange Growers and the National Home Appliance Manufacturers Association also are HMSs as are the federations of churches of different denominations that exist in many cities.

HMSs recognize there is strength in numbers. Each member gives up some authority to make decisions strictly on its own to secure cooperative effort in attaining collective goals. The nature of HMSs also varies widely. AMC and Renault's agreement is formalized and long-term. Cooperative effort among downtown merchants might focus on a single short-run objective, such as getting the city government to finance a new downtown parking area.

**Conflict Relationships.** Firms in a vertical channel are interdependent, but when their goals are incompatible conflict is inevitable. **Channel conflict,** which we will discuss in greater detail later in the chapter, refers to the opposing interests that exist among different levels within a given channel. Competitive and cooperative relationships can occur within, between, or among channels, but conflict relationships are restricted to one channel. A drug manufacturer and its retail pharmacists, for example, might conflict if the manufacturer begins distributing through prescription counters in supermarkets.[4]

horizontal marketing system

channel conflict

## CHANNEL DEVELOPMENT

The channels shown in Figure 13–6 are only a few of the many channels in use. Marketing managers can achieve a differential advantage by developing new channels that better serve their final buyers. Changing shopping habits create opportunity to develop new channels. L'eggs were the first pantyhose to be sold through supermarkets, and Conn organs were the first organs to be sold through department stores.[5]

### Channel Selection Factors

Many manufacturers view their channel strategy as a selection process: alternative channels exist and the task is to select the best one. A better approach is to start with final buyer wants and build the best channel to satisfy them. This helps marketers think of channels as possibilities rather than alternatives.

Among the many factors that affect channel development are characteristics of customers, the product, the company, the middlemen, and the environment. Customer-oriented firms attach great importance to final buyer wants in developing their distribution strategy. (See Figure 13–8.)

**Customer Characteristics.** Unlike consumers, industrial buyers often prefer to deal directly with producers, except when buying small accessory equipment and operating supplies. They also tend to be more concentrated geographically and there are fewer of them for a typical industrial product. These factors favor shorter channels for industrial products.

Changes in customer buying patterns can make existing channels obsolete. More beer is sold through supermarkets and grocery stores

*Figure 13–8. Factors influencing channel development*

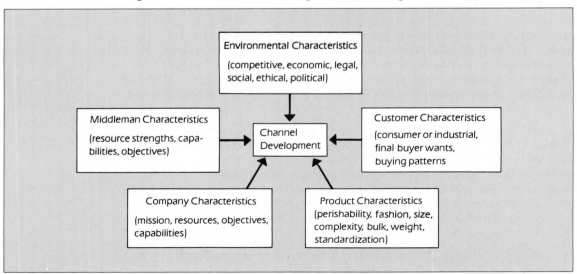

than through bars. Supermarkets also have become an important outlet for house plants, small appliances, lawn care products, and many other nonfood products.

**Product Characteristics.** Product characteristics include perishability, fashion, size, complexity, and standardization. Highly perishable products move through short channels to avoid rehandling and spoilage. Short channels reduce the time a fashion product is in the distribution pipeline from producer to consumer. Low-value, bulky products like cement, sand, gravel, and iron ore move through short channels to reduce transportation and rehandling costs. Complex products like computers move through short channels because they require specialized training and other after-sale services from manufacturers. IBM services its equipment rather than entrust it to middlemen. High-value products also tend to move through short channels. Highly standardized products, however, tend to move through longer channels than those built to individual customer specification.

**Company Characteristics.** A firm's mission, resources, and capabilities also affect channel selection. Toro Company's heavy advertising of its lawn mowers, snow throwers, automatic windup hoses, and other products helped it to get its products into department, discount, and hardware store chains. In 1975 its products were sold through 14,000 dealers; in 1979 they were in 47,000 outlets.[6] Adequate financial resources lessen the need for middlemen who can share the tasks of carrying inventories, granting credit, or providing transportation and warehousing services. Singer can operate its own retail stores, whereas some of its competitors must rely on several types of retailing middlemen to sell their sewing machines.

Companies with wide product mixes like Colgate-Palmolive can afford to do more direct selling to large retailers than smaller firms with narrow product mixes. The smaller firms rely on wholesalers to reach retailers. Colgate-Palmolive's promotion skill also reduces its dependence on middlemen to push retail sales. Firms lacking this capability must rely more on middlemen for promotional push.

**Middlemen Characteristics.** The characteristics of middlemen, such as their particular resource strengths and capabilities, must also be considered. When Mattel, Inc. introduced its Intellivision it chose to distribute the product through major department and chain stores rather than through its traditional toy-store outlets. One reason was the product's high price.[7] Some wholesalers are reluctant to carry inventory and provide credit and delivery to their customers. When suitable middlemen are absent or unwilling to handle a product the manufacturer has to go directly to final buyers. If it lacks the resources and capability to do this, distribution may be impossible.[8]

**Environmental Characteristics.** Environmental factors also affect channel selection. A small canned-foods producer may have trouble convincing wholesalers to stock a new fruit juice because they might be under pressure from present suppliers to keep the new product off the market. Xerox recently abandoned its policy of selling only through its own salesforce and started using outside dealers and distributors to sell its lower-priced equipment. A major reason was the intense competition from Japanese rivals, who sell through networks of distributors and dealers in the United States.[9] Thus the competitive environment must be considered.

The legal environment is another factor. Door-to-door distribution, for example, may be against the law. A distillery cannot sell whiskey through drug and grocery stores in states that operate their own retail alcoholic beverage outlets.

The social, ethical, and political environments must also be considered. Discount stores are generally accepted in metropolitan areas but are still looked down on in some rural areas. The 1973 Supreme Court ruling on obscenity permits, within broad limits, local communities to determine what is obscene. This creates distribution problems for some magazine publishers and film producers.

The economic environment is also important. Aside from the pressure of Japanese rivals, largely because of inflation Xerox also found it was increasingly costly to use its salesforce to sell its small, low-priced equipment to small businesses and professionals, such as doctors, lawyers, and accountants, who have home offices. Thus Xerox is using its own stores to reach these prospective customers.[10] Firms in modern economic systems face fewer problems in developing new channels than firms in traditional societies. This is a big problem in international marketing. A firm may want to avoid going through numerous inefficient wholesalers, but tradition may make more direct distribution impossible. Japanese grocery wholesalers must provide rapid delivery of small orders, extend credit, and sell on consignment to many thousands of small grocery stores. Supermarkets have not edged these independent retailers out of business. The business cycle must be considered, too. During recessions, for example, middlemen may be unwilling to stock new products.

## CHANNEL CONFLICT AND ITS RESOLUTION

Producers who rely on independent middlemen for distribution often assume their wholesalers and retailers are in business to serve the producers' interests. But the middlemen believe they are in business to serve their customers. A wholesaler may think of manufacturers as suppliers and of retailers as customers. But the manufacturer may think the wholesaler is in business to serve it. This can lead to channel conflict.

A channel should function as an integrated system. All members should view themselves as members of a distribution team. It is easier to develop this team spirit in direct than in indirect channel systems.

The chances for conflict are much greater in indirect channels because independent middlemen are present.

## Sources of Conflict

Suppose a manufacturer of small electric motors uses an independent middleman in Wyoming to solicit orders on a commission basis. If the middleman develops the territory, the manufacturer may want to replace him or her with company salespersons. To take another example, suppose Del Monte distributes through an independent wholesaler to grocery stores in a certain city, but one store has become large enough to buy directly from Del Monte. The wholesaler loses a big customer but Del Monte still must depend on the wholesaler for distribution to the smaller stores.

Conflict may also arise over the issue of who is to perform certain functions in a channel. Pushing excessive inventory onto their wholesalers reduces manufacturers' need for storage space and frees some working capital, but the effects on the wholesaler are the opposite.

Conflict often arises over what products wholesalers will stock and how much promotion they will give each one. Manufacturers with wide product lines want wholesalers to stock and promote all items in a line. Wholesalers want to stock fast sellers but cannot give much push to slow movers because they carry many products of many manufacturers.

Another situation that causes conflict is after-sale service. A manufacturer may expect the wholesaler or retailer to maintain a service and repair facility, but middlemen may think that is the manufacturer's job. This is one reason makers of small appliances may set up their own networks of regional service and repair centers. Sometimes a more direct distribution system is the next step.

Poor communication between manufacturers and middlemen can also lead to conflict. Middlemen want to be kept informed of future model changes, price changes, and so on. The introduction of a new model of hair dryer may reduce the value of older models in the middleman's inventory. Unless the middleman is informed in advance so that the old models can be worked out of inventory, or the middleman is permitted to sell the old units at reduced prices without cutting into the profit margin, conflict may develop.

Very high interest rates in early 1980 greatly increased the finance costs auto dealers had to pay. Several Chevrolet dealers formed the Chevrolet Dealers Alliance in an effort to bring their problems to the attention of General Motors. Among the conflict issues were the delivery of too few small cars and the cost of financing new cars already in the dealers' showrooms.[11]

Conflict is inevitable in a channel with independent middlemen. The cooperative relationships among channel members, however, must outweigh the conflicting ones or else the members would not participate. Some degree of conflict may even be beneficial. For example, a manu-

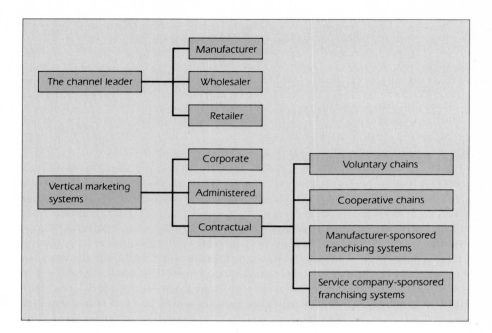

*Figure 13–9. Approaches to resolving channel conflict*

facturer and a wholesaler may have a conflict over the issue of transportation. For years, the manufacturer has shipped in large volumes by rail to the wholesaler. But the wholesaler's customers are placing smaller orders more frequently. The wholesaler's inventory is increasing and a lot of working capital is tied up in unneeded inventory. This conflict could lead to a new method of transportation that would reduce the wholesaler's inventory and also help the manufacturer to even out production scheduling. Truck transportation in smaller volumes might be substituted for rail transportation in larger volumes.

The conflict described above helped overcome the inertia that often develops in channels.[12] The result is a more effective transportation method. This type of constructive conflict is called *functional* conflict. It results in new methods that increase channel efficiency and effectiveness. *Dysfunctional* conflict leads channel members to become uncooperative. The goal is to differentiate between the two types of conflict, reduce dysfunctional conflict, and capitalize on functional conflict. Two basic approaches to dysfunctional conflict resolution are (1) the channel leader and (2) vertical marketing systems. (See Figure 13–9.)

### The Channel Leader

channel leader

The **channel leader** is the most powerful channel member.[13] The leader's task is to manage conflict among channel members. They accept this leadership when they consider it to be in their best interests.

Prior to the Civil War, wholesalers often were leaders. They bought products from overseas and small domestic manufacturers and sold them to small, local retailers. Greater industrialization during the latter decades of the nineteenth century created bigger manufacturing firms and more power for manufacturers. The growth of large retail chains after World War I brought them more power. They assumed traditional wholesaling functions and influenced the design of products.

The locus of power in modern channels is more complicated.[14] Manufacturers have control in cars, and large retail chains have control in food. In other cases it may not be as clear-cut.

**Manufacturers as Leaders.** Several factors favor manufacturers as leaders. Procter & Gamble's success as a consumer products marketer is based on years of experience in understanding the consumer market. Retailers acknowledge and respect its leadership. Manufacturers are in control when considerable research and development is involved in designing and producing a product and when it requires intensive promotion at the national level, such as when Polaroid introduces new cameras. Even giant discount store chains like Woolco and Kmart cannot afford to focus their promotion effort on only one product, but Polaroid can. Large manufacturers also often have more economic power than their middlemen. They are especially powerful in periods of short supplies when they resort to allocating supplies to middlemen. Home insulation materials are an example from recent years.

**Retailers as Leaders.** Several factors favor retailers as leaders. They deal directly with ultimate consumers and are a good source of feedback for manufacturers. It has been suggested that retailers should become the consumer's advocate to entire channels.[15] The difficulty of forecasting and shaping ultimate consumer demand gives retailers even more power. Their knowledge of ultimate consumer wants sometimes enables them to dictate product design to manufacturers. Many also carry their own brands, which gives them considerable power. Giant retailers like Sears and J. C. Penney have economic power over manufacturers that produce their products. Channels for fashion items and household products are often controlled by retailers. Finally, retailers who market mature products incur little risk in carrying their own brands in addition to or in place of manufacturers' brands.

**Wholesalers as Leaders.** Wholesalers, however, still are important in many channels. They stand between manufacturers, who favor long production runs, and small retailers, who often buy in very small quantities. A manufacturer who desires access to a market served by only one grocery wholesaler soon discovers the wholesaler's power.

### Vertical Marketing Systems (VMS)

A **vertical marketing system** (VMS) seeks to remove conflict among channel members by viewing the channel as an integrated system with unified objectives instead of as a loosely organized group of independent firms.[16] This makes possible varying degrees of vertical integration of the channel. Three types of VMSs are (1) corporate, (2) administered, and (3) contractual.

**Corporate Vertical Marketing Systems.** In a corporate VMS there

vertical marketing system

is single ownership of two or more stages in the channel. The ultimate in vertical integration is unified ownership of each stage in the channel. This provides the greatest degree of channel control. Singer makes and distributes its sewing machines through its own retail outlets. Holiday Inns owns a carpet mill and a furniture manufacturing plant. As we saw in Chapter 2, the legality of vertical integration depends on how it is achieved and its effect on competition.

**Administered Vertical Marketing Systems.** In an administered VMS the size and power of the channel leader enable it to plan and coordinate marketing programs for all channel members.[17] The leader does not own the independent members of the channel, however. General Foods and Campbell Soup Company have a lot of power over retailers and enjoy maximum cooperation from them in stocking new product items, giving adequate shelf space to their products, and so on. The Magnavox Corporation's reputation for quality and its consumer advertising enable it to select what it considers to be the best retail outlets. But an administered VMS is harder to manage than a corporate VMS because ownership is not unified.

**Contractual Vertical Marketing Systems.** In a contractual VMS independent channel members are tied together by formalized contracts that spell out their roles in the channel system.[18] Four types are: (1) wholesaler-sponsored voluntary chains, (2) retailer-sponsored cooperative chains, (3) manufacturer-sponsored franchising systems, and (4) service company-sponsored franchising systems.

Wholesaler-sponsored voluntary chains are started by wholesalers. Super Value Stores, Inc. is the largest food wholesaler in the United States. It offers a broad package of services, including accounting, merchandising, site location, store design, and financing to more than 1,500 independent food retailers who voluntarily enter into buying contracts with it. The group's combined buying power enables each member to compete more effectively with big corporate chains like Kroger and Safeway.

Retailer-sponsored cooperative chains function in a similar manner except that the retailers set up their own wholesaling operation. They own and buy from it. Each member receives a patronage dividend based on the volume of its purchases. These are discussed more fully in the next chapter.

Manufacturer-sponsored franchising systems exist at the wholesale and retail levels. The Coca-Cola Company franchises wholesalers (bottlers) to buy its concentrate and produce Coke to sell to retailers in their market areas. Midas Muffler Shops are independently owned retail outlets franchised to buy and install Midas products from the manufacturer.

Service company–sponsored franchising systems serve both consumers and industrial buyers.[19] McDonald's, Burger King, Howard Johnson's, H&R Block, and Avis serve ultimate consumers, and Kelly Services supplies temporary workers to business firms.[20]

In many franchise systems some franchised units are owned by the franchisor. Holiday Inns and Church's Fried Chicken own and operate some of their own units. In other cases ownership in franchised units is shared by the franchisor and the franchisee. In recent years some fast-food franchisors have been buying back franchises from independent franchisees and are operating them. The franchises that remain often are concentrated in large regional chains or mini chains.[21] Finally, some large franchisors operate multiple franchising systems. Both International House of Pancakes and Orange Julius are franchised by International Industries.

## CHANNEL PLANNING

Channel strategy planning is important for manufacturers and middlemen. Wholesalers have to decide on the number and types of retailers through which to distribute. But the closer a channel member is to the ultimate consumer or industrial buyer, the less need it has to develop a channel from scratch.

Resellers, as we have seen, may be the most powerful members in some channels. Sears has power over its more than 12,000 manufacturer-suppliers in the United States because of its huge buying power. Its power is felt by suppliers through Sears's buying decisions. It is the only customer for some of them and if it stopped buying from them, they would be in deep trouble.

Most manufacturers must make many selling decisions. If we rule out direct distribution, a manufacturer must decide on the types and numbers of middlemen to use. They become part of the channel because of the manufacturer's decision to select them and their willingness to join. The job of designing channels typically falls mainly on the manufacturer. Thus we will focus on channel planning for manufacturers.

A manufacturer who decides to use indirect distribution must select independent middlemen. It must decide which type or types of middlemen to use, how many of each type to use, and how to work with resellers in building a channel system.

### Selecting the Type(s) of Middlemen

A manufacturer's ultimate objective in selecting middlemen is to satisfy the final buyer of the product. Sales to middlemen are means to this end. If final buyers are not satisfied, middlemen will stop placing orders. The final buyer's requirements influence the type of retailers selected, and the retailers' requirements influence the type of wholesalers selected. This customer-oriented approach satisfies the manufacturer's final and intermediate customers.

**Multiple Channels.** A manufacturer may want to use multiple channels, or dual distribution, if customers expect the product to be available in different types of outlets.[22] These channels can be competitive or noncompetitive.

For example, some tire makers sell tires directly to car makers as original equipment on new cars and also sell tires to consumers in the replacement market through their company-owned retail stores. These are noncompetitive channels because they reach different market segments. Some tire makers also sell to wholesalers who, in turn, sell to gas stations. This channel is competitive with the manufacturer → manufacturer-owned retail store channel because they serve essentially the same market segment.

Dual distribution policies, however, may involve antitrust questions. Thus one tire maker was sued recently by several states, which alleged the firm sought to fix prices and divide markets between company-owned and independent retail stores.[23]

**Facilitating Middlemen.** Wholesalers and retailers help manufacturers carry out the flow of title to final buyers. But other flows must accompany the title flow. Transportation firms move the products and insurance firms perform the risk-taking function by insuring them. Using indirect channels may slow customer feedback that manufacturers need and so they may use marketing research agencies to perform the information function. Banks help also in performing the financing function.

facilitating
middlemen

These functional specialists are **facilitating middlemen,** or facilitating agencies. Their activities add value and benefits that customers want in the products they buy. A manufacturer could operate its own fleet of trucks rather than use an independent trucking firm. Some functions could also be assumed by retailers and wholesalers instead of by facilitating middlemen. Channel members use facilitating middlemen when they believe the facilitators can perform the functions more economically and efficiently than the channel members.

The types of middlemen selected to carry out the title flow influence the selection of facilitating middlemen. A manufacturer who sells to retailers on consignment may rely more on bank credit to finance its sales than does a manufacturer who sells to wholesalers for cash.

### Determining the Number of Middlemen

The manufacturer's selection of the type of middlemen determines the channel's length. Decisions about the number of middlemen to use at each level in the channel determine its width. (See Figure 13–10.) The intensity of distribution, or a product's market exposure, is a crucial factor in channel planning. Three degrees of market exposure are (1) intensive distribution, (2) selective distribution, and (3) exclusive distribution.

intensive
distribution

**Intensive distribution** means having the product available to buyers in as many outlets as possible, perhaps including vending machines. It gives maximum market coverage. Convenience products are distributed intensively because buyers are unwilling to spend much time shopping for them.

Decisions about the intensity of distribution most directly affect the channel's width. Suppose a marketer of inexpensive cameras wants intensive distribution. If final buyers shop only in camera shops, dis-

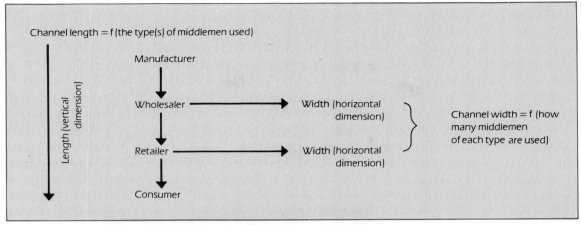

**Figure 13–10.  The vertical and horizontal dimensions of a channel**

tribution through numerous camera shops would be necessary.   If they also shop for cameras in discount, department, and variety stores, those outlets also would have to be included.

Middleman willingness to stock a manufacturer's product is a major factor in achieving intensive distribution.   Middlemen do not want to stock products that may stay in inventory for long periods.   This is one of a middleman's major considerations in deciding to take on new products, especially those produced by small firms with very narrow product mixes.   The manufacturer may have to advertise the product to final buyers so that they will request it from middlemen who, in turn, will place orders with the manufacturer.   Intensive distribution will be hard to achieve if the manufacturer cannot afford the promotion effort.

**Selective distribution** means restricting distribution in an area to middlemen who are selected on the basis of their performance capability. The outlets selected also must be compatible with the product's image. Shopping products, specialty products, and industrial products that require specialized selling effort from middlemen often are distributed selectively.

*selective distribution*

Selective distribution is appealing when a small percentage of customers account for a large part of a manufacturer's total sales.   This is called the iceberg principle, or the 80-20 principle.   A firm may sell 80 percent of its output to 20 percent of its customers.   Limiting distribution to the large accounts cuts selling expenses and, it is hoped, will increase sales to each account.   But care is needed to avoid cutting off accounts with good growth potential.

Selective distribution can benefit middlemen by limiting the number of rival outlets that carry the brand.   This often helps in building cooperation among channel members.   Manufacturers who want intensive distribution sometimes have to settle for selective distribution.   Some

# "You get the best of Seiko only where this sign is displayed.

# When you buy your Seiko anywhere else, someone could be getting the best of you."

*Robert Pliskin*, Robert Pliskin, President
Seiko Time Corporation

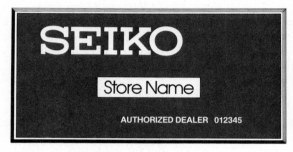

Because Seiko is the world's best-selling quality watch, by far, there are many people, not Authorized Dealers, who will try to sell you a Seiko. And when you buy your Seiko that way, you may not get what you pay for. Regardless of <u>what</u> you pay.

<u>Look for the Authorized Dealer identification. It's a sure sign that you'll always get the best of Seiko.</u>
<u>Or, consider the alternatives:</u>

**1. <u>You get the best selection where you see this sign.</u>**
Only the dealer displaying this sign offers the widest, up-to-date selection. He can even order any Seiko watch that's not in stock. Quickly. Easily.
<u>The unauthorized alternative</u>
The Seiko you buy could be an obsolete model. Perhaps not even made for U.S. distribution. There's even a chance that the watch you buy is not a real Seiko at all, but an imitation designed to exploit Seiko's popularity in the U.S. market.

**2. <u>You get the best warranty where you see this sign.</u>**
Seiko offers the most respected warranty in the industry. But you're only certain of getting that kind of automatic security and protection when you buy your Seiko at an Authorized Dealer.
<u>The unauthorized alternative</u>
You may be buying a watch purchased from an importer who buys from Hong Kong or Taiwan. It may not be covered by a valid Seiko warranty. So you'll have to pay for any servicing, repairs, or adjustments that Seiko makes. It <u>could</u> be covered by the importer's own personal warranty. If you run into trouble, we hope you find him.

**3. <u>You get the highest quality standards where you see this sign.</u>**
When Seiko produces a watch for the U.S. market, certain import indentifica-tion must be stamped or engraved on the inside of each case. Seiko does that <u>before</u> final assembly and <u>before</u> final quality control testing. So the watch you buy is in mint condition, truly representing the best of Seiko technology and craftsmanship.
<u>The unauthorized alternative</u>
When you buy a Seiko not made for the U.S. market, the inde-

pendent importer must open the watch and engrave or stamp the proper identification on the movement and the case to meet U.S. Customs regulations. There goes the protective factory seal. And damage can occur if filings or dust get into the watch itself. In fact, any damage caused by unauthorized tampering with or opening the watch invalidates the Seiko warranty. So you must decide whether you're interested in gambling, or, buying a high quality Seiko watch.

**4. <u>You get the best service and parts where you see this sign.</u>**
Seiko Authorized Dealers have the most knowledgeable, trained personnel.
They'll make sure you end up with the Seiko that's just right for you. They can show you what it does and how easy it is to operate. And should it ever need servicing, the required Seiko parts are available, plus the most admired and efficient service network in the country.
<u>The unauthorized alternative</u>
When the objective is just to make a sale, not necessarily to make a long-term customer, slick salespeople become more important than knowledgeable ones. And if you need any servicing, they could send you to Seiko. Seiko will give you great service of course, but if the watch is not covered by the valid Seiko warranty, you'll have to pay for it. However, if you buy an obsolete watch, or one that's not meant to be sold in the U.S. at all, don't hold your breath while you're waiting for parts. Because not even Seiko can inventory every part for every watch all the time.

## Look for the Authorized Dealer Identification. It's a sure sign that you'll always get the best of Seiko.

# SEIKO

Someday all watches will be made this way.

Seiko Time Corporation, 640 Fifth Avenue, New York, N.Y. 10019

*An ad that reflects a manufacturer's concern about selective distribution*

Source: Seiko Time Corporation

outlets may refuse to carry the product when the manufacturer is not the channel leader or there may be too few outlets of the desired type in an area.

**Exclusive distribution** is the extreme form of selective distribution— one outlet in each market area. Specialty products and installations usually are exclusively distributed. Examples are Rolls-Royce and Mercedes cars, Leica cameras, and Steinway pianos. (See Figure 13–11.)

*exclusive distribution*

Exclusive distribution appeals to manufacturers who want maximum middleman push for their products. Dealers who have no competition from other resellers of the brand in their market areas are expected to do a better job of promoting it. Getting resellers to carry a complete inventory and provide service and repair facilities, when needed, is also easier. The manufacturer's salesforce calls on fewer customers and fewer accounts are carried. This cuts bad debt losses, reduces working capital needs, and may lower total marketing costs. Manufacturer-dealer cooperation is easier to achieve since both work under a contract that spells out their rights and obligations.

Exclusive distribution is also attractive to dealers. The manufacturer's promotion effort benefits dealers exclusively in their market areas. There are no other dealers to underprice an exclusive dealer in its area. Thus inventory may turn over faster. Dealer investment in service and repair facilities creates customer goodwill and greater profit potential.

There are some limitations, however. Convenience products, shopping products, and many types of industrial products do not lend themselves to exclusive distribution. Manufacturers can lose market coverage in an area if the dealer goes out of business or withdraws from the exclusive dealing agreement. Dealers also face the risk that manufacturers will abandon their exclusive distribution policy.

As we saw in Chapter 2, the major problem with exclusive distribution is its legality. Exclusive dealing contracts, territorial restrictions, and tying contracts can be illegal if they tend to lessen competition or create monopoly. The courts tend to be more lenient, however, with new products and smaller firms than with established products and larger firms.

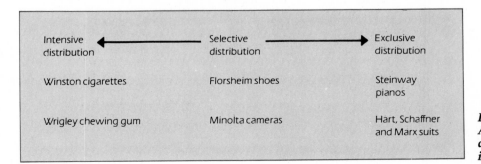

*Figure 13–11.*
*A continuum of distribution intensity*

Several years ago the Federal Trade Commission (FTC) ruled that the exclusive territorial license system in the soft drink industry violated the antitrust laws. These licenses allow a bottler to have a local monopoly for a particular brand of soft drink in its market area. The bottlers, therefore, sought congressional exemption from antitrust challenge as long as there is competition in the area from other brands of soft drinks.

## Working with Middlemen

The systems view of channels focuses on channel members' interdependence, or linkage. Channel conflict results when this linkage is not recognized. Building a channel system used to be the job of the manufacturer's sales manager. Sales personnel were expected to engage in some nonselling goodwill activities with middlemen. Manufacturers now supplement salespersons' efforts to build channel relations by setting up staff departments to foster closer contact and cooperation among channel members. These **trade relations departments** seek to build channel cooperation through providing personnel support, training and development activities, and building dealer motivation.

**trade-relations department**

A manufacturer might provide personnel support by hiring a salesperson to solicit orders from retailers and submit them to wholesalers. This salesperson supplements the wholesaler's selling effort. Training and development activities build sales skills among middlemen and their salesforces. General Electric might send a representative to a retail appliance store to acquaint the salesforce with a new GE appliance's features. Motivational incentives reinforce training and development activities. GE also might offer push money to increase motivation to sell the new appliance. Each salesperson receives a certain amount of money for every unit he or she sells.

## CHANNELS FOR SERVICES

Although marketers include services in the concept of product, services have several distinguishing characteristics, as we saw in Chapter 10. For example, they are intangible, and the market area of service marketers generally is considered to be limited.

Direct selling, however, is not the only channel for service marketers. Agent middlemen are used in channels for insurance and airline tickets, and there are service company–sponsored franchising systems, such as H&R Block and Avis. It has been suggested that marketers should distinguish between production and distribution of services. One author contends that *"any extra-corporate entity between the producer of a service and prospective users that is utilized to make the service available and/or more convenient is a marketing intermediary for that service."* (Italics in original.)[24]

In some cases service marketers have developed new products that include a physical representation of the service they are offering. This makes it possible to use middlemen in distributing the service. Donnelly points out that the bank credit card is an example: "... the bank credit card is a tangible representation of the service of credit though it is not the service itself. As such, it has enabled banks to overcome the inseparability problem and use the retail merchant as an intermediary in the distribution of credit. The credit card has also made it possible for banks to expand their geographic markets by maintaining credit customers far outside their immediate trading areas, since it enables subscribers to maintain an 'inventory' of the bank's credit for use at their convenience."[25]

## THE TOTAL CHANNEL SYSTEM

Where does the channel for steel modular buildings used for storing household goods begin and end? Does it begin with a miner of iron ore, a steel producer, a steel fabricator, or the building's manufacturer?

According to tradition, the channel begins with the modular building manufacturer. A different channel is created whenever the form of a product changes. The steel producer makes rolled sheet steel from iron ore. The fabricator makes the steel into shapes and forms its customers want. The manufacturer puts together a building its customers want and sells it to a retailer who, in turn, sells it to a consumer. Thus we have described four different channels:

iron ore miner → steel producer

steel producer → steel fabricator

steel fabricator → modular building manufacturer

modular building manufacturer → retailer → consumer

Facilitating middlemen are not included in the traditional description of a channel. But although transportation firms, advertising and marketing research agencies, and financial institutions are left out, they may in fact be needed to distribute the product.

The traditional view of channels focuses on transactions between buyers and sellers who are in direct contact. The total systems view focuses on a framework for matching resources in the state of nature with ultimate consumer demand. This matching process occurs through a single integrated marketing system, not a collection of independent producers and middlemen. The channel for the modular buildings starts with the mining of ore and ends with the ultimate consumer. Any institution that increases the efficiency of transforming iron ore into modular buildings and delivering them to consumers is part of the total channel system. This perspective helps in planning channels but is hard to use in a practical way except for highly vertically integrated firms. But it does draw attention to the advantages of the systems view in channel planning.

## REVERSE CHANNELS

As we saw in Chapter 10, the concept of a reverse channel applies to a product recall. Ecological consciousness also has focused attention on the potential of channels to help protect the environment by increasing the efficiency of recycling programs. Recyclable materials can flow in reverse order from consumers or industrial users back to manufacturers.

Reusable soft drink bottles, for example, flow back to the bottler through traditional middlemen like supermarkets. Some manufacturers like Reynolds Aluminum Company operate recycling centers to gather recyclable aluminum. Some breweries that package beer in aluminum cans also operate recycling programs through their distributors. Secondary materials dealers, such as waste paper collectors, are also active in recycling programs.

These operations involve sorting, storage, and transportation costs that may be high in relation to the value of the recycled materials. Furthermore, getting consumers and industrial users to participate in these recycling efforts may be difficult, yet it is necessary because they must take the initiative in starting the reverse flow of materials.

It has been suggested that joint venture recovery centers have some advantages over these traditional reverse flow channels.[26] Consider municipal wastes. Garbage collection routes provide transportation channels so consumers need not change their behavior. They do not have to take their garbage to a recycling center. Government incentives and funding could help manufacturers to set up resource recovery centers by reducing the entrepreneurial risk involved. The volume of materials entering the centers would be high and relatively constant. Furthermore, as technology advances the cost of setting up a recovery center would decline.

## SUMMARY AND LOOK AHEAD

A marketing channel is the series of marketing institutions that facilitates transfer of title to a product as it moves from producer to ultimate consumer or industrial buyer. Channels create utility, improve exchange efficiency, and help match supply and demand. They bring suppliers and buyers together. Middlemen are exchange specialists who perform marketing functions. These functions can be shared among channel members but not eliminated. Channels also help adjust quantity and assortment discrepancies between producers and final buyers.

A channel's vertical dimension (length) is determined by the variety of participants in the channel. There are no middlemen in the most direct channel because producers perform the marketing functions themselves. This gives producers greater control over their products' distribution. Direct channels are more common in industrial products marketing than in consumer products marketing. Middlemen stand between the producer and final buyers in indirect channels. They are very common for convenience products. In vertical channel integration the integrating firm's operations take it closer (forward) to the final buyer or further away (backward) from the final buyer and closer to supply sources.

The number of participants of any one type on the same level in a channel determine its horizontal dimension, or width. The greater or fewer that number, the wider or narrower the channel is. Horizontal channel integration means members on the same level combine under one member's control. A horizontal marketing system involves cooperation between two or more firms on the same level of distribution to accomplish a common goal. Downtown merchants' associations are an example.

A channel is a type of social system in which each member is expected to fulfill certain roles. Competitive, cooperative, and conflict relationships may exist among members. Customer, product, company, middleman, and environmental characteristics must be considered in channel planning.

Dysfunctional channel conflict is undesirable and can be resolved by the channel leader or the vertical marketing system (VMS). The channel leader is the most powerful channel member. It can be a producer or a middleman. Three types of VMS are (1) corporate, (2) administered, and (3) contractual.

If the manufacturer is the leader, it must decide which type or types of middlemen to use, how many of each type to use, and how to work with resellers in building a channel system. Multiple channels may be used. These can be competitive or noncompetitive, depending on whether they seek to serve the same market target.

Intensive, selective, and exclusive are the three degrees of market exposure. Intensive distribution is common for convenience products. Selective distribution is common for shopping and specialty products and industrial products that require specialized selling effort. Specialty products and installations sometimes are distributed exclusively. Trade relations departments seek to build channel cooperation.

The total channel system concept explicitly includes facilitating middlemen and focuses on a framework for matching resources in the state of nature with ultimate consumer demand. The concept is broader than the traditional channel concept but also harder to put to practical use. Reverse channels also have become important as ecological awareness has increased.

In the next chapter we will study retailing and retailers. They are important participants in many consumer products channels.

## REVIEW QUESTIONS

**1.** Do marketing channels create utility? Explain.

**2.** Develop an example that shows how middlemen can enhance exchange efficiency.

**3.** If middlemen can be eliminated, why can't the marketing functions be eliminated?

**4.** How do channels adjust quantity and assortment discrepancies?

**5.** What is meant by the vertical dimension of a channel?

**6.** Why are direct channels more common in industrial products marketing than in consumer products marketing?

**7.** Why are channels for convenience products typically long?

**8.** Contrast forward and backward vertical integration.

**9.** What is meant by the horizontal dimension of a channel and horizontal integration?

**10.** Contrast functional and dysfunctional channel conflict.

**11.** Identify and discuss the two basic approaches to resolving dysfunctional channel conflict.

**12.** Can a retailer serve as a channel leader? Explain.

**13.** Identify and discuss the three major types of vertical marketing systems.

**14.** Contrast competitive and noncompetitive multiple channels.

**15.** Identify and discuss the three degrees of market exposure.

**16.** Contrast the traditional and total system channel concepts.

**17.** Give an example of a reverse channel.

## DISCUSSION QUESTIONS

**1.** Some people believe there is too much vertical integration in some oil companies. They want these firms to sell some of their operations to other firms. Some also believe that American Telephone and Telegraph (AT&T) should sell Western Electric, which makes telephone equipment for AT&T. Do you agree?

**2.** Why do many consumers apparently believe that middlemen increase the prices of the products they buy?

**3.** Why would a manufacturer prefer selective or exclusive distribution over intensive distribution?

**4.** Give an example from your own experience of a firm that created a differential advantage for itself through its distribution strategy.

**5.** Are facilitating middlemen less important in a channel than middlemen who carry out the title flow?

## NOTES

1. See Wroe Alderson, "Factors Governing the Development of Marketing Channels," in *Marketing Channels for Manufactured Products*, ed. Richard M. Clewett (Homewood, Ill.: Richard D. Irwin, 1954).

2. See Robert A. Robicheaux and Adel I. El-Ansary, "A General Model for Understanding Channel Member Behavior," *Journal of Retailing*, Winter, 1976–1977, pp. 13–30.

3. See Bruce Mallen, "Conflict and Cooperation in Marketing Channels," in *Reflections on Progress in Marketing*, ed. L. George Smith (Chicago: American Marketing Association, 1965), pp. 65–85; Larry J. Rosenberg and Louis W. Stern, "Toward the Analysis of Conflict in Distribution Channels: A Descriptive Model," *Journal of Marketing*, October, 1970, pp. 40–46; Bert Rosenbloom, "Conflict and Channel Efficiency: Some Conceptual Models for the Decision Maker," *Journal of Marketing*, July, 1973, pp. 26–30; Adel I. El-Ansary and Robert Robicheaux, "A Theory of Channel Conflict Revisited," *Journal of Marketing*, January, 1974, pp. 2–7; and Douglas M. Lambert and Howard M. Armitage,

"An Information System for Effective Channel Management," *MSU Business Topics*, Autumn, 1979, pp. 13–22.

4. See Gordon R. Foxall, "Marketing and Channel Conflict: Sources and Resolution," *Quarterly Review of Marketing*, Summer, 1977, pp. 4–6; and Michael Etgar, "Sources and Types of Intrachannel Conflict," *Journal of Retailing*, Spring, 1979, pp. 61–78.

5. For discussion of an approach to help channel designers anticipate changes in channel structure, see Bruce Mallen, "Functional Spin-off: A Key to Anticipating Change in Distribution Structure," *Journal of Marketing*, July, 1973, pp. 18–25.

6. "Toro: Transforming Itself to Dominate Home-Care Products," *Business Week*, September 10, 1979, pp. 116, 118.

7. "Mattel Tries to Lure Skeptical Consumers by Selling Computers as High-Priced Fun," *Wall Street Journal*, March 14, 1980, p. 13.

8. Small, technically based firms can enter into new product joint ventures with larger firms that have

marketing capability. See James D. Hlavacek, Brian H. Dovey, and John J. Biondo, "Tie Small Business Technology to Marketing Power," *Harvard Business Review*, January–February, 1977, pp. 106–116.

9. "Xerox, in a Change of Tactics, Turning to Outside Dealers," *Wall Street Journal*, September 5, 1980, p. 32.

10. "Xerox Corp. Plans Chain of Retail Stores in a Bid for Small-Business Customers," *Wall Street Journal*, April 9, 1980, p. 3.

11. "Some GM Dealers, in Rare Move, Prod Company for Help," *Wall Street Journal*, April 18, 1980, p. 5.

12. Some channel innovation, of course, is pioneered by nonmembers of the channel. For examples in the domestic auto industry, see Mel S. Moyer and Neil M. Whitmore, "An Appraisal of the Marketing Channels for Automobiles," *Journal of Marketing*, July, 1976, pp. 35–40.

13. See Adel I. El-Ansary and Louis W. Stern, "Power Measurement in the Distribution Channel," *Journal of Marketing Research*, February, 1972, pp. 47–52; Louis P. Bucklin, "A Theory of Channel Control," *Journal of Marketing*, January, 1973, pp. 39–47; Shelby D. Hunt and John R. Nevin, "Power in a Channel of Distribution: Sources and Consequences," *Journal of Marketing Research*, May, 1974, pp. 186–193; Michael Etgar, "Channel Domination and Countervailing Power in Distributive Channels," *Journal of Marketing Research*, August, 1976, pp. 254–262; Robert F. Lusch, "Sources of Power: Their Impact on Intrachannel Conflict," *Journal of Marketing Research*, November, 1976, pp. 382–390; William P. Dommermuth, "Profiting from Distribution Conflicts," *Business Horizons*, December, 1976, pp. 4–13; Michael Etgar, "Channel Environment and Channel Leadership," *Journal of Marketing Research*, February, 1977, pp. 69–76; and Michael Etgar, "Selection of an Effective Channel Control Mix," *Journal of Marketing*, July, 1978, pp. 53–58.

14. For an interesting discussion of the realities of distribution channels, see Phillip McVey, "Are Channels of Distribution What the Textbooks Say?" *Journal of Marketing*, January, 1960, pp. 61–65.

15. See Mel S. Moyer, "Toward More Responsive Marketing Channels," *Journal of Retailing*, Spring, 1975, pp. 7–19.

16. See Bert C. McCammon, Jr., "The Emergence and Growth of Contractually Integrated Channels in the American Economy," in *Marketing and Economic Development*, ed. Peter D. Bennett (Chicago: American Marketing Association, 1965), pp. 496–515. Also see Johan Arndt, "The Market Is Dying: Long Live Marketing!" *MSU Business Topics*, Winter, 1979, pp. 5–13.

17. See Michael Etgar, "Effects of Administrative Control on Efficiency of Vertical Marketing Systems," *Journal of Marketing Research*, February, 1976, pp. 12–24.

18. See William J. Hannaford, "Contractually Integrated Systems for the Marketing of Industrial Supplies," *Journal of the Academy of Marketing Science*, Fall, 1974, pp. 567–581; and Shelby D. Hunt and Helen D. Jacobs, "Franchising as an Investment Opportunity: An Evaluation," *Marquette Business Review*, Winter, 1976, pp. 135–142.

19. See Michael Etgar, "The Economic Rationale for Becoming a Franchisee in a Service Industry," *Journal of Business Research*, August, 1976, pp. 239–254.

20. For a discussion of what franchisors look for in potential franchisees, see Frank N. Edens, Donald R. Self, and Douglas T. Grider, Jr., "Franchisors Describe the Ideal Franchisee," *Journal of Small Business Management*, July, 1976, pp. 39–47.

21. See Charles M. Lillis, Chem L. Narayana, and John L. Gilman, "Competitive Advantage Variation over the Life Cycle of a Franchise," *Journal of Marketing*, October, 1976, pp. 77–80.

22. See Lee E. Preston and Arthur E. Schramm, Jr., "Dual Distribution and Its Impact on Marketing Organization," *California Management Review*, Winter, 1965, pp. 59–70; and William L. Shanklin, "Dual Distribution as a Source of Channel Conflict," in *Proceedings: The Southern Marketing Association*, ed. Robert L. King (Blacksburg, Va.: Virginia Polytechnic Institute and State University, 1973), pp. 357–361.

23. "Justice Takes Aim at Dual Distribution," *Business Week*, July 7, 1980, pp. 24–25.

24. James H. Donnelly, Jr., "Marketing Intermediaries in Channels of Distribution for Services," *Journal of Marketing*, January, 1976, pp. 55–57, at p. 57.

25. Ibid.

26. John Guiltinan and Nonyelu G. Nwokoye, "Developing Distribution Channels and Systems in Emerging Recycling Industries," *International Journal of Physical Distribution*, January, 1976, pp. 28–38. Also see William G. Zikmund and William J. Stanton, "Recycling Solid Wastes: A Channels-of-Distribution Problem," *Journal of Marketing*, July, 1971, pp. 34–39; and Donald A. Fuller, "Recycling Consumer Solid Waste: A Commentary on Selected Channel Alternatives," *Journal of Business Research*, January, 1978, pp. 17–31.

# Chapter 14

# Retailing

## OBJECTIVES

*After reading this chapter you should be able to*

1. distinguish between retailing and retailer.

2. give an example that shows how retailing adds value to a product item.

3. identify and discuss six bases for classifying retailers.

4. discuss and give examples of scrambled merchandising.

5. identify and discuss nine major retailing decision areas.

6. explain the increasing use of market segmentation by retailers.

7. speculate about the future of retailing.

## KEY CONCEPTS

*Look for these terms as you read the chapter:*

Retailing
Retailer
Consumer Cooperative
Independent Retailer
Retail Chain
Franchising
Merchandise Breadth
Merchandise Depth
Single-Line Retailer
Limited-Line Retailer
Specialty Shop
Scrambled Merchandising
General Merchandise Retailer
General Store
Variety Store
Department Store
Supermarket
Superstore
Discount Store
Nonstore Retailing
In-Home Retailing
Telephone Retailing
Catalogue Retailing
Mail Order Retailing
Automatic Merchandising
Unplanned Shopping Areas
Planned Shopping Centers
Wheel of Retailing

*Depending on where you live, some of these retailers probably are familiar to you: Jordan Marsh (Boston area), Mervyn's (West Coast), Target (Midwest), Winkelman Stores (Detroit area), Woodward & Lothrop (Washington, D.C. area), John Wanamaker (Philadelphia area), Fed-Mart (Southwest), Nordstrom (Seattle area), and Rich's (Atlanta area). Retailing is an important and constantly changing industry. For example, consumers used to order their phones by phone from Bell Telephone Company's business offices. Now many consumers choose the phones they want by shopping in Bell's Phone Center retail stores. Instead of waiting days or weeks for an appointment with their dentist, consumers in a growing number of communities can walk into retail stores in shopping centers to have dental work done without having to wait. Other services that used to be performed only in professional offices but now are increasingly available in retail stores include the services of tax preparers, lawyers, optometrists, chiropractors, and hearing-aid specialists.*

*Nonstore retailing, in which the consumer does not buy from a retail store, is also growing. Sunday newspaper inserts and magazine supplements now are filled with direct response ads for film processing, pantyhose, books, kitchen gadgets, and many other products. Ads on television urge us to pick up the phone and dial toll free to order records, home repair tools, and magazines. Direct mail is being used to retail a growing number of products, such as life and health insurance.*

Retailing is the part of marketing with which consumers are most familiar. Ford, General Electric, General Foods, and Procter & Gamble are huge manufacturers whose names are familiar to all consumers. But few of us deal directly with them because we buy their products in retail stores—car dealerships, appliance stores, discount stores, department stores, and supermarkets.

Retailing is a vital institution in our marketing system. It employs millions of people and provides opportunity for people who want to go into business for themselves. It helps create and deliver our high standard of living. Retailing also is a demanding and dynamic type of business activity in which only efficient retailers survive.

## RETAILING AND RETAILERS

**Retailing** includes all activities involved in selling or renting consumer products and services to ultimate consumers. It includes pricing, advertising, selling, buying, maintaining inventory, and record keeping. Household furniture rental stores and department stores both engage in retailing. A men's clothing store sells and alters suits to fit specific customers. Its offering includes a product and a service. A shop that limits its offering to repairing shoes sells only a service. Sales of industrial products and sales of consumer products to resellers are not retailing.

retailing

Not all firms that engage in retailing are retailers. A **retailer** is a firm that primarily is in the business of retailing. More than half of its sales are to ultimate consumers. A clothing manufacturer that makes a few sales to ultimate consumers through its retail factory outlet is not a retailer. Retailers sometimes are called *dealers* and wholesalers are called *distributors.*

## Retailing's Economic Importance

Over half of our disposable personal income is spent at the retail level, and roughly one out of seven full-time workers is employed in retailing. Many thousands of people also hold part-time jobs in retail stores.

**Efficiency and Concentration.** The efficiency of retailing activities affects the aggregate demand for products in an economy, and the efficiency of individual retailers affects their sales and profits. Thus on both the macro and micro levels the quality and efficiency of retailing operations affects the efficiency of mass distribution.

Retailing is a concentrated business.[1] Large multiunit establishments account for a disproportionate percentage of total retail sales. Table 14–1 highlights several important facts about retailing.

**Value Added by Retailing.** Retailing helps create place, time, possession, and ownership utilities. It also may add form utility, such as when a clothing retailer alters a suit to fit a customer. A retailer's services also help create a product's image because they are part of the total product. This is a major reason some manufacturers practice selective or exclusive distribution. They want only the best retailers to sell their products.

Retailers add value to product items through (1) the services they offer, such as credit, delivery, extended store hours; (2) the image they present, which can enhance the product's image; (3) the personnel they hire, such as salespersons who help identify and solve customer

**Table 14–1.** *Some important facts about retailing*

1. The term *retail establishment* refers to ownership. One retail establishment might include several retail stores.
2. Roughly 88 percent of all retail establishments have only one store. They account for about 60 percent of total retail store sales.
3. Roughly 12 percent of all retail establishments have more than one store. These multiunit establishments (chains) account for about 40 percent of total retail store sales.
4. Roughly half of all retail stores have individual annual sales of less than $50,000. Altogether, they account for less than 6 percent of total retail store sales.
5. Roughly 6 percent of all retail stores have individual annual sales of more than $500,000. Altogether, they account for about 60 percent of total retail store sales.
6. Roughly 80 percent of all retail establishments have fewer than six paid employees.
7. Roughly 75 percent of all retail establishments are sole proprietorships or partnerships.
8. Roughly 3 percent of total retail sales are accounted for by nonstore retailing, such as door-to-door selling and mail order retailing.

problems; and (4) the store's location, perhaps near other stores to facilitate comparison shopping. Retailers put the final touches on product items to make them total products. Car dealers do this when they install accessories and perform dealer "prep" services. They match customer requirements with their merchandise offerings.

## CLASSIFYING RETAILERS

It is hard to develop one approach to classifying retailers. For example, some people think a supermarket is a type of retailing institution in the grocery business, while others think it is a general method or approach to retailing. Consider the term *corporate chain*. Not all chains are corporations and not all corporate retailers are chain organizations.

The following discussion classifies retailers on the basis of (1) form of ownership, (2) organization structure, (3) supplementary service offer-

**Table 14–2.** *Bases for classifying retailers*

*Form of Ownership*

Sole proprietorship
Partnership
Corporation
Consumer cooperative

*Organization Structure*

Independent
Chain
Association of independents
Franchise

*Supplementary Service Offering*

Full service
Limited service
Self-service

*Merchandise Offering*

Single-line
Limited-line
Specialty shop
General merchandise retailer
Scrambled merchandising

*Pricing Strategy*

Normal margin retailer
Discount retailer

*Where Retail Sale Takes Place*

Instore retailer
Nonstore retailer

ing, (4) merchandise offering, (5) pricing strategy, and (6) location of the retail sale.    (See Table 14–2.)

## Form of Ownership

A retail firm can be a sole proprietorship, partnership, corporation, or consumer cooperative.    Although the majority of retail firms are owned by sole proprietors and partners, corporations account for a disproportionate share of total retail sales.

**consumer cooperative**

**Consumer cooperatives** (co-ops) are customer-owned retail outlets. Each consumer-investor receives interest on his or her investment and has one vote in running the co-op, regardless of the amount of investment. Members and nonmembers pay prices similar to those charged by other retailers in the area.    Any profit is returned to the consumer-owners on the basis of their purchases from the co-op.    They can succeed in areas where retailers are inefficient and/or have high markups, but co-ops have not been very important in the United States.    Most that do exist are food co-ops.    Consumers in some low-income neighborhoods have formed them but the failure rate is high.    Co-ops are more popular in some European countries.[2]

## Organization Structure

Regardless of the form of ownership, a retailing operation can be organized as an independent, a chain, an association of independents, or a franchise operation.

**independent retailer**

**Independent Retailers.**    A person or firm that owns and operates one store is an **independent retailer.**    Most retail firms are independents and most independent retailers are sole proprietorships and partnerships. They vary in size from small tobacco shops to large department stores.

Independent retailers enjoy several advantages.    They are in business for themselves and make decisions without required approval from higher-ups.    They often know their customers personally, which helps in keeping up with changing customer wants.    They also can keep a close watch on rival firms in their communities and make quick adjustments to competitive actions.    This flexibility is perhaps their major advantage.    Small independents also can cater to market segments that big retailers consider too small to serve profitably.    Health food stores in some towns are an example.

There are some disadvantages, however.    The failure rate is high. Small independents often suffer from a lack of management skills, financial resources, and accurate and timely records.    It is also easy for them to assume their operations are profitable when, in fact, they might actually be less profitable if the owner had to pay a salary to the spouse and children who may help in running the store.    They also often pay higher prices for the merchandise they buy because they purchase it in small quantities.

**retail chain**

**Chain Retailers.**    Two or more similar, centrally-owned stores (chain stores) make up a **retail chain.**    J.C. Penney Company, for example, owns all the J.C. Penney stores in local communities.  Chains are frequent among variety goods, grocery, and department stores.

Chains like J.C. Penney and Sears are national; chains like Gimbel's are regional.  Some have stores only in one city.  Each store in a chain may have a different name, or several stores in a region may have the same name while those in other regions have different names.  City Stores Company, for example, is a large department store group that includes these department store divisions: Maison Blanche in New Orleans; Richards in Miami; Loveman, Joseph & Loeb in Birmingham, Alabama; B. Lowenstein in Memphis; R.H. White in Worcester, Massachusetts; and Hearn's in New York City.

Chain retailers enjoy many advantages.  Big national chains are diversified geographically.  If the economy in one city turns down, it still has stores in other areas to help spread the risk of doing business.  Chains can buy in large quantities and pass some of the savings on to their customers.  They can afford electronic data processing equipment to handle customer billing, inventory management, and other activities.  Large chains also can hire specialists like advertising copywriters who may be too costly for small retailers.

Large chains also have disadvantages.  They are criticized by people who believe they make it tough for small independents to stay in business.  They sometimes suffer from too much management red tape, which makes them less flexible and responsive to customer wants.  Some focus too much on maximizing sales volume and neglect return on investment.

**Associations of Independents.**  As we saw in the previous chapter, some independents form chains to compete more effectively with corporate chains.  Each store is independently owned, but they cooperate in some aspects of their operations, such as advertising and buying, to achieve some advantages of the chain organization.

In the voluntary chain a wholesaler initiates the association.  These

**Table 14–3.**  *The ten largest retailers in the United States*

| Rank | Company | Sales (in thousands) | Net Income as Percentage of Sales |
|------|---------|---------------------|-----------------------------------|
| 1 | Sears Roebuck (Chicago) | $17,514,252 | 4.6 |
| 2 | Safeway Stores (Oakland) | 13,717,861 | 1.0 |
| 3 | Kmart (Troy, Mich.) | 12,858,585 | 2.8 |
| 4 | J.C. Penney (New York) | 11,274,000 | 2.2 |
| 5 | Kroger (Cincinnati) | 9,029,315 | 0.9 |
| 6 | Great Atlantic & Pacific Tea (Montvale, N.J.) | 7,469,659 | — |
| 7 | F.W. Woolworth (New York) | 6,785,000 | 2.7 |
| 8 | Lucky Stores (Dublin, Calif.) | 5,815,927 | 1.7 |
| 9 | Federated Department Stores (Cincinnati) | 5,806,442 | 3.5 |
| 10 | Montgomery Ward (Chicago) | 5,251,085 | 1.4 |

Source: *Fortune*

chains are most common in grocery retailing but also exist in hardware retailing (Ace), variety store retailing (Ben Franklin), and so on. The independent retailers contract with the initiating wholesaler, who combines their purchases and gets quantity discounts. The wholesaler also may handle their advertising, inventory control, and other functions. The members use a common store name and buy from the wholesaler. The wholesaler gets guaranteed customers, and the retailers get valuable services from the wholesaler.

Retailers initiate the chain in a retailer-sponsored cooperative chain. They join together to set up and operate their own wholesaling operation. These chains are most important in grocery retailing. Examples are Associated Grocers and Certified Grocers. Unlike the wholesaler-sponsored arrangement, members of a retailer-sponsored cooperative chain do not use a common store name.

franchising

**Franchise Operations.** **Franchising** also combines the advantages of independent ownership with those of the chain organization. A franchise is a license to do business granted by a franchisor to a franchisee. The McDonald's Corporation (the franchisor) grants the right to make and sell its hamburgers (a franchise) to independent business persons (franchisees) in designated areas. Some franchisors are owned by parent firms. In fast foods, PepsiCo owns Pizza Hut, Heublein owns Kentucky Fried Chicken, and Pillsbury owns Burger King. Franchising arrangements are very popular in motels, fast foods, car dealerships, gasoline service stations, and clothing stores.

A franchisor who develops an idea for doing business that can be duplicated in many outlets might test market the idea and, if successful, offer franchises to franchisees. The franchisor gives advice and help to franchisees, including finding a good location, providing blueprints for building the shop or store, and giving financial, marketing, and management assistance.

Franchisees own their businesses, but the franchise agreement spells out franchisor and franchisee rights and duties. Franchisees have to adhere to the franchisor's requirements regarding merchandising and operations to preserve uniformity and control.

A franchising agreement offers a franchisee many potential benefits. First, belonging to a recognized franchise organization gives the franchisee's business quick recognition among potential customers. Second, the franchisor provides management training and assistance to the franchisee and his or her employees. Third, the franchisor either makes or buys ingredients, supplies, and parts in large volume and resells them to franchisees, usually at lower prices than they would pay if each franchisee made or bought them independently. Thus the franchisee can enjoy economies in buying. Fourth, franchisors often provide financial assistance to the franchisee. Usually, a franchisee puts up a certain percentage of the cost of land, building, equipment, and initial promotion. The franchiser finances the rest and is paid back out of the revenues the franchisee earns. Fifth, franchisors usually supply the franchisee with various types of promotional aids, such as in-store displays, radio scripts, and publicity releases.

Of course, the agreement also offers a franchisor many potential benefits. First, the franchisor may achieve national and, perhaps, international expansion much faster than by any other approach to expansion. The franchisor's expansion is being partly financed by the franchisees through their payment of royalties and fees. Second, a local franchisee pays a lower rate for newspaper advertising than a national franchisor. The franchisor and the franchisee can share the cost of advertising (cooperative advertising), and both benefit. This also helps the franchisor to avoid wasted coverage—advertising in areas where there are no franchisees. Third, as the owners of their businesses, franchisees may be more motivated to work harder than employees the franchisor might hire. Fourth, whereas the headquarters of a chain store operation must keep payroll, tax, and other records on all of its units and concern itself with local laws regarding sales taxes, licenses, and permits, these are the responsibility of each franchisee.

A franchising agreement's terms can vary greatly but usually provide that the franchisee will (1) pay a flat fee to the franchisor to buy and operate the franchise, (2) pay the franchisor a percentage of the shop or store's gross income, (3) buy supplies and merchandise from the franchisor or, if buying from other sources, buy products of equal quality, and (4) pay a set amount or a percentage of gross receipts into a fund that the franchisor uses to promote the franchised outlets to consumers.

### Supplementary Service Offering

Some retailers provide many services such as delivery, credit, and return privileges because their customers are willing to pay higher prices for them. Other retailers provide very few services because their customers want rock-bottom prices with no service extras. Based on their service offering, retailers are either full-, limited-, or self-service. (See Figure 14–1.)

Full-service retailers charge higher prices to cover the costs of providing their many services. Department stores, for example, provide free delivery, sales clerk assistance, credit, liberal return privileges, and

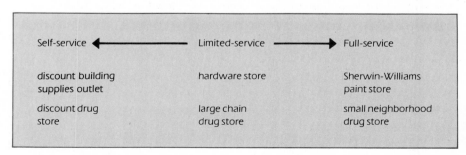

*Figure 14–1.*
*A continuum of retailers' service offering*

lay-aways.   Limited-service retailers offer lower prices and fewer services.   A department store's retail price for a carpet might include
delivery and installation.   A discount store's price might include delivery
but not installation.   Self-service retailers offer practically no services,
for example, self-service gasoline stations.   Self-service retailing has been
growing rapidly over the past several decades.

### The Merchandise Offering

Two basic dimensions of a merchandise mix are breadth (narrow or wide)
and depth (shallow or deep).

merchandise
breadth

Merchandise breadth refers to the number of noncompeting product
lines offered for sale.   Retailers who carry only one or a very few product
lines have narrow **merchandise breadth.**   Singer Sewing Centers, bicycle
shops, and Burger King are examples.   Retailers that carry multiple product lines have wide breadth.   Department stores, for example, carry sporting goods, home appliances, women's, men's, and children's clothing,
jewelry, and other product lines.   (See Figure 14–2.)

merchandise
depth

Merchandise depth refers to the number of brands, models, or styles
carried for each product.   Retailers who carry only one or two brands or
models for each product have shallow **merchandise depth.**   A hardware
store has considerable breadth but lacks depth.   Retailers who carry
multiple brands or models for each product category have considerable
depth.   An example is a TV retailer who carries different models of
Zenith, RCA, Sony, and GE TVs.   (See Figure 14–3.)

specialty shop

**Specialty Shops.**   The ultimate in limited-line retailers are called
**specialty shops.**   Their merchandise offering is extremely narrow and
deep.   Typical examples are tobacco shops, camera shops, meat markets,
bakeries, millinery shops, and furriers.   The products these shops carry
should not be confused with specialty products.   They seldom carry
specialty products.   They specialize in convenience and shopping
products.

limited-line
retailer

**Limited-Line Retailers.**   A retail TV store is a limited-line retailer
in the appliance store category.   A shoe store is a limited-line retailer
in the apparel category.   These **limited-line retailers** have more depth
and less breadth than single-line retailers.

single-line retailer

**Single-Line Retailers.**   Car dealers, shoe stores, appliance stores, food
stores, and furniture stores handle only one basic product line.   These
**single-line retailers** have merchandise depth but little breadth.

Single-line and limited-line retailers account for the majority of retailers.   They tailor their marketing mixes to the wants of carefully
defined market targets.   They stock some items that may move slowly,
which leads to high operating expenses.   A men's shoe store, for example,
stocks many styles and sizes, some of which may move very slowly.
A shoe department in a department store stocks only the faster-moving
styles and sizes.

scrambled
merchandising

**Scrambled Merchandising.**   The retailing practice of carrying product
lines that may appear to be unrelated is called **scrambled merchandising.**

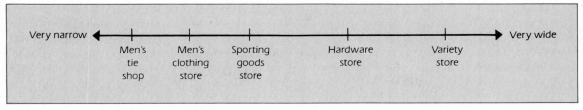

**Figure 14–2. A continuum of merchandise breadth**

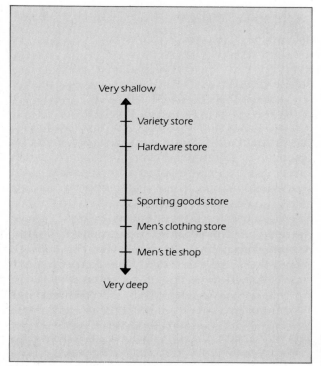

**Figure 14–3.
A continuum of
merchandise depth**

Not only do drugstores carry prescription and over-the-counter drugs but some also carry magazines, toys, hardware, housewares, records, and garden supplies. Nondrug items account for 80 percent of chain drugstore sales.[3] Gasoline stations often stock cigarettes, beer, milk, bread, and many other food products, and grocery stores stock such nonfood items as kitchen utensils, gardening supplies, house plants, small appliances, and apparel items. Scrambled merchandising has become popular over the past several decades. It helps a retailer generate more sales volume, and it fits consumer desire for one-stop shopping.

**General Merchandise Retailers.** General stores, variety stores, and department stores are **general merchandise retailers.** Their merchandise offerings are wider but less deep than those of single- and limited-line retailers.

**general merchandise retailer**

general store

**General stores** are nondepartmentalized stores that sell a wide variety of such staple products as sugar, flour, dried meat, medicines, tobacco, and hardware items. They were very important during the first half of the nineteenth century. The few remaining today are mostly in rural areas and small towns, where the limited concentration of people makes it feasible to serve a broad variety of needs rather than specializing in only a few.

variety store

**Variety stores** used to be called "5 and 10 cent" stores. Ben Franklin and Murphy's are examples. Variety stores have had tough going in recent years, and many variety chains have opened discount stores, such as Kmart and Woolco. Kmart, which used to be called S.S. Kresge, first opened in 1962. By 1977 Kmart units were contributing 96 percent of Kresge's sales and earnings.[4] Thus the corporate name was changed. F.W. Woolworth became the last national variety store chain when W.T. Grant went out of business in 1975.

department store

**Department stores** are large retail firms departmentalized along product lines. They carry wide and deep merchandise lines, such as clothing, furniture, appliances, toys, books, sporting goods, and housewares. A department store really is made up of several limited-line and specialty shops in one building. Some of the most famous names in retailing are department stores—Macy's, Bloomingdale's, and Jordan Marsh.

What manufacturers call product planning, department stores call merchandising. A general merchandising manager decides what general merchandise lines the store will carry. Department managers, called buyers, run the separate departments.[5] Some department stores also have service units—restaurants, optical shops, and beauty salons. Sometimes these are leased to independent entrepreneurs. They carry a narrow and shallow merchandise offering but benefit from the store's ability to generate customer traffic. Department stores account for about 11 percent of total retail sales. Because they are full-service retailers, their operating costs amount to about 35 percent of their sales revenues.

Originally, department stores located close together in downtown areas to aid consumer purchases of shopping products. The post–World War II movement of middle-income families to the suburbs led many stores to open suburban branches. Some of these branches have grown larger and more important than the "main store." Many downtown department stores are supporting efforts to rebuild downtown shopping areas. They cater to tourists, convention goers, central city dwellers, and people who work downtown.[6]

Department store retailing has undergone great change in recent years largely because of environmental change, such as a slower growth in population, a growing singles market, later marriages, and the growing career orientation of many women. Department stores are making greater use of marketing research to cater to their changing customer mix.[7] Many are repositioning themselves to attract younger customers. They also are using demographic and psychographic segmentation and placing renewed emphasis on fashion in their merchandising strategies.[8]

## Pricing Strategy

A retailer's pricing strategy affects its image and the type of customers it will attract. Two general retail pricing strategies are normal-margin pricing and discount pricing.

**Normal-Margin Pricing.** Retailers who practice normal-margin pricing set their prices in line with other retailers in the same line of business. They stress customer service and convenient location instead of price. They may, however, hold special sales of merchandise at reduced prices from time to time. The types of retailers we have discussed are normal-margin retailers.

**Discount Pricing.** Retailers who practice discount pricing stress low prices as their major selling point. They seek to maximize profit by selling great volumes of merchandise at lower prices than normal-margin retailers. Normal-margin retailers are margin oriented. Discount retailers are volume oriented and also offer fewer customer services.

Some retailers operate both normal-margin and discount outlets. For example, F.W. Woolworth Company operates Woolworth variety stores and Woolco discount stores. Mobil Corporation operates Montgomery Ward stores and Jefferson Ward discount stores. Discount pricing is very popular among supermarkets, superstores, and discount stores.

*Supermarkets.* Before the Great Depression of the 1930s Americans bought groceries in small neighborhood grocery stores that provided many services, such as delivery and credit.[9] Their operating costs were high.

First-generation supermarkets started during the depression. They were low-price, self-service, cash-and-carry operations in low-rent areas. Consumers bought canned goods from crates, store fixtures were cheap, and the stores looked like big barns. Most were independents but chains moved in quickly. Some of A&P's stores were built during this period.

*Table 14-4.* Four generations of supermarkets

| Generation | Time | Characteristics |
| --- | --- | --- |
| First | 1930s | low prices, self-service, cash-and-carry, low-rent locations, barn-like stores and cheap fixtures, canned goods in crates |
| Second | 1940s–1950s | larger than first-generation supermarkets, better locations, free parking, more attractive stores and fixtures |
| Third | 1960s | larger than second-generation supermarkets, located in large shopping centers, more attractive stores and fixtures, volume sales of quality merchandise, big volume in nonfood items, very aggressive price competition among themselves for market share, more emphasis on nonprice competition (games, trading stamps, extended store hours) |
| Fourth | 1970s–present | discount supermarkets, lower gross margins than third-generation supermarkets, lower selling prices, less emphasis on nonprice competition, few services, attract customers from nondiscount supermarkets |

Recently, these stores have had a tough time competing with larger, more modern supermarkets and A&P has closed hundreds of them in the past few years.

Second-generation supermarkets of the 1940s and 1950s were larger, in better locations, and offered free parking and a nicer shopping environment. Third-generation supermarkets first appeared during the 1960s. They were even larger and more attractive, and they tended to locate in large shopping centers. They made volume sales of quality merchandise, and a growing percentage of their sales revenues was due to nonfood items.

But during the 1960s supermarkets had just about taken away as much business as they could from fuller-service food stores. Thus they started engaging in aggressive price competition among themselves for market share. Profit margins declined and nonprice competition gradually became more important. Games, trading stamps, and extended store hours increased their costs and prices without improving the profit picture.

As a result, fourth-generation supermarkets are discount supermarkets. Their gross margins are lower than those of third-generation supermarkets. They have eliminated games and trading stamps, cut services to the minimum, and lowered their selling prices. Many of their customers formerly shopped at nondiscount supermarkets. Two rather recent developments are warehouse stores and box stores.[10] Warehouse stores feature a full line of manufacturer brands but customers must mark prices, bag, and carry their purchases out of the store. Box stores are similar but have fewer items and emphasize middleman brands. To avoid the need for refrigeration they generally do not stock refrigerated items.

supermarket

In general, however, modern **supermarkets** are large, departmentalized, self-service retail stores that sell meat, produce, canned goods, dairy products, frozen foods, and such nonfood items as toys, magazines, records, small kitchen utensils, and toiletries.[11] Their main attractions are low prices, good location, and free parking. Roughly one in ten food stores is a supermarket, but they account for about 70 percent of total retail food sales. Their after-tax net profit averages about 1 percent of sales.[12]

*Superstores.* One of the most recent innovations in retailing, the superstore, began in France as the *hypermarché,* or hypermarket, and has spread to the United States. A **superstore** is a giant, one-stop, mass merchandiser of grocery and soft goods that operates on a self-service, low-price basis. Like fourth-generation supermarkets, superstores stock food, laundry, and home cleaning products. But they carry more lines of nonfood items, such as shoe repair, dry cleaning, gasoline, and have departments that sell pharmaceuticals, cosmetics, gifts, toys, and so on. They seek to fill an even broader variety of consumer needs.[13]

superstore

*Discount Stores.* Stores that sell a wide variety of merchandise (such as appliances, cameras, furniture, jewelry, groceries, and clothing) at lower

prices than normal margin retailers are called **discount stores.** They are discount store
large, departmentalized, volume merchandisers who seek high inventory
turnover by stressing low markup. Kmart and Woolco are the largest
and second-largest discount chain stores. Competition is intense between discount stores and normal-margin retailers and among discount
stores themselves. Factory outlets are becoming a very popular type of
discount store. They sell manufacturers' surpluses at lower prices than
conventional discount chains. They also help garment makers by buying
their excess inventory late in the season.

Discount stores began appearing after World War II. But the practice
of selling merchandise at lower than customary prices had existed for
many years prior to the 1940s. For example, some small wholesalers
issued consumers membership cards but did not advertise to consumers.
Consumers typically would shop from manufacturer catalogues and place
orders by model number. Modern discount stores, of course, do not
require shoppers to have membership cards or to order from a catalogue,
and they heavily advertise their low prices and wide variety of merchandise.

To understand discount retailing's tremendous growth after World
War II, we can focus briefly on the retailing of electric household appliances. They were introduced during the 1930s and were sold through
department stores and limited-line appliance stores. These stores advertised the products, provided in-store personal selling effort, and servicing for the manufacturers. Thus they charged high prices to cover
these costs. But after the war, the products were greatly improved in
quality, and manufacturers themselves were offering product warranties
and advertising nationally. This reduced their dependence on these retailers for advertising, in-store promotion, and servicing. The earlier
success of supermarket retailing also had conditioned consumers to accept discount pricing. The big increase in the middle-income group of
consumers, along with their acceptance of discount retailing, convinced
appliance manufacturers to distribute through discounters.

## NONSTORE RETAILING

The retailers we have discussed have at least one element in common—
they are in-store retailers. Their customers come to their stores to shop.
In **nonstore retailing,** customers do not go to a store to buy.[14] Nonstore nonstore retailing
retailing accounts for about 3 percent of total retail sales and it is growing
rapidly. Among the reasons are the high price of gasoline, the growing
number of women employed outside the home who have less time to
shop in stores, the growing number of elderly people who tend to shop
less as age increases, and the presence of unskilled retail salespeople in
stores who cannot provide information about more complex products to
help shoppers make buying decisions. Nonstore retailing also enables
a shopper to buy merchandise that may be unavailable in local stores.[15]
Two types of nonstore retailing are personal and nonpersonal. (See Figure 14–4.)

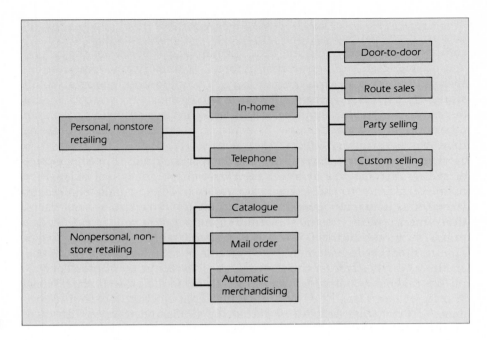

**Figure 14–4.**
**Major types of**
**nonstore retailing**

### Personal, Nonstore Retailing

In personal, nonstore retailing—for example, in-home retailing and telephone retailing—consumers do not go to a store but they have some personal contact with the retailer.

in-home retailing    **In-home retailing** means the sales transaction occurs in a home setting, which enables the seller to offer very personalized service and in-home product demonstrations.    Table 14–5 lists several familiar types of in-home retailing.

In-home retailing ranges from door-to-door cold canvassing to conducting in-home product demonstrations at the prospect's request.    In cold canvassing there is no prior screening, contact, or selection of prospects.    The salesperson goes from door to door searching for customers. Almost one-half of Scott & Fetzer Company's business is due to door-to-door sales of Kirby vacuum cleaners and World Book encyclopedias.[16] Sometimes door-to-door salespersons have leads to help reduce the num-

**Table 14–5.**   *Familiar types of in-home retailing*

| | |
|---|---|
| Door-to-door | Electrolux, Avon, Shaklee, Fuller Brush, and World Book |
| Route sales | Milk, newspapers, and some doughnut and potato chip marketers |
| Party selling | Tupperware, Amway, Beeline, and Sarah Coventry |
| Custom selling | Lawn care and home improvement products |

ber of nonprospects. In some cases, the salesperson may call on prospects because they returned a mailed card, made a phone call, or visited a store and asked for a salesperson to visit their home.

In party-plan selling the salesperson recruits hosts or hostesses to sponsor parties in their homes. They invite friends to a party at which a sales presentation is made. The party sponsor receives free merchandise based on the orders written at the party. Because the invitees know in advance the party's purpose, uninterested ones will not attend, thus reducing the number of nonprospects in attendance. The salesperson can make a single presentation to more prospects than by going door to door.

Both manufacturers and retailers engage in in-home retailing. Avon, World Book, Fuller Brush, and Electrolux are examples of manufacturers that do this. Many department stores will send, on request, salespersons to prospects' homes to make presentations and give estimates and demonstrations of products.

In-home retailing gives salespersons an opportunity to demonstrate products in a very personal manner. They have the prospect's attention and fewer distractions than in a store setting.[17] But this is the most expensive form of retailing. For example, commissions paid to the salesperson typically range between 40 and 50 percent of the product's retail selling price. Think of what that means for Amway, which has about 300,000 salespersons,[18] and Avon, which has nearly one million.[19]

Sales transactions are made entirely over the phone in **telephone retailing.** This contact may be initiated by the seller or the buyer. Some department stores, for example, telephone their customers to inform them of special sales and to take orders for the merchandise.[20] Telephone retailing does not include customers phoning to place catalogue orders or phoning retail stores for information.

telephone
retailing

## Nonpersonal, Nonstore Retailing

In nonpersonal, nonstore retailing consumers do not go to a store and have no personal contact with the seller. The three main types are catalogue retailing, mail order retailing, and automatic merchandising, or vending machines.

In **catalogue retailing** the firm prints a catalogue describing its merchandise and mails it along with ordering instructions to households. The catalogues can be general, specialty, or seasonal. Many consumers also preshop in catalogues before buying in stores.

catalogue
retailing

Big retail chains like Sears and J.C. Penney mail out general catalogues to past catalogue customers and new prospects who request them. They are mailed free of charge to past customers but new prospects may have to pay for them, the cost usually being deducted from the first order they place. Usually there are a fall–winter and a spring–summer catalogue. The merchandise offerings are wide and deep, and the catalogues often run over 1,000 pages. Sears spends $300 million a year on catalogues and circulates more than 325 million of them a year.[21] Orders placed by phone or in person at retail catalogue desks are, however, considered to be in-store sales.

Specialty catalogues like those for stereo equipment, photographic supplies, and guns are targeted to very specific market segments. They offer less breadth but more depth than general catalogues. Seasonal catalogues include Christmas catalogues like the Sears Wish Book. Many products like cheese, wine, nuts, and fruit also are marketed through gift catalogues. Breadth is narrow but there is considerable depth.

Catalogue retailing appeals to people who want to avoid the inconvenience of going to a store, live in rural areas, lack time to shop, or prefer leisurely shopping in their homes. Operating costs and retail prices ordinarily are lower than they are for in-store retailing. But it does require preparing costly catalogues and considerable time passes between printing and receipt by potential buyers. Price changes and new merchandise must be announced in supplementary catalogues. Liberal return privileges are a must, especially when merchandise is not displayed in a catalogue store for consumers to examine.

In 1981, Sears test marketed a new concept in catalogue retailing. It put its summer catalogue on video discs. Each participating household in the two test cities was provided with video equipment and a single disc. Instead of thumbing through the 236-page printed catalogue, they looked at and listened to their TVs to facilitate their at-home shopping.

**mail order retailing**

In **mail order retailing** sales are made by mail to people who place orders after seeing or hearing the product advertised on TV or radio or in magazines or newspapers.[22] Personalized stationery, records, monogrammed T-shirts, and film developing are a few of the many products marketed by mail. The classified ad section in many magazines contains mail order ads. Mail order does not include catalogue sales nor direct mail retailing, in which the seller solicits orders by mailing ads directly to consumers. Many retailers use direct mail advertising; much of it accompanies billing statements from retail stores.[23] It is discussed in Chapter 19.

**automatic merchandising**

**Automatic merchandising** means the product is sold directly to the buyer from a vending machine. Sandwiches, complete meals, cigarettes, newspapers, beverages, flight insurance, cash advances from banks, candy bars, and even fishing worms are sold this way. Advancing technology in machine construction permits the sale of a growing variety of products through vending machines.

Vending machines make it possible to serve customers where and when it is not practical for stores to serve them. Roughly 20 percent of all cigarette sales are made this way. Vending machines play a major role in retailing convenience products and supplement the in-store selling effort of many retailers. Machine maintenance and other operating costs are high and prices generally are higher than in stores. Requirements for successful vending include standardized package sizes, relatively low unit value, and presold branded items with a high turnover rate.

Let's turn now to a discussion of several types of major decision areas for retailers.

## MAJOR RETAILING DECISION AREAS

Major decision areas for retailers include (1) market target selection, (2) store location, (3) store design, (4) store personnel, (5) store image, (6) buying policies, (7) merchandise inventory control, (8) promotion, and (9) credit and collections.

### Market Target Selection

Although some retailers still aim at the mass market, a growing number are practicing market segmentation as they have found it harder to satisfy everyone. Sometimes this requires the retailer to reposition itself. Korvettes once was known as a "bargain hunter's paradise." Then the New York–based retail chain attempted to reposition itself as "promotional department stores." The firm wanted to position itself between Kmart and Woolco on one side, and J.C. Penney, Sears, and Montgomery Ward on the other.[24] Such repositioning, however, is not easy to accomplish. In fact, Korvettes subsequently closed many of its stores and gave up hope of continuing as a merchandiser.[25]

The fastest-growing segment of the retail food industry is the convenience store, such as 7-Eleven, Lil' General, and Minit Markets. Southland Corporation operates more than 6,000 7-Eleven stores and expects to have 12,000 by 1987. Roughly 8 percent of all retail food sales are made by convenience stores, which have focused on a previously neglected segment—people wanting maximum shopping convenience and willing to pay higher prices than in supermarkets.

Compared to supermarkets, convenience stores are smaller, their product assortment is narrower and shallower, and their prices are higher. But their store hours are longer and they are conveniently located. A typical outlet stocks about 3,000 fast-moving impulse items. Roughly 30 percent of their sales are beer and cigarettes and another 30 percent are soft drinks, bakery products, and snack foods.[26]

Retailers must be careful in selecting segmentation variables. Many franchisors traditionally used population as the major variable and excluded towns with less than 50,000 people. Smaller towns were left without outlets. Some franchisors have recognized this and have moved into these smaller towns, where competition is less intense. McDonald's used to think in terms of 50,000 people. Now it has outlets in many smaller towns. Kmart also has opened up many outlets in smaller towns in recent years.

### Store Location

Retailers must select store sites carefully and reevaluate them periodically. Declining neighborhoods cause many retailers to relocate or change their market targets and retailing strategies.[27] What is a good location depends mainly on the type of store. Shoe stores want to locate in areas of heavy foot traffic, whereas gas stations are concerned about car traffic. Most communities have two general types of retail shopping areas, unplanned and planned.

**unplanned shopping areas**

Every community has **unplanned shopping areas** with different types of retail stores that were not located there according to a developer's plan. As several stores began to attract customer traffic, others located nearby. Unplanned shopping areas include downtown shopping areas, secondary shopping areas, and strip shopping areas.

The downtown shopping area usually is in the center of town. It grew as the community grew, usually unplanned. Traffic congestion, lack of parking, movement of people to the suburbs, and urban decay have reduced their importance in many cities.

As a town grows, people move out from the center and neighborhoods result. This attracts retailers to these secondary shopping areas. On-street parking is common and there is little apparent planning of store types. Clothing stores, shoe stores, grocery stores, small hardware stores, and small variety stores are typical.

Strip shopping areas are made up of several stores clustered in a row, usually on one side of the street. Many are close to large apartment buildings where there are a lot of people in a small area. Small restaurants, convenience grocery stores, laundromats, and notions stores are common in this situation.

**planned shopping centers**

**Planned shopping centers** began appearing during the 1950s as many people began moving to the suburbs. Shopping center sites, the number, type, and design of stores, and parking facilities are planned by the developer, who builds and manages the center. Space is leased to tenants (retailers) who are acceptable to the developer. Homart Development Company is a shopping center development firm owned by Sears. Table 14–6 lists several advantages and disadvantages of planned shopping centers. Three types are neighborhood shopping centers, community shopping centers, and regional shopping centers.

The neighborhood shopping center is the smallest type. The main store usually is a supermarket and it is typically accompanied by a hardware store, a beauty salon, a laundry, an appliance store, a drugstore, and a barber shop. A community shopping center might also include a small department store and a variety store.

First-generation regional shopping centers are built around suburban branches of one or two downtown department stores. Limited-line retailers are there to compete with the branches' various departments. Second-generation versions are supercenters. Some have several major anchor department stores, hotels, banks, office buildings, theaters, and even churches in one climate-controlled area. Fountains, pedestrian rest areas, fashion shows, and other coordinated promotional activities are typical.[28]

**Table 14–6.** *Advantages and disadvantages of planned shopping centers*

*Advantages*

1. There is free parking for shoppers.
2. Buildings in the center are carefully planned, designed, and constructed.
3. Maintenance services are provided to tenants in the center.
4. Individual retailers can cooperate in promoting shopping at the center.
5. All tenants must abide by the developer's rules, which helps to develop and maintain an overall uniform shopper image of the center.
6. People in the center are there to shop, not on their way to work as is common of downtown traffic.
7. A center with a good image helps to build the store's image.

*Disadvantages*

1. Some developers do not provide adequate maintenance and upkeep.
2. Some developers plan only for the short run and these centers may be too small soon after they are built.
3. Some small retailers, especially new businesses, may be excluded because they may not help in building customer traffic in the center.
4. Rents usually are high because a lot of space is taken up by parking areas that do not produce any sales per square foot.

In very recent years, discount malls have become popular. They contain a broad variety of stores, all of which offer quality manufacturer brands of a wide variety of merchandise at discount prices.

## Store Design

A store's interior and exterior design affects its image. Care is needed to ensure ease of getting to the store, through the store, and out of the store.[29] Convenience food stores enjoy a strong advantage over many supermarkets in this regard. *Atmospherics* is the term used to refer to a retailer's effort to design a store's physical surroundings to attract target customers.[30] A discount store wants to avoid an atmosphere of exclusiveness, while a prestige dress shop wants exclusivity. Various departments in department stores—the boys wear and women's fashions departments, for example—differ greatly in terms of furniture and fixtures.

Exterior design also should be attractive, inviting, and blend with the store's general surroundings. Consumers often judge stores by their exterior appearance. Thus stores in shopping centers are designed to achieve some degree of uniformity. Good maintenance of the parking lot also helps.

## Store Personnel

A major consumer complaint about retailing is the poor quality of some retail sales personnel. These people are the connecting link between the store and the consumer, and they should be carefully selected and trained to be courteous, helpful, and knowledgeable.

For example, one study found that courtesy "thank you" calls to customers for previous business are beneficial.[31]  Knowledgeable sales personnel can help to build customer loyalty to the store.  Many customers turn to the retailer first instead of the more distant manufacturer to remedy warranty problems, and retail salespersons should be trained to help resolve these problems in order to keep their customers' business.[32]  Effective sales personnel and other employees, such as delivery drivers, can also enhance a store's image.

### Store Image

To a retailer, a store's image is the mental picture, or personality, of the store the retailer tries to project to consumers.  To a consumer, however, a store's image is the attitude he or she has about the store.  Sometimes these images differ.  An exclusive women's clothing store wants to project an image of high fashion, but a consumer may think it has snobbish sales personnel and inflated prices.

J.C. Penney used to think of itself as a retailer to small-town America. It sold its own brands on the basis of price appeal in bargain basement surroundings.  More recently, it has been trying to upgrade its image to that of a chain of moderate-price department stores.  The emphasis is on higher-price fashion in its lines of hardgoods, housewares, and apparel.

Prices, services, quality of merchandise, convenience, breadth and depth of merchandise, store layout, and personnel affect a store's image. Consumers tend to shop in stores that fit their images of themselves, and retailers must project store images that fit the images target customers have of themselves.

In chain organizations both the chain and its individual stores have images.  Individual stores in a chain that has a good image can attract consumers from further away than similar-sized stores in a chain that is perceived as mediocre.[33]  Customers who have a favorable overall image of a chain but whose experiences in one store are unfavorable over time will downgrade their image of the chain.  This is why fast-food franchisors are so careful in selecting and supervising their franchisees.

Four types of stores can be identified based on consumer image: convenience stores, shopping stores, specialty stores, and unrecognized stores.  Consumers perceive convenience stores as readily accessible, and shopping stores as facilitators of shopping effort by carrying wide and deep assortments.  Stores consumers patronize out of habit and to whom they are very loyal are specialty stores.  There is no necessary relationship between this image classification and the classification of products a store carries.  Convenience stores, for example, might carry specialty products.

Retailers seek to develop and enhance good store images.  Some people do not like to shop at large supermarkets because they think the lines at the checkout aisles are too long.  Thus many supermarkets have express checkout aisles that help develop a convenience store image.

# No Hassle Returns.

Included in every gift purchased at Waldoff's is this special guarantee, because we believe that shopping at Waldoff's should make you happy. Happy about what you buy. . .or what you bring back.
Should you make a return or exchange, you'll find that our sales associates will treat you in the same manner as when you made your purchase. . .
No hassle.
No hassle returns.
No hassle exchanges.
No hassle even if you didn't buy it at Waldoff's!
That's right, regardless of where the item was purchased, you can bring it to us and we'll exchange it (provided we carry the identical item). Exchange will be made at our current price for that item.
We're serious when we say that we want our customers to be happy. . .even if they weren't our customers to begin with.

# WALDOFF'S

**NOBODY DOES IT LIKE WALDOFF'S.**

*An ad that seeks to enhance the retailer's image.*

The Sears maintenance agreements that can be purchased with new appliances help develop its specialty store image and customer loyalty, as do the "nation-wide service" and "we service what we sell" themes.

An unrecognized store has no image. A newcomer to a city may have no image of a locally owned department store but the image begins forming after the person sees the store, hears people talk about it, or sees or hears its ads. Advertising and store design are important in developing a good store image. Retailers should study consumer store images periodically to see if the images they want to project are getting across to target customers.

### Buying Policies

Retailers are buying agents for their target customers and must gather information about their wants and offer merchandise that matches those wants. Direct contact with customers helps but retailers are increasingly using marketing research.[34] Their sources of information include consumer surveys; past sales data by product, brand, and department; sales personnel; customer requests for specific merchandise; customer complaints; comparison shopping in rival stores to monitor their offerings; manufacturer and wholesaler marketing research; and magazines, trade publications, and trade associations.

**Selecting Sources of Supply.** "Goods bought well are half sold" is an old retailing adage. Retailers must be careful in selecting their merchandise and suppliers. A large department store's purchasing department buys the supplies and equipment needed to run the store, but buyers in each department buy merchandise for resale. Buyers for small independent stores usually are the owner-managers.

Retailers buy directly from manufacturers when independent wholesalers' services are not needed. Much of this is specification buying. For example, Sears, J.C. Penney, and Montgomery Ward set specifications for their products that manufacturers must meet.

The supplier's salespeople bring information about new merchandise to their customers. Some retailers also go to manufacturing centers to buy. Many apparel retailers go to New York City to visit manufacturers; others buy through resident buyers. These are middlemen who buy merchandise for their principals. Instead of going to New York City, the retailer buys through a resident buyer there.

Big chains practice centralized buying. A buyer, or a buying committee, for each merchandise line buys for all stores in the chain. Individual store managers, however, might have authority to buy certain items on their own to help them cater more carefully to local consumer tastes.

**Negotiating with Suppliers.** Small retailers buying from big manufacturers, or retailers buying merchandise in short supply, do not have much negotiating power over vendors. Ordinarily, however, there is room for negotiating who pays the freight costs, allowable discounts, dating of invoices, timing of deliveries, and merchandise return policy.

But negotiation should recognize the need to build and maintain channel cooperation. In negotiating terms with vendors, retailers should not lose sight of their primary task—putting together a merchandise offering that satisfies their target customers. Ability to do this over the long haul is the essence of retailing.

## Merchandise Inventory Control

Merchandise inventory is the average retailer's biggest asset, and proper management is important to ensure adequate inventory levels and to minimize inventory shrinkage (employee theft, shoplifting, and other causes of lost merchandise). A basic stock list states the minimum quantity of units of staple merchandise to keep in inventory and the quantity to reorder. It is used for stable demand items that do not change much from year to year.

The model stock plan is used for fashion merchandise. It is expressed in dollars instead of units because this merchandise changes from season to season. It breaks down this merchandise by color, size, and type instead of listing specific units.

Retailers use dollar and unit control for inventories. Each buyer in a department store receives a merchandise budget that shows planned and actual sales in dollar amounts. Any differences become evident and buying practices can be changed accordingly. Unit inventory control

**Table 14–7.** *Examples of shoplifting controls for retailers*

1. Encouraging manufacturers to discontinue making bottle caps that are interchangeable on different sizes of bottles.
2. Using price tags that are impossible to switch, such as the plastic string that goes through an item of clothing and can be removed only by cutting. Another example is placing sensitized tags on merchandise and equipping store exits with devices that sound an alarm if a customer leaves with merchandise with sensitized tags. Salesclerks desensitize the tags as the merchandise is paid for.
3. Designing stores that minimize the opportunity for shoplifting, such as stores with fewer exits, fewer partitions, and fitting rooms with doors that do not touch the bottom of the floor.
4. Locating easily shoplifted merchandise away from store entrances.
5. Putting signs in stores that remind shoppers that shoplifting is a crime and the management will prosecute shoplifters.
6. Placing mirrors in isolated store areas.
7. Using closed-circuit television to monitor shopper activity.
8. Hiring security guards and plain-clothes store detectives.
9. Training sales personnel and other store employees to be alert to shoplifting activity; for example, posting reminders at check outs in supermarkets for clerks to check the bottom of the shopping cart for hidden merchandise.
10. Establishing in-store policies to discourage shoplifting, such as limiting the number of garments a customer can take to a fitting room and requiring customers who enter the store with packages to have them checked in and held at a service desk while the customer is shopping.
11. Keeping easily pilfered products like stereo tapes in specially designed display cases that require a clerk with a key to open them.
12. Avoiding the use of ordinary pens to mark down merchandise prices.

helps buyers control merchandise assortments because inventories are in physical units. This helps identify slow- and fast-moving items.

**Inventory Shrinkage.** Inventory shrinkage has occurred when the dollar amount on hand is less than that carried in the inventory records. Many retailers use electronic inventory record-keeping systems to keep track of their inventories. But they do not reveal shrinkage due to shoplifting and employee theft. A physical inventory is needed.

Shoplifting means taking merchandise without paying for it, or paying less than the correct price by switching or altering the price. More than $8 billion worth of merchandise a year is shoplifted from American retailers. The merchandise losses plus extra security precautions add 2 to 3 percent to the cost of merchandise sold by major department stores and drug and grocery chains.[35] Table 14–7 lists several types of shoplifting controls.[36]

Employee theft causes even more shrinkage than shoplifting. Besides outright theft, store employees sometimes do not ring up sales, or cut prices on purchases made by their accomplices. Employee theft controls include establishing an ethic of honesty in managing the store, making reference checks on job applicants, informing employees that the store has a system to detect theft, and prosecuting offenders.

### Promotion

Retail promotion includes all communication from retailers to consumers and between salespersons and consumers. Its objectives are to build and enhance the store's image, build customer traffic, and sell specific products. It includes personal and nonpersonal promotion.

Personal promotion is personal selling—face-to-face communication between salespersons and consumers. Department stores, fashion-clothing stores, and jewelry stores stress it; supermarkets and discount stores stress nonpersonal promotion.

The major type of nonpersonal promotion is advertising. Retailers use such advertising media as TV, radio, newspapers, billboards, and direct mail. Newspapers carry roughly 75 percent of all retail ads in the United States.[37] Other promotion methods include displays, special sales, special giveaways like calendars, and contests. Promotion is discussed in Section VI.

### Credit and Collections

Years ago, many retailers had posters like "Credit Makes Enemies, Let's Be Friends" in their stores. Today, most retailers offer credit. Such credit activities as credit approval, maintaining credit records, billing, and collection must be managed properly. They also must adhere to the federal "truth in lending" law and the Equal Credit Opportunity Act of 1975, which prohibits creditors from discriminating on the basis of sex.

Accounts receivable financing ties up a retailer's working capital. Some of them, especially small independents, routinely sell these accounts to financing specialists known as factors. The factor pays the retailer less than the face value of the accounts but the retailer gets that money immediately.

Competitive pressures force some retailers to offer credit. Bank credit cards like Visa and travel and entertainment cards like Carte Blanche play a major role in retail credit.[38] One study found that regional and local retailers might attract three market segments more effectively by accepting bank credit cards: newcomers to a town, travelers, and persons wishing to carry a minimum of credit cards.[39]

Credit sales account for about 12 to 25 percent of the volume at discount stores and more than 50 percent at most big mass-merchandising chains and department stores.[40] Credit restraints imposed by the government in March 1980, therefore, had a much greater impact on mass-merchandising chains and department stores. Their sales suffered more than those of discount stores.

## THE FUTURE OF RETAILING

Evolutionary changes in retailing have tended to follow a cyclical pattern, which is explained by the **wheel of retailing** theory.[41] According to this theory, the cycle starts with the appearance of an innovator who is a low-margin, low-service, high-volume operator. For example, the discount store appeared and challenged traditional department and appliance stores. Its limited service offering and low-markup, high-volume philosophy contrasted sharply with the full-service, high-markup philosophy of these traditional retailers. The result was lower retailing costs and lower prices for consumers.

Gradually, the innovator takes on more of the characteristics of a mature retailer. Discounters have upgraded their image by carrying higher-quality merchandise, relocating in nicer areas, and adding higher-quality store fixtures. They look more like department stores and their operating costs and prices have gone up. This creates opportunity for other innovative retailers to enter the picture. You may want to review Table 14–4 for a similar pattern among supermarkets. To keep out of the wheel of retailing spiral, an innovative retailer must avoid changes that lead to becoming a traditional retailer. Attention to profit performance and return on investment can help.

Retailers in the future will place more emphasis on professional management—executives who have merchandising and management skills. Cost control will be more important. Retailers have been slower than manufacturers in applying management science techniques because they have not had up-to-the-minute data on sales by department and customer. But modern point-of-sale terminals are remedying this and are being used in a greater variety of stores.[42] A related trend is more emphasis on productivity. Retailing has tended to be highly labor intensive, but as unionization among retail salespersons increases retailers will seek to automate operations.

Some retailers will seek increased productivity through market seg-

wheel of retailing

mentation.[43]    This will increase the number of small specialty shops that cater to carefully defined market segments.    One shop in Orlando, Florida sells snow skis and mountain climbing gear to affluent local customers who want to fly to resort areas fully equipped.    Large-scale mass merchandisers will concentrate on management science techniques to improve buying, merchandising, and distribution efficiency.

The economies of large-scale retail operations will be a factor in further concentration in retailing.[44]    But antitrust law enforcers likely will focus more attention on big retailers to ensure workable competition, and government will take a more active role in protecting consumers in their dealings with retailers.

We will probably also see renewed growth in smaller shopping centers in many areas where overbuilding of large regional shopping centers has occurred.    Higher driving costs also may contribute to this.    Nonstore retailing also will continue to grow.

Cable TV will make teleshopping a reality in perhaps 50 percent of American homes by the early 1990s.    Consumers will tune in to a particular channel and dial a number on an attached phone to see ads for desired product categories.    Other channels might carry ads for new products, supermarket ads, and so on.[45]

Consumers and retailers will see and talk to each other over video phones.    They will call stores and see desired items.    Video phones will help telephone retailers win greater consumer acceptance since both seller and merchandise will be visible.    Ordering, payment, and delivery will be computerized.    Thus the movement of merchandise and information will be substituted for the more costly movement of people.[46]

In some cases, consumers will preshop from mailed catalogues and visit catalogue showrooms to make purchases.    This reduces the need for retail salespersons.    Warehouse showrooms also have been popular in recent years in furniture retailing.    Consumers shop in a display room connected to a giant warehouse. They pay discount prices for merchandise that is available on the spot.    This method of retailing may spread to other types of merchandise.    Superstores will grow in importance because of consumer preference for one-stop shopping.

## SUMMARY AND LOOK AHEAD

Retailing includes all activities involved in selling or renting products and services to ultimate consumers.    To be classified as a retailer more than half of a firm's sales must be made to ultimate consumers.

Retailers can be classified by (1) form of ownership—sole proprietorship, partnership, corporation, consumer cooperative, (2) organization structure—independent, chain, association of independents, franchise operation, (3) supplementary service offering—full-service, limited-service, self-service, (4) merchandise offering—single-line, limited-line, specialty shops, general merchandisers, (5) pricing strategy—normal margin, discount, and (6) where the retail sale takes place—in-store, nonstore.

The basic task of all retailers is creating a merchandise offering that matches target customer wants in depth and breadth. Scrambled merchandising makes it hard to classify modern retailers into truly descriptive categories. Drugstores carry more than drugs and supermarkets carry more than groceries. Furthermore, many retailers like Sears and J.C. Penney are multifaceted retailers. Some of their stores are very similar to department stores, while others are basically catalogue stores. They also engage in in-home, telephone, and catalogue retailing.

Key retailing decision areas include (1) market target selection, (2) store location, (3) store design, (4) store personnel, (5) store image, (6) buying policies, (7) merchandise inventory control, (8) promotion, and (9) credit and collections.

Retailers are increasingly practicing market segmentation and using marketing research. Stores can be located in unplanned shopping areas or in planned shopping centers. More attention is being given to store design, atmospherics, and retail sales personnel development. Based on the consumer's image, retail stores can be classified as convenience, shopping, specialty, or unrecognized stores. Different consumers can have different images of the same store.

A retailer's buying policies are very important. There is a lot of truth to the old adage that "goods bought well are half sold." The selection of suppliers and negotiations with them are crucial aspects of retail management; so are merchandise inventory control, retail promotion, and credit and collections.

Retailing in the future will be characterized by increasing professionalism and effort to control costs and increase productivity. Nonstore retailing also will increase in importance.

The next chapter examines wholesaling and wholesalers. Wholesalers are another major category of middleman.

## REVIEW QUESTIONS

**1.** What is the difference between retailing and a retailer?

**2.** Do retailers add value to the merchandise they sell? Explain.

**3.** What is the basic difference between an independent retailer and a retail chain?

**4.** What is scrambled merchandising? Why do so many retailers practice it?

**5.** Explain how franchising works.

**6.** What does merchandise breadth and depth mean? Give examples.

**7.** What is a single-line retailer?

**8.** Give two examples of general merchandise retailers.

**9.** How do modern supermarkets differ from those of the 1930s?

**10.** How do general stores differ from department stores?

**11.** Contrast the pricing philosophies of discount and normal-margin retailers.

**12.** Contrast supermarkets and convenience food stores.

**13.** Identify and discuss the various types of in-home retailing.

**14.** Contrast catalogue and mail order retailing.

**15.** Contrast unplanned shopping areas and planned shopping centers.

**16.** What can retailers do to control inventory shrinkage?

**17.** Identify and discuss the four types of retail stores based on the consumer's image.

**18.** Can a consumer who has never shopped in a particular store have an image of that store? Explain.

**19.** What can a retailer learn from the wheel of retailing theory?

## DISCUSSION QUESTIONS

**1.** Will consumer cooperatives become more important in the United States as consumers cope with such modern economic realities as inflation?

**2.** What conclusions can you draw from the growth in nonstore retailing?

**3.** Why is the failure rate among retailers so high? What can be done to reduce it?

**4.** Is there too much concentration in retailing?

**5.** Give some examples of consumerism's effects on retailing.

**6.** Speculate on the future of food retailing in the United States.

## NOTES

1. See John F. Cady, "Structural Trends in Retailing," *Journal of Contemporary Business*, Spring, 1976, pp. 67–90.
2. See Donald R. Marion and Bisrat Aklilu, "The Food Co-op Potential," *Journal of Consumer Affairs*, Summer, 1975, pp. 49–59.
3. "Saving Druggists in a Paper Storm," *Business Week*, June 2, 1980, p. 86.
4. "Where Kmart Goes Next Now That It's No. 2," *Business Week*, June 2, 1980, p. 110.
5. See Claude R. Martin, Jr., "The Contribution of the Professional Buyer to a Store's Success or Failure," *Journal of Retailing*, Summer, 1973, pp. 69–80.
6. See Lynne Bershad, "Downtown Resurgence Spurs Department Stores' Comeback," *Chain Store Age Executive*, November, 1979, pp. 30–32.
7. See Doreen Mangan, "Market Research Gaining as a New Retail Sales Tool," *Stores*, May, 1979, pp. 37–40.
8. See Lorraine Baltera, "Focus Selling Efforts on Life Styles, Retailers Told," *Advertising Age*, January 26, 1976, p. 10.
9. For a discussion of the history of supermarkets, see "Supermarkets Owe Success to Marketing Skill," *Marketing News*, June 27, 1980, pp. 10–11.
10. See A. E. Gallo and C. Handy, "Consumers and Warehouse Stores," *National Food Review*, December, 1978, pp. 17–19; and Jacques Neher, "No-Frill Box Stores Move in Fast on Inflation's Heels," *Advertising Age*, August 20, 1979, pp. 3, 60.
11. The large increase in the number of products carried in supermarkets causes problems in allocating shelf space among products and product groups because floor space has not expanded as rapidly. See Charles W. Lamb, Jr., "The Impact of Shelf Space Elasticity on Retailer and Manufacturer Strategy," *Baylor Business Studies*, February–April, 1975, pp. 27–38.
12. For further reading on supermarkets, see David Appel, "The Supermarket: Early Development of Institutional Innovation," *Journal of Retailing*, Spring, 1972, pp. 39–53; Rom J. Markin, "The Supermarket Today and Tomorrow," *Atlanta Economic Review*, October, 1972, pp. 20–24; "Half Century of Supermarkets . . . And What's Ahead," *Chain Store Age*, September, 1975, pp. 63–74; Arieh Goldman, "Stages in the Development of the Supermarket," *Journal of Retailing*, Winter, 1975–1976, pp. 49–64; Danny N. Bellenger, Thomas J. Stanley, and John W. Allen, "Trends in Food Retailing," *Atlanta Economic Review*, May–June, 1978, pp. 11–14; and Robert Kietrich, "Super Market Census—Entering the 80's," *Progressive Grocer*, September, 1979, pp. 34–74.
13. See Walter J. Salmon, Robert D. Buzzell, and Stanton G. Cort, "Today the Shopping Center, Tomorrow the Superstore," *Harvard Business Review*, January–February, 1974, pp. 89–98; and Stanton G. Cort, "The Future of Food Retailing: The Kroger Viewpoint," *Business Horizons*, February, 1977, pp. 48–60.
14. Nonstore retailers sometimes are called direct selling organizations. See Michael Granfield and Alfred Nichols, "Economic and Marketing Aspects of the Direct Selling Industry," *Journal of Retailing*, Spring, 1975, pp. 33–50. For a discussion of in-home shoppers, see Peter L. Gillett, "In-Home Shoppers—An Overview," *Journal of Marketing*, October, 1976, pp. 81–88.
15. See "Socioeconomic Trends Cause High

Growth in Nonstore Marketing Field," *Marketing News*, February 8, 1980, pp. 1, 3.

16. "Customers Cut Buying as Credit Diminishes, Scott & Fetzer Finds," *Wall Street Journal*, April 21, 1980, p. 1.

17. People who sign contracts to buy products from door-to-door salespersons generally have three days within which to cancel the contract without any penalty. For discussion of cooling-off laws, see Dennis H. Tootelian, "Potential Impact of 'Cooling-off' Laws on Direct-to-home Selling," *Journal of Retailing*, Spring, 1975, pp. 61–70.

18. "Amway's Way," *Time*, May 28, 1979, p. 40.

19. "Avon Calling," *Time*, December 4, 1978, p. 72.

20. Telephone marketing's importance is growing as the cost of personal sales visits increases and the cost and problems of delivery of direct mail increase. See Murray Roman, "How Can Telephone Marketing Help You in Direct Selling?" *Direct Marketing*, August, 1975, pp. 34–36.

21. "Mail-Order Marketer Sears Grows to an Institution 'Where America Shops,' " *Marketing News*, April 21, 1978, pp. 1, 16.

22. An FTC trade regulation rule requires mail order firms to fill orders within thirty days or offer consumers their money back. The rule is limited to merchandise and does not cover "services connected with merchandise such as mail-order photo finishing." Also excluded are magazines and other serial deliveries, seeds and growing plants, and orders made on a C.O.D. basis. See "Agency Stamps Regulations on Mail-Order Firms," *Consumer News*, November 1, 1975, p. 1.

23. For a discussion of direct mail advertising as a communication network, see Danny N. Bellenger and Jack R. Pingry, "Direct-Mail Advertising for Retail Stores," *Journal of Advertising Research*, June, 1977, pp. 35–39.

24. "New Marketing Strategy Positions Korvettes as 'Promotional' Chain," *Marketing News*, March 21, 1980, p. 16.

25. "Korvettes Gives Up Plan to Reopen Stores and Will Try to Sell Remaining 23 Sites," *Wall Street Journal*, February 24, 1981, p. 15.

26. "Convenience Stores: A $7.4 Billion Mushroom," *Business Week*, March 21, 1977, p. 61.

27. See Herbert Hand, John Dunkelburg, and W. Palmer Sineath, "Economic Feasibility Analysis for Retail Locations," *Journal of Small Business Management*, July, 1979, pp. 28–35. For discussion of an analytical framework for selecting new store trade areas and adjusting the merchandise mix of existing stores to their present trade areas, see Bert Rosenbloom, "The Trade Area Mix and Retailing Mix: A Retail Strategy Matrix," *Journal of Marketing*, October, 1976, pp. 58–66.

28. See "The First Census of U.S. Shopping Centers," *Chain Store Age Executive*, December, 1978, pp. 23–68.

29. For a discussion of the implications for retail store managers of crowding in retail stores, see Gilbert D. Harrell and Michael D. Hutt, "Crowding in Retail Stores," *MSU Business Topics*, Winter, 1976, pp. 33–39.

30. Philip Kotler, "Atmospherics as a Marketing Tool," *Journal of Retailing*, Winter, 1973–1974, pp. 48–64.

31. J. Ronald Carey, Steven H. Clicque, Barbara A. Leighton, and Frank Milton, "A Test of Positive Reinforcement of Customers," *Journal of Marketing*, October, 1976, pp. 98–100.

32. Robert E. Wilkes and James B. Wilcox, "Consumer Perceptions of Product Warranties and Their Implications for Retail Strategy," *Journal of Business Research*, February, 1976, pp. 35–43.

33. Thomas J. Stanley and Murphy A. Sewall, "Image Inputs to a Probabilistic Model: Predicting Retail Potential," *Journal of Marketing*, July, 1976, pp. 48–53.

34. For a discussion of how free papers (shopper and community newspapers) can be used by local retailers (their advertisers) to survey consumers, see Jay E. Klompmaker, J. Daniel Lindley, and Robert L. Page, "Using Free Papers for Customer Surveys," *Journal of Marketing*, July, 1977, pp. 80–82.

35. "How Shoplifting Is Draining the Economy," *Business Week*, October 15, 1979, p. 119.

36. Also see Robert E. Wilkes, "Fraudulent Behavior by Consumers," *Journal of Marketing*, October, 1978, pp. 67–75; and Peter Nulty, "Sensormatic Collars the Shoplifter," *Fortune*, February 25, 1980, pp. 114–116, 119.

37. "Retailers Buy More Ads on TV, but Many Still Question Results," *Wall Street Journal*, August 14, 1980, p. 19.

38. See Marian Burk Rothman, "Third Party Credit Gaining in Big Stores," *Stores*, September, 1979, pp. 31–36, 56.

39. Jac L. Goldstucker and Elizabeth C. Hirschman, "Bank Credit Card Users: New Market Segment for Regional Retailers," *MSU Business Topics*, Summer, 1977, pp. 5–11.

40. "Discounters Show Stronger Sales Gains than Other Retailers as Buyers Retrench," *Wall Street Journal*, May 29, 1980, p. 42.

41. Professor Malcolm P. McNair developed the wheel of retailing theory. See M. P. McNair, "Significant Trends and Developments in the Postwar Period," in *Competitive Distribution in a Free, High-Level Economy and Its Implications for the University*, ed. A. B. Smith (Pittsburgh: University of Pittsburgh Press, 1958), pp. 1–25. Also see Stanley C. Hollander, "The Wheel of Retailing," *Journal of Marketing*, July, 1960, pp. 37–42; Dillard B. Tinsley, John R. Brooks, Jr., and Michael d 'Amico, "Will the Wheel of Retailing Stop Turning?" *Akron Business and Economic Review*, Summer, 1978, pp. 26–29; and Malcolm P. McNair and Eleanor G. May, "The Next Revolution of the Retailing Wheel," *Harvard Business Review*, September–October, 1978, pp. 81–91.

42. See Louis H. Grossman and John L. Schlacter, "Application of Modern Management Concepts to the Retail Trades," *Journal of Small Business Management*,

January, 1976, pp. 35–41; Michael A. McGinnis and Leland L. Gardner, "Electronic Checkout and Super-market Sales Volume: Some Evidence," *Akron Business and Economic Review*, Summer, 1976, pp. 31–34; John A. Czepiel and Paul Hertz, "Management Science in Major Merchandising Firms," *Journal of Retailing*, Winter, 1976–1977, pp. 3–13; and Sandy Evans, "Research Companies Discover Growing Potential for Studies Based on Supermarket Scanning," *Supermarketing*, May, 1979, p. 32.

43. See Ronald D. Michman, "Changing Patterns in Retailing," *Business Horizons*, October, 1979, pp. 33–38.

44. For a discussion of the factors that affect structural changes in retailing, see Arlie L. Bowling and Joseph F. Hair, Jr., "Structural Changes in Retailing: A Predictive Model," *Marquette Business Review*, Summer, 1975, pp. 55–60. Also see William R. Davidson, Albert D. Bates, and Stephen J. Bass, "The Retail Life Cycle," *Harvard Business Review*, November–December, 1976, pp. 89–96.

45. See Jack M. Starling, "Cable Television: Prospects for Marketing Applications," *Akron Business and Economic Review*, Fall, 1976, pp. 28–35.

46. See Robert E. Stevens, "Retail Innovations: A Technological Model of Change in Retailing," *Marquette Business Review*, Winter, 1975, pp. 164–168.

# Chapter 15

# Wholesaling

**OBJECTIVES**

*After reading this chapter you should be able to*

1. distinguish between wholesaling middlemen and wholesalers.

2. identify and discuss the services (functions) wholesaling middlemen perform for their suppliers and customers.

3. contrast the operations of full-service and limited-service merchant wholesalers.

4. give several examples of limited-service merchant wholesalers.

5. contrast manufacturers' sales branches and sales offices and explain why their share of total wholesale trade has increased in recent years.

6. tell how merchandise agents and brokers differ from merchant wholesalers.

7. identify and classify agent middlemen as regular or irregular representation agents for their principals.

8. compare operating costs as a percentage of sales for merchant wholesalers, manufacturer-owned wholesaling establishments, and merchandise agents and brokers.

9. identify and discuss major decision areas for wholesaling middlemen.

**KEY CONCEPTS**

*Look for these terms as you read the chapter:*

Wholesaling
Merchant Wholesaler
Wholesaling Middlemen
Full-Service Wholesaler
General Merchandise Wholesaler
General-Line Wholesaler
Specialty Wholesaler
Rack Jobber
Limited-Service Wholesaler
Cash-and-Carry Wholesaler
Drop Shipper
Truck Wholesaler
Mail Order Wholesaler
Manufacturers' Sales Branches
Manufacturers' Sales Offices
Manufacturers' Agents
Selling Agent
Commission Merchant
Auction Company
Merchandise Broker
Food Broker
Petroleum Bulk Plants and Terminals
Assemblers of Farm Products
Trade Show
Exhibition
Merchandise Mart

*Anheuser-Busch is the largest brewer in the United States. In recent years it has investigated several possibilities for growth outside the brewing industry. One is the snack business. In testing the attractiveness of entering this business, Anheuser-Busch used its beer wholesalers to distribute the snacks to bars in selected test cities. The firm's distribution system includes 950 beer wholesalers, who have fleets of trucks and sales contacts with bars, restaurants, supermarkets, and liquor stores. It has been said that Anheuser-Busch's distribution system is its most powerful asset.**

Wholesaling is a vital activity in our macro marketing system, and wholesaling middlemen are vital links in marketing channels for many types of products. Nevertheless, wholesaling is less familiar than retailing to most of us and is much misunderstood. When people talk about "eliminating the middleman," they are usually referring to wholesaling middlemen, not retailers. They reason that manufacturers are needed to make products and retailers are needed to sell them to consumers. The need for an intermediate stage(s) in some marketing channels between manufacturers and consumers or industrial users, however, is less obvious, as are the activities wholesaling middlemen perform for their customers and manufacturer-suppliers.

But another often heard phrase, "Hold off buying and I'll see if I can get it for you wholesale," also suggests that the prospective buyer is paying a penalty when buying from a retailer. This penalty usually is considered to be the retailer's markup. These people would like to buy from wholesaling middlemen instead of retailers. In fact, some types of retailers advertise "wholesale prices to everybody." But that does not mean they are wholesaling middlemen or that they are engaging in wholesaling.

In this chapter we will study what wholesaling is and what wholesaling middlemen do—the services (functions) they perform for their customers and manufacturer-suppliers. We also will discuss the many different types of wholesaling middlemen.

## IMPORTANT WHOLESALING CONCEPTS

It is important at the outset to distinguish among the following terms: (1) wholesaling (or wholesale trade), (2) wholesaling firms and establishments, (3) wholesalers and wholesaling middlemen, and (4) wholesaling functions.

### Wholesaling

The broadest view of wholesaling is that it includes all sales transactions, and the activities directly connected to them, except retail sales trans-

*"If Anheuser-Busch Gets Its Way, Saying 'Bud' Won't Say It All," *Wall Street Journal*, January 15, 1981, p. 23.

actions.   Thus wholesaling includes sales to farmers, retailers, government agencies, other wholesaling middlemen, industrial users, commercial users, professional users, and nonprofit organizations.   Manufacturers, wholesaling middlemen, and retailers can engage in wholesaling.

Manufacturers who sell to wholesaling middlemen or industrial users engage in wholesaling.   But manufacturers are in the primary business of producing products.   Their direct sales to industrial users do not show up in wholesale trade statistics unless they sell through their own wholesaling organizations (manufacturers' sales branches and offices). These branches or offices engage primarily in wholesaling, not manufacturing.   We will discuss them in greater detail later in this chapter.

Likewise, broadly speaking, a retailer engages in wholesaling when it sells to customers who buy products for other than personal or household use.   A True Value hardware store engages in wholesaling when it sells nails to a contractor for use in building a house for sale.

This chapter focuses on the narrower concept of wholesaling as a middleman activity.   We will examine the wholesaling activities of firms that are engaged primarily in wholesaling.   For our purposes **wholesaling** involves the activities of firms that sell to retailers, other middlemen, and/or to industrial users but do not sell, except perhaps in small amounts, to ultimate consumers.

**wholesaling**

### Wholesaling Firms and Establishments

A retail establishment is a firm.   Although it may operate one or more stores, the firm is counted as one establishment.   But a wholesaling establishment is a *place* of business.   One wholesaling firm with three outlets counts as three wholesaling establishments.

### Wholesalers and Wholesaling Middlemen

The term *wholesaler* refers to merchant wholesalers.   **Merchant wholesalers** own title to the products they offer for sale.

The term **wholesaling middlemen** includes merchant wholesalers plus other wholesaling middlemen who do not own title to the products

**merchant wholesaler**

**wholesaling middlemen**

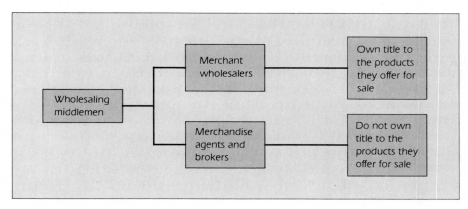

Figure 15–1.
*Two basic categories of wholesaling middlemen*

they offer for sale. Agents and brokers are examples of nontitle-owning wholesaling middlemen. But they are not wholesalers. Only merchant wholesalers are called wholesalers. (See Figure 15–1.)

Merchant wholesalers and merchandise agents and brokers are firms whose primary business is wholesaling. A furniture dealer who advertises "wholesale prices to everybody" actually is a retailer if more than half of its sales revenues are from sales to ultimate consumers. The price at which a product is sold does not determine whether the seller is a retailer or a wholesaling middleman. The classification depends on which type of customer (ultimate consumer or industrial user) accounts for more than half of the firm's sales revenues.

### Wholesale Trade

Wholesale sales are greater than retail sales. You may find this surprising when you consider that wholesale sales do not include a retailer's markup and many products sold at retail never pass through a wholesaling establishment. But the sale of a product at the retail level counts as one sale; that same product, however, may have moved through several wholesaling establishments and have been counted as several wholesale sales. Thus there is some double counting of sales on the wholesale level.

Wholesaling, like retailing, also is a concentrated industry. The share of total wholesale sales made by single establishment firms is declining, while the share made by firms with six or more establishments is increasing. Only about 10 percent of all wholesale establishments sell over $2 million a year. But they account for about 70 percent of total wholesale sales. Manufacturers' sales offices and branches account for the majority of firms that sell more than $2 million a year, while merchant wholesalers account for the fewest. Finally, wholesaling also is concentrated geographically. Roughly half of all wholesale sales are made in the nation's fifteen largest SMSAs.

### WHOLESALING ACTIVITIES

As we said earlier in this text, marketing functions can be shifted and shared among channel members but the functions cannot be eliminated. When a retailer buys directly from a manufacturer, the retailer and/or the manufacturer perform activities that could have been performed by a wholesaling middleman. Thus some firms engage in wholesaling activities although they are not wholesaling middlemen. (See Figure 15–2.)

Wholesaling middlemen perform one or more services for their customers and suppliers. In some channels wholesaling middlemen perform very few services because other channel members have assumed the other services, or functions. When Campbell Soup Company sells directly to Safeway, wholesaling middlemen are bypassed. Instead of having wholesaling middlemen providing credit, delivery, and other services, Campbell and/or Safeway perform them. In general, middlemen who cannot or

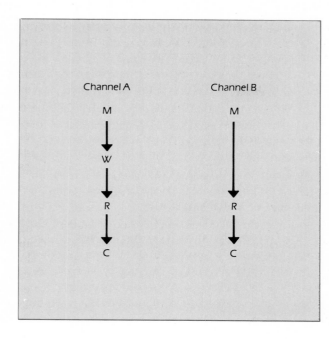

*Figure 15–2.  Bypassing an independent wholesaling middleman*
*The wholesaling middleman is bypassed in channel B, but the manufacturer and/or retailer must perform the functions that would have been performed by the wholesaling middleman.  For example, Safeway can bypass an independent wholesaling middleman by setting up its own wholesaling division.  Safeway's wholesaling division would buy from manufacturers for its retailing division.*

do not perform marketing functions efficiently are eliminated and their functions are assumed by other channel members.

The economic justification for wholesaling middlemen is the services they perform for their suppliers and customers.  Some perform many services; others perform very few.

## Wholesaling Functions for Suppliers

Wholesaling middlemen may help their suppliers perform these types of functions: (1) selling, (2) stocking, (3) financing, (4) gathering market information, and (5) reducing risk.

**The Selling Function.**  A major function wholesaling middlemen perform for manufacturers is the selling function.  Many manufacturers think of their wholesaling middlemen as extensions of their own salesforces.  Sometimes a wholesaling middleman is the only salesperson a manufacturer has in a given territory.  In other cases the wholesaling middleman supplements the manufacturer's salesforce.[1]   The manufacturer's salesforce, for example, may sell to large-volume retailers, while the wholesaling middleman sells to smaller retail outlets that could not be serviced economically by the manufacturer's own salesforce.  This, of course, can lead to channel conflict.

**The Stocking Function.**  Some wholesaling middlemen carry inventory that manufacturers otherwise would have to carry at their factories or regional warehouses.  Wholesaling middlemen stock the variety and quantities of products their customers want.  This enables manufactur-

**Table 15–1.** *Examples of wholesaling functions performed for manufacturer-suppliers*

| | |
|---|---|
| *Selling:* | act as extensions of the manufacturer's salesforce |
| | seek out supply sources and reduce the manufacturer's need for sales personnel |
| *Stocking:* | reduce manufacturers' need to carry large inventories and make heavy investment in warehousing by dispersing inventories instead of concentrating them at factories |
| *Financing:* | reduce warehousing costs |
| | reduce manufacturers' commitment of working capital to inventory |
| | manufacturer conserves working capital by receiving payment for products before they are sold to final buyers |
| | better screening of credit applicants, which reduces bad debts |
| *Market Information:* | may reduce manufacturers' need for market research because of closer contact with manufacturers' final buyers |
| *Risk Reduction:* | assume risk in credit sales to their customers |
| | assume risk of owning title to products |
| | assume risk of carrying inventory |
| | order in advance and help to even out production scheduling |

ers to disperse their inventories instead of, for example, concentrating them at their factories.

**The Financing Function.** Manufacturers may avoid the high fixed cost of building and operating their own warehouses by using wholesaling middlemen. Manufacturers also conserve working capital when they are paid for their products before they are sold to final buyers. They also can do a better job of screening credit applicants when dealing with several wholesaling middlemen rather than many retailers. This helps cut bad debt losses on accounts receivable. By buying ahead, wholesaling middlemen help manufacturers schedule more efficient production runs. This may lower per-unit production and distribution costs.

**The Market Information Function.** A wholesaling middleman's direct contract with retailers who buy the manufacturer's product makes the middleman a good source of information about retailer needs. The same is true of wholesaling middlemen who sell to industrial users.

**The Risk Reduction Function.** Wholesaling middlemen who own their inventory assume the risks of product deterioration and obsolescence and default on credit sales to their customers. They also buy products without knowing for sure if they can resell them. (See Table 15–1.)

### Wholesaling Functions for Customers

Some of the functions wholesaling middlemen may help their customers perform are (1) buying, (2) stocking, (3) gathering market information, (4) financing, (5) reducing risk, (6) contacting, (7) concentrating and dispersing, and (8) management.

**The Buying Function.** Just as wholesaling middlemen help their suppliers perform the selling function, they help their customers perform the buying function. They forecast their customers' requirements and buy products to satisfy them. They offer buying advice to their customers by studying and forecasting buying patterns in their lines of business.

**Table 15–2.** *Examples of wholesaling functions performed for customers*

| | |
|---|---|
| *Buying:* | forecast customer product requirements |
| | buy products to meet those requirements |
| | have sales representatives call on customers |
| *Stocking:* | carry inventory so customers can operate with smaller inventories |
| | help customers avoid over- and underbuying |
| | share with customers economies in operating large-scale warehouses |
| *Market Information:* | provide information about manufacturers and their products |
| | detect developing trends in their industries |
| | keep customers informed of competitive developments |
| *Financing:* | sell on credit |
| | carry inventory |
| | reduce customer need to commit fixed capital to construction and operation of large warehouses |
| *Risk Reduction:* | customers do not have to tie up as much working capital in inventory |
| | make it possible for small firms that might be turned down by manufacturers to buy on credit |
| *Contactual:* | own and transfer title to products without customer need to negotiate directly with manufacturers |
| | enable customers to spend more time on the selling function and less time on the buying function |
| *Concentrating and Dispersing:* | bring together the quantity and assortment of products to meet customer requirements and disperse them to adjust for quantity and assortment discrepancies between manufacturers and customers of wholesaling middlemen: |
| | concentrating—buying in large quantities reduces transportation costs |
| | dispersing—frequent and speedy delivery reduces inventory investment |
| *Management:* | provide advisory services: buying advice, promotional advice, advice on pricing, inventory management, record keeping, personnel training, store layout, point-of-purchase displays |

**The Stocking Function.**   When wholesaling middlemen give buying advice to their customers, they are helping them perform the stocking function.   This advice may help their customers avoid overbuying slow-moving products, which ties up too much working capital in inventory. It also may help avoid underbuying, which results in running out of stock.

**The Market Information Function.**   Closely related to the stocking function is the market information function.   Wholesaling middlemen send buyers to major market areas to see what products are selling and to gather information about manufacturers' plans regarding new product introductions.   Many manufacturers also funnel information about their marketing plans to retailers and industrial users through wholesaling middlemen.

**The Financing Function.**   Wholesaling middlemen who stock products for their customers help them operate with smaller inventories. This reduces the amount of working capital those customers must commit to inventory.   That, along with sales made on credit, means the middlemen provide a financing function for their customers.

**The Risk Reduction Function.**   Wholesaling middlemen who carry inventory and sell on credit also provide a risk reduction function for their customers.   The risk of inventory obsolescence, for example, is borne by the wholesaler.

**The Contactual Function.**   Wholesaling middlemen also help their customers perform the contactual function.   Thus a small grocer can buy products produced by many food manufacturers simply by dealing with one wholesaling middleman.   This allows the retailer to focus more effort on selling and less on buying.

**The Concentrating and Dispersing Functions.**   Wholesaling middlemen bring together the assortment of products their customers want and they disperse them according to customer requirements.   As we saw in the previous chapter, this helps to adjust quantity and assortment discrepancies in channels.

**The Management Function.**   Many wholesaling middlemen also perform a managerial assistance function for their customers.   Customers receive assistance, for example, in managing inventory and developing promotion programs, record-keeping systems, and personnel training programs.   (See Table 15–2.)

## CLASSIFICATION OF WHOLESALING MIDDLEMEN

The Census of Business classifies wholesaling establishments into five groups: (1) merchant wholesalers, (2) manufacturers' sales branches and sales offices, (3) agents and brokers, (4) petroleum bulk plants and terminals, and (5) assemblers of farm products.   The first three groups are, by far, the most important.   The latter two groups account for less than 10 percent of total wholesale trade.

## Merchant Wholesalers

Roughly half of all wholesale sales are made by merchant wholesalers. Roughly two out of three wholesale establishments are merchant wholesalers. These are independent businesses that buy products from manufacturers. They own title to the products they offer for sale and resell products to their customers.

Merchant wholesalers who specialize in industrial products are often called *industrial distributors.* Those who specialize in consumer products are often called *jobbers.* Merchant wholesalers can be divided into two types based on the services, or functions, they perform: full-service (full-function) wholesalers and limited-service (limited-function) wholesalers. (See Figure 15–3.)

**Full-Service Wholesalers.** The most important type of merchant wholesaler in terms of number of establishments and dollar sales volume are **full-service wholesalers.** They perform for their suppliers and customers most or all of the wholesaling functions we have discussed. Their suppliers and customers are willing to pay them for performing these functions efficiently. Smaller manufacturers and retailers, for example, may reason that it is wiser to pay middlemen to do what they can do more efficiently and economically than it is for those manufacturers and retailers to do it themselves.

**full-service wholesaler**

Full-service wholesalers can be further classified by the lines of prod-

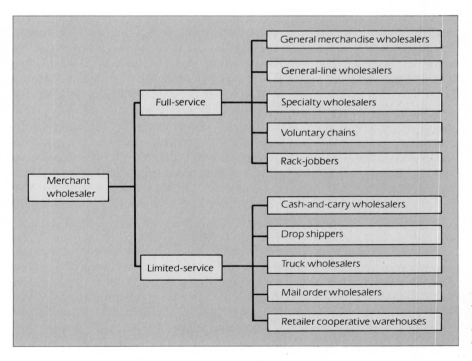

*Figure 15–3. Merchant wholesalers classified by service offering*

ucts they stock: (1) general merchandise wholesalers, (2) general-line wholesalers, and (3) specialty wholesalers.

**general merchandise wholesaler**

**General merchandise wholesalers** stock a wide assortment of unrelated product lines like drug sundries, hardware, electrical supplies, auto equipment, plumbing supplies, nonperishable foods, detergents, and cosmetics. Their major customers are small grocery and department stores and small nonbusiness organizations. They were very important in serving general stores, but their importance declined as the general store was largely replaced by other retailers who carry more specialized product mixes.

Industrial distributors like the mill supply house sell primarily to industrial users rather than to retailers. Some stock up to 70,000 items to serve industrial users in various industries.

**general-line wholesaler**

**General-line wholesalers** carry a complete stock of items in a complete line. Examples are drug wholesalers, grocery wholesalers, and hardware wholesalers. In consumer products marketing, general-line wholesalers serve single- and limited-line retail stores. A plumbing supply house is an example in industrial products marketing. General-line wholesalers are the single most important type of wholesaler in terms of dollar sales volume.

**specialty wholesaler**

**Specialty wholesalers** specialize in one particular part of a line of products. A specialty wholesaler in the foods line, for example, might stock only frozen foods. They deal with fewer manufacturers than general merchandise and general-line wholesalers. Thus they can provide more promotional support for their manufacturer-suppliers. They often set up displays in retail stores and can provide valuable advice and assistance to retailers based on their in-depth experience with a very narrow range of merchandise. Specialty wholesalers in industrial marketing also provide detailed product knowledge and service to their customers.

Two other types of full-service merchant wholesalers are wholesaler-sponsored voluntary chains and rack jobbers. We discussed wholesaler-sponsored voluntary chains in Chapters 13 and 14. The initiating wholesaler provides many valuable services for retail members.

**rack jobber**

♦ **Rack jobbers,** or service merchandisers, developed when supermarkets began expanding into high-margin nonfood items, such as paperback books, small toys, health and beauty aids, hardware, records, and school supplies. They contract with supermarkets and small department, discount, drug, and variety stores to handle items these stores normally do not stock themselves. Rack jobbers stock displays (racks or shelves) with these products and regularly call on retailers to restock the racks and shelves and to take back damaged or slow-moving products. Rack jobbers absorb these costs, not the retailers.

Rack jobbers relieve retailers of the need to order, price, display, and keep inventory records on the racked items. The merchandise usually is provided to the retailer on a consignment basis. The rack jobber collects from the retailer only after the merchandise is sold. In effect, they rent space from retailers to whom they pay a commission on products that are sold.

**Limited-Service Wholesalers.** Wholesalers who peform fewer services for their customers than full-service wholesalers are called **limited-service wholesalers.** They may offer their customers lower prices for foregoing wholesaler services.[2] Their appeal depends on whether the customer can perform the services not offered by the limited-service wholesaler. The following are examples of this type of merchant wholesaler: (1) cash-and-carry wholesalers, (2) drop shippers, (3) truck wholesalers, (4) mail order wholesalers, and (5) retailer cooperative warehouses.

**Cash-and-carry wholesalers** began in the grocery business during the Great Depression when many grocers were cutting operating expenses by giving up some wholesaler services for lower wholesaler prices. Instead of buying from general-line wholesalers, some grocers started buying from the new cash-and-carry wholesalers, who eliminated frills like free delivery and credit.

Cash-and-carry wholesalers usually stock a limited line of products, mostly staples and fast turnover items. Their customers tend to be small retailers and small industrial buyers who buy frequently and in small quantities. Small grocers and small building contractors are examples. Cash-and-carry wholesalers also are important in filling emergency orders for larger retailers and industrial buyers. Some full-service wholesalers have separate departments to serve customers who want to buy all or some of their requirements on a cash-and-carry basis.

**Drop shippers,** also called desk jobbers, take orders from their customers and give them to manufacturers, who ship directly to the drop shipper's customers. Drop shippers buy in their own name (take title), assume the risk of owning products, arrange for transportation, and may extend credit. Since they do not store, handle, or deliver the products, their operating costs are lower than those of full-service wholesalers.

Drop shippers deal mainly in bulky products. They eliminate the need for costly rehandling of products at the wholesale level. They often are used when there is no quantity discrepancy between the manufacturer and the drop shipper's customer, such as a firm that buys lumber or coal in rail carload quantities. Thus there is no need for intermediate bulk breaking (breaking down larger shipments into smaller shipments).

Drop shippers have detailed knowledge of demand conditions in their lines of business. Thus they are valuable to their suppliers because drop shippers know which firms need to buy those suppliers' products. Likewise, drop shippers have detailed knowledge of supply conditions in their lines of business. Thus they are valuable to their customers because drop shippers know which firms have products their customers need. Drop shippers are experts in negotiating sales and they handle all the details of getting the products to their customers.

**Truck wholesalers,** also called wagon, or truck, jobbers, operate rolling warehouses and sell a limited line of products directly from their

limited-service
wholesaler

cash-and-carry
wholesaler

*good for small retailers*

drop shipper

truck wholesaler

trucks to their customers. They often specialize in perishable or semi-perishable fast-selling products. They call on their accounts regularly, which enables their customers to buy in small quantities.

Truck wholesalers handle products like potato chips, candy, dairy products, and tobacco. They combine the personal selling and delivery functions when they call on small grocers. Some truck jobbers call on service stations and car repair shops to sell items like fan belts. The many services they offer to customers who buy in small quantities lead to high operating expenses for truck wholesalers.

mail order<br>wholesaler

**Mail order wholesalers** operate like catalogue retailers and many sell to ultimate consumers. These wholesalers are often used mainly to reach small retailers in remote areas. Products typically sold through them include jewelry, cosmetics, car parts, hardware, stereo equipment, and sporting goods.

We discussed retailer-sponsored cooperative chains in Chapters 13 and 14. These retailers get together and form a buying group to make purchases from manufacturers and wholesalers. Some of these groups go one step further and operate their own warehouse. This is a limited-service wholesaling establishment.

### Manufacturers' Sales Branches and Sales Offices

A growing volume of wholesale sales is accounted for by manufacturer-owned wholesaling establishments. There are two types: manufacturers' sales branches and manufacturers' sales offices.

**manufacturers' sales branches**

**Manufacturers' sales branches** are owned and operated by manufacturers. They are separated physically from manufacturing plants and are set up in areas of high demand for the manufacturers' products. They carry inventory and are very important in serving retailers and industrial users.

**manufacturers' sales offices**

**Manufacturers' sales offices** are similar to sales branches except that sales offices do not carry inventory. A sales office serves as a regional office for the manufacturer's salesforce in that area. It has a listed phone number that target customers can call for information. This helps the manufacturer keep in touch with them. Sales offices are very important in serving industrial buyers because buyers can place orders quickly and take delivery directly from the manufacturer.

These manufacturer-owned facilities provide such services as delivery, credit, and promotional assistance to their customers. Buyers who do not want these services, however, may prefer to buy directly from the factory.

Manufacturers who set up sales branches and sales offices are vertically integrating forward. Because they set them up in areas of high demand, operating expenses tend to be lower than for some independently owned wholesaling establishments. Roughly 13 percent of wholesaling establishments are manufacturers' sales branches and offices, but they account for about 37 percent of total wholesale sales. (See Figure 15–4.) Their growing share of wholesale trade is due largely to the fact that

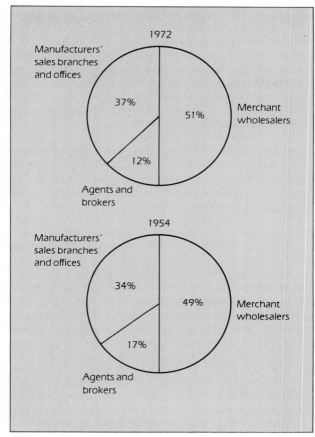

Figure 15–4.
Relative shares of
total wholesale
trade by major
types of wholesaling
establishments

Source: *U.S. Census of Business, Wholesale Trade*

many manufacturers want to exercise greater control over the distribution of their products.   As market potentials in sales territories increase, manufacturers tend to replace agent middlemen with sales branches and offices.   This, of course, can lead to channel conflict.

## Merchandise Agents and Brokers

Unlike the merchant wholesalers we have discussed, merchandise agents and brokers do not own title to the products they sell, although they may physically handle them.[3]   Merchandise agents and brokers facilitate the buying and selling functions by bringing buyers and sellers together. Agent middlemen specialize by product lines and/or by customer types but perform fewer functions than merchant wholesalers.   Some agent middlemen represent their principals (manufacturers) on a regular basis while others represent their principals on an irregular basis.   (See Figure 15–5.)

**Regular Representation Agents.**   Two major types of regular, or con-

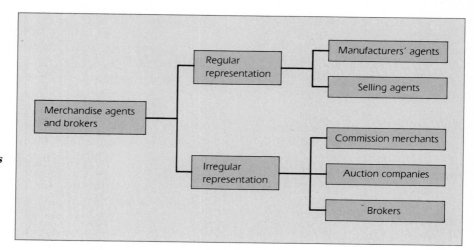

**Figure 15–5. Merchandise agents and brokers classified by the regularity with which they represent their principals**

tinuous, representation agent middlemen are manufacturers' agents (or manufacturers' representatives) and selling agents (or sales agents).

manufacturers' agents

A **manufacturers' agent** is an independent wholesaling middleman who sells on a commission basis for several manufacturers of related, but noncompeting, products. The agent sells a part of each principal's output in a specified territory at prices and terms set by each principal. The cost per sales call, therefore, is spread over several products and principals.

Manufacturers' agents are common in channels for many industrial and consumer products, such as machinery and equipment, electrical and plumbing supplies, metals, specialty foods, furniture, and automotive supplies. Their commission rate ranges from 2 to 20 percent and averages around 7 percent. Products sold in large volumes carry the lower commission rates.

Small manufacturers who lack marketing expertise to distribute their products often use manufacturers' agents to handle the wholesaling job. They also are helpful to manufacturers who cannot afford to maintain company salesforces, because these agents are paid a commission only on the products they sell. A firm that wants to introduce a new product that is unrelated to its established line of products might use these agents for the new product and continue selling the established line through the company salesforce. Likewise, a firm that wants to expand distribution to a new territory where the sales potential cannot justify using company sales personnel could use manufacturers' agents to pioneer acceptance there.

Some manufacturers are using these agents in some territories because of the rising costs of maintaining their own salesforces. Recession and cost-profit squeezes are two reasons some firms have switched to these agents. Thus an increasing number of manufacturers' agents are handling a growing volume of products.

selling agent

**Selling agents** are similar to manufacturers' agents except they handle competing product lines, handle their principals' entire output of the product or products they represent, operate nationally, not in restricted sales territories, and handle the entire marketing task for their principals.

Selling agents are mini-marketing departments for their principals because they develop marketing strategies and programs for them. Sometimes they help finance their principals, which gives them considerable control over them. The selling agent's importance in wholesaling, however, is declining because most manufacturers want more control over their marketing programs than is possible when using a selling agent.

**Irregular Representation Agents.** Manufacturers' agents and selling agents work for their principals on a continuing basis. Some manufacturers use other agent middlemen to sell a specific inventory of products in single, one-time transactions. These agents include commission merchants, auction companies, and brokers.

**Commission merchants,** or commission houses, have physical control of their principals' products, provide storage, and negotiate sales between principals and buyers. They are common in agricultural marketing, especially grain and livestock.

commission<br>merchant

A grain producer who wants to sell in a distant central market might ship grain to a commission merchant there. The merchant stores the grain and shows samples to potential buyers. The principal usually sets a minimum asking price but the commission merchant tries to get a higher price because his or her commission is a percentage of the selling price. Once a sale is negotiated, the commission merchant deducts the commission and sends the balance to the principal.

**Auction companies** provide a place for storing their principals' products so potential buyers can inspect them. This place usually is a low-cost building, such as a shed, but it enables buyers and sellers to conduct transactions. Sales are made to the highest bidder and the auction company charges a fixed fee or a commission for its services. They are common in marketing used cars, livestock, tobacco, furs, fruits and vegetables, and antiques.

auction company

**Merchandise brokers** do not physically handle products but they do bring buyers and sellers together. Many work out of offices in their homes because their main product is information. Sellers wanting information about potential buyers or buyers wanting information about products available for purchase often use brokers. Brokers receive a commission from their principals (sellers or buyers), usually about 2 percent. In a given transaction a broker represents either a seller or a buyer, not both. Brokers are common in marketing real estate, canned foods, and machinery. Their main job is bringing buyers and sellers together and negotiating terms most favorable to their principals. Principals decide, however, whether to accept or reject deals negotiated by their brokers.

merchandise<br>broker

One special type of broker is the **food broker.** A salmon cannery, for example, might can salmon during the harvesting season and use a food broker to help market the output. The principal tells the broker

food broker

**Table 15–3.** *Three major categories of wholesaling middlemen*

| | DISTINGUISHING CHARACTERISTICS | GENERAL TYPES | SPECIAL TYPES |
|---|---|---|---|
| **MERCHANT WHOLESALERS** | Independently owned<br>Title taking<br>Often called jobbers (consumer products)<br>Often called industrial distributors (industrial products) | Full-service wholesalers (classified by product line specialization):<br>  General merchandise (mill supply house)<br>  General-line (drugs, hardware, grocery)<br>  Specialty wholesaler (frozen foods, produce)<br>Limited-service wholesalers:<br>  Cash-and-carry<br>  Drop shipper<br>  Truck wholesaler<br>  Mail order wholesaler<br>  Retailer cooperative warehouse | Wholesaler-sponsored<br>Voluntary chain<br><br>Rack jobber |
| **MERCHANDISE AGENTS AND BROKERS** | Independently owned<br>Nontitle taking | Regular representation agents:<br>  Manufacturers' agents<br>  Selling agents<br>Irregular representation agents:<br>  Commission merchants<br>  Auction companies<br>  Merchandise brokers | Food brokers |
| **MANUFACTURER-OWNED FACILITIES** | Owned and operated by manufacturers<br>Separated physically from manufacturing plants | Sales branch (carries inventory)<br>Sales office (no inventory—serves as a regional sales office for company salesforce) | |

what price is desired and the broker searches for buyers. Once the output is sold to grocery wholesalers and supermarket chains, the agent-principal relationship ends.

Over the years, many food brokers have evolved into institutions that do more for their principals.[4] They resemble manufacturers' agents in that they operate in specified territories on a continuous representation basis. But they do more to help their principals develop and implement marketing strategy. A typical grocery products manufacturer can achieve national distribution by dealing with less than 100 of these food brokers. Their usual commission is 5 percent of sales. (See Table 15–3.)

## Petroleum Bulk Plants and Terminals

Although they are basically merchant wholesalers or manufacturers' sales branches, **petroleum bulk plants and terminals** are listed separately in the Census of Business because of their specialized plant facilities. They resell petroleum products, such as gasoline, kerosene, fuel oils, liquefied petroleum gases, and other bulk petroleum products to petroleum retailers, other wholesaling middlemen, and industrial users.

*petroleum bulk plants and terminals*

When these facilities are owned by oil companies they operate like manufacturers' sales branches. Others are owned independently and are similar to merchant wholesalers. They resell mainly to small petroleum retailers. There are about 30,000 such establishments and they account for about 5 percent of total wholesale trade.

## Assemblers of Farm Products

Although they are merchant wholesalers, **assemblers of farm products** are listed separately in the Census of Business because of their methods of operation. Unlike other wholesaling middlemen, they buy in small quantities from many producers and sell in large quantities to fewer customers. Their functions are performed in the very early stages of the distribution process.

*assemblers of farm products*

Assemblers deal mainly in grain, cotton, livestock, fruits and vegetables, and seafood. They buy (assemble) these products in local producing areas from small farmers and fishers and combine the output for economical handling and transport. They move the products to central markets for sale to other wholesaling middlemen or to industrial users, such as food processors. There are about 11,000 assemblers' establishments and they account for about 2 percent of total wholesale trade.

## Other Wholesaling Institutions

Several other important types of wholesaling institutions are not wholesaling middlemen, but they are important centers of wholesaling activities. These include trade shows, exhibitions, and merchandise marts.

**Trade shows** are sponsored periodically by competing manufacturers to display their merchandise and to solicit orders from the industrial buyers, wholesalers, and retailers who attend. The shows often are held in hotels or auditoriums.[5] They are very common in apparel wholesal-

*trade show*

ing. Some other objectives manufacturers have for holding trade shows include meeting potential customers, developing a mailing list, introducing new products, demonstrating nonportable equipment, building goodwill, discovering new uses for existing products, and observing competitive offerings.

**exhibition**

**Exhibitions** are similar to trade shows but the exhibitors do not solicit orders. The goal is to make it easier for the manufacturers' sales personnel to make sales when they call on people who attended the exhibit and inspected the products. Exhibitions often are held in conjunction with trade association meetings.

**merchandise mart**

**Merchandise marts** are large buildings in major cities where manufacturers can lease space to display their products for retailer inspection on a year-round basis. They often have space for setting up temporary displays and may be used for trade shows and exhibitions. Merchandise marts are similar in purpose to shopping centers for ultimate consumers.

## WHOLESALING MIDDLEMEN: COSTS AND PROFITS

Table 15–4 reveals several important characteristics of several types of wholesaling middlemen. Merchant wholesalers have the highest operating expenses as a percentage of sales because they assume the risks that

**Table 15–4.** *United States wholesale trade by type of operation*

| Type of Operation | Number of Establishments (in thousands) | Operating Expenses as % of Sales |
|---|---|---|
| Merchant wholesalers | 290.0 | 13.9 |
| Manufacturers' sales branches | 33.0 | 11.0 |
| Manufacturers' sales offices | 15.0 | 4.1 |
| Manufacturers' agents | 17.0 | 7.1 |
| Selling agents | 1.7 | 3.2 |
| Commission merchants | 6.9 | 3.8 |
| Auction companies | 1.8 | 2.5 |
| Merchandise brokers | 4.8 | 3.2 |

Source: *1972 Census of Wholesale Trade.*

go along with owning title to the products they offer for sale. They also provide many services for their customers.

Manufacturers' sales branches have higher operating expenses as a percentage of sales than manufacturers' sales offices because offices do not carry inventory. A major reason sales branches have lower operating expenses than merchant wholesalers is that manufacturers set up sales branches only in areas where customers are relatively concentrated.

The data pertaining to operating expenses as a percentage of sales are only averages for the different types of wholesaling middlemen. They may vary among firms in each category and among different types of products. Table 15–5 gives some representative figures on net profit as a percentage of net sales, after deducting federal income taxes, for several types of wholesaling businesses.

Let's turn now to a discussion of several types of major decision areas for wholesaling middlemen.

**Table 15–5.** *Median net profits in selected lines of wholesaling*

| Line of Business | Net Profits as Percentage of Net Sales* |
|---|---|
| Air heating and air conditioning | 2.84% |
| Automotive parts and supplies | 3.55 |
| Beer and ale | 2.91 |
| Chemicals and allied products | 3.63 |
| Commercial machines and equipment | 4.18 |
| Confectionery | 1.98 |
| Dairy products | 1.71 |
| Electronic parts and equipment | 3.73 |
| Fresh fruits and vegetables | 1.74 |
| Groceries, general line | 1.10 |
| Industrial machinery and equipment | 3.27 |
| Meats and meat products | 1.47 |
| Petroleum bulk stations and terminals | 1.91 |
| Scrap and waste materials | 4.17 |
| Tires and tubes | 2.60 |
| Tobacco and tobacco products | .95 |

*Profit after full depreciation of fixed assets; after reserves for federal income and excess profit taxes; after reduction in the value of inventory to cost or market, whichever is lower; after charge-offs for bad debts; after miscellaneous reserves and adjustments; but before dividends or withdrawals.

Source: *Dun's Review*

## MAJOR DECISION AREAS FOR WHOLESALING MIDDLEMEN

Major decision areas for wholesaling middlemen include (1) market target selection, (2) location, (3) warehouse design, (4) personnel, (5) image, (6) product, (7) inventory control, (8) promotion, and (9) credit and collections.

### Market Target Selection

Market research and cost analysis have become more crucial aspects of wholesaling management as managers recognize that a profitable sales volume is more important than volume for the sake of volume. This realization is influencing their selection of market targets. Some are pruning their customer lists—eliminating customers who buy in small volume on an occasional basis—to cut costs and enable them to focus greater attention on those customers whose business accounts for most of their profit. They are becoming more selective in their choice of customers.

### Location

The selection of warehouse sites can be a big problem for multiestablishment wholesaling middlemen, especially merchant wholesalers who carry inventory. Many are turning to linear programing to help them select locations that minimize costs while providing the desired level of customer service. We will discuss this in greater detail in the next chapter.

### Warehouse Design

Perhaps one of the more obvious changes in wholesaling is the middleman's effort to derive greater efficiency from warehouse operations. Mechanized warehouses have supplanted labor-intensive operations in many cases. Mechanized and automated materials-handling systems and order-picking systems are also helping to reduce costs and increase customer service, as we will see in the next chapter.

### Personnel

Modern wholesaling middlemen, especially full-service merchant wholesalers, increasingly are recognizing the desirability of staffing their organizations with professionals. Some grocery wholesalers, for example, now have personnel who advise their grocer customers on store design, layout, and point-of-purchase displays. Many are investing in training programs to upgrade the sales and managerial skills of their personnel.[6]

### Image

Many people have suspected that wholesaling middlemen, perhaps more than any other channel member, are responsible for the higher prices that ultimate consumers and industrial buyers pay. The middlemen are also aware of this image—especially grocery wholesalers. Wholesaling middlemen are seeking to improve their images by updating their service offerings, practicing cost control, and focusing their resources and capabilities more specifically on target customer requirements. Many are working through their trade associations to educate the public about their role in marketing channels.

## Product

Wholesaling middlemen face three major product-related decisions: (1) depth and breadth of the product mix, (2) purchasing policies, and (3) supplementary service offering.

**Depth and Breadth.** A wholesaling middleman's decisions about the depth and breadth of its product mix are largely influenced by its financial resources. A general-line wholesaler's product mix, for example, is broader and deeper than a cash-and-carry wholesaler's. But a cash-and-carry wholesaler offers more breadth and depth than a rack jobber.

The availability of greater financial resources often leads a wholesaling middleman to expand its mix in depth and/or breadth. A broader product mix may lend greater stability to the firm by appealing to a wider mix of customers. Greater depth within fewer product lines, however, may bolster the firm's image as a knowledgeable and valuable source of supply and information for a certain category of customers.

**Purchasing.** A wholesaling middleman's purchasing decisions largely determine the type of business the firm is in. A growing number of firms have come to recognize that their primary mission is to satisfy their customers' buying requirements. They are practicing professional purchasing. In some cases, customers are providing them with more detailed analyses of their requirements. Supermarkets that have Universal Product Code scanners, for example, can provide their wholesalers with detailed information regarding the products and quantities they need. This helps to take some of the guesswork out of the wholesaler's purchasing activities. Many large wholesaling middlemen also are practicing centralized purchasing to help cut costs. Merchant wholesalers especially are practicing strict controls to help ensure that their suppliers will not overload them with unnecessary inventory financed at high interest rates.

**Supplementary Service Offering.** A wholesaling middleman's supplementary service offering can help it create a differential advantage. Some industrial buyers want to buy some of their major equipment on an installed basis. When manufacturers cannot or are unwilling to provide installation and service, some wholesaling middlemen are willing to assume these services. Sometimes the offering of such services requires complex negotiation between the manufacturer, the wholesaling middleman, and the buyer. In other cases, some wholesaling middlemen are unbundling their service offering. Some full-service wholesalers used to offer numerous services to all their customers. When a customer did not want a particular service, the customer still paid for it. This is part of the reason limited-service wholesalers appeared. Some full-service wholesalers now offer a basic bundle of widely required services and charge extra for additional services.

### Inventory Control

Wholesaling middlemen, like retailers and manufacturers, are recognizing the need to exercise careful control over inventory levels. Many are becoming much more selective about the products they stock. A growing number use electronic data processing systems to help control inventory costs. These systems also help to identify unprofitable products that may be considered for deletion. We will discuss inventory control in greater detail in the next chapter.

### Promotion

Wholesaling middlemen also use promotion to communicate with their customers, and even their customers' customers. Grocery wholesalers, for example, often advertise to consumers in an attempt to increase demand in retail stores for the products they stock. Sometimes they send salespersons to their retailer customers to solicit orders. The cost of maintaining a salesforce is increasing for wholesaling middlemen, and many are encouraging their customers to use automated reorder systems, as many wholesalers themselves do. This frees salespersons from routine order taking and allows them to devote more time to function as problem-solving consultants for customers. We will discuss this in greater detail in Chapter 18.

### Credit and Collections

In an age of costly credit, wholesaling middlemen increasingly are aware of the cost of carrying accounts receivable. Although financing their customers and suppliers still is a function of wholesaling middlemen in many channels, many are analyzing on a customer-by-customer basis the effects on profit of offering credit. Some, for example, are refusing to sell to small, slow-paying customers. Some are reducing the period of time they will sell on credit without charging interest. In some cases, wholesaling middlemen are seeking to shift away from credit to offering their customers various types of management assistance. Some believe this is a more lasting way to differentiate their offerings from those of rivals.

### THE FUTURE OF WHOLESALING

Small, inefficiently managed, family-run wholesaling establishments will have an increasingly difficult time surviving. They will have to adopt newer planning and control techniques and procedures, and practice better management.

Manufacturers' agents and selling agents must sharpen their skills to meet the challenge of manufacturers' sales branches and offices. They will have to make the economic advantages of using their services even more obvious to manufacturers.

Limited-service wholesalers must keep in touch with changing customer requirements regarding just how limited they want their limited-service wholesalers' offerings to be. Full-service wholesalers, perhaps more than any other group, must recognize the potential that vertical marketing systems, especially the corporate variety, have to eliminate them.

Wholesalers' keys to survival are sharper management skills, willingness to adapt to a changing environment, cost control, and an ability and willingness to develop creative and uniquely satisfying service offerings for their customers and suppliers.

## SUMMARY AND LOOK AHEAD

Wholesaling involves the activities of firms that sell to retailers, other middlemen, and/or industrial users but do not sell, except perhaps in small quantities, to ultimate consumers. Wholesaling middlemen include title-owning merchant wholesalers and nontitle-owning merchandise agents and brokers. Only merchant wholesalers can be called wholesalers.

Like retailing, wholesaling is a concentrated industry. The share that single establishment (one outlet) firms have of total wholesale sales is declining, while that of multiunit establishments is increasing. Roughly half of all wholesale sales are made in our fifteen largest SMSAs.

Wholesaling middlemen may perform any or all of the following functions for their manufacturer-suppliers: (1) selling, (2) stocking, (3) financing, (4) gathering market information, and (5) reducing risk. They also perform functions for their customers: (1) buying, (2) stocking, (3) gathering market information, (4) financing, (5) reducing risk, (6) contacting, (7) concentrating and dispersing, and (8) providing management assistance and advice. The three major categories of wholesaling middlemen are (1) merchant wholesalers, (2) manufacturers' sales branches and sales offices, and (3) merchandise agents and brokers.

Full-service and limited-service merchant wholesalers are independent businesses that own title to the products they offer for sale. Full-service wholesalers can be classified by the lines of products they stock: (1) general merchandise wholesalers, such as the mill supply house, (2) general-line wholesalers, such as the grocery wholesaler, and (3) specialty wholesalers, such as the frozen foods wholesaler. Wholesaler-sponsored voluntary chains and rack jobbers are two examples of other full-service wholesalers. Limited-service wholesalers offer fewer services to their customers and suppliers and include cash-and-carry wholesalers, drop shippers, truck wholesalers, mail order wholesalers, and retailer cooperative warehouses.

Manufacturers' sales branches and sales offices account for a growing volume of wholesale trade. Sales branches carry inventory but sales offices do not.

Merchandise agents and brokers are independently owned wholesaling establishments that do not own title to the products they help their manufacturer-principals to sell. Manufacturers' agents and selling agents are regular representation agents. Commission merchants, auction companies, and merchandise brokers are irregular representation agents. Modern food brokers are a special case because they have evolved to resemble manufacturers' agents.

Trade shows, exhibitions, and merchandise marts are not wholesaling middlemen but are important centers of wholesaling activities.

In general, merchant wholesalers have the highest operating costs as a percentage of sales because they own title. Full-service wholesalers account for the majority of merchant wholesalers' sales. Manufacturers' sales offices have lower operating expenses than sales branches because offices do not carry inventory. Operating expenses are very low for agent middlemen, such as auction companies and merchandise brokers, whose primary function is bringing buyers and sellers together.

Major decision areas for wholesaling middlemen include (1) market target selection, (2) warehouse location, (3) warehouse design, (4) personnel, (5) image, (6) product mix, (7) inventory control, (8) promotion, and (9) credit and collections.

A wholesaling middleman's survival hinges on the ability to continue performing needed functions efficiently and economically. This requires constant attention to new techniques for modernizing their operations.

The topic for the next chapter is physical distribution. As we indicated in this chapter, some of the ways wholesaling middlemen can modernize their operations are discussed there.

## REVIEW QUESTIONS

**1.** Are wholesalers and wholesaling middlemen the same thing? Explain.

**2.** Can a retailer engage in wholesaling activity? Explain.

**3.** Identify and discuss the functions wholesaling middlemen might perform for their suppliers.

**4.** Identify and discuss the functions wholesaling middlemen might perform for their customers.

**5.** How do assemblers of farm products differ from other wholesaling middlemen?

**6.** What is the basic difference between merchant wholesalers and merchandise agents and brokers?

**7.** Identify and discuss the three basic types of full-service wholesalers based on the product lines they carry.

**8.** Identify and discuss five types of limited-service wholesalers.

**9.** Why would a customer use a drop shipper?

**10.** What is the major difference between manufacturers' sales branches and manufacturers' sales offices?

**11.** Why are manufacturer-owned wholesaling establishments increasing their share of wholesale trade?

**12.** Identify and discuss two types of regular representation agent middlemen.

**13.** Identify and discuss three types of irregular representation agent middlemen.

**14.** Is it correct to say that many modern food brokers are very similar to manufacturers' agents? Discuss.

**15.** Why do merchant wholesalers tend to have higher operating expenses as a percentage of sales than merchandise agents and brokers?

**16.** Which type of merchant wholesaler accounts for the majority of merchant wholesaler sales, full-service or limited-service wholesalers?

**17.** Identify and discuss briefly nine major areas of decision making for wholesaling middlemen.

**18.** What are the keys to survival of a particular type of wholesaling middleman?

## DISCUSSION QUESTIONS

**1.** "The cost of distributing products would be reduced if more manufacturers vertically integrated forward and set up their own wholesaling establishments." Do you agree?

**2.** Drop shippers do not have to store or deliver products because they do not physically handle them. Why are not all merchant wholesalers drop shippers?

**3.** Suppose you are a manufacturers' agent. A manufacturer wants you to handle its product in a new sales territory. You suspect the manufacturer will drop you after you develop the territory enough so that the manufacturer can use its own salespersons there. Would you do a good job of developing that territory?

**4.** "Wholesaling middlemen who have high operating expenses are destined to be eliminated from marketing channels." Do you agree?

## NOTES

1. For discussion of the importance to manufacturers of researching and motivating their distributors, see Irving D. Canton, "Do You Know Who Your Customer Is?" *Journal of Marketing*, April, 1976, pp. 83–85. Also see Frederick E. Webster, Jr., "The Role of the Industrial Distributor in Marketing Strategy," *Journal of Marketing*, July, 1976, pp. 10–16.
2. See Don Markwalder, "The Changing Status of Wholesaling," *Business and Economic Dimensions*, September–October, 1972, pp. 15–18.
3. Merchandise agents and brokers are also referred to as functional middlemen.

4. See Kenneth J. Lacho, "Food Broker Search for Product Line Additions," *Atlanta Economic Review*, October, 1972, pp. 49–53.
5. See Suzette Cavanaugh, "Setting Objectives and Evaluating the Effectiveness of Trade Show Exhibits," *Journal of Marketing*, October, 1976, pp. 100–103.
6. See Don Knowles, "Marketing: Don't Sell It Short," *Industrial Distribution*, September, 1978, p. 101.

# Chapter 16

# Physical Distribution

**OBJECTIVES**

*After reading this chapter you should be able to*

1. explain the growing importance of the physical distribution (P-D) function and P-D management.

2. contrast the total P-D concept to traffic management.

3. give examples of cost tradeoffs in P-D management.

4. discuss the significance of the flow concept to warehousing management.

5. state the basic goal of inventory management.

6. contrast ordering cost and carrying cost.

7. give examples of innovations in materials handling.

8. identify and discuss the four legal forms of transport.

9. identify and discuss the relative advantages of the five modes of transportation.

**KEY CONCEPTS**

*Look for these terms as you read the chapter:*

Physical Distribution
Total Cost Concept of Physical Distribution
Distribution Center
Public Warehouse
Carrying Cost
Ordering Cost
Economic Order Quantity
Materials Handling
Unitization
Containerization
Order Processing
Common Carrier
Contract Carrier
Private Carrier
Exempt Carrier
Modes of Transportation
Freight Forwarder

*In the latter part of 1980 and into 1981 the midwestern United States was experiencing a serious drought. The lack of adequate rainfall was causing severe problems for marketers of grain, coal, and crude oil because they rely heavily on barge transportation to move their products to customers. The water level of the Mississippi River was way below normal and barges were running aground. To help alleviate the problem, barge operators were only partially loading their barges, a practice that resulted in higher transportation costs per ton of product moved.*

*Meanwhile, the American auto industry was in such a slump that excess inventories of finished cars were building up. Thus some car makers closed several of their plants or slowed their assembly lines in order to cut back production and reduce the inventory burden. The goal was to achieve a better balance between production and sales. High interest rates made it even more important to avoid carrying excess inventories.*

Before the Industrial Revolution, manufacturers bought and placed raw materials into production only after customers had placed orders for finished products. There were few problems in managing inventories of raw materials, goods in process, and finished products because they, in effect, were already sold. No great distances separated manufacturers and their customers because products were produced in small, local plants. The major transportation problem was its availability because there were few alternatives from which to choose.

With the arrival of mass production in anticipation of orders, however, the problem of inventory management arose. As the market area served by the manufacturer increased, plant and warehouse location decisions became more important. Furthermore, the fuller development of the nation's transportation system presented the shipper with a greater number of transportation alternatives. The need for physical distribution (P-D) management became apparent.

In this chapter, we will examine physical distribution activities, the major institutions that perform them, and how firms manage the physical distribution of their products.

## WHAT IS PHYSICAL DISTRIBUTION?

To some firms physical distribution (P-D) means moving finished products from the end of the production line to customers. A more systems-oriented view is that **physical distribution** involves moving (1) raw materials from their sources to the beginning of the production process, (2) raw materials, semimanufactured products, and finished products within and among plants, (3) finished products through warehouses and middlemen, and (4) finished products to final buyers. (See Figure 16–1.)

**physical distribution**

P-D activities include (1) transportation, (2) warehousing, (3) materials handling, (4) inventory control, (5) plant and warehouse location, (6) order processing, (7) customer service, (8) market forecasting, and (9) protective

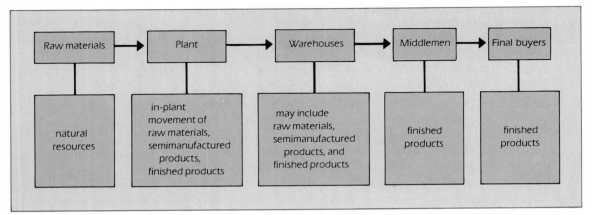

*Figure 16–1.   The total physical distribution concept*

packaging.   These activities cross departmental lines and require coordination to carry out the firm's channel strategy.[1]

Some firms refer to P-D as logistics or materials management.   *Logistics* is a military term.   The problems military organizations face in scheduling production and distribution of matériel and coordinating their movement with personnel are similar to those manufacturers face in producing and distributing products.   Many of the quantitative and computer techniques that businesses use to manage their P-D activities were, in fact, developed by the military.[2]

Many modern firms are using simulation techniques to increase efficiency in managing their P-D activities.   Several years ago, for example, Electrolux Corporation was considering moving its warehouse out of Atlanta.   A computer simulation enabled the firm to compare several months of freight bills from its Atlanta warehouse with those that would be generated by other possible sites.   The warehouse was moved to Charlotte, North Carolina after the simulation showed that the move would save money.[3]

### The Growing Importance of P-D

The P-D function used to involve little more than traffic management—finding the cheapest method of transporting finished products to customers.   A traffic manager scheduled traffic and reported to the production manager.   The goal was to coordinate production scheduling with shipments of finished products.   Customer wants often were overlooked and they often failed to receive the service they wanted.   This production-oriented view of P-D was the norm well into the present century. It still exists in some firms today.

**Distribution Economies.**   American manufacturing history reflects management's effort to minimize production costs.   Mass production economies stem from declining unit production costs as production runs are lengthened.   But much less attention was given to the per-unit costs of getting products to final buyers through marketing channels. Whereas per-unit production costs tended to go down, per-unit distribution costs often tended to stay the same or go up. Thus for many firms the potential to increase profitability through P-D technology is greater than it is in production technology.[4] Past neglect of the P-D function means there is a lot of room for improvement, especially since the advent of the energy problem.[5] On the average, P-D costs still account for roughly half the cost of marketing, and as much as half of P-D costs may be transportation costs.[6]

**Mechanization and Automation.** Substituting machinery for labor helped reduce per-unit production costs, but little attention was given to these substitution possibilities in P-D activities. Thus P-D remained highly labor-intensive. Because unionized transportation and warehouse workers, for example, receive relatively high wages, many firms are now realizing that huge cost savings are possible from mechanizing and automating some P-D activities.

**Inventory Cost.** Manufacturers, wholesalers, and retailers are more aware of the cost of carrying inventories. High interest rates increase the cost of borrowed funds tied up in inventory. Many retailers and wholesalers use computerized inventory control systems so that they can operate with smaller inventories. This pushes some of the stocking function backward in marketing channels to manufacturers, who must increase their P-D efficiency or commit more working capital to inventory.

**Shortages.** Intermittent shortages of some raw materials and finished products increase the importance of effective P-D management. It can help stretch available supplies among customers by minimizing the volume of products lying idle in storage throughout the distribution pipeline.

**The Company Mission.** A firm's P-D management efficiency can affect top management's concept of the company mission. Firms that want to grow by selling their products in distant markets may have to meet or beat local marketers' prices in those areas. Low cost, dependable transportation to those markets may be a requirement for market entry.

**The Marketing Concept and P-D.** A major factor in explaining P-D management's growing importance is greater acceptance of the marketing concept. For the P-D function, this means providing customers the level of P-D service they want—timely deliveries, avoiding out-of-stock situations, correct invoicing of orders, and delivery of undamaged products. A growing number of meat packers, for example, are shipping cattle carcasses split into cuts and boxed at the plant. Supermarkets often prefer this to receiving carcass beef because it requires less labor at the supermarket.

Although the broader view of P-D generally has been neglected in the past, some firms have always paid attention to some P-D activities. Marketers of iron ore, coal, and lumber sell bulky products whose transportation costs account for a big percentage of their delivered selling prices. Transportation cost is critical in determining the geographical scope of their markets. Likewise, marketers of perishable and fragile products like fresh fruits and vegetables and fine china have been concerned about speedy and damage-free deliveries. But even these firms focused mainly on transportation instead of the broader view of P-D.

## THE TOTAL P-D CONCEPT

The total P-D concept recognizes the diversity of P-D activities and the need to coordinate them under a P-D manager.[7] This avoids dividing up and assigning P-D activities to different executives, such as assigning traffic to the production manager and inventory control to the finance manager.

Earlier in this text we referred to the systems view of management. P-D provides a good example of how this concept can be applied to achieve an optimum overall blend of P-D activities. Three key concepts are part of this systems view of P-D: (1) the total cost concept, (2) the cost tradeoff concept, and (3) the optimization concept. (See Figure 16–2.)

### The Total Cost Concept

**total cost concept of physical distribution**

The **total cost concept of physical distribution** focuses on the cost of all P-D activities as a whole instead of viewing them independently. The goal is to minimize total P-D costs, subject to a constraint of providing a predetermined level of customer service. The firm sets a customer-oriented level of service and then seeks to minimize the cost of providing it.[8]

### The Cost Tradeoff Concept

Implementing the total cost concept requires that P-D managers recognize the necessity for cost tradeoffs because the goals of different P-D activities often conflict. Suppose we want to provide next-day delivery to cus-

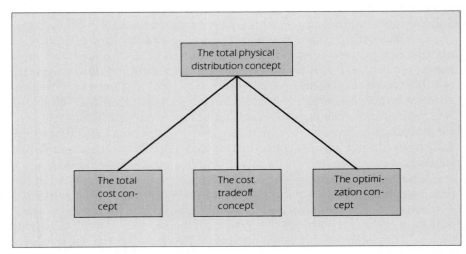

*Figure 16–2. Concepts underlying the total systems view of physical distribution*

tomers and also minimize freight costs. The desired level of service (next-day delivery) conflicts with the transportation goal (cost minimization).[9] Salespersons want quick delivery to customers, whereas the traffic manager wants minimum freight bills. A possible cost tradeoff would be second-day delivery to customers for lower transportation costs. If customers accept that service reduction, the tradeoff will be profitable.

Consider other examples of cost tradeoffs. Transportation rates per unit of product moved tend to decrease as volume increases. One firm may willingly increase warehousing costs in order to concentrate enough volume of product at the plant to get a lower freight rate. Another firm may willingly pay higher freight rates to avoid tying up working capital in inventory and fixed capital in a warehouse.

Another tradeoff involves order quantity and order frequency. Some firms place frequent small orders, whereas others place fewer large orders. The larger the quantity ordered, the less often orders have to be placed. This cuts order-preparation costs and the receiving department has fewer shipments to keep track of. But warehousing and inventory costs will go up because more units of product must be inventoried.

All tradeoff decisions require careful thought. High interest rates and declining consumer demand in the first half of 1980 led many retailers to cut inventories. They pushed the inventory function backward in the channels. They were willing to experience more stockouts to save on inventory costs. Retailer desire to cut inventories caused problems for manufacturers' advertising programs. Retailers also focused more attention on high turnover products, which made it tougher for manufacturers to introduce new products.

## The Optimization Concept

Underlying the total P-D concept is P-D management's desire to optimize overall P-D performance. Optimization is a condition in which the various P-D activities are balanced in such a way that overall P-D costs are minimized while the predetermined level of customer service is provided. Achieving this optimal result is tough, however, because (1) top management may think other objectives are more important than P-D objectives, (2) different P-D activities may be assigned to different departments, which makes coordinating them difficult, and (3) some firms are reluctant to specify the level of customer service they will provide.

Top management in some firms looks at P-D merely as a service function. A warehouse manager may be told to store products as they roll off the production line (without any input in decision making about the length of production runs) and to be ready to fill orders at the salesforce's request (without any input in decision making about order size). In cases like this, the P-D department often is not operated as a profit center to which costs are assigned. It is a service function operated for the convenience of production, finance, and marketing managers.

It is hard to coordinate P-D activities when they are assigned to different departments. Inventory management may be assigned to production and order processing may be assigned to accounting. Management also may fail to set a specific level of customer service. Thus P-D performance may vary according to the department or person performing each activity. The result is that suboptimization usually occurs in P-D management. Overall P-D costs are not minimized subject to the customer sevice constraint. This will likely continue until top management recognizes P-D's role in helping the firm achieve its objectives and concentrates P-D activities under one executive.

## THE P-D SYSTEM

Raw materials processors, manufacturers, and middlemen face P-D decisions. So do ultimate consumers. Some consumers, for example, buy large quantities of frozen foods and store them in home freezers. Others buy only for current consumption.

Freight carriers, warehouse operators, and many other marketing specialists also are parts of P-D systems. How a product is distributed may be affected by their decisions. Ideally, P-D planning should be done from a systems view. But because many firms make up a typical marketing channel, total, system-wide planning is rare. Vertically integrated firms like a steel company that mines its own iron ore and sells through its own outlets come close to system-wide P-D planning.

Our discussion focuses on P-D planning in the individual firm. Although P-D factors sometimes dominate channel strategy development, P-D planning usually occurs after other channel decisions have been made. In recent years, however, it seems that P-D considerations have been entering into many marketing decisions, including decisions about pruning the product mix.[10] We will discuss several major subsystems of the P-D system—warehousing, inventory control, materials handling, order processing, and transportation. These subsystems, of course, are interdependent.

### The Warehousing Subsystem

P-D activities have one unifying goal—to develop and maintain a steady flow of products. Ideally, as we saw in Chapter 13, this flow begins with raw materials in the state of nature and ends with manufactured products in the hands of ultimate consumers or industrial users. Activities of many independent firms normally are involved in this flow.

**Storage.** Although maintaining a steady flow of products is desirable, there are valid reasons for interrupting the flow.[11] Grain is produced seasonally but some must be stored for off-season consumption. Swimsuits and lawnmowers are consumed seasonally but produced year-round. Storage interrupts the flow from producer to final buyer but makes longer and more efficient production runs possible. Production cost savings may be greater than the storage costs.

Storage also provides time utility to products. It helps firms balance supply (production) and demand (consumption). Even when products are consumed as they are produced, firms usually store some output in case actual demand exceeds forecasted demand.

Storage also may be needed to add form utility to products. Bananas need time to ripen and beer needs time to age. Other reasons for storage include stockpiling in case of strikes by supplier and transportation workers and anticipated materials shortages and/or price increases. Some firms incur storage costs to get bigger quantity discounts on their purchases. Clearly, there are advantages to storing products. But there also are costs, such as insurance, taxes, obsolescence, warehouse operation, and interest on borrowed funds and/or the opportunity cost of funds (that is, the lost opportunities of using the funds elsewhere) invested in stored products.

**Warehousing.** Products are stored because they are not needed for immediate consumption. Warehousing serves as a valve to regulate the flow of products through a marketing channel. Storage is static; the focus is holding. Warehousing is dynamic; the focus is moving (throughput).[12] Effective warehousing makes the flow concept of P-D operational.

From a macro view, the purpose of inventories is to coordinate production and demand. Big changes in inventory levels may be a major factor in the business cycle. Firms produce to meet current demand and to build inventories for future orders during expansionary phases. But production falls below the current level of sales as firms reduce inventories during contractionary phases.

Individual firms also try to coordinate production and sales through inventory management. This includes decisions about the size, location, handling, and transporting of inventories. A useful starting place in warehousing planning is determining the number, location, and ownership of warehouses. Because these decisions are affected by the number and location of plants, plant location also is part of P-D planning.

*Plant Location.* Plant location decisions affect production and distribution costs and, therefore, the market areas a firm can serve profitably. Plants locate near raw material or supply sources when the product loses weight during production. They tend to locate near customers when the product gains weight during production. Other plant location factors include the quality and quantity of available labor, water supply, energy resources, and state and local taxes. The cost of transporting a product to market limits its market area. A firm that wants to sell in a distant market cannot price its product higher than local competitors there unless the product is significantly differentiated.

Warehousing's importance to a firm depends a lot on the distance between supply sources and markets. If they are far apart, the warehousing subsystem is very important. But if production is close to supply sources and markets, the warehousing subsystem is much less important. When plant locations are fixed, the warehousing decision involves finding locations between plants and markets for inventories of finished products.

*Warehouse Location.* Finished products can be concentrated at the plant or at a centrally located warehouse, dispersed to many warehouses each of which serves customers in its local area, or dispersed to a few large warehouses and concentrated there for shipment to customers.

A centralized inventory requires building and stocking one warehouse. Because all products the firm markets are in one warehouse, order changes can be handled easily and fewer customers will receive only partial shipments. Inventory control is easier with only one warehouse. Warehousing cost per unit of product should be low because the large-scale operation makes it economical to use mechanical and automated equipment to handle products and process orders.

On the other hand, a centralized inventory means slow delivery to customers on the fringes of the distribution area. Total transportation cost is also high.

A compromise between total centralization or total decentralization of inventory is the **distribution center**. It is planned around markets to maintain an efficient flow of products from producer to customers. The goal is to move products (throughput), not store them. Order taking, order filling, delivery activities, and so on are coordinated in one building. Orders are processed rapidly because modern handling equipment, sci-

**distribution center**

***Figure 16–3.   The distribution center concept***
*This manufacturer of home appliances has three plants.   One produces dishwashers, one produces refrigerators, and one produces washing machines. Each plant ships its product in volume quantities to the distribution center, where order taking, order filling, and delivery activities are coordinated and the products flow to large retail chain buyers in the Southeast.*

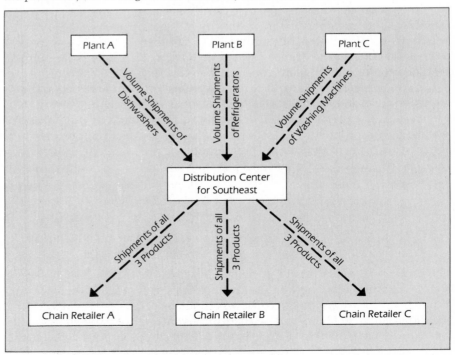

entific inventory management, and computer technology make automation practical. This reduces costs, improves customer service, and speeds inventory turnover. (See Figure 16–3.)

Middlemen also use distribution centers. For example, many supermarket, fast-food, convenience food, and department store chains use them. One result in some cases is to reduce a particular store's dependence on local wholesalers.

Marketers who decide to concentrate their inventories in one warehouse must select a specific site. Those who decide to disperse their inventories must decide how many warehouses to operate and select a site for each of them. Many variables enter into these decisions. Examples include inbound freight cost and delivery schedules, customer buying patterns and service requirements, the availability and cost of alternative modes of transportation, and construction or rental costs and taxes in various locations. Computer simulation techniques, as we suggested earlier, are being used to help in making these decisions.

*Warehouse Ownership.* Warehousing strategy requires an investment decision. Building and operating a private warehouse (branch warehouses) require a big investment. If those funds could be invested elsewhere more profitably, the firm should consider using **public warehouses.** These are independently owned, profit-seeking businesses that offer services to firms and individuals. Because the user pays only for space used, public warehousing is a variable cost as opposed to the largely fixed cost of building and operating branch warehouses. Table 16–1 lists several types of public warehouses and Table 16–2 discusses the services they offer.

Public warehousing appeals to firms with seasonal or otherwise lim-

public warehouse

**Table 16–1.** *Major types of public warehouses*

| | |
|---|---|
| *General Merchandise* | Used for products that do not require specialized storage facilities. |
| *Special Commodity* | Used for specific commodities, such as cotton, grain, and fur. |
| *Bonded* | A type of general merchandise or special commodity warehouse. Used for products subject to excise taxes or import duties, such as alcoholic beverages and tobacco. The operator is bonded to ensure payment of those taxes or duties. Payment is due when the products are removed. |
| *Cold Storage* | Used for frozen foods, meats, certain drugs, and other products that require refrigeration. |
| *Household Products* | Used for storing personal property, such as furniture. |
| *Field* | The owner of merchandise inventory can place part of it in a field warehouse. The warehouse custodian takes control but not title to the merchandise and issues a warehouse receipt to the owner. The owner can use this receipt as collateral for a bank loan. |

**Table 16–2.** *Services offered by public warehouses*

| | |
|---|---|
| *Storage* | The seller can stockpile products until needed for delivery to customers. |
| *Break Bulk and Reshipping* | The seller ships in carload or truckload lots to the warehouse. The warehouse breaks bulk and delivers to the seller's local customers. |
| *Stock Spotting* | The seller locates inventories of finished products near large customers rather than at the plant. The warehouse provides local delivery upon receipt of orders from those customers. |
| *Management and Labor Expertise* | Public warehouses are specialists in performing P-D activities. |
| *Financing* | Public warehouses issue warehouse receipts that can be used by their customers as collateral for bank loans. |

ited warehousing needs and those lacking funds and personnel to operate branch warehouses. Small firms that do not need aggressive selling effort often use them instead of local salesforces. Some other firms use them instead of traditional wholesalers. These examples show that P-D factors may, in fact, strongly influence channel strategy.

High interest rates, rising real estate costs, and the cost-profit squeeze make public warehouses attractive. They can extend their customers' capabilities. Some will package their customers' products. Delaying packaging until products are nearer to customers can reduce costs because unpackaged products usually are cheaper to transport than packaged products. Funds tied up in packaging also add nothing to profits until the products are sold.

Rising labor and real estate costs encourage greater effort to increase warehouse labor productivity and space utilization by using mechanized and automated equipment. Careful cost analysis is needed in decisions about automating warehouse operations. Such analysis has led many firms to close obsolete warehouses, and public warehouses are phasing out smaller, less efficient facilities.

## The Inventory Control Subsystem

Minimizing working capital tied up in inventory while providing the specified level of customer service is the goal of inventory management. If cost were not a factor, a firm would carry enough inventory to fill all customer orders on short notice. But the required investment in inventory increases at an increasing rate as the level of customer service increases. (See Figure 16–4.) Suppose a firm can fill 90 percent of all orders from a $200,000 inventory. Raising this percentage to 95 might require a $300,000 inventory. This must be considered in setting the specified level of customer service.[13] To help hold down distribution costs some firms are working closer with middlemen and final buyers to

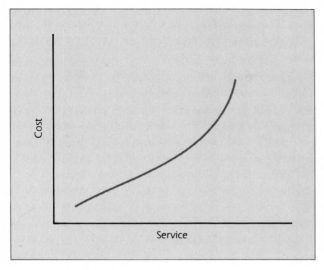

*Figure 16–4. The sales and cost dimensions of inventory management*
*Notice that the required investment in inventory increases at an increasing rate as the level of customer service increases. Service level here refers to the percentage of orders the firm can fill from its current inventory.*

determine what service levels are acceptable to them in the light of rapidly rising energy costs.

**Carrying Cost.** One major inventory cost is **carrying cost.** This includes the costs of storage, record keeping, insurance, taxes, handling, depreciation, damage, interest, and obsolescence. As the size of each individual order placed increases, inventory carrying cost increases. The costs of rented warehouse space and insurance on inventory are easy to compute, but the opportunity cost of funds committed to inventory and obsolescence costs are tougher to compute.

Financing inventory with borrowed money requires interest payments, whereas the use of internally generated funds does not. But a firm that ignores the opportunity cost of using those funds will invest too much in inventory. Obsolescence is a major carrying cost for fashion products but it cannot be determined before it occurs. The chances of its occurrence, however, must be considered in computing carrying cost.

**Ordering Cost.** Another major inventory cost is **ordering cost**—the cost of placing an order. Ordering cost decreases as the size of each individual order increases. One large order is cheaper to process and handle than many small orders and there may be quantity discounts.

The **economic order quantity** is the amount that should be ordered each time to minimize total cost (carrying cost and ordering cost). (See Figure 16–5.) But the EOQ is not necessarily the quantity that will be ordered. If the EOQ is 460 units and sellers accept orders only in multiples of 100, the firm probably will order 500 units. If the firm produces the product for itself and its most efficient production run is 490 units, then 490 units probably will be produced.

**Order Timing.** The timing of orders is another decision. Suppose the usage rate is 5 units per day and order lead time (time between place-

carrying cost

ordering cost

economic order quantity

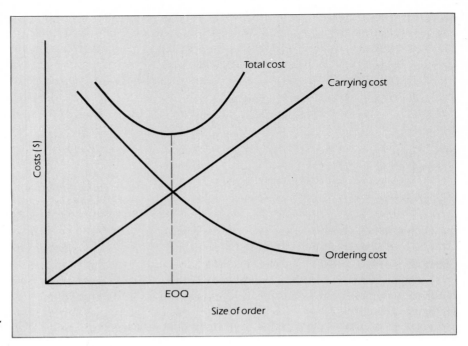

**Figure 16–5.**
**The economic order**
**quantity (EOQ)**

ment and receipt) is fifteen days. An order would be placed when the inventory fell to 75 units (the reorder point). These 75 units are the firm's *basic stock.*

Order lead time varies, however, because of strikes, transportation problems, and supplier out-of-stock situations. If an order is received in ten days, the firm will be overstocked. If it is received in twenty days, the firm will experience stockouts. Thus most firms also carry *safety stock* to offset variations in order lead time.

The usage rate also may vary. If it is 3 units per day, the firm will be overstocked. If it is 7, the firm will experience stockouts. Inventory carried as a hedge against usage rate variation is called *seasonal stock.*

**Inventory Control.** Inventories are controlled by setting upper and lower limits. The firm's desired level of customer service determines the upper limit. It sets the percentage of orders that can be filled from inventory on hand. The lower limit depends on how fast inventories can be replenished by more production or buying from suppliers. When inventory on hand reaches the lower limit (the reorder point), an order is placed to replenish it. Some firms use computers to handle reordering details.

Different factors affect the upper and lower limits for inventories of finished products, goods in process, and raw materials. Finished products inventories are managed with a view to all marketing mix elements. An upcoming ad campaign or a temporary price cut may favor an increase in the upper limit. The greater the number of customers, the less frequent model changes are, and the greater the efficiency of long production runs, the higher the upper limit for goods-in-process inventories. The more distant and undependable suppliers are and the greater the risk of product shortages, the higher the upper limit for raw materials inventories.

To evaluate inventory management a firm could compare its inventory turnover rate with those of other firms in its industry. But a high turnover rate could be achieved by keeping small inventories and ignoring ordering costs and out-of-stock costs. Some firms set a desired rate of return on inventory investment. Regardless of the evaluation approach, the desired level of customer service should not be sacrificed for cost savings.

Rising costs and supply problems tend to lengthen the order cycle. This makes safety stocks more desirable. But high interest rates increase carrying cost and favor smaller inventories. Rapid inflation, however, reduces the real cost of carrying inventory because its value tends to increase along with the price level.[14] In some cases product availability may be the big problem. This is why the purchasing function is so important, especially when sellers allocate products among customers.

Good inventory management can help product managers. Accurate inventory turnover and cost data can help determine which stage of their life cycles products are in. This helps identify declining products, which may make cost elimination possible.

### The Materials Handling Subsystem

**Materials handling** involves the activities of moving products within plants, warehouses, and transportation terminals. High labor costs and new warehousing tools make the selection of materials handling equipment a crucial decision. Tradeoffs exist here also. Using high-stacking equipment increases the usage of cubic capacity in high-ceilinged warehouses, but it may be costly in terms of equipment, extra time needed to move loads, and packaging.

materials
handling

**Handling Efficiency.** The design of warehouses and materials handling equipment should complement each other and be compatible with transportation decisions. Flexibility also is important because of changing equipment technology and changes in the products being handled. Materials handling decisions also must be coordinated with activities performed by outsiders, such as freight carriers and wholesaling middlemen.

Products often must be moved manually between floors in multistory warehouses, whereas single-story warehouses permit greater use of mechanical and automated equipment. Thus many downtown multistory warehouses have been replaced by single-story suburban warehouses. Incoming shipments are checked for damage and to determine if the order has been filled properly before they are moved to storage areas. When an order is received, order picking, assembly, and preparation for shipment are necessary.[15]

Order size decisions are also important in materials handling. Setting minimum order sizes along with a discount structure that encourages

*An ad illustrating the importance of utilizing cubic capacity in a modern warehouse*

Source: Lyon Metal Products, Inc.

customers to place preferred-size orders reduces manual handling.   Orders too small to handle by a fork-lift truck require costly manual handling.

**unitization**

    **Unitization,** or unitizing, is a technique for increasing the efficiency of handling small packages.   The basic idea is that it is easier and cheaper to move one large package than several smaller ones.   Unitization usually involves palletization, or combining several small packages and strapping them to a pallet for movement. In shrink palletizing the entire unit is covered with plastic film. The plastic is heated and then cooled so it shrinks and holds the products together for shipment. Unitized pallets move faster and cheaper than individual items handled separately. Damage and pilferage are also reduced.

**Containerization** is a materials handling system that encloses a shipment of products (perhaps several unitized loads) in a container, seals it, and transports it from shipper to receiver without rehandling the individual products in the container. The container usually is eight feet wide by eight feet high and ranges in length from ten to forty feet. Piggyback, birdyback, and fishyback are examples of containerized freight movement systems. In piggyback, trailers are trucked for short hauls and transferred to rail flatcars for long hauls. Containers are also loaded on cargo planes (birdyback) and aboard ships (fishyback). Containerization cuts transit time, loading and unloading time, handling costs, damage, and theft. It also makes intermodal transportation practical, such as piggyback. We will discuss these concepts again later in this chapter.

containerization

## The Order Processing Subsystem

The accuracy, reliability, and speed with which orders are received, handled, and filled are crucial customer service factors. **Order processing** activities include order receipt, credit approval, invoice preparation, and collection of accounts receivable. These activities also cross departmental lines.

order processing

Fast and accurate filling of orders reduces the time customers must wait to receive shipments. Speed and reliability are important. The more reliable a seller is in meeting delivery dates the better its customers can manage their inventories. This often is a major factor in a buyer's choice of suppliers. Considerable progress is also being made in automating order processing activities.

Coordination between sales and office personnel is a must. The longer salespersons wait to submit orders to office personnel, the less efficient the system becomes. Delays are very serious when supplies are tight and inflation is pushing prices up. Once received in the office, an order must be invoiced quickly, order picking instructions must be sent to the warehouse, and transportation instructions must be sent to the traffic department. Variability in the timing of these activities causes unreliable delivery and customer complaints. P-D managers also should be able to give customers up-to-date information about the status of their order. Customer relations suffer when sellers tell customers they do not know when their shipments will arrive.

## The Transportation Subsystem

Transportation is needed to move raw materials to production points, semimanufactured products among manufacturing points, and finished

*An ad illustrating the importance of coordinating customer service activities with inventory management and production scheduling*

Source: 3M Company.

products to resellers or final buyers. One source reports that "in 1979, U.S. manufacturers spent $209 billion to move goods, an increase of 9% from the previous year and their third-largest expense after labor and materials."[16]

Freight transportation means moving products through time and space (distance). But distance in miles to a market and transportation cost to that market may have little relationship. A shipper on a navigable waterway may pay a railroad the same amount for a 500-mile movement that an inland shipper pays for a 300-mile movement. The inland shipper lacks the option of using barge transportation and cannot use that as leverage in negotiating rates with the railroad. Distance is an economic concept for P-D managers.

Suppose a product must be delivered by truck to a buyer in New Orleans. There are five potential suppliers, one in New Orleans and the others in Houston, Memphis, Atlanta, and Little Rock. The New Orleans supplier is closest to the buyer. But if the buyer is satisfied with second-day delivery and all suppliers can provide this, all are equidistant in terms of time. The ability of the four suppliers to sell to the buyer depends on whether they can meet or beat the New Orleans supplier's delivered price.

**Legal Forms of Transport.** The four legal forms of transport are (1) common carriers, (2) contract carriers, (3) private carriers, and (4) exempt carriers.

**Common carriers** are for-hire carriers that serve the general public on a fee basis without rate or service discrimination. They are regulated by the government. They operate under a government franchise, must accept freight from any shipper, must maintain regular service, and normally need permission to change their routes and rates. Railroads and many truck lines are examples of common carriers.

**common carrier**

**Contract carriers** do not maintain regular routes nor are they regulated as closely by the government. They are for-hire carriers who move freight for shippers under contracts negotiated with them. Rates and services are negotiated between each shipper and the carrier. Some common carriers also engage in contract carriage. Many truck lines and barge companies are contract carriers.

**contract carrier**

**Private carriers** are not for hire. They move their own freight in their own or leased equipment and they are free from rate and service regulation. A firm might undertake private carriage if it moves freight in volumes like those moved by common and contract carriers and if it believes it can provide better service at the same or lower cost. Many oil companies, for example, operate their own fleets of oil tankers. Thus a firm also faces a make-or-buy decision in transporting its products.

**private carrier**

**Exempt carriers** are not regulated. Certain geographic areas are classified by the Interstate Commerce Commission (ICC) as exempt zones within which anyone can perform transport service without rate regulation. Bulk commodities, such as many agricultural products, are exempted specifically from ICC regulation for some carriers, as are some shipper associations, such as agricultural cooperatives.

**exempt carrier**

**Modes of Transportation.** The five **modes of transportation** are (1) railroads, (2) motor carriers, (3) airlines, (4) pipelines, and (5) water carriers.

**modes of transportation**

*Railroads.* Railroads moved most of the freight in the United States during the nineteenth and early twentieth centuries. But when trucks appeared, they began taking away much of the railroads' traffic in manufactured products. As we will see later in this chapter, railroads were

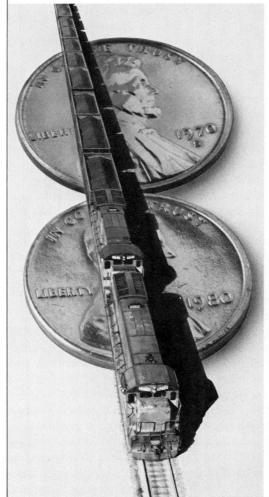

# Myth:
Railroads charge too much to move coal.

# Fact:
Rail costs are a smaller share of the delivered price of coal today than they were 10 years ago.

The United States has enough coal to break our energy dependence on imported oil. Now, when this vital resource is needed more than ever, America's freight railroads are being accused of charging too much to move coal, thus impeding the nation's shift from oil to coal.

Nothing could be further from the truth. Coal prices and electric utility rates have risen much faster than railroad coal rates. Ten years ago, rail transportation charges averaged 39 percent of the delivered price of coal. Today, they average only 25 percent of the delivered price.

Naturally, specific rates may be higher or lower than average depending on such factors as the distance the coal is moved.

America's freight railroads are the most reliable and cost-efficient way to move most coal from where it's mined to where it's needed—to generate electricity and fuel our industries. Today, that's more important than ever.

For more information, write: Coal, Dept. A1, Association of American Railroads, American Railroads Building, Washington, D.C. 20036.

# Surprise:
Railroads move a ton of coal for an average charge of less than 2¢ a mile.

*An ad illustrating the major inherent advantage of rail transportation—low-cost movement of bulk commodities*

Source: Association of American Railroads.

the first mode of transportation to come under federal rate and service regulation. This often placed them at a disadvantage in competing for nonbulk freight. For many years, therefore, railroads focused on moving bulk commodities. Their major inherent advantage has always been low cost, long-haul (over 300 miles) transportation for heavy and bulky commodities that have a relatively low value in relation to weight. Examples are coal, sand, gravel, steel, iron ore, lumber, and grain.

Deregulation in recent years, along with a variety of innovations in equipment, services, and operating procedures, are helping the railroads to increase their traffic in farm products other than grain and manufactured products, as well as bulk commodities. Better service for their customers is the goal of modern railroads. They are targeting their service offering to carefully selected types of shippers, updating equipment, and providing faster service, reduced damage claims, specialized handling equipment and rolling stock, computerized terminals, and automated equipment.

Railroads charge shippers a higher rate per 100 pounds of freight for less-than-carload (l.c.l.) than for car-load (c.l.) shipments. Pool car service, however, enables small shippers to combine (pool) their shipments to fill a rail car. The cargo moves the entire distance at the lower c.l. rate when all shippers' customers are located in the same area. When they are located in different areas the c.l. rate applies all the way to the first customer. Then the shipment is broken down for movement to other customers at the l.c.l. rate. This service helps shippers who are transporting the same basic product. But when different types of products are shipped in the same car, it is called mixed car service. All products move at the rate applicable to the product that has the highest rate, but it is a c.l. rate.

The diversion in transit privilege permits shippers to change the destination of their shipments after the train has left the terminal. A Florida orange grower could send a carload from Florida toward New York City and divert it to Chicago if the Chicago market price for oranges was higher. The shipper pays a small fee for this service but pays the through rate from Florida to Chicago.

The processing in transit privilege is important for agricultural commodities and industrial raw materials that must be moved from source points to intermediate processing points and then to final buyers. If the products are moving in the same general direction (no backtracking), the through rate applies to the entire movement. There are no separate rates for the raw material shipment and the processed products shipment. Grain can move from Washington state to Minneapolis for processing into flour. The flour then moves from Minneapolis to New York. The shipper pays the through rate from Washington state to New York.

Heavy, bulky commodities still provide railroads most of their freight revenues and they are anxious to strengthen their competitive advantage in moving these products. A unit train moves one bulk commodity for one shipper from one point to another without stopping in between. A trainload of coal can be transported from a coal mine directly to an electric generating station. The rail cars may be unloaded by automated devices that do not require the train to come to a complete stop. Once unloaded, the train returns empty to the coal mine for another load. It operates like a giant conveyor belt.

Landbridge service enables railroads to pick up containerized freight from ships in Pacific coast ports and deliver it to ships in Atlantic coast ports for overseas movement. This combination of ship-rail service eliminates time-consuming routing through the Panama Canal and speeds service, reduces receivers' inventory requirements and warehousing costs, and can open new markets to both American- and foreign based firms.

Aerated cars haul dry bulk cargoes like flour, cement, and plastic pellets. They operate on the vacuum cleaner principle and "inhale" their cargo when loading and "exhale" it when unloading, thereby eliminating the need for packaging. Snowy freight cars have a 2-inch coating of foam insulation that keeps pre-cooled perishable products at the desired temperature enroute without ice or expensive mechanical refrigeration devices, thereby helping railroads to increase their freight in perishable products like fruits and vegetables. Hot slab gondola cars haul slabs of hot steel from steel plants to rolling mills, in effect, making rail service a part of the steel industry's production line. Enclosed auto rack cars are fully enclosed or shielded bi-level and tri-level auto-rack cars to protect new automobiles from vandalism and theft of parts while enroute by rail from factories to dealers throughout the country. Railroads now haul more than half the traffic in new autos.

*Motor Carriers.* The major inherent advantages of trucks are speed and flexibility, especially for small loads over short distances. The interstate highway system provides very direct truck connections between many cities. Automated terminals, team driving (which reduces downtime on the road), and mechanical handling equipment help in providing speedier service.

If 50 tons of grain are transported 100 miles, the total movement is 5,000 ton-miles. Truck lines typically receive more revenue per tonmile than railroads because trucks move more high-value manufactured products and their operating costs per ton-mile generally are higher.

Trucks also benefit from intermodal carriage, especially piggyback. With fishyback, loaded trailers are trucked to ports and loaded onto barges or ships. The trailers are off-loaded at the destination port and trucked to a receiving terminal for distribution.

Some firms can penetrate new market areas with truck transportation. Retailers and wholesalers can also operate with smaller inventories when speedy transportation is available. Faster transportation reduces the need for products in the distribution pipeline.

*Air Freight.* The volume of air freight has increased greatly in recent years but still accounts for less than 1 percent of total ton-miles shipped in intercity commerce. (See Table 16–3.) Air freight is the highest quality type of transportation available. Speedy service is the major advantage but air freight also exposes cargo to less potential for damage, pilferage, deterioration, and obsolescence.

Fashion merchandise, fragile and highly perishable products, emergency shipments, and expensive and intricate industrial products account for the bulk of air freight. Shipper acceptance of the total cost concept

**Table 16–3.** *Estimated distribution of United States intercity freight traffic for selected years, in billions of ton-miles*

| Carrier | Billions of Ton-miles 1980 | Percentage of Total | | | | |
|---|---|---|---|---|---|---|
| | | 1980 | 1970 | 1960 | 1950 | 1929 |
| Railroads | 932 | 37.3 | 39.8 | 44.1 | 56.2 | 74.9 |
| Trucks | 565 | 22.6 | 21.3 | 21.7 | 16.3 | 3.3 |
| Great Lakes | 113 | 4.6 | 5.9 | 7.6 | 10.5 | 16.0 |
| Rivers and canals | 307 | 12.3 | 10.5 | 9.2 | 4.9 | 1.4 |
| Oil pipeline | 575 | 23.0 | 22.3 | 17.4 | 12.1 | 4.4 |
| Air | 5 | 0.2 | 0.2 | — | — | — |
| Totals | 2,497 | 100.0 | 100.0 | 100.0 | 100.0 | 100.0 |

Source: *Yearbook of Railroad Facts.*

Note: Ocean coastal traffic between United States ports is not included above. Also, *intracity* freight traffic is not included. Because trucks move the great bulk of intracity freight volume, the table above understates the importance of trucks in the total freight picture.

of P-D has benefited air freight a great deal. Although it is the most expensive mode in terms of rates, overall distribution costs may be reduced by using air freight.[17] The low damage factor may mean lower packing and insurance costs. Air freight may also enable a firm to close some distant warehouses that are costly to operate. Without it, some products might be impossible to market in some areas. Live Maine lobsters and Hawaiian orchids would have more limited geographical markets. Cargo Air Lines, Ltd. (C.A.L.) was set up in 1976 by Israeli farmers to transport their fruit and vegetables to European markets. The firm leases the planes. On return trips to Israel the planes are loaded with European products. C.A.L.'s rates run only about 2 percent higher than sea rates from Europe to Israel.[18]

*Pipelines.* Pipelines, the most invisible mode of transportation, are second only to railroads in ton-miles of intercity freight. Pipelines are used mainly to transport natural gas, crude petroleum, and petroleum products from production fields to refineries. From there, these products usually move to consumption points by ships, barges, railroads, and trucks. Intermodal transfer often is necessary because the economics of pipeline operation limit the area that can be served directly by the pipeline. Natural gas, of course, is piped from production fields to distributors in local market areas.

Service is very dependable because pipelines are not affected much by weather and labor strikes. Pipelines are the least labor-intensive mode and maintenance expenses are low. Pipeline technology also is advancing. Batch processing permits movement of different products in the same pipeline. This increases pipeline utilization and helps keep rates down. Another innovation is the slurry pipeline. Coal, for ex-

# 9,436 miles and they didn't crack under the strain.

Recently, an outside source ran a secret test to find out whether Western's Cargo Coddlers really coddle cargo as well as we say.

They took two dozen fresh eggs and packed them in one of our regular Speedpak containers. Then they shipped the Speedpak from Los Angeles to Seattle to Anchorage to Seattle to Los Angeles to Miami and back to Los Angeles. Total miles: 9,436. Approximate number of Cargo Coddlers who handled the Speedpak en route: 45.

The Speedpak was then opened before a blue ribbon audience of Western executives. The result? Not one broken egg. Not even a crack. Proof Western AirCargo people are exactly as advertised — cargo coddlers.

If you want that kind of coddling for your cargo, call the Cargo Coddlers. They're crackerjacks, not crackers. And we've got the proof.

**Western AirCargo**
Hawaii/Alaska/Western USA/Florida/Canada/Mexico

*An ad illustrating the high quality of air freight*
Source: Western Airlines.

ample, is pulverized into a powder and mixed with water for pipeline movement.

Probably the most famous pipeline is the 800-mile Alyeska line, which moves crude oil from Prudhoe Bay oil fields in northern Alaska to the city of Valdez in southern Alaska. Environmentalists' questions about potential for leaks and damage to the permafrost had to be answered before it went into operation in 1978.

*Water Transportation.* Water transportation is the oldest mode. Two types of water carriers are ocean vessels and barges. Ocean vessels move freight in international commerce, on the Great Lakes, and between ports in the United States. The volume of coastal traffic between American ports has declined since World War II largely because of diversion of much of that traffic to railroads.

Towboats and tugboats move barges on inland waterways. This traffic has grown slowly but steadily during recent decades. The major inherent advantage is low cost for low-value bulk commodities. Because that is also true for railroads, there is a lot of competition between barges and railroads for moving products such as coal, petroleum products, and steel. Barges also compete with pipelines for moving crude petroleum and petroleum products.

Barges, like railroads, can realize considerable economies of scale. The extra fuel cost incurred in adding several more rail cars behind a locomotive or several more barges to a towboat or tugboat is small relative to the extra freight revenues that can be earned.

Modern barge lines use specialized barges like covered-hopper, dehumidified, and refrigerated barges to move products that used to be unsuited to barge movement. Most barge traffic is also unregulated because of the high incidence of private carriage and the exemption from Interstate Commerce Commission (ICC) regulation of common carriers that haul exempted bulk commodities.

Containerization also affects water transportation. Loaded trailers often move by truck and/or rail to port cities where they are fishybacked on containerships to overseas ports. Loaded barges are towed on inland waterways to ocean port cities where they are lifted or floated onto barge-carrying ocean vessels. The barges are off-loaded at overseas ports and towed on the inland waterways to receivers. These ships can load and unload their cargo in less than twenty-four hours, whereas conventional cargo ships usually spend half their time in port discharging and taking on cargo. (See Table 16–4.)

Barge transportation is the lowest-cost method of moving some bulk commodities, but it is slow and subject to seasonal interruption. Service on some waterways stops in the winter because of ice. Thus some steel producers barge iron ore from supply points to their mills during good weather and store it there for use year-round. When the storage costs are less than the transportation savings, the total cost of distribution is reduced.

Unless shipper and receiver are located on navigable waterways, intermodal transfer is necessary. Thus a lot of barge traffic involves joint movement by barge-rail and barge-pipeline. Sometimes all three modes are combined for a coordinated barge-rail-pipeline movement.

**Supplementary Carriers.** The P-D manager also may use supple-

**Table 16–4.** *Cost and quality of the different modes of transportation*

| Cost and Quality Factors | Rail | Truck | Air | Pipe-line | Water (ocean & inland) |
|---|---|---|---|---|---|
| Transportation cost | medium | high | highest | low | lowest |
| Door-to-door transit time | medium | fast | fastest | slow | slowest |
| Dependability in meeting schedules | medium | good | very good | best | fair |
| Scope of products economically transportable | broad | medium | narrow | narrowest | broad |
| Major inherent advantages | low cost for long hauls of bulk com-modities | speed and door-to-door ser-vice | fastest and highest quality transport | low-cost, dependable transpor-tation | low cost for long hauls of bulk com-modities |
| Necessity of inter-modal transfer for door-to-door transit | often* | no | practi-cally always | often* | often* |
| Ability to reach shippers over widespread areas | very good | best | very good | very limited | very limited |
| Products ideally suited to move-ment | low-value bulk commod-ities | high-value manu-factured products | high-value perish-able products | petroleum natural gas | low-value bulk com-modities |

*Except when shipper and receiver are located on rail spurs (for rails); when they are connected by pipeline (for pipeline); when they are located on navigable waterways (for water carriers).

mentary carriers, mainly for small shipments. These include (1) freight forwarders, (2) the United States Postal Service, (3) United Parcel Service (UPS), (4) bus service, and (5) shipper cooperatives.

**freight forwarder**    Common carriers who sell the services of railroads, airlines, water carriers, and truckers are called **freight forwarders.** They do not own transportation equipment except perhaps pick-up and delivery trucks. They pick up less-than-truckload (l.t.l.) or less-than-carload (l.c.l.) ship-ments at their customers' plants or warehouses, consolidate them into truckload or carload shipments, and arrange for delivery at destination points. Their margin is the difference between the l.t.l. or l.c.l. rates they charge their customer and the t.l. or c.l. rates they pay to the carrier. They may also make special charges for service extras. Forwarders serve as their customers' traffic manager and secure better transportation ser-vice for them.

Foreign freight forwarders are important in international marketing. Many exporters rely on them to handle their export documentation problems and to deliver their products to overseas customers. They handle roughly 75 percent of all the general cargo that leaves United States ports.

The U.S. Postal Service handles a large volume of freight through its parcel post service and also offers Express Mail, a next-day delivery service. Retailers and wholesalers, for example, often mail merchandise to their customers. United Parcel Service (UPS) is privately owned and offers shippers pick-up service. But its service areas are more limited than the Postal Service's. Bus service is provided by intercity bus lines, such as Greyhound and Trailways. They transport a large volume of small packages.

Shippers' cooperatives are somewhat like freight forwarders. The members set up a facility to collect their shipments and hire a local pick-up carrier to move the products to a terminal for loading. At the destination terminal, the products are picked up and delivered to customers by local pick-up carriers. Each shipper's share in the cooperative's transportation bill is based on its shipment's percentage of total weight.

**Transportation Rates.** Transportation traditionally has been a heavily regulated industry. The first regulatory commission in the United States, the Interstate Commerce Commission (ICC), was created in 1887 to regulate railroads. Later, pipelines, motor carriers, and inland water carriers were brought under ICC regulation. Other regulatory bodies include the Federal Maritime Commission and the Civil Aeronautics Board. Regulation covers rates and services.

Transportation regulation has been a controversial issue. Some people believe that the various regulatory agencies should be replaced by one superagency; some others favor doing away with regulation entirely. In very recent years, considerable deregulation has taken place, beginning with the airlines in 1978. Subsequent deregulation has focused on trucks and railroads. The goal is to spark greater intermodal and intramodal competition by reducing or eliminating rate and service regulation.

Many shippers audit their freight bills to make sure they are not being overcharged. Some have internal freight bill auditors. Others use outside specialists who do the job for a percentage share in any rebates they get for their clients on carrier overcharges. New computer service businesses are building data banks of freight rates that consider all possible combinations of origins, destinations, products, weight, and type of carrier to help their clients save on freight bills.

Modern P-D managers are alert to opportunities to cut freight costs. Perhaps a minor change in a product item or package design will result in lower freight rates. Detailed cost studies also may show that another mode, private carriage, or changing warehouse locations would reduce the freight bill.


## ORGANIZING FOR P-D

Unless top management implements the total P-D concept, P-D activities will tend to be spread among different departments. No single executive is likely to be accountable for managing the firm's P-D activities, including coordinating them within the channel system and keeping an eye on costs and customer service.

Implementing the total P-D concept in a firm is similar to implementing the marketing concept.[19] It takes time and may require change in the organization's structure.[20] There is no one best way of organizing to implement the total P-D concept. Some firms create a manager of P-D who reports directly to the marketing manager and is accountable for coordinating all P-D activities. Other firms, however, may want to elevate the P-D executive's status. He or she may report directly to the firm's chief executive officer. Thus the marketing manager and the manager of P-D are coequal.


## SUMMARY AND LOOK AHEAD

Physical distribution, or logistics, involves moving raw materials from their sources into manufacturing plants; moving these materials, semi-manufactured products, and finished products within plants and among warehouses; and moving finished products to middlemen and/or final buyers. P-D activities include transportation, warehousing, materials handling, inventory control, plant and warehouse location, order processing, customer service, market forecasting, and protective packaging. Implementing the total P-D concept is the key to integrating and coordinating these activities. The total P-D concept views P-D activities from a systems perspective. The goal is to set a desired level of customer service and minimize the cost of providing it. The total cost concept, the cost tradeoff concept, and the optimization concept underlie the total P-D concept.

The total cost concept advocates taking a broad view of the total cost of performing P-D activities. The cost tradeoff concept recognizes that cost increases for performing some P-D activities may be desirable if they lead to lower overall P-D costs because of the cost savings possible in performing other P-D activities. Optimizing total P-D performance takes precedence over optimizing the performance of each separate activity.

The unifying goal of the various P-D subsystems is to develop and maintain a steady flow of products. Storage is desirable when it adds time utility to products, however. Effective warehousing reduces the costs of unnecessary storage, such as excess working capital tied up in inventory. It enables firms to coordinate their production and sales. Plant location, warehouse location, and warehouse ownership are important decisions. The warehousing subsystem is crucial when plants and markets are separated by great distances.

A firm can concentrate its inventory of finished products at the plant, at one centralized warehouse, at numerous warehouses located throughout its market area, or at a smaller number of larger warehouses called distribution centers. Warehousing strategy also involves an investment decision. Privately owned branch warehouses require a firm to invest in building and operating warehouses. Public warehousing is an attractive alternative to many firms because they pay only for the space they use.

Inventory management's goal is to minimize the working capital tied up in inventory while providing the specified level of customer service. The two major costs here are carrying cost and ordering cost. Carrying cost goes up as the order size increases while ordering cost decreases as the order size increases.

Materials handling involves moving products within plants, warehouses, and transportation terminals. Unitization and containerization help reduce P-D costs. Order processing activities include order receipt, credit approval, invoice preparation, and collection of accounts receivable. Efficient performance builds customer satisfaction and enhances the firm's image.

In P-D, distance is an economic concept. The four legal forms of transport are common, contract, private, and exempt carriers. The five modes are rail, truck, air, pipeline, and water carrier. Railroads are most important in ton-miles of intercity traffic. Each mode, however, has its relative advantages. Intermodal service, such as piggyback, birdyback, and fishyback, improves service to shippers because it combines the advantages of two or more modes.

Like the marketing concept itself, the total P-D concept has its effects on the firm's organizational structure. Some firms have created new executive-level positions staffed by P-D professionals.

In the next section we will study promotion—the third element in the firm's marketing mix.

## REVIEW QUESTIONS

**1.** Explain the growing importance of P-D management.

**2.** How does the total P-D concept differ in perspective from traffic management?

**3.** What goal underlies the total cost concept of P-D?

**4.** Give two examples of possible cost tradeoffs in P-D management.

**5.** What problems might a firm encounter in trying to optimize overall P-D performance?

**6.** Why is total, system-wide P-D planning easier for a vertically integrated firm?

**7.** Why might storage of products be necessary?

**8.** What is a distribution center?

**9.** Why would a firm use public warehouses?

**10.** What is inventory carrying cost? What is its relationship to order size?

**11.** What is ordering cost? What is its relationship to order size?

**12.** Define: (a) basic stock, (b) safety stock, and (c) seasonal stock.

**13.** How can unitization and containerization improve materials handling efficiency?

**14.** Give examples of order processing activities.

**15.** Identify and define the four legal forms of transport.

**16.** Identify the five modes of transportation and the relative advantages of each.

**17.** Why are l.c.l. and l.t.l. freight rates higher per unit of product moved than c.l. and t.l. rates?

**18.** What is intermodal transportation service? Give three examples.

**19.** What is a freight forwarder?

## DISCUSSION QUESTIONS

**1.** What is the significance of the flow concept of P-D?

**2.** How might a firm's implementation of the marketing concept affect its management of P-D activities?

**3.** How might rising energy costs affect private carriage?

**4.** Large supermarkets offer low prices on products purchased by the truckload or railcar load directly from the manufacturer. Will this practice become more common among other retailers and wholesalers as they try to hold prices down?

## NOTES

1. See Bert Rosenbloom, "Using Physical Distribution Strategy for Better Channel Management," *Journal of the Academy of Marketing Science*, Winter–Spring, 1979, pp. 61–70.

2. See Arthur M. Geoffrian, "Better Distribution Planning with Computer Models," *Harvard Business Review*, July–August, 1976, pp. 92–99; Ronald H. Ballow, "Computer Models in Transportation-Distribution," *Transportation Journal*, Winter, 1976, pp. 72–85; Stephen K. Keiser and Robert L. Paretta, "Quantitative Aids and Physical Distribution Management: A Study of Current Practice," *Transportation Journal*, Fall, 1977, pp. 67–72; Francis J. Quinn, "A Worldwide, Computerized Network," *Traffic Management International*, Spring, 1978, pp. 21–25; and Jack W. Farrell, "Computerization: A Whole New Ball Game," *Traffic Management*, June, 1978, pp. 26–28, 31–32.

3. "Saving Money When Freight Rates Are Computerized," *Business Week*, February 25, 1980, p. 114.

4. See James L. Heskett, "Logistics—Essential to Strategy," *Harvard Business Review*, November–December, 1977, pp. 83–96.

5. See William D. Perreault, Jr. and Frederick A. Russ, "Physical Distribution Service: A Neglected Aspect of Marketing Management," *MSU Business Topics*, Summer, 1974, pp. 37–45. For discussion of the energy problem's impact on physical distribution management, see Barbara J. Bagley and S. Lynn Diamond, "The Energy Problem: Short-term Solutions, Long-range Plans," *Traffic Management*, April, 1978, pp. 27–35, 38–40, 42–45; Douglas M. Lambert and James R. Stock, "Physical Distribution and Consumer Demands," *MSU Business Topics*, Spring, 1978, pp. 49–56; and James R. Stock, "The Energy/Ecology Impacts on Distribution," *International Journal of Physical Distribution and Materials Management*, 1978, pp. 249–283.

6. "New Distribution Strategies Needed to Combat Skyrocketing Energy Costs," *Marketing News*, February 8, 1980, p. 14.

7. See Douglas M. Lambert, James F. Robeson, and James R. Stock, "An Appraisal of the Integrated Physical Distribution Management Concept," *International Journal of Physical Distribution and Materials Management*, 1978, pp. 74–87.

8. See Robert Lekashman and John F. Stolle, "The Total Cost Approach to Distribution," *Business Horizons*, Winter, 1965, pp. 33–46. In one survey it was found that 83 percent of the responding firms were operating their physical distribution activities within the total cost concept. See D. L. Bates and John E. Dillard, Jr., "Physical Distribution: Current Application of Theory," *Transportation Journal*, Winter, 1975, pp. 28–30.

9. For fuller discussion of the customer service aspect of physical distribution, see William D. Perreault and Frederick A. Russ, "Quantifying Marketing Tradeoffs in Physical Distribution Policy Decisions," *Decision Sciences*, April, 1976, pp. 186–201.

10. "New Distribution Strategies Needed to Combat Skyrocketing Energy Costs," *Marketing News*, February 8, 1980, p. 14.

11. See C. G. Chentnik, "Storage in PDM," *Transportation & Distribution Management*, July–August, 1975, pp. 42–46.

12. See Kenneth B. Ackerman and Bernard J. LaLonde, "Making Warehousing More Efficient," *Harvard Business Review*, March–April, 1980, pp. 94–102.

13. For discussion of the effect on required inventory of an increase in the in-stock service level, see Warren Blanding, "Logistical Ineptness as an Alternative to Regulation," *Transportation & Distribution Management*, March–April, 1976, pp. 18–20, 49. For discussion of an approach to quantifying the cost of

failing to maintain in-stock service levels, see Harvey N. Shycon and Christopher R. Sprague, "Put a Price Tag on Your Customer Servicing Levels," *Harvard Business Review*, July–August, 1975, pp. 71–78.

14. Inflation, however, has increased dramatically the potential cost savings from using sophisticated inventory models. See James Don Edwards and Roger A. Roemmich, "Scientific Inventory Management," *MSU Business Topics*, Autumn, 1975, pp. 41–46.

15. Order picking involves taking products from their storage areas in warehouses upon receipt of orders for their shipment. A lot of progress has been made in automating this activity. See Richard L. Speaker, "The Basics of Bulk Order Picking," *Transportation & Distribution Management*, September–October, 1975, pp. 40–44.

16. "Saving Money When Freight Rates Are Computerized," *Business Week*, February 25, 1980, p. 111.

17. See James Hulbert and John Binkley, "Selling Strategy and Air Freight Decisions," *Transportation Journal*, Summer, 1977, pp. 61–69.

18. "Non-profit Israeli Airfreight Company Thrives," *Traffic Management*, June, 1978, p. 22.

19. See David P. Herran, "Managing Physical Distribution for Profit," *Harvard Business Review*, May–June, 1979, pp. 121–132.

20. See Les Cisneros and Colin Barrett, "Within the Management Structure," *Distribution Worldwide*, June, 1978, pp. 40–46.

# Section VI
# **Promotion**

Promotion is communication by an organization with its many publics. These publics include present and potential customers, employees, suppliers, creditors, rival firms, special interest groups, and government. Promotion is an important part of a marketing strategy and includes professional selling, advertising, sales promotion, and public relations and publicity. A successful promotion effort must be geared to the target groups the firm is trying to communicate with. It also must be guided by specific objectives, planned carefully, and evaluated in terms of accomplishing those objectives.

Chapter 17 describes the communication process, the elements of promotion, factors that influence the promotion mix, and how the promotion effort is managed. Sales promotion and public relations and publicity are discussed in detail.

Chapter 18 discusses professional selling. This is personal promotion.

Chapter 19 examines advertising. This is mass selling. There is no face-to-face contact between a salesperson and a prospective buyer.

# Planning and Managing the Promotion Effort

OBJECTIVES
*After reading this chapter you should be able to*

1. give a model of the communication process and discuss its elements.

2. give examples of the goals of promotional activities.

3. identify the elements of the promotion mix.

4. give examples of sales promotion directed to consumers, company salespersons, middlemen, and dealer salesforces.

5. identify several approaches to evaluating sales promotion effectiveness.

6. distinguish between public relations and publicity.

7. identify several approaches to evaluating the effectiveness of publicity.

8. describe the factors that determine the promotion mix.

9. identify and discuss the activities involved in managing the promotion effort.

10. identify and discuss several methods for determining the promotion budget.

KEY CONCEPTS
*Look for these terms as you read the chapter:*
Communication
Message
Communication Channel
Receiver
Feedback
Noise
Promotion Mix
Advertising
Professional Selling
Sales Promotion
Coupons
Cents-Off Offers
Samples
Money-Refund Offers
Premiums
Consumer Contests
Consumer Sweepstakes
Additional Product Deals
Trading Stamps
Consumer Exhibitions
Sales Contests
Point-of-Purchase Displays
Dealer Contests And Premiums
Public Relations
Publicity
Push Philosophy
Pull Philosophy
Gravity
Promotion Campaign

*Effective promotion effort requires planning and management. Part of the effort involves research.*

*Consider a recent survey conducted by Benton & Bowles, Inc., a New York–based advertising agency. The mail survey, entitled "Men's Changing Role in the Family of the '80s," revealed that, of the men sampled, 32 percent shop for food; 74 percent take out the garbage; 47 percent cook for the family; 53 percent wash the dishes; 29 percent do the laundry; 28 percent clean the bathroom; 39 percent vacuum the house; and 80 percent take care of the children (in households with children under age twelve).*

*Based upon the survey results, Benton & Bowles expects, for example, that recipe ads may appear in magazines like* Esquire *and* Playboy *and television commercials for dishwashing detergents may appear on Monday Night Football. Ads for household products also are likely to portray men in domestic roles.* [*]

Companies communicate with people whether they try to or not. Anything visible, such as salespersons' behavior, store location, and the product's physical form tells something about the firm. Customers also tell others about their experiences with the firm and its products. A firm could decide to ignore the communication process and focus solely on developing and producing products. But it probably would find that many people would be unaware of the firm and its products; others probably would have distorted ideas about what the firm does or the qualities of its products. Many people who could use the firm's products, therefore, would not buy them. This is why most firms try to control the communications about themselves and their products.

Promotion is the communication efforts of manufacturers, middlemen, or nonprofit organizations. It is one of the four marketing mix elements that a firm uses in marketing its products.

In this chapter we will discuss how the communication process works, the purposes of marketing communications, the factors that influence it, and the various types of promotion. Sales promotion and public relations and publicity are emphasized.

## HOW COMMUNICATION WORKS

communication

**Communication** is the process of influencing others' behavior by sharing ideas, information, or feelings with them. Figure 17–1 shows the basic elements in the communication process.

### The Source

The source is the sender of the message. For example, Procter & Gamble is the source of many ads on TV during daytime TV dramas (soap operas).

---

[*] "Large Numbers of Husbands Buy Household Products, Do Housework," *Marketing News*, October 3, 1980, pp. 1, 3.

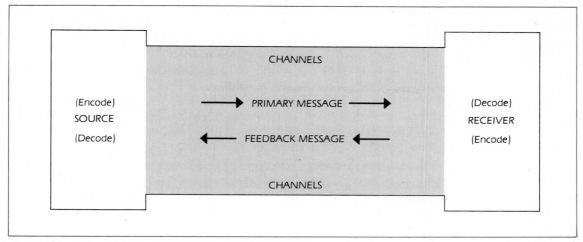

**Figure 17–1. Elements of the communication process**

Effective communication requires the source to (1) identify the intended receiver's characteristics and what change in behavior is desired, (2) formulate the message and place it in a form the receiver can interpret (encoding), (3) select the channel(s) that can best reach the receiver and carry the message, and (4) interpret feedback from the receiver (decoding) and determine what changes may be needed to improve the communication process. Who the intended receiver is and how well the source knows the intended receiver affect how the source does these things.

## The Message

**Messages** are made up of symbols that represent objects or experience. Most symbols, like words, can have more than one meaning. Thus symbols selected for messages usually should be familiar to intended receivers and arranged in the simplest structure possible. Several years ago the California Milk Advisory Board ran ads in magazines featuring a young woman in sportswear. The ad talked about "the milk-white look" in fashion and the virtues of drinking milk. Consumer, women's, and black groups complained that the ads presented women as racist sex objects and the theme was replaced by "Time for milk."[1]

*message*

## The Communication Channel

**A communication channel** is anything that will carry a message; salespersons, TV, and radio are examples. They vary in the amount of information they carry and the people they reach. A salesperson can communicate a greater volume of more complex information to a receiver than an ad on TV. He or she also communicates with one person who may be carefully selected as a good prospect to buy. TV reaches a far greater number of people, some of whom may not be good prospects to buy. Effective channels reach intended receivers and carry the message.

*communication channel*

The primary communication channel is the channel selected to carry the message. But secondary channels also may carry information. The salesperson's voice is the primary channel in a personal selling situation, but the salesperson's nonverbal behavior (body language) also gives the prospect considerable information. Secondary channels can reinforce or destroy the primary channel's message. The salesperson's body language, for example, may indicate to the prospect that the salesperson really does not believe the claims he or she is making for the product.

### The Receiver

receiver

The **receiver,** a potential customer perhaps, is an active participant in communication who (1) on the basis of knowledge and experiences assigns meanings to (decodes) messages received and (2) reacts to the decoded meaning by asking questions, making comments, or buying. It is impossible to communicate with someone who is unwilling and/or unable to decode your message. The meanings a receiver assigns to a message depend on many factors, such as the message's relationship to the receiver's goals, competing messages, previous experiences, and how accurately the message was received. Pert shampoo ads in 1980 discussed the product's benefits in allowing one's hair to bounce and also behave. That message would have been difficult for consumers in the 1950s to decode because the most popular hair styles required that hair be held rigidly in place.

### Feedback

feedback

How a receiver reacts to the meaning he or she assigns to a message is called **feedback.** Feedback, the second stage of communication, flows from the receiver back to the source. It can occur only if the source is geared to receive it.

Feedback often is hard to interpret because it is not necessarily meant to communicate to the source. But it does suggest what changes are needed to improve the communication process. Field sales reports, inquiries to ads, consumer research, and sales figures are sources of feedback for marketers. Whirlpool's Cool-Line enables users of its products to call the company for information about Whirlpool appliances. A growing number of marketers are recognizing the value of this type of feedback and are establishing channels to encourage and receive it.

### Noise

noise

Ineffective communication often is attributed to noise. **Noise is anything that interferes with the communication process.** Vacuum cleaner salespersons in department stores must contend with other instore activities that distract prospects' attention when making product demonstrations. Door-to-door salespersons do not have to contend with these instore distractions but must cope with in-house distractions. Ads prepared without an understanding of consumer concerns about a product can create noise. Ads for microwave ovens that stress short cooking time are not received well by people concerned about radiation leakage.

A receiver's assigned meanings to symbols also may be different from what the source intended because of differences in their backgrounds. This is especially true in promoting ethnic products. Different messages carried through primary and secondary channels also confuse receivers. A restaurant may stress wholesome food in its ads. But a person who eats there and smells mildewed carpets will doubt the wholesomeness of the food.

## GOALS OF PROMOTIONAL ACTIVITIES

A firm's promotional goals depend on its specific situation. One goal of a new firm might be "to develop consumer and middleman awareness of the firm and its products." This is a very general, long-run goal. A more specific and useful statement might be "to develop consumer and middleman awareness of the firm so that at least 50 percent of them will know who we are and what we have to offer by the end of our first two years in business." Another of its objectives may be short run in nature, "to achieve a monthly sales volume of $100,000 on product X within the next six months."

Like the overall marketing objectives, promotion objectives should be stated clearly and specifically and a time frame should be given for their accomplishment. Otherwise, there is no basis for determining when to begin an evaluation of promotional effectiveness or upon what bases to evaluate performance. The role of each promotion mix element in achieving the objectives also should be stated specifically.

Table 17–1 lists several generalized statements of promotion objectives. In practice, they would be stated more specifically along the lines we discussed above. These objectives are discussed in the following paragraphs.

### Creating Awareness

All firms want to make target customers aware of the firm and/or its products. People cannot include unknown brands on their deficits lists

**Table 17–1.** *Examples of generalized promotion objectives*

1. To create target customer awareness of the firm and/or its products.
2. To provide information to target customers.
3. To explain company actions to people outside the market target.
4. To induce people to try products.
5. To induce middlemen to stock and push a product.
6. To retain loyal customers.
7. To increase the amount or frequency of product usage by present and new users.
8. To help the firm learn who its customers are and/or what they think of the firm or product.
9. To reduce sales fluctuations.

(see Chapter 4), nor will they gather information about unknown brands. Every year many firms go out of business simply because target customers never hear about them or what they have to offer. Product awareness also can play a major role in distribution strategy. Wholesaling middlemen, for example, are unwilling to stock products that are unknown to retailers, consumers, and/or industrial buyers.

### Providing Information

Consumers, middlemen, and industrial buyers often want specific information about complex products—construction, ingredients, and uses. Marketers must provide informative ads about the firm, product warranty, and service facilities. Informative ads, brochures, folders, and store demonstrations also help inform target customers about changes in well-accepted products, packaging, or brand name. BankAmericard's change to Visa, and Master Charge's change to MasterCard are examples. If information is unavailable or not usable, the brand may not be considered for purchase, especially when usable information is available about other brands.

### Explaining Company Actions

Companies often must explain their actions to people who feel those actions affect their welfare. Failure to do this can lead to misinterpretation, distrust, or open hostility. The nuclear accident at Three Mile Island several years ago resulted in some loss of public confidence in nuclear energy. It had a very direct effect on firms that use nuclear plants to generate electricity and firms that build the plants. Oil companies and electric and gas utilities spend a lot of money telling the public what they are doing to cope with dwindling energy supplies. Firms with common interests often form associations to plan and finance these communications efforts. The National Association of Manufacturers and the National Association of Appliance Manufacturers are trade associations that explain their members' activities to the general public.[2]

### Inducing Product Trials

A lot of promotion seeks to induce people to try products. The aim is to motivate rather than inform market targets. Getting action rather than awareness often requires different promotional appeals. Coupons, reduced prices, samples, and contests are examples of efforts that can help in getting people to make trial purchases. When Chrysler Corporation was on the brink of bankruptcy several years ago it started referring to itself as "The New Chrysler Corporation" to convince people it was a changed company. Part of the problem was its reputation among some consumers for allegedly making poorly engineered, gas-guzzling cars.

### Inducing Middlemen to Stock a Product

Wholesalers and their salesforces must be persuaded that consumer demand exists or can be stimulated. Retailers also want information on

ONE OF THE LARGEST
BANKS IN THE WORLD
IS TAKING A NEW PATH
TO INTERCEPT THE FUTURE.

Historic symbol of Bankers Trust—The pyramid atop our Wall Street building.

## WHAT WE DID AND WHY.

We have concentrated the entire resources of our world-class bank in four major financial areas. They are wholesale commercial banking, fiduciary services, money and securities markets, and corporate financial services.

We chose these core businesses because they represent our special strengths. Now we are dedicated to expanding and developing them even further. To the highest degree.

We have also decided to focus our strongest capabilities on selected markets. That way we can readily coordinate and bring to bear all four of our core businesses on a customer's requirements.

We have reorganized Bankers Trust and redefined its priorities because (while it is tempting to think otherwise) one bank, no matter how large, can no longer be all things to all customers.

If the requirements of business today suggest a specialized cluster of complementary banking services, the pressures of tomorrow will demand it.

We have always been structured to meet our customers' current needs. Now we are structured to meet their needs of tomorrow as well.

Bankers Trust
Company
Worldwide

With wholly owned subsidiaries in Canada:
B.T. Capital Services Ltd., Toronto
B.T. Financial Services Ltd.,
Toronto and Vancouver

Headquarters at 280 Park Avenue, New York, N.Y. 10017
International Banking Subsidiaries in the United States: Chicago, Houston, Los Angeles and Miami. Overseas Branches:
LONDON, BIRMINGHAM, MILAN, PARIS, TOKYO, SEOUL, SINGAPORE, BAHRAIN, NASSAU and PANAMA CITY.
An International Banking Network of branches, subsidiaries, affiliates and representative offices in over 30 countries on 6 continents.

Member Federal Deposit Insurance Corporation © Bankers Trust Company

*An ad explaining a company's actions*

Source: Bankers Trust Company.

the promotion efforts manufacturers and wholesalers will undertake to stimulate consumer demand. Communicating with middlemen requires different information and appeals than communicating with final buyers because middlemen buy for resale. They want to know about cooperative advertising arrangements in which manufacturers share promotion costs with middlemen, replacement of stale stock, shelf space requirements, point-of-purchase displays, and historical sales data.

### Retaining Loyal Customers

Marketers must communicate regularly with customers who use their brands to discourage brand switching. As we saw in Chapter 5, consumers often tend to generalize their experiences with one brand to other brands in the product category. Thus the leading brand may become a generic name. Consumers also tend to get tired of using the same brand and will try new brands. Both situations require the marketer to (1) remind customers that the brand is still available, (2) show customers that the brand's benefits are superior to those of rivals, (3) reinforce the brand name's cueing function (see Chapter 5) through discrimination training, (4) inform customers of changes in the brand that make it better than rivals, and (5) offer added values for using the brand, such as T-shirts, sailboats, drink coolers, or bar sets.

### Increasing Amount and Frequency of Use

Insurance company and savings and loan association ads tell us how much life insurance and savings we should have at different income levels and stages in the family life cycle. They are seeking to stimulate light users to use more. Ads encouraging people to drink orange juice at nonbreakfast meals and use breakfast cereals as party snacks also seek to induce more frequent use. Individually packaged servings of Kellogg's cereals and two-tablet dosages of Alka-Seltzer help ensure consumers will use the full amount each time they use the product. As we saw in Chapter 10, Arm & Hammer has been very successful in finding new uses for baking soda, and Johnson & Johnson appeals to adults to use its baby shampoo and baby powder.

### Learning about Customers

Magazine ads sometimes include direct response coupons that help the advertiser determine whether a given magazine reaches target customers and possible market segments that have been overlooked. Follow-up letters and questionnaires to present customers also help marketers learn more about their customers. These communications have both research and promotional goals and may be a joint effort of a firm's marketing research and advertising departments. The same is true of warranty cards that accompany many consumer products. A new Konica camera comes with a card that requests information about the purchaser and place of purchase. The buyer does not have to return the card for warranty purposes but the information requested helps Konica to learn more about its final buyers.

### Reducing Sales Fluctuations

Some firms market products that have fluctuating demand patterns. Sales may vary from day to day, week to week, or month to month.

Sometimes sales are affected by climate, season, and holidays. This can create problems with production scheduling, shipping, inventory management, and financial and personnel requirements.

Some resort hotels promote heavily in their off-seasons to attract people and cut back on promotion during peak seasons to prevent stimulating more demand than can be accommodated. Several years ago, to help reduce peak admittances during weekdays, a hospital offered people who checked in on the weekend for elective surgery a free vacation in Las Vegas. Many colleges promote preregistration and preadvisement programs to reduce peak loads during regular registration and advisement.

Tyson Foods, Inc., a large poultry producer, is promoting its chicken-based wieners, chicken-corn dogs, and other precooked snack and convenience foods to consumers to help reduce its dependence on the cyclical commodity poultry business.[3] This illustrates the interdependence of marketing mix elements. The decision to stimulate sales of branded products meant the firm had to promote them to consumers and middlemen.

Airlines promote the economy of flying, AT&T promotes long-distance calling, and electric utilities promote the use of electricity during periods of relatively low demand. Retailers try to even out their Christmas sales by promoting lay away sales well in advance of Christmas. Manufacturers and retailers also promote sales of air conditioners and lawnmowers in the fall and winter and sales of coats and heaters in the spring and summer to help even out demand patterns. Usually these efforts also include price reductions.

## PROMOTION MIX ELEMENTS

In Chapter 12 we saw that packaging can play a very important promotional role as a "silent salesperson." Therefore, it logically could be included among the elements in a firm's promotion mix. Marketers also use advertising, professional selling, sales promotion, and public relations and publicity to accomplish their promotional goals. These types of promotion effort are the elements in the **promotion mix.** (See Figure 17–2 on page 488.)

**promotion mix**

### Advertising

Any paid form of nonpersonal communication through the mass media about a product or idea by an identified sponsor is **advertising.** The mass media used include magazines, direct mail, radio, television, billboards, and newspapers. Sponsors may be a nonprofit organization, political candidate, company, or an individual. Advertising differs from news, public relations, or publicity in that an identified sponsor pays for placing the message in the media. Advertising is used when sponsors want to communicate with a number of people who cannot be reached economically and effectively through personal means. It is discussed more fully in Chapter 19.

**advertising**

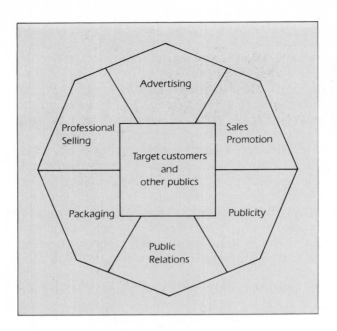

*Figure 17–2.*
*Elements in the*
*promotion mix*

### Professional Selling

professional
selling

Personal, face-to-face contact between a seller's representative and those people with whom the seller wants to communicate is **professional selling.** Nonprofit organizations, political candidates, companies, and individuals also use personal contact to communicate with their publics.

Retail and door-to-door sales are two types of personal contact with customers that usually are not considered part of professional selling. But they serve the same communication functions for retailers that professional salespersons serve, for example, in industrial marketing firms. A lower level of planning, problem solving, and communications skills is required for these salespeople than for professional salespeople. The costs for training, managing, compensating, and providing other benefits for a professional salesforce also are much greater than those for door-to-door salespersons. The number of people who can be reached through professional selling, however, is limited. Professional selling is discussed in more detail in the next chapter.

### SALES PROMOTION

sales promotion

**Sales promotion** includes activities that seek to directly induce a desired response by target customers, company salespersons, middlemen, or their salesforces. These activities add value to the product and/or serve as incentives to motivate a desired response.

Sales promotion may be a firm's primary promotional effort or it may supplement and complement professional selling, advertising, public relations and publicity, and packaging.[4]   In either case, all promotion mix elements are interrelated and interdependent.   Sales promotion activities range from short-run effort to move excess stock to long-run effort to inform target customers at the point of purchase.   Several examples of sales promotion objectives are listed in Table 17–2.

Point-of-purchase (P.O.P.) displays complement and supplement advertising.   Anheuser-Busch's "pick-a-pair" ads encourage consumers to buy two six-packs of Bud.   P.O.P. displays in supermarkets reinforce this, perhaps with a display featuring a picture of Ed McMahon and Doc Severinsen as they appeared on the TV commercial on "The Tonight Show."   But when Publishers Clearing House runs ads on TV telling consumers to watch the mail for their sweepstakes entries, the advertising supplements and complements the primary promotion effort—sales promotion.

A marketer must consider these factors in selecting sales promotion methods: (1) sales promotion objectives, (2) target customer characteristics, (3) product characteristics, (4) marketing channel characteristics, (5) the legal and regulatory environment, (6) the competitive environment, and (7) the economic environment.   Consider the following examples.

If the goal is to stimulate middlemen to increase their sales effort, a contest offering prizes for dealer salespersons makes more sense than a contest for consumers.   Target customer characteristics, such as age and education, could influence a manufacturer's decision about the type of consumer contest to sponsor.   A product's size, packaging, perishability, weight, volume, bulk, and cost could affect the desirability of mailing free samples.

The choice between point-of-purchase displays or instore product

**Table 17–2.** *Examples of sales promotion objectives*

1. To encourage trial purchases of new products by consumers.
2. To encourage shoppers in a retail store to drop coins in a container placed there by the local humane society.
3. To encourage middlemen to increase their order size.
4. To encourage consumers to buy several units of the product at one time.
5. To encourage a middleman's salesforce to give extra selling effort to a mature product.
6. To encourage retailers to devote more shelf space to the product.
7. To encourage wholesalers to cooperate in a manufacturer's effort to generate more feedback from retailers.
8. To encourage voters to vote for a particular candidate.
9. To encourage company sales personnel to increase sales effort for a new product.
10. To encourage retailers to devote more shelf space to a product.
11. To acquaint consumers or industrial users with product modifications.
12. To identify new consumers or industrial users.
13. To develop a mailing list.
14. To attract more attendance at a rock concert.
15. To build customer loyalty.
16. To encourage brand switching by consumers.
17. To encourage off-season purchases by retailers.
18. To gain entry into new retail outlets.

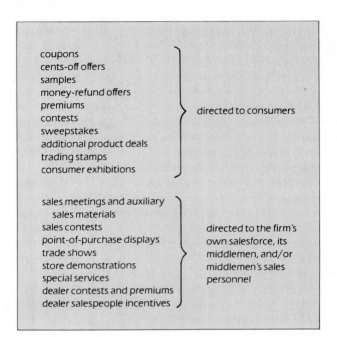

coupons
cents-off offers
samples
money-refund offers
premiums
contests
sweepstakes
additional product deals
trading stamps
consumer exhibitions
} directed to consumers

sales meetings and auxiliary
  sales materials
sales contests
point-of-purchase displays
trade shows
store demonstrations
special services
dealer contests and premiums
dealer salespeople incentives
} directed to the firm's own salesforce, its middlemen, and/or middlemen's sales personnel

*Figure 17–3.
Examples of sales
promotion*

demonstrations might depend on whether a channel is direct or indirect and the number and variety of middlemen.   The legal and regulatory environment might be a factor in choosing between a consumer sweepstakes and coupons because some states outlaw consumer sweepstakes. The competitive environment might discourage a manufacturer from offering push money to dealer salesforces if the manufacturer expects that will induce better-financed rivals to offer even more push money.   Recession and inflation may increase the attractiveness of using coupons and money-refund offers to help consumers stretch their buying power.

Sales promotion can be directed to consumers, company salespersons, middlemen, and dealer salesforces.   (See Figure 17–3.)

### Sales Promotion Directed to Consumers

Sales promotion methods range far and wide.[5]   Jostens, Inc., a marketer of high school rings and yearbooks, sponsors workshops on building school spirit to help sales of its products.   Its salespeople give away pennants and posters and help school administrators and student leaders develop ideas for pep rallies.[6]

Specific types of sales promotion directed to consumers include (1) coupons, (2) cents-off offers, (3) samples, (4) money-refund offers, (5) premiums, (6) contests, (7) sweepstakes, (8) additional product deals, (9) combination product deals, (10) trading stamps, and (11) consumer exhibitions.

**coupons**

**Coupons** have increased in popularity in recent years as consumers use them to stretch their incomes.[7]   A typical coupon reduces the retail price of a product at the checkout counter by ten cents, but some offer much larger reductions. They are placed in magazines, newspapers, or are mailed to consumers. When a manufacturer offers a reduced price to retailers, they are expected to cut their prices to consumers; but some do not. Coupons, however, enable the manufacturer to pass a price reduction directly to the consumer.

In 1979, manufacturers distributed about 81.2 billion coupons; only about 4 percent were redeemed.[8] Problems for manufacturers in the use of coupons relate to fraudulent use and variable redemption rates. For example, redemption rates often are as much as three or four times higher in more affluent than in less affluent neighborhoods. Some retailers complain that the handling fee manufacturers pay them, typically five cents per coupon, is too low. Some manufacturers have raised it to seven cents.

Consumers who receive coupons by mail or in magazines or newspapers often lose, misplace, or ignore them. Carol Wright is a registered trade name of a cooperative coupon distribution service that mails coupons six times a year to 21 million frequent users of several grocery product categories. It tested a new distribution system in eighty supermarkets in Los Angeles in 1980. Representatives stood at supermarket entrances and handed shoppers flip-through coupon booklets in an effort to stimulate same-day purchases and increase the coupon redemption rate. The checkouts also were equipped with Universal Product Code scanners to give immediate sales feedback to participating companies and retailers.[9]

**Cents-off offers** are printed on, attached to, or included in the product's package and constitute a reduction in the product's retail price. A package of Swiss Miss hot cocoa mix may have a coupon printed on the package that a consumer can use for the next purchase of the brand. Alka-Seltzer has attached coupons to some of its packages that can be removed and used for the current purchase of Alka-Seltzer. Attached coupons probably are more likely to stimulate initial trial purchases than are printed-on coupons. Meow Mix has placed coupons with a rub-off spot in the package. When removed, the coupon shows the value of the offer, such as forty cents or even a year's supply.

**cents-off offers**

**Samples** are free packages of the product, either the normal size or a specially designed trial size for sampling purposes. Production and distribution costs are high and many recipients will not try free samples. To counteract these disadvantages, Sales/Marketing Assistance Corporation has a staff of 10,000 part-time workers who pass out samples for their clients in retail stores in 150 markets. This helps build product awareness among consumers for these clients.

**samples**

**Money-refund offers** return an amount of money to consumers who mail in a proof-of-purchase of a product. New brands of cereal often include these offers on the package.

**money-refund offers**

One type of **premium** is a continuous offer to redeem some proof-of-purchase for merchandise. This can help build brand loyalty. Several

**premiums**

# THE ORE-IDA FAMILY FAVORITES SWEEPSTAKES IS NO SMALL POTATOES.

### Here's your chance to win one of 5,601 exciting prizes with a total retail value over $75,000.

**GRAND PRIZE**
1980 Volkswagen Rabbit Convertible. Fuel Injection. Front-Wheel Drive. 5-Speed Gearbox. AM/FM Stereo Tape. The ultimate in air-conditioning is free.

**FIRST PRIZE**
15 Whirlpool Upright Freezers. 19.6 cu. ft. capacity, with adjustable temperature control, no-frost cooling system and a super storage door.

**SECOND PRIZE**
40 "Corda"™ Dinnerware sets by Thomas, Div. of Rosenthal USA Ltd. A complete 53 piece set for eight with an exciting modern design. Dishwasher safe and oven proof.

**THIRD PRIZE**
70 Maxim™ Convection Ovens. Broils, roasts, bakes. Cooks uniformly and in less time than regular ovens. Self-cleaning. Porcelain exterior.

**FOURTH PRIZE**
175 Revere Ware Copper Clad 7 pc. Stainless Steel Cookware sets. Includes 1- and 2-quart covered sauce pans, 4½-quart Dutch Oven and a 9" skillet.

**FIFTH PRIZE**
300 West Bend® 12" Automatic Skillets. SilverStone® non-stick durable surface, accurate electric temperature control, dishwasher safe and immersible.

**SIXTH PRIZE**
5000 Ore-Ida Menu Magic Cookbooks. Entrees, Side Dishes, Appetizers, Snacks. Over 80 scrumptious recipes using Ore-Ida frozen potatoes.

## OFFICIAL RULES—NO PURCHASE NECESSARY

1. On an official entry blank or a plain 3" x 5" piece of paper, hand print your name, address and zip code. Include with your entry the orange and brown ORE-IDA logo from any package of ORE-IDA frozen potatoes or the words "ORE-IDA" hand printed on a plain 3" x 5" piece of paper. The official entry blank cannot be mechanically reproduced.

2. Enter as often as you wish, but each entry should be mailed separately to: ORE-IDA FAMILY FAVORITES SWEEPSTAKES, P.O. Box 2706, Westbury, New York 11591. All entries must be received by September 30, 1980.

3. Winners will be selected in random drawings conducted by National Judging Institute, Inc., an independent judging organization, whose decisions are final on all matters relating to this sweepstakes. All prizes will be awarded and winners notified by mail. Only one prize to a family or household. No substitutions or exchanging of prizes. Liability for taxes is the responsibility of individual winners. Winners may be asked to execute an affidavit of eligibility and release.

4. Sweepstakes open to all residents of the U.S., except employees and their families of Ore-Ida Foods, Inc., the H.J. Heinz Company, their affiliates, subsidiaries, advertising agencies, and Don Jagoda Associates, Inc. The offer is void wherever prohibited and subject to all Federal, State, and local laws. No purchase necessary.

5. For a list of major winners, send a stamped, self-addressed envelope to: Family Favorites Winners, P.O. Box 2758, Westbury, New York 11591.

## ENTRY BLANK

How to Enter: Print your name, address and zip code below. Include with your entry the orange and brown ORE-IDA logo from any package of ORE-IDA frozen potatoes, or the words "ORE-IDA" hand printed on a plain 3" x 5" piece of paper. Mail to ORE-IDA FAMILY FAVORITES SWEEPSTAKES, P.O. Box 2706, Westbury, New York 11591.

Name_____

Address_____Apt.____

City_____State_____Zip____

**ALL ENTRIES MUST BE RECEIVED BY SEPTEMBER 30, 1980.**

*A consumer sweepstakes*

Source: Ore-Ida Foods, Inc.

brands of coffee include this type of offer. In some cases, consumers who do not have the required number of proofs can get the premium by paying some cash in addition to surrendering the proofs they have.

Another type of premium is an item placed in or on the product's package or given to customers by a merchant. CrackerJack is the classic example. Bic pens have been used as premiums with Bic lighters. Some detergent packages also have towels in them.

**Consumer contests** require consumers to compete for prizes by demonstrating a skill, such as writing an essay or jingle or baking a cake. Contests also may be used in conjunction with coupons. They can stimulate sales and increase store traffic. But as a sales promotion technique, contests cannot require a purchase as a condition of entry. Contests also are prohibited in some states.

consumer contests

In a **consumer sweepstakes** consumers merely put their names on a form to be included in a drawing for prizes. They are more common and attract more participants than contests. Examples include Publishers Clearing House Sweepstakes and *Reader's Digest* Sweepstakes. Sweepstakes often are accompanied by direct mail and TV advertising. Like contests they can stimulate sales, increase store traffic, cannot require a purchase as a condition of entry, and are prohibited in some states.

consumer sweepstakes

**Additional product deals** give the consumer extra product for the regular price. Scope, Listerine, and Lavoris bottles, for example, might contain eight free ounces. "One-cent" sales are another example. Rexall drugstores often feature such sales. Consumers pay the regular price of featured products and get a second unit for one cent.

additional product deals

Some retailers also give **trading stamps.** For example, a grocer might give one stamp for each ten cents of groceries a customer buys. Customers can redeem the stamps at the stamp maker's (such as Top Value) redemption centers for products or for cash. Some consumers believe they are getting an extra bonus or that the stamps represent a reduction in price. This can be the case if competition from other retailers prevents the retailer from passing on to consumers the costs of offering stamps. They can help a retailer differentiate its offering from rivals, at least in some market segments. During the 1960s, numerous gas stations offered trading stamps. Overall, they probably are a less popular sales promotion technique now.

trading stamps

Marketers sometimes collectively sponsor **consumer exhibitions** of their products. Typical examples are boat shows and sporting goods shows. These can be very helpful to manufacturers in introducing new products.

consumer exhibitions

## Sales Promotion Directed to the Salesforce, Middlemen, and Their Salesforces

Sales promotion directed to salespeople, wholesalers, and retailers includes (1) sales meetings and auxiliary sales materials, (2) sales contests, (3) point-of-purchase displays, (4) trade shows, (5) store demonstrations, (6) special services, (7) dealer contests and premiums, and (8) dealer salespeople incentives.

**Sales Meetings and Auxiliary Sales Materials.** Sales meetings and auxiliary sales materials support the company salesforce with product information, skills, and aids—such as product models—which they can use in sales interviews with customers. Sales meetings provide motivation for a salesforce by giving them recognition or a disguised vacation by holding it in a resort area.

**Sales Contests.** Sales contests offer cash incentives, merchandise, or vacations for company salespeople who reach certain goals in their territories. Some **sales contests** may be a continuing program to encourage salespeople to establish new accounts, or a temporary effort to help introduce a new product.

sales contests

**Point-of-Purchase Displays.** Manufacturers often provide retailers with store signs, display racks, brochures, banners, and other printed materials. These **point-of-purchase displays** direct consumers to the manufacturer's product and help explain it without the aid of a salesclerk. A shopper in a discount store, supermarket, or large drugstore, for example, can view Timex watches in an attractive display case that revolves at the touch of a button.

point-of-purchase<br>displays

**Trade Shows.** As we saw in Chapter 15, many manufacturers exhibit their products at trade shows for middlemen. Company representatives can write orders or get leads for salespeople to call on later.

**Store Demonstrations.** Manufacturers also can arrange with retailers for a special store demonstration of their products. Manufacturers supply highly trained representatives for these shows. Many cosmetics firms periodically send representatives to retail stores to show consumers how to use their products and to answer questions.

**Special Services.** Manufacturers also offer special services for retailers. Labels with the store's name, prepricing of merchandise at the plant, buy-back agreements, special packaging, and special colors or sizes can increase the attractiveness of the manufacturer's products to retailers. Another example is the dealer listing in which the manufacturer prepares an ad that promotes a product and lists the names of its retailers that sell the product.

**Dealer Contests and Premiums.** Manufacturers often sponsor contests for and offer premiums to their salespeople. **Dealer contests and premiums** are very similar to those provided for the company's own salespeople. They usually involve more expensive incentives, however, such as vacations or new cars.

dealer contests<br>and premiums

**Dealer Salespeople Incentives.** Incentives to dealer salespeople often are less expensive forms of promotions to the dealers. Push money, for example, is money provided by the manufacturer for dealer salespeople. On items like color TVs it may be as much as $20 in addition to the normal commission paid by the dealer. The dealer salesperson gets the regular commission plus an extra amount of money supplied by the manufacturer. Supplies of the company's product also may be given to the dealer's salespeople for their personal use to help ensure their familiarity with it.

## Evaluating Sales Promotion Effectiveness

Sales promotion directed to consumers can be evaluated by sales performance, laboratory panels and field surveys, and experiments.

Sales performance can be measured before, during, and after the sales promotion activities. These activities generally can produce a short-run boost in sales but marketers often prefer a lasting sales boost. Procter & Gamble does not want a couponing program to create $10 million of Crest sales now solely at the expense of $10 million of Crest sales over the next four months.

A marketer who has access to market share data might note the firm's share prior to the promotion. If the share goes up while the activities are being conducted, they are producing some results. But if the share drops down to its original level shortly after the activities cease, there has been little carry-over effect. Most marketers, however, do not want to risk spacing sales promotion activities far enough apart to permit this type of evaluation. The major problem with the sales performance approach to evaluation is that it attributes all sales increases to sales promotion activities.

Consumer panels can be questioned regarding their likes and dislikes concerning the sales promotion activities, whether or not the activities caused them to switch to the marketer's brand, and, if so, if they intend to continue buying the brand. A field survey could extend the evaluation to a larger number of people and include measuring the percentage of the target audience that was reached. Experiments might include running two types of sales promotion activities at the same time and comparing results. An example is comparing coupon redemption rates in newspapers and magazines.

## PUBLIC RELATIONS AND PUBLICITY

Modern firms also are concerned about the effects of their actions on people outside their market targets. These people may have little contact with the firm but feel it affects their welfare in some way. Unless the firm understands their concerns and communicates its goals and interests, they may misinterpret, distort, or be openly hostile to the firm's actions. Communication to correct erroneous impressions, maintain goodwill of the firm's many publics, and explain the firm's goals and purposes is called **public relations** (P-R).

**public relations**

Unlike the other promotion mix elements, public relations is concerned primarily with people outside the market target, although it may include them. Government agencies, communities in which plants are located, consumerists, environmentalists, stockholders, and college professors are some of the groups reached by a firm's public relations efforts. Lobbying in Congress and state legislatures to help pass legislation favorable to the firm and to help defeat legislation unfavorable to the firm is part of a public relations department's activities.  P-R personnel also advise top management about societal changes that may affect the firm and actions that might help to improve the firm's public image.  In recent years, top executives have been participating more directly in P-R activities to help improve the image of business.

Companies conduct their P-R programs through direct contact, publicity, and institutional advertising.

### Direct Contact

Direct contact with a public includes letters, plant tours, visits by public relations personnel, and company-sponsored events.  Employers who recruit on college campuses may write personal letters to professors explaining their management philosophy and required qualifications for student interviewees.  Kraft, a major advertiser on TV, distributed reprints of its policy statement on violence in TV programing to marketing professors.  Plant tours often are scheduled by breweries and soft drink bottlers.  Visits by P-R personnel include speakers at civic and service club meetings to explain their firms' goals and policies that may be of interest to the local community.  Company-sponsored events include sponsorship of craft fairs and youth athletic programs and Kool's hot air balloon race.

### Publicity

publicity

**Publicity** is news published in the mass media about a firm and its products, policies, personnel, or actions.  P-R activities in most larger firms are handled out of their public relations departments, not their marketing departments.  Thus marketing-related P-R activities, such as generating publicity for new products, is only part of a P-R department's responsibilities.  Some firms set up publicity units in their marketing departments and use advertising agencies or public relations firms to help ensure that marketing-related P-R activities will not be overlooked.  Smaller firms may have one or two people handling publicity.  Table 17–3 highlights some of the major differences between publicity and advertising.[10]

Publicity has several advantages over other promotion techniques: (1) it may reach people who ordinarily do not pay attention to advertising, sales promotion, and salespersons, (2) it has greater credibility than ad-

**Table 17–3.** *How publicity differs from advertising*

1. Publicity is not paid for by the firm.
2. Publicity has no identified sponsor.
3. The firm does not control the content of the coverage, although it may have initiated the media interest and supplied the information included.
4. The firm cannot schedule repetitions of publicity materials.
5. Publicity is presented as news by the media rather than as a persuasive ad and, therefore, may have more credibility than advertising that ordinarily is set apart from broadcast programs or editorial content in print media.

vertising, (3) it is relatively inexpensive and provides coverage that would cost many advertising dollars, and (4) it can provide more information than advertising.

**Publicity Tools.**   Publicity can originate with the firm or the media. Annual model changeovers in the auto industry are traditional and media editors are likely to accept and use related publicity materials from the automakers.   A shopping center developer who announces the planned construction of a new mall in a particular city is likely to be contacted by local newspapers and TV stations for information.   These events have high interest value and a news angle.   But events having less news value in the opinion of media editors require more skill on the publicist's part to create a story.   Celebrities, for example, may have to be present at sponsored events to generate enough interest to merit media editors' attention.   Effective publicists have good working relationships with media people and can prepare materials for them that have a good chance of being used.

Firms try to influence the information in media coverage by providing news releases, a packet of background information for feature articles, press conferences, editorials for newspapers and magazines, and tapes and films for radio and TV.   Perrier water, for example, received a lot of publicity before its actual full-scale introduction in the United States. This carefully orchestrated publicity helped create attention and interest and paved the way for other promotional activities in introducing the product.

A news release, usually one typed page, contains information the firm wants disseminated along with the name, address, and phone number of the person to contact for more information.   Feature articles are longer and are prepared for specific publications.   Media are invited to press conferences to hear news of an upcoming major event.   Letters to the editor are sent to newspapers and magazines, perhaps in response to materials that appeared in those media.   Radio and TV stations are given tapes and films for airing.

Media people decide whether any of the material is published or aired. They may use it as supplied, alter or change it completely, or throw it away.   Marketers cannot control publicity but they can set up programs and guidelines for generating usable publicity materials.[11]

**Negative Publicity.**   Another implication of free publicity is that some of it can damage company and/or brand images.   Companies try to avoid unfavorable publicity by using careful quality-control procedures, providing use limitation information on product labels, and conducting in-plant safety and training programs.   But it is almost impossible to eliminate all potentially damaging events.   Thus most firms set up policies for handling news coverage related to such events.[12]   News of a product recall, for example, can be accompanied by company statements telling consumers what to do to get the product repaired or replaced. It is wise to cooperate with the media in giving speedy and fair coverage to unfavorable events.[13]   Impeding regulatory agency and news media access to information likely will start damaging rumors and hurt future efforts to secure favorable publicity from the media.

After a McDonnell Douglas DC10 was involved in a crash in 1979 the planes were grounded by the government. The accident and the grounding created negative publicity for the firm. A government investigation found the accident was caused by faulty maintenance, not a design flaw in the plane. The company wanted to start an ad campaign soon after to counter the negative publicity, but several airlines that flew the plane objected. They figured people would forget the crash. But McDonnell Douglas began an ad campaign in the summer of 1980 that emphasized that the DC10 was the most tested plane in the sky and reminded people of the company's role in the space program.

**Evaluating Publicity's Effectiveness.** Preparing publicity materials costs money even though the media time and space are free. This alone is reason enough for firms to evaluate publicity's effectiveness. The most common approach is to count the number of exposures in the media, such as how many press releases, feature articles, photographs, and films, were published or aired during a given period of time.

Ad agencies and public relations firms clip printed publicity materials from newspapers and magazines and keep track of minutes of air time on radio and TV for broadcast publicity for their clients. They also often convert this space and time to an equivalent amount of advertising cost to give the client some idea of the value of publicity.

Firms that do not use ad agencies or public relations firms can keep track of printed media publicity generated by hiring a clipping service. It will clip and send relevant printed publicity materials to the client. But there are no similar independent services for broadcast materials.

## Institutional Advertising

Some types of institutional advertising are a part of public relations. A chemical firm may show how it avoids polluting the environment, while another firm may show it is a good member of the community by awarding grants of money to the city library. These ads mainly attempt to create or enhance a positive company image rather than encourage consumers to buy its products. But some institutional ads seek to do both. National or regional firms with large publics are more likely to use these ads than small local firms. We will discuss institutional advertising in greater detail in Chapter 19.

## FACTORS DETERMINING THE PROMOTION MIX

Most firms use a combination of elements in their promotion mixes. Each should reinforce the messages of the others.[14] In the final analysis, the ultimate test of any promotional strategy is whether it gets the desired results. Factors that influence the use and emphasis placed on each mix

**Table 17–4.** *Factors that influence development of the promotion mix*

| | |
|---|---|
| 1. Product-related factors | a. amount and complexity of product information |
| | b. product's stage in its life cycle |
| | c. product type and unit price |
| 2. Consumer-related factors | a. size and characteristics of the market target |
| | b. type of buying decision |
| 3. Firm-related factors | a. marketing channel and promotion philosophy |
| | b. branding strategy |
| | c. pricing strategy |
| | d. budget |
| | e. company personnel |
| 4. Situation-related factors | a. visibility of the firm in its environment |
| | b. competitors' actions |

element include (1) product-related factors, (2) consumer-related factors, (3) firm-related factors, and (4) situation-related factors. (See Table 17–4.)

### Product-related Factors

Three product-related factors affect the promotion mix: (1) amount and complexity of product information to be communicated, (2) the product's stage in its life cycle, and (3) product type and unit price.

**Amount and Complexity of Product Information.** To get across simple ideas or make consumers aware of a product whose features are easily observed more emphasis usually is placed on advertising. It also is used for products that are familiar to consumers. The messages are relatively simple and easily understood.

To demonstrate complex ideas more emphasis is placed on professional selling and sales promotions, such as printed brochures, demonstrations, and point-of-purchase displays. Professional salespeople and product demonstrations convert complex information about home computers and microwave ovens, for example, to a form consumers can understand. Such personal contact also enables consumers to experience the product and ask questions. Figure 17–4 shows the relationship between amount and complexity of information and the selection of promotional tools.

**Product's Stage in the Life Cycle.** The goals and tools used for the promotion effort differ in each stage of a product's life cycle. During introduction and growth, promotion must create awareness and induce trial purchases. Extensive advertising, sales promotions such as coupons, cents-off offers, free samples, and publicity help to reach consumers. Professional selling also helps to reach middlemen to ensure adequate

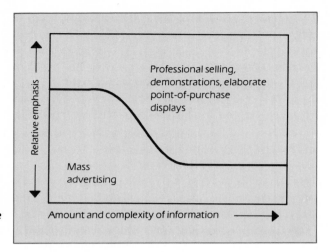

*Figure 17–4.
The relationship
between amount
and complexity of
information and the
selection of
promotional tools*

distribution. During maturity, effort shifts to differentiating the brand by showing its advantages relative to rival brands. Establishing brand loyalty is a major concern. As the product passes to the saturation stage, the focus shifts to retaining market share, fighting off the effects of rivals' new brands, and combating price cuts. Marketers of leading brands engage in discrimination training to prevent their brand names from becoming generic. Product improvements may be introduced to combat or discourage introduction of new brands, especially dealer brands, and to extend the brand's life. These product changes may require new promotion campaigns.

Marketers usually reduce promotion in the decline stage. But they may continue aggressive promotion to a particularly loyal segment of customers. Otherwise, much of the promotion is left to middlemen because the manufacturer's profit margin no longer will support the heavy promotion expenditures of earlier stages.

**Product Type and Unit Price.** The interaction of product type (consumer or industrial) and unit price affects the promotion mix, as shown in Figure 17–5. Heavy emphasis is placed on advertising for relatively inexpensive consumer products. Items with a high unit price receive more professional selling support because consumers want more detailed and personalized information. Professional selling is more important at all price levels for industrial products but receives even greater emphasis at the higher unit price levels. Again, the need for more accurate and tailored information for large purchases probably accounts for this.

### Consumer-related Factors

Two consumer-related factors influence the promotion mix: (1) size and characteristics of the market target and (2) type of buying decision.

**Size and Characteristics of the Market Target.** Nonpersonal forms of promotion, such as advertising, sales promotion, and publicity, are

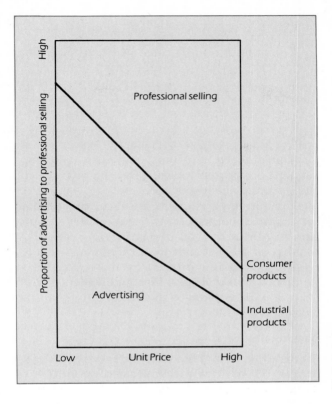

*Figure 17–5.*
*Interaction between*
*type of product,*
*unit price, and*
*promotion activity*

favored as the size of the market target increases. But as it increases in size, the people in the target become more heterogeneous with respect to demographic and lifestyle characteristics. This makes nonpersonal forms of promotion less effective. Beyond a certain point, therefore, marketers usually engage in market segmentation and product differentiation. Even if the product remains the same, the promotion efforts may be radically different. Regional TV ads for nationally distributed products may be used as well as different ads in various regional magazines. Nonpersonal forms of promotion tailored for each segment can be used as long as the sizes of the different segments are relatively large.

The choice of a promotion mix for products with a relatively small market target depends on whether people in it are relatively similar. If so, special-interest or local mass media may be used. If not, personal contact through sales or sales letters may be used.

**Type of Buying Decision.** The second consumer-related influence on the promotion mix is the type of buying decision involved—programed or nonprogramed. Consumers making programed decisions are not receptive to information. If they make programed purchases of the firm's brand, promotion focuses on calling attention to the brand at the point of purchase, reminding them that the brand remains better than others, and combating the introductory campaigns of new brands. If they make programed purchases of rival brands, promotion might focus on appeals like "if you're tired of your brand, try ours."

The promotion mix must be heavily informative and tailored to the consumer's primary concerns when nonprogramed decisions are being made. The effects of rivals' promotional campaigns also must be considered because consumers usually are not biased in their use of information about alternative brands. Reassuring the consumer after the decision through individualized communications like a personal letter may help reduce cognitive dissonance, which we discussed in Chapter 4.

Convenience, shopping, specialty, and unsought products require different promotion mixes. But the buying decision for a product may change and place it in a different category. The introduction of similar rival brands may switch it from a specialty product to a shopping product. For example, nothing on the market was an adequate substitute for the Shower Massage when it was first introduced. But Norelco, Pollinex, and several other brands were then brought out, which made the Shower Massage a shopping product for many consumers. The same was true for Rival Crock Pots and Waring blenders. Shifts in a product's classification require changes in the content, goals, and elements of the promotion mix.

### Firm-related Factors

A promotion mix must take into account these preexisting firm-related factors: (1) marketing channel and promotion philosophy, (2) branding strategy, (3) pricing strategy, (4) budget, and (5) company personnel.

**Marketing Channel and Promotion Philosophy.** Three marketing channel possibilities are illustrated in Figure 17–6. Regardless of the

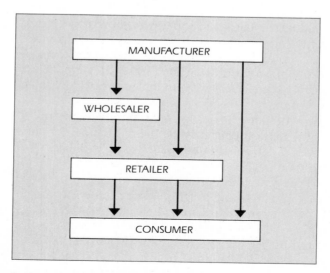

*Figure 17–6.*
*Marketing channels*

channel used, a firm can use three types of promotional philosophies: (1) push, (2) pull, and/or (3) gravity.

With a **push philosophy** promotional effort is directed to the next lower level of the channel whether it is wholesale or retail. Once the next lower level of the channel accepts the product, it in turn will promote to the next lower level.

**push philosophy**

With a **pull philosophy** the manufacturer tries to stimulate consumer or industrial user demand by directing promotion effort directly to ultimate consumers or industrial users. This helps create demand for the firm's product throughout the channel.

**pull philosophy**

In 1980 Johnson Products Company, maker of Ultra Sheen and Afro Sheen, introduced Precise, a patented professional product that is used only in beauty salons. If the firm had selected a push approach, it could have promoted the product to middlemen who sell to operators of beauty salons or to the operators themselves. But the firm chose the pull approach and directed the advertising to consumers. It wanted to maintain the product's professional prestige and encourage consumers to request Precise when they went to beauty salons. That would "force" the salons to stock the product.[15]

A firm that wants to use a push philosophy must develop a marketing channel that includes wholesaling firms that have their own salesforces and/or a network of retailers who will promote the product aggressively. A manufacturer has less control over promotion to final buyers with a push than with a pull philosophy. The push approach is weighted heavily to professional sales and sales promotion. Advertising is limited to trade publications and print media that reach decision makers at the wholesale or retail level.

A pull philosophy allows the manufacturer to control how the product is presented to consumers. Advertising is stressed and is produced, placed, and paid for by the manufacturer. Pull is more appropriate when the manufacturer wants to create a strong corporate image. But it requires considerable knowledge of market targets and expertise in reaching them with appealing themes.

**Gravity** involves concentrating on producing a superior product and depending only on word-of-mouth to sell it. Satisfied customers— whether a wholesaler, retailer, consumer, or industrial buyer—are expected to create demand for the product.

**gravity**

A gravity approach is appropriate when a manufacturer has long-term contracts for products marketed under dealer brands. A new firm that lacks excess capacity and funds for expansion also might use this approach. Some manufacturers use gravity to reinforce a company image of high quality and exclusivity. But a manufacturer has to produce exceptionally high-quality or unique products to use gravity. Some surgeons, attorneys, CPAs, and other marketers of services use gravity when they want to limit the number of patients or clients.

Most firms use various combinations of push and pull. Colgate-Palmolive may emphasize pull by using heavy consumer advertising but also may use push by maintaining a salesforce to call on middlemen to make sure they are stocking enough of the product to meet consumer demand. An industrial marketer may rely primarily on a professional salesforce because its customers are fewer and more geographically concentrated. But it also may direct advertising to them through trade publications. Mass media also may be used to help create a favorable impression of the firm in the public as well as the buyer's mind.

**Branding Strategy.** A firm that selects an individual branding strategy commits itself to heavy promotional expenditures to introduce a new brand. An image must be created for each brand to gain acceptance at each level of the marketing channel. Sales promotion, concentrated efforts of a professional salesforce, and massive advertising are needed to establish the brand.

Family branding requires less promotion effort to introduce a new product. Perhaps only a small amount of advertising to create consumer awareness will be needed because the new product capitalizes on the family brand's image. Consumers may try it because of their satisfaction with other products with the family brand name. Scotch brand adhesives are an example.

**Pricing Strategy.** Pricing strategy also can affect promotion mixes. Some firms try to create a prestige image for a product or retail store through promotion so they can charge premium prices. They must control how the product or store is promoted to consumers. Thus they stress advertising. Anheuser-Busch, for example, stresses advertising for Michelob in building its prestige image. Getting retailers to honor a manufacturer's suggested retail price often requires the manufacturer to invest heavily in advertising. This is one reason Levi Strauss advertises Levi's. But a professional salesforce usually is emphasized in marketing many costlier industrial products and selectively distributed consumer products.

**Budget.** Firms choose among promotion elements on the basis of the relative costs of reaching each intended receiver. Maintaining a professional salesforce, for example, is more expensive per person reached than advertising. Sales promotions may be expensive or relatively low cost depending on the type used. Public relations generally is considered a necessary part of doing business and its budget often is considered separately from a firm's promotion budget.

Most marketers try to optimize their return on promotion dollars. The mix most firms settle for always is less than ideal because there usually is a tradeoff between the funds available, number of people in the target, quality of the communication needed, and the relative costs of the different promotion elements. Generally, the cost per person reached is higher for professional sales, personal contact P-R, and sales promotions like samples and demonstrations than for advertising, other sales promotions, and publicity.

**Company Personnel.** A fifth firm-related factor is the expertise and peculiarities of a firm's personnel. Some firms lack experience with certain promotion elements and do not use them. Powerful executives may favor using certain elements because of previous results that have little to do with effectiveness per dollar of promotion expenditure. A casual remark like "Oh, your company makes . . ." by a stranger who saw an ad on TV may create a bias in favor of TV advertising.

### Situation-related Factors

Situation-related factors that affect the promotion mix stem from the firm's environment. They are (1) visibility of the firm in its legal, political, and social environment and (2) competitors' actions.

**Visibility of the Firm.** Some firms are more visible to the public because of their products, relative position in an industry, or their potential impact on the physical, economic, or political life of their communities. A manufacturer of industrial ball bearings is less visible in a highly industrialized area than a manufacturer of a nationally distributed consumer product in a less industrialized area. More people are more concerned about the actions of highly visible firms. Thus these firms spend relatively more on P-R. This is also true for firms that have large market shares; their executives are perceived as spokespersons for their industries. Firms whose actions are essential to or are potentially harmful to the public welfare, such as chemical, transportation, pharmaceutical, petroleum, and steel companies and public utilities, also spend heavily on P-R. Some firms prefer to maintain a low profile and downplay publicity.

**Competitors' Actions.** Rivals' promotional activities also affect the mix. Firms often have to match or counter the promotional activities of rivals to maintain or increase their market share. General Foods' Maxwell House had to counter Folger's introduction on the East Coast and Coke had to answer the Pepsi Challenge.

## MANAGING THE PROMOTION EFFORT

All firms want a promotion program in which all elements work together to produce a high level of understanding between the firm and its publics. Such a program results from the efforts of a team of executives and their

*Figure 17–7. Organization of the promotion effort*

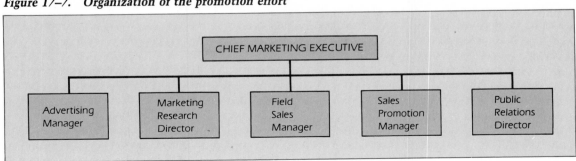

staffs. Figure 17–7 shows how the marketing arm of the company can be organized to produce such a program. This team takes the following steps: (1) sets promotion objectives and selects a promotion mix, (2) plans the promotion effort, (3) determines budget size and allocates it among the promotion mix elements, (4) implements the promotion program, and (5) evaluates the promotion program.

### Setting Promotion Objectives

Successful promotion campaigns depend largely on how their objectives are stated. Promotion objectives should be realistic and specific and include the criteria by which success or failure will be judged, including the time frame for accomplishing them. They take into account all the factors we have discussed, including marketing research, and are consistent with top management's concept of the firm's mission.

promotion
campaign

A **promotion campaign** is an interrelated series of promotional activities designed to communicate with target groups of people to produce changes in behavior. Unless objectives are stated clearly, it is impossible to evaluate promotional effectiveness. Table 17–5 gives some examples of these objectives.

### Planning the Promotion Effort

Once objectives are set, the next steps are to (1) determine which promotion elements are most appropriate to reach the target, (2) determine exactly what each element must do and who will be accountable for what, and (3) construct a coordinated work sequence for the promotion elements with a schedule of when each step will be completed.

Figure 17–8 presents a small section from the middle of a schedule for a firm introducing a new dog food. Notice that each step specifies the promotion element, the target group, and the purpose of the action. This spells out which element will do what and when. A coordinated schedule also provides a framework for an integrated team effort to reach

**Table 17–5.** *Comparison of poorly stated and effectively stated promotion objectives*

---

*Poorly Stated Objectives*

---

1. To create good acceptance of our firm by consumers.
2. To market our product with dignity.
3. To increase the market for our product.

---

*Effectively Stated Objectives*

---

1. To retain the cuing value of our trademark through discrimination training.
2. To create awareness of our new product in 40 percent of the 16–21 age group this year.
3. To increase market share for our brands by 5 percent in the coming year.
4. To position our product over the next three years as the best one on the market in the 18–34 age group.

---

promotion objectives, to fine tune what is to be done, and to estimate the budget required.

## Determining the Promotion Budget

Many approaches can be taken in setting the promotion budget; for example: (1) establishing a percentage of current or forecasted sales, (2) spending all available funds, (3) matching the expenditures of a major competitor, (4) estimating return on investment, (5) setting an arbitrary amount and seeing what can be done with it, and (6) deciding on promotion objectives and setting the budget accordingly.[16]

**Percentage of Current or Forecasted Sales.** The budget can be figured by taking a percentage either of last year's sales or the forecasted sales for the coming year. A slight variation is to use a fixed amount per unit of product and multiply it by the forecasted number of units to be sold in the coming year. This approach is rigid and leads to overspending during expanding markets and underspending during declining markets. It also confuses cause and effect. Basing a promotion budget on current sales, for example, means that promotional funds are a function of sales.[17]

**Spending All Available Funds.** Small firms often use for promotion whatever funds remain after expenses and allowance for a reasonable profit. This method reflects management's desire to maintain liquidity but does not consider promotion as a capital investment for which a firm might reasonably borrow money. The budget also is not related to the firm's promotion objectives.

**Matching Expenditures of a Major Competitor.** Matching the expenditures of a major competitor assumes the rival knows what it is doing and that your firm's needs are the same. A variation is to use the average percentage of sales devoted to promotion in the industry. This recognizes the activities of rivals but does not tie budgets to promotion objectives or recognize differences in the firms' promotional effectiveness.

**Return on Investment.** The return on investment approach treats promotion as a capital investment. The underlying logic is that since an organization's funds are limited, the allocation of those funds should be based on their projected return on investment. Thus the use of funds

| May 1–2 | Training for salespeople and distribution of sales aids. |
| May 5 | Sales letters and brochures to wholesalers and retailers to prepare them for salespeople. |
| May 15– June 15 | Salespeople contact wholesalers and retailers to explain introductory promotional campaign and take initial orders. |
| June 30– July 30 | National newspaper and television blitz. |

*Figure 17–8. Partial schedule for introducing a new dog food*

for promotion must compete with their use for other purposes, such as building a new plant or buying new equipment. Use of this approach to determining the promotion budget is limited in practice, however, because of the difficulty of estimating the return on dollars spent on promotion.

**Arbitrary Amount.** Deciding how much you want to spend and then seeing what you can get for the money is a highly arbitrary method. It basically is a function of the marketer's feelings toward consumers and the promotion process. This approach sometimes leads to overspending for small firms. Owners, for example, may receive benefits that are unrelated to the firm's objectives, such as compliments on their appearance in TV commercials.

**Budget by Objectives.** Perhaps the most effective approach is to (1) determine the objectives you want to accomplish, (2) determine the mix of promotion elements that will produce these results, and (3) estimate carefully the cost of each element in the mix.

Different objectives will require different mixes, and costs will vary accordingly. But objectives and the mix can be adjusted to fit resources. The budget figures arrived at can be compared to the figures arrived at by using any of the other approaches. Any budget and the objectives it is supposed to support must be flexible to adjust to changing market conditions. Flexibility in allocating funds to different mix elements allows greater use of those that prove to be more effective as the program is implemented.

### Implementing and Evaluating the Promotion Program

Once the objectives and budget have been set and funds have been allocated to the different mix elements, implementation is necessary. Sales and advertising management become the centers of activity. These are discussed in the next two chapters.

There is no objective way to determine for sure whether a firm's promotion program is worth the money invested in it. But very few firms are willing to risk not communicating with their many publics. Attempts to use such objective techniques as return on investment are themselves subjective because many factors influence sales. In the final analysis, evaluation of the total promotion effort is a subjective judgment based on objective data like sales data, market share, and subjective feedback from customers and the salesforce. We will discuss evaluation of advertising and salesforce effectiveness in greater detail in the next two chapters.

Several types of feedback, however, signal the need for changes in promotion programs. These include programs that (1) stimulate more demand than the firm can meet, (2) confuse middlemen or final buyers, (3) damage company or brand images, (4) create expectations that cannot be met, and (5) fail to reach their targets.

## SUMMARY AND LOOK AHEAD

Communication is the process of influencing others' behavior by sharing ideas, information, or feelings with them. The basic elements of the communication process are the source, message, channel, receiver, and feedback. Noise is anything that interferes with the communication process. Marketers must understand the process to communicate effectively with their market targets and other publics. We usually refer to the communication efforts of manufacturers, middlemen, or nonprofit organizations as promotion—an element in the marketing mix.

Examples of promotional goals are making target customers aware of the firm and its products, providing information, inducing trial purchases, and explaining company actions. Four types of promotion effort are (1) advertising, (2) professional selling, (3) sales promotion, and (4) public relations and publicity. These constitute the promotion mix.

Advertising is any paid form of nonpersonal communication through the mass media about a product or idea by an identified sponsor. Professional selling, on the other hand, involves direct, face-to-face contact between a representative of the firm and those people with whom the firm wants to communicate. Sales promotion is activities that seek to induce directly a desired response from target customers, company salespersons, middlemen, or their salesforces. These activities add value to the product and/or serve to motivate a desired response.

Public relations (P-R) is communication to correct erroneous impressions about the firm or to maintain and build its goodwill. Unlike advertising, professional selling, and sales promotion, P-R primarily is concerned with communicating with people outside the market target. P-R programs can be conducted through direct contact, publicity, or institutional advertising. Publicity is news or information about the firm or its products that is not paid for by the firm. It is presented by the media as news.

Factors that influence the use and relative emphasis on the various promotion elements are (1) product related, (2) consumer related, (3) firm related, and (4) situation related. Product-related factors include (1) amount and complexity of product information to be communicated, (2) product's stage in the life cycle, and (3) product type and unit price. Consumer-related factors include (1) size and characteristics of the market target and (2) type of buying decision. Firm-related factors include (1) type of marketing channel and promotion philosophy, (2) branding strategy, (3) pricing strategy, (4) budget, and (5) expertise and peculiarities of company personnel. Finally, situation-related factors include (1) visibility of the firm in the environment and (2) competitors' activities.

Managing the promotion effort requires (1) setting promotion objectives and selecting a promotion mix, (2) planning the promotion effort, (3) determining budget size and allocating it among promotion mix elements, (4) implementing the promotion program, and (5) evaluating the promotion program. Special attention must be given to the sales and advertising efforts.

In the next chapter we will discuss professional selling—personalized promotion—in greater detail.

## REVIEW QUESTIONS

**1.** Identify and discuss the elements of the communication process.

**2.** What functions does the source of communication perform?

**3.** What is the difference between primary and secondary communication channels?

**4.** Identify and discuss four general promotional goals.

**5.** Identify and discuss the elements in the promotion mix.

**6.** Identify and discuss five types of sales promotion directed to consumers and five types directed to the salesforce, middlemen, and their salesforces.

**7.** What advantages does publicity have over other public relations techniques? What about disadvantages?

**8.** What four general types of factors influence the use and emphasis placed on each element in a promotion mix? Give examples of each.

**9.** Contrast push and pull promotion philosophies.

**10.** What are the characteristics of a good promotion objective? Give an example.

**11.** Identify and discuss four approaches to determining the promotion budget.

**12.** What subjective criteria tell a firm that the promotion program needs revision?

## DISCUSSION QUESTIONS

**1.** Select and bring to class an ad that creates noise by using words most people will not understand.

**2.** Bring examples of different types of sales promotions to class. Be prepared to explain the purpose of each.

**3.** What might indicate that a firm's public relations efforts are ineffective?

**4.** How does the type of consumer decision involved with a product affect the promotion effort?

**5.** Would most consumers prefer lower prices to sales promotions like coupons and consumer sweepstakes?

## NOTES

1. "Advertising for Trouble," *Time*, March 20, 1978, p. 63.

2. It has been suggested that consumerism and environmentalism are factors that should lead industry trade associations to direct their public relations activities to the general public. See Ronald N. Levy, "The Role of Publicity in Association Public Relations," *Public Relations Journal*, March, 1977, pp. 14–17.

3. "Tyson Foods: Putting Its Brand on High-Margin Poultry Products," *Business Week*, August 20, 1979, pp. 48–49.

4. Aggregate expenditures on sales promotion exceed those on advertising. See Roger A. Strang, "Sales Promotion—Fast Growth, Faulty Management," *Harvard Business Review*, July–August, 1976, pp. 115–124.

5. See B. C. Cotton and Emerson M. Babb, "Consumer Response to Promotional Deals," *Journal of Marketing*, July, 1978, pp. 109–113.

6. "Jostens: A School Supplier Stays with Basics as Enrollment Declines," *Business Week*, April 21, 1980, pp. 124, 129.

7. For discussion of the factors that influence coupon redemption, see Ronald W. Ward and James E. Davis, "Coupon Redemption," *Journal of Advertising Research*, August, 1978, pp. 51–58.

8. "Coupon Gimmicks Spread as Manufacturers

Look for Attention-Getting Ideas," *Wall Street Journal,* February 21, 1980, p. 1.

9.  " 'Carol Wright' to Distribute Coupons at Supermarket Doors," *Marketing News,* February 22, 1980, p. 12.

10.  For further discussion of the relationship between marketing and public relations, see Philip Kotler and William Mindak, "Marketing and Public Relations," *Journal of Marketing,* October, 1978, pp. 13–20; and Jonathan N. Goodrich, Robert L. Gildea, and Kevin Cavanaugh, "A Place for Public Relations in the Marketing Mix," *MSU Business Topics,* Autumn, 1979, pp. 53–57.

11.  See Irwin Ross, "Public Relations Isn't Kid-Glove Stuff at Mobil," *Fortune,* September, 1976, pp. 106–114.

12.  See Katherin Marton and J. J. Boddewyn, "Should a Corporation Keep a Low Profile?" *Journal of Advertising Research,* August, 1978, pp. 25–31.

13.  See R. Seymour Smith, "How to Plan for Crisis Communications," *Public Relations Journal,* March, 1979, pp. 17–18.

14.  See John Peters, "Good PR Strategy Can Reinforce All Efforts in Communications," *Industrial Marketing,* February, 1976, pp. 50–55.

15.  Bernard F. Whalen, "Beleaguered Johnson Products Company Plans War with Cosmetology Giants," *Marketing News,* February 22, 1980, p. 7.

16.  See Malcolm A. McNiven, "Plan for More Productive Advertising," *Harvard Business Review,* March–April, 1980, pp. 130–136.

17.  For a different perspective, see Donald S. Tull, James H. Barnes, and Daniel T. Seymour, "In Defense of Setting Budgets for Advertising as a Percent of Sales," *Journal of Advertising Research,* December, 1978, pp. 49–51.

# Chapter 18

# Professional Selling

**OBJECTIVES**

*After reading this chapter you should be able to*

1. identify the basic objectives of personal selling.

2. identify and discuss the steps in the personal selling process.

3. contrast five traditional approaches to selling.

4. identify and discuss several factors that favor a customer-oriented professional approach to selling.

5. explain how professional salespersons serve their employers and customers.

6. describe the structure and goals of a sales interview.

7. identify four types of professional sales calls and their purposes.

8. compare a customer-oriented sales approach to the traditional approaches.

9. identify and discuss several important sales interview skills.

10. contrast four types of professional sales jobs.

11. identify and discuss seven important decision areas in sales management.

**KEY CONCEPTS**

*Look for these terms as you read the chapter:*

Prospecting
Qualifying
Approach
Close
Stimulus-response Selling
Sales-call Ratio
Need Satisfaction Selling
Mood Selling
Successive Commitment Selling
Formulized Selling
Balanced Selling Effort
Customer-oriented Selling
Territory Screening
Sales Interview
Initial Contact Calls
Regular Customer Calls
Follow-up Calls
Service Calls
Regular Dealer Salesperson
Missionary Salesperson
Industrial Salesperson
Professional Sales
Geographical Territorial Organization
Product Specialization
Task Specialization
Market Target Specialization

*Personal selling includes sales jobs that range from retail salesclerks to highly trained professional salespersons who sell complex data processing systems. Retail salesclerks sometimes are hired and put on the job with little effort to train them. This probably is one reason so many of them use the same ineffective approach to selling prospective customers, "May I help you?" Some retailers, however, are recognizing the need for more effective training and are providing it. Companies like Xerox or IBM, on the other hand, may invest $60,000 to $75,000 to train a professional salesperson.\* He or she requires detailed product knowledge and professional selling skills.*

*Consider the copier industry. At one time Xerox had the market practically to itself. But as Japanese rivals entered the market with lower-priced copiers, Xerox started losing market share at the lower end of the market. The Japanese firms adopted a somewhat different approach to marketing. Unlike Xerox, which used its own salesforce to call on prospective buyers, they relied on their dealers to sell the copiers.*

*In more recent years, as we saw in Chapter 13, Xerox has begun marketing its lower-priced copiers through its own stores. Meanwhile, some Japanese rivals are seeking to penetrate the market for more sophisticated and costlier copiers and are finding it necessary to invest more in training their dealers to sell them.*

Personal selling effort is necessary for any individual or organization that seeks to accomplish marketing objectives. In this chapter we will discuss the nature of the personal selling process and how personal selling differs from other promotion mix elements. We will present several traditional approaches to personal selling along with their relative advantages and disadvantages.

The focus will then shift to a discussion of factors that are resulting in greater emphasis on professional selling and the nature of customer-oriented professional selling. We also will discuss professional sales jobs and the nature of sales management.

## EVERYBODY DOES IT

Business firms use personal selling to sell products, college students use it to get dates or additional money from their parents, college recruiters use it to attract students, and the American Cancer Society uses it in soliciting contributions. Politicians also use personal selling to win votes, graduating college students use it in marketing themselves to campus recruiters, some physicians use it in persuading their patients to begin a regular program of exercise, and the Pope uses it to sell the idea of brotherhood. Everybody practices personal selling.

---

\*"Japan, Hoping to Duplicate Its Success in Auto Field, Battles Xerox for U.S. Sales," *Wall Street Journal*, January 15, 1981, p. 42.

Personal selling is different from other promotion mix elements in that it involves personalized face-to-face contact between a salesperson and a prospective buyer. Door-to-door salespersons for Electrolux and Avon, salespeople in retail stores, and IBM sales engineers are engaged

## Figure 18–1. Sales reps now earning $27,000 a year: survey

Average annual income of experienced sales representatives hit $27,000 in 1979, having doubled since 1969, according to the Dartnell Institute of Financial Research, Chicago.

That statistic is one of many found in the Institute's recently released *20th Biennial Survey of Salesmen's Compensation.* More than 350 sales managers, reporting the income of 26,000 sales reps, contributed information for the survey.

According to Dartnell, the experienced sales rep working on straight commission fares best—earning an average of $32,135 a year. Reps working for a combination salary and commission or bonus averaged $28,456 annually, and sales reps on straight salary earned $22,265.

Semi-experienced sales reps earned $21,400, an increase of nearly 17% over the 1977 figure set during the previous survey, and sales trainees are now paid $15,030, a 10% increase.

The combination plan of salary and incentive was far and away the most popular with companies (54% use this method), followed by straight salary plans (26%), and commission-only plans (20%).

Some of the highlights reported in the survey include the cost of a sales call, now estimated to be $71.90, a jump of 22% over the 1977 figure. The normal expenses incurred by sales personnel (travel, lodging, meals, etc.) also increased 14% over the last two years.

Dartnell, which surveyed sales managers in the U.S. and Canada, also found that the total average field expense per sales rep is now $10,618. The cost of training a sales rep (salary, trainer's salary, program costs, etc.) has hit $12,452, an increase of 13% over the cost set in 1977.

The Institute also provides in its survey a composite of the "average" American sales representative. According to its research, he or she:
—is 37 years old;
—is a college graduate (or has some college training);
—has been with the company 7.5 years;
—is most likely to quit after 4.5 years, if at all;
—costs $12,452 to train;
—is paid for travel expenses;
—spends 16.3 hours a week in nonselling company activities;
—earns $27,000 a year;
—is paid mostly on a salary/incentive basis; and
—costs the company $71.90 to make a sales call.

In Canada, the average earnings of an experienced sales rep are $23,976. Those on a salary plan earn an average of $20,485, those on straight commission earn $25,912, and reps on a combination plan earn $25,127.

A semi-experienced Canadian rep earns $18,772, and a trainee makes $14,700 during that particular period. The salary and incentive plan is most popular with Canadian companies (45%), followed by straight salary plans (37%), and commission plans (18%).

Cost of training a sales rep in Canada is $11,400 and the cost of an average sales call is $55.83, up 20% over 1977. Total average field expense per sales rep is $11,348 ($730 more than in the United States).

The survey, which also describes compensation plans according to industry type, is 325 pages and costs $89.50. For more information, contact the Dartnell Corp., 4660 Ravenswood Ave., Chicago, IL 60640, (312) 561-4000.

Source: *Marketing News.*

in personal selling. It is the oldest type of promotional effort and companies spend more money on it than on any other element in the promotion mix. Millions of Americans are employed part-time and full-time in personal selling.

Other promotion mix elements are targeted to groups of people. When Schlitz and Budweiser advertise on TV they know some people will not be prospective buyers. Likewise, billions of coupons printed in newspapers and magazines are not used by people who are not interested in the couponed products. Salespersons can do a better job of weeding out nonprospects. Personal selling is a highly personalized type of promotion in which the salesperson tailors the message to the prospect's situation, answers questions, and deals with objections.

Because of its highly personalized nature, however, personal selling generally is the most costly element in the promotion mix. Total spending on personal selling exceeds that for advertising and sales promotion. Professional sales representatives are costly to train and each sales call represents a considerable expense to the firm. (See Figure 18–1.)

## THE PERSONAL SELLING PROCESS

The basic objectives of personal selling are (1) to find prospective customers, (2) to convert them to customers, and (3) to keep them as customers. The activities in the personal selling process vary among salespersons depending on the type of sales job and the particular selling situation. But it generally includes these steps: (1) prospecting, (2) qualifying, (3) preparing the preapproach, (4) approaching the prospect, (5) making the sales presentation, (6) handling objections, (7) closing the sale, and (8) following up the sale.

### Prospecting

**Prospecting** means getting leads. A lead is the name of a person or organization who might use the salesperson's product. Important internal sources of leads are company records and personnel in the service, advertising, and credit departments. External sources include trade journals, business sections of local newspapers, present customers, trade shows, trade association directories, and mail-in or telephone requests for information from prospects who have seen or heard the firm's ads.

prospecting

### Qualifying

**Qualifying** involves gathering additional information about prospects to determine if they can benefit from buying the product, can afford it, and are qualified to make the buying decision. Unqualified prospects are eliminated after careful evaluation and qualified ones may be ranked in terms of their buying potential.

qualifying

### Preparing the Preapproach

Preapproach preparation is part of the salesperson's homework before making contact with the prospect. It involves gathering more specific information about the prospect and his or her product needs, background, and company and personal characteristics. This information helps in selecting a method of approach and presentation.

### Approaching the Prospect

approach

The **approach** is the manner chosen by the salesperson to establish initial contact with a prospect. If the prospect's business is in a seasonal lull the salesperson may call in person without having set up an appointment. Otherwise, the salesperson might schedule an appointment over the phone with the prospect or the prospect's secretary. Careful preparation of the approach helps ensure a good first impression on the prospect.

### Making the Sales Presentation

In making the sales presentation, the salesperson first must get the prospect's attention quickly and creatively to prepare the way for building interest and desire for the product. Demonstrations and visuals help show prospects how the product can help them solve a problem. The productivity of a presentation, for example, can be increased by using portable, self-contained overhead projectors to help demonstrate product benefits. We will discuss several approaches to the sales presentation later in this chapter.

### Handling Objections

Normally, a prospect will have some objections to buying the product. Some salespersons want to discuss possible objections before the prospect voices them. This is risky because some of those objections may not have even occurred to the prospect. Encouraging prospects to voice objections helps the salesperson deal with them in a positive fashion. Salespersons cannot cope with objections when prospects do not voice them. Advertising often helps salespersons deal with objections. For example, Curtis-Mathes's advertising theme, "The most expensive television set you can buy—and darn well worth it," helps to dispel a prospect's objection about price. Thus the salesperson in a retail store may not have to devote much time to this aspect in the sales presentation.

### Closing the Sale

close

The **close** is the point in the sales presentation at which the salesperson attempts to clinch the sale. Many attempt trial closes at one or more places in the presentation. For example, after demonstrating the product the salesperson might ask the prospect about a desired delivery date. If the prospect supplies a desired date, the salesperson knows the sale is made. If the prospect raises objections, another attempt at closing is necessary.

## Following Up the Sale

After closing a sale, an effective salesperson will follow up to make sure the order was delivered on time, the product arrived damage free, and, if necessary, was installed properly. Subsequent checks on product performance also help ensure customer satisfaction, build goodwill, and may lead to repeat business. Following up is part of the effort to implement the marketing concept at the organization's sales level. The following discussion focuses specifically on the sales presentation.

## TRADITIONAL APPROACHES TO HANDLING SALES PRESENTATIONS

Five traditional approaches to handling sales presentations are (1) stimulus-response selling, (2) need satisfaction selling, (3) mood selling, (4) barrier (successive commitment) selling, and (5) formulized selling.

## Stimulus-Response Selling

Basically, **stimulus-response selling** is a canned sales approach in which the salesperson presents a memorized sales talk, including a number of key words (stimuli) to produce a favorable response by the prospect. Thus in selling to a retailer a salesperson might use words such as "high profit margin" and "high turnover."

**stimulus-response selling**

Constructing a stimulus-response sales presentation involves listing all the prospect's possible buying motives. Then the product's features are translated into selling points to show what each will mean to the prospect. The fact that a ball-point pen has a Diamite ball point may have little meaning to a prospect. It must be translated into selling points like "won't skip" or "won't leak" to be meaningful and influence the prospect's buying behavior. This is called "benefitizing" the product. After all product features have been benefitized, a sales presentation is written and each salesperson memorizes and uses it on all prospects. If all buying motives have been identified correctly, those for any one prospect will be covered in the sales presentation.

The major advantage of this approach to selling is low-cost sales training. It can generate a sales volume for simple-decision products with a minimum of training time and costs.[1] It is most suitable for door-to-door and telephone selling and as a training technique for beginning salespersons, who will quit using it after developing product knowledge and sales skills.

Stimulus-response selling is not suitable for complex decision products. The salesperson cannot adjust the presentation to a prospect's situation. Prospects often become impatient with parts of the sales presentation that do not apply to them. The only feedback the salesperson wants is an indication that the prospect is willing or unwilling to buy—the salesperson does not want and cannot handle questions or objections. This approach usually leads to a very low **sales-call ratio** (the

**sales-call ratio**

number of sales made to the number of calls made). A ratio of 1:10, for example, means that only 1 sale was closed in 10 calls.

### Need Satisfaction Selling

**need satisfaction selling**

**Need satisfaction selling** recognizes that the main reason people buy comes from within the person, not from outside stimuli. The salesperson has to discover the prospect's needs and show how the product will satisfy them. Most applications of this approach to selling involve four steps that relate to Maslow's need hierarchy, which we discussed in Chapter 5. (See Figure 18–2.)

Salespersons using this approach do not try to cover all possible buying motives and product features. They use appeals to broad-based need clusters early in the presentation to determine which needs are important and then they concentrate on these. An example of an appeal to the safety need cluster for a life insurance salesperson might be, "I'm sure you sometimes worry about what would happen to your spouse and children if anything should happen to you." An alternate appeal might be, "It's hard to know what the future will bring, isn't it?" A positive response by the prospect indicates that safety is an important need.

After appeals to all the broad-based need clusters are made, the salesperson discusses the product in terms of specific needs within each cluster that received a positive response. Emphasis by the salesperson on relieving worry about accidents and preparing for retirement could benefitize life insurance in terms of the specific needs in the safety cluster.

The words a salesperson uses to benefitize the product must fit the prospect's frame of reference and situation. In discussing a typewriter with an office manager, the emphasis might be on eliminating several operations by typists, expressed as "increased productivity." In discussing the typewriter with a typist, the emphasis might be on "makes correcting typos a lot easier."

This approach can produce excellent results when the salesperson is sensitive, understands motivation, and knows the product. It emphasizes internal motivation, benefitizing the product from the prospect's

*Figure 18–2. Steps in need satisfaction selling*

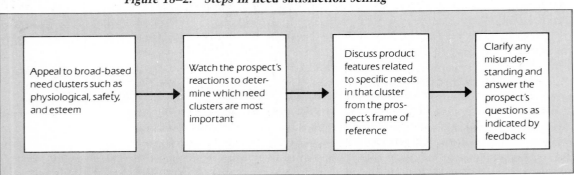

frame of reference, and feedback to determine what the salesperson does in the presentation. In practice, however, salespersons often use canned statements for each need cluster and are unable to assess prospect needs accurately. Nevertheless, the need satisfaction approach is the central idea of the customer-oriented professional selling approach we will discuss later in the chapter.

### Mood Selling

**Mood selling** assumes that what a salesperson says is less important than how the prospect feels about the salesperson, product, and firm. These feelings are determined by the emotional climate the salesperson creates in the selling situation. Two types of mood selling are respect selling and clown selling.

**mood selling**

In respect selling, the salesperson tries to create an atmosphere of sincere concern for the prospect's welfare. He or she must feel the salesperson is a trusted friend. Prospects who do not buy deny the sincerity of the salesperson's friendship. It is a high-pressure technique. In clown selling, the salesperson tries to create a happy atmosphere by telling jokes and funny stories. To keep the salesperson coming back the prospect must continue to buy.

The key to effective use of either approach is the salesperson's ability to maintain the role established with the prospect. Behavior that does not fit this role creates doubts in the prospect's mind. Mood selling's major contribution is its recognition of the importance of establishing a good working relationship with prospects. But it basically is playacting. One simply cannot be sincerely concerned about a prospect's welfare or bubbling with happiness all the time. Yet the salesperson must maintain that role with the prospect. This can lead to feelings that no one really knows or likes the salesperson as he or she really is. The result can be loneliness and despair.

### Barrier, or Successive Commitment, Selling

In **successive commitment selling,** the salesperson views the selling process as a series of prospect commitments to the buying decision. These commitments are "yes" or other agreement responses with the salesperson's statements. In order not to buy, the prospect must admit he or she lied every time he or she agreed with the salesperson. As we saw in Chapter 4, a person who behaves inconsistently in terms of previous behavior experiences psychological tension, or cognitive dissonance. Most people will avoid this discomfort by trying to behave consistently. It is very inconsistent not to buy after agreeing with the salesperson's presentation.

**successive commitment selling**

Two basic forms of this approach are the traditional barrier approach and the never-ending spiral. The traditional barrier approach sometimes is used in selling life insurance. Table 18–1 is an excerpt from such a presentation that shows the attempt to lead the prospect to buy a deferred payment life insurance policy.

**Table 18–1.** *Use of the traditional barrier approach in selling life insurance*

| | |
|---|---|
| S12 | I'm sure you don't have a lot of extra money now since you are in school and have a small child. (pauses) |
| P12 | That's for sure. |
| S13 | Yet you do need basic coverage in case something happens to you. Isn't that right? |
| P13 | Yeah. |
| S14 | A policy that would give you the coverage you need right now but would let you pay for it as your income increases would be an ideal solution, wouldn't it . . . ? |
| P14 | Yes it would . . . |

Products with many optional features or components like cars or stereo components systems lend themselves to the never-ending spiral approach. The salesperson starts with a basic model at a reasonable price and adds options or components one at a time. As each trade-up is added the salesperson gets the prospect's agreement that it adds value to the total product. This continues until the prospect stops agreeing. Successive commitment also is a high-pressure technique. The

**Table 18–2.** *The formulized selling approach*

| Stages | Mental States | Prospect Decisions |
|---|---|---|
| **Prospecting, qualifying, and preparing the preapproach**<br>(Continually searching for and qualifying leads and gathering information on the prospect's background, personal characteristics, and product needs.) | | |
| **Preapproach**<br>(Setting up initial contact with the prospect by making an appointment either in person or by phone.) | **Attention**<br>(If the prospect is contacted directly, the salesperson may have to get attention by giving a general idea of the call's purpose and the benefits the prospect can expect. Otherwise, this mental stage becomes a part of the approach stage.) | |
| **Approach** | **Attention/interest**<br>(Getting the prospect's attention and interest by making a forceful statement, such as "I want to help you increase your profits by $25,000 this year." Reduce the prospect's tension in dealing with a stranger by such statements as, "I'm not going to try to sell you anything today.") | **See and hear**<br>(The salesperson must get an observable commitment by the prospect to continue the sales presentation.) |

salesperson does not want the prospect to consider other ways of handling the buying problem. The goal is to get a buying commitment right now or else the prospect probably will not buy. Once away from the salesperson the prospect thinks of other ways of handling the buying decision. If the prospect does buy, however, it is also likely that this will occur and he or she may become dissatisfied with the purchase. Thus in 1974 the Federal Trade Commission imposed a "cooling off" rule that requires door-to-door salespersons to give written notice to customers placing orders of $25 or more that they can cancel their purchase, without penalty, within three days.

Notice in Table 18–1 that the prospect participates very little in the selling process. The salesperson is in control and may learn very little about the prospect's needs.

## Formulized Selling (A.I.D.A.)

The **formulized selling** approach assumes that (1) every successful sales presentation has certain identifiable stages, (2) in each stage the salesperson must create certain mental states in the prospect's mind and get certain overt commitments from the prospect, and (3) if the salesperson

formulized
selling

**Table 18–2.** *The formulized selling approach Cont.*

| Stages | Mental States | Prospect Decisions |
|---|---|---|
| **Demonstration** (Information giving: (1) telling the prospect what he or she is going to see or experience, (2) letting the prospect operate, touch, feel, or see the product, explaining the important features while the prospect is experiencing it and the benefits of each, and (3) summarizing what the prospect has experienced, touched, felt, or seen.) | **Desire** (Showing how the product will work in the prospect's situation— what it will do—to stimulate desire for the product.) | **Advantages and disadvantages** (When the prospect tries the product certain advantages and disadvantages will be VOICED. The salesperson encourages the prospect to VOICE these thoughts.) |
| **Handling objections** (Encouraging the prospect to voice any problems or objections in using the product. This gives the salesperson a chance to deal with them. Objections or doubts not voiced by the prospect are the ones that usually cause the prospect not to buy.) | **Confidence** (Handling doubts or objections helps create confidence in the prospect that the product or proposal is the best alternative to use in the prospect's situation.) | **Proposition, firm, and salesperson** (Three aspects of a buying situation about which a prospect must have confidence and about which objections might be raised are the product, the salesperson's firm, and the salesperson.) |
| **Closing** (Getting a buying commitment from the prospect in the form of a definite order for a certain amount, at a set price, to be delivered at a certain date.) | **Action** (The mental state of doing something about his or her situation, deciding or moving ahead, is the goal of the salesperson.) | **Now** (Placing the order now, not sometime in the future. Buying now means the prospect can be reaping the benefits of the decision that much sooner.) |

does what is supposed to be done in each stage the prospect will buy. Table 18–2 is an outline of formulized selling that identifies the stages of the sales presentation, the mental states to be created in the prospect's mind, and the prospect decisions the salesperson must get.

This approach gives the salesperson an organized way to plan and assess the presentation. Demonstrating the product helps in communicating product benefits to prospects. Voicing objections and doubts involves prospects in applying the product to their situation and gives the salesperson a chance to clarify any confusion. Of course, it may not be necessary to create attention, interest, and desire in prospects who tentatively have decided that they need a product marketed by a certain company. But the salesperson must not assume that once a prospect's attention is gained that he or she need not worry about it any more. The prospect can be distracted. Keeping his or her attention should be a concern throughout the presentation.

Notice in Table 18–2 that the prospect is involved actively in the selling process only in the objection stage. Prospect objections and questions are delayed or minimally answered in the early stages. This limits communication from prospects and may lead salespersons to discuss the product in ways that are irrelevant to prospects. Another disadvantage of this approach is the idea that a properly given sales presentation always leads to a sale. This can damage a salesperson's morale, especially if the prospect has decided not to buy immediately. The prospect may want to think it over before deciding, but the salesperson may feel that he or she has done something wrong. A final weakness is that the stage of the formula the customer is in determines the salesperson's behavior. In most instances, the salesperson's major concern is feedback from the prospect to determine when to move to the next stage in the formula.

## A NEW VIEW OF SELLING

As we saw in the previous chapter, professional selling is a part of personal selling but excludes retail salespersons and door-to-door salespersons. Our primary emphasis in the remainder of this chapter also is on professional selling. Professional selling may also be called customer-oriented selling.

As we saw in Chapter 1, salespeople were basically perceived as movers of inventory during the hard-sell era. Modern professional salespeople are perceived quite differently.[2] They are highly trained professionals who help their target customers solve problems. They often serve as consultants to their employers and customers. In many firms they are among the highest-paid employees. Furthermore, people with professional selling backgrounds are in top management in many firms. In the first three months of 1980, marketing/sales accounted for the greatest volume of executive jobs filled. Salaries were in the $45,000 to $65,000 range.[3]

Five major factors help explain the greater emphasis on professional selling: (1) a need for more accurate communication, (2) the development of the total product concept, (3) a desire for greater market penetration, (4) the need for a balanced selling effort, and (5) the need to cope with shortages.

### Accurate Communication

Building and maintaining a salesforce is costly but may be the best way to communicate effectively with target customers, especially about complex and/or new products. Mass advertising can reach many people at a low cost per contact but is limited in the amount and complexity of information it can deliver. For example, a recent study found that TV viewers miscomprehend some portion of everything they watch on TV.[4] Advertising's effectiveness is limited by lack of direct feedback and the need to present information that can be understood by people with different backgrounds and circumstances. A salesperson can tailor the presentation to each prospect.

### The Total Product

The salesperson's presentation can provide a basis for differentiation among similar brands in a product category. Knowledgeable salespersons who can work at the prospect's level and establish a problem-solving relationship help differentiate their offerings from those of rivals. A salesperson who does not lead prospects to believe the product will do things it will not, follows up sales to make sure the product is performing satisfactorily, and makes and keeps firm delivery dates builds customer satisfaction with the product and company.

### Market Penetration

Most firms today want to achieve deep and profitable market penetration. An industrial products marketer, for example, wants to sell its product to every account that can be serviced profitably. Salespersons must work to develop their territories to the fullest extent possible. Getting new accounts requires them to search for leads, look for new uses for the product, and maintain close contact with people who can provide information about changes in their territories that are important to their marketing manager. Those who adjust their behavior to each prospect will develop more of the potential market for their firms' products.

### Balanced Selling Effort

Professional salespersons establish and maintain a long-term relationship with their firms' markets. They are the key contact between the firm and its customers. To maintain the required type of relationship a **balanced selling effort** is needed. Salespersons must be concerned about more than merely selling present products to present customers.

**balanced selling effort**

These other responsibilities can be divided into four major areas. First, salespersons must maintain regular contact with buyers of existing products, help introduce new products, and discover unfulfilled needs. Second, they must develop new accounts through prospecting activities. Third, they must perform a service function for their target customers: they are marketing consultants who help prospects solve problems. Fourth, they must follow up sales to old and new accounts to ensure that products are performing properly. Design errors, quality control problems, and unique customer situations make follow-up a necessary part of a salesperson's job in keeping customers satisfied after the sale.

### Shortages

When demand outstrips supplies of raw materials and manufactured products, resource planning and forecasting of needs become crucial. During acute shortages, a firm must decide which customers will be served. This includes assessing what alternative products and/or sources can relieve some customer problems and informing customers of them. In some cases, it may be necessary to refuse customers even though alternative products or sources are not available. Doing this while maintaining a working relationship with that customer requires salespersons who are highly skilled in human relations.

### CUSTOMER-ORIENTED SELLING

customer-
oriented
selling

With **customer-oriented selling,** the focus is on the prospect rather than a formula, series of commitments, or canned sales presentation. Professional salespersons serve their employers and customers by functioning as (1) territorial market managers, (2) educators, (3) communications specialists, (4) helpers in problem solving, (5) human relations experts, and (6) feedback mechanisms.

### Territorial Market Manager

Professional salespersons make many of the same decisions at a territorial level that marketing managers make at the company-wide level.[5] Although they have no direct control over sales volume, they can prepare daily, weekly, and monthly plans based on factors they can control, such as the number and type of sales calls for their assigned territories.[6]

A daily plan, for example, includes whom to call on that day, type of call, what to discuss, and any materials that must be taken to the sales interview. (See Figure 18–3.) This enables salespersons to evaluate their daily performance. Reviewing these plans over weeks and months can help increase selling effectiveness by, for example, modifying the call mix.

Salespersons must also plan their territorial coverage. Call frequency, geographical location, and customer preferences affect travel time. Salespersons can divide territories into easily covered units by using zones or sections and establishing a call frequency that maintains a working relationship with the prospect.

territory
screening

**Territory screening** is a continuous process of prospecting and de-

DAILY PLAN

DATE:
PLACE:
PHONE:
ROOM NO.:

| TIME | PERSON | COMPANY ADDRESS PHONE | PURPOSE OF CALL | TYPE OF CALL | MATERIALS NEEDED |
|------|--------|------------------------|------------------|--------------|-------------------|
|      |        |                        |                  |              |                   |
|      |        |                        |                  |              |                   |
|      |        |                        |                  |              |                   |
|      |        |                        |                  |              |                   |
|      |        |                        |                  |              |                   |
|      |        |                        |                  |              |                   |
|      |        |                        |                  |              |                   |
|      |        |                        |                  |              |                   |
|      |        |                        |                  |              |                   |
|      |        |                        |                  |              |                   |
|      |        |                        |                  |              |                   |
|      |        |                        |                  |              |                   |

*Figure 18–3. A salesperson's daily plan*

veloping new accounts. This requires a personal record-keeping system that should at least include a prospect file and a current customer file. (See Figure 18–4.)

**Educator**

Several of the salesperson's tasks come under the education function. They inform prospects about product features and their meaning. Making highly technical new product information meaningful to an industrial

CURRENT CUSTOMER FILE

Name of Co.:                                              Classification:
Address:
Phone:
Person to Call On:
_____

Personal Information:

_____

Call Data:

| DATE | COMMENTS | REMINDER |
|------|----------|----------|
|      |          |          |
|      |          |          |
|      |          |          |
|      |          |          |
|      |          |          |
|      |          |          |
|      |          |          |
|      |          |          |
|      |          |          |
|      |          |          |
|      |          |          |
|      |          |          |
|      |          |          |
|      |          |          |
|      |          |          |
|      |          |          |
|      |          |          |
|      |          |          |
|      |          |          |

buyer may require assessing the prospect's level of education, product knowledge, and readiness to learn. Choice of words, use of visual materials, and demonstration techniques are important.

Equally important is offering new ways for prospects to think about problems. A prospect may have faced a problem before being approached by the salesperson. Thus it is likely the prospect has developed habitual ways of looking at the situation. The salesperson must help the prospect look at the situation in a different way in order to formulate alternative approaches to solving the problem. This often gives the salesperson an opportunity to show how a product can help solve the problem.

Salespersons who sell to retailers must know how to demonstrate new uses for existing products and offer new ways of marketing them, including how to display and promote them. Salespersons also perform an educational function in sales training. Experienced salespeople demonstrate their techniques at sales meetings. Beginning salespersons often travel with experienced ones to get pointers on sales planning, sales techniques, and filing company reports.

### Communications Specialist

Professional salespersons need information-getting skills, information-giving skills, and consultant skills to communicate effectively with their prospects.

Information-getting skills are needed to get prospects to talk about their situations and problems so the salesperson can present product information from the prospect's frame of reference. This, of course, also requires information-giving skills. Consultant skills are important because salespersons often act as communications consultants for buyers. For example, retailers sometimes expect a manufacturer's representative to help them prepare advertising campaigns, the cost of which is shared by the manufacturer and the retailer.

### Helper in Problem Solving

Prospects are in a problem-solving situation whenever they consider a new product. This is true whether they already are aware of it or become aware of it because of a salesperson's call. When the problems relate to the salesperson's product, the task is to help the prospect define the situation clearly and to consider alternatives. It is not the salesperson's job to make a decision for the prospect. Only the prospect knows enough about the situation to make the decision. Prospects also often expect help in solving problems that are not related directly to the salesperson's products. Providing this help increases trust and establishes a basis for possible future sales to those prospects.

Of course it is easier to talk about helping prospects solve problems than it is to do it. Generally, effort in the early part of a sales interview

◀  *Figure 18–4.  A salesperson's current customer file*

# Amaizo's dextrin expertise.

## It'll solve one sticky problem after another.

As one of the largest dextrin producers in the industry, we know that providing you with uniform quality and a multitude of solubilities and viscosities in over 25 different dextrins, just isn't enough in today's marketplace.

That's why we back our extensive product research and development with a thorough "hands-on" knowledge of your processing procedures and end use applications.

Call an AMAIZO "Dextrin Expert" and he'll show you how to meet modern adhesive requirements and improve productivity. He'll evaluate your needs, both in our labs and in your plant...suggest effective starting formulations...even anticipate potentially costly problems before they occur.

As the Complete Provider of dextrins to the adhesive industry, we've made a firm commitment to improve your products and profits, right down the line. And that's a promise we'll stick to.

*"The Complete Provider"*
*Building better products*
*with nature's building blocks*

Seventy Five Years

AMAIZO
American Maize-Products Company
Corn Processing Division
113th Street & Indianapolis Boulevard
Hammond, Indiana 46326
**Call toll free (800) 348-9896**
**In Indiana, call (219) 659-2000**

98† American Maize-Products Company

*An ad that depicts the salesperson's role as a helper in problem solving.*

Source: American Maize-Products Company.

focuses on separating symptoms from problems, separating objective and subjective facts, and identifying what can be changed and what cannot.

A department store owner may identify low sales in the sporting goods department as a problem, but the manufacturer's salesperson may help the retailer to see that low sales result from poor displays or old stock. Low sales are a symptom of the real problem—poor displays or old stock.

Subjective fact is how a person feels about a situation. Objective fact is what is actually taking place. The retailer may blame low sales on the personnel by saying, "They're the laziest, most uninterested bunch I've ever seen. All they do is stand around and gossip." The subjective facts are the retailer's feelings that personnel are lazy, uninterested gossips. The objective facts are that they stand around, talk to each other, and perhaps do not wait on customers. The salesperson must help the retailer deal with both sets of facts. Perhaps the employees have not been trained properly to sell the products.

The salesperson also must identify what parts of the prospect's situation are changeable and which are fixed. Those that cannot be changed rule out many ways of solving a problem. The best solution may be to fire the sporting goods department manager. But if this person is a relative, the best alternative may be to retrain the salesclerks to increase their productivity.

### Human Relations Expert

Professional salespersons need a high level of human relations skills. Ideally, the salesperson-prospect relationship should be one of warmth, honesty, trust, and confidentiality.[7] This is especially important in times of shortages. When a firm cannot produce enough output to meet demand, salespersons must work with customers so they will understand and remain customers. Salespersons play a major role in implementing a demarketing strategy.

### Feedback Mechanism

Salespeople are a vital part of a firm's marketing information system. They hear about problems customers are having with the firm's products and can provide valuable feedback on customer comparisons of rivals' products, prices, and services, modifications needed in existing products, effectiveness of mass advertising and other promotional efforts, and changes needed in marketing channels.

Let's look now at the conduct of a customer-oriented sales interview.

## THE CUSTOMER-ORIENTED SALES INTERVIEW

Customer-oriented salespersons think in terms of **sales interviews** instead of sales presentations. The emphasis is on two-way communication. This helps them to tailor accurate and useful communication for each

sales interview

prospect, which is important because prospects will be at different points in the buying decision process.

Each contact with a prospect is viewed as part of a continuing relationship. These salespersons know people buy on the basis of their needs, not pressure. Pressure would only damage their relationship with the prospect and lead to a loss of future sales. This way of looking at the prospect-salesperson relationship has been called one of high perceived-repeat-sale potential and low sales aggressiveness.[8] A sale today to a prospect who really does not need the product will cost the salesperson more in the long run than not making the sale. They see themselves as professionals who have knowledge, skills, and an ethical code of behavior.

### Types of Sales Calls

As shown in Table 18–3, professional salespeople make four basic types of sales calls based on the purpose of the call: (1) initial contacts, (2) regular customer calls, (3) follow-up calls, and (4) service calls.

**initial contact calls**

**Initial contact calls** are the first face-to-face contact a salesperson has with a prospect. They may be either cold calls or by appointment. Cold calls help in fully developing a territory. They also build flexibility into a daily plan because they can be omitted if necessary. But they may use up valuable time if the salesperson has to wait to see prospects. Initial

**Table 18–3.** *Types and purposes of sales calls*

| *Type of Call* | *Purposes of Call* |
|---|---|
| *Initial contact call* | 1. To verify information obtained through prospecting.<br>2. To gather new information about the prospect to see if the product can be used.<br>3. To give the prospect information about the firm's products verbally and/or through printed materials. |
| *Regular customer call* | 1. To get information about changes in the customer's situation, problems, or attempts at solving problems.<br>2. To provide information and help the customer consider alternative courses of action and their consequences.<br>3. To understand the customer's situation from the customer's point of view.<br>4. To make the sale if it appears to be appropriate for the customer's situation. |
| *Follow-up call* | 1. To handle any problems the customer is having with the product.<br>2. To communicate concern for the customer and to build trust in the salesperson and his or her firm.<br>3. To make auxiliary sales. |
| *Service call* | 1. To provide requested service on the product.<br>2. To gather feedback.<br>3. To gather additional information about the customer's other needs. |

contacts by appointment reduce wasted time but at the cost of losing flexibility.

Salespersons make **regular customer calls** on established customers or prospects that have been called on before. They usually are by appointment and at regular intervals. These calls are sales interviews.

regular customer calls

A nonprofessional salesperson's relationship with a customer often ends with the sale, especially for products with a low repeat-sale potential. But professional salespersons make **follow-up calls** on previous sales to help ensure after-the-sale satisfaction. These calls are often made without an appointment and can help build flexibility into the daily plan.

follow-up calls

Salespersons make **service calls** in response to customer requests for service, anticipated problems with the product, or new developments that will affect the performance of products bought for resale. For example, salespersons make service calls on a retailer when they are notified that a design error in the product requires immediate modification. Occasionally, salespeople make service calls on customers who are having problems with a competitor's products. These often lead to sales. Both follow-up and service calls are important as a feedback mechanism for the salesperson's company.[9]

service calls

### Structure of the Sales Interview

A sales interview can be divided into three phases based on the amount of talking by the salesperson and the prospect and the goals the sales-

**Table 18–4.** Structure of a sales interview

| Initial | Middle | Conclusion |
|---|---|---|
| Salesperson 25% of talking | Salesperson 48% of talking | Salesperson 40% of talking |
| Customer 75% of talking | Customer 52% of talking | Customer 60% of talking |
| 5 minutes | 35 minutes | 20 minutes |

**Table 18–5.** Goals of the sales interview

| Initial | Middle | Conclusion |
|---|---|---|
| 1. social amenities<br>2. establishing set (in initial contact)<br>3. getting prospect to start talking about his or her situation<br>4. verifying information obtained from prospecting or other activities<br>5. determining whether to continue interview | 1. getting reactions and information from prospect<br>2. giving information<br>3. suggesting alternatives | 1. answering questions<br>2. summarizing the previous discussion<br>3. making arrangements for future contacts<br>4. completing details of sale or service to customer<br>5. social amenities |

person is trying to accomplish. While the length and nature of these phases may vary for different types of sales calls, they follow the same general format. Table 18–4, on page 531, depicts the structure of a one-hour sales interview with a regular customer. The salesperson does less talking than the customer in the initial and closing phases but becomes more active in the middle phase.

While the percentages and duration will vary by prospect, salesperson, and type of sales call, they illustrate the importance of the salesperson's listening skills. Professional salespersons do not try to control the interview because more information can be obtained by listening than by talking.

The salesperson also tries to accomplish different things in different parts of the interview. This accounts for the differences in interaction patterns in the various phases. (See Table 18–5 on page 531.)

The initial phase may be very brief in a regular customer call and consists of the social amenities and an open-ended question, such as, "What's been going on since I saw you last month?" On the other hand, in a cold-call initial contact the salesperson has to establish set. This means establishing the purpose of the call as learning about the prospect,

**Table 18–6.** *Interviewing responses*

| Response | Definition | Examples of Use |
|---|---|---|
| Minimal social stimuli | Responses that tell the prospect you are listening and to continue. Include "uh huh," "yes," "I see," and "oh." | P\*: I've thought a lot about it recently . . . there are many things about . . . (Salesperson nods) that it's hard to know . . . <br> S\*\*: Yes. |
| Repetition of final word or phrase | Salesperson repeats exactly the last word or phrase of what the prospect just said. | P: The answer just can't be that simple, uh, I'm exaggerating a little, but I can't be sure . . . (pause) <br> S: Just can't be sure. |
| Paraphrasing | A restatement of the context of a prospect's statement using different words to highlight what the salesperson thinks is important. | P: At present we don't know exactly what benefits package we're going to offer in negotiations but we think employee demands will concentrate on health care, vacation pay, and sick leave. <br> S: Employee demands are still unclear, but health care will be one aspect of the benefits package. |
| Reflection of feeling | A labeling of prospect's feelings that are expressed or implied by behavior. | P: We're losing money . . . we supply the meat at the same contract price even though our costs are rising 1 percent a month. It's a stupid way to do business, but that's where we are. <br> S: You feel squeezed and angry about your present contracts. |

verifying the accuracy of information obtained by prospecting, and asking an open-ended question. As the prospect talks, the salesperson gains insight into the prospect's knowledge level, needs, and situation.

After assessing the prospect's readiness for product information, the salesperson becomes more active. This middle phase may be very short in an initial contact. If the product is highly technical, the salesperson may leave several brochures with the prospect. The middle phase in a regular customer call may take up 80 percent of the time they are together. Demonstrations and detailed discussion help show how the product fits the customer's situation. The middle phase in follow-up and service calls deals with problem solving or gathering information about the causes of customer problems.

In concluding an interview, salespersons want to check on their listening skills to be sure they fully understand what has been discussed. This is called *summarizing*. Either party may summarize. It also provides a basis for agreement about what can be done next—whether it is to buy the product, set up another appointment, or make delivery arrangements. If it is obvious during the middle phase that the customer is ready to buy, the conclusion will be short since summary is unnecessary.

**Table 18–6.** *Interviewing responses Cont.*

| *Response* | *Definition* | *Examples of Use* |
|---|---|---|
| Summarization | A summary of the ideas and emotions from the prospect's discussion of his or her situation. | S: So far, I've followed what you said. You need four new machines, eight operators' manuals, and financing for two years. |
| Tacting response leads | Gets prospect to discuss something just mentioned or other occasions when something has occurred. | P: We've been thinking about leasing, but that's a big headache.<br>S: Tell me exactly what you mean by leasing. I'm not sure I know what you mean by leasing. |
| Developmental questions | Open-ended questions that cannot be answered by "yes" or "no". | P: We are considering several alternatives, but none seem really good.<br>S: What sorts of things have you considered? |
| Evaluative questions | Ask the prospect for feedback about ideas or information provided by the salesperson. | S: Have I omitted anything? Is that an accurate statement of your situation? Does that sound reasonable? |
| Suggesting alternatives | Introduces ideas for the prospect's consideration in a way that prospect can reject or accept as his or her own. | P: We'll just have to forget the new equipment. Our cash for capital investments is all earmarked.<br>S: I wonder if a rental–option to buy arrangement would be possible in your situation? |

* (P) Prospect
** (S) Salesperson
Adapted from *Journal of the Academy of Marketing Science*, Spring, 1976.

### Interviewing Skills

Getting prospects to talk about their situation and tailoring an interview based on that discussion requires interviewing skills. Table 18–6 lists and defines interviewing responses and gives examples of their use. Practicing these skills is an important part of a professional sales training program.

## PROFESSIONAL SALES JOBS

Professional salespeople can be divided into four groups based on whom they call on and the characteristics of their work: (1) regular dealer salespersons, (2) missionary salespersons, (3) industrial salespersons, and (4) people who sell to professionals.

### Selling to Regular Dealers

regular dealer
salesperson

**Regular dealer salespersons** may work for a manufacturer and call on middlemen, or for a wholesaler and call on retailers. They usually are assigned a small territory and call on their customers frequently. They check the dealer's stock, advise about display and advertising, introduce new products, handle complaints, write orders, and help train salesclerks to sell the company's products. Their major concern is repeat sales so they do not pressure their customers to buy.

Regular dealer salespeople usually are paid a salary plus a small commission on sales. Most spend each night at home and become friends with their customers. General Foods and R. T. French Company are examples of firms that maintain a regular dealer salesperson salesforce.

### Selling to Middlemen

missionary
salesperson

**Missionary salespersons** do not take orders but call on retailers and wholesalers to encourage them to stock their employers' products. They build business by helping wholesalers and retailers improve their marketing techniques. They are marketing consultants to these middlemen. Their territories are usually much larger than those of regular dealer salespersons because their call frequency is lower. Missionary salespersons spend an average of two or three nights a week away from home. They usually are paid a somewhat higher salary than regular dealer salespersons and earn commissions or bonuses based on the sales volume in their territories.

Missionary salespersons must have a thorough knowledge of marketing, wholesale and retail operations, and be able to form working relationships quickly. Armstrong Cork and Shell Oil are examples of firms that maintain missionary salesforces.

### Selling to Industrial Buyers

industrial
salesperson

**Industrial salespersons** usually work for manufacturers or wholesalers and sell to industrial buyers.[10] Most of these buyers have purchasing agents who are especially concerned about product features, firmness of delivery dates, unvarying, quality, and after-sale service. They expect the salesperson to help solve their buying problems. Thus these salespersons must possess technical information about the product and offer advice on how to use it. A technical background often is necessary in addition to sales skills. Salespeople for mining equipment firms, for example, often have an engineering background.

As we saw in Chapter 7, purchasing agents are generally thought to be more objective in their buying decisions than retailers and wholesalers because they often work from detailed specifications supplied by using departments in their firms. But as products are more similar, other less objective factors influence their decisions. Well-trained professional salespersons should have an advantage in these situations.

In many cases, industrial salespersons are assisted in their selling efforts by technical specialists, such as engineers or scientists. A marketer of electrical equipment may have a staff of engineers who provide services to the company's salesforce. One of the firm's salespersons may have learned that a prospective buyer is seeking proposals from vendors on a new drive system for a shearing line. The salesperson may need an engineer's help in developing a proposal for the buying firm. The engineer probably will go to the prospect's place of business and discuss product specifications with the prospect's production and engineering personnel. Eventually, it may be the sales engineer who supervises the actual installation of the new machine in the buyer's plant. Although the salesperson identified the prospect and expressed a desire to bid on the new machine, the engineer's services were needed in helping the salesperson to solve the buyer's problem.

Industrial salespeople usually have large territories and spend more time away from home than missionary salespeople. They may spend only 39 percent of their time in face-to-face selling. The rest is used in traveling to interviews, waiting for interviews, making reports, attending meetings, and making service calls.[11] They usually have high incomes and often are paid a straight commission on sales.

## Selling to Professionals

Medical doctors, architects, and college professors are professionals who determine what their clients or students will buy. The salespeople who call on them often are called detail salespersons, and their work often resembles that of missionary salespersons. But there are enough differences to warrant treating them as a separate category of **professional sales.** professional sales They must do three things: (1) establish a strong personal relationship with the professional, (2) provide samples, brochures, and other services, and (3) be continually on the lookout for new product developments, new uses for existing products, and new products.

These salespeople really do not sell because the people they call on do not buy the company's product. A drug salesperson makes calls on physicians to show new products and distribute samples. The salesperson hopes that the physician will specify the firm's brands when writing prescriptions for patients. In the end, professionals make decisions based on their professional judgment. Thus most salespeople who call on them avoid overt persuasion by relying heavily on samples, printed information, and promotional reminders like coffee cups, pens, paperweights, and calendars.

Salespersons who sell to professionals must be knowledgeable about the professionals' field to converse intelligently with them. Many pharmaceutical companies used to hire medical school dropouts and publishers used to hire former college teachers who had not completed their degrees as college textbook salespersons. More recently, some of these firms are finding it easier to teach marketing graduates technical information than to teach marketing skills to people with technical backgrounds. Salespeople in this category usually are paid a salary plus bonus.

## SALES MANAGEMENT

Salesforce management, as we said in the previous chapter, is vital in implementing the promotion program. A salesforce must be managed effectively if it is to contribute to a firm's overall marketing effort. Important decision areas in sales management are (1) organizing the salesforce, (2) recruiting and selecting the salesforce, (3) training and developing the salesforce, (4) compensating the salesforce, (5) setting up sales territories, (6) motivating the salesforce, and (7) supervising and evaluating the salesforce.

### Organizing the Salesforce

How the salesforce is organized affects the quality of the firm's communication with its customers. Different approaches are appropriate for different types of firms that deal with different types of customers. The key is to match the organizational structure with the type of communication the firm needs.

A professional salesforce can be organized by (1) geographical territories, (2) product, (3) task, and/or (4) market targets.

**geographical ter-ritorial organization**

In **geographical territorial organization** each salesperson is assigned a territory and sells all the firm's products to all customers in that territory. It is common among firms that have a small number of closely related, nontechnical products. This allows the firm to assess the costs of doing business in each territory and ensures adaptability to changing conditions in each of them. It also helps salespersons in developing long-term working relationships with customers. This increases their credibility as a source of new ideas and information for customers.

**product specialization**

In **product specialization** some salespeople sell one or a few products to customers in a territory, while other salespeople may sell other company products to the same customers. Salespeople, therefore, become very knowledgeable about their products. Overlapping territories, however, are a problem for firms whose products are closely related. Customers may become confused when several salespeople from the same firm call on them. It also is costly to the marketer. For example, Swift & Company at one time had as many as six salespersons from its various subsidiaries calling on the same customer.[12]

**Task specialization** usually is found in large firms. Some salespeople may serve established customers in their territories, while a smaller group develops new accounts. Newly established accounts are turned over to the salesperson in whose territory the new account is located. The advantage here is that the communication skills needed to establish new accounts differ from those needed to maintain existing accounts.

task special-<br>ization

With **market target specialization** the salesforce is divided by market targets and each salesperson calls on only one target group. This approach often is used for complex and technical products whose use varies by market target. This allows wide application of the product in a variety of settings. American Telephone and Telegraph shifted their communications specialists to market target specialization to meet the competitive challenges of smaller firms that specialize in certain markets. Some textbook publishers have one group of sales representatives for junior and community colleges and another group for colleges and universities. NCR's sales personnel also specialize by market target. Data processing needs, for example, vary among firms in retailing, banking, and manufacturing.

market target<br>specialization

### Recruiting and Selecting the Salesforce

Recruiting is the process of attracting applicants for sales positions. For most firms it should be an on-going process instead of effort that is engaged in only when vacancies open up. This helps ensure an adequate number of recruits from which to select. Methods of recruitment include word of mouth, newspaper ads, announcements in trade publications, conventions, referrals by present company employees, public and private employment agencies, and vocational, technical, and college recruiting.

Selection procedures are guided by criteria that either have been validated as predictors of success or are believed to be important. Examples include aptitude tests, interest inventories, prior sales experience, college degree and grade-point average, role playing, and interviews. Selection criteria and procedures should be validated and those that are ineffective as predictors of selling success should be dropped. This is required by equal opportunity legislation. Many firms also are affirmative action recruiters.

Most firms use a sequential selection procedure in which unsuitable applicants may be rejected at one of several steps in the selection process. Figure 18–5 shows the sequence used by one firm that recruits nationally on college campuses. This procedure reduces the time and money spent on unsuitable applicants.

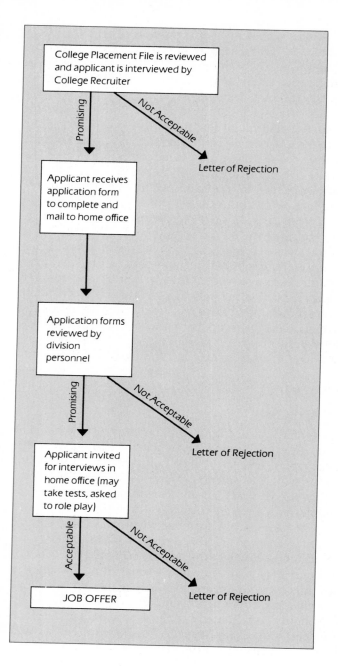

Figure 18–5.
Sequential selection
procedure

## Training and Developing the Salesforce

Sales training used to focus on product knowledge and practice in making sales presentations to prospects. Door-to-door salespersons especially were expected to learn through experience and little effort was given to

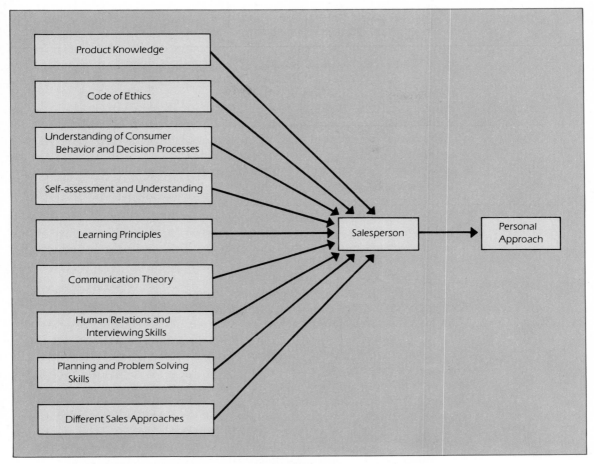

Figure 18–6. *Subjects included in sales training programs*

training them. With the increasing professionalization of selling and the development of video tape facilities, sales training has been broadened. Figure 18–6 shows the knowledge areas usually covered in modern sales training programs. These programs assume salespeople will use the knowledge and skills they acquire to develop their own individual approach to selling.[13]

### Compensating the Salesforce

Salespeople may be compensated in three basic ways: (1) straight commission, (2) straight salary, and (3) a combination of salary and incentive, such as commission and bonus, or other benefits. Each is used in different types of selling situations.[14]

**Straight Commission.** Straight commission often is used by firms with limited resources or in high-ticket industrial sales, such as construction and electronic health care and laboratory equipment. Insurance, real estate, and door-to-door consumer products salespersons are also often paid on straight commission.

Commissions usually are stated as a flat percentage of sales. But some firms use variable percentages that reflect the different profit margins of various product lines. Straight commission rewards salespersons on the basis of productivity but may not provide the balanced selling effort most firms want. Salespersons tend to concentrate on large accounts, high-commission items, and the immediate sale rather than long-range development of new accounts, service, and follow-up activities that are so important to a balanced selling effort. Turnover also tends to be higher under this system. This limits the resources a firm can invest in training beginning salespersons. Also, the sales manager has less control over personnel because they receive no salary.

**Straight Salary.** Straight salary gives the sales manager greater control over the salesforce. It also creates willingness on the part of the salesperson to devote time to the nonselling activities necessary for a balanced selling effort because they are paid on the basis of time. Salespeople are less concerned about an immediate payoff and are more interested in long-range development of good working relationships with target customers. But apart from periodic merit increases and keeping their jobs, straight salary is not as effective in motivating the salesforce to maximum effort.

**Combination Plans.** Combination plans of salary, commission, and other benefits are the most widely used form of compensation among firms with a professional salesforce. Although varying widely in details, most plans include a salary that covers the professional salesperson's living expenses. This frees them from worry about having money to pay the mortgage and grocery and utility bills. Commissions usually are figured on a percentage of sales over quota. Other benefits may include a company car, expenses, medical and life insurance, contests, prizes, and bonuses for special achievements.[15]

Combination plans relieve the salesperson of anxiety about daily living expenses, offer incentives related directly to productivity, provide benefits that are not taxable income, and encourage salespersons to do the nonselling activities that lead to a balanced selling effort.

### Setting Up Sales Territories

An important factor in compensating and motivating professional salespeople is setting up sales territories.[16] Poor servicing of existing accounts, lack of new accounts, low sales for some product lines, high travel expenses, high turnover of sales personnel, and wide, unaccounted-for differences in sales volume among territories are symptoms of the need to redraw territorial lines. Motivational factors also must be considered. A big complaint among some salespersons is that they build sales in a territory and then the sales manager breaks it into two or three territories. This can undermine morale and reduce the salesperson's compensation.

**Table 18–7.** *Guidelines for establishing sales territories*

1. A salesperson should not have to spend more than two or three nights a week away from home to cover the territory.
2. The number of established customers in a territory should be somewhat less than the salesperson can call on and maintain the call frequency demanded by the product.
3. A territory will provide adequate income for the salesperson and have growth potential.
4. A suitable plan for salespersons to live near the geographical center of their territories should be developed.
5. Travel routes in a territory will be arranged to keep mileage and traveling time to an acceptable minimum.
6. The potential volume of a territory will cover direct expenses of maintaining a salesperson there plus an acceptable profit margin.
7. Territorial lines will be observed by sales personnel—sales in a territory are credited to that territory's salesperson regardless of who makes the sale.

Table 18–7 lists several guidelines for establishing sales territories.

The guidelines in Table 18–7 affect the size of a firm's salesforce. But salesforce size is a dynamic variable. It will change as the firm's market conditions and marketing objectives change.[17]

## Motivating the Salesforce

Selling can be a frustrating type of work. Outside salespersons also spend most of their time away from the company and are on their own much of the time. Motivating them to make cold calls can be a big problem. In addition to financial rewards, therefore, nonfinancial incentives can help motivate them.[18] Examples include conventions, formal sales meetings, and trips.

## Supervising and Evaluating the Salesforce

Regional or district sales managers are important in managing the sales effort. They are resource persons for sales personnel in their regions or districts. A sales manager's main task is to provide a supportive climate and the resources needed to build salesperson effectiveness.[19] Among these resources are additional training, personal counseling, help in defining problems and generating solutions, technical assistance, additional support from other promotion mix elements, and emotional support.[20] Sales managers continually evaluate the performance of their personnel to identify and provide solutions to problems that help maintain a balanced selling effort. Activity reports, sales figures, and open lines of communication help sales managers collect the information they need to use a variety of quantitative and qualitative bases for evaluating sales personnel. Table 18–8 lists some of these evaluation criteria.

The sales manager's goal is to help a salesperson do a better job of selling. Suppose a salesperson is developing some new accounts that

**Table 18–8.** *Bases for evaluating salesperson performance*

---

*Quantitative*

---

1. Sales volume by product, customer group, or type of call.
2. Sales volume as a percentage of quota or market share.
3. Gross margin by product line, customer group, or order size.
4. Number, average size, and ratio of sales to calls.
5. Number of new accounts, lost accounts, and number of accounts with overdue payments.
6. Days worked, number and type of sales calls, and whom they were made on.
7. Ratio of selling time to nonselling activities.
8. Types and number of nonselling activities, such as display setups, letters, and service calls.
9. Direct selling expenses as a total, as a percentage of sales volume, as a percentage of quota, or as a return on investment.

---

*Qualitative*

---

1. Personal characteristics.
2. Quality of salesperson's time management, prospecting, and sales interviews.
3. Knowledge of product, competitors, and customers.
4. Quality of salesperson's relationships with customers.

---

Source: Stanton and Buskirk, *Management of the Salesforce*, 5th ed.

buy once and do not buy again. The manager checks the salesperson's activity reports and finds that the salesperson is calling on these customers. It may indicate that the salesperson is overly aggressive and selling to customers who really do not need the company's products. Perhaps this person enjoys the challenge of the initial sale but does not like calling on customers on a continuing basis. In either case, the one-sale phenomenon indicates a need for additional sales training. Likewise, increased buying levels followed by small purchases by a customer with a history of regular buying patterns, spending too much time with certain customers, failure to develop new accounts, and loss of long-term regular customers may be signs that a salesperson needs help from the sales manager.

## SUMMARY AND LOOK AHEAD

Business and nonbusiness organizations and individuals use personal selling to accomplish their objectives. This element of the promotion mix differs from others in that it involves personalized, face-to-face contact between a salesperson and a prospective buyer. It is the oldest type of promotional effort and companies spend more on it than on any other element in the promotion mix.

The basic objectives of personal selling are (1) to find prospective customers, (2) to convert them to customers, and (3) to keep them as customers. Thus the personal selling process includes (1) prospecting, (2) qualifying, (3) preparing the preapproach, (4) approaching the prospect,

(5) making the sales presentation, (6) handling objections, (7) closing the sale, and (8) following up the sale.

Five traditional approaches to handling sales presentations are (1) stimulus-response, (2) need satisfaction, (3) mood, (4) barrier, and (5) formulized. Each approach contributes to our understanding of personal selling.

Several factors have contributed to a new view of selling that, like the marketing concept, focuses on the customer's needs. These include the need for more accurate communication, development of the total product concept, desire for greater market penetration, need for a balanced selling effort, and need to cope with product shortages in some selling situations. This new view of selling views the salesperson as a professional—a consultant to target customers in identifying and solving their problems. Instead of a short-run relationship with their clients, they work toward building a long-term relationship based on mutual respect.

Professional salespersons are market managers of their territories, educators, communications specialists, helpers in problem solving, human relations experts, and feedback mechanisms to their companies. Four types of sales calls are (1) initial contacts, (2) regular customer calls, (3) follow-up calls, and (4) service calls.

Professional salespersons are concerned about repeat sales to their established customers. They do not use high-pressure sales techniques that often lead to a present sale at the expense of long-run mutual respect between them and their clients. They also view their calls on prospects as interviews.

Sales management activities focus on (1) organizing the salesforce, (2) recruiting and selecting salespersons, (3) training and developing the salesforce, (4) compensating the salesforce, (5) setting up sales territories, (6) motivating the salesforce, and (7) supervising and evaluating the salesforce.

In the next chapter, we will discuss advertising and its role in communicating with target customers.

## REVIEW QUESTIONS

**1.** What are the basic objectives of personal selling?

**2.** Identify and discuss the steps in the personal selling process.

**3.** What does prospecting involve?

**4.** What is the difference between a lead and a qualified prospect?

**5.** Identify and contrast the five traditional approaches to handling sales presentations.

**6.** Which of the five traditional approaches to handling sales presentations is closest to customer-oriented professional selling? Explain.

**7.** What major factors underlie the trend to more professionalism in selling?

**8.** Identify and discuss the functions customer-oriented professional salespersons perform.

**9.** What information is included in a current customer file?

**10.** Identify and discuss the communications skills required for professional selling.

**11.** Discuss the significance of subjective fact and objective fact in the salesperson's role as a problem solver.

**12.** Why do professional salespersons have to be good listeners?

**13.** Identify and contrast four types of sales calls.

**14.** Contrast sales presentations and sales interviews.

**15.** Explain the meaning of high perceived-repeat-sale potential and low sales aggressiveness.

**16.** Identify and discuss four types of professional selling jobs.

**17.** Identify and discuss briefly the seven major decision areas in sales management.

**18.** Identify and contrast four bases for organizing a salesforce.

**19.** Identify and contrast the three basic approaches to compensating a salesforce.

## DISCUSSION QUESTIONS

**1.** How would you benefitize a microwave oven for a prospect?

**2.** Do you believe "salespersons are born, not made"?

**3.** What are the differences and similarities between professional salespersons and salesclerks in retail stores?

**4.** Is the concept of a balanced selling effort compatible with the marketing concept?

**5.** How can salesforce performance affect a firm's effort to implement a demarketing strategy without damaging the firm's image?

## NOTES

1. For fuller discussion of the canned sales presentation, see Marvin A. Jolson, "The Underestimated Potential of the Canned Sales Presentation," *Journal of Marketing*, January, 1975, pp. 75–78; Jim D. Reed, "Comments on the Underestimated Potential of the Canned Sales Presentation," *Journal of Marketing*, January, 1976, pp. 67–68; and Marvin A. Jolson, "A Reply to Reed," *Journal of Marketing*, January, 1976, pp. 68–70.

2. See James O'Hanlon, "The Rich Rewards of the Salesman's Life," *Forbes*, October 16, 1978, pp. 155–162, and Hugh D. Menzies, "The New Life of a Salesman," *Fortune*, August 11, 1980, pp. 173–174, 177–178, 180.

3. "Marketing Briefs," *Marketing News*, June 27, 1980, p. 2.

4. "From ¼ to ⅓ of What is Viewed on Television is Miscomprehended," *Marketing News*, June 27, 1980, p. 1.

5. See Michael S. Heschel, "Effective Sales Territory Development," *Journal of Marketing*, April, 1977, pp. 39–43; and Thomas A. Witty, "Focusing the Sales Effort," *Sales and Marketing Management*, September 17, 1979, pp. 57–60.

6. See Charles M. Futrell, "Sales Force Job Attitudes, Design, and Behavior," *Journal of the Academy of Marketing Science*, Winter, Spring, 1979, pp. 101–107.

7. It has been suggested that different types of sales behavior are needed under different market conditions. See Peter W. Pasold, "The Effectiveness of Various Modes of Sales Behavior in Different Markets,"

*Journal of Marketing Research*, May, 1975, pp. 171–176. Also see Paul J. Halvorson and William Rudelius, "Is There a Free Lunch?" *Journal of Marketing*, January, 1977, pp. 44–49; and Alan J. Dubinsky, Eric N. Berkowitz, and William Rudelius, "Ethical Problems of Field Sales Personnel," *MSU Business Topics*, Summer, 1980, pp. 11–16.

8. Barry J. Hersker, "The Ecology of Personal Selling," *The Southern Journal of Business*, July 1970, pp. 41–46.

9. The increasing cost of industrial sales calls has led many industrial marketers to give more attention to inside selling, which does not require travel. See "A Case for Inside Sales," *Industrial Distribution*, September, 1979, pp. 89–90. Also see Norman A. Hart, "Industrial Press Advertising," *Quarterly Review of Marketing*, Spring, 1978, pp. 14–16; and William R. Swinyard, "How Many Ad Exposures Is a Sales Call Worth?" *Journal of Advertising Research*, February, 1979, pp. 17–21.

10. A good organizational climate is very important for the morale of industrial salespersons. See Gilbert A. Churchill, Neil M. Ford, and Orville C. Walker, Jr., "Organizational Climate and Job Satisfaction in the Salesforce," *Journal of Marketing Research*, November, 1976, pp. 323–332. For discussion of industrial sales as a career for women, see Leslie Kanuk, "Women in Industrial Selling," *Journal of Marketing*, January, 1978, pp. 87–91; and John E. Swan, Charles M. Futrell, and

John T. Todd, "Same Job—Different Views: Women and Men in Industrial Sales," *Journal of Marketing*, January, 1978, pp. 92–98. Also see Dan H. Robertson and Donald W. Hackett, "Saleswomen: Perceptions, Problems, and Prospects," *Journal of Marketing*, July, 1977, pp. 66–71; and Paul Busch and Ronald F. Bush, "Women Contrasted to Men in the Industrial Sales Force: Job Satisfaction, Values, Role Clarity, Performance, and Propensity to Leave," *Journal of Marketing Research*, August, 1978, pp. 438–448.

11. "Marketing Observer," *Business Week*, September 26, 1977, p. 158.

12. "A Meatpacker Discovers Consumer Marketing," *Business Week*, May 28, 1979, p. 168.

13. Companies tend to follow one of two approaches to training costs for sales trainees: (1) minimum investment or (2) return on investment. With the latter approach, the emphasis shifts from training costs for trainees to the profit realized from investing in the total salesforce. See James F. Carey, "Paying the Sales Trainee," *Sales and Marketing Management*, August 23, 1976, pp. 43–49. Also see Bernard M. Kessler, "New Selling Skills for Today's Changing Marketplace," *Training and Development Journal*, November, 1977, pp. 38–41; and Frank W. Bonheim, "Dual Purpose Training," *Training and Development Journal*, May, 1978, pp. 40–42.

14. Overall, there has been some movement away from straight commission to salary or, more often, to a combination of salary plus commission. There also is greater effort to tailor compensation plans to specific management objectives. See "Sales Force Compensation," *Sales and Marketing Management*, August 23, 1976, p. 64. For discussion of the evolution of a highly motivating sales compensation plan, see Leon Winer, "A Sales Compensation Plan for Maximum Motivation," *Industrial Marketing Management*, March, 1976, pp. 29–36. Also see John K. Moynahan, "Sales Compensation Plans: Some Important Points You Should Forget," *Sales and Marketing Management*, July 10, 1978, pp. 66–67.

15. See Jacob Gonik, "Tie Salesmen's Bonuses to Their Forecasts," *Harvard Business Review*, May–June, 1978, pp. 116–122.

16. For discussion of an eight-step process for developing the expected potential of each salesperson in a territory, see A. Parasuraman, "Assigning Salesmen to Sales Territories: Some Practical Guidelines," *Industrial Marketing Management*, December, 1975, pp. 335–344.

17. For a review of models related to determining salesforce size, designing sales territories, and allocating selling effort, see A. Parasuraman and Ralph L. Day, "A Management-Oriented Model for Allocating Sales Effort," *Journal of Marketing Research*, February, 1977, pp. 23–33.

18. See Stephen X. Doyle and Benson P. Shapiro, "What Counts Most in Motivating Your Sales Force?" *Harvard Business Review*, May–June, 1980, pp. 113–140.

19. See Paul Busch, "The Sales Manager's Bases of Social Power and Influence upon the Sales Force," *Journal of Marketing*, Summer, 1980, pp. 91–101.

20. For discussion of the use of management by objectives in salesforce management, see Donald W. Jackson, Jr. and Ramon J. Aldag, "Managing the Sales Force by Objectives," *MSU Business Topics*, Spring, 1974, pp. 53–59. For discussion of salesforce motivation, see Rom Markin and Charles Lillis, "Sales Managers Get What They Expect," *Business Horizons*, June, 1975, pp. 51–58.

# Chapter 19

# Advertising

**OBJECTIVES**

*After reading this chapter you should be able to*

1. contrast product and institutional advertising.

2. contrast pioneering, competitive, and retentive advertising.

3. give an example of comparative advertising and cooperative advertising.

4. identify four major media characteristics used for comparing media.

5. identify the major advertising media and compare them in terms of relative advantages and disadvantages.

6. discuss the copywriting process.

7. give examples of advertising concepts.

8. identify the different parts of a magazine advertisement.

9. discuss timing and scheduling of advertisements.

10. explain why a firm with an advertising department might also use an advertising agency.

11. discuss approaches to evaluating advertising effectiveness.

12. state and discuss several major criticisms of advertising.

**KEY CONCEPTS**

*Look for these terms as you read the chapter:*

Product Advertising
Comparative Advertising
Institutional Advertising
Cooperative Advertising
Media
Reach
Qualitative Selectivity
Geographical Selectivity
Frequency
Cost-per-Thousand (CPM)
Print Media
Broadcast Media
Direct Advertising Media
Location Advertising Media
Copywriting
Ad Concept
Layout
Timing
Scheduling
Advertising Department
Advertising Agency
Account Profile
Puffery
Corrective Advertising

*See if you can fill in the missing names:*

1. "_____ Adds Life"
2. "_____ , the Wings of Man"
3. "Weekends Were Made for _____"
4. "_____ Are Not Just for Dancing"
5. "_____ , the King of Beers"
6. "_____ , We Are Driven"
7. "Nothing Beats a Great Pair of _____"
8. "_____ , Where America Shops for Value"
9. "_____ , When You Care Enough to Send the Very Best"
10. "Choosy Mothers Choose _____"
11. "_____ , the San Francisco Treat"
12. "Is It Live or Is It _____ ?"
13. "_____ , the Sunshine State"
14. "Fill It to the Rim with _____"

*The answers are 1) Coke, 2) Eastern, 3) Michelob, 4) Danskins, 5) Budweiser, 6) Datsun, 7) L'eggs, 8) Sears, 9) Hallmark, 10) Jif, 11) Rice A Roni, 12) Memorex, 13) Florida, and 14) Brim. These advertisers exerted a lot of effort to teach you these slogans.*

Advertising is primarily one-way mass communication and does not have many of the self-correcting qualities of other promotion mix elements. It can also be expensive and involves a high risk of wasting company resources if it is handled improperly. To reduce this risk everyone involved in advertising planning and creation must have a thorough knowledge of the firm's product—what it does; how it compares with rivals' in function, price, and appearance; how well it is made; and how it can be identified. They must also know the market target, including demographic characteristics, developmental tasks or needs the product satisfies, and who makes the buying decisions.

Effective advertising must (1) have clearly stated, measurable objectives for changing how target customers feel, think, or act; (2) be coordinated with and reinforce, supplement, or explain the information provided by professional selling, public relations, and sales promotion; (3) include a plan of evolving change to coincide with changes in the market; (4) create an identity or "look" that distinguishes the firm and/or its products from rivals; (5) be a part of a sound marketing plan; and (6) reach target customers at points in the decision making process in a form that will be accepted and used.

To create an ad the advertiser makes decisions about (1) the type of advertising, (2) which media to use, (3) the creative concept, and (4) scheduling and timing. Each is discussed in this chapter along with some criticisms of advertising.

# THE NATURE OF ADVERTISING

Advertising is a powerful promotional tool for informing, persuading, and reminding target customers about organizations and their products.[1] Business and nonbusiness organizations and individuals advertise their offerings to their market targets.

Advertising has been practiced since ancient times.[2] Town criers walked the streets of ancient Athens announcing upcoming sales of goods, thus serving as the forerunners of radio ads. Contrary to popular belief, advertising even exists in the Soviet Union. When excess supplies of some products are produced, the Soviets may use advertising to help stimulate demand for them.

From Table 19–1 we see that some of the largest advertisers in the United States each spend many millions of dollars on advertising. Table 19–2 shows the percentages of sales that firms in selected industries spend on advertising. Federal, state, and local governments also spend hundreds of millions of dollars each year on advertising. But as we will see later in the chapter, some people raise questions about the social desirability of advertising.

We defined advertising in Chapter 17 as any paid form of nonpersonal communication through the mass media about a product or idea by an identified sponsor. Two types of advertising can be distinguished based on what is advertised in the ad: (1) product advertising and (2) institutional advertising. Some ads are of both types. Retail advertising, for example, may include both product and institutional advertising.

## Product Advertising

product advertising

**Product advertising** focuses on selling products offered by a manufacturer, a wholesaler, or a retailer. It may be directed at channel members, consumers, or industrial users.

**Table 19–1.** *Advertising expenditures of the top 10 national advertisers*

| Rank | Company | Total Advertising (millions of $) | Advertising as Percentage of Sales |
|---|---|---|---|
| 1 | Procter & Gamble Co. | $614.9 | 5.7% |
| 2 | General Foods Corp. | 393.0 | 6.5 |
| 3 | *Sears, Roebuck & Co. | 379.3 | 2.1 |
| 4 | General Motors Corp. | 323.4 | 0.5 |
| 5 | Philip Morris, Inc. | 291.2 | 3.5 |
| 6 | * Kmart Corp. | 287.1 | 2.3 |
| 7 | R. J. Reynolds Industries | 258.1 | 2.9 |
| 8 | Warner-Lambert Co. | 220.2 | 6.8 |
| 9 | American Telephone & Telegraph Co. | 219.8 | 0.4 |
| 10 | Ford Motor Co. | 215.0 | 0.5 |

*Does not include local retail advertising. For example, Sears spent $330 million on local retail advertising in newspapers during the year.
Source: *Advertising Age.*

**Table 19-2.** *Percentage of sales spent on national advertising by selected companies, by industry group*

| Industry | Company | Percentage |
|---|---|---|
| **Airlines** | Trans World Corp. | 1.4% |
| | Delta Air Lines | 1.3 |
| **Appliances, TV, radio** | RCA Corp. | 2.1 |
| | General Electric Co. | 0.6 |
| **Automobiles** | Chrysler Corp. | 1.0 |
| | American Honda Motor Co. | 1.2 |
| **Chemicals** | Du Pont | 0.7 |
| | Union Carbide Corp. | 0.6 |
| **Communications, entertainment** | CBS, Inc. | 3.9 |
| | Time, Inc. | 4.1 |
| **Drugs** | SmithKline Corp. | 8.0 |
| | Miles Laboratories | 13.1 |
| **Food** | McDonald's Corp. | 3.8 |
| | Kellogg Co. | 5.0 |
| **Gum & candy** | Mars, Inc. | 7.8 |
| | Wm. Wrigley Jr. Co. | 9.6 |
| **Photographic equipment** | Eastman Kodak Co. | 1.1 |
| | Polaroid Corp. | 3.7 |
| **Retail chains** | Kmart Corp. | 2.3 |
| | J.C. Penney Co. | 1.1 |
| **Soaps, cleansers (and allied)** | Colgate-Palmolive Co. | 2.7 |
| | Clorox Co. | 12.8 |
| **Soft drinks** | PepsiCo, Inc. | 4.2 |
| | Coca-Cola Co. | 3.4 |
| **Telephone service equipment** | American Telephone & Telegraph | 0.4 |
| | International Telephone & Telegraph | 0.8 |
| **Tobacco** | Philip Morris, Inc. | 3.5 |
| | Liggett Group | 5.6 |
| **Toiletries, cosmetics** | Bristol-Myers Co. | 7.7 |
| | Gillette Co. | 6.4 |
| **Wine, beer, and liquor** | Heublein, Inc. | 8.8 |
| | Jos. Schlitz Brewing Co. | 8.0 |

Source: *Advertising Age.*

Any ad's specific objectives, or those of a series of ads in an advertising campaign, are determined by the overall promotional plan and vary by stage of the product life cycle.    Product advertising can be divided into three categories based on its objectives: (1) pioneering, or informative, (2) competitive, or persuasive, and (3) retentive, or reminder.

**Pioneering Product Advertising.**    Pioneering product advertising seeks to create awareness and understanding and develop primary demand for a new product category. It provides information in the early stages of the adoption process. It is especially necessary when potential buyers must learn a new use system. Ads must create awareness of the new product, teach potential buyers how to use it, and induce channel members to stock it. Microwave ovens, food processors, woks, and hot-air corn poppers were new product categories and potential customers had to learn new use systems.

**Competitive Product Advertising.** Competitive product advertising focuses on stimulating selective demand, or demand for a particular brand within a product category. Once products reach the growth stage of their life cycles competitive product advertising helps to create a brand image and target customer recognition of the brand name or trademark; to compare the brand's characteristics, price, or benefits to rival brands; to motivate target customers to buy the brand and increase usage by light users; to increase demand by attracting new users.

Competitive product advertising is easy to recognize by its persuasive emphasis. Its aim is to stimulate purchases either immediately or over the long run. These ads may stress a brand's unique qualities and benefits, stimulate desire for it, tie its use to cultural values and myths, and/or stimulate immediate purchase through fear appeals.

For many years, some competitive product ads featured differences between the advertiser's brand and unnamed brands (X, Y, and/or Z). The Federal Trade Commission (FTC) believed comparative advertising might provide more useful information to consumers and so authorized **comparative advertising,** in which the advertiser compares the advertised brand to rival brands that are identified by brand name.[3] Firms that claim superior benefits for their brands in comparative ads have to be prepared, however, to produce research and test results to support their claims.[4]

comparative advertising

Ideal Toy Company used comparative advertising in introducing Maniac. Ideal knew it could not adequately describe the product during a thirty-second TV spot ad, so it said the product was similar to Simon, which had been introduced earlier by Milton Bradley, but had advantages of its own.[5]

**Retentive Product Advertising.** Retentive, or reminder, product advertising is used when a product reaches the brand-preference or insistence stage among a large number of target customers. It is most common during the maturity stage of the product life cycle.

Retentive product advertising does not necessarily mean the advertiser is satisfied with the brand's present market share. This type of advertising can summarize major benefits claimed for the brand in ads over a number of years and thus serve a similar purpose to summary statements in the closing of a professional sales interview. Retentive ads also can be used as an effective postpurchase communication to help customers evaluate their decisions and reduce dissonance, to introduce

*The silk print and repp ties are by C.F. Hathaway.*

### Nonsense! says Hathaway
### to those who would tamper with tradition.
### This is the classic oxford button-down.

There is an art to the classic button-down, as practised by Hathaway, that can easily elude the maker of humdrum shirts.

The buttons for the collar tips, for instance, must be placed just so. If too far apart, they will cause the collar to bulge where it shouldn't. If too close together, they will give the collar a rumpled, slovenly look.

Shown in the picture above are two classic Oxford button-down shirts from the C.F. Hathaway Co. Examine them closely and you will see for yourself the proper roll of a button-down collar: a gentle, sculptured curve.

They are the very latest state of a very traditional art.

Source: Hathaway Shirt Co.

*An example of retentive product advertising*

new uses for existing products, and to reinforce the discrimination training of earlier competitive product advertising.

## Institutional Advertising

**Institutional advertising** focuses on the image of a product category, a company, a nonprofit organization, or an industry association rather than

*institutional advertising*

*An example of institutional advertising*

Source: American Gas Association.

a specific brand. This type of advertising can create and maintain a corporate or family brand image among target customers and channel members, supplement public relations activities by building goodwill among noncustomer publics, counter adverse publicity or government action that might damage the organization, and generate demand for a product category.

For example, during the 1970s chemical companies generally were perceived by some people to be poor corporate citizens because of concern about hazardous waste dumps, product safety, health questions, and spills.   As part of their public relations efforts to help change things, many chemical companies developed ad themes focusing on some of the issues raised.   Examples are Dow Chemical Company's "Common Sense—Uncommon Chemistry," Monsanto's "Without chemicals, life itself would be impossible," and Du Pont's "You and Du Pont.   There's a lot of good chemistry between us."

Advocacy advertising is a type of institutional advertising in which the advertiser takes a position for or against a point of view.[6]   Mobil Oil Corporation, for example, has run ads critical of governmental regulation of the oil industry.

**Pioneering Institutional Advertising.**   A newly organized charitable organization might use pioneering institutional advertising to inform the public of a rare disease that has received little attention and explain its approach to combating it.   The National Aeronautics Corporation, which started in business in 1945 as a manufacturer of navigation and communication devices, dropped those products in the early 1960s, switched to manufacturing health-care machinery, and changed its name to Narco Scientific, Inc.[7]   Pioneering institutional advertising would be useful in situations like this to inform potential new customers about a firm's new mission.

**Competitive Institutional Advertising.**   Competitive institutional advertising is often used when different product categories compete for the same market segment.   Some of these ads seek to stimulate an immediate buying response, while others point out the advantages of an industry association's product.   Ads promoting Florida oranges, wool clothing, milk, and glass containers seek to generate demand for a product category.   The sponsoring associations believe all member companies will benefit.   Thus the Florida Orange Growers Association advertises that "orange juice is not just for breakfast anymore" in an attempt to gain a position in the highly competitive soft drink, tea, and coffee market.

**Retentive Institutional Advertising.**   Retentive, or reminder, institutional advertising can summarize information presented or comparisons made in previous pioneering or competitive campaigns.   Texaco's theme, "We're working to keep your trust," reinforces the theme of earlier years, "You can trust your car to the man who wears the star."

## Retail Advertising

Advertising by retailers is often considered a special type of advertising. Retailers use both product and institutional advertising.   They use product advertising to move excess stock or attract attention to special promotions by featuring brand name products.   In **cooperative advertising** a manufacturer pays part of a retailer's cost of advertising the manufacturer's product in the retailer's local market.   General Electric, Maytag, and many canned-food products manufacturers engage in cooperative ad-

cooperative
advertising

vertising with their retailers. Cooperative advertising arrangements vary.[8] Some manufacturers pay a higher percentage of the advertising cost than others. Some provide the ad for the retailers, while others do not. Retailers benefit from the lower cost of preparing ads, which also may be better than those that could be produced locally. The manufacturer benefits from more knowledgeable placement of ads in each local market, perhaps at a lower cost. The product also may develop a local identity, which is harder to obtain with national advertising. A possible problem for the manufacturer is lack of coverage in a local market when a retailer rejects a cooperative campaign.

Institutional advertising by retailers helps increase customer traffic through the store by focusing the advertising on the store image rather than on specific products. Examples are "Sears, Where America Shops for Value" and "Penneys, the Fashion Place."

We discussed communication channels in Chapter 17. The following section deals with communication channels for advertisers.

## MEDIA SELECTION

media

**Media** are communication channels through which advertising messages are transmitted to target groups. They include newspapers, magazines, radio, and TV. Advertisers must decide which medium or media to use for delivering their messages and also select particular vehicles within each medium. For example, if the selected medium is magazines, should the ads be placed in *Time, TV Guide,* and/or *Reader's Digest?* These are vehicles within the magazine medium. In this chapter we will use *medium* generally to include both the medium and vehicles within that medium.

Media decisions involve a careful fit between advertising objectives, medium and vehicle characteristics, target receiver characteristics, information to be communicated, and funds available for advertising. Important media characteristics to evaluate in comparing media are (1) reach, (2) frequency, (3) cost, and (4) constraints.

### Reach

reach

The number and characteristics of the people to whom a medium can provide access during a given period of time is called **reach.** More specifically, it is the number of people seeing an ad one time during a stated time period. The number of people a medium reaches usually is stated in terms of audience size or circulation.

qualitative
selectivity

Selectivity is desirable in choosing among media. There are two types: (1) qualitative selectivity and (2) geographical selectivity. The more alike members of a medium's audience are in one or more characteristics that are important to the advertiser, the greater its **qualitative selectivity.** Many media offer demographic and behavioral profiles of their audiences. *Playboy,* for example, publishes a demographic profile of its readers in some of its issues. Many newspapers also do this periodically. A women's dress manufacturer that wants to advertise to larger-sized women would think *BBW* (formerly *Big Beautiful Women*) magazine offers more qualitative selectivity than *Cosmopolitan.*

The greater a medium's ability to reach people in selected geographical areas, the greater its **geographical selectivity.** *Southern Living* offers more geographical selectivity than *Better Homes and Gardens. Atlanta* magazine offers even more geographical selectivity than *Southern Living.* This is important when a high percentage of a marketer's target customers are clustered in either widely separated or very condensed locations.

But using highly selective media can be dangerous if the marketer has not clearly defined the market target. The ads could miss (not reach) important market segments. This is why careful market research is desirable before making media decisions.[9]

**geographical selectivity**

## Frequency

The number of times the same people in a target group are exposed to an ad during a certain period of time is called **frequency.** In some media, such as radio and TV, repetition must be scheduled and paid for. In some others, such as a direct mail catalogue or outdoor advertising (billboards), an ad is relatively long lived and a potential customer may see it several times at no additional cost to the advertiser. Frequency is discussed in more detail later in this chapter.[10]

**frequency**

## Costs

Media cost is based on the number of people reached, frequency, and the expense of producing the ad. Rates are quoted in standard units, such as line rates for newspapers, page rates for magazines, and spot rates for broadcast media (TV and radio). This allows advertisers to make rough cost comparisons between different media.

Rates for one newspaper may be higher than for another that has lower circulation and/or less coverage of specific market segments. National magazines and network TV and radio can reach people nationwide. Local newspapers and regional magazines have a much smaller geographical scope. But media with nation-wide reach can be useful to advertisers whose target audiences are limited to people in a single region, state, or city. The advertiser can use local spot ads on radio and TV instead of network coverage.

The price of placing an ad does not tell if it is a good buy. Comparisons usually are made by a cost ratio that is used for all media, with some variations. **Cost-per-thousand (CPM)** is computed by the following formula:

**cost-per-thousand (CPM)**

$$CPM = \frac{\text{cost of purchase unit} \times 1{,}000}{\text{number of prospects reached}}$$

The purchase unit (lines in newspapers or seconds of time on radio) makes no difference in the formula as long as the same unit is used for each vehicle in a medium.

### Constraints

Each medium places constraints on the advertiser that may make it unsuitable for certain purposes. Government regulations, creative demands, consumers' relationship with the medium, competitive considerations, and the minimum cost of entry are all factors that must be considered.

**Government Regulations.** As we saw in Chapter 2, the Wheeler-Lea Act of 1938 gives the Federal Trade Commission power to regulate the advertising industry to prevent fraud and deceit. The prohibition on fraudulent and deceitful advertising applies to all media. Other regulations apply only to specific media. Some areas covered by government regulations are listed in Table 19–3.

Some media also have their own regulations. Prior to 1972, for example, the TV industry banned advertising of menstrual products. Its liquor ban still stands. Up until 1979 *Reader's Digest* also banned alcoholic beverage advertising.

**Creative Demands.** The creative demands of ads favor some media over others. Some ideas are best expressed in words; others require pictures. Color, movement, sound, smell, or feel are important qualities of some products but are unimportant for others. Innovations have made it possible to convey more about certain products. For example, microencapsulation ("scratch and sniff") adds impact to print media for colognes, and audio discs in magazines allow readers to sample recordings.

Another factor that limits media selection is the immediacy (lead time) required for ads. Production time for TV, magazine, and outdoor ads is much longer than for newspapers and radio, which have the lowest lead time for producing ads—often as little as twenty-four hours. This is important for firms whose advertising must change often, such as local department stores and supermarkets.

**Consumers' Relationship with the Medium.** How a medium fits into a consumer's lifestyle often determines whether it is appropriate for advertising certain types of products. Radio is an important part of teenagers' lifestyle, especially from 3:00 to 10:00 p.m., and for working people during morning and evening drive time. TV has tended to be somewhat

*Table 19–3.* *Examples of government regulations of media*

1. What products may be advertised through different media: no cigarettes on TV.
2. The information ads must contain: car ads must include EPA mileage estimates and cigarette ads must include nicotine and tar levels.
3. The placement and number of ads that can be used: billboards along interstate highways and the number of ads per hour of TV programing.
4. Product claims: specific claims must be backed up by test results and research; the term *health food* cannot be used in advertising food products.

more conservative than other media because of its central role in the homes of most families.

Media also vary in terms of the trust consumers place in information obtained through them. Newspapers generally are seen as more believable (credible) than radio and TV and are more appropriate for complex and detailed information.[11] All media limit the effectiveness of advertising by their programing content, which sets the context for ads.[12] A cigarette ad next to a magazine article on lung cancer or a beer ad during a sophisticated comedy on TV may reduce the ad's effectiveness. A medium's social class image may also rule out ads for products that do not share the same image. Advertising fine china or crystal in *True Story* or on a country and western radio station probably would be ineffective.

**Competitive Considerations.** Competitors' media strategy also limits an advertiser's media selection. A firm that wants to meet a rival's advertising head on generally must use the same media. Marketers of brands with dominant market shares might try to block rivals from using the same media by, for example, buying up huge blocks of prime time on TV (although they conceivably could be charged with an antitrust violation). Advertisers who wish to avoid direct confrontation may reach selected market segments through more selective media, often at less cost. Thus some marketers of pantyhose use direct mail or mail order rather than compete with L'eggs on TV.

**Minimum Cost of Entry.** The size of an advertiser's budget limits the selection of media. The minimum cost of entry (the cost of producing and placing one ad in the medium) varies among media and depends on the cost of producing ads and the smallest unit of purchase possible. Radio and newspapers generally have the lowest entry costs. Advertisers with limited budgets often select media with lower entry costs to increase ad frequency even if other media may be more desirable in accomplishing advertising objectives. Other factors that affect the selection of a cost-efficient media mix are included in the following discussion of the major advertising media.

## MAJOR ADVERTISING MEDIA

Advertising media can take some rather exotic forms, such as skywriting. New media also appear from time to time. Advertisements on movie screens were once such a new form, but research has showed that many consumers consider this practice offensive. One firm recently began placing advertising posters in theater lobbies. Advertisers who want to reach persons 18–34 years old are expected to find these posters helpful because persons in that age group are not heavy readers of newspapers and magazines, nor do they watch much TV. But they do attend movies frequently.[13]

The major types of advertising media, however, are (1) print, (2) broadcast, (3) direct, and (4) location. Table 19–4 shows the estimated annual

**Table 19–4.** *Expenditures on advertising in the United States, by medium, 1980*

| Medium | Millions of Dollars |
|---|---|
| Newspapers | |
| Total | $15,615 |
| National | 2,335 |
| Local | 13,280 |
| Magazines | |
| Total | 3,225 |
| Weeklies | 1,440 |
| Women's | 795 |
| Monthlies | 990 |
| Farm Publications | 135 |
| Television | |
| Total | 11,330 |
| Network | 5,105 |
| Spot | 3,260 |
| Local | 2,965 |
| Radio | |
| Total | 3,690 |
| Network | 185 |
| Spot | 750 |
| Local | 2,755 |
| Direct Mail | 7,655 |
| Business Publications | 1,695 |
| Outdoor | |
| Total | 610 |
| National | 400 |
| Local | 210 |
| Miscellaneous | |
| Total | 10,795 |
| National | 5,690 |
| Local | 5,105 |
| Total | |
| National | 30,435 |
| Local | 24,315 |
| Grand Total | 54,750 |

Source: *Advertising Age.*

ad expenditures for selected years by type of medium. Table 19–5 summarizes the relative advantages and disadvantages of the major media.

### Print Advertising Media

print media

Mass **print media** stimulate one sensory mode directly. They lack the impact of other media, such as TV, that stimulate several sensory modes. But more information can be communicated more accurately through

**Table 19–5.**  *Relative advantages and disadvantages of major media*

| Medium | Advantages | Disadvantages |
|---|---|---|
| Newspapers | immediacy<br>flexibility<br>low-cost entry<br>preshopping reference<br>  source<br>local image and coverage<br>high believability<br>geographical selectivity | short life<br>little pass-along readership<br>little repeat exposure to<br>  single insertion ads<br>poor color reproduction<br>considerable clutter<br>direct stimulation of only<br>  one sensory mode |
| Magazines | long life<br>high pass-along readership<br>quality color reproduction<br>qualitative selectivity<br>geographical selectivity | considerable clutter<br>very expensive to stimulate<br>  more than one sensory<br>  mode<br>production of ad is the re-<br>  sponsibility of the adver-<br>  tiser or its advertising<br>  agency |
| Radio | mass usage<br>qualitative selectivity<br>geographical selectivity<br>low cost<br>short lead time<br>spoken word may be easier<br>  to understand than the<br>  printed word<br>flexibility | stimulates only one sen-<br>  sory mode<br>listeners pay casual<br>  attention<br>limited to simple messages<br>short life |
| Television | mass usage<br>stimulates sight and<br>  hearing<br>can show motion | limited qualitative<br>  selectivity<br>clutter<br>high cost<br>short life |
| Direct mail and<br>  mail order | qualitative selectivity<br>geographical selectivity<br>intensive coverage<br>low cost<br>flexibility | junk mail image<br>costly mailing lists |
| Outdoor | geographical selectivity<br>high repeat exposure<br>flexibility<br>low cost | very limited qualitative<br>  selectivity<br>growing scarcity of good<br>  locations<br>limited to short and simple<br>  messages |
| Transit | geographical selectivity<br>qualitative selectivity<br>low cost<br>flexibility<br>high repeat exposure | limited to short and simple<br>  messages |

them than others, except for some direct advertising media, such as a direct mail catalogue.

Print media include newspapers and magazines. Each has its advantages and disadvantages. Newspapers cannot convey as much or as complex information as magazines because readers spend less time reading newspapers. Magazines also are more likely to be kept for future reference by readers and passed along to others (pass-along readership).

**Newspapers.** Newspapers can be classified as daily or weekly with local or national distribution.[14] Local newspapers are geographically selective, and national newspapers and those of a religious, ethnic, or foreign language nature are qualitatively selective.[15] Some qualitative selectivity is also possible in communities with two or more newspapers that are targeted to different market segments and by varying the section and/or page placement of an ad within a newspaper. Placing sporting goods ads in the sports section probably provides more qualitative selectivity than placing them in the entertainment section. Ads on the front page of a section offer less qualitative selectivity than ads within sections, but they are likely to be read by casual readers.

Local retailers use newspapers because of their reach, use as a pre-shopping reference source, and local identity. Advertisers can be confident of the exposure they are purchasing because circulation figures are verified by a circulation audit company like the Audit Bureau of Circulations. Most newspapers quote contract prices that offer a volume discount over single insertion prices, which are called standard, or flat, rates. One reason national manufacturers engage in cooperative advertising with their local retailers is that local advertisers pay lower rates than national advertisers.

Newspaper advertising is a low-cost entry medium because the cost of preparing an ad and the cost of a single run are low. Rates usually are quoted by the milline—the theoretical cost of one line of advertising to a circulation of one million people. A line is a column wide and ¼-inch deep. Although page sizes vary among newspapers, column width is constant. The milline rate is:

$$\frac{\text{cost of one line} \times 1,000,000}{\text{actual circulation of the paper}}$$

Some newspapers also quote rates in cost-per-thousand as is common among other media.

Newspaper ads enjoy high credibility because they appear in a news context.[16] They also offer immediacy and flexibility few other media can match.

There are three major limitations of newspaper advertising. First, ad life is very short. Readers usually do not keep newspapers for future reference, there is little pass-along readership, and single insertion ads have very little repeat exposure. Special inserts, such as a supermarket's insert, however, have a longer life.

Second, the quality of color reproduction is inferior to that of magazines and is very expensive. To overcome this limitation, advertisers who want high-quality color must use special inserts or Sunday supplements. Most newspapers also accept inserts printed and furnished by the advertiser on a charge-per-insertion basis. Locally produced Sunday supplements feature local and national advertising, while nationally syndicated ones like *Family Weekly* and *Parade* feature national advertising.

Third, although clutter is found in all media, it abounds in newspapers. Many ads on one page may compete for attention. To increase attention the advertiser may have to buy extra space, often white space, to help isolate the ad from others on the page.[17]

**Magazines.** The number of general-interest magazines has declined over the years, while the number of special-interest magazines has increased. Special-interest magazines offer more qualitative selectivity. However, some general-interest magazines do have demographic editions that are targeted, for example, to students, teachers, or businesspersons. Some also are departmentalized and have features to attract different market segments. This strengthens their qualitative selectivity.

Magazines can also be classified by the target group for which the content is tailored: consumers, businesses, and farmers. Consumer magazines range from large-circulation, general-interest magazines like *Reader's Digest, People,* and *Time* to lower-circulation, special-interest magazines like *Hot Rod, Weight Watchers,* and *Jogging.* Business publications include magazines of broad scope like *Business Week* and *Fortune* and those targeted to specific industries (*Men's Wear*) or a type of occupation (*Journal of Purchasing*). *Farm Journal* is a broad-interest national magazine, but most national farm publications specialize by type of farm activity, such as dairy, beef, or poultry. Most farm publications, however, are regional or state-wide because content must reflect differences in climate, soil, and crops.

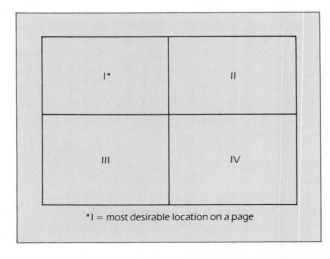

Figure 19–1.
The desirability of different page positions for ads less than a full page

Most magazines are published monthly.  Weekly magazines like *People* and *Us* are the second-largest group.  Low publication frequency reduces repeat exposure, except for repeated exposures to an ad in a single issue.  This can be important to marketers introducing new products.  It also means long lead times, which can limit the advertiser's responsiveness to changes in market conditions.

Most magazines are national but some are regional (*Southern Living*) and some are local (*New York, Atlanta*).  National magazines can increase geographical selectivity through split runs of ads for products in regional editions.  Thus you may see an ad for your local bank in *Time* magazine.

Magazines usually have a single rate structure for all advertisers but may offer volume discounts.  Base rates are determined by the CPM formula, which includes a guaranteed circulation.  Premiums are charged for color, preferred page positions for partial-page ads, and location of the ad within the magazine. Figure 19-1 shows the desirability of different page positions for ads less than a full page.  The CPM for magazine ads usually is higher than for newspaper and radio.

### Broadcast Advertising Media

broadcast media

**Broadcast media** (radio and TV) differ from print media in creative potential and pose special problems for advertisers.

**Radio.**  Radio reaches practically every home and car in the United States.  Most stations are regional or local.  Most communities have several stations that tailor their program formats to certain market segments.  Thus it is hard to get full coverage of a local area on one station.  Radio is very qualitatively and geographically selective.

About 63 percent of the roughly 7,000 radio stations in the United States are AM.  FM stereo stations usually offer more programing and cluster their ads to provide more uninterrupted music.  The program format of both AM and FM stations, however, generally consists of music and local news.  Radio stations can be identified by their music or ethnic appeal: rock, classical, easy listening, country and western, jazz, and ethnic, such as Spanish-language and black.

Radio stimulates one sensory mode and ads usually cannot contain much information because people pay only casual attention.  Most advertisers try to get across simple messages through announcements or musical jingles.  Production time for simple ads is short, which allows advertisers to change their ads often and quickly.  Thus radio is a very flexible medium.

Most radio stations do not charge advertisers for preparing ads.  Broadcasting rates are usually determined by the CPM method, with the number of homes being reached by a station verified by independent firms like Mediastat.  Advertisers can buy program sponsorships, most of which center on local weather or news, or spots.  A spot is a certain amount of time (15, 20, 30, 60 seconds) between programs; several may be aired during a programing break.  The advertiser pays for repeated exposures.   A spot's life is short so repetition is important.   Some stations give volume discounts to advertisers.

**Television.**   Television also reaches practically all homes in the United States.   It basically is a nonselective medium because most programing is provided by three major national networks and most stations are network affiliates.   Local and syndicated programs account for a small percentage of programing.   Cable TV brings distant stations into many local communities.   Some independent stations, such as WTBS in Atlanta, use satellites to reach cable systems over large areas of the nation.   Some of these stations may develop into new networks as their original programing increases.

In buying national programs or spots, advertisers must select time periods or types of programs that appeal to target customers.   The size and demographic characteristics of audiences are verified by firms like A.C. Nielsen.   An advertiser's own marketing research department or that of its ad agency may research other audience characteristics.[18] Identifiable market segments by type of program and time of day include: daytime (homemakers and preschool children), Saturday morning (children), weekend afternoons (adult males), sports programs (adult males), and feature movies (young adults).

Sponsorship of a popular program provides a large audience but is costly and hard to obtain.   Networks usually provide participation plans that allow several national advertisers to sponsor such programs.   Ad rates for new episodes of shows that become big hits can double.   Spots may be purchased network-wide or market-by-market.   A sixty-second spot on CBS during the 1980 Super Bowl cost $468,000.   Some firms specialize in placing nonnetwork spots for regional and national advertisers.

TV ads are short-lived but often have more impact than radio ads because they stimulate both sight and hearing.   Advertisers can show their product in use (motion).   On the other hand, clutter can be a problem because TV ads are clustered during station breaks and program interruptions.[19]   Back-to-back ads tend to reduce effectiveness.[20]

Production costs depend on the ad's complexity.   Some ads simply consist of one or more slides of the product and an announcer who provides the audio (voice-over).   These may be produced by the station free of charge if the advertiser buys a set minimum amount of air time. Direct-response commercials for products like phonograph tapes, records, and household gadgets are of this type and are not scheduled for prime time.   They are a growing source of revenue for TV stations.   Complex ads may take several months to produce and usually are prepared by the advertiser's ad agency.   Cost can run up to a quarter of a million dollars, or more.

### Direct Advertising Media

Marketers try to communicate directly with potential customers when they use **direct advertising media.**   They can be highly selective and

**direct advertising media**

*An ad explaining the Direct Mail/Marketing Association's Mail Preference Service.*

Source: Direct Mail/Marketing Association.

convey complex information tailored to the receiver's situation. Examples are (1) direct mail, (2) mail order, and (3) unmailed direct.

**Direct Mail and Mail Order.** Direct mail can have a format of any size or shape that is unbound and offers one or, at most, a few products for sale. Examples are sales letters and leaflets. Mail order usually takes a bound catalogue format with information, illustrations, and order forms for a much larger number of products.

Both offer selectivity, intensive coverage, low cost, and flexible format. The cost may seem high when comparing CPM with other media, but the ratio of buying responses to the cost of reaching those buyers usually is much higher. People who buy by direct mail also tend to be consistent in their buying by mail.[21] Mailing list accuracy regarding addresses and prospect characteristics is crucial.

Because of complaints from some people about unsolicited mail, the Direct Mail/Marketing Association set up a Mail Preference Service in 1971. Notice in the above ad that people who do not want to receive direct mail advertising can request a NAME-REMOVAL form. Others can request an ADD-ON form if they want to receive more of it.

**Unmailed Direct.** Unmailed direct includes handbills, booklets, and leaflets that are distributed by hand, either door-to-door or in parking lots at shopping centers or sporting events. Other examples include advertising specialties (novelties), directory advertising, and house organs.

Advertising specialties like pencils, calendars, key chains, book matches, and T-shirts feature the firm's name and perhaps a short advertising message.[22] They can be a highly selective medium when distributed only to target customers. They are most effective for retentive product or institutional advertising.

Membership directories of professional organizations and college student directories usually include ads. Directory advertising can be very selective and repeated exposure tends to be high. People who are ready to buy often use the "Yellow Pages" to preshop.

Firms such as airlines and motel chains use house organs to reach customers. These range from a magazine format to directory-type publications. Customers often are encouraged to take these publications with them.

### Location Advertising Media

**Location advertising media** includes outdoor and transit advertising.

*location advertising media*

**Outdoor Advertising.** Outdoor advertising is an industry term that refers to poster panels, painted bulletins, signs, and electric spectaculars.

A poster panel is a permanent structure on which printed paper is glued, and they are rented for thirty days or longer. Some are lighted. Painted bulletins (displays) last longer and usually are rented on a yearly basis. The ad is painted on a structure similar to that of a poster panel, on the side of a building, or on a panel that can be moved to other locations. Some are animated and lighted. Multisided bulletins have triangular louvers turned by electric motors every few seconds. This provides three different sides for presenting messages. Their attention-producing value increases because of closure, which we discussed in Chapter 5.

Signs appear in numerous forms along roadways and other high-traffic locations. They are maintained by the advertiser or, at its expense, by an outdoor advertising firm. Electric spectaculars are nonstandardized, permanent displays used to mark the location of a business or for advertising in heavy-traffic locations. Examples are the signs on Las Vegas hotels and advertising spectaculars along Broadway in New York City.

Outdoor advertising generally is a nonselective medium but some selectivity is possible by choosing locations target customers travel past regularly. For example, blue-collar workers can be reached near entrances to industrial parks. But local ordinances and federal restrictions have contributed to a growing scarcity of good locations. Nevertheless, since 1969 outdoor advertising has been growing by 10 percent a year.

**Transit Advertising.** Transit advertising firms rent space on buses, cabs, subways, and commuter trains. Rates usually are quoted on a monthly basis and vary by amount of traffic carried. Geographical selectivity is high and demographic studies by these firms give advertisers some qualitative selectivity, especially for ethnic products. Transit advertising includes car cards, traveling displays, and terminal posters and displays.

Car cards are inside the vehicle and are aimed at riders. Traveling displays are on the outside of the vehicle. The audience is larger but exposure time is much less. Terminal displays may involve slides, video loops, and other visuals. They and terminal posters are placed in waiting areas and can be coordinated with car cards and traveling displays.

## THE CREATIVE PROCESS

copywriting

**Copywriting** is the process of creating an ad. It includes (1) selecting an appeal(s), (2) formulating the ad concept(s), (3) developing the ad elements, and (4) providing technical directions for production. (See Figure 19–2.)

### Selecting an Appeal

Selecting the appeal(s) to use in an ad is usually based on both market research and creative intuition. Suppose research shows that what women want most in a hair coloring product is not to have their hair look artificially colored.[23] They want natural looking hair. But if rival firms' research reveals the same want, ads for the various brands might claim "You will look natural with (brand name) hair color." There is no differentiation among the brands.

But when Clairol introduced Nice 'n Easy it used language that helped to differentiate the brand. The ad featured a young woman saying, "It lets me be me." In effect, the ad said the woman's beauty was already there but Clairol was just helping to bring it out. Once an appeal(s) is selected the next step is to formulate the ad concept.

### Formulating the Ad Concept

ad concept

The **ad concept** (theme) is a rough idea of a situation (context) that can be used to organize the ad elements. Examples are given in Table 19–6.

**Figure 19–2. The copywriting process**

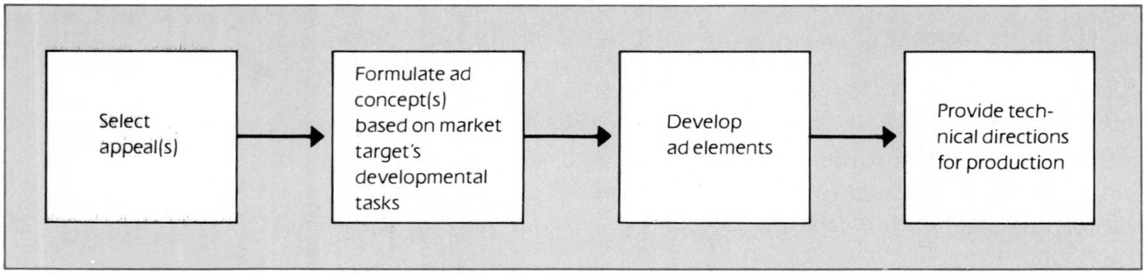

**Table 19-6.** *Examples of ad concepts*

1. *Testimonials and endorsements: Cheryl Tiegs and Cover Girl*
2. *Case histories and slice-of-life (what actually happened to real people): Allstate homeowners insurance*
3. *Associating the product with other objects of symbolic meaning: "Speidel . . . Can you tell the difference between solid gold and Speidel gold overlay?"*
4. *Tying the product to a cultural myth: DeBeers's "A diamond is forever"*
5. *Using closure and other principles of perception: "Volkswagen does it again"*
6. *Showing product uses and recipes: "The good cooks at Kraft"*
7. *Fantasy or exaggeration: Jontue, "Sensual . . . but not too far from innocence"*

Several concepts might be developed to appeal to different market segments or to be used in different media. Also, different versions of the same concept may lead to a series of ads.

## Developing the Ad

The technical terms for the various parts of an ad vary among media but they perform roughly the same functions. The Kraft ad on page 568 illustrates the different parts of a magazine ad: headline, illustration, copy, and signature.

The headline usually states the ad's central idea, elicits an emotion, or poses a question. It must attract attention. The illustration should also attract attention, and it should communicate information quickly, dramatize a product benefit, and provide an atmosphere, or context, for the ad. A good illustration can communicate such concepts as prestige (Mercedes Benz ads), strong emotion (Allstate life insurance ads), and sensuous luxury (Black Velvet whisky ads) far more easily and effectively than words.

Composing ad copy is a very exacting exercise in the use of language. Each word must help convey the message simply and clearly. Copy usually expands on the idea of the headline and illustration and provides evidence to support the major claim(s) of the headline. The signature usually is composed of the brand name, trademark, and slogan to reinforce brand identification.

## Providing Technical Direction

**Layout** basically is a print media or outdoor term but we take it to include    layout
the structuring process that occurs in broadcast media also. An ad's layout is the actual arrangement of its various parts to form a cohesive unit. It is guided by well-accepted principles. Marketers rely on technical personnel, such as art directors or designers, for layout work. They work in advertising departments and ad agencies.[24]

Layout for a print ad takes the form of an artist's rough sketch that includes the locations of all ad elements. Further refinements include printing directions, such as size and kind of type. In radio, layout is a

**1. The headline**
(*"The Top of the Morning"*)

**2. The illustration**
(*cup and cheese*)

**3. The copy**
(*printed material*)

**4. The signature**
(*KRAFT trademark and "Our Pride. Your Joy."*)

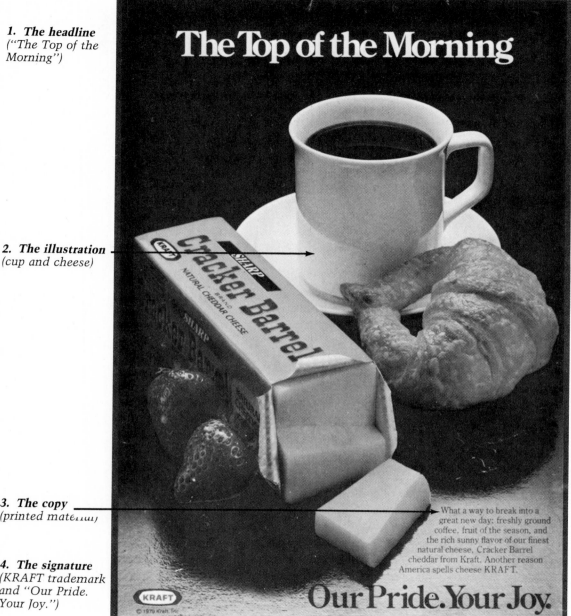

# The Top of the Morning

What a way to break into a great new day: freshly ground coffee, fruit of the season, and the rich sunny flavor of our finest natural cheese, Cracker Barrel cheddar from Kraft. Another reason America spells cheese KRAFT.

## Our Pride. Your Joy.

Source: Kraft, Inc.

script that includes the words to be spoken, directions for music and sound effects, and other audio directions. For TV, the layout (design) is a story board. This is a series of sketched frames showing actions, spoken words, and technical directions for taping the ad.

## TIMING AND SCHEDULING

Two major decisions in planning when ads will appear are timing and scheduling.

### Timing

**Timing** involves determining when an ad will first appear and how long it will run. Factors that affect the timing decision are (1) the product's life cycle, (2) the advertiser's ability to meet demand the ad may stimulate, and (3) the target audience's exposure to other promotional activities, including those of rivals.

*timing*

Advertising and other promotional efforts usually are designed to reach the market target in a desired sequence and must be coordinated. Consider a manufacturer's promotion to retailers. The retailer may receive a direct mail piece, see an ad in a trade magazine, receive a call by a salesperson, and be offered point-of-purchase displays by the manufacturer. A similar planning process is necessary when several media are used in an advertising campaign. Radio, outdoor, magazine, and newspaper ads must reach their targets in the desired sequence.

### Scheduling

**Scheduling** involves determining the frequency of an ad and the time of day it will run. The primary concerns are (1) selecting the times during the day or week when it will reach target customers and (2) determining the number of repetitions (same ad reaching the same consumer).

*scheduling*

Earlier in this chapter we discussed audience characteristics at different times of the day for broadcast media. Little is known about other media in this regard. Newspapers, however, often find differences between readers of morning and evening daily papers and between readers of daily and Sunday editions. These differences are important when placing ads in a local market.

Each repetition of an ad increases the chances target customers will see it, the amount of information they will learn and remember, and the probability of its hitting while target customers are making a buying decision. Repetition increases reach and is especially desirable during new product introductions and for ads that contain complex information.[25] The scheduling techniques discussed in Table 19–7 represent a tradeoff between desired frequency, patterns of demand for the product, and advertising cost.

As we saw in Chapter 5, ads gradually lose their attention-producing ability because of adaptation. Frequency of repetition affects an ad's life span. The higher the frequency, the faster the ad will lose attention-producing value. Also, ads have longer lives with flighting schedules. They recover attention-producing value after being rested for a while. Decisions about dropping an ad should be based on research on the ad's impact. Using an ad that no longer produces attention may alienate people who are tired of it.

**Table 19–7.** *Advertising scheduling techniques*

| | |
|---|---|
| *Even Schedule* | The same size (print media) ad or length (broadcast media) ad is placed at regular intervals (daily, weekly, or monthly).   This schedule is common for products with fairly stable demand patterns.   Food ads, for example, often appear in a local newspaper on a particular day of the week. |
| *Alternating Schedule* | Ads of different sizes or lengths are run at regular intervals.   A full-length TV ad may run for 60 seconds while a shorter version may run for 20 seconds.   The longer ad contains all the information about the product.   The shorter ad focuses on only one idea.   This allows the advertiser to get more frequency with a given budget.   It also may be used to lengthen the period over which an ad will run or to reduce advertising cost. |
| *Variable Schedule* | This involves intermittent periods of high frequency and increased size or length of ads.   These schedules are common for products with predictable periods of peak demand. Flighting and saturation schedules are two types of variable schedules.   Flighting means concentrating ads during periods of high demand with little advertising during periods of low demand.   This is common in advertising toys, luggage, greeting cards, antifreeze, and swimming pools. |
| | Saturation schedules are common during the introductory stage of a product's life cycle.   The goal is to achieve maximum reach and high frequency during a concentrated period to create maximum impact.   A saturation schedule may be followed by an even schedule. |

## MANAGING THE ADVERTISING EFFORT

The advertising manager is part of the team that decides the firm's promotion goals.   Once these are determined, the advertising manager (1) plans and coordinates the advertising program with other promotion mix elements, (2) directs the execution of the advertising campaign(s) done by in-house advertising personnel, (3) selects and works with independent ad agencies, and (4) evaluates advertising effectiveness.

### Advertising Departments

In very small firms advertising is handled by one or two people.   They develop basic themes and rely on copywriters and other specialists who work for local media to produce, place, and schedule ads.

Larger firms usually must decide whether to have an advertising department handle advertising and/or rely to varying degrees on independent ad agencies.   An **advertising department** exists within the advertiser's own company.   It may be headed by an advertising manager, who participates in all phases of advertising production and media placement and reports to the firm's marketing manager.   Personnel might include cre-

**advertising department**

ative and technical specialists who create and implement ad campaigns. Sometimes they may turn to outside free-lance specialists for help.

## Advertising Agencies

An **advertising agency** is a firm that offers its services to clients (advertisers). Ad agencies range from very small, one-person firms to big agencies like J. Walter Thompson Company. Most large agencies are located on Madison Avenue in New York City, but thousands of smaller ones are found throughout the United States.

**advertising agency**

Large ad agencies generally have a creative department that develops and produces ads, a media department that handles media selection and placement, a research department that researches audience characteristics, and a business department that handles the agency's business affairs. Each client (or account) is handled by an account executive. Some multiproduct firms use different ad agencies for different products.

Among the reasons many firms with in-house advertising departments use outside ad agencies are (1) ad agencies are staffed by specialists who have wide advertising experience, (2) ad agencies may introduce more objectivity into decision making because they are outsiders, and (3) an ad agency may work harder for its client because it can easily be replaced by a rival agency.

Ad agencies basically are compensated by the media, not the client. If an advertiser contracts with an agency for $800,000 of broadcast media time, the agency bills the client for $800,000 and deducts a 15 percent commission ($120,000) for itself and remits $680,000 to the media. This commission system is changing but the basic principle still holds.[26] If, however, an ad agency performs special services for clients, such as marketing research, it tacks on extra fees.

The firm's advertising manager serves as a liaison with the ad agency. While the ad agency handles the production and placement of major media advertising, the firm's advertising department handles other auxiliary sales promotion activities. The ad manager also coordinates ad campaigns for different products in multiproduct firms.

**Agency Selection.** In selecting an ad agency the advertising manager must communicate to prospective agencies the firm's history, overall promotion strategy, specific campaign objectives, product characteristics, market research information on target customers' needs and how they use or can use the product, campaign budget and its tentative division among different media, the desired sequencing of promotional activities, and the desired services the agency is to provide, specifying the role of the firm's in-house ad department in the campaign.

This information is called the firm's **account profile.** It enables the advertiser to approach and negotiate with prospective ad agencies. It also helps agencies to discuss intelligently the prospective client's advertising needs. The actual selection process varies among companies. Many invite a number of agencies to make private competitive presentations of their preliminary ideas for the ad campaign.

**account profile**

A commitment to go with an agency should include a contract or a letter of agreement that spells out the duties the agency will perform for which brands, method of compensation, billing procedures, and client audit of accounts, ownership of ideas and client approval of strategy and copy, and duration and conditions for ending the relationship.

## Evaluating Campaign Effectiveness

The end product of an ad manager's efforts with in-house and ad agency personnel is a campaign made up of ads in different media. Evaluating campaign effectiveness always is tough. Good ads may be ineffective because other marketing mix elements and other promotion mix elements are not coordinated properly with the campaign.

Evaluating campaign effectiveness helps the advertising manager to determine how well advertising is coordinated with other promotion and marketing mix elements and if the campaign's objectives have been achieved, and to appraise the relative effectiveness of different ads, media, and media decisions. Effectiveness can be evaluated before (pretest), during, and/or after (post-test) the campaign.

**Criteria for Measuring Effectiveness.** Criteria for measuring ad effectiveness vary among firms. But evaluation must be tied to the objectives the ads were designed to achieve. Using sales volume of an advertised product as the criterion of ad effectiveness attributes all sales increases or decreases to advertising. It ignores the roles of other promotion and marketing mix elements and environmental changes. Examples of other major objectives an ad may be designed to accomplish are to create awareness, to give target customers product information that will be remembered, to change how target customers think or feel about a product, and to stimulate target customers to action. Two basic ways of determining whether an ad campaign has accomplished or probably will accomplish its objectives are (1) laboratory experiments and (2) field experiments and surveys.

Laboratory experiments can be used to pretest different versions of an ad or to check how effective an ad has been (post-test). A simple experiment to pretest effectiveness of different ads designed to create awareness is to show them in a dummy magazine to groups of people. Each group is given a check list and asked to indicate products they remember seeing advertised in the magazine. Some products not advertised in the magazine also are included as a correction factor. The recognition scores for each ad can then be compared. The same experiment can be used as a post-test if the magazine is an actual issue instead of a dummy.

Recall tests measure ad effectiveness in giving information about a product. An interviewer may ask subjects to tell what they remember about an ad. A more sophisticated method involves the subject's matching important phrases taken from ads with the advertised products. These also can be pretests or post-tests.

Semantic differential scales and projective experiments measure the effects of alternative ads on the way people think or feel about the product. Different versions of the ad are given to different groups who rate them on a number of scales that describe the product or how they think people will think and feel about it. Differences in the ratings are attributed to the different versions of the ad. These also can be pretests or post-tests.

Laboratory techniques to measure an ad's ability to stimulate action range from measures of changes in eye pupil size to choosing a product they would like to try. There is doubt, however, whether any of these measures can predict buying behavior in the marketplace.

Field experiments and surveys differ from laboratory methods because they attempt to measure ad effectiveness in real-life situations. One of the best known methods of measuring awareness and effectiveness in getting across information people will remember is the Starch Readership Report. A sample of people who recently have read a magazine are surveyed to see if they remember seeing the ad, what they looked at, and if they read at least half of the written material.

Field measures of an ad campaign's ability to stimulate action include sales tests and inquiry tests. In sales tests two market areas that are closely matched by characteristics and buying patterns are selected. One receives the ad and the other does not. Any differences in sales between them are attributed to the ad. In inquiry tests the number of responses people make to ads that offer a sample of the product, a booklet, or a cents-off coupon is used to evaluate the ad's stimulation value. It is hard to say, however, whether the ad would produce the same result without the sales promotion.

Advertising touches our lives every day. Some people believe it touches us too often and tries to persuade us too much. Let us look at some of these criticisms.

## CRITICISMS OF ADVERTISING

Advertising is criticized severely by some consumers, government agencies, and businesspeople. Some attack it as an institution, while others focus on specific advertisers and ads. Thus criticism exists on the macro and micro levels.[27]

On the micro level advertising certainly is not beyond reproach. A majority of consumers may consider some ads to be misleading, deceptive, or unacceptable. Some ads may be offensive to certain people while, at the same time, helpful to other people. Our society is a heterogeneous mixture of people with different ethical and social values, abilities, and educational levels. Advertising, therefore, never can be tailored exactly to each person's situation because it is a mass selling approach to promotion. But ads that target customers perceive as offensive, deceptive, or otherwise unacceptable probably will not achieve the advertiser's objectives.

The following discussion examines these questions: (1) Does advertising lead to monopoly and higher prices? (2) Does advertising brainwash consumers? (3) Does advertising misrepresent the truth? (4) Does advertising cause economic waste? (5) Does advertising make consumers materialistic? (6) Does advertising stereotype consumers? and (7) Does advertising ignore good taste?

## Does Advertising Lead to Monopoly and Higher Prices?

Some people believe the large ad budgets of big firms keep smaller firms from entering competition. They contend advertising helps create monopolies that can charge very high prices. It is clear that many smaller firms have succeeded despite the mass advertising of giant rivals. But it is impossible to determine how many smaller firms never got started simply because the ad budgets of giant rivals were too big an obstacle to entry. Advertising plans clearly aimed at preventing rivals from entering a market, however, may be construed as a violation of the antitrust laws.

A firm may enjoy economies of scale in producing and marketing its product if advertising increases the demand for it. If these economies more than offset the advertising cost, the firm could pass some of the savings to consumers by lowering prices. Heavy advertising of pocket calculators, digital watches, and CB radios probably contributed to economies of scale and lower prices for consumers.

We discussed the role of advertising in nonprice competition earlier in this text. It is interesting that advertising as a way of stimulating price competition among professionals like doctors, lawyers, and accountants is encouraged by the Federal Trade Commission.[28] The American Institute of Certified Public Accountants has voted to permit its members to advertise, and the American Bar Association's commission on advertising publishes a how-to manual on advertising for lawyers.

## Does Advertising Brainwash Consumers?

Some critics believe marketers use advertising to create consumer tastes and preferences. Persuasive advertising, they argue, makes consumers mere pawns of mass advertisers. But the high failure rate of new products proves that advertisers are not in complete control. Advertising cannot manipulate people against their will. Although much of it seeks to persuade us to do certain things, it cannot brainwash us. You may want to review the discussion of subliminal advertising in Chapter 5.

## Does Advertising Misrepresent the Truth?

puffery

**Puffery** is exaggeration in claims made about a product.[29] Practically all advertisers use superlative terms like *best* in describing their brands.[30] But the limits on permissible puffery have narrowed over the years. Ads that misrepresent the truth beyond mere puffery are misleading, deceptive, and/or fraudulent and are illegal.[31]

corrective advertising

In recent years, the FTC has used **corrective advertising** as a remedy for allegedly deceptive advertising.[32] One case involved Listerine anti-

# "I think that ad is lying."

## If you think that an advertisement is misleading or untruthful, here's what you can do about it.

Most advertisers work very hard to make sure their advertising is completely honest and truthful. But if you ever see an advertisement or a commercial that you think takes liberties with the truth or makes questionable claims, there's something you can do about it.

Write to the National Advertising Review Board.

If truth or accuracy in a national ad or commercial is your concern (not matters of taste or matters of editorial or program content), the advertiser will be asked for substantiation of the claims made.

Where justified, advertisers will be requested to modify or discontinue any claim for which there is not adequate support.

You will be notified of the results of the investigation and they will be reported in a monthly press release.

### NARB IS SELF-REGULATION

The NARB was formed in 1971 out of the conviction that self-regulation of advertising is preferable to government regulation. It is faster. No tax dollars are required to support it.

The NARB is sponsored by four leading advertising and business organizations: The American Association of Advertising Agencies, the American Advertising Federation, the Association of National Advertisers, and the Council of Better Business Bureaus. Its board of directors consists of representatives of advertiser companies, advertising agencies, and members representing the public sector.

Since its inception, more than 1,300 inquiries regarding national advertising have been reviewed.

Advertisers have cooperated in providing substantiation of the advertising in question.

More important, not one advertiser has refused to modify or discontinue advertising found to be misleading.

NARB is self-regulation that works.

If you would like further information or if you see advertising that you feel is untruthful...

**write to:
National Advertising Review Board, 845 Third Avenue, New York, New York 10022.**

*An example of self-regulation in the advertising industry.*
Source: National Advertising Review Board.

septic, which had for years claimed that it helped prevent colds and sore throats. Because the maker could not substantiate these claims to the FTC's satisfaction, it had to run $10 million of corrective ads on TV for two years informing consumers that the product does not prevent colds and sore throats.

The FTC may go beyond requiring corrective advertising and try to prevent what it considers unfair advertising. Among present and potential targets for FTC action are ads aimed at children and the less educated and ads that encourage consumers to buy energy-inefficient products.[33]

Advertisers, ad agencies, and the media have made considerable voluntary progress in eliminating misleading advertising. As the ad on page 575 explains, the National Advertising Review Board plays an active role in self-regulation.[34] But it is the relatively few advertisers that still engage in outright deception that do great damage.

### Does Advertising Cause Economic Waste?

Some critics say the advertising efforts of rivals cancel each other and much of it is so superficial and meaningless that it produces no economic benefits. But when demand for a certain product category cannot be increased and brands in that category are very similar, marketers engage in nonprice competition. They know overall demand for the product category will not increase in proportion to their advertising expenditures. But advertising is a tool for engaging in nonprice competition.

### Does Advertising Make Consumers Materialistic?

The argument that advertising makes consumers materialistic, makes them want things they really do not need, has been heard for many years. Materialism, these critics argue, stresses acquisitiveness and a false set of values. It allegedly makes possession of products an end in itself.

Our macro marketing system's objective is to satisfy consumers' wants as individual consumers define them. If we resorted to satisfying only basic survival needs, we might end up living in caves, wearing animal skins, and eating wild berries. If we view possession of products as a means to an end, instead of an end in itself, one could argue that having them frees people to achieve higher-level needs. Labor-saving products like automatic dishwashers, power lawnmowers, and home computers "free" us to pursue higher ends, such as attending the opera or devoting time and effort to combating social problems.[35]

### Does Advertising Stereotype Consumers?

Broadcast programing, editorial content in print media, and advertising often are criticized for stereotyping consumers.[36] Some women complain that many ads depict them as sex objects or in demeaning "housewife" roles. Men, on the other hand, are very seldom depicted doing household chores when, in fact, many men do them. Lifestyles and sex roles are changing so rapidly in our society that some ads may depict people in outmoded stereotypes.

## Does Advertising Ignore Good Taste?

Some critics say advertising is guilty of using poor taste. Erotic appeals for products ranging from cosmetics to drill presses and fear appeals for deodorants and mouthwashes are often cited.[37] Also cited are ads that insult our intelligence with monotonous and repetitive themes and unbelievable situations. Advertisers are also often attacked for damaging the environment with billboards, invading consumers' privacy with junk mail, and for sponsoring broadcast programs that some consumers feel are in very bad taste.

There are, however, wide differences of opinion concerning what constitutes good and bad taste. Taste in advertising is subjective just as in music, dress, and personal behavior. In some cases, critics are attacking the product being advertised and, in the process, the advertising comes under criticism. For example, some people feel feminine hygiene products should not be advertised on TV. Although a specific ad for such a product might be very tastefully done, the ad is criticized as a result of its association with the product.

## SUMMARY AND LOOK AHEAD

Advertising, a mass communication element of the promotion mix, has been practiced by business and nonbusiness organizations and individuals since ancient times. Advertising is any paid form of nonpersonal communication through the mass media by an identified sponsor about a product or idea.

Product advertising focuses on selling products; institutional advertising focuses on the image of a product category, a company, a nonprofit organization, or an industry association rather than a specific brand. Retail advertising is often considered to be a special type of advertising. Product, institutional, or retail advertising can be pioneering, competitive, or retentive.

Advertising media are the communication channels the advertiser selects to reach the intended audience. Media decisions involve a careful fit among (1) advertising objectives, (2) medium and vehicle characteristics, (3) target receiver characteristics, (4) information to be communicated, and (5) funds available for advertising. Media are selected on the basis of their characteristics, such as reach, frequency, costs, and constraints. The major media that advertisers use are print, broadcast, direct, and location. Each medium has its relative advantages and disadvantages.

The process of creating an ad is called copywriting. Effective copywriting requires a thorough knowledge of the product, the consumer, and advertising media. The steps in the copywriting process are (1) selecting an appeal, (2) formulating the ad concept, (3) developing the ad elements, and (4) providing technical directions for production.

Once an ad is constructed and the media are selected the advertiser must decide when the ad will first appear and how long it is to run. This is called timing. Determining how often and the time of day ads are to run is called scheduling. An advertiser may increase the impact and life span of an ad by using different types of schedules. Three types are even, alternating, and variable.

The firm's advertising manager plans and coordinates the advertising program with other promotion mix elements, directs the execution of the advertising campaign, selects and works with the ad agency, and evaluates advertising effectiveness. An advertising department exists within the advertiser's own company, whereas advertising agencies are outside firms that offer their services to clients (advertisers).

Advertising is criticized by many people. Some attack it as an institution (macro level) while some others attack specific advertisers and ads (micro level).

The next section of the text discusses price. This is another element in the marketing mix.

## REVIEW QUESTIONS

1. Identify and define the two types of advertising based on what is being advertised in the ad.

2. Identify and define the three categories of product and institutional advertising based on the objectives of the advertising.

3. In which stage of a product category's life cycle is pioneering advertising most likely to be used? Explain.

4. What is comparative advertising?

5. What is cooperative advertising?

6. Identify and discuss the four media characteristics that should be evaluated in comparing media.

7. Distinguish between qualitative and geographical selectivity.

8. Identify the four major types of media and give examples of each.

9. What are the major advantages and disadvantages of the following media: (a) newspapers, (b) magazines, (c) radio, (d) television, (e) mail order and direct mail, (f) outdoor, and (g) transit?

10. Identify and discuss three types of direct advertising.

11. Give two examples of outdoor advertising.

12. Identify and discuss the four steps in the copywriting process.

13. Identify the four parts of a print ad and tell their functions.

14. What factors affect the timing and scheduling of ads?

15. What is the difference between an advertising department and an advertising agency?

16. What is an account profile?

17. Give an example of the use of a laboratory experiment to test the effectiveness of an ad.

18. Contrast criticism of advertising on the macro and micro levels.

## DISCUSSION QUESTIONS

1. Is comparative advertising ethical?

2. Is advertising by government agencies a waste of the taxpayers' money?

3. Would you rather place an ad in a weekly or a monthly magazine?

**4.** Why do some companies use advertising specialties?

**5.** Find an example of each of the commonly used ad concepts listed in this chapter.

**6.** In view of the major criticisms of advertising, is it justifiable?

## NOTES

1. For discussion of how a firm might appraise its advertising opportunity, see Charles H. Patti, "Evaluating the Role of Advertising," *Journal of Advertising*, Fall, 1977, pp. 30–35.

2. For discussion of the history of advertising in the United States, see Thomas Fleming, "How It Was in Advertising: 1776–1976," *Advertising Age*, April 19, 1976, pp. 1, 27–35.

3. See Anthony C. Chevins, "A Case for Comparative Advertising," *Journal of Advertising*, Spring, 1975, pp. 31–36; William L. Wilkie and Paul W. Farris, "Comparison Advertising: Problems and Potential," *Journal of Marketing*, October, 1975, pp. 7–15; V. Kanti Prasad, "Communication-Effectiveness of Comparative Advertising: A Laboratory Analysis," *Journal of Marketing Research*, May, 1976, pp. 128–137; Philip Levine, "Commercials That Name Competing Brands," *Journal of Advertising Research*, December, 1976, pp. 7–16; Stanley I. Tannenbaum, "Put Consumerism to Work for You—Use Ad Comparisons," *Marketing News*, December 17, 1976, pp. 1, 5; Stephen W. Brown and Donald W. Jackson, "Comparative Television Advertising: Examining Its Nature and Frequency," *Journal of Advertising*, Fall, 1977, pp. 15–18; Aimée L. Morner, "It Pays to Knock Your Competitor," *Fortune*, February 13, 1978, pp. 104–111; Subhash C. Jain and Edwin C. Hackleman, "How Effective Is Comparison Advertising for Stimulating Brand Recall?" *Journal of Advertising*, Summer, 1978, pp. 20–25; Charles W. Lamb, Jr., William M. Pride, and Barbara A. Pletcher, "A Taxonomy for Comparative Advertising Research," *Journal of Advertising*, Winter, 1978, pp. 43–48; Marianne M. Jennings, "New FTC Policy Statement Encourages Comparative Ads," *Marketing News*, October 19, 1979, p. 8; Michael Etgar and Stephen A. Goodwin, "Planning for Comparative Advertising Requires Special Attention," *Journal of Advertising*, Winter, 1979, pp. 26–32; and Peter M. Ginter and Jack M. Starling, "A Twofold Analysis of Comparative Advertising Effectiveness," *Akron Business and Economic Review*, Spring, 1979, pp. 12–18.

4. See Kenneth A. Coney and Charles H. Patti, "Advertisers' Responses to Requests for Substantiation of Product Claims: Differences by Product Category, Type of Claim and Advertising Medium," *Journal of Consumer Affairs*, Winter, 1979, pp. 224–235; and Dorothy Cohen, "The FTC's Advertising Substantiation Program," *Journal of Marketing*, Winter, 1980, pp. 26–35.

5. "Should an Ad Identify Brand X?" *Business Week*, September 24, 1979, p. 161.

6. See S. Prakash Sethi, "Issue-Oriented Corporate Advertising: Tax Treatment of Expenditures," *California Management Review*, Fall, 1976, pp. 5–13; Louis Banks, "Taking on the Hostile Media," *Harvard Business Review*, March–April, 1978, pp. 123–130; and S. Prakash Sethi, "Institutional/Image Advertising and Idea/Issue Advertising as Marketing Tools: Some Public Policy Issues," *Journal of Marketing*, January, 1979, pp. 68–78.

7. "Narco Scientific: A Costly Shift out of Aviation and into Health Care," *Business Week*, November 5, 1979, p. 154.

8. See Ed Crimmins, "How Cooperative Advertising Helps Sales—Participation from Our Smaller Dealers," *Sales and Marketing Management*, October 11, 1976, pp. 75–77.

9. See Larry Percy, "How Market Segmentation Guides Advertising Strategy," *Journal of Advertising Research*, October, 1976, pp. 11–22.

10. See Howard Kamin, "Advertising Reach and Frequency," *Journal of Advertising Research*, February, 1978, pp. 21–25.

11. See Ernest F. Larkin, "Consumer Perceptions of the Media and Their Advertising Content," *Journal of Advertising*, Spring, 1979, pp. 5–7.

12. See John H. Murphy, Isabella C. M. Cunningham, and Gary B. Wilcox, "The Impact of Program Environment on Recall of Humorous Television Commercials," *Journal of Advertising*, Spring, 1979, pp. 17–21.

13. Bernard F. Whalen, "Movie Theater Posters Introduced as Ad Medium," *Marketing News*, June 27, 1980, pp. 1, 2.

14. The suburban press, the fastest-growing segment of the newspaper industry, is very effective in reaching people in the suburbs. See Jonathan M. Kramer, "Benefits in the Use of Suburban Press for Large Metropolitan Buys," *Journal of Marketing*, January, 1977, pp. 68–70.

15. For discussion of religious publications as an advertising medium, see Arthur W. Van Kyke, "Stop Killing Us with Kindness," *Journal of Marketing*, July, 1976, pp. 90–91.

16. See Ernest F. Larkin and Gerald L. Grotta, "Consumer Attitudes toward the Use of Advertising Content in a Small Daily Newspaper," *Journal of Advertising*, Winter, 1976, pp. 28–31.

17. See E. S. Lorimor, "Classified Advertising: A Neglected Medium," *Journal of Advertising*, Winter, 1977, pp. 17–25.

18. One study has indicated that radio and television audiences exhibit distinctive psychographic characteristics. See Jesse E. Teel, William O. Bearden, and

Richard M. Durand, "Psychographics of Radio and Television Audiences," *Journal of Advertising Research,* April, 1979, pp. 53–56.

19. See Peter H. Webb and Michael L. Ray, "Effects of TV Clutter," *Journal of Advertising Research,* June, 1979, pp. 7–12.

20. Time compression is an electronic procedure that can be used to speed up a television commercial. For example, a thirty-second spot can be viewed in twenty-four seconds with no noticeable loss of voice pitch. Time compression may result in an increase in attention power of television commercials. See James MacLachlan and Priscilla LaBarbera, "Time-Compressed TV Commercials," *Journal of Advertising Research,* August, 1978, pp. 11–15.

21. See Patrick Dunne, "Some Demographic Characteristics of Direct Mail Purchasers," *Baylor Business Studies,* July, 1975, pp. 67–72.

22. See William H. Bolen, "Consumer Attitudes toward Specialty Advertising," *Atlanta Economic Review,* August, 1971, p. 35.

23. This example is taken from "Today's Ads Need More Creativity, Less Reliance on Science, Research," *Marketing News,* June 13, 1980, p. 5. William Bernbach, chairman of the executive committee, and Doyle Dane Bernbach discussed the Clairol ad appeal during a luncheon address at the Advertising Research Foundation's 26th Annual Conference in New York.

24. For discussion of eight rules for evaluating advertising creativity, see John M. Keil, "Can You Become a Creative Judge?" *Journal of Advertising,* Winter, 1975, pp. 29–31.

25. A single advertising exposure, however, can be effective. See Robin T. Peterson and Charles H. Gross, "What Effect from a Single Advertisement?" *Journal of the Academy of Marketing Science,* Summer, 1978, pp. 222–227.

26. See "How Agencies Should Get Paid: Trend Is to 'Managed' Systems," *Advertising Age,* January 17, 1977, pp. 41–42.

27. See Leo Bogart, "Is All This Advertising Necessary?" *Journal of Advertising Research,* October, 1978, pp. 17–26.

28. See John R. Darling, "Attitudes towards Advertising of Accountants," *Journal of Accounting,* January, 1977, pp. 48–53; Paul N. Bloom and Stephen E. Loeb, "If Public Accountants Are Allowed to Advertise," *MSU Business Topics,* Summer, 1977, pp. 57–64; Paul N. Bloom, "Advertising in the Professions: The Critical Issues," *Journal of Marketing,* July, 1977, pp. 103–110; and John F. Darling and Donald W. Hackett, "The Advertising of Fees and Services: A Study of Contrasts between, and Similarities among, Professional Groups," *Journal of Advertising,* Spring, 1978, pp. 23–24.

29. See Ivan L. Preston, "The FTC's Handling of Puffery and Other Selling Claims Made by 'Implication,'" *Journal of Business Research,* June, 1977, pp. 155–181; Richard L. Oliver, "An Interpretation of the Attitudinal and Behavioral Effects of Puffery," *Journal of Consumer Affairs,* Summer, 1979, pp. 8–27; Terence A. Shimp, "Social Psychological (Mis) Representations in Television Advertising," *Journal of Consumer Affairs,* Summer, 1979, pp. 28–40; and Bruce G. Vander Bergh and Leonard N. Reid, "Puffery and Magazine Ad Readership," *Journal of Marketing,* Spring, 1980, pp. 78–81.

30. In one study it was found that the believability of advertised product claims and the credibility of the source may be enhanced if the advertiser does not claim superiority of its product on all attributes. See Robert B. Settle and Linda L. Golden, "Attribution Theory and Advertiser Credibility," *Journal of Marketing Research,* May, 1974, pp. 181–185.

31. See David M. Gardner, "Deception in Advertising: A Conceptual Approach," *Journal of Marketing,* January, 1975, pp. 40–46; Gary M. Armstrong and Frederick A. Russ, "Detecting Deception in Advertising," *MSU Business Topics;* Spring, 1975, pp. 21–31; and H. Keith Hunt, "Decision Points in FTC Deceptive Advertising Matters," *Journal of Advertising,* Spring, 1977, pp. 28–31.

32. See Marianne M. Jennings, "FTC Will Order Corrective Ads on Case-by-Case Basis," *Marketing News,* June 13, 1980, p. 16.

33. See Pat L. Burr and Richard M. Burr, "Television Advertising to Children: What Parents Are Saying about Government Control," *Journal of Advertising,* Fall, 1976, pp. 37–41. Also see Seymour Banks, "Children's Television Viewing Behavior," *Journal of Marketing,* Spring, 1980, pp. 48–55.

34. See Priscilla A. LaBarbera, "Advertising Self-Regulation: An Evaluation," *MSU Business Topics,* Summer, 1980, pp. 55–63.

35. See Jack Z. Sissors, "Another Look at the Question: Does Advertising Affect Values?" *Journal of Advertising,* Summer, 1978, pp. 26–30.

36. See Del I. Hawkins and Kenneth A. Convey, "Advertising and Differentiated Sex Roles in Contemporary American Society," *Journal of the Academy of Marketing Science,* Winter, 1976, pp. 418–428; Cyndy Scheibe, "Sex Roles in TV Commercials," *Journal of Advertising Research,* February, 1979, pp. 23–27; and Roger A. Kerin, William J. Lundstrom, and Donald Sciglimpaglia, "Women in Advertisements: Retrospect and Prospect," *Journal of Advertising,* Summer, 1979, pp. 37–43.

37. See Clifford Elliot and G. Creighton Frampton, "The Use of Fear Messages in Advertising," *Akron Business and Economic Review,* Winter, 1977, pp. 16–21.

# Section VII
# Price

Even well-designed products that are distributed and promoted effectively may not sell if they are not priced right. A product's price, the amount of buying power the target customer has to give up to buy the product, can be the most important or the least important element in its marketing mix. If the price is too high or even too low the product will not sell.

Chapter 20 introduces the environment for pricing decisions. We will discuss various pricing objectives that underlie pricing decisions and develop a basic approach marketers can follow in setting list prices on their products.

Chapter 21 discusses several specific approaches to determining list prices. Some marketers are cost-oriented pricers, some are demand-oriented pricers, and some seek to balance supply and demand factors in setting their list prices.

Chapter 22 focuses on the actual day-to-day administration of prices—how list prices are adjusted to remain flexible and responsive to company and customer requirements. Some examples of list price adjustments are discounts and the many ways freight costs from sellers to buyers can be handled.

# Pricing Objectives and Approach

**OBJECTIVES**

*After reading this chapter you should be able to*

1. discuss the importance of prices on the macro and micro marketing levels.

2. give an example of the price-quality relationship.

3. contrast price and nonprice competition.

4. identify and discuss four general types of pricing objectives.

5. identify and discuss six steps in setting list price.

6. state the law of demand.

7. contrast a change in demand with a change in quantity demanded.

8. discuss the concept of price elasticity of demand.

9. identify and discuss three price-level options for firms with downsloping demand curves.

10. contrast skim-the-cream and penetration pricing strategies.

11. discuss the nature of the contemporary pricing environment.

**KEY CONCEPTS**

*Look for these terms as you read the chapter:*

List Price
Price-Quality Relationship
Price Awareness
Price Consciousness
Profit Maximization Objective
Target Return Objective
Market Share Objective
Price Stabilization Objective
Price Signaling
Stay-out Pricing Objective
Shake-out Pricing Objective
Law of Demand
Expected Price
Change in Demand
Change in Quantity Demanded
Price Elasticity of Demand
Skim-the-Cream Pricing
Penetration Pricing

*Price can play a relatively minor or a relatively major part in marketing strategy. For example, Michelin radial tires traditionally were priced above the average price of other radial tires because many people perceived them as a superior product. But as other radial makers increased the quality of their tires, it became harder for Michelin to command an above-market price. Thus it is doing something it had not done before—advertising the price of its tires.*

*On the other hand, the coal industry traditionally included many small producers. In recent years, however, many big oil companies have been seeking to position themselves in this industry because of plentiful supplies. Thus they are buying out many small coal producers. One result may be a higher price for coal as the small producers, who engaged mainly in price competition, go out of business.*

Our economy basically is a market-directed economy in which product prices are determined mainly by the forces of supply and demand. Although other factors like government regulations and the money supply also affect prices, supply and demand forces are the major determinants.

We do know, however, that when General Motors introduces its new cars each year they are sent to dealers with price stickers on them. This sticker price is a basic, or list, price. It is the type of price we will study in this and the following chapter. The price a buyer actually pays for a new GM car may be lower than the list price because of haggling between the car salesperson and the buyer, or it may be higher if the particular model is in heavy demand. This actual price is the list price after adjustments made to cope with demand and supply conditions at the point of sale. This aspect of pricing is discussed in Chapter 22.

Price setting in the real world is a complex procedure. The list price a firm sets on its product depends on many factors such as demand, costs, company objectives, competitors' prices, and the stage of the business cycle. To a marketer, price is only one element in the marketing mix—perhaps the most important or the least important. But unless the right product, in the right place, at the right time is priced "right," it will not be sold. Price also must return an adequate profit or else the seller cannot survive over the long run. This sometimes happens when a marketer miscalculates cost.

## PRICE AND PRICING

Our discussion of utility and value in Chapter 1 indicated that when something has utility it can satisfy wants. It is a product. A product's value in exchange is (1) its ability to command another product in return for giving up ownership of it to someone else and (2) a quantitative expression of how many units of each product are required to carry out the exchange.

This approach to valuing products exists mainly in barter economies, in which products are swapped directly for each other. Thus one acre of land might be swapped for fifteen cows.    In a money economy, however, a product's value usually is expressed in money terms.    The price of a product is the amount of money a buyer must pay the seller to complete a sales transaction.    But barter may also exist.    Some American airlines, for example, trade seats on their planes for jet fuel.    This is especially appealing to airlines that are short on cash.[1]

Two cautions are in order concerning the concept of price.    First, seller and buyer must be sure they are talking about the same product. If a price is quoted for a car in a TV commercial, an accompanying statement explains exactly what the price is for—"Price is for the model shown with four-cylinder engine, manual transmission, AM radio.    Tax and license tag not included.    Other options available."    Seller and buyer also should have the same total product in mind.    A newspaper ad for a window air conditioner quoted at $399.99 should specify whether the price includes delivery, installation, and other product-related services that may accompany the product item.

The second caution involves the difference between tentative pricing and actual price paid.    Sellers engage in tentative pricing when they set an original offering price for their products.    This is called a basic price, or a **list price.**    Having priced a new car for $9,648.39, the Ford Motor Company attaches a price sticker to the window and sends the car to a Ford dealer in Miami, Florida.    The dealer may end up selling the car to a consumer for $8,850.    If no buyers are willing to pay the sticker price (list price), it will be lowered in order to sell the car.    In 1980, American car makers were offering direct rebates to buyers of their larger models, even after dealer discounts, to move huge inventories of these cars.    The recession had dealt a serious blow to new car sales and many people who were buying chose imported cars, many of which sold at higher than list prices.

list price

## HOW IMPORTANT IS PRICE?

In our economic system, relative prices guide the allocation of scarce resources among alternative uses.    Price is the mechanism that facilitates exchange.    Prices, therefore, are very important on the macro marketing level.    But they are just as important on the micro level in transactions between sellers and buyers.    Unless a seller and a buyer can agree on a price, a sales transaction will not occur.

### Price and the Seller

Firms that compete in purely competitive markets do not set their prices. A product's market price is set by industry-wide forces of supply and demand, and no individual seller can influence that price.    A firm that wants to sell must sell at the market price.    Practically all firms in our economy, however, set their own list prices.

**Pricing Freedom.**    A firm's pricing activities are subject to more local, state, and federal regulation than any of its other marketing activities.

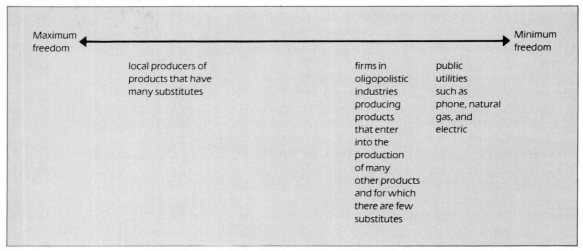

*Figure 20–1. A continuum of pricing freedom (freedom from government regulation of the firm's pricing activities)*
Note: The imposition of government price controls would restrict the pricing freedom of all firms.

But these regulations do not affect all firms equally.[2]   No local hamburger vendor has ever been called in for talks with government officials to justify a price hike.   But executives of big steel firms occasionally have been called in for "jawboning" sessions with government officials to convince them to roll back their announced price hikes.   (See Figure 20–1.)

Unlike hamburger, the price of steel affects the prices of many other products that require steel in their production.   Soon after one steel company announces a price hike that other steel producers will likely follow, automakers announce how much their prices will go up.   There is a snowball effect in that price hikes in one industry lead to price hikes in others.   This may pose problems for government in fighting inflation.

**Costs and Revenues.**   Marketers seek to match effective demand with supply.   In the process they incur costs.   Product, place, and promotion elements in the marketing mix often are viewed as cost factors. The price element must be "right" if the firm is to recover these costs plus a satisfactory profit from sales revenues.   Well designed, efficiently distributed, expertly promoted products simply will not sell if prices are not "right."   To a buyer the "right" price of a product is equal to or less than its perceived value.[3]

**Competitive Factors.**   Price also is a major factor in determining a firm's market share, its company and brand images, and its competitive position.   Consider the beer industry.   After Prohibition was repealed in 1933, there were over 700 breweries in the United States; today, there are less than 70.   Large breweries' aggressive pricing policies helped them increase market share at the expense of smaller rivals.[4]

Consumers also tend to rely on price as an indicator of a product's

Boodles, the ultra-refined British gin, is an unparalleled pleasure.
Both as a martini pleasure and as a pleasure with tonic.
It is produced from the world's costliest methods and imported from Britain.
Boodles provides such a perfect martini and mixing experience,
that it is well worth its price. The price of perfection.

## Boodles. The world's costliest British gin.

Source: General Wine and Spirits Co.

*An ad reflecting
the price-quality
relationship
(prestige pricing)*

quality, especially when they lack information or have trouble evaluating
quality based on other attributes.   When this **price-quality relationship**
exists, the consumer's perception of a product's quality varies directly
with its price.[5]   Within reasonable limits, the higher the price, the higher
the perceived quality.   Many marketers use this in their ads.   Examples

**price-quality
relationship**

are Préférence by L'Oreal, "Sure it costs more . . . but I'm worth it," and Curtis-Mathes TVs, "The most expensive television set you can buy, and darn well worth it."

Pricing strategy also plays a role in shaping a firm's image. This is especially apparent at the retail level. Neiman-Marcus sets relatively high prices to build and maintain its image of exclusiveness. Discounters, on the other hand, set their prices low to build an image of helping customers save money.

Pricing strategy can also help in positioning a firm relative to its rivals. The appeal of low-priced quality merchandise played a major part in the entry of supermarkets into food retailing. Budget motels such as 8 Days Inn also found a niche in the motel industry by offering low-priced lodging.

**Nonprice Competition.** Price can play a major or a minor role in a firm's marketing strategy. Marketers who stress nonprice elements, such as product differentiation and market segmentation, in their marketing mixes deemphasize price as a competitive tool. Advertising often seeks to draw target customers' attention away from price. Marketers that deemphasize price believe a firm's pricing strategy often is the easiest marketing mix element for rivals to copy. They also believe the differential advantage they might achieve through superior product design and effective advertising is harder for rivals to match. This nonprice competition focuses mainly on nonprice elements in the marketing mix.

The importance marketers attach to prices depends a lot on the existing economic environment. Consumers tend to pay less attention to prices during good economic times. But when rapid inflation, lack of job security, and recession exist, consumers tend to become more concerned about prices as they try to maintain their standard of living. Thus marketers give more attention to pricing.[6]

### Price and the Buyer

A marketer's pricing strategy must consider potential buyers' expectations and behavior. One fact is crucial in looking at prices from the buyer's perspective: buying power is limited and buyers try to get the greatest expected utility from it. For many products, such as housing, cars, and home appliances, price has another dimension in addition to initial acquisition cost—high energy costs have increased the effective cost of using these products. This use cost may be considered an important part of a product's total cost by some consumer segments.

price awareness

**Price Awareness and Price Consciousness.** The buyer's ability to remember prices is called **price awareness.** Popular economic theory assumes that buyers are aware of and can recall the prices they pay for the products they buy.

price consciousness

The buyer's sensitivity to price differentials is called **price consciousness.** Popular economic theory also assumes that buyers are sensitive to price differentials—that they will search for and buy lower-priced brands that they perceive to be as good as higher-priced brands.[7] At this point you may want to review the discussion of Weber's law and social class in Chapters 5 and 6.

The view of buyer behavior expressed in economic theory probably applies more to industrial buyers than to ultimate consumers. Purchasing agents are accountable for securing the best prices on the products they buy for using departments in their firms. These departments usually submit detailed product specifications to the purchasing agent, whose job is to find the seller who offers the total product at the lowest price.

As we saw in the discussion of consumer behavior, ultimate consumers do not always behave in a similar fashion. A consumer who is in the process of buying a refrigerator, for example, may not know exactly the type he or she wants and is very interested in gathering additional information about available product features. There is no user department to specify exactly what to buy. Product features may be more important than price during the early stages of shopping.

During the shopping process consumers form a more specific idea of what they want and may become more concerned about prices of acceptable alternatives. Price-conscious buyers are more unwilling to pay higher prices for product extras than less price-conscious buyers. Thus manufacturers of cameras, home appliances, cars, and numerous other products offer various versions at various prices. Many large retailers like Montgomery Ward have discount operations in addition to their regular stores.

There is some tendency for increasing affluence to make consumers less price conscious, especially when buying grocery items. But even here the success of dealer brands and generic items in many supermarkets suggests that the economic realities of inflation and recession tend to make at least some consumers more price conscious. Perhaps the major, and fundamental, pricing constraint marketers face in their pricing decisions is the value buyers place on their offerings. We will discuss this later in the chapter.

## PRICING OBJECTIVES

Marketers should decide their pricing objectives before attempting to set prices on their products. But many firms are reluctant to discuss their pricing objectives with outsiders or to put them in writing. One reason is fear that the objectives might spark an antitrust investigation. Another reason is some firms merely take whatever price they can get for their products. Price really is not a controllable element in their marketing mixes.

### Conflict over Pricing Objectives

Considerable conflict can exist among departments when a firm sets its pricing objectives. Salespersons may favor low prices to build sales volume, whereas finance people may favor high prices to earn more sales revenue per unit. Conflict also may arise from outside the firm. An

**Table 20–1.**  *Examples of general types of pricing objectives*

1. Profitability objectives:
    profit maximization
    satisfactory profit
    target return (short or long run)
2. Sales volume objectives:
    maximize sales
    market share
3. Image building objectives:
    prestige image
    leadership image
4. Preventing competition objectives:
    price stabilization
    elimination of competition

objective of gaining deep market penetration by featuring a low price may alienate middlemen who want high margins. These conflicts must be resolved before the marketing manager can set pricing objectives, guided by top management's concept of the firm's mission.

General types of pricing objectives include (1) profitability, (2) sales volume, (3) image building, and (4) preventing competition. These are not mutually exclusive objectives, nor are they the only objectives possible.[8] A firm's pricing objectives are influenced by time and circumstances. Some objectives are short run, whereas others are long run in nature. As we said earlier, American automakers had huge inventories of cars in 1980. Although their long-run pricing objective may have been to earn a stated rate of return on investment or to gain a certain market share, their short-run objective was to move inventory and speed up cash flow by using price rebates. (See Table 20–1.)

### Profitability Objectives

Two basic types of pricing objectives are tied directly to profitability: (1) profit maximization and (2) target return.

**Profit Maximization.** Classical economic theory assumes that firms set their prices to maximize profit. If all firms tried to do this, society's resources probably would be optimally allocated. But few firms, especially large ones, will admit that this is their objective because many people associate a **profit maximization objective** with high prices, excess profits, monopoly power, and exploitation of buyers.

A firm that is maximizing its profits is not necessarily making excess profits. The few so-called natural monopolies (public utilities) in our economy are regulated by government to ensure they do not take advantage of consumers. But we have other safeguards against firms' making excess profits. If a firm restricts supply to increase price, other firms probably will enter the industry or consumers may switch to substitute products, postpone purchases, or perhaps even stop using the product.

**profit maximization objective**

If there are barriers to entry into the industry, the public will demand government regulation of firms in the industry.

A firm that does have a goal of long-run profit maximization may accept short-run losses. For example, a firm may want to expand distribution into a new market area that currently is served by rivals. It may have to absorb high freight charges on shipments to the area, offer very low prices, and spend heavily on promotion to attract buyers. The firm may incur initial losses upon entering the new area, but it expects future profit on sales there will justify the expansion. This long-run perspective is more likely to be taken by larger firms, however.

The profit maximization objective pertains to a firm's entire product mix, not separate product items. Supermarkets often feature leader items like milk, coffee, sugar, and soft drinks at prices that may not even cover their costs. They are not maximizing profit on these "loss leaders" but expect to sell a lot of higher-margin items to consumers who come to buy the leaders. Because these loss leaders help to increase overall sales and profits, they could be called profit leaders.

A variation of the profit maximization objective is the goal of earning a satisfactory profit. Professional managers in large corporations who want to earn an amount of profit that will satisfy the stockholders are "satisficers," not maximizers.

**Target Return.** Many firms state their profitability objectives in terms of earning what they consider to be an acceptable rate of return on their net sales or investment in the firm. A **target return objective** sets a profit goal against which earned profit is compared to gauge performance. This simplifies the problem of determining profit performance in multiproduct firms and those that have several operating divisions. Products and divisions that do not meet the target can be identified and steps can be taken to improve performance, perhaps by deleting the product or closing the division. This is why General Motors sold its home appliance division (Frigidaire) to White Consolidated Industries.

target return
objective

Target returns also can be expressed in short- or long-run terms. Retail stores and wholesalers often use a short-run target rate of return on net sales. They set their markup percentages to cover their costs plus a desired profit percentage. Large, multidivision firms that are perceived to be industry leaders tend to set long-run target rates of return on their investment. This is in line with their high degree of public visibility and the potential for governmental action if their prices seem to be inflationary.

## Sales Volume Objectives

Sales volume objectives are common in sales-oriented firms that tend to equate increased sales with increased profit. Although it is incorrect to equate the two, the sales orientation still persists in some firms, especially when executive salaries and bonuses are tied to sales instead of profit.

The cost-profit squeeze of recent years has shown that sales can go up but there may be little, if any, profit improvement, especially if the costs of doing business are skyrocketing. The marketing concept has played a role in helping to reconcile the sales volume objective with the profit objective. Some firms, therefore, set a lower limit on what they consider an acceptable profit and try to maximize sales subject to that profit constraint. This gives a profit base to sales volume objectives.

The fast-food industry is a recent example of an industry that is focusing on sales volume. Competition among firms in the industry is becoming more intense because many areas are saturated with outlets. It is becoming harder for many of them to tie growth prospects to opening new outlets. Thus growth for many firms focuses on greater sales per existing outlet. Burger King added specialty sandwiches to attract dinner traffic and McDonald's added breakfast to build early morning traffic. The goal is to increase sales and profit per outlet.

**Market Share Objectives.** Some firms tie their sales volume objective to their market share.[9] It usually is easier to determine whether a firm's market share has remained the same, gone up, or declined than it is to determine, for example, if it is maximizing profit. Industry trade association data and surveys can help in determining a firm's market share.

The impact of even a small increase or decrease in market share can be significant. For example, a 1 percent increase in market share for a firm in the cigarette industry adds about $100 million to its sales.[10] Consequently, market share data are watched very closely by cigarette makers. The same is true in the breakfast cereal industry. A 1 percent market share in this industry equals $20 million in annual sales volume.[11]

market share objective

A **market share objective** also may be more meaningful than a target rate of return. A firm can be achieving its target rate of return year after year, but if total industry sales are growing, the firm may be losing its relative position in the industry. It may be getting a decreasing share of a larger and larger market even though it continues to earn what it considers a satisfactory target rate of return on investment.

Market share objectives are popular among larger, multiproduct firms, and executive salaries and bonuses often are tied to market share performance. Larger firms seek to maintain their existing shares or possibly reduce them if they fear an antitrust investigation. Smaller and more aggressive firms are more interested in increasing their market share. Prior to the huge increase in share of the American auto market accounted for by foreign automakers, General Motors was less anxious to increase its market share than AMC (American Motors Corporation).

Regulatory agencies and commissions often use market share data also. Procter & Gamble, Colgate-Palmolive, and Lever Brothers together have an 85 percent share of the laundry detergent business. After a six-year study, the Federal Trade Commission decided there was no evidence of anticompetitive behavior that would warrant antitrust action by the commission.[12]

Market share objectives are related to sales volume, but in a relative way. They are expressed in relation to rivals. Market share alone, however, does not ensure any profit. Increasing market share by selling at profitless prices very seldom is a desirable goal except in the very short run. Some large, multiproduct firms will do this when introducing a new brand. Their immediate goal is to build market share. This strategy is often called buying a market share.

### Image Building Objectives

Some firms rely on their pricing strategy to help build and maintain a company image.[13] As we said earlier, some retailers set high prices to build a prestige image. A manufacturer's image among middlemen also can be important in reaching its final buyers, especially for new and smaller firms that rely on middlemen for distribution. The manufacturer may be guided by a primary objective of allowing satisfactory margins for middlemen in setting prices.

Manufacturers who are leaders in their industries often want to set prices that rivals consider "fair." This is very common in oligopolistic industries. It helps the firm maintain its respected leadership position and reduces the likelihood of a price war among rivals.

During periods of very high inflation, some firms have on occasion raised prices out of fear the government will impose price controls. When the controls are not imposed, their prices are out of line with marketers who did not raise their prices. This has forced some of the price hikers to trim their effective prices through such sales promotions as coupons and cents-off offers. Some firms, however, want to develop an image of holding the line on prices. While some supermarkets reprice all items on their shelves when the cost of newly ordered merchandise goes up, others apply the higher price only to the merchandise they buy at the higher price and stress that in their advertising.

### Preventing Competition Objectives

Two fundamentally different types of pricing objectives seek to prevent competition. Price stabilization seeks to stabilize prices among rivals in an industry. Elimination seeks to reduce the number of firms that compete by eliminating some from the industry.

**Price Stabilization.** In industries in which a price leader tries to set a price that rivals can live with, **price stabilization objectives** are common. This is important when rivals sell highly standardized products and rapidly changing supply and demand conditions could cause pricing havoc. Rivals, therefore, set their prices to maintain some type of stable relationship between their prices and the leader's price. This lends stability to pricing practices because each firm is able to meet the competition. The number of competitors is unaffected but spirited price competition is avoided. Competitors are willing to follow the leader's leadership. This is common in construction materials, plumbing supplies, and certain kinds of office equipment.

Traditionally, it is not illegal for firms to follow an industry's price leader in setting their prices as long as they do not get together and agree

price stabilization objective

to do this.   But there is some interest among antitrust law enforcers to require firms to set prices according to their own costs.   The legality of price signaling, another common practice in a price leadership situation, also is under scrutiny.   **Price signaling** means the price leader lets it be known through public speaking engagements and interviews when and how much price should be increased.

**price signaling**

**Elimination.**   Elimination objectives also seek to prevent price competition, but the pricer's goal is to eliminate one or more present or potential rivals. A **stay-out pricing objective** involves setting a low price to discourage the entry of new firms.   The low price supposedly will not attract rivals, who will think the profit potential is inadequate.   This reasoning may be sound if the product sells in very limited quantities and those units that are sold do not yield much profit.   But if the product sells in large quantities, rivals might try to make a profit through volume selling, even if per-unit profit is rather small.   A stay-out pricing objective conceivably could result in a firm's being charged with attempting to monopolize commerce.

**stay-out pricing objective**

A **shake-out pricing objective** also leads a firm to set a low price to force inefficient rivals out of the industry.   This also can be illegal if it develops into predatory pricing deliberately to eliminate smaller rivals. In recent years, marginal firms have disappeared in many industries as competition heated up.   These include firms that produced smoke alarms, pocket calculators, and digital watches.

**shake-out pricing objective**

## SETTING LIST PRICE

There is no one, generally accepted, single series of steps that marketers follow in setting prices.   The following steps, however, make up a logical approach: (1) estimate demand, (2) forecast probable competitive reactions, (3) consider company mission and marketing objectives, (4) prepare preliminary pricing strategy over the product's life cycle, (5) select the list price, and (6) establish pricing policies that allow for adjusting list price in individual transactions.   We will discuss the first four steps in this chapter.   Step five is discussed in the next chapter, and step six is covered in Chapter 22.   (See Figure 20–2.)

*Figure 20–2.  An approach to setting list price*

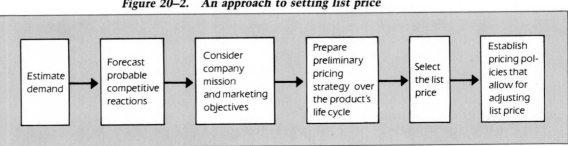

**Table 20–2.** *Demand schedule for disposable razors*

| Price per Unit | Quantity Demanded (units) |
|---|---|
| $.80 | 5 |
| .60 | 10 |
| .40 | 15 |
| .20 | 25 |

## Estimate Demand

The demand for a product is the number of units buyers will buy at a set price. Many factors underlie the demand for a product, such as population, buying power, the availability and prices of substitute products, and buyer preferences. The following concepts are important in estimating demand: (1) the law of demand, (2) a change in demand, (3) a change in quantity demanded, and (4) demand elasticity.

**The Law of Demand.** A product's demand schedule is an estimate of the number of units buyers will purchase at different prices. For most products more units are demanded at lower prices than at higher prices. This **law of demand** can be shown in graphic form as a demand curve. Table 20–2 is a demand schedule and Figure 20–3 is the related demand curve for disposable razors.

law of demand

Underlying the law of demand is the principle of diminishing marginal utility. We can understand this with an example. As you acquire additional units of a product, the amount of additional satisfaction each one adds to your total satisfaction is less than the previous unit's. Suppose you have six sweaters in your wardrobe. The purchase of the sixth

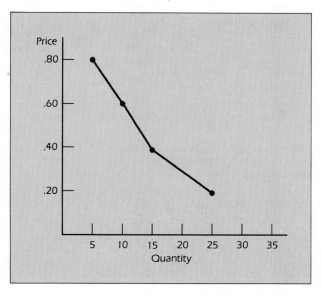

**Figure 20–3.**
**Demand curve for disposable razors**

sweater gave you less additional satisfaction than the first. Although you are better off having six sweaters than only one, you are not six times better off. As the marginal utility (incremental satisfaction) of each additional sweater diminishes, you are willing to pay less to get them.

The demand for prestige products, however, does not conform to the law of demand. They tend to sell better at higher prices than at lower prices. Boodles Gin (see the ad earlier in this chapter) is an example of a prestige product. Within reasonable limits, more units are likely to be demanded at higher than at lower prices. We will discuss prestige pricing in more detail in Chapter 22. People consciously or unconsciously value products in their minds. They have a ballpark figure of what a product is worth, especially when it is a new brand within an already established product category. They may have a tougher time valuing a totally new product, but even here there usually are some substitutes or experiences to serve as a basis for comparative valuing.

**expected price** We call this ballpark figure or, perhaps more accurately, this price range the potential buyer's **expected price.**

Target customers will consider a product priced below the expected range to be low in quality and may refuse to buy it. They also may consider a product priced above the expected range to be overpriced and not buy it. Manufacturers who use indirect marketing channels are interested in their middlemen's views concerning expected price. Mid-

**Table 20–3.** *Examples of changes in quantity demanded and changes in demand*

| Situation | Effect on Demand or Quantity Demanded |
|---|---|
| 1. Eastern Airlines reduces the price of its tickets and sells more tickets. | 1. An increase in quantity demanded for Eastern Airlines tickets. |
| 2. A rapid rise in the price of beef leads to reduced sales of beef and greater sales of Hamburger Helper despite no price change for Hamburger Helper. | 2. A decrease in quantity demanded for beef and an increase in demand for Hamburger Helper. |
| 3. A price cut by steel producers leads to reduced sales by aluminum producers. | 3. An increase in quantity demanded for steel producers and a decrease in demand for aluminum producers. |
| 4. Sony's advertising campaign increases its TV sales without changing the price per unit. | 4. An increase in demand for Sony TVs. |
| 5. Maytag cuts the price on its washing machines to reduce its inventory and sells more units. | 5. An increase in quantity demanded for Maytag washing machines. |
| 6. Polaroid reduces the price of its cameras and sells more cameras and more film despite no change in the price of film. | 6. An increase in quantity demanded for Polaroid cameras and an increase in demand for Polaroid film. |

dlemen have a keen sense for knowing the prices their customers will be willing to pay for a product.

**Change in Demand.** A **change in demand** means that more or fewer units of a product are bought even though its price is not changed. Price remains stable but buyers will buy more or fewer units than they previously bought. An increase in demand occurs when they buy a greater number of units; a decrease in demand occurs when they buy a smaller number. Thus the demand for Hamburger Helper increased as the price of meat skyrocketed several years ago. The price of meat changed but the price of Hamburger Helper was unchanged.

change in demand

**Change in Quantity Demanded.** A **change in the quantity demanded** of a product, on the other hand, is caused by a change in its price. An increase in quantity demanded occurs when a reduction in price leads to more sales of a product; a decrease in quantity demanded occurs when

change in quantity demanded

**Figure 20–4. Change in demand and change in quantity demanded**
**Left side:** *The original demand curve is $D_0$. The shift to the right is a change in demand—an increase in demand without changing the price per unit. The shift to the left is also a change in demand—a decrease in demand without changing the price.*
**Right side:** *At price $P_0$ the quantity demanded is $Q_0$. When price is lowered to $P_1$, the quantity demanded increases to $Q_1$. When price is raised to $P_2$, the quantity demanded decreases to $Q_2$. These are not changes in demand (shifts in the curves); they are changes in quantity demanded (movements along the same curve).*

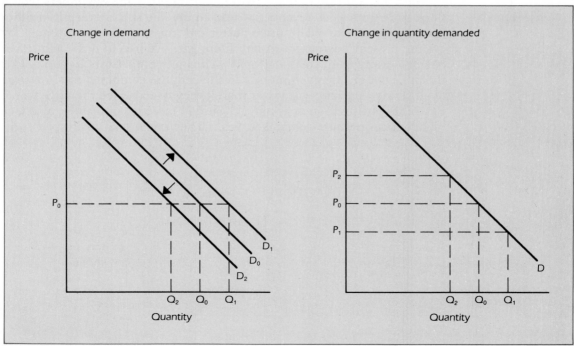

a price increase leads to fewer sales of a product.    Table 20–3 and Figure 20–4, on pages 596 and 597, help to clarify the difference between a change in demand and a change in quantity demanded.

**Demand Elasticity.**    Another important concept is **price elasticity of demand.** This refers to the effect price changes have on the quantity demanded of a product and the firm's sales revenue.    The total sales revenue (TR) a firm receives from selling its product equals the price per unit (P) times the number of units sold (Q): TR = P × Q.

The demand for a product is price elastic when (1) a price cut causes TR to increase or (2) a price hike causes TR to decrease.    The price cut causes such a large increase in the quantity sold that the lower price received per unit is more than offset by the revenues received from the greater number of units sold.    The price hike, on the other hand, gives the firm more revenue per unit sold but the quantity sold falls off so much that total revenue decreases.    (See Figure 20–5.)

The demand for a product is price inelastic when (1) a price cut causes TR to decrease or (2) a price hike causes TR to increase.    In other words, the quantity bought stays relatively steady regardless of the price charged.    TR goes down when price is cut because the quantity sold does not increase enough to make up for the lower price per unit.    TR goes up when price is raised because the number of units sold does not decrease enough to offset the higher price received for the units that are sold.    (See Figure 20–6.)

Before the energy crunch gasoline service stations often had price wars.    One station in an area would cut its price and customers would flock to it.    Its sales revenues would go up, but at the expense of other stations' revenues.    The price cutter did not increase its revenues by getting present customers to buy more gas.    It had to draw additional business away from rival stations.    Thus all competitors had to match the price cut or lose customers.    In the end, the combined total revenue of all service stations was lower than if they had avoided the price war.[14]

Public utilities, such as natural gas and electric companies, also face highly price-inelastic demand curves.    They know that raising price will

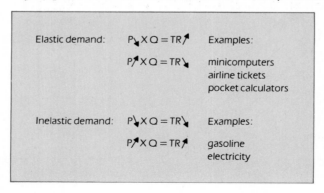

*Figure 20–5.*
*Price elasticity of*
*demand*

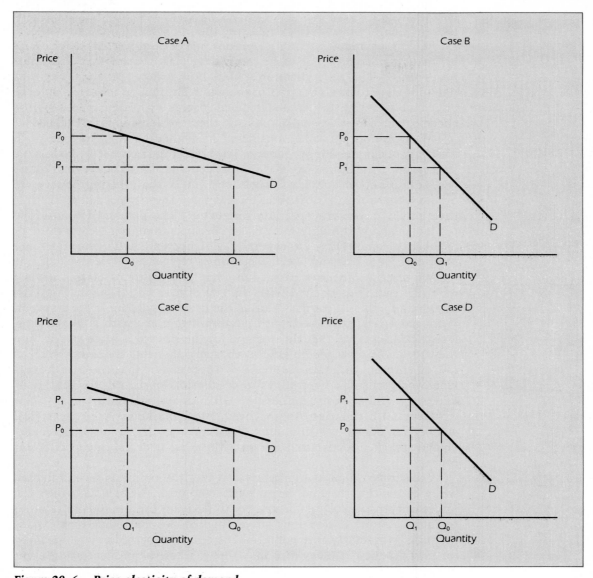

**Figure 20–6. Price elasticity of demand**
*In case A the decline in price from $P_0$ to $P_1$ leads to a large increase in
quantity demanded ($Q_0$ to $Q_1$). In case B the decline in price from $P_0$ to $P_1$
leads to a much smaller increase in quantity demanded ($Q_0$ to $Q_1$). Demand
in case A is much more elastic than in case B.*

*In case C the increase in price from $P_0$ to $P_1$ leads to a large decrease in
quantity demanded ($Q_0$ to $Q_1$). In case D the increase in price from $P_0$ to $P_1$
leads to a much smaller decrease in quantity demanded ($Q_0$ to $Q_1$). Demand
in case C is much more elastic than in case D.*

lead to greater revenues. They are regulated by government agencies to prevent them from unfairly exploiting the inelastic demand situation.

*Judging Demand Elasticity.* A crude rule of thumb is that the demand for luxury products tends to be more price elastic than the demand for necessities. This generalization applies more to broad product categories like food than to product types or brands. The demand for food is more price inelastic than the demand for sliced bacon. The demand for Swift's sliced bacon is even less price inelastic than the demand for sliced bacon.

Many factors must be considered in evaluating the probable price elasticity of demand for a product. The greater the number of substitutes for a product, the more price elastic is its demand. This is why marketers use promotion to convince target customers that their products are unique—there are no substitutes for them. If they succeed in doing this, their products become specialty products. The demand for multiuse products usually is highly price elastic because there is a greater number of substitutes for them. In general, the higher a product's price the more price elastic its demand because customer buying power is limited.

We discussed rites of passage in Chapter 6. Buying class rings is a purchase that is associated with the rite of passage for graduating high school and college seniors. But as the price of gold multiplied several years ago, many seniors stopped buying rings made with gold. Manufacturers discovered that the demand for the rings was price elastic, and they began switching from gold to cheaper substitute materials, such as nickel, chrome, and stainless steel. To help ensure that potential buyers would not consider these alloys to be inferior substitutes for gold, marketers gave them exotic names like Ultrium and Siladium.[15]

**Demand Estimation Approaches.** Most marketers take a practical approach to demand estimation. They consider the factors we have discussed and then focus attention on estimating sales volume at different prices.

Consumer products marketers consider the opinions of middlemen when estimating the final buyer's expected price. They also study the prices of competitive brands and try to position their brands in relation to them. Some use various survey approaches and laboratory experiments to gain insight into potential customers' expected price, especially for new products. They also may test market the product at different prices in different markets.

Marketers of more complex industrial products like installations and accessory equipment may send representatives into potential buyers' plants to demonstrate and discuss the product or product concept with engineers. Purchasing agents are a useful source of information for cheaper and less complex industrial products.

After defining the market target's probable expected price range, the marketer estimates demand at each price within the range. If demand is thought to be highly price elastic, the product probably will be priced at the lower end of the range. This should help to build sales volume and bring in greater sales revenues. But final decisions of this nature must be postponed until we have considered the other steps in our approach to pricing. The lower price may appear to be the wisest choice at this stage but the expected reaction of rivals and the firm's resources must be considered. Perhaps the low-price, large-volume approach would be unrealistic if plant capacity is severely limited. The firm may not be able to produce enough to meet the demand.

### Forecast Probable Competitive Reactions

Only a pure monopolist can price its product without regard to competitors because it has no rival firms or products. But even a monopolist runs the risk that a potential rival will develop a substitute product. Thus all firms must consider the reactions of present and potential rivals to their pricing decisions.

As we said in Chapter 2, all firms engage in generic competition. Each is seeking a share of aggregate buying power. Marketers also face competition from existing and new brands within their product's category and outside that category. Glass manufacturers compete with each other and with plastics, aluminum, and steel producers for market share in the beverage container business. Much of this competition centers on price because, in many uses, these products are substitutable.

Motels used to compete mainly with hotels for customers. But as rates at traditional motels like Holiday Inn and Ramada Inn increased, budget motels like Scottish Inn and 8 Days Inn entered the industry. Thus some traditional motels have cut their rates. Holiday Inn has even offered discount coupons in *People* magazine. Marketers of recreational vehicles also are competing with motels, at least in some market segments.

A typical bathroom in a new home used to have a ceramic tile floor and shower-tub enclosure. But as the price of the tile increased, along with the labor cost to install it, a shift to vinyl floor coverings, wallpaper, fiberglass tub enclosures, and imitation marble occurred.

Forecasting rivals' reactions to a firm's pricing strategy is made even tougher when there are shortages in some industries. The energy crunch led to an explosive demand for fiberglass insulation that exceeded the industry's production capacity. Thus new substitute insulation materials and processes have been developed to compete with fiberglass.

The marketing research department, company salespersons, and careful observation of rivals' actions can help a firm anticipate what rivals will do in response to its pricing decisions. This intelligence gathering is even more important during a period of general inflation, especially in industries where entry is easy and profit potential is attractive.

**The Price Level.** Marketers of products with downsloping demand curves have three pricing options: they can set prices (1) at the market level, (2) above the market level, or (3) below the market level. Two major factors affect how a product is priced relative to its rivals: (1) the degree to which it is differentiated and (2) how long that differentiation can be protected. The more a product is differentiated, the more freedom

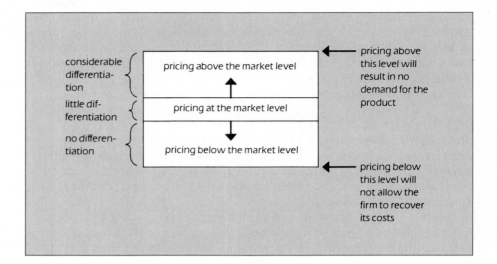

*Figure 20–7. Three pricing options for marketers facing downsloping demand curves*

the marketer has to price above the market level. The longer this differentiation can be protected, the longer the freedom lasts. (See Figure 20–7.)

A poorly differentiated product may sell at or below the market level. Price may be the only basis for competing with the more effectively differentiated brands. But because rivals can match a lower price more easily than any other differentiating factor in a marketing mix, some marketers avoid setting prices below the market price.

*Pricing at the Market Level.* Pricing at the market level amounts to a strategy of meeting competition. It is common in oligopoly where rivals sell a fairly homogeneous product. Market level pricing is practical when a marketer wants to avoid price competition or when there is little differentiation among rival offerings. The pricing of premixed cement in a local market is a common example of this pricing strategy.

*Pricing above the Market Level.* A product that most target customers perceive as superior can be priced above the market level. It occupies a very well-insulated niche in the market. Bayer aspirin is an example. Michelin tires and Shaklee vitamins used to be priced above the market level, but rivals who offered lower prices cost them market share. Thus Michelin and Shaklee prices no longer are as much above the market level as they used to be.

Comparing prices of brands in a product category and making judgments about whether a price is at, below, or above the market level is unwise, however, unless their total marketing mixes are considered. Only if their marketing mixes are identical and they appeal to the same market target should we refer to a price as being at, above, or below the market level. Bayer aspirin users may not think the brand is priced above the market level; they may think the brand is in a class by itself— a specialty product.

*Pricing below the Market Level.* Pricing below the market level is common when a firm wants to stress price in the marketing mix. This is the discount retailer's strategy. Again, however, the discounter's total market offering may not be competing with those of conventional retailers.

Some small firms price below the market level to compete with larger rivals. They may enjoy a combined market share that the big firms consider unimportant. Thus the large firms do not retaliate by lowering their prices. Sometimes they cannot retaliate. Budget motels, for example, can price below the market because their investment and overhead expenses are much lower than full-service motel chains. The same is true for cut-rate car rental firms and smaller firms that compete with American Telephone and Telegraph Company for long distance telephone calls.

The recent increase in popularity of ceiling fans is due largely to high energy costs for cooling homes and perhaps a touch of nostalgia. Until recently, perhaps only five or six firms made ceiling fans. By the early 1980s, there were more than seventy brands on the market and many of the newer entrants stressed low price as their differentiating factor.

## Consider Company Mission and Marketing Objectives

Marketers should not lose sight of their firms' mission and marketing objectives in setting prices. There is a tendency, however, among some to approach pricing as a mechanical exercise of adding up costs and tacking on a desired profit. The other marketing mix elements do not lend themselves as much to this type of treatment.

How aggressively a firm will price its product depends in part on top management's desired market share. Several years ago Sears decided to open budget shops and mark down merchandise prices in its stores to recapture customers it had lost to discounters. Sears's sales went up but its profits went down.

Price also must be compatible with other marketing mix elements. Marketers like Magnavox and Sony want to maintain a high-quality product image and will not be overly aggressive in pricing their products. Adequate middleman margins also must be provided in indirect channels. Some marketers do differentiate their brands through superior product design and more effective distribution but fail to capitalize on it in setting price. They may underprice their brands out of fear customers may reject them in favor of lower-priced rival brands.

## Prepare Preliminary Pricing Strategy over the Product Life Cycle

A marketing manager should project a new product's life cycle and prepare preliminary pricing strategy over the cycle before setting its list price. Pricing is not a matter of setting one list price for a product's entire life.

**Introductory Stage.** A new product almost always enjoys its greatest degree of differentiation during the introductory stage of its life cycle. Demand usually is more price inelastic than at any other stage mainly because there are fewer perceived substitutes than will exist later as rival versions (me-too, or parity brands) are introduced.

Two opposite pricing strategies for introducing a new product are (1) skim-the-cream pricing and (2) penetration pricing.

*Skim-the-cream Pricing.* In **skim-the-cream pricing** the introductory price is set relatively high in the range of expected prices to skim the top off the market. It attracts buyers at the top of the product's demand curve. This is a low-risk approach that the marketer hopes will permit the recovery of high research and development costs more quickly and the development of more insight about the demand for the product. Early marketers of microwave ovens, food processors, CB radios, videotape recorders, home smoke detectors, and home security alarms used the skimming strategy.

Many pharmaceutical firms invest heavily in research and development to develop new drugs. The patent on a new drug lasts for seventeen years but before the drug can be marketed it must be approved by the Food and Drug Administration. The testing period can run for several years. But it is during the period of patent protection that a drug firm expects to recoup the major part of its research and development and other costs plus a profit through skim-the-cream pricing. The loss of patent protection often results in rivals' introducing generic versions with a price appeal.

A marketer who uses the skimming strategy and finds few customers buying the product can lower price to be more in line with their expected price. The demand turns out to be more price elastic than was expected. This is less risky than starting with a low price and having to raise it because excessive demand is straining production capacity or the price is too low to permit recovery of costs plus a satisfactory profit.

A skimming strategy assumes that layers of customers can be peeled off one at a time. After those who are willing to pay the initial high price have bought, price can be lowered to appeal to the next layer. This process can continue through the life cycle, accompanied by other marketing mix changes. For example, as price comes down product distinctiveness no longer will be the main appeal in promotion. Distribution also may become less selective. Eventually the product may even be appealing to price-conscious buyers. Polaroid Corporation often uses a skimming strategy in pricing its new cameras. It introduces a high-priced model and follows it up later with lower-priced versions. (See Figure 20–8.)

The marketer, however, may decide to offer price reductions during the introductory stage to speed the product's adoption rate. This is called *introductory price dealing.* The price cuts cease after the product has gained satisfactory initial acceptance. Polaroid sometimes accomplishes this through trade-in allowances on older models of its cameras.

skim-the-cream
pricing

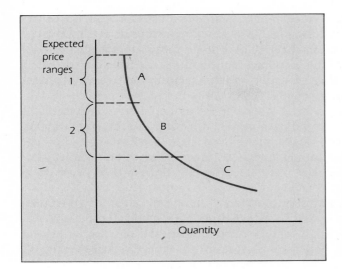

**Figure 20–8. Skim-the-cream pricing**
*If the original skimming price is within expected price range 1, the marketer will peel off customers along the A portion of the demand curve. If the price is lowered within expected price range 2, the marketer will peel off the second layer of customers along the B portion of the demand curve.*

The main problem with cream skimming is that the high initial price may attract rivals. Other firms see the product is selling well at a relatively high price and they may introduce rival versions. Thus by the time the marketer is ready to peel off the second or third layer of customers, rival brands may be on the market.

*Penetration Pricing.* In **penetration pricing** the initial price is set low in the expected range because (1) demand is thought to be highly price elastic or (2) the segment of customers willing to pay a price in the upper range is too small. A low introductory price may enable a marketer to gain deep market penetration quickly. Large volume sales could lead to declining unit production and distribution costs during the early life cycle stages. Since per-unit profit is not high and the firm attracts a large number of customers rapidly, rivals may be discouraged from entering. Texas Instruments, Inc. often has used this strategy in marketing its products.

penetration
pricing

**Growth, Maturity, and Decline Stages.** Pricing strategy over the rest of the life cycle is influenced mainly by the marketer's ability to preserve the brand's differential advantage. Usually price changes are needed as a product goes through its life cycle, perhaps even within a particular stage of the cycle. A skimming price that fails to attract sufficient customers, for example, may have to be changed to a penetration price in the introductory stage. Some household kitchen gadgets are priced this way.

A change in consumer tastes, the appearance of substitutes, and changes in costs are only a few reasons for changing price. The timing of price changes also is important. Reductions may have to tie in with special promotion efforts and hikes may be necessary due to higher costs. If rival brands' prices are rising, a decision must be made whether to remain in line by raising price also.

Factors that make a price change desirable also tend to make other marketing mix changes desirable. As a product moves into late maturity, for example, promotion may have to play down the product's prestige and play up its low price. This also may require more intensive distribution. Examples of products that have followed this strategy include small chain saws, portable electric typewriters, and CB radios.

Competition tends to focus more on price as a product moves through its life cycle because of eroding nonprice differential advantage. Price cutters, latecomers, and dealer brands enter the market. Middlemen also may pressure the manufacturer to lower price. Sometimes the manufacturer has to practice more selective distribution to have any real control over price.

A brand that is very similar to others will have to sell at a comparable price. But there will be downward pressure on this market price if rivals compete mainly on a price basis. A brand also will have to be priced below market if it is perceived as inferior to others. Price changes, however, may make it possible to recycle mature or declining brands. If demand is highly price elastic, a price cut may lead to greater profit.

## THE CONTEMPORARY PRICING ENVIRONMENT

Long-run, target-rate-of-return pricing works best when economic conditions are relatively stable. This permits operating plants at near-capacity levels and accurate cost and demand forecasts. But during recent years, American marketers have had to cope with environmental changes that may be causing them to shift away from long-run, target-rate-of-return pricing to short-run, aggressive pricing to hold or increase market share.[16] Coping with sluggish demand, rapidly rising costs, and strong competition from foreign firms has caused some firms to operate far below their capacities. They have been thrust into active price competition for market share.

Experience suggests that once a firm loses market share it is very hard to recapture it. Whether American automakers will be able to recapture lost share from foreign makers remains to be seen. Firms that stress a market share pricing objective expand their productive capacity which, in turn, tends to make it harder for potential rivals to enter the industry. Experience also suggests that firms with larger market shares tend to have larger profit margins because they are well known by customers and realize economies of scale in their operation.

The effects of a shift from long-run, target-return pricing to more aggressive, short-run, market-share-oriented pricing will be felt at the macro marketing level. Sudden drastic changes in demand in an industry, for example, could lead to much quicker price adjustments. Increased demand will lead to price hikes faster, and decreased demand will lead to more rapid price cuts as firms seek to capitalize on these changes in the short run.

The result is greater price instability in the economy. Large firms that practice aggressive pricing will not be content to set prices that rivals can live with as is true under a condition of price leadership. Inefficient rivals probably will have to leave the industry, which means ownership of American industry would become more concentrated.

## SUMMARY AND LOOK AHEAD

In a money economy a product's price is the amount of money a buyer must pay a seller to complete a sales transaction. Price is a major determinant of a firm's sales revenue, market share, competitive position, and its company and brand images. Consumers also often use price as an implied indicator of product quality.

In the real world nonprice competition often centers on product differentiation, market segmentation, or ad campaigns. How active price is in a marketing mix depends largely on environmental conditions. Buyers tend to become more price conscious, or sensitive to price differentials, during periods of economic uncertainty. Thus price competition usually is stronger during these periods than when business conditions are stable at a high level of consumer demand.

Pricing objectives should be decided before setting list prices. Four general types of objectives are (1) profitability, (2) sales volume, (3) image building, and (4) preventing competition.

Profit maximization and target return are profitability objectives. Many people associate profit maximization with high prices and so many firms are unwilling to state such a goal in writing. Target return objectives can be stated as a rate of return on investment or net sales.

Sales volume objectives are common in sales-oriented firms. Large firms often state this objective in terms of desired market share.

Image building objectives might focus on the company or its products. Firms that rely on middlemen for distribution might set prices with an eye to providing good margins for middlemen. Price leaders want to set prices rivals can live with.

Two different types of preventing competition objectives are price stabilization and elimination. Price stabilization objectives are popular with price leaders. Elimination objectives seek to eliminate one or more present or potential rivals from the industry.

A logical approach to setting list price includes these steps: (1) estimate demand, (2) forecast probable competitive reactions, (3) consider company mission and marketing objectives, (4) prepare preliminary pricing strategy over the product's life cycle, (5) select the list price, and (6) establish policies for adjusting list prices in individual transactions.

The law of demand, change in demand, change in quantity demanded, and price elasticity of demand are basic concepts in estimating demand. The anticipated reactions of present and potential rivals also must be considered in setting list price. Marketers with downsloping demand curves can price at, above, or below the market level.

A firm's mission and its overall marketing objectives also are relevant in pricing decisions. A firm that seeks to increase its market share dramatically will be more aggressive in its pricing than a firm that is content with its present market share.

The marketer also should project a product's life cycle before setting its price. Two opposite strategies in launching a new product are skim-the-cream and penetration pricing. A skimming price is set relatively high in the expected price range to peel off layers of customers on the product's demand curve. A penetration price is set low because demand is thought to be highly price elastic or the segment of customers willing to pay a high price is too small.

The contemporary pricing environment may favor more aggressive pricing for market share. Underlying factors include rapid inflation, excess production capacity, difficulty in forecasting costs and demand, and intense competition from foreign firms.

The focus in the next chapter is on the fifth step in our approach to pricing, setting the list price.

## REVIEW QUESTIONS

1. What is the price-quality relationship?

2. What is a price-conscious buyer?

3. Why do some marketers refuse to state publicly a profit maximization objective?

4. How do profit satisficers differ from profit maximizers?

5. Identify four general types of pricing objectives and give an example of each.

6. Contrast a stay-out pricing objective with a shake-out pricing objective.

7. Identify the six steps in our approach to setting price.

8. Does the demand for all products obey the law of demand? Explain.

9. Contrast a change in demand with a change in quantity demanded.

10. What is the significance of expected price to a marketer in pricing a new product?

11. How is a firm's total revenue affected when it raises the price of a product that has a highly price-elastic demand?

12. How does the presence of a large number of substitutes affect a product's price elasticity of demand? Give an example.

13. Assume the demand for a product is highly price elastic. Would the marketer be more likely to price at the lower or the higher price in the expected price range? Explain.

14. Why might a firm want to price its product below the market level?

15. Contrast skim-the-cream and penetration pricing strategies.

16. Why is price competition among brands in a product category likely to intensify during later stages of its life cycle?

17. Why is long-run, target-rate-of-return pricing more likely during stable economic periods?

## DISCUSSION QUESTIONS

1. Which is better for consumers, price competition or nonprice competition?

2. Is it possible for a product to be underpriced?

3. Can a person be price conscious in buying some products and practically ignore price in buying other products?

**4.** Is a firm exploiting consumers when it uses skim-the-cream pricing in introducing a new product?

**5.** Why do firms with large market shares tend to have larger profit margins than those with very small market shares?

## NOTES

1. "Barter Deals Become the New Airline Fuel," *Business Week*, July 7, 1980, pp. 20–21.

2. No firm, however, is totally beyond the reach of potential regulation. For example, one study suggests that pharmaceutical manufacturers and retail pharmacies should consider the potential for greater scrutiny of their pricing practices by state and federal agencies. A major reason is the increasing involvement of government in funding health care plans. See Charles M. Futrell, "Prescription Drug Costs Based on Income and Area of Residence," *Baylor Business Studies*, August–October, 1975, pp. 21–25.

3. See Benson P. Shapiro and Barbara B. Jackson, "Industrial Pricing to Meet Consumer Needs," *Harvard Business Review*, November–December, 1978, pp. 119–127.

4. Edwin C. Hackleman, Jr. and Sandra K. Siegert, "Another Look at the Beer Industry," *Marquette Business Review*, Fall, 1975, pp. 108–116.

5. See Peter C. Riesz, "Price versus Quality in the Marketplace, 1961–1975," *Journal of Retailing*, Winter, 1978, pp. 15–28; and Steven M. Cox, "The Relationship between Price and Quality in Situations of Repeated Trial," *University of Michigan Business Review*, May, 1979, pp. 24–29.

6. See Alan J. Resnik, Peter B. B. Turney, and J. Barry Mason, "Marketers Turn to 'Countersegmentation,'" *Harvard Business Review*, September–October, 1979, pp. 100–106.

7. One study found that American motorists were conscious of and responsive to price differentials among competing gasoline service stations prior to the 1973 oil embargo. But during the embargo buyers did not care about price. Availability was their big problem. When gasoline supplies returned to normal, however, consumers did not resume their price sensitivity in choosing service stations. See William S. Penn, Jr. and Harold W. Fox, "Puzzling Price Latitude at Service Stations," *Business Economics*, March, 1977, pp. 12–16.

8. See Robert F. Lanzillotti, "Pricing Objectives in Large Companies," *American Economic Review*, December, 1958, pp. 921–940; and Robert E. Hampel, "Pricing Policies and Profitability," *Management Accounting*, July, 1977, pp. 53–56.

9. For discussion of various strategies to increase, maintain, or decrease market share, see Paul N. Bloom and Philip Kotler, "Strategies for High Market Share Companies," *Harvard Business Review*, November–December, 1975, pp. 63–72.

10. "Decision of Lorillard's Judge to Stress Low-Tar Cigarets Sustained by Public," *Wall Street Journal*, March 27, 1980, p. 16.

11. "Kellogg: Still the Cereal People," *Business Week*, November 26, 1979, p. 83.

12. "Detergent Firms Cleared as FTC Ends Long Study," *Wall Street Journal*, May 13, 1980, p. 8.

13. It has been suggested that retail stores should consider their overall price image as well as the pricing of individual items. Price images are relatively stable and do not change rapidly despite special price promotions. See Harry Nystrom, Hans Tamsons, and Robert Thams, "An Experiment in Price Generalization and Discrimination," *Journal of Marketing Research*, May, 1975, pp. 177–181.

14. For discussion of the usefulness of the pricing mechanism to achieve reduced gasoline consumption, see John F. Willenborg and Robert E. Pitts, "Gasoline Prices: Their Effect on Consumer Behavior and Attitudes," *Journal of Marketing*, January, 1977, pp. 24–31.

15. "Classy Rings," *Time*, May 19, 1980, p. 81.

16. This section is largely based on "Flexible Pricing," *Business Week*, December 12, 1977, pp. 78–81, 84, 88.

# Chapter 21

# Setting List Price

## OBJECTIVES

*After reading this chapter you should be able to*

1. identify and discuss three basic pricing orientations.

2. identify and contrast the various cost-oriented approaches to pricing.

3. identify and define seven types of cost and explain their behavior as output fluctuates.

4. draw graphs that depict total cost, average cost, and marginal cost curves.

5. explain why a firm might use the marginal cost approach to pricing.

6. identify the conditions under which a firm might use the incremental cost approach to pricing.

7. compute a breakeven point in units and draw a breakeven chart.

8. demonstrate how demand can be introduced into breakeven analysis.

9. distinguish among total, average, and marginal revenue.

10. discuss the theoretical approach to price setting and its limitations for marketers.

11. give an example of demand-oriented pricing.

12. distinguish between markon and markup.

## KEY CONCEPTS

*Look for these terms as you read the chapter:*

Full Cost Pricing
Average Cost Pricing
Marginal Cost Pricing
Incremental Cost Pricing
Target Return Pricing
Breakeven Pricing
Total Fixed Cost (TFC)
Total Variable Cost (TVC)
Total Cost (TC)
Average Total Cost (ATC)
Average Fixed Cost (AFC)
Average Variable Cost (AVC)
Marginal Cost (MC)
Breakeven Point (B.E.P.)
Total Revenue (TR)
Average Revenue (AR)
Marginal Revenue (MR)
Gross Margin
Markon
Markup
Stock Turnover Rate

*One of the industries hardest hit by foreign competition in recent years is the steel industry. Foreign producers, especially the Japanese, sell considerable quantities of their steel in the United States at lower prices than those charged by American producers. One reason they can do this is that their mills are newer and operate at lower cost.*

*More recently, however, another competitor of big American steel mills has appeared. These are small mills that specialize in producing only a few products, unlike the big mills, which produce many products. The small mills have set up operations using the latest technology and operate at much lower fixed costs than their big rivals. Thus they can set lower prices on their products than the big mills.*

Marketers take different approaches to setting list prices for their products. These range from imitating rivals' prices to setting price on the basis of a detailed analysis of cost and demand factors.

There are many simple approaches to pricing. Some antique shops set list prices solely on what they think the traffic will bear. Some other firms set list prices solely on cost. In many cases, list prices are set in relation to both cost and demand factors. A retailer of women's dresses, for example, might add to the cost of a dress a certain percentage over cost to cover operating expenses and profit. This percentage may be set after a careful study of the retailer's costs and an analysis of demand, or it could be the traditional percentage rivals use in pricing their merchandise.

Manufacturers usually pay closer attention to costing their products because they do not buy finished products for resale. They often use sophisticated cost accounting systems to keep track of manufacturing costs. This helps in setting their list prices. But manufacturers also have to consider demand.

From a long-run perspective, a firm has to set its prices to fall within a range in which cost is the floor and the highest price the most anxious buyer is willing to pay is the ceiling. But as we will see in this chapter, there are different types of costs that can be used in setting list prices.

## APPROACHES TO SETTING LIST PRICE

Unfortunately, there is no one best approach to setting list prices. Some marketers stress a cost orientation while others focus more on demand. Some try to bring supply and demand forces together by using an approach based on microeconomic theory.[1] Thus we will look at prices based on (1) costs, (2) a balance between supply and demand, and (3) demand.

### Prices Based on Costs

Most marketers take a cost-oriented approach to pricing their products. Because no firm can stay in business over the long run unless the price it gets for its product covers the firm's costs, marketers put a lot of emphasis on cost data. Cost accounting systems collect these data and report them to marketing decision makers. The bottom line on the

**Table 21–1.** *Cost-oriented approaches to pricing*

full cost pricing

average cost
   pricing

marginal cost
   pricing

incremental cost
   pricing

target return
   pricing

breakeven pricing

| | | |
|---|---|---|
| 1. **Full cost pricing** | Price equals total cost plus something for profit. |
| 2. **Average cost pricing** | Price is set according to the average total cost curve, which includes a provision for profit. |
| 3. **Marginal cost pricing** | Price is set to cover only the marginal cost (the change in total cost from producing one more unit) of that unit. |
| 4. **Incremental cost pricing** | Price is set according to the costs that are relevant to a particular order. |
| 5. **Target return pricing** | Price is set to provide a profit target expressed as a percentage or as a dollar amount of return on sales or investment. |
| 6. **Breakeven pricing** | The minimum selling price is established at the breakeven point, where total cost equals total revenue. |

income statement is preceded by deductions of costs from net sales to arrive at a net profit figure. Thus costs set a floor below which a firm cannot price its product and expect to stay in business as a going concern.

Cost-oriented pricing approaches range from the very simple to the very complex. We will begin with the full cost approach, or simple cost-plus pricing. (See Table 21–1.)

**Simple Cost-plus Pricing.** The simplest cost-plus pricing approach results in a selling price for each unit of product that equals its total cost plus something extra for profit. Suppose a home builder wants to price new houses 20 percent above total costs. The firm is building ten identical new houses and total labor and materials costs are expected to be $400,000. The builder also figures overhead costs such as office rent, depreciation on equipment, insurance, and telephone at $100,000. Total costs, therefore, are $500,000 and the desired profit is $100,000 (20 percent of $500,000). Cost plus profit equals $600,000 and each house is priced at $60,000.

This full cost approach to pricing is simple but does not reflect the fact that different types of cost behave differently. Suppose the builder builds and sells only five houses instead of ten and assumes the profit earned will be cut in half. Total sales revenue is 5 × $60,000, or $300,000. The overhead costs will be the same as if all ten houses had been built and sold. Office rent, telephone cost, and insurance will not go down simply because fewer houses were built and sold. But labor and materials costs will go down. Instead of $400,000, those costs will be 5 × $40,000, or $200,000. Thus total costs are $100,000 + $200,000, or $300,000. The entire proceeds from selling five houses must go to cover costs. There is nothing left over for profit.

**More Sophisticated Cost-plus Pricing.** A more careful analysis of costs reveals that different types of cost behave differently as output increases or decreases. The following costs are important in pricing decisions:

1. **TFC (Total Fixed Cost):** The sum of all costs that remain fixed in total regardless of output volume. Examples are rent, fire insurance premiums, executive salaries, and telephone.

2. **TVC (Total Variable Cost):** The sum of all costs that vary in total with output volume. Examples are total wages paid to assembly line workers and the total cost of materials used to make a product.

3. **TC (Total Cost):** The sum of TFC and TVC. Changes in TC are due to changes in TVC since TFC is constant.

4. **ATC (Average Total Cost):** TC divided by the number of units of output (Q) associated with these costs.

$$ATC = \frac{TC}{Q}$$

5. **AFC (Average Fixed Cost):** TFC divided by the number of units of output associated with these costs.

$$AFC = \frac{TFC}{Q}$$

Although TFC remains fixed, per-unit fixed costs (AFC) decrease as output increases because a constant number is being divided by an ever-increasing number of units of output.

6. **AVC (Average Variable Cost):** TVC divided by the number of units of output associated with these costs.

$$AVC = \frac{TVC}{Q}$$

Within a narrow range of production, AVC may tend to remain constant. Thus if the first unit requires $1 of labor and $1.25 of materials, it contains $2.25 of variable costs. This $2.25 per unit might remain constant for a short while. But beyond a certain level of output we might get quantity discounts on materials, which might lead to a reduction in AVC. It also may go up if output expands enough to require paying overtime wages.

7. **MC (Marginal Cost):** The change in TC resulting from the production of one more unit of output.

$$MC = \frac{\Delta TC}{\Delta Q}$$

If TC is $500 for twelve units and $520 for thirteen units, the MC of the thirteenth unit is $20.

An understanding of the behavior of costs is essential in making marketing decisions. Several years ago McDonald's expanded its product offering by adding breakfast to the menu. This enabled the restaurants

total fixed cost (TFC)

total variable cost (TVC)

total cost (TC)

average total cost (ATC)

average fixed cost (AFC)

average variable cost (AVC)

marginal cost (MC)

**Table 21–2.** Types of costs

| Quantity (Q) | Total Fixed Cost (TFC) | Average Fixed Cost (AFC) $\frac{TFC}{Q}$ | Total Variable Cost (TVC) | Average Variable Cost (AVC) $\frac{TVC}{Q}$ | Total Cost (TC) TFC + TVC | Average Total Cost (ATC) $\frac{TC}{Q}$ | Marginal Cost (MC) $\frac{\Delta TC}{\Delta Q}$ |
|---|---|---|---|---|---|---|---|
| 0  | $200 | $      | $  0 | $     | $200 | $      | $   |
| 1  | 200  | 200.00 | 50   | 50.00 | 250  | 250.00 | 50  |
| 2  | 200  | 100.00 | 79   | 39.50 | 279  | 139.50 | 29  |
| 3  | 200  | 66.67  | 104  | 34.67 | 304  | 101.33 | 25  |
| 4  | 200  | 50.00  | 126  | 31.50 | 326  | 81.50  | 22  |
| 5  | 200  | 40.00  | 147  | 29.40 | 347  | 69.40  | 21  |
| 6  | 200  | 33.33  | 167  | 27.83 | 367  | 61.17  | 20  |
| 7  | 200  | 28.57  | 187  | 26.71 | 387  | 55.29  | 20  |
| 8  | 200  | 25.00  | 209  | 26.13 | 409  | 51.13  | 22  |
| 9  | 200  | 22.22  | 239  | 26.56 | 439  | 48.78  | 30  |
| 10 | 200  | 20.00  | 284  | 28.40 | 484  | 48.40  | 45  |
| 11 | 200  | 18.18  | 351  | 31.91 | 551  | 50.09  | 67  |
| 12 | 200  | 16.67  | 445  | 37.08 | 645  | 53.75  | 94  |

to open earlier in the morning and helped to spread their fixed costs over more hours of operation. Steel makers know that operating their mills below 80 percent of capacity is risky because of their high fixed costs. When demand falls off they are likely to make price cuts to help keep their mills operating nearer to capacity. They are also willing to accept higher inventory carrying cost to avoid the high costs of stopping and restarting their operations.

Broiler producers are also geared to high fixed-cost operations. A decrease in demand for chicken in one year may cause prices to fall, but the producers cannot simply cut back production without considering the effects on costs. Per-unit costs tend to rise sharply when output drops.

Table 21–2 illustrates the costs we have discussed. TFC stays constant but AFC declines as output increases. Also, TVC increases but AVC declines and then rises with production of the ninth unit. The increase in AVC may be due to paying overtime wages.

TC = TFC + TVC. TC increases as output increases. ATC declines and begins to rise with the eleventh unit. Although AFC declined throughout the entire range of production, AVC begins to rise with the ninth unit. In other words, the declining AFC is more than offset by the rising AVC, starting with the eleventh unit. Thus ATC increases with the eleventh unit. Unless each unit can be sold at a price that covers its marginal cost, the firm will incur a loss on its sale. MC declines but turns up before the ATC turns up.

Figure 21–1 shows the total cost curves—TC, TVC, and TFC—that

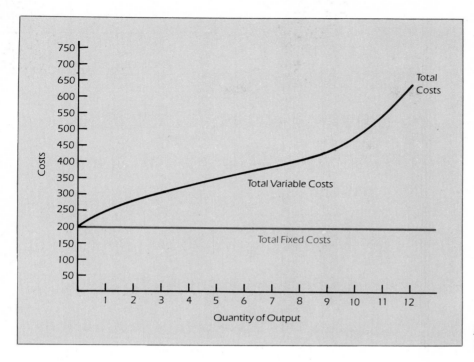

*Figure 21–1.*
*Total cost curves*

correspond to the data in Table 21–2. TVC is the area between TC and TFC. Our discussion assumes a short-run situation. Over the long run, there are no fixed costs; all costs are variable. Thus there would be no TFC line.

Figure 21–2 shows the average cost curves. These are per-unit cost curves—ATC, AVC, AFC, and MC. The MC crosses the AVC and ATC from below at their minimum points. In the short run, a firm might continue to sell its output even if the price it receives falls below the ATC. If it did not sell, it would receive no revenue but its fixed costs would still go on. Any price above AVC covers the variable costs of producing each unit and contributes something to help cover fixed cost. Notice that the AFC curve declines throughout its range.

As long as price is greater than AVC but less than ATC, the sale of the unit helps the firm minimize its operating loss. But if price falls below AVC the firm probably should shut down. This means the firm's short-run supply curve is that part of its MC curve above its intersection with the AVC curve.

Other, more sophisticated cost-oriented pricing approaches are (1) the average cost approach, (2) the marginal cost approach, (3) the incremental cost approach, (4) the target return approach, and (5) the breakeven approach.

*The Average Cost Approach.* Suppose a firm wants to earn a $10,000 profit next month. It could treat this desired profit like a fixed cost and

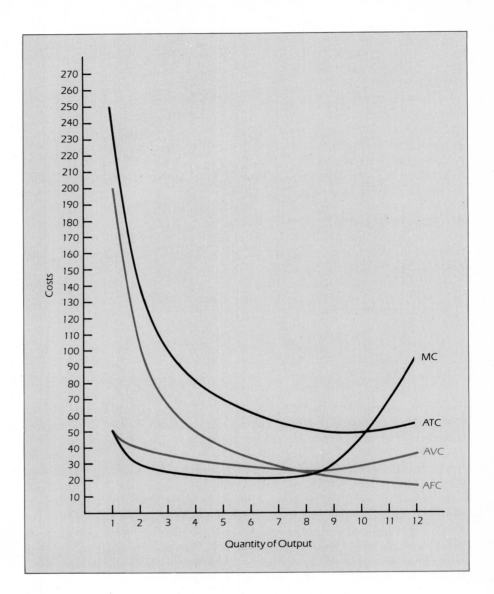

Figure 21–2.
Average cost and
marginal cost
curves

add it to the AFC curve if the firm states the profit goal in cents per unit.
If the firm expects to sell x units next month (based on the quantity sold
last month), it locates that point on the horizontal axis of the cost graph.
Above that point on the ATC curve, the firm looks across to the vertical
axis for the price per unit that would yield the desired profit per unit.

Look at Table 21–2 and Figure 21–2 and assume that the desired profit
is built into the fixed or variable cost curves. If the firm expects to sell
eight units, the selling price will be $51.13 (the ATC). If it expects to
sell ten units, the selling price will be $48.40. But if sales fall short of

expectations, the profit goals will not be realized because the AFC will be higher than expected because fewer units were sold. If more units are sold than expected, the firm will make extra profit because AFC continues to decline throughout its entire range.

*The Marginal Cost Approach.* Sometimes firms will set a price that covers only their marginal cost. As we said earlier, marginal cost is the change in TC resulting from the production of one more unit of output. Remember also that a firm's short-run supply curve is that part of its MC curve above its intersection with the AVC curve. In Table 21–2 the firm might sell the tenth unit at $45 rather than the full cost of $48.40. It may be willing to do this (1) if the buyer will purchase other products from the firm at a price that will cover full costs, (2) if the firm wants to sell the product to avoid storage costs, or (3) if selling the product will enable the firm to avoid laying off workers because of lack of sales. Firms that operate employee cafeterias as a fringe benefit often use the marginal cost approach in pricing the food.

*The incremental cost approach.* Consider the following example:

| | | |
|---|---|---|
| *Sales (100,000 units at $20)* | | *$2,000,000* |
| Costs: | | |
| Variable | $1,000,000 | |
| Fixed | 500,000 | |
| Total | | 1,500,000 |
| *Net profit* | | $ 500,000 |

Suppose this manufacturer is approached by a buyer who wants to order 20,000 units and is willing to pay $250,000, or $12.50 per unit. Should the firm accept the order?

Total cost per unit of the original 100,000 units is $15. The buyer, however, is willing to pay only $12.50. Under the full cost approach to pricing the offer would be refused. But the $12.50 per unit would enable the seller to cover the variable cost of producing the item ($10 per unit) and leave $2.50 over to apply to fixed costs. Thus it may be willing to accept the order if (1) the variable cost per unit will remain the same or decline, (2) no other buyer is willing to pay more, (3) accepting the order will not change TFC, and (4) accepting the order will not affect sales to regular customers.

This incremental cost approach to pricing considers only those costs that are relevant to a particular order. Accepting the order would result in the following income statement. Notice the $50,000 in incremental profit.

| | | |
|---|---|---|
| *Sales (100,000 units at $20)* | | |
| *( 20,000 units at $12.50)* | | *$2,250,000* |
| Costs: | | |
| Variable | $1,200,000 | |
| Fixed | 500,000 | |
| Total | | 1,700,000 |
| *Net profit* | | $ 550,000 |

*Target return approach.*   In the target return approach to pricing the profit target can be set as a percentage or as a dollar amount of return on sales or investment.   This approach also assumes the last period's sales volume will be achieved in the coming period.

Suppose:

1.  sales volume = 20,000 units
2.  TFC = $100,000
3.  total investment = $80,000
4.  desired rate of return on investment = 15 percent
5.  AVC = $10

The 15 percent rate of return on $80,000 is $12,000, which is added to TFC.   TFC plus the desired return is $112,000.   Dividing that by 20,000 units results in a fixed cost and target return per unit of $5.60. Adding variable cost per unit of $10, we have a total cost plus target return per unit of $15.60.   That is the price per unit that should be charged.

**breakeven point (B.E.P.)**<br>**total revenue (TR)**

*Breakeven Approach.*   A firm's **breakeven point (B.E.P.)** is that point at which its total revenue equals its total cost (TR = TC).

**Total revenue (TR)** is the price per unit times the number of units sold (TR = P × Q).   To simplify the discussion of breakeven analysis we will assume all costs are either fixed or variable and AVC is constant. Breakeven analysis helps a firm determine the level of sales at which TR will equal TC, given the product's per unit selling price.

Suppose:

1.  selling price per unit = $1.75
2.  AVC = $1.25
3.  TFC = $15,000

For each unit sold at $1.75, $1.25 goes to cover variable cost.   This leaves 50 cents to cover fixed costs.   Since TFC is $15,000, 30,000 units must be sold to cover TFC ($15,000 ÷ $0.50).   The B.E.P. in units, therefore, is 30,000.   The 50 cents available from the sale of each unit to cover TFC is called the fixed cost contribution per unit.   The formula for the B.E.P. in units is

$$\frac{\text{TFC}}{\text{FC contribution per unit}}$$

By definition, the B.E.P. is where

$$
\begin{aligned}
\text{TR} &= \text{TC} \\
\text{P} \times \text{Q} &= \text{TFC} + \text{TVC} \\
\$1.75 \times \text{Q} &= \$15,000 + \$1.25\,(\text{Q}) \\
\$.50\text{Q} &= \$15,000 \\
\text{Q} &= 30,000 \text{ (B.E.P. in units)} \\
\$1.75 \times 30,000 &= \$52,500 \text{ (B.E.P. in dollars)}
\end{aligned}
$$

Figure 21–3 is a breakeven chart.   The TFC curve is horizontal.   The

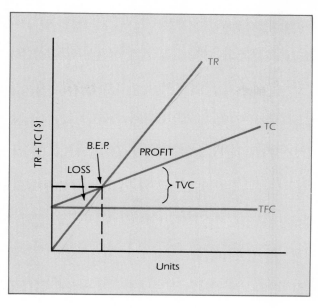

*Figure 21–3.*
*Breakeven chart*
*with one TR curve*

area between the TFC and TC curves is TVC.   The B.E.P. is where the
TR and TC curves cross.   Profit increases rapidly beyond the B.E.P. because TFC is covered at the B.E.P.   The only cost that must be covered
on each unit beyond the B.E.P. is variable cost.   The TR curve is a straight
line because we are assuming each unit is sold at the same price.   This
price could have been determined by any of the pricing approaches we
have discussed.

Using only one TR curve means any number of units can be sold at
the set price.   This is unrealistic because the demand curve (AR) would
have to be horizontal (perfectly elastic) at that price.

Each of the TR curves in Figure 21–4 on page 620 is based on a
different selling price.   The steeper the curve, the higher the price.   Thus
the B.E.P. associated with $TR_1$ requires that fewer units be sold to break
even than the B.E.P. associated with $TR_3$.   Demand, however, still is
ignored because each TR curve assumes that the related demand curve
is perfectly elastic at those prices.

Suppose the sales forecast tells us that quantities A, B, C, and D are
associated with the prices assumed in $TR_1$, $TR_2$, $TR_3$, and $TR_4$, respec-
tively.   (See points A, B, C, and D in Figure 21–4.)   Connecting these
points gives us a curve indicating the TR that will be received at each
price and quantity.   This is not the usual downsloping demand curve
but a TR curve.

The B.E.P. associated with $TR_1$ lies above point A, the B.E.P. associated with $TR_4$ lies above point D, but the B.E.P. associated with both
$TR_2$ and $TR_3$ lies below points B and C.   Clearly, point C is higher above
the TC line than point B.   Thus the best selling price is the one associated
with $TR_3$ if we assume the firm wants to maximize profit.   This is

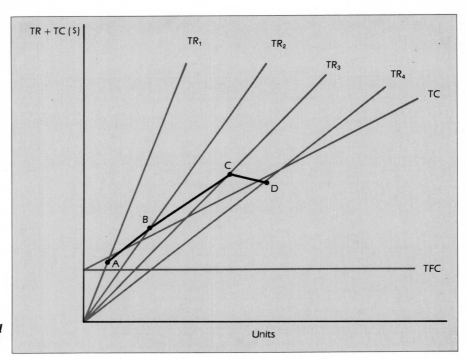

**Figure 21–4.**
**Introducing demand**
**into breakeven**
**analysis**

because point C is at the greatest vertical distance above the TC curve. Unlike the other cost-oriented pricing approaches, the flexible breakeven approach allows us to introduce demand into the analysis.

### Prices Based on a Balance Between Supply and Demand

The economic theory of price determination assumes a firm sets its prices to maximize its profits. This approach to price determination is based on balancing supply and demand. It requires a consideration of revenue curves as well as cost curves.

**Revenue curves.** In addition to total revenue (TR), which was introduced earlier, two other revenue curves are important:

<table>
<tr><td>average revenue (AR)</td><td>1. AR (Average Revenue): TR divided by the number of units that were sold to produce that revenue</td></tr>
</table>

$$AR = \frac{TR}{Q}$$

<table>
<tr><td>marginal revenue (MR)</td><td>2. MR (Marginal Revenue): The change in TR due to the sale of one more unit</td></tr>
</table>

$$MR = \frac{\Delta TR}{\Delta Q}$$

**Table 21-3.** *Marginal revenue and price*

*If the AR (price) is $80 and two units are sold, TR = $160 (two units @ $80 each). If, in order to sell one more unit, price must be lowered to $70, TR = $210 (three units @ $70 each). Although the third unit sells for $70, the net benefit from selling three units rather than two is $50. This $50 is the MR from selling the third unit. Notice the sixth unit. Its price is $40 but the MR is negative. Thus, the sale of the sixth unit causes TR to decline.*

| Quantity (Q) | Price (AR) (P) | Total Revenue (TR) | Marginal Revenue (MR) |
|---|---|---|---|
| 0 | $100 | $  0 | $ |
| 1 | 90 | 90 | 90 |
| 2 | 80 | 160 | 70 |
| 3 | 70 | 210 | 50 |
| 4 | 60 | 240 | 30 |
| 5 | 50 | 250 | 10 |
| 6 | 40 | 240 | − 10 |
| 7 | 30 | 210 | − 30 |
| 8 | 20 | 160 | − 50 |
| 9 | 10 | 90 | − 70 |

In pure competition each firm's demand curve (AR curve) is perfectly elastic (horizontal) at the price set by industry forces of supply and demand. (See Figure 21–5 on page 622.) The firm can sell its entire output at the market price. Only in pure competition is a firm's demand curve perfectly elastic and the same as its marginal revenue (MR) curve. Otherwise, the AR curve is downsloping. The MR curve is below the AR curve and falls faster than the AR curve. A downsloping AR curve means that in order to sell one more unit of product, the price of all units sold must be lowered. This is shown in Table 21–3.

**Profit Maximizing Pricing.** A firm that wants to maximize its profit will produce that quantity of units where MR = MC. The optimum price is the point on the AR curve above the point where the MR and MC curves cross. Figure 21–5 shows the output at which profit will be maximized and the optimum price for firms operating in different market structures.

The situation in oligopoly is less clear. Because there are few sellers the actions of each affect total industry sales and profits and their division among rivals. The rivals make decisions that either maximize their combined profits or uniquely benefit each firm.

Rivals will try to maximize their combined profits when they recognize their interdependence. This usually occurs when (1) their brands are very similar, (2) their market shares are roughly equal, (3) there are major entry barriers to the industry, (4) one firm is dominant, (5) the price that maximizes industry profit is stable or increasing, or (6) they have a similar view of their industry's future.

Otherwise, rivals will seek to maximize their individual profits. When they do not recognize their interdependence, each firm's demand

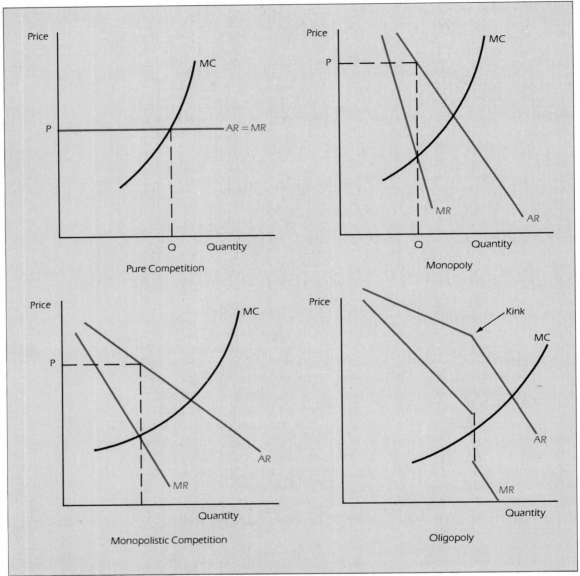

**Figure 21–5. Profit maximization output and price**

curve is more price elastic than the industry's. If one firm cuts price and the others do not follow, its TR may increase a great deal even though industry sales remain the same. This is why each firm tries to anticipate the others' reactions to its pricing decisions. If rivals are not expected to retaliate, the price cutter will take sales from them.

*Kinked Demand Curves.* Oligopolists often face kinked demand curves. The part of the AR curve above the kink in Figure 21–5 is highly elastic. The part below the kink is highly inelastic. The MR curve has two parts and is discontinuous at the kinked price. If the MC curve crosses the MR curve in its discontinuous portion, the firm will hold its price at the kinked level. Raising its price above the kink (into the elastic part of its demand curve) would lower its TR. Thus a price increase by one firm that is not matched by rivals will cost it lost sales. A price decrease that is matched by rivals means all sellers will have lower total revenues. This is why prices in oligopoly situations with kinked demand curves tend to be stable.

Oligopoly prices often stay at the kinked price through price leadership. Cutting prices may lead to price wars and less TR for all rivals. Thus one firm may serve as the price leader and rivals will stay in line with its price. The leader sets a price rivals can accept without having to engage in illegal price-fixing agreements. The leader usually is the firm that has the best record for forecasting demand and cost conditions in the industry.

**Evaluation of Price Theory.** Marketers encounter several problems in using price theory to set prices. The theory assumes a firm's goal is to maximize profit, and price changes are the only way it can attract more customers. It ignores nonprice competition. The revenue and cost curves we have discussed are hard to develop in the real world. Sometimes the data needed to develop them are almost impossible to get or the cost of getting the data may outweigh its value in pricing decisions. Price theory is of very limited value to multiproduct firms that have to price several, often related, products. Marginal analysis also assumes firms make decisions on a unit base, but most firms do not. A manufacturer of golf balls might make decisions on the basis of 10,000 dozen golf balls. Nevertheless, the theory does provide some useful insight into pricing.

## Prices Based on Demand

Our discussion of oligopolists holding their prices at the kinked price suggests they are adhering to the customary price in their industry. Marketers of many types of products must contend with customary prices. A classic example is the price of a standard chocolate candy bar. The five-cent candy bar was around for many years before rising costs pushed the price up. This is a source of concern for candy marketers because demand is price elastic.

Suppose Jiffy Homebuilders has been selling houses in the $60,000 to $70,000 price range. Despite rising materials and labor costs it wants to continue selling in that price range because its appraisal of demand suggests that those houses will continue to be in great demand. Like the candy makers, Jiffy is caught in a cost-profit squeeze. They must either cut costs or be willing to operate at less profit, or even a loss. To cut costs candy makers might reduce the size of their candy bars and/or use cheaper ingredients. Jiffy might use cheaper lumber and plumbing fixtures and prefabricated materials to cut labor and materials costs.

Although we usually think of costs determining selling prices, these cases show that a marketer's desired selling price, based on its analysis of demand, may determine how much cost can be built into products. We will return to this in the next chapter's discussion of value augmentation.

Demand factors also are in evidence in the flexible breakeven approach we discussed earlier. The total revenue curves used in the analysis should reflect the marketer's knowledge of customer behavior. Those customers could be grouped into segments based on the similarity of their responses to different prices. This helps a marketer in developing demand curves for different market segments. Past sales data can be correlated with selling prices in developing those schedules. Controlled pricing experiments also may help in developing demand schedules. Although the data are somewhat subjective, these experiments may be necessary in pricing new products.

## PRICING BY MIDDLEMEN

Cost-plus pricing probably is the most widely used approach among retailers and wholesalers in setting initial offering prices on their merchandise. But if customers do not buy at these prices, they will be lowered. Another indication of middleman concern with demand considerations in pricing is their tendency to set different percentage markups on different products. Supermarkets, for example, apply a lower markup percentage on highly competitive items like sugar and coffee than on meat, fruits, and vegetables.

### Markup and Markon

gross margin

Sam's Novelty Shop buys an item for $1.00 and Sam wants to make $.25 over cost for his gross margin. **Gross margin** is net sales minus the cost of goods sold. Stated differently, it is his operating expenses plus profit. Sam will sell the item for $1.25.

markon

To find Sam's **markon** (percentage based on his cost):

$$\text{Markon} = \frac{\$ \text{ amount added to cost}}{\$ \text{ cost}}$$

$$= \frac{\$.25}{\$1.00}$$

$$= 25 \text{ percent}$$

markup

To find Sam's **markup** (percentage based on selling price):

$$\text{Markup} = \frac{\$ \text{ amount added to cost}}{\$ \text{ selling price}}$$

$$= \frac{\$.25}{\$1.25}$$

$$= 20 \text{ percent}$$

Markon percentages can be converted to markup percentages with this formula:

$$\text{Markup} = \frac{\%\ \text{markon}}{100\% + \text{markon}\ \%}$$

$$= \frac{.25}{1.25}$$

$$= .20$$

Markup percentages can be converted to markon percentages with this formula:

$$\text{Markon} = \frac{\%\ \text{markup}}{100\% - \text{markup}\ \%}$$

$$= \frac{.20}{.80}$$

$$= .25$$

Using an across-the-board markup for all products in a store simplifies pricing but ignores demand factors. Most retailers, therefore, use flexible markups. Slow-moving items have higher markups than fast-moving items. Discounters use lower markups to increase inventory turnover and sales. They use flexible markups that vary with the stock turnover rate.

The **stock turnover rate** is the number of times per year the average inventory (beginning + ending inventory ÷ 2) is sold. The lower the turnover rate, the greater the inventory carrying cost. An inventory that has a turnover rate of 1 ties up five times as much working capital as one that has a turnover rate of 5. A low turnover rate could result from carrying an assortment of products that is not satisfying target customers. In general, products that have a seasonal demand pattern, have a very low repeat purchase frequency, or are slow sellers, will have a relatively low stock turnover rate.

**stock turnover rate**

Use this formula to find the stock turnover rate when inventory is carried at cost:

$$\frac{\$\ \text{cost of goods sold}}{\text{average inventory at cost}}$$

Use this formula to find the stock turnover rate when inventory is carried at selling price:

$$\frac{\$\ \text{net sales}}{\text{average inventory at selling price}}$$

## SUMMARY AND LOOK AHEAD

Marketers can base list prices on (1) costs, (2) a balance between supply and demand, or (3) demand. The cost orientation is the most traditional approach because marketers realize that cost is the floor below which price cannot fall if the firm is to survive as a going concern. But cost approaches to pricing vary in terms of complexity. The simple full cost approach, for example, does not recognize the fact that different types of costs behave differently as output fluctuates. More sophisticated cost-oriented approaches do.

Cost-oriented pricers should understand (1) total fixed cost (TFC), (2) total variable cost (TVC), (3) total cost (TC), (4) average total cost (ATC), (5) average fixed cost (AFC), (6) average variable cost (AVC), and (7) marginal cost (MC).

TFC is the sum of all costs that remain fixed in total regardless of output volume. AFC is the fixed cost per unit of output. AFC decreases as output expands. In the long run, however, all costs are variable. TVC is the sum of all costs that vary in total as output fluctuates, and AVC is TVC divided by the number of units of output. Within a narrow range of output, AVC may be relatively constant. TC is TFC + TVC. ATC is TC divided by the number of units of output. MC is the change in TC that results from producing one more unit of output.

An understanding of these different types of costs enables a marketer to price a product on the basis of something other than full costs. Several options include the average cost approach, the marginal cost approach, the incremental cost approach, and the target return approach. Break-even analysis helps in determining the sales volume needed for a firm to break even (TR = TC).

The economic theory of price determination incorporates both cost and demand factors. Its use requires an understanding of several concepts of revenue in addition to cost concepts: (1) total revenue (TR), (2) average revenue (AR), and (3) marginal revenue (MR). TR is the product's price times the number of units sold. AR is TR divided by the number of units that were sold to produce that revenue. MR is the change in TR due to the sale of one more unit. The theory assumes the firm wants to maximize profit. It often is hard to make practical use of it because the theory presumes detailed knowledge of cost and demand factors and is especially difficult for multiproduct firms to use.

In demand-oriented pricing price is set in relation to demand. The concept of customary price is important in this approach. The flexible breakeven approach introduces demand into breakeven analysis.

In the real world list prices often must be adjusted in individual sales transactions. Discounts off list prices are an example. This enables the firm to administer its prices on a day-to-day basis. We will discuss these adjustments in the next chapter.

## REVIEW QUESTIONS

1. What is the major drawback of the full cost approach to pricing?

2. Define: (a) TFC, (b) TVC, (c) TC, (d) ATC, (e) AFC, (f) AVC, and (g) MC.

**3.** Is it possible for AVC to remain constant within a narrow range of production? Explain.

**4.** What is the firm's short-run supply curve?

**5.** Describe a situation that might lead a manufacturer to take the marginal cost approach to pricing.

**6.** Contrast the full cost and incremental cost approaches to pricing.

**7.** What is the meaning of fixed cost contribution per unit in breakeven analysis?

**8.** Explain how demand can be introduced into breakeven analysis.

**9.** What major assumptions underlie the economic theory of price determination?

**10.** How does one locate the optimum selling price when using the economic theory of price determination?

**11.** Under what conditions will rivals in an oligopolistic industry seek to maximize their combined profits?

**12.** What is the significance of a kinked demand curve?

**13.** What is a customary price? Give an example.

**14.** Why do retailers often use flexible markups?

**15.** What is the difference between markon and markup?

## DISCUSSION QUESTIONS

**1.** Why are all costs variable in the long run?

**2.** What are the relative advantages of price leadership for the firms in an industry and for consumers?

**3.** During periods of economic instability would a firm more likely use the full cost approach or the marginal cost approach to pricing?

**4.** Firms with high fixed costs have high breakeven points. The airline industry is an example. How does this affect the airlines' approach to pricing?

## NOTES

1. For discussion of several commonly used pricing models, see Kent B. Monroe and Albert J. Della Bitta, "Models for Pricing Decisions," *Journal of Marketing Research*, August, 1978, pp. 413–429.

# Chapter 22

# Price Administration

## OBJECTIVES
*After reading this chapter you should be able to*

1. give examples of several types of discounts and allowances.

2. discuss value augmentation as an approach to adjusting price.

3. give examples of geographic price policies.

4. distinguish between one price and flexible price policies.

5. give examples of psychological pricing.

6. contrast competitive bidding and negotiated contracts.

7. outline the relative advantages of leasing to lessors and lessees.

8. discuss several approaches to setting a transfer price.

9. discuss and give examples of professional pricing.

10. discuss pricing in nonbusiness organizations.

## KEY CONCEPTS
*Look for these terms as you read the chapter:*
    Cumulative Quantity Discount
    Noncumulative Quantity Discount
    Trade, or Functional, Discount
    Seasonal Discount
    Cash Discount
    Cash Rebate
    Brokerage Allowance
    Promotional Allowance
    F.O.B. Shipping Point Pricing
    Uniform Delivered Pricing
    Zone Pricing
    Basing Point Pricing
    Freight Absorption Pricing
    One Price Policy
    Flexible, or Variable, Price Policy
    Psychological Pricing
    Prestige Pricing
    Leader Pricing
    Variable Leader Pricing
    Bait Pricing
    Odd Pricing
    Unit Pricing
    Price Lining
    Competitive Bidding
    Negotiated Contracts
    Leasing
    Transfer Price
    Professional Pricing
    Ethical Pricing

American automakers have faced stiff competition in recent years from foreign firms, especially the Japanese. In the late 1970s and into 1980, Detroit's automakers tended to offer discounts to dealers on slow-moving big cars in an effort to stimulate sales. They also tended to hike prices on the faster-selling small cars to get more profit per car sold.

But in 1981 some American car manufacturers started giving discounts on some of the smaller cars. General Motors, for example, reduced the suggested retail selling price of the Chevette by $100. Apparently, the manufacturers were willing to make less profit per car sold in the hope of increasing their share of the small car market against imports. Some also were adjusting downward the interest rates charged on credit purchases to help offset the depressing effect on sales of high interest rates.

Some companies like Xerox started marketing reconditioned machines in order to offer lower prices to their customers. Discounts also were being offered by some airlines to build traffic, and manufacturers of cars, home appliances, smoke detectors, kitchen gadgets, and other products were offering rebates to customers in order to help stimulate sales.

A product's list price is the reference point in day-to-day pricing decisions. But list prices often are adjusted to remain flexible and responsive to company and customer requirements. This is necessary if the firm is to practice creative rather than purely mechanical pricing.

List prices are adjusted through discounts and allowances, price promotions, value augmentation, and freight charges. In some cases, list prices have little meaning because they are routinely discounted. Among the many important pricing decisions is the choice between a one price and a flexible price policy. Should one price be quoted to all target customers or should different prices be quoted to different target customers?

Psychological pricing also is important in contemporary marketing, especially in retailing. Supermarkets, for example, use so-called loss leaders to attract shoppers who want to get a bargain. Competitive bidding and negotiated contracts are especially important in industrial marketing. Leasing, an alternative to buying a product outright, also is an option some marketers may offer their customers.

We will discuss these topics along with intracompany pricing, professional pricing, ethical pricing, and pricing in nonbusiness organizations.


## DISCOUNTS AND ALLOWANCES

Discounts and allowances are reductions from list prices that enable marketers to adjust their actual prices without changing their published list prices. Industrial marketers, for example, often revise their discount sheets to adjust their list prices rather than print new catalogues. The following are examples of discounts and allowances: (1) quantity discounts, (2) trade discounts, (3) seasonal discounts, (4) cash discounts, (5) cash rebates, (6) trade-in allowances, (7) damaged goods allowances, (8) brokerage allowances, (9) promotional allowances, and (10) push money allowances.

## Quantity Discount

Marketers offer quantity discounts to encourage customers to place larger orders or to remain loyal buyers. This discount can be based on the dollar value of purchases or on the number of units purchased.

A **cumulative quantity discount** applies to purchases made during a period of time. The buyer's purchases are totaled up at the end of the

cumulative
quantity
discount

| Noncumulative | |
|---|---|
| Cases Purchased on Individual Order | Discount Percentage |
| 1–10 | 0.0 |
| 11–25 | 2.0 |
| 26–40 | 3.5 |
| over 40 | 6.0 |

*A buyer who places a single order for twelve cases gets a 2 percent discount from list price on that particular order. But suppose the buyer places fifty orders for ten cases each over the period of a year. Under a noncumulative quantity discount, the buyer would not receive any quantity discount during the year.*

| Cumulative | |
|---|---|
| Cases Purchased during Year | Discount Percentage |
| 1–50 | 0.0 |
| 51–125 | 2.0 |
| 126–250 | 4.0 |
| over 250 | 7.0 |

*With a cumulative quantity discount, the buyer's purchases are added up over the year and the discount percentage applies to the total volume of purchases made during the year. The buyer above purchased five hundred cases during the year and would be entitled to a 7 percent discount from list price.*

*Figure 22–1.
Noncumulative and
cumulative
quantity discounts*

period and the discount received depends on the quantity (dollars or units) bought during that period. The discount percentage usually increases as the quantity purchased increases. This type of discount has a promotional impact because it rewards a customer for being a loyal buyer. It could be called a patronage dividend.

A **noncumulative quantity discount** applies to a single order rather than the total volume of orders placed during a period of time. The larger the order, the larger the discount. It rewards the buyer for placing large orders and assuming part of the seller's storage function. Some of the transportation, order processing, and other cost savings are passed on to the buyer. (See Figure 22–1.)

noncumulative
quantity
discount

### Trade Discount

A **trade, or functional, discount** is a reduction in list price granted to a channel member for performing marketing functions. Suppose a manufacturer quotes trade discounts of 30 percent and 10 percent. This is a chain discount. The price to wholesalers is the retail price less discounts of 30 and 10 percent. Notice in Figure 22–2 that each discount percentage is figured on the amount remaining after the preceding percentage has been deducted. A chain discount of 30 and 10 percent, therefore, does not mean a total discount of 40 percent.

If the retail price is $200, the wholesaler's selling price to the retailer is $140 ($200 less 30 percent). The manufacturer's selling price to the wholesaler is $126 ($140 less 10 percent). The percentages vary by industry, product turnover rate, and according to the functions expected of the middleman. Trade discounts are granted on the basis of the middleman's position in the channel. Every retailer in a manufacturer's channel system qualifies for the same trade discount. A wholesaler is not entitled to a retailer's trade discount and vice versa.

trade, or
functional,
discount

---

**Given:** *Retail selling price of an item is $200.*
*Manufacturer quotes a chain discount of 30 and 10 percent.*

The wholesaler gets the 30 and 10 percent discount and is supposed to keep the 10 percent and pass on the 30 percent to the retailer.

Retailer pays wholesaler:

$200 less 30 percent
$200 less $60
$140

Wholesaler pays manufacturer:

$140 less 10 percent
$140 less $14
$126

*Figure 22–2.*
*Figuring a chain*
*discount*

**Legality of Quantity and Trade Discounts.** We discussed the legal environment of marketing in Chapter 2. You may want to review that part of the chapter pertaining to pricing, especially price discrimination, brokerage allowances, and promotional allowances.

Marketers should be prepared to justify their discount schedules. Under the Robinson-Patman Act, quantity discounts are legal if the resulting price differentials do not exceed the cost differentials in manufacturing and selling the product to buyers who are in competition with each other. This cost defense is hard to assert convincingly for a cumulative quantity discount. Although not easy to do, the cost defense stands a better chance of success in defending a noncumulative discount.

Neither the Clayton Act nor its Robinson-Patman amendment discusses trade discounts specifically. But several court cases seem to uphold the legality of offering separate discounts to separate classes of buyers as long as the discounts are offered in return for services rendered (marketing functions performed). One discount can be offered to wholesalers and another to retailers. All retailer buyers must be offered the same discount and all wholesaler buyers must be offered the same discount.

### Seasonal Discount

seasonal discount

A **seasonal discount** may be used to induce buyers to place orders in advance of need. A swimming pool builder may offer such a discount to a person who is willing to have the pool built during the winter. This helps the builder keep workers employed during the off season and improves the firm's cash flow. Carrier may give a seasonal discount to an appliance dealer who places an order for air conditioners in November. Early ordering by the buyer enables Carrier to push the storage function forward in the channel along with the risk of price changes. The discount may be granted in cash or as extended credit by forward dating of invoices. Seasonal discounts help manufacturers even out their production scheduling and run their plants more efficiently. Hotels and motels in many areas offer lower off-season rates to help them cover their fixed costs.

One version of the seasonal discount is the off-hour discount. The season in this case is a part of the day or week when demand is low and the seller wants to stimulate sales. Examples are special discounts offered to airline passengers for taking late-night flights, lower rates on long-distance phone calls placed at night and on weekends, lower rates charged to industrial customers by public utilities for shifting consumption to nonpeak demand hours, and bargain matinees at movie theaters.

### Cash Discount

cash discount

A **cash discount** rewards customers for paying their bills promptly. Terms of "2/10, net 30" mean the buyer can take a 2 percent discount off the invoice price by paying within 10 days of the invoice date. The buyer gets a 2 percent discount for paying the bill 20 days sooner than it is due. Since there are 18 periods of 20 days in a year during which the buyer could earn the 2 percent, the annual percentage rate is 38 percent.   Many buyers will borrow money to take advantage of cash discounts.

Marketers use cash discounts for promotional reasons, to help cut bad debt losses, and to speed up the collection of accounts receivable. They can extend the credit period by forward dating their invoices. Terms of "2/10, net 30 e.o.m." (end of month), for example, mean the discount period for an invoice dated March 3 runs until April 10.   The invoice is treated as if it were prepared on the first day of the month following the invoice date, April 1, instead of March 3.   Terms of "2/10, net r.o.g." (receipt of goods) mean the discount period does not begin until the buyer receives the goods.   Cash discounts are computed after deducting any trade, seasonal, and quantity discounts from the list prices.

Some retailers offer cash discounts to customers who pay cash instead of using credit cards.   These retailers list a single price and offer a percentage discount for cash sales or list two separate prices, one for cash and one for credit transactions.

For many years, five beer wholesalers in the Fresno, California area allowed their retailers to buy on thirty-day, interest-free credit.   When they agreed to stop this and require cash on delivery, several retailers took the wholesalers to court alleging they were trying to fix prices.   The case went all the way to the U.S. Supreme Court, which said that granting interest-free credit was the equivalent of a discount and an agreement to end the practice was the same as agreeing to eliminate discounts.   This is illegal because it constitutes price fixing.[1]

## Cash Rebates

Manufacturers of consumer products sometimes use **cash rebates** to stimulate sales of products such as cars, smoke detectors, small electric appliances, automatic coffee makers, and CB radios.   The retailer sells the product to consumers and they send the coupon to the manufacturer requesting the rebate.   Thus rebates are a type of couponing effort by manufacturers.   Many car dealers will allow car buyers to apply the rebate as a full or partial down payment.   Rebates help increase inventory turnover when sales are sluggish and often are used during the latter stages of a product's life cycle to stimulate purchases by late adopters and laggards.

cash rebate

Rebates also may involve income tax implications for manufacturers. An automaker who grants rebates can deduct them from corporate taxable income.   The rebate may be preferable to simply reducing the list price by a like amount because in the latter case there would be no expense to record and benefit from.   The rebate also can be used for a limited time only to stimulate an immediate consumer response.

## Trade-in Allowance

Buyer-seller negotiation of adjustments to list prices might involve the value of a trade-in.   The Xerox Store ad which follows shows a trade-in offer.   Notice that this particular offer has an expiration date and includes

# There's $200 on your desk!

Bring in your old typewriter, regardless of its make, age or condition, and save $200 on a new Xerox self-correcting typewriter. And, depending on the brand and model, we'll give you even more. Up to $600!

And what a typewriter! The Xerox 590 or the 585 office typewriter that saves you time and money because it's self-correcting. And gives all your paper work a sharp, professional look.

So trade in that old typewriter and trade up to a Xerox, while this offer lasts.* Sorry, only one trade-in typewriter allowance per purchase.

**\*Offer expires March 28, 1981**

## The Xerox Store
It's like a supermarket for small businesses.

**Aurora at Parker & Havana,
2393 South Havana St. 695-8660
University Hills West,
2555 South Colorado Boulevard 692-0414**
Open 9 AM to 6 PM Monday-Saturday.
**16th Street and Champa on the Mall 825-2386**
Open 8:30 AM to 5 PM weekdays.

**XEROX**
XEROX® is a trademark of XEROX CORPORATION

*An ad offering a trade-in allowance*

Source: Xerox Corporation.

trade-ins of rival brands. The allowance enables the store to adjust the actual price a customer pays without reducing list price.

A construction company that owns a piece of heavy equipment and a consumer who owns a three-year-old car both might place an inflated value on these products. Marketers of new models place a much lower value on these used products. Thus some new car buyers prefer to sell their used cars themselves rather than negotiate a trade-in value with the new car dealer. They believe they can get a higher price for their used cars and avoid getting confused on the new car's real price.

Marketers who accept trade-ins sometimes develop a lucrative business in reconditioning and marketing them. Many new car dealers also sell secondhand (or preowned) cars. Xerox Corporation recently started offering its customers the option of buying reconditioned machines that sell at lower prices than new units.

## Damaged Goods Allowance

Another allowance off list price is the **damaged goods allowance.** The allowance indicates that the bundle of services the buyer gets is something less than that provided by an undamaged unit. Sears, for example, sells at marked-down prices appliances that are dented, scratched, or otherwise damaged. Price-conscious market segments are attracted to this merchandise.

**damaged goods allowance**

## Brokerage Allowance

As we saw in Chapter 15, brokers are agent middlemen who do not take title to the products they sell. They are allowed a discount off list price much like the trade discount offered to wholesalers and retailers. A wholesaler or retailer legally cannot receive a **brokerage allowance.** It also is illegal for manufacturers to pay brokerage fees to a buyer. A large retail chain, for example, that performs for itself the services formerly performed by an independent broker legally cannot demand a brokerage allowance from the manufacturer. In practice, however, these allowances sometimes are disguised as promotional allowances to keep large chains as customers.

**brokerage allowance**

## Promotional Allowances

**Promotional allowances** are reductions from list prices granted by sellers to compensate buyers for performing promotional services. Del Monte, for example, may grant a certain amount of money for each case of its catsup wholesalers or retailers buy. They are supposed to use the money in promoting the catsup. These allowances help build cooperation among channel members.

**promotional allowance**

## Push Money Allowances

As we saw in Chapter 17, push money (PM) is cash or prizes manufacturers or wholesalers offer their dealers and dealer sales personnel for aggressive

*"It's simple, sir. You pay full fare and the person in line behind you pays one-half fare."*

Source: *Chicago Tribune*—New York News Syndicate, Inc.

selling effort.   It can help stimulate sales of new products, slow-moving products, and high-markup products.

## PRICE PROMOTIONS

As we also saw in Chapter 17, manufacturers use many types of sales promotions that basically are price promotions.   They appeal to middlemen and ultimate consumers.   In recent years airlines have heavily promoted discount fares.   Many of these fares impose restrictions on the passenger because the airlines want to avoid shifting regular fare passengers, who must fly to scheduled appointments, to discount fare passengers.   The discounts are intended to attract people who otherwise might not fly.

## VALUE AUGMENTATION

Some marketers adjust their prices up or down by varying the value they add to the basic product.   This gets at the crucial difference between the basic product and the total product. For example, a tract housing builder's houses will follow the same basic floor plan. But by varying the quality of interior features, such as wallpaper, carpet, and appliances, the price may be tailored to fit a potential buyer.

In early 1980 Chrysler Corporation developed a "guarantees" program to help stimulate sales by offering its buyers added value without raising prices. Its new car buyers got a thirty-day/1,000-mile money-back guarantee. The buyer could return the car to the dealer if he or she were dissatisfied and get a refund. Additional features included no charge for scheduled maintenance for two years and motor club membership for two years. People who test-drove a new Chrysler product and bought it or another manufacturer's directly competitive model within a certain time period were paid $50. This helped to attract prospects to Chrysler dealers.

Another example of a product whose value has been augmented is the CAT (computerized axial tomography) scanner, a sophisticated x-ray machine that costs about $500,000 per unit. Installation and operating costs also run into hundreds of thousands of dollars. Thus smaller hospitals generally cannot afford them. But several years after the product was introduced several health care companies started installing the scanners in large vans and driving them periodically to small hospitals.[2] These firms augmented the manufacturers' product and made it feasible for small hospitals to use the equipment.

### The Cost-Profit Squeeze

The cost-profit squeeze of recent years has caused marketers, especially those whose products have a highly price-elastic demand, to consider making adjustments in the product offering. They know they cannot indefinitely pass on their cost increases as price increases to customers without reducing sales of their products.

One approach is to alter the product's quantity and/or quality. Ideally, this alteration would not be enough of a change to be noticed by customers (see Chapter 5). Examples of quantity changes are fewer sheets of paper in a notebook or on a roll of paper towels. Examples of quality changes include magazines published on cheaper paper, soft drink bottlers using a high-fructose corn sweetner as a partial substitute for more costly sugar, and manufacturers of appliances using plastic rather than metal components.

Another approach is to change the bundle of services that accompanies the product. For example, a growing volume of toys and furniture is sold unassembled to buyers who are willing to perform some labor to save money. In other cases, marketers are charging extra for services that used to be included in the product's price. Thus the phone company may want to charge people for directory assistance calls and a service station may want to charge for air to inflate tires. Other examples include department stores charging extra for delivery and gift wrapping, hotels eliminating free parking for registered guests, and insurance companies writing home and auto policies with higher deductibles.

## GEOGRAPHIC PRICE POLICIES

List prices can also be adjusted by the manner in which freight cost from the seller to the buyer is handled. This cost can be paid by the seller, by the buyer, or shared between them.

### F.O.B. Shipping Point Pricing

When a seller quotes prices f.o.b. (free on board) at the seller's plant or warehouse, the seller pays for loading the freight onto the carrier, at which time title passes to the buyer. **F.o.b. shipping point pricing** means that the buyer assumes the risks in transporting the products and pays the entire freight charge.

*f.o.b. shipping point pricing*

This approach limits a seller's market area because distant buyers will favor nearby suppliers to avoid paying high freight charges. Customer goodwill also suffers when a buyer pays a high freight charge because the seller routed shipments improperly. Quoting prices can be tough for firms that offer a wide product mix to widely scattered customers. Buyers do not know in advance what their delivered prices will be. But the seller receives the same amount of revenue on all sales to customers who buy in the same quantity. This is true regardless of a buyer's location.

### Delivered Pricing

Buyers know in advance what their delivered prices will be when sellers quote delivered prices. Types of delivered pricing include (1) uniform delivered pricing, (2) zone pricing, and (3) basing point pricing.

*uniform delivered pricing*

Under **uniform delivered pricing,** or postage-stamp pricing, all quoted prices include a fixed average freight charge because the seller averages total transportation costs for serving all customers. All buyers pay the same average transportation charge and all are quoted the same delivered price. Thus nearby buyers pay more than the actual cost of shipping to them. They pay phantom freight charges. Distant buyers, on the other hand, pay less than the actual cost of shipping to them because the seller absorbs some of the freight cost. This approach is practical when freight cost is low in relation to a product's value. It also enables sellers to quote only one price in their national advertising.

*zone pricing*

**Zone pricing** is a type of uniform delivered pricing in which buyers in a given zone pay the same delivered price but buyers in different zones pay different delivered prices. A seller who quotes prices that are "slightly higher west of the Mississippi River" is using a two-zone pricing system. Any number of zones could be used, however. Zone pricing is more practical than totally uniform delivered pricing (or one-zone pricing) when the freight cost is large in relation to a product's value. Phan-

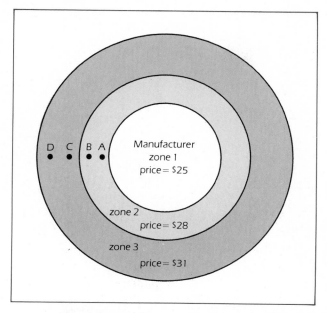

*Figure 22–3. Zone pricing*
*The delivered price for customers A and B in zone 2 is $28.*
*The delivered price for customers C and D in zone 3 is $31.*
*The delivered price for customers in zone 1, where the manufacturer is located, is $25.*

tom freight charges and absorption of freight charges by the seller still exist under zone pricing. (See Figure 22–3.)

**Basing point pricing** started in the steel industry, which developed in the Pittsburgh area. Each steel producer quoted prices f.o.b. shipping point, which meant distant buyers paid higher prices than local buyers. This stimulated construction of new mills in places like Chicago and Birmingham, Alabama that were closer to steel buyers in those areas. Thus Pittsburgh mills could sell in the Chicago area only if they absorbed the freight difference between the Chicago and Pittsburgh mills. Sellers often wanted to broaden their market areas to spread their fixed costs over a wider range of production. But because total industry demand tended to be highly price inelastic, price competition would develop and reduce all rivals' revenues.

**basing point pricing**

Thus steel industry leaders set up a basing-point pricing system known as Pittsburgh-plus. All mills quoted delivered prices that assumed the steel was being shipped from Pittsburgh. A steel buyer in Jackson, Mississippi logically would buy from a Birmingham mill even though the delivered price would be identical to that from a Pittsburgh mill. The Pittsburgh mill benefited by being able to sell to more distant customers. The Birmingham mill benefited because it could charge its buyer in Jackson phantom freight from Pittsburgh. This meant extra profit for the Birmingham mill. (See Figure 22–4.)

A single basing point pricing system restricts competition. The steel industry eventually went to a multiple basing point system. Some customers, however, still paid phantom freight because even though the mills they bought from were closer to them, the mills were not basing

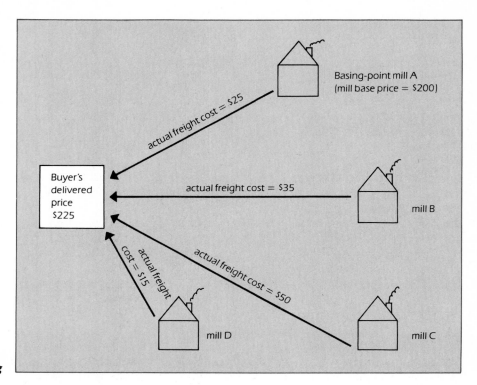

Buyer's delivered price $225

actual freight cost = $25

Basing-point mill A
(mill base price = $200)

actual freight cost = $35

mill B

actual freight cost = $15

actual freight cost = $50

mill D

mill C

*Figure 22–4.*
*Basing point pricing*

points.    The legality of the basing-point system still is not entirely clear. Collusion among rivals to set up such a system is illegal.    Even in the absence of collusion, the system can be illegal.    It appears that the presence of phantom freight charges is enough to make the legality questionable.

### Freight Absorption Pricing

**freight absorption pricing**

A firm that wants to penetrate distant markets to maintain or increase market share can practice **freight absorption pricing** to meet delivered prices of rivals in those areas.    The seller grants locational discounts to some customers by absorbing freight costs.    This may benefit customers, who no longer would be restricted to buying from local suppliers.    Those local suppliers might become inefficient if they were insulated from distant rivals.

Expanding its market area may enable a firm to spread its fixed costs. But freight absorption pricing is practical over the long run only when the profit from the new business at least offsets the cost of absorbing freight into those market areas.    In general, this practice is legal when used in a nonpredatory manner to meet competition.

Several years ago, there was a glut of eggs on the market due to overproduction and the market price was tumbling.    Producers in the southeastern states typically had lower feed prices than producers in the western states.    Thus southeastern producers were willing to absorb freight costs into areas such as Denver and Phoenix, which traditionally were served by egg producers in the West.[3]

## PRICE FLEXIBILITY

A marketer also has to decide whether to sell a product at the same price to all buyers or at different prices to different buyers. The choice is between a one price policy and a flexible price policy.

### One Price Policy

All customers who buy a seller's product under the same conditions, in the same quantities, and at the same time pay the same price under a **one price policy.** This makes it easy to administer prices and eliminates the risk of losing customer goodwill due to differential price treatment. But there is no room for tailoring the price to the customer. This can be a big problem, especially in industrial marketing where prices often are negotiated between buyer and seller. A one price policy is common among most retailers in the United States. There are, of course, some exceptions, such as antique shops and new car dealers, where prices are subject to seller-buyer negotiation.

*one price policy*

### Flexible Price Policy

Different customers who buy a seller's product under the same conditions, in the same quantities, and at the same time pay different prices under **a flexible, or variable, price policy.** Price is a more active marketing mix element. Thus when American car manufacturers began to experience stiff competition on the West Coast from Japanese imports, many adopted a flexible price policy. They charged their West Coast dealers less for subcompacts than they charged their dealers elsewhere in the country.

*flexible, or variable, price policy*

A flexible price policy enables industrial products salespersons to tailor their prices to a prospect's situation. As we said, the one price policy is most common in retailing, but there are exceptions other than antique shops and new car dealers. A small appliance retailer, for example, may put the same list price on all refrigerators of a certain make and model, but the price a buyer pays depends on his or her bargaining skill. Flexible pricing exists in practically all sales transactions that involve trade-ins.

The main drawback of flexible pricing is the potential loss of customer goodwill if some buyers learn they paid more than other buyers. Salesforce productivity also declines when salespersons devote too much effort to haggling over price. They may make price adjustments routinely whether it helps to close sales or not.[4]

## PSYCHOLOGICAL PRICING

**Psychological pricing** attempts to influence buying decisions by setting prices that are emotionally pleasing to buyers. It is especially common

*psychological pricing*

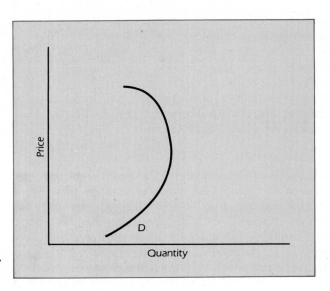

*Figure 22–5.*
*A demand curve for*
*a prestige product*

in retailing.   Examples are (1) prestige pricing, (2) leader pricing, (3) variable leader pricing, (4) bait pricing, (5) odd pricing, (6) unit pricing, and (7) price lining.

### Prestige Pricing

prestige pricing

Our discussion of prestige products in Chapter 20 indicated that sales of some products go up as price increases.   In **prestige pricing** prices are set high to benefit from the price-quality relationship that exists in many consumers' minds.   Figure 22–5 shows a demand curve for a prestige product.   Within a certain range the higher the price, the greater the quantity demanded.[5]   But when price rises too high the product is considered overpriced and quantity demanded falls off.   When price falls too low the product is suspected of lacking quality.

### Leader Pricing

leader pricing

The opposite of prestige pricing is **leader pricing.**   As we saw in Chapter 20, a grocer uses loss leaders like sugar and milk to build customer traffic. The grocer hopes that low prices on these items will attract customers who will buy other products that carry higher margins.

Several years ago, some fast-food restaurants added salad bars to help build customer traffic.   This required extra spending on condiments and labor.   The salad bars attracted some customers but often added more to costs than to profits.   Thus many of those restaurants soon discontinued them.   Care is needed in selecting leader items.

### Variable Leader Pricing

variable leader
pricing

Most supermarkets practice **variable leader pricing,** which means they feature different items as specials during different weeks.   The items

Section VII   PRICE

featured in the current week depend on what the store selected as specials in past weeks and what rivals are expected to feature this week. Supermarkets, therefore, can be differentiated on the basis of their leaders. Ideally, these products can be featured as specials many times during a year because they cannot be stocked up (hoarded) conveniently by shoppers. Because households with freezers can stock up on some specials more easily than those without freezers, supermarkets often place purchase limits on their specials.

## Bait Pricing

Bait pricing can also build customer traffic. A furniture store might advertise a recliner chair at a very low price to attract shoppers. But a shopper who comes to inspect the chair will be talked out of buying it by a salesperson who points out its faults and the advantages of buying a higher-priced chair. Bait-and-switch schemes are illegal in interstate commerce. But as they usually occur at the retail level in a limited area, the federal law may not apply. Many states, however, also have laws against **bait pricing.**

bait pricing

## Odd Pricing

**Odd pricing** means setting prices that end in odd numbers, such as $.49 and $29.95.[6] It is assumed that sales revenues will be greater than if the prices were set at $.50 and $30. Odd pricing developed as a cash control device to discourage employees from pocketing cash. Salesclerks had to ring up sales on cash registers to make change. Although many retailers still practice odd pricing, research suggests that buyers do not see such prices as significantly lower. Prestige products like exclusive men's suits are not priced this way. You would expect such a suit to be priced at $600 instead of $599.99.

odd pricing

## Unit Pricing

Many supermarkets use **unit pricing.** The price for each brand and package size is shown on a shelf label in terms of dollars and cents per pound or per pint, and so on.[7] Consumers can do a better job of comparison shopping and make more informed purchase decisions if they use unit prices when shopping.

unit pricing

## Price Lining

Retailers traditionally have practiced **price lining.** This means they buy products that fit into set price lines and target each line to a particular market segment. Thus an apparel retailer might sell dresses in three price lines—$25.95, $35.95, and $45.95. The retailer then buys dresses to fit those price lines. Products in the different lines are perceived to be of different quality. (See Figure 22–6 on page 644.)

price lining

Price lining simplifies the customer's buying process. For example, a woman shopping for a $35.95 dress has only to choose which particular dress she wants to buy in that price line. It also helps retailers. They

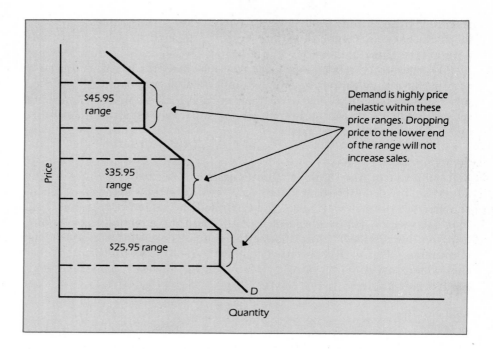

**Figure 22–6.**
**Price lining**

Within the figure:

$45.95 range

$35.95 range

$25.95 range

Price

Quantity

D

Demand is highly price inelastic within these price ranges. Dropping price to the lower end of the range will not increase sales.

can offer customers a wider assortment in each price line. Price lining can also help reduce markdown sales, simplify buying procedures, and increase stock turnover.

Sears advertises many of its products as "good," "better," or "best" rather than advertising specific price lines. "Good" chain link fence material will be "good" three years from now. But if Sears emphasized only the price, consumers might be confused as the price increased because of inflation. The same might be true of Sears's suppliers who make products to fit different price/quality lines established by Sears.

Products in a given line sometimes compete with each other. Sears, for example, must consider price spreads carefully when setting prices on three models of food blenders. Too little spread may cause consumers to doubt that real differences exist among them. Too much difference, however, may create opportunity for rivals to fill the price gaps with their brands. Buyer expectations and the nature of rival offerings must be considered. Sears's bottom-of-the-line model generates traffic, whereas the top-of-the-line model enhances the firm's image. In most cases, the middle-of-the-line model sells the most.

Products in a given line also may be complementary. Polaroid might set a low price on a camera if it thinks demand is price elastic. This means greater sales of cameras. The film could be priced high if the camera were useless without the film and if there were no direct substitutes for either the camera or film. If the camera were unique but rival brands of film were available, Polaroid could price the camera high and the film low. It might price both items independently if substitutes were available for both.

Prices must be related to each other if the products in a given line are targeted to the same market. This is not necessary when they are targeted to different markets. Goodyear, for example, prices the tires it sells through its retail outlets independently of those it sells to automakers as original equipment on new cars.

Usually it is hard to allocate fixed costs over a product line. This is why judgment is needed in setting prices on each product. A common approach is to collect variable costs on a product basis through a carefully designed cost accounting system and use those costs as the price floor. A markup is then added to the floor. The markup percentage depends on such factors as the product's demand elasticity and the nature of competition. Because of huge inventories of larger cars during the late 1970s and into the 1980s, American automakers were more likely to apply lower markup percentages to their large cars than to faster-selling smaller cars.

## COMPETITIVE BIDDING

Sellers often compete on a bid basis in pricing products for industrial buyers.[8] The sale could involve a construction project, a physical product, and/or a service. **Competitive bidding** requires the seller to have a good cost accounting system for analyzing costs. Fixed and variable costs must be estimated carefully to avoid a loss if a bid is accepted and turns out to be too low.

competitive bidding

Detailed knowledge of buyer requirements also is necessary. The buyer may prepare detailed specifications that are compiled by the firm's purchasing officer, using department, and technical personnel.

Suppose Apex Plumbing Company wants to bid on a job. Ideally, it wants to know if other firms will bid, how many will do so, which firms will bid, and their probable bid prices. Apex wants to submit the lowest bid that will enable it to achieve its pricing objective. Suppose that objective is to maximize expected profit. Apex can use a probability approach in its bidding strategy. Its cost estimate for the job is $150,000 and the owner wants to submit a bid of $400,000. Apex's bidder, however, wants to submit a bid of $500,000. Assume that the probability of winning the contract is 60 percent for the lower bid and 45 percent for the higher bid. The formula for expected profit is

$$\text{Expected Profit} = P \text{ (bid price} - \text{cost estimate)}$$

P is the probability of winning the bid. The expected profit on the low bid is $150,000 and $157,500 on the high bid. Apex, therefore, should bid $500,000.

## NEGOTIATED CONTRACTS

negotiated
contracts

Some buyers prefer **negotiated contracts** to competitive bidding. The buyer requests bids from several bidders but the one selected is not necessarily the lowest. The bid selected is the one the buyer finds most attractive in terms of the total offering. The buyer and the selected bidder then negotiate a contract. Buyers often negotiate contracts when they want to consult with bidders in developing specifications.

In recent years, inflation has caused severe problems for many building contractors because construction costs are more difficult to predict. Some construction jobs, therefore, are being handled through the fast-track design procedure. This involves concentrated effort on speeding up design work, cutting construction timetables, and cutting nonessentials from a building's design.[9]

Inflationary periods also pose a problem for marketers who sell products under long-term contracts. A price set in one year may turn out to be too low in the future. Some marketers handle the problem by charging the price that prevails when the product is shipped. Another approach is to include an escalator clause in the sales contract that ties price to industrial indexes.[10]

## LEASING

leasing

**Leasing** is an arrangement in which a lessor grants use of a product to a lessee for a period of time in return for stated regular payments. The lessee rents, not owns, the product. Thus leasing is an alternative to purchasing. Some consumers lease cars, musical instruments, furniture, appliances, TVs, and household maintenance and repair products. They rent the services these products provide. Business and other organizations lease computers, trucks, photocopying and word processing equipment, and cars.

### Lessor Benefits

A lessor might choose to lease its product rather than sell it outright for a variety of reasons. Heavy research, development, and production costs associated with a product may require such a high price that very few customers could afford to buy it. This is why the earliest computers were leased rather than sold. Another reason is the lessor may find it easier to make sales of complementary products needed to operate the leased product. Thus IBM sells paper and punch cards to its lessees. Lessors of sophisticated products generally require considerable financial resources because the costs are not recovered as quickly as they are from an outright sale. For example, suppose IBM sells a computer to a customer during a particular month. The sale will generate more revenue for IBM than leasing thirty-five computers in that same month.[11]

## Lessee Benefits

A lessee also can enjoy several benefits from leasing: (1) it may eliminate the need to borrow funds to buy the product, which can be very important when interest rates are high, borrowing power is limited, or better uses exist for the funds that otherwise would be committed in an outright purchase, (2) a lessee can replace leased equipment with more modern equipment without the losses involved in selling obsolete equipment, (3) lease payments may offer a tax advantage because they are a deductible business expense, (4) maintenance and repair service usually is provided as part of the lease payment, and (5) equipment can be leased only when needed unlike purchased equipment, which may lie idle for extended periods of time. But the cash payments on a lease often are considerably higher than financed purchase payments and use restrictions may be imposed on the equipment by the lessor.

## INTRACOMPANY PRICING

Many firms that use a profit center system to evaluate performance of different departments also face a pricing decision. A profit center is a part of the firm to which revenues and costs are assigned.

Suppose a firm makes a component part that it uses in producing its main product. The department that makes the component is a profit center and has to set a price to charge the using department. This intracompany price is called a **transfer price.**[12] Many approaches can be taken to setting this price. It might be set to reflect the price the firm would have to pay if it bought the part from an outside supplier. If the firm also sells some of these parts to other firms, that price could be used. The transfer pricing problem also exists in firms that produce parts in one country and export them to their overseas assembly plants.

transfer price

## PROFESSIONAL PRICING

Professionals like doctors and lawyers often practice **professional pricing.** They are bound by ethical codes in setting their fees, or prices. These codes are based on the premise that standard fees are more appropriate than fees based on the amount of time spent with individual patients or clients. For example, a routine doctor's office visit might be priced at $25 regardless of how much time the physician spends with the patient. In recent years, some professionals, such as CPAs, physicians, lawyers, and dentists, have begun to advertise their fees for specific types of services and consultation time. This has been encouraged by the Federal Trade Commission. In some cases, such advertising has led to price competition among professionals for customers.

professional
pricing

Whenever the demand for a product is extremely price inelastic, there is the potential for the seller to exploit the buyer. This is why govern-

**ethical pricing**

ment agencies regulate rates charged by public utilities. But a pharmaceutical firm could charge a very high price for life-extending drugs. Firms such as these practice what they call **ethical pricing** and do not take undue advantage of the highly price-inelastic demand for their products.

## PRICING IN NONBUSINESS ORGANIZATIONS

Nonbusiness organizations also make pricing decisions. The United States Postal Service, for example, has to set prices for different classes of mail. Under the full cost method, each piece of mail would require a postage charge to cover the full cost of delivering it. In practice, the rates on first-class mail help to cover the losses realized from third-class mail. Policymakers appear to believe society is best served by these rates. This, of course, means any deficits must be made up from other sources of revenue.

Earlier in the chapter we referred to uniform delivered pricing as postage-stamp pricing. All customers pay the same delivered price regardless of their locations. This is the case, for example, with first-class mail. A first-class postage stamp on a letter will take it to a receiver across the street or across the nation.

The pricing of some public services can be a means to an end. The cost of car inspections often is set low to encourage car owners to comply with local or state laws designed to keep unsafe cars off the road. High parking fines in congested downtown areas discourage people from taking their cars there. This policy may also help to increase the use of mass transit.

## SUMMARY AND LOOK AHEAD

List prices are adjusted to enable a firm to respond to company and customer requirements. Discounts are reductions from list prices. Cumulative quantity discounts apply to purchases over a period of time and help develop customer loyalty. Noncumulative quantity discounts apply to a single order and encourage customers to place larger orders. Trade, or functional, discounts are granted to middlemen for performing marketing functions. Seasonal discounts encourage buyers to buy in advance of need, while cash discounts reward customers for timely payment of their invoices. Cash rebates may speed inventory turnover when sales are sluggish.

Allowances are also reductions from list prices. Examples are trade-in and damaged goods allowances. Brokerage allowances are granted to brokers for performing marketing functions. Promotional allowances are granted to middlemen for performing promotional services for the manufacturer.

Price promotions are a combination of price and promotion elements in the marketing mix. These can be directed at middlemen and/or ultimate consumers. Marketers can also adjust their prices up or down by varying the value they add to the basic product. Within limits, the more a product's value is augmented, the higher the price the seller can charge.

Freight cost can be paid by the seller or buyer, or shared between them. F.o.b. shipping point pricing means the buyer pays the entire freight cost. With delivered pricing, the buyer knows in advance what the delivered price will be. Zone pricing means all customers within a particular zone pay the same delivered price, but customers in different zones pay different prices. The presence of phantom freight charges may be enough to make the basing point pricing system of questionable legality. Freight absorption pricing is legal when used in a nonpredatory manner to meet competition.

A major pricing decision is the choice between a one price and a flexible price policy. Different customers who buy the product under the same conditions, in the same quantities, and at the same time may pay different prices under a flexible price policy. They pay the same price under a one price policy.

Psychological pricing means setting prices that are emotionally pleasing to buyers. Examples are prestige pricing, leader pricing, variable leader pricing, bait pricing, odd pricing, unit pricing, and price lining. Psychological pricing is most prevalent in retailing.

Competitive bidding and negotiated contracts are important in industrial marketing. Intracompany pricing involves setting a transfer price. This often is necessary when one department in a firm produces a part that is used to make the firm's main product.

Leasing is an alternative to outright purchase of a product. It offers potential advantages to lessors and lessees.

Professional pricing is the approach used by physicians, lawyers, and other professionals in setting their fees. Ethical pricing is important when a product's demand is extremely price inelastic.

Pricing in nonbusiness organizations often is viewed as a means to an end. Examples include the pricing of postal services and of car inspections by local or state governments.

The next chapter discusses marketing's international dimension.

## REVIEW QUESTIONS

**1.** Contrast a cumulative and a noncumulative quantity discount.

**2.** Assume the retail price of a product is $100 and the manufacturer quotes trade discounts of 30 percent and 10 percent. What price will the wholesaler pay to the manufacturer? What price will the retailer pay to the wholesaler?

**3.** Why do some manufacturers offer seasonal discounts?

**4.** Explain the meaning of "3/10, net 30." Why do some marketers offer cash discounts?

**5.** Explain the concept of value augmentation from a pricing perspective.

**6.** What are the relative advantages and disadvantages of f.o.b. shipping point pricing?

**7.** What is phantom freight?

**8.** Why did steel producers adhere to the old Pittsburgh-plus basing point pricing system?

**9.** Why would a firm practice freight absorption pricing?

**10.** Contrast a one price policy and a flexible, or variable, price policy.

**11.** Contrast prestige, leader, and bait pricing.

**12.** Why might a retailer practice price lining?

**13.** Contrast competitive bidding and negotiated contracts.

**14.** What are the relative advantages to lessors and lessees of leasing?

**15.** What is a transfer price? Give an example.

**16.** Give an example in which ethical pricing might be used.

## DISCUSSION QUESTIONS

**1.** Would it be advisable for a department store to offer cumulative quantity discounts to its customers? What about a supermarket?

**2.** Why would a consumer products manufacturer use a cash rebate instead of reducing its prices to wholesalers and retailers?

**3.** Which type of geographic price policy helps most to maintain price competition among firms in an industry?

**4.** Is flexible pricing socially responsible?

**5.** Is price competition among providers of professional services preferable to professional pricing?

## NOTES

1. "Top Court Keeps Stringent Stance on Price-Fixing," *The Wall Street Journal*, May 28, 1980, p. 4. For further discussion of price fixing, see Jeffrey Sonnenfeld and Paul R. Lawrence, "Why Do Companies Succumb to Price Fixing?" *Harvard Business Review*, July–August, 1978, pp. 145–157.

2. "CAT Scanners Put on Wheels to Cut Costs," *The Wall Street Journal*, July 1, 1980, p. 23.

3. "Overproduction of Eggs Indicates Prices Should Remain Low for Rest of the Year," *The Wall Street Journal*, July 17, 1980, p. 28.

4. See R. Ronald Stephenson, William L. Cron, and Gary L. Frazier, "Delegating Pricing Authority to the Sales Force: The Effects on Sales and Profit Performance," *Journal of Marketing*, Spring, 1979, pp. 21–28.

5. See Zarrel V. Lambert, "Product Perception: An Important Variable in Price Strategy," *Journal of Marketing*, October, 1970, pp. 68–76; and Arthur G. Bedeian, "Consumer Perception of Price as an Indicator of Product Quality," *MSU Business Topics*, Summer, 1971, pp. 59–65.

6. See Zarrel V. Lambert, "Perceived Price as Related to Odd and Even Price Endings," *Journal of Retailing*, Fall, 1975, pp. 13–22.

7. See Kent B. Monroe and Peter J. La Placa, "What Are the Benefits of Unit Pricing?" *Journal of Marketing*, July, 1972, pp. 16–22; and Hans R. Isakson and Alex R. Maurizi, "The Consumer Economics of Unit Pricing," *Journal of Marketing Research*, August, 1973, pp. 277–285.

8. For discussion of the decision to bid, see Stephen Paranka, "Question: To Bid or Not to Bid? Answer: Strategic Prebid Analysis," *Marketing News*, April 4, 1980, p. 16.

9. "Speedy Construction Schedules Are Used by Building Planners to Outrun Inflation," *The Wall Street Journal*, July 1, 1980, p. 38.

10. Bruce H. Allen, Ronald L. Tatham, and David R. Lambert, "Flexible Pricing Systems for High Inflationary Periods," *Industrial Marketing Management*, October, 1976, pp. 243–248.

11. "IBM Net Rose 14% in 2nd Period, Breaking a Slump," *The Wall Street Journal*, July 14, 1980, p. 4.

12. See David R. Lambert, "Transfer Pricing and Interdivisional Conflict," *California Management Review*, Summer, 1979, pp. 70–75.

# Section VIII
# The International Dimension

Marketers in today's complex and changing world must stay alert to new market opportunities and challenges. Our final chapter discusses international marketing. For many marketers, overseas markets can be the source of market opportunity. Some firms find it easier and more profitable to export products they market at home than to develop new products for sale at home. But this strategy requires the firm to get involved in varying degrees in international marketing. They may have to adapt their entire marketing mixes to the environments that exist in their foreign markets. In fact, this involvement may alter their company missions as they become multinational companies instead of purely domestic companies.

# Chapter 23

# International Marketing

**OBJECTIVES**

*After reading this chapter you should be able to*

1. distinguish between international trade and international marketing.

2. tell what a multinational company is and how it differs from a firm that limits its overseas operations to exporting.

3. discuss the environment of multinational marketing and give examples of how environmental factors affect marketing decisions in multinational companies.

4. identify and discuss four basic company orientations to the world.

5. contrast indirect, semidirect, and direct exporting and give examples of each type.

6. identify and discuss four types of overseas operations.

7. contrast wholly owned subsidiaries and joint ventures.

8. give examples that demonstrate the need for international marketers to be adaptive in developing marketing mixes.

**KEY CONCEPTS**

*Look for these terms as you read the chapter:*

International Trade
Balance of Trade
International Marketing
Multinational Company (MNC)
Theory of Comparative Advantage
Regional Trading Bloc
Indirect Exporting
Semidirect Exporting
Combination Export Manager
Manufacturers' Export Agent
Webb-Pomerene Export Association
Piggyback Exporting
Direct Exporting
Foreign Licensing
Foreign Assembly
Contract Manufacturing
Joint Venture
Dumping

*Baseball is an American sport but nearly 95 percent of all baseball gloves used in the United States are made in the Far East even though most are made from American cowhide. Mounds and Almond Joy candy bars, Baskin-Robbins ice cream, S.O.S. soap pads, Keebler biscuits, Pepsodent toothpaste, Calgon bath oil, Canon cameras, Honda and Datsun cars, Savin copiers, Foster-Grant sunglasses, Perrier water, Sony TVs, Seiko watches, One-A-Day vitamins, and Adidas, Puma, and Tiger running shoes all have one element in common: they are manufactured by foreign-based firms.*

*Henry Ford sold the Model A in Europe in 1903 and started manufacturing cars in Europe in 1912. Volkswagen manufactures cars in Pennsylvania. French Rossignol skis are made in Vermont, West German cuckoo clocks are made in Virginia, Sony TVs are made in California, and Italian shoes are made in New Hampshire. Tengelmann Group of West Germany owns a large chunk of A&P, while Chicago-based Jewel Companies owns a large chunk of Aurrera, Mexico's largest retailer. Yoshinoya Company, one of Japan's largest fast-food chains, has opened Beef Bowl outlets in the United States, while McDonald's, Pizza Hut, and many other American-based fast-food chains have opened outlets in Japan and many other countries.*

One of the most important developments in business in the post–World War II period is the tremendous growth in international business. Purely domestic firms limit their search for market opportunity to their home markets. But international marketers look to overseas markets also.

Involvement in overseas business can range from occasionally exporting excess output to overseas buyers all the way to setting up production plants and sales subsidiaries in foreign countries. Some American firms, for example, limit their overseas involvement to exporting products made in the United States to foreign buyers. Some American-based firms, such as Ford, Xerox, IBM, PepsiCo, and General Electric, have operations spread throughout the world. They actually manufacture products in foreign countries. These are called multinational companies (MNCs), or global enterprises.

Many MNCs are based in foreign countries. For example, you may use Shell gasoline, eat Nestlé chocolate, look at TV programs on a Sony television, or drive on Michelin radial tires. All these products are made by foreign-based MNCs. They may have production and marketing operations in the United States, but they still are foreign-based firms.

In this chapter we will discuss why some firms get involved in exporting, why some set up foreign operations, and how their operations differ from those of purely domestic firms.

## INTERNATIONAL TRADE AND
## INTERNATIONAL MARKETING

It is important at the outset to distinguish between international trade and international marketing and to gain insight into the nature of a multinational company.

### International Trade

**International trade** refers to the movement of products across national borders, the imports and exports of nations. The United States sells (exports) and also buys (imports) more than any other country. Exports now account for about 12 percent of our Gross National Product (GNP), compared to about 6 percent in 1970.[1] These are much smaller percentages than for many other nations, such as Belgium, the Netherlands, and Japan. Our share of total world exports has declined as countries like Japan and West Germany, whose economies were devastated during World War II, have rebuilt and become major exporting nations.

The United States is totally dependent on imports for some products like chromium and coffee and is becoming more dependent on imports

*international trade*

**Figure 23–1. The United States balance of trade, selected years (in billions of dollars)**

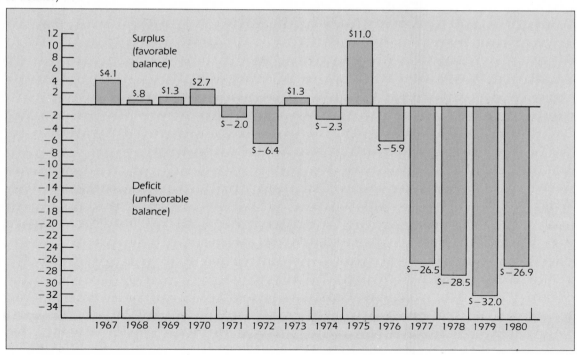

Source: *Survey of Current Business.*

*An ad that focuses on the role productivity plays in international trade*

Source: Westinghouse Electric Corporation.

of products like petroleum. Other imports, such as wines, cars, and cameras, are not critical but add to our enjoyment of life. Some American firms also rely heavily on exports for profit.

balance of trade

A country's **balance of trade** is the difference between the money values of its exports and imports. For many decades prior to the 1970s, our balance of trade was favorable in almost every year. Exports were greater than imports. But in the 1970s we began to have unfavorable balances of trade in many years. Imports were greater than exports.

This has been due to the long-term increasing productivity of many foreign firms (see the Westinghouse ad), their ability to compete more effectively with American firms due in part to lower labor costs in many other countries, and our growing dependence on high-priced imported oil. (See Figure 23–1 on page 655.)

## International Marketing

In consumer-controlled economies business firms account for most imports and exports. Business firms, not countries, do the buying and selling. But there are some exceptions. For example, an American farm machinery maker might sell tractors to our government for overseas distribution under a foreign aid grant. The firm did not deal directly with the foreign country nor with a firm in that country. Our government may also negotiate sales by American firms to foreign buyers of military equipment.

State-controlled economies view foreign trade mainly as an instrument of foreign policy. Politics plays a big part in their trade with other countries, especially with consumer-controlled economies.[2] Communist nations trade through government-owned state trading companies.[3]

**International marketing** means marketing in more than one country. It includes exports and other flows of resources across national borders. Ford engages in international marketing when it exports cars from the United States or when it builds a plant in Mexico to make cars for Mexicans. The sales of Ford's Mexican plant do not show up as exports from the United States. But Ford did export from the United States other resources, such as money to build the plant and technological and managerial skills to run it.

**international marketing**

Nonbusiness organizations also engage in international marketing. UNICEF, for example, is a global charity, and many churches send missionaries abroad to seek converts. Many American universities also seek to attract foreign students.

## Multinational Companies (MNCs)

A **multinational company (MNC)** is based in one country (the parent, or home, country) and conducts production and/or marketing activities in one or more foreign countries (host countries). Some are global enterprises that have operations throughout the world. Examples of American-based MNCs are IBM, Ford, Procter & Gamble, and Coca-Cola. Foreign-based MNCs include Nestlé, Unilever, Royal Dutch Shell, Nissan Motor Company, and Honda Motor Company. (See Table 23–1 on page 658.) To simplify the discussion in this chapter we will discuss MNCs from the perspective of American-based MNCs.

**multinational company (MNC)**

American-based MNC shipments of component parts from the United States to their overseas subsidiaries for assembly into finished products count as exports from the United States. These intracompany sales account for a growing percentage of our exports—somewhere between 25 and 50 percent.[4]

**Table 23–1.** The 10 largest industrial corporations outside the United States (ranked by sales)

| Rank | Company | Country | Industry | Sales ($000) |
|---|---|---|---|---|
| 1 | Royal Dutch/Shell Group | Neth.–Britain | Petroleum | $59,416,560 |
| 2 | British Petroleum | Britain | Petroleum | 38,713,496 |
| 3 | Unilever | Britain–Neth. | Food products | 21,748,583 |
| 4 | ENI | Italy | Petroleum | 18,984,960 |
| 5 | Fiat | Italy | Motor vehicles | 18,300,000 |
| 6 | Francaise des Pétroles | France | Petroleum | 17,305,220 |
| 7 | Peugeot-Citroën | France | Motor vehicles | 17,270,104 |
| 8 | Volkswagenwerk | Germany | Motor vehicles | 16,765,683 |
| 9 | Phillips' Gloeilampenfabrieken | Netherlands | Electronics, appliances | 16,576,123 |
| 10 | Renault | France | Motor vehicles | 16,117,376 |

Source: *Fortune.*

## Societal Dimensions

theory of comparative advantage

The **theory of comparative advantage** helps explain why nations trade. The general idea is that each country should specialize in producing products in which it has the greatest comparative advantage and import those in which it has the greatest comparative disadvantage. Standards of living would rise if all nations did this because of the international specialization of labor. Nations generally do not abide by this theory, however. It might mean, for example, that the United States should specialize in producing agricultural products because we are very efficient in agriculture. But most people associate high standards of living with the industrialized nations. Mutual trust among all nations also would be necessary because they would be highly interdependent.

MNCs must make many decisions regarding their marketing strategies in host countries. A major one is whether the firm should adapt to each host country's environment or try to be innovative by bringing in outside ways of doing things.[5] MNCs often act as agents of cultural change, but this may or may not be desirable.

For example, should American-based manufacturers of toothpaste, mouthwash, and deodorant try to persuade host-country nationals to use these products or use them more often?  Should MNCs try to change cultural values regarding birth control or breast feeding?  American fast-food companies, such as McDonald's, Dairy Queen, Kentucky Fried Chicken, Shakey's, Pizza Hut, and Mister Donut, have already changed eating habits of some people in Japan.  But often there is resistance to cultural change.  Thus the French are trying to rid their language of American terms that have crept into their everyday conversation.

The impact of MNCs on society is being examined and debated here and abroad.  Some Americans are concerned about the growth of foreign investment in the United States, such as Arabs owning farmland.  Some are concerned about the "export" of American jobs to overseas subsidiaries of American-based MNCs when unemployment in the United States is at a high level.[6]  Congress passed the Foreign Investment Act of 1974 to gain more information about the effects of foreign investment in the United States.  Other nations also are concerned about the social and economic effects of direct investment by foreign-based MNCs in their countries.

## THE ENVIRONMENT OF MULTINATIONAL MARKETING

Firms that operate in only one country should at least be aware of present and potential foreign competitors.  But MNCs need a much deeper understanding of home and host country environments.  These factors are important: (1) the economic environment, (2) the competitive environment, (3) the technological environment, (4) the sociocultural environment, and (5) the political-legal and ethical environment.

### The Economic Environment

A major concern is a host country's current and projected level of economic development.  Developed countries, less developed countries, underdeveloped countries, emerging nations, and Third World nations are designations that describe a country's stage of economic development.

*Figure 23–2.  A continuum of economic development*

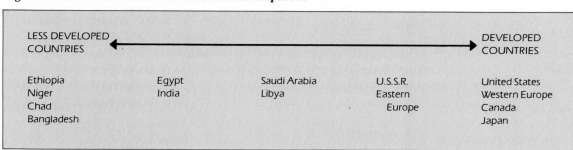

Figure 23–2 on page 659 shows that economic development is a relative concept. It is a process. For convenience, we will refer to the more economically advanced countries as developed countries and the less economically advanced ones as less developed countries, or LDCs.

Countries can be ranked in terms of their economic development by using GNP per capita. This statistic is also a measure of the standard of living. Some LDCs have per capita GNPs of less than $100 a year and illiteracy rates above 90 percent. Some also have a bimodal income distribution—there are a few wealthy households and many, many poor ones. The middle-income group, the one that buys most of the consumer products in developed countries, is practically absent. These countries also usually have dual economies. There may be modern showcase cities, but poverty exists on their outskirts.

Care is needed in evaluating countries as potential markets. For example, Mexico's oil revenue may help it to develop a middle class. In some LDCs marketers of prestige products can find some very wealthy consumers. These countries also offer potential to marketers of low-priced necessities, especially some food products.

**Marketing's Role in Economic Development.** As suggested earlier, LDCs that want to develop their economies tend to consider industrialization the key to better educational opportunities, more responsive government, better health care, and elimination of social inequities. Political leaders, however, often are product-oriented in their thinking and stress better techniques for producing products and increasing output. They assume a country must industrialize before concerning itself with marketing and consumption. But as we said in Chapter 1, mass production requires mass consumption. Effective production systems require effective distribution systems. The Chinese are recognizing this as they move toward greater industrialization.

### The Competitive Environment

In analyzing potential host countries, MNCs must consider the number of competitors, their size and marketing strategies, and each country's potential for economic development. Entering a promising LDC and investing resources in establishing the firm's niche before rivals recognize the potential can be very profitable. Introducing new production and marketing techniques also may help the country develop its economy more fully. Local firms may try to imitate these methods, thereby increasing their efficiency and ability to compete. But if local firms cannot compete, they may sell out to MNCs. This does less to stimulate their economy's development and contributes to skepticism regarding foreign-based firms.

### The Technological Environment

A country's level of technological development affects the attractiveness of doing business there and the type of operations that are possible.

Marketers in developed nations often take for granted modern transportation, communication, data processing facilities, and adequate energy supplies that may be absent in some LDCs.

A poor transportation system increases production and physical distribution costs. Poor communications facilities may rule out advertising on TV, radio, and in magazines and require more costly personal selling. Absence of modern data processing facilities makes it harder to plan, coordinate, and control a foreign subsidiary's operations and integrate them with the parent firm's operations.[7] Inadequate energy supplies cause production scheduling and inventory management problems.

During recent years there has been a lot of discussion of technology transfer, especially from the United States to the Soviet Bloc.[8] Soviet countries have demonstrated keen interest in acquiring American technology, especially computer technology. This transfer often has political implications. When the cold war heats up, as occurred in 1980 after Soviet troops moved into Afghanistan, firms are pressured to slow or even halt this technology transfer. Of course, we also stand to benefit from the transfer of foreign technology to our country. The CAT scanner discussed in Chapter 22, for example, was developed by a British firm.

## The Sociocultural Environment

MNCs must adapt to different cultures in each host country and, perhaps, to different subcultures within a country. Executives of MNCs must be capable of practicing cultural empathy.[9] They must understand the cultural environments in their host countries. Considerable differences may exist between an MNC's home and host countries with respect to language, aesthetics, religion, cultural values and attitudes, social structures, and customs and taboos. (See Figure 23–3 on page 662.)

**Language.** There are almost 3,000 languages in the world. Americans speak and write in the English language. In a bilingual country some people speak and write in one language while others use another language. Canada is an example. Some Canadians use English, others use French. Language differences sometimes foster even deeper divisions among a country's people. People in Quebec, for example, think of themselves as set apart from the English-speaking majority of Canadians and have strong separatist feelings, despite the fact that formal separation was voted down in 1980.

There are more than 200 different dialects in India, and because many people are illiterate they often have a tough time communicating with each other. A similar problem exists in China. The language problem causes problems for marketers in designing ad campaigns and product labels. Even when people use the same written language, there can be problems with the spoken language. Americans put gas in their cars; the English put petrol in theirs.

**Aesthetics.** Aesthetics refers to concepts of beauty and good taste. Many Americans, for example, think suntans are attractive and give a person a youthful, healthy appearance. Suntanning booth franchises in

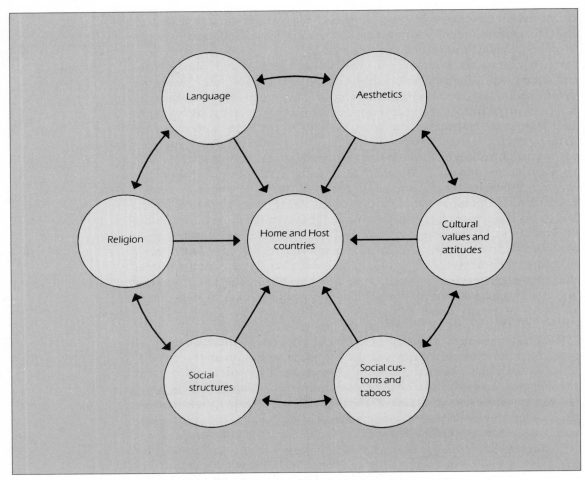

*Figure 23–3.  Elements of the sociocultural environment*

the United States enable customers to get tanned faster and keep their tans year-round.  The Japanese, however, think suntans are unattractive.

The meaning of something as basic as color can also vary.  Purple is associated with death in many Latin American countries, black is the mourning color in the United States, and white is the mourning color in Japan.  Green is the national color of Egypt but is associated with jungle sickness in Malaysia.  A marketer selling to people in those countries would not want to use green packages.

**Religion.**  Religious beliefs affect our general outlook on life and buying behavior.  They affect how and when we shop, the products we buy, and our ideas about affluence, materialism, sexual equality, and family roles.  The Christmas season is a major sales period in countries with a heritage of Christianity.  But religious holidays are not popular occasions for buying products in many other religions. Orthodox muslims do not drink alcoholic beverages but Turkish muslims do. Women do not participate much in household buying decisions in countries where the women's rights movement is opposed on religious grounds.[10] Some religions place a high value on the extended family unit. Joint buying decisions among extended family units are quite different from those of nuclear family units. A marketer who wants to do business in Northern Ireland must understand the strong hostility between Catholics and Protestants.

**Cultural Values and Attitudes.** As we have suggested, many of our cultural values and attitudes spring from religious beliefs. Thus Americans and Western Europeans place a much higher value on material well-being and are more likely to buy status symbols than are people in India. But other cultural values relate to other aspects of our lives. The Latin American male, for example, is expected to be very masculine, or "macho." Some cultures consider the elderly to be wisest, while other cultures place a much higher value on youth. The cultural value of personal cleanliness is strong in the United States and may help explain the huge amount of money we spend on bath soap, deodorant, and mouthwash. Americans also are more likely to take the risk of buying a new product than are people in more tradition-bound societies.

**Social Structures.** Multiple-earner families in the United States are creating a more affluent segment of consumers. But in some cultures it is not acceptable for women to work outside the home. As we saw in Chapter 6, there is a social class structure in the United States, but it is less rigid than that in many other countries. Ad campaigns stressing the idea of upward social mobility are less likely to be effective in those countries. The youth and elderly subcultures in the United States are less apparent in some Asian nations and LDCs.

**Customs and Taboos.** Customs and taboos vary widely among cultures as the following discussion suggests. Practically all Swedes, but very few French people, eat crackers. The English like their beer at room temperature but Americans like it cold. The French serve wine with most of their meals, while Americans drink milk, tea, water, or soft drinks. White-collar workers in Latin America do not wash their cars themselves as do some white-collar American workers. The Japanese take off their shoes before entering the house. Americans wipe their shoes on a doormat. In Russia men often greet each other with a kiss but that is not socially acceptable in the United States. Salespersons who insist on setting definite times for sales calls often will spend a lot of time waiting for Arab and Latin American prospects, who are less time bound than Americans.

## The Political-Legal and Ethical Environment

Each nation adopts its own internal system of government, policies, and laws and determines how it will deal with other nations. Governments that believe in free trade encourage domestic firms to do business overseas and welcome foreign investment and imports. They do not overly restrict imports or discriminate against foreign-based firms that do business in their countries.[11]

In general, our government supports the concept of free trade. But when heavy imports of some products lead to layoffs of American workers, there is pressure to limit imports. Examples from recent years include imports of steel, shoes, TV sets, cars, and clothing. There also is pressure to regulate overseas activities of American-based MNCs. Mounting political pressure in the United States to restrict imports of Japanese-made cars probably played a part in Honda Motor Company's and Nissan Motor Company's decision to build plants in the United States. Also, in 1981, an agreement was reached with the Japanese to reduce their exports of cars to the United States. Some people also believe MNCs contribute to domestic unemployment by manufacturing overseas instead of exporting products made in the United States.

Some governments openly oppose free trade. Communist nations want to be self-sufficient, and they restrict foreign trade to avoid interdependence with noncommunist nations. They trade mostly with each other. The volume of their trade with noncommunist nations fluctuates with changes in the international relations between East and West.[12]

A major task of government in some newly formed African nations is to instill in the people a feeling of nationalism. This may lead it to restrict imports and the entry of foreign-based firms. Firms wanting to do business there may have to form a partnership with the government. They may become involved in activities that appear to be illegal or unethical to observers in the firms' home countries.[13] They may, for example, have to pay commissions to sales agents who really are government officials in order to set up operations in some countries.[14]

Business activity tends to thrive under conditions of political stability. MNCs must assess the past history of political stability and current trends before entering a foreign market. Each country has its special interest groups and their goals and activities have to be considered. The consumerism movement, for example, is much stronger in some Western European nations than in the United States.

Government policies can promote and/or restrict an MNC's operations. Several years ago, IBM decided to leave India rather than abandon its policy of insisting on total ownership and control of its overseas subsidiaries. The Indian government wanted IBM to allow Indians to have partial ownership and control. Coca-Cola was willing to go along with partial ownership but refused a request to give the Indian government the secret formula for Coke. Coke also was blacklisted from the Arab world in 1967 after awarding a franchise to an Israeli bottler. The firm, however, was permitted to reenter Egypt in 1978.

regional trading bloc

Regional trading blocs exist in many areas of the world. A **regional trading bloc** is a group of countries that formally agrees to reduce trade barriers among themselves. The European Economic Community, or the Common Market, is an example. There are no tariffs among member countries but there is a common tariff applied to products from non-member countries. A West German firm can export products to France without paying a tariff, but an American exporter would have to pay the French tariff. The American firm could avoid the tariff by setting up manufacturing operations in one or more Common Market countries. Eastman Kodak's British unit produces Ektacolor paper and its French unit produces movie film and supplies for the entire Common Market.[15]

One risk all MNCs face is the risk of expropriation. Because each host country is sovereign, the government can take over ownership of plants with or without compensating the foreign-based company for the property it expropriates.[16]

## THE FIRM LOOKS AT THE WORLD

Firms can be categorized by their orientation to the world: (1) ethnocentric (home country orientation), (2) polycentric (host country orientation), (3) regiocentric (regional orientation), or (4) geocentric (global orientation).[17] (See Figure 23-4.)

### Ethnocentric Orientation

Two types of ethnocentric orientation are (1) domestic only and (2) predominantly domestic.

**Domestic Only.** Many firms limit operations to their domestic markets. The earliest American firms exported raw materials to England and imported manufactured products. But the westward movement opened up a huge domestic market for them. An abundance of natural resources for producing products, a growing population at home, and a political philosophy of noninvolvement with other nations led them to focus almost exclusively on the American market. Even today, most American firms retain their domestic-only orientation. A major reason is the belief that too much red tape is involved in international mar-

*Figure 23-4.* *A continuum of perspectives firms may take in viewing the world*

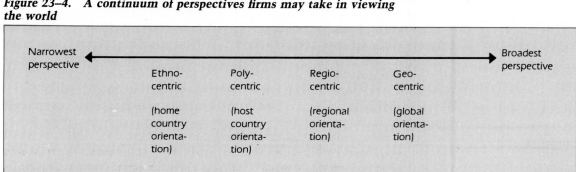

Adapted from *Journal of Marketing.*

keting.[18]   It has been estimated that roughly 20,000 American firms export products.   About 1 percent of them account for about 85 percent of all exports from the United States and most of this group are large MNCs.[19]

**Predominantly Domestic.**   Some American firms look to overseas markets to absorb the output they cannot sell at home.   Because the products were produced for sale in the United States, these exporters have the best chance of selling them in Western European countries and Canada, where consumer tastes and preferences are similar to ours.   They make little or no effort to adapt their products and other marketing mix elements to suit foreign tastes.

### Polycentric Orientation

If a predominantly domestic firm's profit potential in foreign markets becomes at least as attractive as that in the domestic market, it may begin exporting products tailored to foreign tastes.   It may set up production and marketing facilities in those countries.   The underlying belief is that social systems, buying patterns, and legal systems vary so much among nations that it is best to let local people in each country manage the firm's operations there.   This is a host country orientation. Marketing mixes in the home and host countries may vary in minor or major ways.

### Regiocentric Orientation

The polycentric orientation may cause problems in planning, coordinating, and controlling operations in the home and host countries.[20]   Some firms, therefore, try to group host countries by region.   There are some market segments in Latin America that are alike except that people in the segments live in different countries.   Were it not for these political boundaries these people could be treated as one market segment.   The regiocentric orientation makes this possible, especially for MNCs that market to members of a regional trading bloc.

### Geocentric Orientation

The geocentric, or global, orientation is an extension of the regiocentric orientation.   The firm pushes national borders aside and looks at the entire world as one big source of market opportunity.   But because of significant cultural, social, economic, political, and legal differences among nations, this orientation may be more useful in functional areas like production and finance than in some marketing activities because marketing is more culture bound.

This orientation enables a firm to enjoy more fully the benefits of synergism in its operations.   Loosely translated, synergism means the whole is greater than the sum of its parts.   Thus the MNC becomes more than one parent firm in a home country and a loose association of subsidiaries in host countries.   It becomes a unified system for matching its resources and capabilities with market opportunities on a global scale.

In the next section we will discuss the various methods of conducting international marketing.

## METHODS OF CONDUCTING INTERNATIONAL MARKETING

Except for domestic-only firms, a firm can have various degrees of involvement with international marketing. At one extreme is the firm whose products end up overseas without any effort on its part; at the other extreme are large MNCs that have production and marketing operations spread throughout the world.[21]

### Exporting

Exporting is a low-risk approach to entering foreign markets. Firms export products for a variety of reasons.[22] Those whose products are in the maturity stage of their life cycle at home may find growth markets overseas. For example, practically every American household has a refrigerator. Additional sales depend mainly on the new household formation rate and the replacement rate. But in some overseas markets the product is in the growth stage. One reason Perrier decided to export its bottled water to the United States was the product's maturity in Western Europe. Some firms find it less risky and more profitable to diversify by exporting their present products instead of developing new products for domestic consumption. Firms whose products have seasonal demand patterns may want to shift their off-season output to foreign markets where the product is in season. Another reason for exporting is less competition in some foreign markets.

There are various degrees of involvement in exporting. Some firms'

*Figure 23–5. A continuum of involvement in exporting*

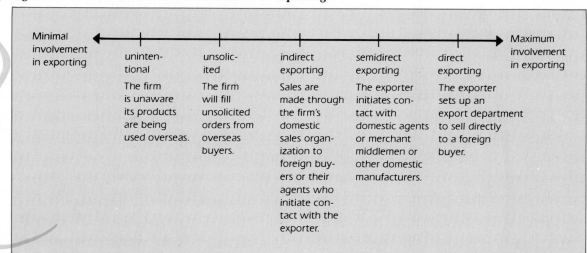

products are exported without their knowledge. A supplier of component parts to International Harvester may have its parts end up on tractors that are sold overseas. The supplier, therefore, could be said to be engaging in unintentional exporting. Some firms occasionally receive and fill unsolicited orders from overseas buyers. They are engaging in unsolicited exporting. But many firms are more actively involved in exporting. They engage in either (1) indirect exporting, (2) semidirect exporting, or (3) direct exporting. (See Figure 23–5 on page 667.)

**Indirect Exporting.** Indirect exporting means a firm exports some products but these foreign sales are treated like domestic sales. They are made through the firm's domestic sales organization because there is no separate export department. Examples of **indirect exporting** are given in Table 23–2.

**Semidirect Exporting.** In indirect exporting foreign buyers or their agents usually initiate contact with the exporting firm. But in **semidirect exporting** the American exporter usually initiates the contact through agent and merchant middlemen or other manufacturers in the United States. Semidirect exporting can be handled through (1) combination export managers (CEMs), (2) manufacturers' export agents (MEAs), (3) Webb-Pomerene export associations (WPEAs), or (4) piggyback exporting.

A **combination export manager** is a domestic agent middleman that serves as the export department for several noncompeting manufacturers. CEMs contact foreign customers and negotiate sales for their manufacturer clients for a commission that ranges between 10 and 20 percent,

*margin terms:*
indirect exporting

semidirect exporting

combination export manager

*Table 23–2.* *Examples of indirect exporting*

| | |
|---|---|
| 1. Resident buyers in the United States | Foreign manufacturers, middlemen, and governments have resident buying offices in the United States to buy American-made products. |
| 2. Buyers for export | Agent middlemen buy products at the request of their overseas buyer-principals, such as manufacturers, middlemen, and governments. They usually specialize in buying particular lines of products. |
| 3. Export merchants | American-based merchant wholesalers who buy products from American manufacturers, ship them overseas, and handle the marketing there, either through their own sales organizations or through other middlemen in the overseas markets. |
| 4. International trading companies | These large importing and exporting firms often have world-wide buying and selling operations. They accumulate and distribute products from marketers in many countries. Many have buying offices in the United States. Mitsui and Mitsubishi are two large Japanese trading companies. Mitsubishi is a family of more than forty related but separate Japanese firms. |

depending on the services they perform. They are similar to selling agents in domestic marketing.

A **manufacturers' export agent** is another domestic agent middleman. Unlike a CEM, an MEA does not serve as the client's export department. They do not have long-term working relationships with their manufacturer clients, and they cover only one or two foreign markets. A manufacturer could deal with one CEM but might have to deal with several MEAs to achieve the same coverage in foreign markets. MEAs are similar to manufacturers' agents in domestic marketing.

The Webb-Pomerene Act of 1918 permits American firms that compete in the home market to collaborate in exporting. If the association's activities do not tend to lessen competition in the American market, they are not prosecutable under our antitrust laws. This makes it easier for American firms to compete with cartels overseas. Cartels are combinations of firms (or countries) that agree to limit competition among themselves. They are illegal in the United States but are legal in many other countries.[23] Regional trading blocs also are a type of cartel.

A **Webb-Pomerene export association** can operate in many ways. For example, it could limit cooperation to overseas advertising, it could handle the export of members' products, or it could serve as a merchant wholesaler for its members in foreign markets. WPEAs account for about 5 percent of American exports.

**Piggyback exporting** is another type of cooperative exporting. A manufacturer with export facilities and overseas marketing channels (the carrier) handles the foreign wholesaling of one or more other firms' (the riders) noncompetitive, but complementary, products. This helps the carrier put together a more complete product mix and gives the rider fairly easy access to foreign markets. The carrier might sell the rider's products on a commission basis or buy them outright and sell them under the carrier's brand.

**Direct Exporting.** The exporter does not have to handle the export task alone in indirect and semidirect exporting. But in **direct exporting** the manufacturer sets up an export department to sell directly to a foreign firm. The exporter contacts foreign buyers and performs market research, physical distribution, and export documentation for itself. Thus in 1911 General Motors set up the General Motors Export Company to handle its exports to Europe.

Direct contact with foreign buyers gives the exporter greater control over the marketing of its products but requires getting involved in the environment of foreign countries. It may help a firm to diversify into other export markets or get more involved in multinational operations.

France's Michelin tire company, for example, entered the American market with exports from its European factories. It contracted to supply Sears with radial tires for the replacement market and to supply Ford with Michelin radials for Lincolns in the original equipment market. This exporting experience paved the way for Michelin to build tire plants in South Carolina.

**Margin notes:**
manufacturers' export agent

Webb-Pomerene export association

piggyback exporting

direct exporting

**Table 23–3.** *How a direct exporter might achieve distribution within a foreign market*

| | |
|---|---|
| 1. Manufacturers' representatives | Overseas agent middlemen who sell related but non-competitive products for a limited number of principals. They often have a continuing relationship with their overseas principals but do not arrange for shipping and seldom take physical possession of the products they sell. |
| 2. Import jobbers | Merchant middlemen who buy products directly from the exporter and resell to wholesalers, retailers, and industrial users in their countries. A manufacturer might sell to several import jobbers in a given country because they do not have exclusive territorial rights in their countries. |
| 3. Dealers | Merchant middlemen who work with exporters on a continuing basis because they have exclusive selling rights in their areas. Manufacturer-dealer relationships often are set up as franchisor-franchisee. |
| 4. Wholesalers and retailers | These middlemen in foreign countries often engage in direct importing. Large retailers sell to ultimate consumers but also frequently wholesale to smaller retailers the products they import. |
| 5. Foreign sales subsidiaries | The exporter exports its products to its own foreign sales subsidiary. This approach may be taken when the exporter and the foreign market are large enough to justify the investment. This is a type of direct foreign investment because the firm actually is present in the foreign country. |

Direct exporting, however, does not mean direct distribution. Direct exporting refers to the manner in which a product enters a foreign market, not the way it is distributed within that market. A product can reach a foreign market through direct exporting but its marketing channel in the country might be very indirect.

In planning for distribution *within* a foreign country direct exporters can turn to the U.S. Department of Commerce, Dun & Bradstreet, Inc., and other exporters for information about available agents and distributors. Often the exporter will also make a personal visit to observe first-hand their character and reputation in the trade before selecting specific middlemen. Direct exporters can achieve distribution within foreign markets by dealing with various types of middlemen or by setting up a foreign sales subsidiary. These are discussed in Table 23–3.

### Overseas Operations

The spirit of nationalism, especially in newly emerging nations, often leads to laws that require foreign firms to build plants or contract with local firms there to produce products in those countries rather than export finished products to them. Local production creates jobs, and the government can exercise greater control over the firm's operations. Most LDCs want to use their natural resources in developing domestic industry rather than export them to produce products in the industrialized nations for reexport.[24] By setting up its own plants or contracting with local firms to produce their products, MNCs can avoid the high tariffs that countries often impose on imported finished products.

Industrialized nations also sometimes pressure foreign-based exporters to set up operations in their countries. Our government has applied pressure to induce Japanese car manufacturers to set up operations in the United States. Beretta, an Italian gunmaker, started manufacturing its handguns in the United States when our government restricted imports of small-sized guns.

Entry methods other than exporting also may enable a firm to make more profit. The following are types of overseas operations: (1) foreign licensing, (2) foreign assembly, (3) contract manufacturing, and (4) overseas production subsidiaries. (See Figure 23–6.)

In **foreign licensing,** an American firm (the licensor) grants a foreign firm (the licensee) the right to use the licensor's manufacturing processes, trademark, patent, or merchandising know-how in return for a fee or royalty. The licensor exports manufacturing and marketing know-how and property rights instead of physical products. The licensee handles production and/or marketing in its market. The Gerber Company and Spalding, for example, entered the Japanese market through licensing. They got involved in foreign operations with little, if any, additional investment in plant and equipment, nor did company personnel have to be sent overseas to manage operations.

foreign licensing

Licensing also has enabled some American firms to enter some communist nations. PepsiCo sells its concentrates to the Russians, who bottle the product under license for sale in the Soviet Union. Coca-Cola does the same in China.

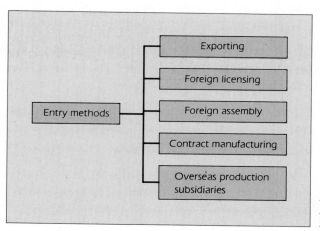

*Figure 23–6.*
*Methods of entering*
*foreign markets*

There are some potential problems with licensing. If the agreement is not prepared carefully the licensor might be helping to create a strong competitor in the licensee's country and in other countries where the licensee sells. Some licensees also have been known to sit on their rights—not produce or market the product in order to help sales of their own rival products.

Franchising, as we saw in Chapter 14, is a popular type of licensing arrangement in consumer products industries. McDonald's, Kentucky Fried Chicken, and Holiday Inn, for example, have expanded to foreign countries through franchising.[25]

**foreign assembly**

In **foreign assembly,** the MNC exports component parts to foreign countries for assembly into the finished product rather than the finished product. Sony televisions and Honda motorcycles, for example, are assembled in the United States for sale here. The firm doing the assembling can be an overseas subsidiary, a licensee of the MNC, or a local firm there. Tariffs on unassembled products are lower than those on assembled products.

**contract manufacturing**

In **contract manufacturing,** the MNC contracts with local firms in foreign markets to make the product. The MNC handles the marketing, usually through its foreign sales subsidiaries. Procter & Gamble, for example, contracts with local producers in some countries to produce its products, but P&G handles the marketing.

Some MNCs, however, prefer to set up their own **overseas production subsidiaries** and produce their products themselves in their host countries. No local licensee or contractor is involved.

## Ownership of Overseas Operations

An MNC must make an investment decision in setting up production and/or marketing operations overseas. They may be owned 100 percent by the MNC or only partially owned. Furthermore, the MNC might buy into or buy outright an existing firm there or build operations from the ground up. Thus when the Clorox Company decided to enter Spain, it purchased the leading producer of bleach in that country.

Some American firms invest in foreign firms mainly to receive interest and dividend payments but do not want to participate in managing these overseas firms. These are portfolio investments. But an MNC may invest in a foreign operation to exercise some direct control over its decision making. This direct foreign investment can give an MNC total or partial ownership of a foreign operation. Sales of overseas subsidiaries in which American firms hold majority ownership add up to four or five times the dollar volume of our exports.

**Wholly Owned Subsidiaries.** A wholly owned subsidiary of an MNC is owned outright by the MNC; there are no local part owners. This gives the MNC greater control over its subsidiaries and makes coordinating their operations easier. The host country, however, still has some control because it can require the subsidiary to hire local nationals and restrict how much profit it can send to its foreign owners.

The majority of overseas investments of American-based MNCs are wholly owned. But there is a strong trend toward requiring some ownership by local nationals. Mexico, for example, limits to 49 percent the amount of new investment that can be foreign owned. Its local content requirements also specify that parts made in Mexico must account for 65 percent of the value of cars sold there and 50 percent of the value of trucks. Ford has manufacturing plants in Mexico and has an advantage over Japanese automakers, who do not. Japanese cars, therefore, are a rarity in Mexico.[26] During recent years, there has also been growing economic, political, and emotional reaction to foreign control of Canadian corporations.[27]

**Joint Ventures.** In international business a **joint venture** means a partnership in which the partners share ownership and control of the venture's operations and property rights. The partners can be (1) two foreign firms doing business in a host country, (2) a foreign firm and a government agency, or (3) a foreign firm and a locally owned firm. A growing number of host countries require joint ventures as a condition of entering their markets. They are very important in East-West trade.[28] The first foreign showroom and retail store in China opened in Peking in 1980. It is a joint venture between K. Hattori & Company (the Japanese maker of Seiko watches) and Peking Watch and Spectacle Company.[29]

Joint ventures offer several advantages. A local partner may have well-established marketing channels and a good reputation that can benefit a foreign firm. Firms with production know-how can benefit from joint ventures with firms that have strong financial positions and marketing know-how. The partners, however, must work hard to make the venture work. Cultural and other environmental differences between home and host countries can be very important.[30]

joint venture

## ADAPTING TO INTERNATIONAL MARKETING

Like purely domestic marketers, MNCs seek to identify and exploit market opportunity by matching their resources and capabilities with the requirements of selected market targets.[31]

### Analyzing Foreign Market Opportunity

In analyzing market opportunity, overseas firms that are making a first attempt at international marketing seek overseas markets for their existing products. Market studies help to focus on those countries that appear to offer the most potential, given the firm's objectives, resources, and capabilities. Then the firm begins developing its strategy for entering the foreign market(s).

The decision to enter a foreign market is not a commitment to remain there indefinitely. The entry decision is based on research that suggests greater market opportunity exists there than in either the firm's home country or other foreign countries. If a review of operating results after entry indicates that this is not valid, the firm may decide to withdraw from that market and focus more effort on market opportunity at home or in other countries. As in purely domestic marketing, it is necessary to allow adequate time for phasing in the effort and to monitor performance continuously in the light of environmental change.

Many firms take a low-risk approach to initial entry, such as indirect exporting, to develop a better feel for the market before making a greater commitment of resources to it. As more information becomes available, the firm may increase its commitment to the market. One possible drawback to this approach, however, is that another firm may enter with a greater degree of commitment and make a greater impact on the market.

### International Marketing Research

Population, GNP, and other secondary data about foreign markets are available from the United Nations. The *United Nations Statistical Yearbook* contains data on more than 200 countries, and there are other regular publications available, such as the *Economic Survey of Latin America*. Drug manufacturers can obtain useful data from the United Nations World Health Organization, and farm equipment makers will find the Food and Agriculture Organization useful. Other international and regional organizations also are available as data sources. The Organization for Economic Cooperation and Development (OECD), for example, publishes reports on business in the industrialized Western nations. Regional trading blocs are another source.

Marketers can also obtain data from governments in their target countries. Many have embassies in the United States that supply information to interested firms. Nongovernmental sources include the Chamber of Commerce of the United States and international trade clubs, banks, ad agencies, and shipping companies. Care is needed in using secondary data, however. Some countries may be able to provide only crude estimates even for population, GNP, and personal income. More detailed data, such as analyses of buying patterns by income class, may be unavailable or outdated.

After using the available secondary data, the marketer must decide whether to collect primary data. As in domestic marketing, the costs, risks, and expected benefits must be considered. In many LDCs gathering primary data is very costly and risky because of the scarcity of research agencies and the likelihood that familiar research techniques may not be suitable. High illiteracy rates, poor postal and telephone service, language problems, and a general suspicion of people who ask questions, for example, make telephone, mail, and personal interviews difficult. Many firms, therefore, rely on interviewing other executives who do business in these countries and sending their own executives overseas for a firsthand look at the market.

American research techniques can be more easily adapted for use in the more developed nations. The MNC can conduct the research for

# In Europe as in the U.S.,
# Travel advertising goes further using TIME.

Would you like to find out more about a specific part—or all—of your market? A highly regarded survey* provides a wide assortment of the latest marketing as well as readership data in your field.

One finding of the survey—a finding which has been market-tested with travel clients—is that target markets are best reached when TIME is included on any European advertising schedule.

For example, a leading airline gave us a detailed brief and asked us to analyse groups ranging from a market of 1,672,000 to a more selective market of only 472,000. Of the different advertising schedules analysed (all of equal budgets), the highest coverage was obtained from those including TIME. In fact, these gave a clear lift of 9% to 24% over those schedules without TIME.

If you would like to see details of this one airline's example, or have a copy of the Pan European Survey, please let us know. We can do a similar analysis for you.

# The news magazine for the internationally minded.

The Pan European Survey sponsored by The Economist • International Herald Tribune • Newsweek • Scientific American • TIME. © Time Inc. 1981

**An example of a source of data on international markets**
Source: Time, Inc.

itself or use research firms there. These firms may be local firms or overseas branches of large American research firms.[32]

### Product Decisions

The product often requires modification to suit different customer needs. Some Europeans wash their clothes in very hot water, which requires built-in heaters on their washing machines. Nestlé markets light instant coffee for Americans and dark instant coffee for Italians. Other product considerations are (1) packaging, (2) labeling, (3) branding, (4) warranties, and (5) after-sale service.

Consumer products in many countries move through very long channels, and transportation is often crude. This may require stronger packaging materials. Differences in tastes regarding package shapes, colors, and sizes are also important. Americans prefer tightly sealed packages for many items, but some foreign consumers insist on opening the package to examine the contents before buying.

Labeling decisions are affected by language, laws, literacy rates, and local customs. Multilingual labels and package inserts are necessary in multilingual countries. Labeling laws may require informative labels. Pictures can help where illiteracy rates are high. (However, the Gerber baby on the Gerber label was interpreted by some consumers to mean the jars contained ground-up babies.) Differences in systems of weights and measures also must be considered.

Branding decisions can be risky. A sugar refinery's shipment to Iraq was not accepted until the firm removed its trademark, a six-pointed star that very closely resembled Israel's national symbol, from the bags. Citizens in some countries sometimes register popular foreign trademarks in their own names. When the foreign firm enters that country, it must either pay the owner to use the trademark, change it, or stay out of the market. Local firms also may package and brand their products to look like prestigious foreign brands. McDonald's, for example, had no franchisees in the Middle East, but two Israelis opened a MacDavids in Tel Aviv to serve American tourists and status-conscious Israelis. It listed "big macs" on its menus. McDonald's claimed the founders were using trademarks that McDonald's had registered in Israel. An Israeli judge ruled MacDavid's could continue to use its name if it was written as one word but could not use "big mac" on menus or packaging to describe its hamburgers.[33]

An MNC can (1) offer the same warranty world-wide, (2) offer one warranty for all foreign markets and a separate one for the home market, or (3) customize the warranty for each country. An American automaker that offers the same warranty world-wide can expect problems in countries with dirt roads for highways. But Volkswagen's standardized world-wide warranty has played a big part in its market success.

After-sale service policies are important if the firm wants to avoid the reaction of "you can't get service on those foreign-made products." Japanese exporters of machine tools learned quickly that American man-

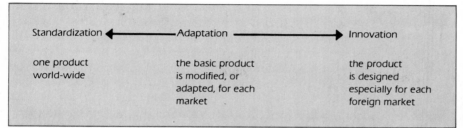

Figure 23–7.
*A continuum of product strategies for international marketers*

ufacturers used the machines around the clock to maximize equipment utilization. Breakdowns were a big problem and the Japanese had to modify their products and strengthen their service policies to fit the tougher use conditions in the United States.

Three basic product strategies for international marketers are (1) standardization, (2) adaptation, and (3) innovation. (See Figure 23–7.)

**Product Standardization.** Product standardization means selling the identical product in all countries. It is the least costly strategy because there is no need for special market research or product modification. Economies of scale are possible in producing and marketing the product. Whether this will be a profitable strategy depends on the product's suitability to its different market targets. The "made in USA" image used to be an almost certain guarantee of sales, but the image of American products has declined in some foreign markets in recent years.[34] Even many Americans apparently believe Japanese-made cars are superior to American-made cars.

Source: *Dunagin's People,* Field Newspaper Syndicate.

*"Of course, when we open our plant in the United States, we will have to overcome the Made-In-America Syndrome."*

In their rush to enter Western European markets after World War II, some American home appliance manufacturers shipped large-capacity refrigerators with freezer compartments there. But these products did not make much headway in Italy and France because homemakers in those countries considered shopping a social event. Many shop daily or even several times a day for groceries, and they had little need for large refrigerators.

**Product Adaptation.** Product adaptation means modifying the product to suit local tastes. It involves greater costs but may also result in greater profit. This strategy is often used when the product performs the same function in different countries but use conditions are different. Reducing the size of the American refrigerators, for example, made them more suitable to Italian and French use conditions. In recent years, Japanese-based Matsushita Electric, Sharp, and Sanyo Electric have been producing and marketing small-sized refrigerators in the United States. This helps them to avoid head-on competition with American manufacturers, who produce larger models.

**Product Innovation.** Heavy investment in research and development and innovation help American firms enter many foreign markets.[35] In some cases simple product modification is not enough. The product may have to be made especially for the foreign market target. General Motors' Basic Transportation Vehicle is a light, easy-to-assemble, short-distance hauler that was developed to meet the needs of people in LDCs for low-cost basic transportation. NCR developed a crank-operated cash register for sale in some LDCs. These are examples of backward product innovation.

## Distribution Decisions

The factors that affect channel decisions in the United States also operate in foreign countries. The major differences between domestic and foreign channels are mainly environmental.

Middlemen in most countries tend to be either very large or very small. Many small wholesalers buy and sell from each other many times before products even reach the retail level in Japan. Japan's land area is about 4 percent that of the United States, but there are almost as many wholesaling establishments in Japan as there are in the United States, 340,000 versus 370,000.[36] Wholesaling in Finland, on the other hand, is dominated by large firms. Japanese public policy is also more restrictive regarding the growth of large retailing establishments than is the case in the United States.[37]

Middlemen in small countries tend not to specialize by product lines as much as middlemen in the United States. The size of the market limits their ability to specialize. There also is resistance to changing distribution structures and patterns in many countries. This is another factor that makes joint ventures with local nationals attractive to many foreign-based firms.

**Physical Distribution.** Large MNCs must manage their global logistics. But transportation, warehousing, order-processing, and materials-handling facilities vary greatly among and within countries and by product type. Supertankers are used to take on oil in many Middle East ports, but general cargo may be unloaded manually and transported by very small trucks or wagons. Government regulations concerning physical distribution activities also vary.

One especially important facilitating middleman is the foreign freight forwarder. They handle about 75 percent of the general cargo that moves from United States ports. Forwarders consolidate small shipments into larger ones and arrange for overseas transportation. They also handle all the complicated paperwork required by governments in exporting and importing products.

## Promotion Decisions

An MNC's promotion strategy also has to consider the relative merits of standardization and adaptation.[38]

**Advertising.** The attitudes of consumers, government, competitors, and middlemen must be considered in advertising decisions. Consumers in some countries believe firms that advertise their products are trying to cover up product faults. Government may prohibit advertising altogether, prescribe its content, or determine the types of products that can be advertised. In Saudi Arabia, for example, advertising is permitted only in print media.[39] Competitors in some countries consider advertising to be nothing more than entertainment for consumers, and middlemen cannot always be counted on to cooperate in promoting a manufacturer's products.

There also are problems in preparing ads. Western European nations appear to be reemphasizing their national identities, so promotional programs must be attuned more carefully to each host country.[40] American ads can be translated into foreign languages, but there will be problems if the translator is not up to date on the idioms and dialects of the foreign language. Pepsi's "Come Alive" theme of several years ago came out as "Come alive out of the grave" in Germany. Ads directed to Orientals in Hong Kong must appear in English and Chinese. If they appear only in Chinese, the Orientals may think the product is inferior. Ad themes and appeals also must fit the target audience's culture. Bare feet, for example, have strong sexual connotations in the Far East.

Media selection decisions often require adaptation. The use of print media is greatly limited in countries with high illiteracy rates. Government regulations can also affect media selection. Hard liquor, for example, cannot be advertised on TV in the United States but is allowed in Japan. Many countries do not have television, and some newspapers will not accept advertising. TV ads in some countries must be contracted one year in advance of their appearance, and it is not unusual for as many as fifty TV commercials to be bunched together for one showing. Circulation figures for magazines and newspapers often are suspect. This makes it harder to select the proper media mix.[41]

The firm may also have to select an ad agency. It can use an agency in its home country, separate local agencies in each host country, or a large multinational agency with branches in the advertiser's host countries. American-based ad agencies have been opening foreign branches for many years. The most popular means of entry has been the purchase of existing agencies in foreign countries.[42]

**Personal Selling.** Personal selling is more culture bound than advertising because of face-to-face contact between the salesperson and the prospect. Most sales of consumer products are made by local nationals. But expensive industrial products often are sold to local nationals by foreign salespersons. A few examples will show the need to practice cultural empathy in the personal selling effort.

Salespersons in some German-speaking countries should avoid smiling when shaking hands with prospects because the prospects may consider it too affectionate. The French do not say "thanks" in response to praise. If an American salesperson responds to a compliment with thanks, the client may interpret it as ridicule. Using first names in the sales presentation is also considered offensive by the French. A salesperson who talks in a loud voice may be perceived as angry by the Chinese. In the Middle East and Latin America people stand much closer together while talking than in the United States. One of the worst things an industrial salesperson can ask an Arab businessman is "How are the wife and children?"

## Pricing Decisions

MNCs must cope with the problem of fluctuating exchange rates, which has to do with the value of one currency in relation to others. For example, when the German Deutschemark goes up in value (appreciates) relative to the U.S. dollar, German-made products become more expensive in the United States. But American-made products become cheaper in Germany. Fluctuating exchange rates cause international marketers problems in quoting prices, especially industrial marketers who are negotiating long-term contracts.

Among the other more obvious differences between foreign and domestic pricing are currency differences, tariffs, special taxes, international shipping costs, export credit terms, and, usually, less control over middleman margins. Barter trade arrangements especially are common in international marketing.[43] Many communist countries prefer barter deals because it enables them to avoid paying for their imports with hard currency.

**Export Pricing.** Besides manufacturing costs, exporters must evaluate demand in each foreign market along with the competitive environment and government regulations. This often results in different prices for domestic and foreign buyers, and there may be different prices in different export markets. Table 23–4 lists several reasons exporters

**Table 23–4.** *Factors favoring lower f.o.b. factory prices on exports*

1. Lower buying power in the foreign market requires lower selling prices to sell there.
2. Competition in the foreign market is very strong.
3. Add-ons to the f.o.b. price such as tariffs and shipping costs are high.
4. Export pricing is based on variable costs and domestic pricing is based on full costs.
5. In the case of consumer products the foreign government sets price ceilings and the export price must be low enough to enable middlemen to add their margins and still meet the prescribed retail price.

may set their f.o.b. factory prices lower on export sales than on domestic sales.

**Dumping** can be a problem.   This means shipping substantial quantities of a product to a foreign country at prices that are below either the home-market price of the same product or the full cost (including profit) of producing it.   Under the United States Antidumping Act, firms that complain of foreign dumping must show that the prices of the dumped goods are lower in the United States than in their home markets and that American producers are being directly harmed by the alleged dumping. If the U.S. Department of Commerce finds that dumping has occurred, it can impose a countervailing duty on the dumped products to wipe out the foreign firm's price advantage.   Japanese makers of TV sets and steel, for example, have been accused of dumping in some recent years.

**dumping**

**Pricing for Overseas Subsidiaries.**   Many American-based MNCs are organized into product divisions and an international division.   The product divisions sell their products to the international division, which, in turn, sells to the firm's overseas subsidiaries.   These intracompany sales require the setting of transfer prices when the separate divisions are operated as profit centers.[44]

Product divisions want to set high transfer prices, but the international division wants to pay low transfer prices.   Each wants its operation to show a profit, and this often leads to conflict.   This is another case where the systems view is essential.

The international division also has to set transfer prices for overseas subsidiaries.   Those in low-tax countries tend to get low transfer prices, while those in high-tax countries tend to get high transfer prices.   The MNC wants subsidiaries in low-tax countries to show more profit than those in high-tax countries.   The U.S. Internal Revenue Service, U.S. customs officials, and tax and customs officials overseas can regulate transfer prices when they are being used to avoid taxes and/or customs duties.

**Pricing Within Foreign Markets.**   Once the product enters the foreign country, pricing decisions become domestic pricing decisions.   MNCs that distribute their products through wholly owned subsidiaries with local salesforces must set prices for final buyers in each host country. Their pricing problems are very much like those of purely domestic marketers.   But MNCs that distribute through foreign middlemen in their host countries exercise less control over pricing to final buyers.

## SUMMARY

International trade involves the movement of products across national borders—the imports and exports of nations. The United States is the world's largest exporter and importer, but our exports account for a relatively small percentage of our GNP when compared to many other countries. Also, our share of total world exports has been declining. Some American industries depend heavily on export sales, some products would be absent in our country were it not for imports, and some imports add to our enjoyment of life.

In consumer-controlled economies most trade is the result of buying and selling activities of business firms. In communist countries, however, foreign trade is handled through government-owned state trading companies.

International trade is concerned only with flows of products between countries. International marketing is concerned with other types of resource flows as well as product flows. These include financial resources, property rights, and technological and managerial skills.

A multinational company (MNC) is a firm based in one country with production and/or marketing operations in one or more foreign countries (host countries). Large MNCs are global enterprises. Some MNCs are American-based, but many are based in other countries. There is a lot of controversy surrounding these global enterprises. Some people, for example, believe they are not subject to enough social control.

International marketers have to contend with domestic and foreign environments. Their ability to adapt and innovate in those environments is a basic determinant of their success. Knowing when to adapt and when to innovate also is important. MNCs can act as agents of cultural change, but there often is cultural resistance to change.

The United States government generally supports the concept of free trade, but there are exceptions. Whenever our national interests, or those of firms, industries, or other special interest groups are threatened by foreign competition, our government will tend to take action to stem the flow of imports into our country and/or exercise greater control over American-based MNCs.

Four basic orientations a firm can take in viewing the world are (1) ethnocentric, (2) polycentric, (3) regiocentric, and (4) geocentric. Most MNCs probably take a polycentric view, but regional trading blocs make a regiocentric view more realistic for some firms.

Firms engage in exporting for a variety of reasons, such as those related to the product life cycle, diversification, and production considerations. We can classify exporting as indirect, semidirect, or direct. The more direct, the more important it is for the marketer to understand the environment of its host countries.

Foreign licensing, foreign assembly, contract manufacturing, and overseas subsidiaries are examples of overseas operations that represent a greater commitment and more involvement in international marketing than does exporting. Ownership of these operations can be total or partial. Joint ventures have become more important in recent years. The desire of many countries for their trade to benefit them is a major reason for this.

The standardization versus adaptation decision must be faced whenever a firm does business overseas. For firms that restrict their involvement to occasional exports of surplus output, this issue is not too important. But the more a firm takes on the characteristics of an MNC, the more important the standardization-adaptation decision in managing the marketing effort.

## REVIEW QUESTIONS

**1.** Contrast international trade with international marketing.

**2.** Explain how an MNC might act as an agent of cultural change.

**3.** Why is cultural empathy important for international marketers?

**4.** "Marketers can forget about the less developed countries because they do not offer any market opportunity." Do you agree? Why or why not?

**5.** What is a regional trading bloc?

**6.** How do the domestic-only and predominantly domestic versions of the ethnocentric orientation differ? Are there any similarities? Explain.

**7.** Identify and discuss four reasons a firm might engage in exporting.

**8.** Contrast indirect, semidirect, and direct exporting.

**9.** Contrast combination export managers (CEMs) and manufacturers' export agents (MEAs).

**10.** What is a Webb-Pomerene export association?

**11.** How does piggyback exporting benefit the rider and the carrier?

**12.** Does direct exporting mean the same thing as direct distribution? Explain.

**13.** What is an import jobber?

**14.** Contrast foreign licensing, foreign assembly, and contract manufacturing.

**15.** Why have joint ventures increased in popularity in recent years?

**16.** Give several examples of the potential differences between marketing research conducted in the United States and that conducted in a less developed country.

**17.** Identify several considerations in adapting the product element of the marketing mix to the environment in a foreign country.

**18.** What alternatives does an MNC have in selecting an ad agency in a host country?

**19.** Under what circumstances would an MNC probably set a lower f.o.b. factory price on export sales than on domestic sales?

**20.** Discuss transfer pricing in an MNC with overseas sales subsidiaries.

## DISCUSSION QUESTIONS

**1.** Is international trade really beneficial to American consumers?

**2.** Is technology transfer between East and West desirable?

**3.** What are some of the problems an MNC with subsidiaries in numerous host countries might encounter in its efforts to act in a socially responsible manner in its decision making?

**4.** Is direct foreign investment in the United States by foreign firms desirable?

**5.** How might politics affect the operations of an MNC?

**6.** What might motivate a group of countries to form a regional trading bloc?

## NOTES

1. "Trade Is Playing Fast-Growing Role in Economic Picture of the U.S.," *Wall Street Journal*, November 13, 1980, p. 48.

2. Comparative marketing is the study of the similarities and differences between two or more marketing systems or parts of systems. See Eugene D. Jaffe, "Comparative Marketing Revisited," *Marquette Business Review*, Winter, 1976, pp. 143–153.

3. See Robert E. Weigand, "Selling Soviet Buyers," *MSU Business Topics*, Spring, 1976, pp. 15–21.

4. "The Reluctant Exporter," *Business Week*, April 10, 1978, p. 56.

5. See William H. Newman, "Adapting Transnational Corporate Management to National Interests," *Columbia Journal of World Business*, Summer, 1979, pp. 82–88.

6. See Franklin R. Root and Bernard Mennis, "How U.S. Multinational Corporations, Unions, and Government View Each Other and the Direction of U.S. Policies," *Journal of International Business Studies*, Spring, 1976, pp. 17–30.

7. See William K. Brandt and James M. Hulbert, "Patterns of Communications in the Multinational Corporation: An Empirical Study," *Journal of International Business Studies*, Spring, 1976, pp. 57–64.

8. See Eric W. Hayden, "Technology Transfer to the Soviet Bloc," *MSU Business Topics*, Winter, 1976, pp. 11–23.

9. See Theodore O. Wallin, "The International Executive's Baggage: Cultural Values on the American Frontier," *MSU Business Topics*, Spring, 1976, pp. 49–58.

10. See Susan P. Douglas and Christine D. Urban, "Life-Style Analysis to Profile Women in International Markets," *Journal of Marketing*, July, 1977, pp. 46–54; and Marianne A. Ferber and Helen M. Lowry, "Women's Place: National Differences in the Occupational Mosaic" *Journal of Marketing*, July, 1977, pp. 23–30.

11. See Yves L. Doz and C. K. Prahalad, "How MNCs Cope with Host Government Intervention," *Harvard Business Review*, March–April, 1980, pp. 149–157; and Louis Kraar, "The Multinationals Get Smarter about Political Risks," *Fortune*, March 24, 1980, pp. 86–88, 92, 95, 98, 100.

12. The term *transideological corporation* has been applied to corporations that are owned and operated jointly by a Western firm and a communist country. See Howard V. Perlmutter, "Emerging East-West Ventures: The Transideological Enterprise," *Columbia Journal of World Business*, September–October, 1969, pp. 39–50. Also see Herbert E. Meyer, "This Communist Has a Capitalist Accent," *Fortune*, February, 1977, pp. 134–148; Charles S. Mayer, "Marketing in Eastern Socialist Countries," *University of Michigan Business Review*, January, 1976, pp. 16–21; and Ronald

E. Hoyt, "East-West Trade Growth Potential for the 1980s," *Columbia Journal of World Business*, Spring, 1978, pp. 59–70.

13. See Harold W. Berkman, "Corporate Ethics: Who Cares?" *Journal of the Academy of Marketing Science*, Summer, 1977, pp. 154–167.

14. See Jack Kaikati, "The Phenomenon of International Bribery," *Business Horizons*, February, 1977, pp. 25–37. Also see Hurd Baruch, "The Foreign Corrupt Practices Act," *Harvard Business Review*, January–February, 1978, pp. 32–50.

15. "As Recession Bites, Many Multinationals Get Lift from Abroad," *Wall Street Journal*, July 23, 1980, pp. 1, 12.

16. See James K. Weekly, "Expropriation of U.S. Multinational Investments," *MSU Business Topics*, Winter, 1977, pp. 27–36.

17. Yoram Wind, Susan P. Douglas, and Howard V. Perlmutter, "Guidelines for Developing International Marketing Strategies," *Journal of Marketing*, April, 1973, pp. 14–23.

18. See James K. Weekly and Edward J. Bardi, "Managerial Perceptions of Exporting Problem Areas," *Baylor Business Studies*, January, 1976, pp. 17–27.

19. "The Reluctant Exporter," *Business Week*, April 10, 1978, pp. 54, 60.

20. See James M. Hulbert, William K. Brandt, and Raimar Richers, "Marketing Planning in the Multinational Subsidiary: Practices and Problems," *Journal of Marketing*, Summer, 1980, pp. 7–15.

21. The "internationalization" of American firms' operations has been called the Third Industrial Revolution. See David S. Leighton, "The Internationalization of American Business—The Third Industrial Revolution," *Journal of Marketing*, July, 1970, pp. 3–6.

22. See A. H. Kizilbash and C. A. Maile, "Export Marketing in a Changing Economic Environment," *Journal of Small Business Management*, January, 1977, pp. 1–6.

23. See Robert T. Jones, "Executive's Guide to Antitrust in Europe," *Harvard Business Review*, May–June, 1976, pp. 106–118.

24. See: Andre van Dam, "Marketing in the New International Order," *Journal of Marketing*, January, 1977, pp. 19–23.

25. See Bruce J. Walker and Michael J. Etzel, "The Internationalization of U.S. Franchise Systems: Progress and Procedures," *Journal of Marketing*, April, 1973, pp. 38–46; and Donald W. Hackett, "The International Expansion of U.S. Franchise Systems: Status and Strategies," *Journal of International Business Studies*, Spring, 1976, pp. 65–75.

26. "As Recession Bites, Many Multinationals Get Lift from Abroad," *Wall Street Journal*, July 23, 1980, p. 1.

27. See David Barrows and Peter Lyman, "Foreign

Ownership and Corporate Behavior in Canada," *MSU Business Topics*, Spring, 1975, pp. 13–20.

28.  See Jeffrey M. Hertzfeld, "New Directions in East-West Trade," *Harvard Business Review*, May–June, 1977, pp. 93–99.

29.  "Watch Store Makes Timely Appearance in Downtown Peking," *Wall Street Journal*, March 11, 1980, p. 26.

30.  See Richard W. Wright, "Joint Venture Problems in Japan," *Columbia Journal of World Business*, Spring, 1979, pp. 25–31.

31.  For discussion of marketing opportunities in Islamic countries, see Mushtaq Luqmani, Zahir A. Quraeshi, and Linda Delene, "Marketing in Islamic Countries: A Viewpoint," *MSU Business Topics*, Summer, 1980, pp. 17–25.

32.  See Eugene D. Jaffe, "Multinational Marketing Research—The Headquarters Role," *Akron Business and Economic Review*, Winter, 1975, pp. 9–16.

33.  "'big mac' Court Attack Lost by Israeli MacDavid's," *Times-Picayune*, January 12, 1979, sec. 3, p. 2.

34.  See Akira Nagashima, "A Comparison of Japanese and U.S. Attitudes toward Foreign Products," *Journal of Marketing*, January, 1970, pp. 68–74; and Akira Nagashima, "A Comparative 'Made In' Product Image Survey among Japanese Businessmen," *Journal of Marketing*, July, 1977, pp. 95–100.

35.  See Peter S. Chang, "A Suggestive and an Alternative Pattern of Foreign Trade: The Role of Research and Development Examined," *Marquette Business Review*, Summer, 1975, pp. 69–77; and Vern Terpstra, "International Product Policy: The Role of Foreign R&D," *Columbia Journal of World Business*, Winter, 1977, pp. 24–32.

36.  "Japan: The Distribution Knot Strangling Consumers," *Business Week*, September 18, 1978, pp. 44, 49.

37.  See Hirotaka Takeuchi and Louis P. Bucklin, "Productivity in Retailing: Retail Structure and Public Policy," *Journal of Retailing*, Spring, 1977, pp. 35–46;

and Mitsuaki Shimaguchi and William Lazer, "Japanese Distribution Channels: Invisible Barriers to Market Entry," *MSU Business Topics*, Winter, 1979, pp. 49–62.

38.  See Ulrich S. Wiechmann, "Integrating Multinational Marketing Activities," *Columbia Journal of World Business*, Winter, 1974, pp. 17–23; Robert T. Green, William H. Cunningham, and Isabella C. M. Cunningham, "The Effectiveness of Standardized Global Advertising," *Journal of Advertising*, Summer, 1975, pp. 25–28; Dean M. Peebles, John F. Ryans, Jr., and Ivan R. Vernon, "Coordinating International Advertising," *Journal of Marketing*, January, 1978, pp. 28–34; James Killough, "Improved Profits from Transnational Advertising," *Harvard Business Review*, July–August, 1978, pp. 102–110; and Saul Sands, "Can You Standardize International Marketing Strategy?" *Journal of the Academy of Marketing Science*, Winter, Spring, 1979, pp. 117–134.

39.  Jack G. Kaikati, "The Marketing Environment in Saudi Arabia," *Akron Business and Economic Review*, Summer, 1976, pp. 5–13.

40.  See S. Watson Dunn, "Effect of National Identity on Multinational Promotional Strategy in Europe," *Journal of Marketing*, October, 1976, pp. 50–57.

41.  See David A. Ricks, Jeffrey S. Arpan, and Marilyn Y. Fu, "Pitfalls in Advertising Overseas," *Journal of Advertising Research*, December, 1974, pp. 47–51.

42.  See Arnold K. Weinstein, "The International Expansion of U.S. Multinational Advertising Agencies," *MSU Business Topics*, Summer, 1974, pp. 29–35.

43.  See Jack G. Kaikati, "The Reincarnation of Barter Trade as a Marketing Tool," *Journal of Marketing*, April, 1976, pp. 17–24; Robert E. Weigand, "International Trade without Money," *Harvard Business Review*, November–December, 1977, pp. 28–30; and Robert E. Weigand, "Apricots for Ammonia," *California Management Review*, Fall, 1979, pp. 33–41.

44.  See Seung H. Kim and Stephen W. Miller, "Constituents of the International Transfer Pricing Decision," *Columbia Journal of World Business*, Spring, 1979, pp. 69–77.

# NAME INDEX

# SUBJECT INDEX

*This Continues
Page II Credit listing.*

Jersey. p. 90—*Pepper . . . and Salt*, by Chuck Vadun, as seen in *The Wall Street Journal.* Reprinted with permission. p. 91—*Statistical Abstract of the United States, 1979,* 100th ed. (Washington, D.C.: U.S. Bureau of the Census, 1979), p. 440.

**Chapter 4:** p. 104—Reprinted with permission of Whirlpool Corporation, Benton Harbor, Michigan. p. 111—Reprinted with permission of Macmillan Publishing Co., Inc. from *Difussion of Innovations.* Copyright © 1962 by the Free Press of Glencoe, a division of Macmillan Publishing Co., Inc.

**Chapter 5:** p. 118—A. H. Maslow, "A theory of Human Motivation," *Psychological Review,* July 1943, pp. 370–396. p. 121—Adopted from Donald H. Blocher *Developmental Counseling,* (New York: Ronald Press, 1966). p. 125—*The Better Half* by Vinson, Reprinted courtesy of the Register and Tribune Syndicate, Inc. pp. 127–128—Reprinted with permission of Xerox Corporation and Needham, Harper, and Steers.

**Chapter 6:** p. 143—W. D. Wells and G. Gubar, "Life Cycle Concept in Marketing Research," *Journal of Marketing Research,* November 1966, pp. 353 ff. Adapted by permmision of American Marketing Association. p. 144—Adopted from James H. Myers and William H. Reynolds, *Consumer Behavior and Marketing Management,* (Boston: Houghton Mifflin, 1967) p. 245. Reprinted with permission. p. 146—Harry L. Davis and Benny P. Rigaux, "Perception of Marital Roles in Decision Processes," *The Journal of Consumer Research* (June 1974), p. 54. Reprinted with permission. p. 152—From *Consumer Behavior,* Second Edition by James F. Engel,

David T. Collatt, and Roger D. Blackwell. Copyright © 1968, 1973, by Holt, Rinehart and Winston, Inc. Adapted by permission of Holt, Rinehart and Winston. And from W. Lloyd Warner, Marchie Meeker, and Kenneth Eels, *Social Class in America: The Evaluation of Status* (New York: Harper & Row, 1960). Copyright © 1960 by Harper & Row, Publishers, Incorporated. Reprinted by permission. p. 155—Reprinted with permission of DeBeers and N. W. Ayer. pp. 158–159—"How Marketers can Cater to Voluntary Simplicity Segment," *Marketing News,* March 21, 1980, p.3. Reprinted with permission of American Marketing Association.

**Chapter 7:** p. 173—Reprinted with permission of AMP Incorporated, Harrisburg, Pennsylvania. p. 175—Reprinted with permission of Ryder Truck Rental Inc., Miami, Florida.

**Chapter 8:** p. 205—Reprinted with permission of The Procter & Gamble Company, Cincinnati, Ohio. p. 208—Reprinted courtesy of Standard Brands Foods, Division of Standard Brands Incorporated. p. 211—Russell I. Haley, "Benefit Segmentation: A Decision-Oriented Research Tool," *Journal of Marketing* (July 1968) p. 33. Reprinted with permission of American Marketing Association. p. 215—Reprinted with permission of IBM Corporation, Armonk, New York. p. 221—From Philip Kotler, *Marketing Management:* Analysis, *Planning, and Control,* 3rd ed. © 1976, p. 129. Adapted by permission of Prentice-Hall, Inc., Englewood-Cliffs, N.J.

**Chapter 9:** p. 231—Reprinted with permission of Xerox Corporation and Needham, Harper, and Steers. p. 233—Reprinted with permission of Donnelly Marketing. p. 243—

Reprinted with permission of Booz, Allen & Hamilton, Inc.

**Chapter 10:** p. 278–279—Reprinted with the permission of General Motors Corporation.

**Chapter 11:** p. 304—© 1980. Reprinted by permission of *The Wall Street Journal* and Brenda Burbank. p. 306—Reprinted from the July 7, 1980 issue of *Business Week* by special permission © 1980 by McGraw-Hill, Inc., New York, NY 10020. All rights reserved. p. 310—Reprinted with permission of 3M Corporation. p. 312—Reprinted with permission of the Boeing Company p. 313—Copyright © 1962, by the Foundation for the School of Business at Indiana University. Reprinted by permission. p. 314—Reprinted with the permission of General Motors Corporation. p. 316—Reprinted by permission from *Sales & Marketing Management* magazine. Copyright 1973, pp. 33–36. p. 320—Reprinted by permission of the *Harvard Business Review.* Excerpt from "Exploit the Product Life Cycle" by Theodore Levitt (November–December 1965). Copyright © 1965 by the President and Fellows of Harvard College. All rights reserved. p. 321—Reprinted with permission of Pfizer, Inc. p. 322—Reprinted with permission of Johnson & Johnson. p. 324—Courtesy of Arm & Hammer Division, Church & Dwight Co., Inc.

**Chapter 12:** p. 337—Reprinted with permission of Fiskars Manufacturing. p. 344—Reproduced courtesy of General Foods Corporation. p. 346—Reprinted with permission of Beatrice Foods Co. p. 348—Reproduced courtesy of Owens-Illinois, Inc. p. 350—Reprinted with permission of General Wine and Spirits Company. p. 354—Reprinted by permission of *The Wall Street Journal.*

**Chapter 13:** p. 382—Reprinted with permission of Seiko Time Corporation.

**Chapter 14:** p. 395—"The Fortune Directory of the Fifty Largest Retailing Companies," *Fortune,* July 14, 1980, pp. 154–155. Reprinted with permission. p. 411—Reprinted with permission of Milton Waldoff.

**Chapter 15:** p. 433 and p. 438—*1972 Census of Wholesale Trade,* Volume 1, (Washington, D.C. U.S. Bureau of the Census, 1972), p.8. p. 439—Reprinted with the special permission of Dun's Review, November 1980, Copyright 1980, Dun & Bradstreet Publications Corporation.

**Chapter 16:** p. 460—Reprinted with permission of Lyon Metal Products, Inc., Aurora, Illinois. p. 462—Reprinted with permission of 3M Corporation. p. 464—Reprinted with permission of the Association of American Railroads. p. 467—*Yearbook of Railroad Facts,* (Washington, D.C.: Association of American Railroads, 1981), p. 36. Reprinted with permission. p. 468—Reprinted with permission of Western Airlines, Los Angeles, California.

**Chapter 17:** p. 485—Reprinted with permission of Bankers Trust Company. p. 492—Reprinted with permission of Ore-Ida Foods, Inc.

**Chapter 18:** p. 514—*Marketing News,* February 22, 1980, p. 3 Reprinted with permission of the American Marketing Association. p. 528—Reprinted with permission of American Maize-Products Company. p. 533—Table based on material in "A Behavioral Science Approach to Effective Sales Presentation" in the Spring 1976 *Journal of the Academy of Marketing Science.* p. 542—*Management of the Sales Force,* 5th ed., by